SUSE Linux Enterprise Server Administration (Course 3112): CLA, LPIC-1 & Linux+

3112

Novell Training Services

www.novell.com

AUTHORIZED COURSEWARE

D0025476

SUSE Linux Enterprise Server Administration (Course 3112): CLA, LPIC-1 & Linux+

Novell.

COURSE TECHNOLOGY
CENGAGE Learning·

SUSE Linux Enterprise Server Administration (Course 3112): CLA, LPIC-1 & Linux+

Novell and Jason Eckert

Vice President, Editorial: Dave Garza

Executive Editor: Steve Helba

Acquisitions Editor: Nick Lombardi

Managing Editor: Marah Bellegarde

Product Manager: Natalie Pashoukos

Editorial Assistant: Sarah Pickering

Vice President, Marketing: Jennifer Ann Baker

Marketing Director: Deborah S. Yarnell

Associate Marketing Manager: Erica Ropitzky

Production Manager: Andrew Crouth

Senior Content Project Manager: Kara A. DiCaterino

Senior Art Director: Jack Pendleton

Library of Congress Control Number: 2011929267

ISBN-13: 978-1-111-54003-6

ISBN-10: 1-111-54003-9

Course Technology
20 Channel Center Street
Boston, MA 02210
USA

Cengage Learning is a leading provider of customized learning solutions with office locations around the globe, including Singapore, the United Kingdom, Australia, Mexico, Brazil, and Japan. Locate your local office at:
international.cengage.com/region

Cengage Learning products are represented in Canada by Nelson Education, Ltd.

For your course and learning solutions, visit **www.cengage.com/coursetechnology**

Purchase any of our products at your local college store or at our preferred online store **www.cengagebrain.com**

Visit our corporate website at **cengage.com**

Course Technology, a part of Cengage Learning, reserves the right to revise this publication and make changes from time to time in its content without notice.

The Novell and SUSE names and trademarks are the exclusive property of, and are licensed from Novell Inc. Linux is a registered trademark of Linus Torvalds.

Printed in the United States of America
1 2 3 4 5 6 7 15 14 13 12 11

Contents

Preface

Open source software such as Linux has radically changed how the computer industry approaches software development. One of the largest changes since 2000 was Novell's switch to SUSE Linux as their main enterprise platform. Today, there are millions of Linux users, administrators, and developers, and this trend continues as companies adopt Linux and open source technologies. To provide benchmarks for hiring, many vendors such as CompTIA, Novell, Red Hat, and the Linux Professional Institute (LPI) have released Linux certification exams geared toward different skill sets required for common Linux job functions. One of the most common entry-level Linux certifications is LPI Level 1 (LPIC-1), which tests Linux skills in many different areas of usage and systems administration. Using carefully constructed examples, questions, and practical exercises, the *SUSE Linux Enterprise Server Administration (Course 3112): CLA, LPIC-1 & Linux+* text introduces you to the concepts required to successfully use and administer a Linux system as well as prepare for the two LPIC-1 certification examinations.

The Intended Audience

This book is appropriate for anyone who wishes to learn how to administer, use, or develop programs for SUSE Linux. The concepts introduced in this book do not assume prior Linux experience and are geared toward the objectives on the two LPIC-1 certification exams. Furthermore, many of the concepts and procedures introduced in this book are transferable to most other Linux distributions.

Section Descriptions

Section 1, " Use the Linux Desktop and the Command Line Interface," examines how to navigate and use the GNOME desktop and command line interface in SUSE Linux Enterprise Server (SLES) 11. As well, this section discusses how to perform configuration of accessibility settings and locale information in SLES 11.

Section 2, " Install SUSE Linux Enterprise Server 11," discusses the configuration of disks and file systems as well as the installation of SLES 11. This section also introduces the File System Hierarchy Standard (FHS).

Section 3, " Administer SUSE Linux Enterprise Server 11 with YaST," discusses the procedures used to administer various components of SLES 11 using the graphical Yet Another Setup Tool (YaST) utility. In addition, this section examines the structure of the X Window System and its configuration.

Section 4, "Administer SLES 11 with the Command Line Interface," walks through the procedures used to administer software, libraries, users, groups, permissions, file systems, backups, and hardware using various commands within SLES 11.

Section 5, " Manage Processes, Jobs, and Runlevels," covers the tools and procedures used to manage and schedule processes on a Linux system. Additionally, this section discusses how to manage system initialization and runlevels, as well as the tools that can be used to monitor and troubleshoot an SLES 11 system.

Section 6, " Configure the Network," discusses the structure of the TCP/IP protocol suite as well as the tools and procedures that can be used to configure and troubleshoot

TCP/IP network interfaces within SLES. This section concludes with a discussion of firewall configuration using iptables.

Section 7," Configure Applications and Services," examines the configuration of key network services, including Samba, Apache, FTP, e-mail, CUPS, DNS, NTPD, xinetd, and Squid.

Section 8, "Understand Security-Related Tools," discusses the tools and procedures that can be used to secure an SLES 11 system. Focus is placed environment, remote access, authentication, and file-related security.

Features

To ensure a successful learning experience, this book includes the following pedagogical features:

- **Section Objectives:** Each section in this book begins with a detailed list of the concepts to be mastered within that section. This list provides you with a quick reference to the contents of the section, as well as a useful study aid.

- **Screenshots, Illustrations, and Tables:** Wherever applicable, screenshots and illustrations are used to aid you in the visualization of common installation, administration, and management steps; theories; and concepts. In addition, many tables provide command options that may be used in combination with the specific command being discussed.

- **Exercises:** Exercises are found at the end of each chapter. They contain specific step-by-step instructions that enable you to apply the knowledge gained in the section.

- **End-of-Chapter Material:** The end of each chapter includes the following features to reinforce the material covered in the section:

- Chapter Summary: Gives a brief but complete summary of the section

- Key Terms List: Lists all new terms and their definitions

- Review Questions: Test your knowledge of the most important concepts covered in the section

- Discovery Exercises: Include theoretical, research, or scenario-based projects that allow you to expand on your current knowledge of the concepts that you learned in the section

On the DVDs: On the DVDs included with this text you will find a copy of SUSE Linux Enterprise Server 11, SLES 11 VMWare Server, a Student Manual PDF, a PDF of the Self-Study Workbook, and Self-Study Files.

INSTRUCTOR'S MATERIALS

The following supplemental materials are available when this book is used in a classroom setting. All of the supplements available with this book are provided to the instructor on a single CD.

Electronic Instructor's Manual: The Instructor's Manual that accompanies this textbook includes additional instructional material to assist in class preparation, including suggestions for classroom activities, discussion topics, and additional projects.

Solutions: Answers to all end-of-chapter materials are provided, including the Review Questions, and, where applicable, Discovery Exercises.

ExamView®: This textbook is accompanied by ExamView, a powerful testing software package that allows instructors to create and administer printed, computer (LAN-based), and Internet exams. ExamView includes hundreds of questions that correspond to the topics covered in this text, enabling students to generate detailed study guides that include page references for further review. The computer-based and Internet testing components allow students to take exams at their computers, and also save the instructor time by grading each exam automatically.

PowerPoint presentations: This textbook comes with Microsoft PowerPoint slides for each chapter. These are included as a teaching aid for classroom presentation, to make available to students on the network for chapter review, or to be printed for classroom distribution. Instructors, please feel at liberty to add your own slides for additional topics you introduce to the class.

Figure Files: All of the figures in this textbook are reproduced on the Instructor's Resource CD in bitmapped format. Similar to the PowerPoint presentations, these are included as a teaching aid for classroom presentation, to make available to students for review, or to be printed for classroom distribution.

LAB REQUIREMENTS

The following hardware is required for the Discovery Exercises at the end of each section and should be listed on the Hardware Compatibility List available at *www.novell.com/linux/:*

- Pentium 4 or later CPU

- 2 GB RAM (4 GB RAM recommended)

- 40 GB or greater hard disk

- A DVD drive (or a combination CD/DVD drive)

- Network Interface Card

- Internet connection

Similarly, the following lists the software required for the Discovery Exercises at the end of each section:

- SUSE Linux Enterprise Server 11

ACKNOWLEDGMENTS

First, I wish to thank the staff at Cengage Learning and Novell for an overall enjoyable writing experience. More specifically, I wish to thank my Product Manager, Natalie Pashoukos, for her coordination and insight, Frank Gerencser, of triOS College for freeing me up to work on this project, and the Starbucks Coffee Company for providing me with the raw materials that were ultimately converted into the text within this book. Readers are encouraged to e-mail comments, questions, and suggestions regarding

SUSE Linux Enterprise Server Administration (Course 3112): CLA, LPIC-1 & Linux+ to Jason W. Eckert: jason.eckert@trios.com

Introduction

This textbook is based on Novell authored courseware *Novell's Guide to the LPIC-1 Certification Using SUSE Linux Enterprise Server 11 (Course 3112)*, which Novell sells and distributes to commercial and academic institutions, as well as self-study customers.

Utilizing the strength of Novell's original content, software, and hands-on exercises, Course Technology has reformatted and enhanced the text for an academic audience. Additional end of chapter exercises, student labs, and instructor tools - including test banks, PowerPoint slides, and suggested solutions - have been added to produce quality courseware based on Novell's SUSE Linux. The *Novell's Guide to the LPIC-1 Certification Using SUSE Linux Enterprise Server 11* (3112) course has two main goals:

1. To teach practical Linux skills, using SUSE Linux Enterprise Server 11,

2. To prepare for the LPI Level One Certification exam.

Novell, Linux Professional Institute, and CompTIA have teamed up to offer you the chance to earn three Linux certifications: the Novell Certified Linux Administrator, the Linux Professional Institute LPIC-1, and CompTIA Linux+ Powered by LPI.

By passing the LPI Level One Certification, you also fulfill the requirements of Novell Certified Linux and Administrator and CompTIA Linux+ Powered by LPI.

The topics covered in this course are based on the April 2009 revision of the LPI Level One Objectives, published on the LPI Web site (http://www.lpi.org/eng/certification/the_lpic_program/lpic_1).

The main focus of the course is teaching you the actual skills needed to administer a SUSE Linux Enterprise Server 11 while at the same time covering the knowledge needed to pass the LPIC Level One exam. To achieve this, the manual contains the technical and background information, while the workbook contains exercises to practice administrative tasks.

Student Kit Deliverables

The contents of your student kit include two DVDs. The first DVD is your course DVD and contains the following:

- *Novell's Guide to the LPIC-1 Certification Using SUSE Linux Enterprise Server 11 (Course 3112)* Student Manual

- *Novell's Guide to the LPIC-1 Certification Using SUSE Linux Enterprise Server 11 (Course 3112)* Self-Study Workbook

- *Novell's Guide to the LPIC-1 Certification Using SUSE Linux Enterprise Server 11 (Course 3112)* Self-Study Files

- SLES 11 VMWare Server

The second DVD contains a full evaluation version of SUSE Linux Enterprise Server 11. To accomodate this academic deliverable, the original software has been modified from CD to DVD and is distributed on an "AS IS" basis. Please note that this software is for classroom use only and is not to be used in a production environment.

To download a fully functional, supported, and upgradeable version of the SUSE Linux Enterprise Server and other Novell Open Source products, visit www.novell.com/downloads.

The *Novell's Guide to the LPIC-1 Certification Using SUSE Linux Enterprise Server 11* Course CDROM contains an empty VMware image that is used in Section 2 to practice the installation of SUSE Linux Enterprise Server 11.

Most of the exercises are performed on the SUSE Linux Enterprise Server 11 (hostname: da-host) installed on the actual hardware. In addition to da-host, the virtual SUSE Linux Enterprise Server 11(hostname: da1) installation created in Section 2 is used subsequently in exercises in the Workbook that require two computers.

NOTE: Instructions for setting up a self-study environment are in the 3112_setup.pdf on the Course CD.

Course Design

The course design is explained under the following headings:

- Course Objectives
- Audience
- Certification and Prerequisites
- Agenda

Course Objectives

This course teaches you how to perform the following SUSE Linux Enterprise Server 11 administrative tasks:

- Use the Linux Desktop and the Command Line Interface
- Install SUSE Linux Enterprise Server 11
- Administer SUSE Linux Enterprise Server 11 with YaST
- Administer SLES 11 with the Command Line Interface
- Manage Processes, Jobs, and Runlevels
- Configure the Network
- Configure Applications and Services
- Understand Security-Related Tools

These are tasks common for a beginning to intermediate SUSE Linux Enterprise Server 11 administrator in an enterprise environment.

Audience

This course is designed to teach basic to intermediate Linux skills to students who are either entirely new to Linux or have 6 to 12 months of experience with Linux, as this is the target audience for the LPI Level One, Novell Certified Linux and Administrator and CompTIA Linux+ Powered by LPI certification exams.

A student new to Linux can use the course to get started with Linux and to get the needed skills to administer SUSE Linux Enterprise Server 11. He or she should gain practical experience after the course before taking the LPIC-1 exam. A student who already has a Linux background with 6 to 12 months of practical experience can use this course to review the topics of the LPIC-1 exam objectives and to prepare for the test.

Certification and Prerequisites

While existing Linux knowledge would be helpful, it is not absolutely required. Students should have good knowledge of using a graphical user interface, such as Microsoft Windows Vista/Windows 7 or Mac OS X, and should be familiar with PC basics, including partitions, file systems, directories, files, and fundamental TCP/IP networking concepts as well as basic administration know-how in a Windows environment.

This course can be used as preparation towards the following certifications:

- LPI Level One, Novell Certified Linux and Administrator, CompTIA Linux+ Powered by LPI

- Novell Certified Linux Professional 11

LPI Level One, Novell Certified Linux and Administrator, CompTIA Linux+ Powered by LPI

This course helps you prepare for the LPIC-1 exam. The exam is delivered in testing centers around the world. Registration the steps required to become certified are listed on the LPI Web site (http://www.lpi.org/eng/certification/faq/procedure_for_taking_exams).

The following illustrates the training/testing path for Novell CLA 11:

Figure Intro-1   *Novell CLA 11 LPI Certification Path*

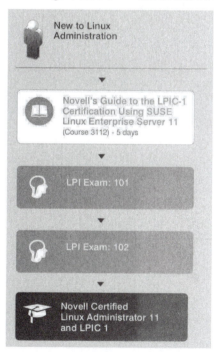

Courtesy of Novell, Inc.

Novell Certified Linux Professional 11

This course can be used as the first course toward the Novell Certified Linux Professional 11 (Novell CLP 11) Certification. Unlike a multiple choice test, the Novell CLP 11 exam is a practical exam, called Practicum, requiring the examinee to perform actual system administration tasks. The Practicum is a hands-on, scenario-based exam where you apply the knowledge you have learned to solve real-life problems—demonstrating that you know what to do and how to do it.

The practicum tests you on objectives in the skills outlined in the following three Novell CLP 11 courses:

■*SUSE Linux Enterprise 11 Fundamentals* - Course 3101

(The topics of the 3101 course are included in *Novell's Guide to the LPIC-1 Certification Using SUSE Linux Enterprise Server -* Course 3112.)

■*SUSE Linux Enterprise 11 Administration* - Course 3102

(Some of the topics of the 3102 course are covered in this 3112 course but not all of them.)

■*SUSE Linux Enterprise Server 11 Administration* - Course 3103

As with all Novell certifications, course work is recommended. To achieve the certification, you are required to pass the following:

- LPIC-1/Novell Certified Linux Administrator exam

- Novell CLP 11 Practicum (050-721)

The following illustrates the training/testing path for Novell CLP 11 (CLA 10 or CLA 11 are a prerequisite for CLP 11):

Figure Intro-2   *CLP 11 Certification Path*

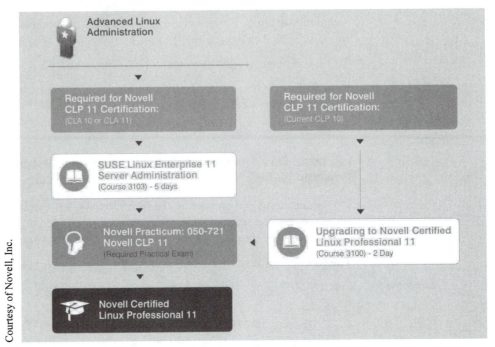

Courtesy of Novell, Inc.

NOTE: For more information about Novell certification programs and taking the Novell CLP 11 Practicum, see http://www.novell.com/training/certinfo

Agenda

The following is the agenda for this course:

Table Intro-1   *Agenda*

Section	Duration
Introduction	00:30
Section 1: Use the Linux Desktop and the Command Line Interface	03:00
Section 2: Install SUSE Linux Enterprise Server 11	03:00
Section 3: Administer SUSE Linux Enterprise Server 11 with YaST	02:00
Section 4: Administer SLES 11 with the Command Line Interface	05:00
Section 5: Manage Processes, Jobs, and Runlevels	03:30
Section 6: Configure the Network	03:30
Section 7: Configure Applications and Services	07:00
Section 7: Configure Applications and Services (contd.)	03:00
Section 8: Understand Security-Related Tools	02:00

Exercise Conventions

When working through an exercise, you will see conventions that indicate information you need to enter that is specific to your server.

The following describes the most common conventions:

- *italicized text*: This is refers to your unique situation, such as the hostname of your server.

  For example, supposing the hostname of your server is da50 and you see the following

  hostname.digitalairlines.com

  You would enter

  da50.digitalairlines.com

- 172.17.8.*xx*: This is the IP address that is assigned to your SUSE Linux Enterprise Server 11.

  For example, supposing your IP address is 172.17.8.50 and you see the following

  172.17.8.*xx*

  You would enter

  172.17.8.50

- Select: The word *select* is used in exercise steps with reference to menus where you can choose between different entries, such as drop-down menus.

- Enter and Type: The words *enter* and *type* have distinct meanings.

  The word *enter* means to type text in a field or at a command line and press the Enter key when necessary. The word *type* means to type text without pressing the Enter key.

  If you are directed to type a value, make sure you do not press the Enter key or you might activate a process that you are not ready to start.

- Key combinations: Ctrl+Alt+F1 indicates that all three keys should be pressed at the same time. Ctrl, Alt, F1 indicates that the three keys should be pressed and released one after the other.

SUSE Linux Enterprise Server 11 Information

The copy of SUSE Linux Enterprise Server 11 you receive in your student kit is a fully functioning copy of the SUSE Linux Enterprise Server 11 product.

The following information will help you to get the most out of SUSE Linux Enterprise Server 11:

- SUSE Linux Enterprise Server 11 Support and Maintenance
- Novell Customer Center
- SUSE Linux Enterprise Server 11 Online Resources

SUSE Linux Enterprise Server 11 Support and Maintenance

To receive official support and maintenance updates, you need to do one of the following:

- Register for a free registration/serial code that provides you with 60 days of support and maintenance.
- Purchase a copy of SUSE Linux Enterprise Server 11 from Novell (or an authorized dealer).

You can obtain your free 60 day support and maintenance code at http://www.novell.com/products/server/eval.html

---

NOTE: You will need to have a Novell login account to access the 60 day evaluation.

Novell Customer Center

Novell Customer Center is an intuitive, Web-based interface that helps you to manage your business and technical interactions with Novell. Novell Customer Center consolidates access to information, tools, and services such as the following:

- Automated registration for new SUSE Linux Enterprise products
- Patches and updates for all shipping Linux products from Novell
- Order history for all Novell products, subscriptions, and services
- Entitlement visibility for new SUSE Linux Enterprise products
- Linux subscription renewal status
- Subscription renewals via partners or Novell

For example, a company might have an administrator who needs to download SUSE Linux Enterprise software updates, a purchaser who wants to review the order history, and an IT manager who has to reconcile licensing. With Novell Customer Center, the company can meet all these needs in one location and can give users access rights appropriate to their roles.

You can access the Novell Customer Center at http://www.novell.com/customercenter

SUSE Linux Enterprise Server 11 Online Resources

Novell provides a variety of online resources to help you configure and implement SUSE Linux Enterprise Server 11:

- http://www.novell.com/products/server

  This is the Novell home page for SUSE Linux Enterprise Server 11.
- http://www.novell.com/documentation/sles11

  This is the Novell Documentation Web site for SUSE Linux Enterprise Server 11.
- http://support.novell.com/linux

  This is the home page for all Novell Linux support and it includes links to support options such as Knowledgebase, downloads, and FAQs.
- http://www.novell.com/coolsolutions

  This Web site provides the latest implementation guidelines and suggestions from Novell on a variety of products, including SUSE Linux Enterprise.

SECTION 1   Use the Linux Desktop and the Command Line Interface

This section helps you to get to know some of the basic features of SUSE Linux Enterprise Server 11 (SLES 11). You are introduced to the GNOME desktop environment and the Linux command line interface (CLI).

Objectives

1. Use the GNOME Desktop Environment

2. Configure Accessibility Settings

3. Access the Command Line Interface from the Desktop

4. Work with the Linux Shell

5. Use Command Line Tools to Work with Files and Directories

6. Apply Locale and Time Zone Settings

Objective 1   Use the GNOME Desktop Environment

GNOME is an intuitive desktop environment that supports drag and drop. Numerous programs are specifically designed for GNOME. Using these programs requires an understanding of how to navigate in GNOME.

To use the GNOME desktop environment, you need to know how to do the following:

- Log In
- Understand Login Screen Options
- Log Out
- Shut Down
- Identify GNOME Desktop Components
- Manage Icons in GNOME
- Use the GNOME File Manager (Nautilus)
- Work with GNOME

Log In

If computer users want to work with a multiuser-capable operating system, they must first identify themselves to the operating system. For this purpose, they need

- A **login string** or **username**
- A **password** (usually assigned by the system administrator when a new user is added)

When the computer is booted and ready for work, the following login dialog appears:

Figure 1-1   *Login Dialog*

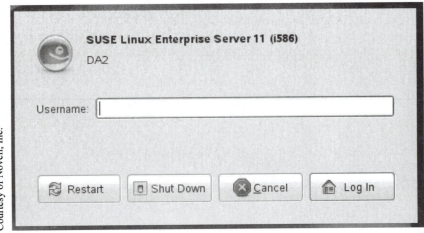

Courtesy of Novell, Inc.

Understand Login Screen Options

In the lower left corner of the login screen, you will notice four options:

- **Restart.** Restarts the system.

NOTE: Only root is allowed to reboot the system. Enter the root password when prompted.

- **Shut Down.** Shuts down your computer.
- **Cancel.** Cancels the login.
- **Log In.** Select this after entering the password.

  1. Type a username and press Enter.
  2. Type your password and press Enter again.

     If the login is successful, the following GNOME desktop environment appears:

Figure 1-2   *Gnome Desktop*

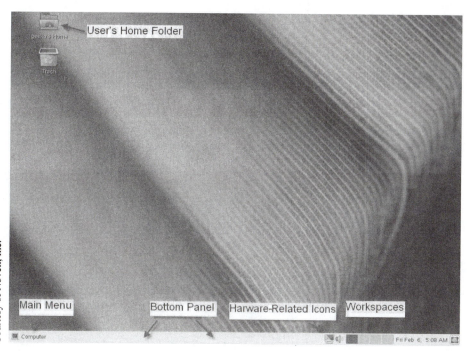

Courtesy of Novell, Inc.

Log Out

When you are ready to log out of the system, do the following:

1. Open the **Computer** menu (also called *main menu*) in the bottom panel.

Figure 1-3   *Computer Menu*

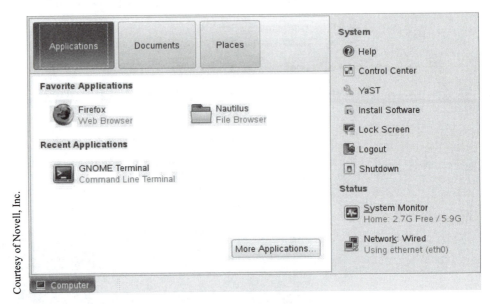

Courtesy of Novell, Inc.

2. From the System panel on the right side, select **Logout**.

   A confirmation dialog appears.

Figure 1-4   *Log Out Confirmation*

Courtesy of Novell, Inc.

3. Select **Log Out** to end the session or **Switch User** to open a new login dialog to allow another user to log in.

NOTE: After logging in as a new user, you can switch back to the previous login by pressing Ctrl+Alt+F7. To return to the login of the new user, press Ctrl+Alt+F8. If you use Switch User and use the same user name as the one already logged in, you are simply returned to your desktop. Press Ctrl+Alt+F8 to get back to the login dialog.

Shut Down

Older computers that do not have power management and cannot switch themselves off can be switched off manually when the following message appears:

```
Master Resource Control: runlevel 0 has been reached
```

If you switch the machine off too soon, this could lead to loss of data.

NOTE: You should always shut down your computer before you turn it off.

1. Go to the **Computer** (main) menu at the bottom of the screen.

2. Select **Shutdown** from the System panel on the right side.

    The following dialog is displayed:

Figure 1-5   *Shut Down Confirmation*

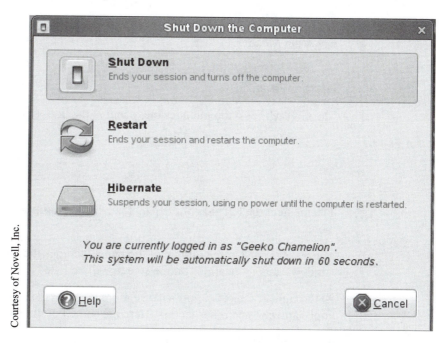

Courtesy of Novell, Inc.

3. Click **Shut Down**.

    You will be asked to authenticate as root; by default, only root has the permission to shut down the system on SLES 11.

Figure 1-6   *Root Password Dialog*

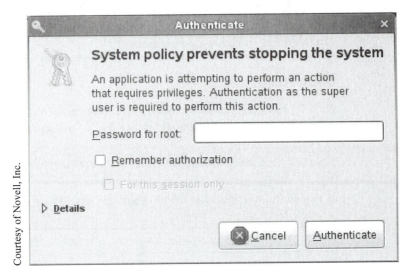

Courtesy of Novell, Inc.

4. Enter the root password and click **Authenticate**.

Identify GNOME Desktop Components

This section explains the components on the

■ Bottom Panel

■ Main Menu

Bottom Panel

The GNOME desktop includes one panel at the bottom of the screen.

Figure 1-7   *GNOME Panel*

Courtesy of Novell, Inc.

The menu at the left side of the panel is labeled **Computer**. It is called the main menu.

The empty space in the middle of the panel includes the task manager. All opened windows and applications on the screen will be listed here.

At the right of the panel you will see more icons. Which icons are present depends on your hardware and other factors. Here are some possible icons:

■ Monitor. Lets you configure display settings.

■ Battery. Power management for laptops.

■ Speaker. Volume control.

■ Clock. Shows date and time.

- **Board.** Minimizes all open windows or shows them again on the desktop.

- **Workspaces.** Workspaces are discreet areas in the GNOME Desktop in which you can work.

Main Menu

You can start a program by double-clicking the icon on the desktop, but normally programs are started from the main menu.

Figure 1-8   *Main Menu*

Courtesy of Novell, Inc.

At the top of the left frame you see three menu buttons, representing three different filters:

- **Applications**

  This is the default view, showing favorite and recent applications.

- **Documents**

  Shows documents you have been working on recently.

- **Places**

  Shows favorite places like servers, file system, and desktop.

The left frame displays a button labeled **More Applications**. When you select this button, the application browser appears.

Figure 1-9   *Application Browser*

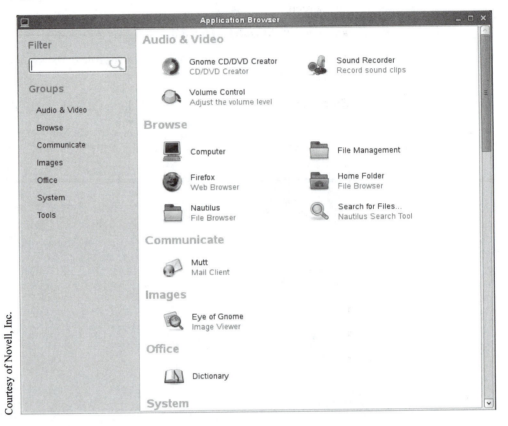

Courtesy of Novell, Inc.

Application Browser

The right frame of the application browser shows a list of the most important installed applications. The applications are grouped and you can see a list of the groups in the left frame. Select a group to see only the applications that belong to this group.

The Filter option adds even more flexibility. Enter a part of the name of the application you want to start in the **Filter** text box in the left frame. The filtered applications are shown immediately in the right frame. For example, type *file* and the right frame will show all applications that have the string "file" in their executable or in their description.

System Menu

The right frame of the main menu displays seven system options:

- **Help**. Starts the online help.

- **Control Center**. Starts the GNOME Control Center where you can configure your desktop.

- **YaST**. Starts the YaST system administration tool. YaST allows you to easily administer many aspects of SUSE Linux Enterprise Server 11.

- **Install Software**. Shows a list with the available software on your registered installation media.

- **Lock Screen**. Locks the screen. You have to enter your password to unlock the screen.

- **Logout**. Must be selected to log out of the system.

- **Shutdown**. Allows you to shut down or reboot the system after prompting for the root password.

Status Menu

At the bottom of the right frame you can open the Status Monitor to see the status of your hard drives, network, and processes. When you click the **Network** icon, you are prompted for the root password to open the YaST Network dialog where you can change the network configuration.

Manage Icons in GNOME

You can manage icons on your desktop in different ways. For simplicity, we will describe only the most important methods.

You can find icons in the following three areas on your desktop:

- Desktop Icons
- Panel Icons
- Main Menu Icons

Desktop Icons

To create an icon for an application on your desktop, do the following:

1. Select the item in your application menu.

2. Drag it to a free space on your desktop and release the mouse button.

   Notice there is a small plus icon by the mouse pointer when moving the icon. This indicates that a copy of the icon will be created.

To create a new folder on the desktop, do the following:

1. Right-click a free space on your desktop. A context menu appears:

Figure 1-10 *Desktop Context Menu*

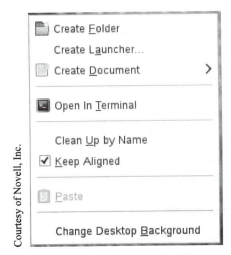

Courtesy of Novell, Inc.

At the top of the pop-up menu are three menu options that can be used to create a new icon:

- **Create Folder.** This creates a new and empty folder icon.

- **Create Launcher.** Creates a new application launcher.

- **Create Document.** Creates an empty document.

2. Select **Create Folder**.

3. When the icon appears, enter the folder's name.

Figure 1-11 *New Folder Name*

Courtesy of Novell, Inc.

To create a new Launcher

1. Right-click the desktop.

2. Select **Create Launcher**. A dialog appears:

Figure 1-12   *Create Launcher Dialog*

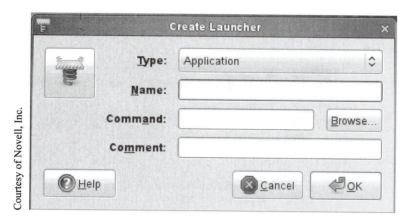

Courtesy of Novell, Inc.

3. Enter the following information:

    ■ **Type.** Type of file to be launched.

    ■ **Name.** Name and label of the launcher.

    ■ **Command.** Command that should be executed when double-clicking the launcher icon.

    ■ **Comment.** (Optional) Tool tip that appears when you hover the mouse pointer over the icon.

    ■ **Icon.** (Optional) Icon representing the launcher you are creating.

4. Click **OK**.

Depending on your installed software, various document types are available in this menu. Immediately after a default installation, however, you can create only an empty text file. To create a new document, do the following:

1. Right-click on the desktop.

2. Select **New Document**.

3. When the icon appears, enter the text file's name.

Figure 1-13   *New Document Name*

Courtesy of Novell, Inc.

Panel Icons

To add new programs to the bottom panel, do the following:

1. Right-click a free area of the panel.

2. Select **Add to Panel**.

3. From the dialog that appears, select the application you want to add.

4. Right-click its icon to add the program to the panel.

Figure 1-14   *Add to Panel Dialog*

Courtesy of Novell, Inc.

To remove a program from the control panel, do the following:

1. Right-click the program's icon in the bottom panel.

2. Select **Remove From Panel**.

To move icons in the panel, do the following:

1. Hold down the right mouse button.

2. Select **Move** from the Context menu.

Main Menu Icons

Only the user root is allowed to add a new entry to a menu. Normal users are only allowed to declare favorite applications. To add icons to your favorites, do the following:

1. Open the main menu in the panel.

The menu appears.

2. Select **More Applications**.

3. Select an application item in the right frame with the right mouse button.

4. Select **Add to Favorites** from the pop-up menu.

Use the GNOME File Manager (Nautilus)

GNOME provides its own file manager, called Nautilus.

Figure 1-15   *Nautilus File Browser*

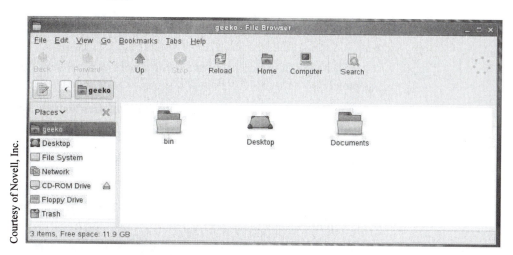

To start Nautilus, do one of the following:

■   Select the *username's* **Home** icon on the desktop.

    or

■   Select **Nautilus** from the main menu.

By default, Nautilus is marked as a favorite application. Normally, Nautilus shows the content of the user's home directory after starting. The right frame of the Nautilus window shows the content of the current directory.

You can see your current position in the location bar below the tool bar. All higher directories are shown as buttons. Select one of these buttons to switch into the higher directory.

The Nautilus Side Panel

The left frame is called *Side Panel*.

Figure 1-16   *Nautilus Side Panel*

Courtesy of Novell, Inc.

At the top of the side panel is a menu where you can select the content of the side panel:

- **Places.** Shows the most important directories and devices to store files.

- **Desktop.** Lists the contents of the desktop.

- **File System.** Shows the file system folders.

- **Network.** Shows any network locations.

- **CD-ROM Drive.** Shows the contents of any media in any CD-ROM drives present.

- **Floppy Drive.** Shows the contents of any media in any floppy drives present.

Exercise 1-1   *Work with GNOME*

In this exercise, you add a panel icon to and remove a panel icon from the bottom panel and you explore your GNOME desktop and learn how to use the GNOME File Manager Nautilus.

You will find this exercise at the end of the chapter.

(End of Exercise)

Objective 2   Configure Accessibility Settings

The Linux operating system includes a variety of accessibility tools. In this objective, you learn how to do the following:

■ Configure Keyboard Accessibility

■ Configure Visual Accessibility

Configure Keyboard Accessibility

Linux includes accessibility tools that address users who have physical impairments that may make it difficult for them to use a mouse or keyboard. The following are addressed here:

■ Using AccessX

■ Using On-Screen Keyboards

■ Using Mouse Gestures

Using AccessX

The AccessX application is included with the X Window software. It provides a graphical interface for configuring the following keyboard accessibility settings:

■ **StickyKeys**: This feature enables users to lock modifier keys such as Ctrl and Shift. This allows users to complete keyboard tasks that normally require two or more fingers with just one finger.

■ **MouseKeys**: This feature provides key sequences that can be used to move the mouse cursor on the screen and send mouse clicks to the application.

■ **SlowKeys**: This feature configures the keyboard so that the user must hold a key down for a configured period of time before the keystroke is sent; thus preventing accidental keystrokes from being sent.

■ **ToggleKeys**: This feature sounds an audible alert whenever Caps Lock and/or Num Lock is on.

■ **RepeatKeys**: This feature gives the user extra time to release a pressed key before sending multiple keystrokes to the application.

■ **BounceKeys** (also called **Delay Keys**): This feature is used to prevent the system from accepting unintentional keystrokes by inserting a delay between keystrokes.

The way you configure AccessX settings varies from Linux distribution to distribution. For most distributions, including SLES and SLED, you access the system Control Center and select the option to configure **Keyboard Preferences**. The interface used to configure these settings on a SLES 11 server system is shown below:

Figure 1-17   *Configuring Keyboard Accessibility Options*

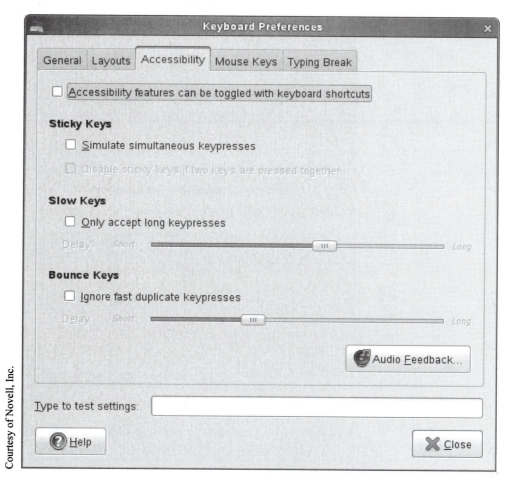

Likewise, mouse accessibility options are configured by selecting the **Mouse Preferences** option from the system Control Center. This is shown below:

Figure 1-18 *Configuring Mouse Accessibility Options*

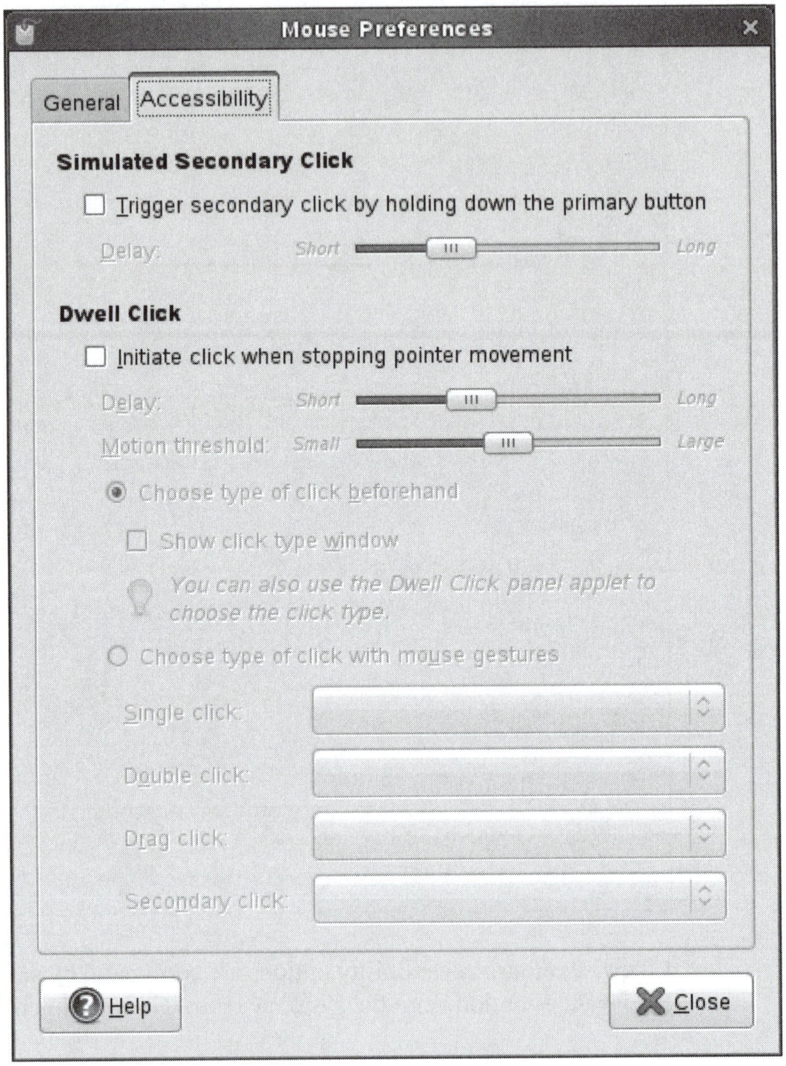

Courtesy of Novell, Inc.

These accessibility options can also be configured by selecting **Assistive Technologies** from the Control Center. When you do, the following is displayed:

Figure 1-19 *Accessing Assistive Technologies Preferences*

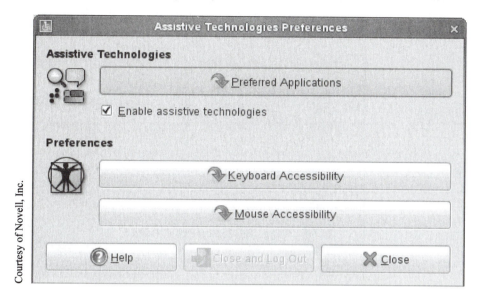

Courtesy of Novell, Inc.

The *Keyboard Accessibility* and *Mouse Accessibility* buttons in this screen take you to the screens shown in Figure 1-17 and Figure 1-18.

Using On-Screen Keyboards

In addition to keyboard and mouse accessibility tools, Linux also provides you the option of using an *on-screen keyboard*. An on-screen keyboard allows you to use a mouse (or any other pointing device) to select keys on a virtual keyboard. Some commonly used on-screen keyboard applications include the following:

- GTkeyboard

- GNOME Onscreen Keyboard (GOK)

- Dasher

You can configure an on-screen keyboard on SLES or SLED by accessing the Control Center and selecting Assistive Technologies > Preferred Applications. When you do, the following is displayed:

Figure 1-20   *Configuring Preferred Applications*

Courtesy of Novell, Inc.

In the Mobility drop-down list, select the on-screen keyboard you want to use; then select **Close**. In the figure above, the GNOME OnScreen Keyboard (GOK) has been selected and configured to run at startup.

NOTE: The GNOME OnScreen Keyboard can also be started manually by entering gok at the shell prompt.

The GOK on-screen keyboard is shown below:

Figure 1-21   *Using the GOK On-Screen Keyboard*

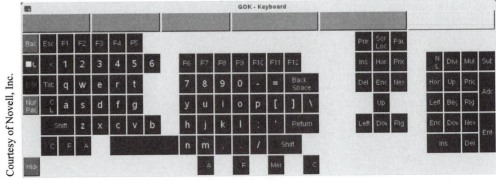

Courtesy of Novell, Inc.

Using Mouse Gestures

You can also configure mouse gestures in Linux. Essentially, gestures are the mouse equivalent of keyboard shortcuts. Using mouse gestures, you can configure Linux to complete a specified task when you move the mouse in a certain pattern.

For example, you could configure the system so that clicking and dragging to the left causes your Web browser to navigate back to the previous page viewed while clicking and dragging to the right causes it to navigate forward.

NOTE: To be able to use mouse gestures on most Linux distributions, you need to first install the **mousetweaks** software, available from (http://live.gnome.org/Mousetweaks/Home).

You can configure mouse gestures on a SUSE Linux Enterprise Desktop or Server system by doing the following:

1. Select **Computer** > **Control Center** > **Assistive Technologies** > **Mouse Accessibility**.

   The following is displayed:

Figure 1-22   *Configuring Mouse Gestures*

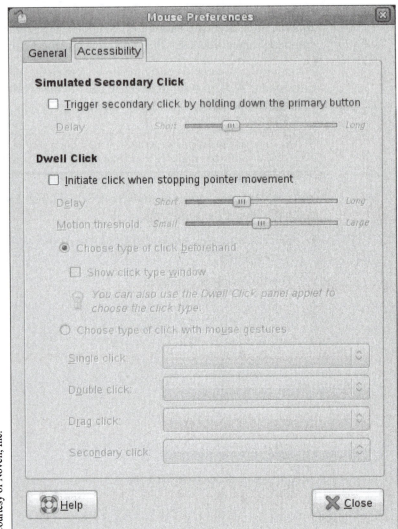

Courtesy of Novell, Inc.

2. Mark **Initiate Click When Stopping Pointer Movement**; then mark **Choose Type of Click with Mouse Gestures**.

3. Configure your desired actions using the following drop-down lists:

   ■ Single Click

   ■ Double Click

   ■ Drag Click

   ■ Secondary Click

4. Select **Close**.

Configure Visual Accessibility

In addition to keyboard accessibility features, Linux also provides tools for the visually impaired. The following are discussed here:

- Using Screen Readers and Magnifiers

- Using Braille Devices

- Using High-Contrast and Large-Text Desktop Themes

Using Screen Readers and Magnifiers

A *screen reader* application translates the text displayed on the screen into audio information that is "spoken" audibly for the user. Some applications do this through the computer's sound interface while others require speech synthesizer hardware. Some of the more commonly used screen readers include the following:

- **Emacspeak**: Provides a text-based interface for users who are visually impaired.

- **Jupiter Speech System**: Provides a screen reader for the Linux console.

- **Speaker**: Provides a screen reader plugin for the Konqueror file manager and Web browser environment.

- **Orca**: Provides a scriptable screen reader. It also incorporates various combinations of speech, braille, and magnification. Unlike many other screen readers, Orca works with the GNOME desktop.

A *screen magnifier* enables users that are partially sighted to enlarge areas of the screen, similar to using a physical magnifying glass. A wide variety of screen magnifiers are available for the Linux platform, including UnWindows and Xzoom. However, one of the most popular is Orca.

To run Orca, you can enter `orca -e magnifier` at the shell prompt. If you want it to run every time the system starts, access the Control Center and select **Personal** > **Assistive Technologies** > **Preferred Applications**. Select **Orca with Magnifier** from the Visual drop-down list and mark **Run At Start**; then select **Close**. This is shown in the figure below:

Figure 1-23   *Configuring a Screen Magnifier*

Courtesy of Novell, Inc.

NOTE: You can also select **GNOME Magnifier without Screen Reader** from the Visual drop-down list.

Once started, you can use the Orca Configuration GUI to customize the behavior and features of Orca. This can be done by selecting **Preferences** in the Orca window. The first thing you need to do is to configure the **Key Bindings** tab, shown below:

Figure 1-24   *Configuring Orca Key Bindings*

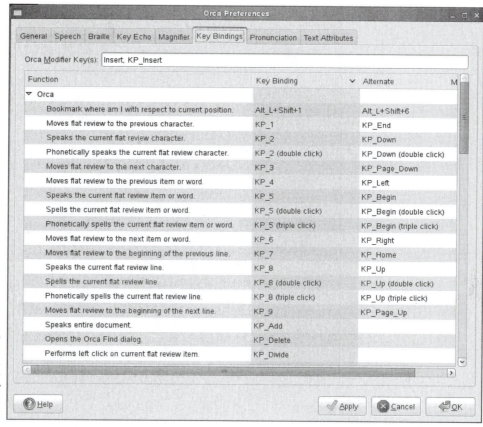

First, you need to specify your Orca Modifier key. This is the key that you press and hold in conjunction with other keys to give commands to Orca. By default, this is the Insert key on desktop systems and the Caps Lock key on notebook systems.

Once done, you can then configure the key bindings table for common Orca tasks. This table provides a list of Orca operations and the keys that are bound to them. The *Function* column provides a description of the operation. The *Key Binding* column lists the keystrokes required to invoke the operation. The *Alternate* column can be used to configure an alternate means for invoking the operation.

Next, you can configure screen magnification by selecting the Magnifier tab. When you do, the following is displayed:

Figure 1-25   *Configuring Orca Magnifier Settings*

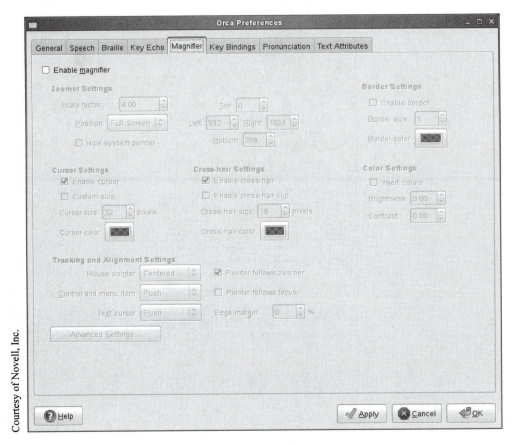

Courtesy of Novell, Inc.

To enable the magnifier feature of Orca, mark **Enable Magnifier**. Once enabled, you can then customize how the magnifier works using the following settings:

- **Zoomer Settings**: Determines magnification characteristics.

- **Border Settings**: Determines if a window border is visible for the magnifier and the size of the border in pixels.

- **Cursor Settings**: Determines the size and color of the magnifier's cursor. You can set the following:
  - Enable cursor
  - Custom size
  - Custom color

- **Cross-Hair Settings**: Determines the magnifier's optional area-targeting cursor. You can configure the following:
  - Enable cross-hair
  - Enable cross-hair clip
  - Cross-hair size
  - Cross-hair color

- **Color Settings**: Allows you to adjust the color of the magnified region. You can configure the following:

  - Invert colors

  - Brightness

  - Contrast

- **Tracking and Alignment Settings**: Controls the tracking of the mouse cursor. You can configure the following:

  - Mouse pointer

  - Pointer follows zoomer

  - Control and menu item

  - Text cursor

To enable screen reader functionality, select the Speech tab. When you do, the following is displayed:

Figure 1-26   *Configuring a Screen Reader*

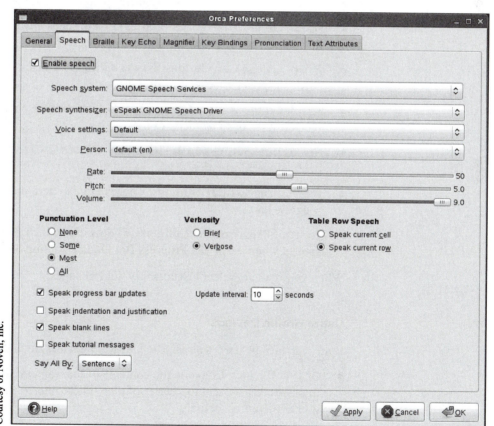

Courtesy of Novell, Inc.

You can configure the following on this tab:

- **Enable speech**: Determines whether or not Orca will use a speech synthesizer.

- **Speech System and Speech Synthesizer**: Determines the speech system Orca will use. GNOME-speech and Emacspeak are two of the most commonly used systems. After selecting a speech system, you can then select an available speech synthesizer.

- **Voice Settings**: Allows you to use multiple voices to identify different types of text in an application, such as hyperlinks or upper-case text.

- **Punctuation Level**: Allows you to adjust the amount of punctuation spoken by the synthesizer.

- **Verbosity**: Determines the amount of information to be spoken. For example, if set to **Verbose**, the synthesizer will speak shortcut keys for menu items. If set to **Brief**, shortcut keys are not spoken.

- **Table Row Speech**: Determines the way Orca reads table information.

- **Speak Blank Lines**: Determines whether blank lines will be spoken.

- **Speak Multicase Strings As Words**: Causes Orca to break multi-case words into separate words.

- **Speak Tutorial Messages**: Provides spoken tutorial messages.

- **Speak Object Mnemonics**: Causes Orca to speak any mnemonic associated with the object that has the focus (for example Alt+A).

- **Break Speech Into Chunks Between Pauses**: Causes Orca to insert brief pauses between spoken pieces of information.

- **Speak Child Position**: Causes Orca to announce the position of the item with the focus if it resides in a menu or a list.

- **Speak Indentation and Justification**: Causes Orca to speak justification and indentation information.

- **Speak Progress Bar Updates**: Causes Orca to periodically speak the status of progress bars.

- **Restrict Progress Bar Updates To**: Specifies which progress bars should be spoken when the Speak Progress Bar Updates option has been enabled.

When you're done, select **OK** to apply your changes.

Using Braille Devices

Linux can also be used with Braille hardware devices, including the following:

- **Braille Display**: Converts the contents of the standard display terminal into impulses that are sent to a series of pins. These pins form Braille symbols that the user experiences tactilely.

- **Braille Embosser**: Prints a hard copy of a text document using embossed Braille characters.

BRLTTY is a Linux service (daemon) which provides access to the Linux console in text mode for users using Braille displays. It drives the braille display and provides screen review functionality.

You can use Orca with BRLTTY to enhance the Braille functionality of the system. This can be done by selecting Preferences in the Orca window and selecting the Braille tab, shown below:

Figure 1-27   *Configuring Braille Settings in Orca*

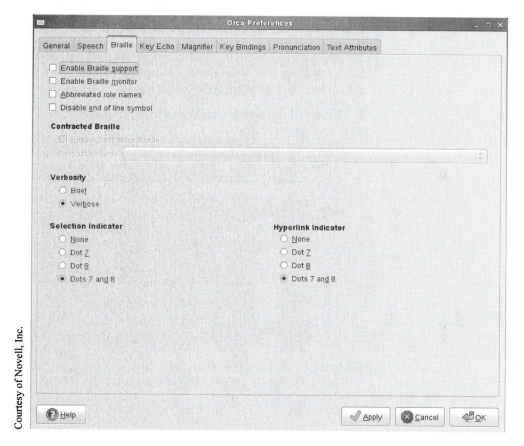

You can configure the following settings on this tab:

- **Enable Braille Support**: Configures Orca to use a Braille display.

NOTE: BRLTTY must be running on the system.

- **Enable Braille Monitor**: Enables an on-screen Braille monitor so you can visually see what's happening on the Braille display device.

- **Abbreviated Role Names**: Abbreviates role names on the Braille display.

- **Disable End of Line Symbol**: Configures Orca to not present the $l end-of-line characters.

- **Contracted Braille**: Configures Orca to use contracted Braille.

- **Verbosity**: Determines the amount of information that will be Brailled.

- **Selection Indicator**: Determines how selected text on screen will be underlined in Braille.

- **Hyperlink Indicator**: Determines how hypertext on screen will be underlined in Braille.

When you're done, select **OK** to save your changes.

Using High-Contrast and Large-Text Desktop Themes

You can also use high-contrast and large-text desktop themes to support visually impaired users. On SUSE Linux Enterprise systems (both Desktop and Server), this can be done by completing the following:

1. Select **Computer** > **Control Center** > **Appearance**.

NOTE: You can also right-click the desktop and select **Change Desktop Background > Theme**.

The following is displayed:

Figure 1-28   *Configuring Desktop Themes*

Courtesy of Novell, Inc.

2. Scroll down through the list of themes and locate themes that use high-contrast and/or large print, as shown below:

Figure 1-29   *Identifying High Contrast and Large Print Themes*

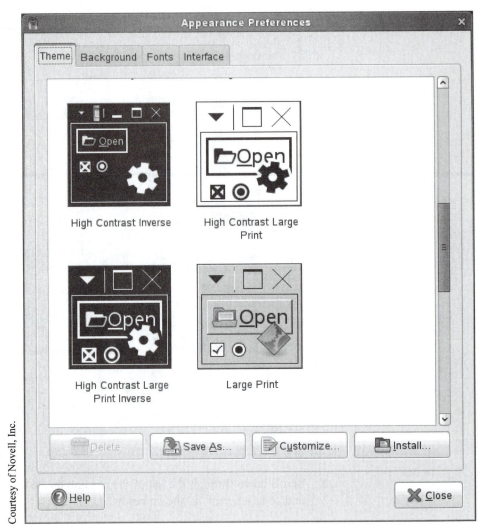

Courtesy of Novell, Inc.

3. Select the *theme* you want to use; then select Close.

TIP: You can use the Install option in this screen to install a custom theme you've created manually or downloaded from the Internet.

Objective 3   Access the Command Line Interface from the Desktop

A classic multi-user environment can be implemented by connecting several terminals (dialog stations)—monitor and keyboard units—to the serial interface of a single computer.

You can still connect several terminals to the serial interface in a Linux system; however this is hardly ever done anymore. To simulate such serial terminals, *virtual terminals* were created in Linux. With virtual terminals, you can work in Linux as if you had several classic terminals available at the same time.

By default, six virtual terminals are available. You can access them by holding Ctrl+Alt+F1 to Ctrl+Alt+F6. When you switch to a virtual terminal, a login prompt appears:

```
Welcome to SUSE Linux Enterprise Server 11 (i586) - Kernel
2.6.27.19-5-pae (tty1).


da1 login:
```

You can determine the terminal currently being used from the tty*x* number (tty1–tty6—tty is an abbreviation for *teletype*, which is another word for terminal).

From the virtual terminals, Alt+F7 returns you to the graphical user interface.

Instead of switching to the virtual terminals, you can access a terminal emulation window directly from the desktop: Right-click on the desktop and select **Open in Terminal**.

You can also start a terminal emulation from the main menu by clicking **More Applications** and selecting **GNOME Terminal** or **XTerm** from the **System** application group. If the KDE desktop environment is installed, you can also use KDE's terminal emulation, **Konsole**.

Figure 1-30   *GNOME Terminal*

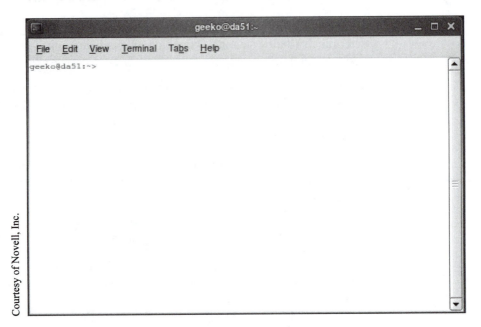

Courtesy of Novell, Inc.

The terminal appears inside a window with options (such as font and background color) you can select to modify the display of the terminal.

Exercise 1-2   **Access the Command Line Interface**

In this exercise, you practice switching to a virtual terminal and then switching back to the graphical user interface. You also log in to and out of a virtual terminal.

You will find this exercise at the end of the chapter.

(End of Exercise)

Objective 4   Work with the Linux Shell

The shell is the program that takes commands from the user, executes the command, and writes the output of these programs back to the screen. If you did the exercises in this course so far, you have already gained some familiarity with the shell, which is the program that runs within virtual terminals or terminal emulation windows.

This objective covers the Bash (Bourne Again Shell), which is the default shell in SUSE Linux Enterprise Server 11 (SLES 11), in more detail. To use the shell efficiently and effectively, you need to

- Understand Command Shells
- Use the Command Line Efficiently
- Work with Variables and Aliases
- Use Piping and Redirection
- Use the vi Editor to Edit Files
- Understand Shell Scripting Basics
- Work with the Linux Shell

Understand Command Shells

Because you cannot communicate directly with the Linux operating system kernel, you need to use a program that serves as an interface between the user and the operating system. In UNIX, such a program is called the shell.

The shell accepts a user's entries, interprets them, converts them to system calls, and delivers system messages back to the user, making the shell a command interpreter.

To understand command shells, you need to know the following:

- Types of Shells
- Bash Configuration Files

Types of Shells

UNIX has a whole series of shells, most of which are provided by Linux in freely usable versions. The following are examples of some popular shells:

- The Bourne Again shell or `bash` (`/bin/bash`). The standard Linux shell with many advanced features.
- The Bourne shell (`/bin/sh`, a symbolic link to `/bin/bash`). When called as /bin/sh, bash behaves as the original Bourne shell does.
- The Korn shell (`/bin/ksh`). Known for its rich scripting capabilities.
- The TC shell (`/bin/tcsh`). Enhanced C shell with file name completion and command line editing.
- The C shell (`/bin/csh`, a symbolic link to `/bin/tcsh`). Its syntax is modeled after the C programming language.

The various shells differ in the functionality they provide.

Every shell can be started like a program and you can switch at any time to a different shell. For example, you can switch to the TC shell by entering `tcsh` at the Bash prompt; you can switch to the Korn shell by entering `ksh`.

Unlike most other programs, an interactive shell does not terminate on its own. You need to enter the `exit` command at the shell prompt to return to the previous shell.

A shell is started at a text console right after a user logs in. This is called the login shell. Which shell is started for which user is determined in the user database.

The standard Linux shell is Bash, so we will only cover Bash in this objective.

Bash Configuration Files

To customize Bash for an interactive session, you need to know about the configuration files and about the order in which they are processed.

To understand how shells work, you need to know the difference between the following:

- Login Shells
- Non-Login Shells

Like most other Linux distributions, SLES 11 has a default setup that ensures users do not see any difference between a login shell and a non-login shell. In most cases, this is achieved by also evaluating the `~/.bashrc` file when a login shell is started.

Login Shells

A login shell is started whenever a user logs in to the system. In contrast, any shell started from within a running shell is a non-login shell. The only differences between these two are the configuration files read when starting the shell.

A login shell is also started whenever a user logs in through an X display manager. Therefore, all subsequent terminal emulation programs run non-login shells.

The following files are read when starting a login shell:

1. `/etc/profile` is a system-wide configuration file read by all shells. It sets global configuration options. This configuration file will be read not only by the Bash, but also by other shells.

   `~/.profile` is a file created for each new user by default on SLES 11. Any user-specific customizations can be stored in it.

2. `/etc/bash.bashrc` makes some useful configurations for the Bash. For example:

   - Appearance of the prompt
   - Colors for the `ls` command
   - Aliases

For your own system-wide bash configurations, use the `/etc/bash.bashrc.local` file that is imported from `/etc/bash.bashrc`.

`~/.bashrc` is a configuration file in which users store their customizations.

Non-Login Shells

When you use the `su` command to switch to user root, you will receive root's default shell, but it will be as a non-login shell.

The only way to exit a non-login shell is with the `exit` command.

The following files are read when a non-login shell is started:

- `/etc/bash.bashrc`
- `/etc/bash.bashrc.local`
- `~/.bashrc`

If you change any settings and want them to be applied during the same shell session, the changed configuration file needs to be read in again.

The proper way to read in a changed configuration file and to apply the changes to the current session is by using the `source` internal shell command, as in the following example:

```
source  ~/.bashrc
```

You can also use the "short form" of this command, which happens to be included in many configuration files, where it is used to read in other configuration files, as in the following (with a space between the period and the tilde):

```
.  ~/.bashrc
```

Use the Command Line Efficiently

A command on the command line is executed by typing the command name and pressing Enter. Depending on the command, options (usually a hyphen followed by one or more letters [such as `-lh`] or two hyphens and a word [such as `--help`]) and parameters (such as a file name) can be included on the command line to influence the behavior of the command.

Bash offers many features to facilitate its use in daily work. You can use the following to help make entering shell commands and administering SLES 11 much easier:

- Entering Commands at the Shell Prompt
- Completion of Commands and Filenames
- History Function
- Useful Commands
- Find Help for Commands

Entering Commands at the Shell Prompt

You can run a command from the shell prompt by entering the name of the command. However, depending upon where the binary executable file is located, you may also need to provide the path to the command.

When you specify a command to run, the Bash shell looks for the corresponding executable file in the directories contained in the PATH environment variable.

NOTE: Environment variables are addressed in detail later in this course.

You can view a list of directories contained in the PATH environment variable using the `echo $PATH` command at the shell prompt. An example is shown below:

```
geeko@da1:~/Desktop> echo $PATH
/home/geeko/bin:/usr/local/bin:/usr/bin:/bin:/usr/bin/X11:/usr/
X11R6/bin:/usr/games:/usr/lib/mit/bin:/usr/lib/mit/sbin
```

If the executable you want to run resides in a directory that is in the PATH environment variable, you can run it by simply entering its name at the shell prompt.

If, however, the executable you want to run resides in a directory that is not included in the PATH environment variable, you must manually specify the path to the file in the command. For example, if you need to run a file named `runme` in the `/home/geeko/` directory, you would need to enter `/home/geeko/runme` at the shell prompt.

It's important to remember that the Bash shell does **not** look in the current directory for the command. Even if you were to use the `cd` command to change the `/home/geeko` directory, you must still specify the path to the `runme` file to execute it from the shell prompt. However, because it resides in the current directory, you can simply add `./` to the front of the command.

You can also use the `exec` command to run a program. For example, if you had a program named runme, you could execute it by entering `exec runme` at the shell prompt (assuming path to the runme file is included in the PATH environment variable). This command isn't actually used that often as it is usually just as easy to run the command directly from the shell prompt, as discussed above.

However, the `exec` command does have a useful feature. When you run a command directly from the shell prompt, the new process it creates runs alongside the shell itself. However, using exec, new process created by the command replaces the shell. When you exit out of the application, it is as if the shell itself was terminated.

Completion of Commands and Filenames

The Bash supports a function of completing commands and filenames. Just enter the first characters of a command (or a filename) and press the Tab key. The Bash completes the name of the command.

If there is more than one possibility, the Bash shows all possibilities when you press the Tab key a second time. This feature makes entering long filenames very easy.

History Function

Bash stores the commands you enter so you have easy access to them. By default, the commands are written in the `.bash_history` file in the user's home directory. In SUSE Linux Enterprise Server 11, the size of this file is set to a maximum of 1,000 entries.

You can display the content of the file by using the `history` command.

You can display the commands stored in the history cache (one at a time) by using the arrow keys. The Up-arrow shows the previous command; the Down-arrow shows the next command. After finding the desired command, edit it as needed, then execute it by pressing Enter.

When browsing the entries of the history, you can also select specific commands. Type one or more letters, and press PageUp or PageDown to display the preceding or next command in the history cache beginning with this letter.

You can also search the history for a part of a command (not necessarily the beginning of the command). Press Ctrl+r and start typing the characters—the most recent matching command is displayed. Press Ctrl+r again to find an earlier matching command. Press Enter to execute the command displayed, or Tab to edit it before executing it.

Useful Commands

Throughout this course you will be introduced to many of the command line tools available. The following commands are useful when working with the Bash:

- su Command
- xargs Command

su Command

If you are working with a shell, you can become root user by entering the `su -` (switch user) command and the root password. The root user is comparable to the Administrator user in Windows. You have to log in as root to perform system administration tasks. The root user is the superuser and the only account with all the privileges needed to do anything in the system.

- When you enter `su`, you switch to root and stay in the same directory.
- When you enter `su -`, you switch to root's home directory.

You can check to make sure you are root by entering `id` or `whoami`. To quit the root administrator shell, enter the `exit` command.

If you want to switch to a user other than root, add the new user name, such as `su - tux`. If you are currently logged in as a normal user, you are prompted for the new user's password. If you are currently logged in as root, you are not prompted for the password.

xargs Command

Due to a limit imposed by the Linux kernel, the maximum length of a Bash command line is 128 kB. If, for instance, you want to delete all the files in a directory containing lots of files, you could encounter the following error message:

```
geeko@da2:/tmp/lotsoffiles> ls | wc -l
400000
geeko@da2:/tmp/lotsoffiles> rm *
bash: /bin/rm: Argument list too long
geeko@da2:/tmp/lotsoffiles>
```

NOTE: The wc (word count) command is used to count characters, words, or lines.

There are different ways to work around this.

One possibility is to use find with the -exec option. (The find command is covered in more detail in Use the find Command.) The time command is included in this example to measure the time the find command takes:

```
geeko@da2:/tmp/lotsoffiles> ls | wc -l
400000
geeko@da2:/tmp/lotsoffiles> time find -type f -exec rm {} \;
real    17m17.109s
user    4m18.224s
sys     12m49.244s
geeko@da2:/tmp/lotsoffiles>
```

The disadvantage of this approach is that it takes quite some time, as the rm command is called separately for each file.

A faster way is to use the xargs command. It breaks down a long command line into chunks of 128 kb, and passes each 128 kb section as an argument to the command listed after xargs:

```
geeko@da2:/tmp/lotsoffiles> ls | wc -l
400000
geeko@da2:/tmp/lotsoffiles> time ls | xargs rm
real    0m26.628s
user    0m1.892s
sys     0m24.794s
geeko@da2:/tmp/lotsoffiles>
```

As you can see, this is *much* faster because rm is executed only 21 times, instead of 400,000 times when using the find command with the -exec option.

Find Help for Commands

Within the SUSE Linux Enterprise System, there are three main areas where you get help for commands. You need to be able to

- Access and Use man Pages
- Use info Pages
- Use System Documentation

Access and Use man Pages

The most important command for help is `man` (an abbreviation of manual or man page). To display the man page of the `man` command, open a command prompt and enter: `man man`.

If the English man pages are not shown automatically with the `man` command, you can display the English version of the man page by using the option `LANG=en_EN`.

For example, to display the English version of the man page for the `man` command, enter the following: `LANG=en_EN man man`.

Using the parameter `LANG=en_EN` switches to the English language for the requested man pages only.

NOTE: All manual pages are available in English and many have been translated into other languages. Because these translations are often incomplete or not maintained, we recommend using the English versions.

The header of each manual page contains the command name at the left and right sides and the section number to which the manual page belongs. In the center of the header is the name of the section. The last line usually contains the date of the last changes.

The section numbers indicate the following subject matters:

Table 1-1   *Manual Page Section Numbers and Topics*

Section	Contents
1	Executable programs and shell commands (user commands)
2	System calls
3	Functions and library routines
4	Device files
5	Configuration files and file formats
6	Games
7	Macro packages and file formats
8	System administration commands

An individual manual page is usually divided into the following parts:

Table 1-2 *Sections Within Manual Pages*

Part	Contents
NAME	Name and short description of the command
SYNOPSIS	Description of the syntax
DESCRIPTION	Detailed description of the command
OPTIONS	Description of all available options
COMMANDS	Instruction that can be given to the program while it is running
FILES	Files connected in some way to the command
SEE ALSO	Hints on related commands
DIAGNOSTICS	Possible error messages of the program
EXAMPLES	Examples of calling up a command
BUGS	Known errors and problems with the command

Manual pages are, by default, displayed by the `less` command. Therefore, you can navigate within a manual page with the same keys that are used when viewing text files with the `less` command:

Table 1-3 *Keys that Can Be Used with Less*

Key Command	Description
Space	Page one screen forward.
b	Page one screen backward.
PageDown	Page half a screen forward.
PageUp	Page half a screen backward.
Down-arrow, Enter	Jump one line forward.
Up-arrow	Jump one line backward.
End	Go to end of the manual page.
Home	Go to beginning of the manual page.
/expression	Search forward from the current cursor position for *expression*; matching line is displayed as first line on the screen.
?expression	Search backwards from current cursor position for *expression*; matching line is displayed as first line on the screen.
n	Move to next instance of expression in the search.
N	Move to previous instance of expression in the search.
q	End display of the manual page.

For example, entering the following displays general information about the `crontab` command:

```
man 1 crontab
```

Entering the following displays information about the configuration file for the `crontab` command (the configuration file is also named crontab):

```
man 5 crontab
```

It is especially important to know to which section a command belongs when there is more than one manual for a command.

If you just enter `man crontab` without the number of the section, a dialog allows you to choose which manual page you want to look at.

You can display a brief description of all the available manual pages for a command or utility by using the `whatis` command, as in the following:

```
geeko@da2:~> whatis uname
uname (1)              - print system information
uname (2)              - get name and information about current kernel
uname (1p)             - return system name
uname (3p)             - get the name of the current system
geeko@da2:~>
```

Depending on the distribution, `whatis` reads different databases. On SLES11 it uses the manual index that is created with the `mandb` command, on other distributions it uses whatis files created with the `makewhatis` command.

If you enter `man -k keyword` or `apropos keyword`, a list of manual pages in which the keyword appears in the NAME section is displayed. For example:

```
geeko@da2:~> man -k printf
asprintf (3)              - print to allocated string
bitmap_scnlistprintf (9) - convert bitmap to list format ASCII string
bitmap_scnprintf (9)     - convert bitmap to an ASCII hex string
bitmap_scnprintf_len (9) - return buffer length needed to convert
dprintf (3)              - print to a file descriptor
format (n)               - Format a string in the style of sprintf
...
```

NOTE: In SLES 11, the manual pages are located in the /usr/share/man/ directory.

Use info Pages

Many programs no longer use the man pages. Instead, the help information can be found in information files which can be accessed with the `info` command.

In SUSE Linux Enterprise Server 11, the info files are located in the `/usr/share/info/` directory.

The following is the beginning of the info file for the `info` command:

Figure 1-31   *The info Command*

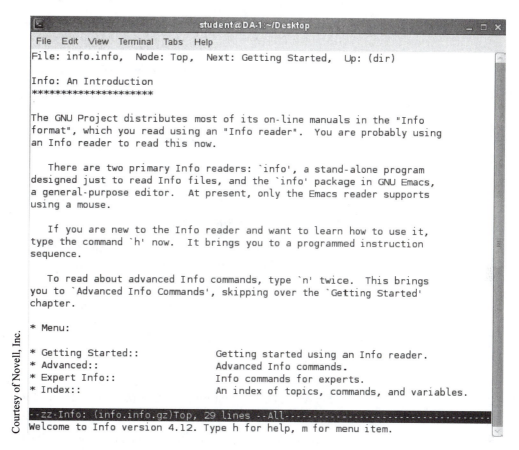

Courtesy of Novell, Inc.

The following are advantages of the info file format:

- It uses a structured document setup.

- Specific sections can be reached directly from the table of contents.

- Specific sections can be linked.

The following are the most commonly used key commands for the info command:

Table 1-4   *Keys Used Within the info Command*

Key Command	Description
Space, PageDown	Page down one screen.
Backspace, PageUp	Page up one screen.
b	Move cursor to the beginning of current info page.
e	Move cursor to the end of current info page.
Tab	Move cursor to the next reference (*).

Key Command	Description
Enter	Follow the reference.
n	Move to the next info page of the same level (Next:).
p	Move to the previous info page of the same level.
u	Move one level higher.
l	Move back to the last text displayed; end help.
s	Search in the info page.
h	Display help.
?	List a summary of commands.
q	End display of info document.

Use System Documentation

In addition to the manual and info pages that come with most of the command line programs, for many programs additional information is available in the /usr/share/doc directory:

- **/usr/share/doc/packages/**. This directory contains many subdirectories named as the program they refer to. Usually you find in these subdirectories license information, change logs, readme files, and similar information for the respective program.

- **/usr/share/doc/manual/**. This directory contains the SUSE Linux Enterprise Server 11 administration and other manuals relevant for the system administration of your Linux system.

- **/usr/share/doc/release-notes/**. This directory contains the release notes that are displayed at the end of the installation.

- **/usr/share/doc/licenses/**. This directory contains the GPL and LGPL license texts.

Work with Variables and Aliases

Two features make working with the Bash more powerful:

- Variables

- Aliases

Variables

With shell and environment variables, you are able to configure the behavior of the shell and adjust its environment to your own requirements.

The convention is to write variables such as PATH in uppercase letters. If you set your own variables, they should also be written in capitals for the sake of clarity.

Environment variables are used to control the behavior of a program that is started from a shell. Shell variables, on the other hand, are used to control the behavior of the shell itself.

Some important environment variables include the following:

- **USER.** The login name of the actual user.

- **HOME.** The user's home directory.

- **PATH.** When a program is called up, the program is searched for in the directories specified here (each separated by ":"). The order in which directories are listed is important, since they are searched in turn.

  The path elements are defined in the /etc/profile file as well as in files in the /etc/profile.d/ directory.

- **PS1.** This variable specifies what the primary prompt, such as geeko@da1:~> looks like. This variable is set in /etc/bash.bashrc.

- **PS2.** This variable specifies the secondary prompt string, such as "> ", which is also the default value used by Bash unless set differently in one of the Bash configuration files.

- **EDITOR.** This variable defines which editor is started, for instance when switching from less to an editor by pressing the v key.

  In SLES11 EDITOR is not set by default, but an entry is already prepared in ~/.bashrc that you can edit according to your needs.

- **PAGER.** This variable determines which program is used as pager, for instance, when viewing manual pages.

  This variable is set to less by default in /etc/profile.

- **PRINTER.** This variable can be used to store the name of the default printer. It is not set by default in SLES11, you can specify a value for it in ~/.bashrc as needed.

To display the value of all environment variables, enter env at the shell prompt, as shown below:

```
geeko@da2:~ > env
LESSKEY=/etc/lesskey.bin
ORBIT_SOCKETDIR=/tmp/orbit-geeko
INFODIR=/usr/local/info:/usr/share/info:/usr/info
NNTPSERVER=news
MANPATH=/usr/local/man:/usr/share/man
HOSTNAME=da1
XKEYSYMDB=/usr/share/X11/XKeysymDB
SHELL=/bin/bash
TERM=xterm
HOST=da1
HISTSIZE=1000
...
```

To display the value of a single shell or environment variable, enter `echo $variable`, as in the following:

```
geeko@da2:~ > echo $HOME
/home/geeko
```

To set the value of a variable or to create a new variable, use the syntax `variable=value`, as in the following:

```
da2:~ # MYVAR=myvalue
da2:~ # echo $MYVAR
myvalue
da2:~ #
```

The value can be a number, a character, or a string. If the string includes a space, you have to write the value in full quotes, as in the following:

```
da2:~ # MYVAR="my value"
da2:~ # echo $MYVAR
my value
da2:~ #
```

You can use the `unset` command to remove the value assigned to a variable. For example, to delete the value assigned to MYVAR in the example above, you would enter `unset MYVAR` at the shell prompt.

Variables set by the user in local Bash configuration files, such as `~/.bashrc`, take precedence over the values the system administrator has set, for instance, in `/etc/profile` or `/etc/profile.local`.

Aliases

Defining aliases allows you to create shortcuts for commands and their options or to create commands with entirely different names. Aliases can save you a lot of typing by assigning short names to long commands.

In SUSE Linux Enterprise Server 11, whenever you enter the `dir`, `md`, or `ls` command, for instance, you will be using aliases.

You can find out about the aliases defined on your system with the `alias` command. This will show you that

- `dir` is an alias for `ls -l`
- `md` is an alias for `mkdir -p`

To see whether a given command is an alias for something else, use the `type` command. For each command specified, `type` will tell you whether it is a built-in shell command, a regular command, a function, or an alias.

For regular commands, the output of `type` lists the path to the corresponding executable. For aliases, it lists the elements aliased:

```
geeko@da2:~> type -a ls
ls is aliased to `/bin/ls $LS_OPTIONS'
ls is /bin/ls
```

The above example shows that `ls` is an alias although, in this case, it is only used to add some options to the command.

The `-a` option was used with `type` to show both the content of the alias and the path to the original `ls` command. The output shows that `ls` is always run with the options stored in the `LS_OPTIONS` variable.

These options cause `ls` to list different file types in different colors (among other things).

Most of the aliases used on a system-wide basis are defined in the `/etc/bash.bashrc` file. Aliases are defined with the `alias` command and can be removed with the `unalias` command.

For example, entering `unalias ls` removes the alias for `ls`, causing `ls` to stop coloring its output.

The following is the syntax for defining aliases:

```
alias aliasname="command options"
```

An alias defined in this way is only valid for the current shell and will not be inherited by subshells, as in the following:

```
geeko@da2:~> alias ps="echo Hello"
geeko@da2:~> ps
Hello
geeko@da2:~> bash
geeko@da2:~> ps
 PID TTY        TIME CMD
 858 pts/0   00:00:00 bash
 895 pts/1   00:00:00 bash
 ...
```

To make an alias persistent, you need to store the definition in one of the shell's configuration files. In SUSE Linux Enterprise Server 11, the `~/.alias` file is created for personal aliases defined by each user.

This file is read in by `~/.bashrc`, where a command is included to that effect. Aliases are not relevant to shell scripts, but they can be a real time saver when using the shell interactively.

Use Piping and Redirection

Linux has three standard data channels:

Figure 1-32   *Standard Input, Output, and Error Output*

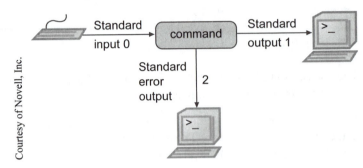

- **Standard input (stdin).** The currently running program reads the input from this channel (usually the keyboard).

- **Standard output (stdout).** The program sends its output to this channel (usually the monitor).

- **Standard error (stderr).** Errors are issued through this channel (usually the monitor).

These input and output channels (also referred to as file descriptors) are assigned the following numbers:

Table 1-5   *Input and Output Channel Numbers*

Channel	Number Assigned
Standard input (stdin)	0
Standard output (stdout)	1
Standard error output (stderr)	2

Each channel can be redirected by the shell. For example, stdin can come from a file or stdout and stderr can be directed to a file. The following are the redirection characters:

Table 1-6   *Input/Output Redirection*

Redirection Character	Description
< file	Redirects standard input.
> file	Redirects standard output (> without a preceding number is just an abbreviation for 1>), overwrites file.
>> file	Redirects standard output, appends to file.
2> file	Redirects standard error output.

The following is an example of a standard input, standard output, and standard error output:

```
geeko@da2:~ > ls /opt /recipe
/bin/ls: /recipe: No such file or directory
/opt:
gnome kde3
```

If the standard error output is redirected to /dev/null, only the standard output is displayed on the screen:

```
geeko@da2:~ > ls /opt /recipe 2> /dev/null
/opt:
gnome kde3
```

To redirect standard output and standard error output to a file (such as list), enter the following:

```
ls /opt /recipe > list 2>&1
```

First, the standard output is redirected to the list file (> list); then the standard error output is directed to the standard output (2>&1). The & refers to the file descriptor that follows (1 for the standard output).

You can display the contents of the list file by using the cat command, as in the following:

```
geeko@da2:~> cat list
/bin/ls: /recipe: No such file or directory
/opt:
gnome
kde3
```

This option of process communication is available not only in the shell, but can also be used in programs directly. All known files in the system can be used as input or output.

Occasionally, you might want to use a file as input for a program that expects input from the keyboard. To do this, the standard input is redirected, as in the following:

```
geeko@da2:~ # echo "Hello Tux,
>
> how are you?
> Is everything okay?" > greetings
geeko@da2:~ # mail tux < greetings
```

First, the text is redirected to the greetings file through the > command. The e-mail program, mail, receives its input from the greetings file (not the keyboard), and then the e-mail program sends the e-mail to the user tux.

The output of one command can be used as the input for another command by using the pipe ("|"):

```
command1 | command2
```

In a pipe, a maximum of 4 KB of not-yet-processed data can exist. If the process creating the output tries to write to a full pipe, it is stopped and only allowed to continue if the writing process can be completed. On the other side, the reading process is stopped if it tries to read an empty pipe.

```
geeko@da2:~ > ls -l /etc | less
```

Occasionally the user might want output from a command displayed on the screen and written to a file. This can be done using the `tee` command:

```
ls -l | tee output
```

In this example, the output of the command is displayed on the screen as well as written to the `output` file.

To redirect the output of several consecutive commands on the command line, the commands must be separated with semi-colons and enclosed in parentheses:

```
(command1; command2; ...)
```

```
geeko@da2:~> (id ; ls ~) > output
geeko@da2:~> cat output
uid=1000(geeko) gid=100(users)
groups=14(uucp),16(dialout),33(video),100(users)
bin
Desktop
Documents
output
public_html
geeko@da2:~>
```

The shell starts a separate subshell for processing the individual commands. To redirect the linked commands, the shell must be forced to execute the command chain in the same subshell by enclosing the expression in parentheses.

Upon completion, every program returns a value that states the success of the execution. If this return value is 0, the command completed successfully. If an error occurred, the return value is greater than 0. (Depending on the program, different return values indicate different errors.)

You can use the `echo $?` command to display a return value.

The return value can be used to trigger the execution of another command:

Table 1-7 *The && and || Operators*

Link	Result
command1 && command2	command2 is only executed if command1 is completed without any errors.
command1 || command2	command2 is only executed if command1 is completed with an error.

The following illustrates using both "||" and "&&":

```
geeko@da2:~> ls recipe || ls ~
/bin/ls: recipe: No such file or directory
bin  Desktop  Documents  output  public_html  test
geeko@da2:~> ls recipe && ls ~
/bin/ls: recipe: No such file or directory
geeko@da2:~>
```

The recipe file does not exist and the `ls recipe` command leads to an error. Because of this, the `ls ~` command is executed in the first line, but not in the fourth line.

Use the vi Editor to Edit Files

Even if the vi editor needs some getting used to, it is nevertheless necessary for a Linux system administrator to at least know its basic functions to be able to open, edit, and save configuration files. If the system is unusable for some reason, the vi editor might be the only editor available within, for instance, a rescue system.

In SUSE Linux Enterprise Server and Desktop, `vim` (vi improved) by Bram Moolenaar is the standard vi editor. When you enter `vi`, vim is started via a link to it.

You can start vi by entering `vi` or `vim`, followed by various options, and the name of a file to edit, as in the following example:

`vi exercise`

If a file does not yet exist, it is created.

You can move the cursor with the `k`, `j`, `h`, and `l` keys (k - one line up, j - one line down, h - to the left, l - to the right) or by using the arrow keys (Up, Down, Left, and Right).

In contrast to many other editors, vi is mode-oriented. When vi is first started, it is in command mode. Anything you enter in this mode is considered a command. You must switch to input mode before you can type any text. This can be frustrating to users who are unfamiliar with vi.

In addition to switching modes, you must learn which keys perform which actions because you cannot use the mouse. However, the number of commands needed for everyday work is fairly small, and you can get used to them quickly.

To enter text, you must first switch the editor to input mode by typing `i` (insert) or pressing the Insert key. At the bottom of the screen, you will see the message -- INSERT--.

Press Esc once to take you back to the command mode. From command mode you can switch to command-line mode by entering ":". The cursor jumps to the last line after ":" and waits for a command entry.

A command will only be carried out in command-line mode after you press Enter. Then you are automatically back in command mode.

The following is a summary of the available modes:

- **Command mode**: When vi starts, it is automatically in this mode. In command mode, vi can be given commands. The i command puts it into insert mode and the : command switches it to command-line mode.

- **Insert mode**: In this mode, vi accepts all input as text. Return to command mode with Esc.

- **Command-line mode**: In this mode, vi accepts commands from the vi command line. Pressing Enter causes the command to be executed and automatically returns to the command mode.

You can use the following commands in command mode:

Table 1-8 *Commands in vi in Command Mode*

Command	Result
i or Insert	Switches vi to insert mode.
x or Delete	Deletes the character where the cursor is.
dd	Deletes the line in which the cursor is located and copies it to the buffer.
D	Deletes the rest of the current line from the cursor position.
yy	Copies the line in which the cursor is located to the buffer.
p, P	Inserts the contents of the buffer after/before current cursor position.
a	Append after cursor.
A	Append after line.
C	Change to the end of the line.
cc	Change the whole line.
ZZ	Saves the current file and ends vi.
u	Undoes the last operation.
/pattern	Searches forward from the cursor position for *pattern*.
?pattern	Searches backward from the cursor position for *pattern*.
n	Repeats the search in the same direction.
N	Repeats the search in the opposite direction.
h	Moves the cursor left one character.
l	Moves the cursor right one character.
j	Moves the cursor down one line.
k	Moves the cursor up one line.
0	Moves the cursor to start of current line.

If you want to use a command for several units, place the corresponding number in front of the command. For example, 3x deletes three characters, 5dd deletes five lines, and 7yy copies seven lines to the buffer.

You can use the following commands in command-line mode:

Table 1-9   *Commands in vi in Command-Line Mode*

Command	Result
:q	Ends vi (if no changes were made).
:q!	Ends vi without saving changes in the file.
:wq or :x	Saves the current file and ends vi.
:w	Saves the current file.
:w *file*	Saves the current file under the name *file*. (Note: You continue editing the original file, not the new file.)
w!	Overwrites the current file.
e!	Forgets changes since last write.

NOTE: If you want to configure vi, you have to edit the ~/.vimrc file. By default, this file does not exist. You can find vimrc template files in the /usr/share/doc/packages/vim/ directory that you can copy to ~./.vimrc and edit according to your needs.

Understand Shell Scripting Basics

Bash is not only an interactive command interpreter, it also includes a script programming language. Shell scripts are used during system start and to start and stop services. An administrator can significantly reduce his workload by writing scripts that take care of tasks that involve several steps. Moreover, these scripts can then be scheduled to run automatically using the cron and at tools covered later in this course.

To write a simple shell script and to understand scripts you find in the SUSE Linux Enterprise Server 11 system, you have to understand the following:

- Elements of a Shell Script

- Running BASH Commands in a Script

- Reading User Input

- A Simple Script

- Control Structures

- Writing Functions

Elements of a Shell Script

A shell script is basically an ASCII text file containing commands to be executed in sequence. To allow this, it is important that permissions for the script file are set to r (readable) and x (executable) for the user that runs it.

However, the execute permission is not granted by default to newly created files. To assign this permission, you need to use a command such as the following:

```
chmod +x script.sh
```

NOTE: You can also execute the script from another shell with a command such as the following:

```
bash script.sh
```

In this case it is not necessary to make the script executable.

On SUSE Linux Enterprise Server 11, /bin/sh is a link to /bin/bash. When invoked as sh script.sh, some Bash features are not available and your script might not work as intended if it relies on some of these features.

If you want to be able to run the script by using its name alone, the directory where the script is located must be listed in the $PATH variable. If there is a bin directory in the home directory of a user, this directory is included in $PATH by default in SUSE Linux Enterprise Server 11.

Shell scripts in a directory that is not listed in $PATH must be started with the full path name or a relative path name such as ./script.sh.

When naming script files, it is a good idea to add an .sh extension to the filename. Linux doesn't require it, but it ensures that the file can easily be recognized by the system administrator as a shell script.

If you do not add the suffix, you need to make sure the filename is not identical to existing commands. For example, a common mistake is to name a script "test" which interferes with the test command line tool.

Within a script, empty lines and lines starting with a # character are ignored. The # character is used to add comments to your script. As a general practice, you should add a comment in the beginning, giving a brief overview of what the script is supposed to do, and also add comments throughout your script to explain what a line or section does. This makes it much easier for you and others to understand the script when you go back to it after some time to modify it.

The first line of a script defines the shell used to execute the script. This line is sometimes referred to as the she-bang line. Only this first line is interpreted despite the fact it starts with a # character. It has the following syntax:

```
#!/bin/bash
```

All subsequent lines of the script are either comments (starting with a # character) or actual commands.

Running BASH Commands in a Script

Scripts can be used to do many things, such as displaying text on the screen or running shell commands. The commands contained within the script are executed in the order they appear.

Reading User Input

In addition to running a sequence of commands, you can also have your scripts ask the user a question and then capture the user's response for processing. This is done using the `echo` command in conjunction with `read variable_name` command.

The `echo` command is used to present the user with a question. The `read variable_name` command is used to pause the script, present a prompt on the screen, and read the information the user supplies into a variable. For example:

```
#!/bin/bash
#An example of reading user input.
echo "What is your name?"
read MYNAME
echo "Greetings " $MYNAME
exit 0
```

In this example, the user is asked to enter his or her name with the `echo` command. Then the `read` command is used to read the user input into a variable named **MYNAME**. The `echo` command is then used to display the value in the variable on the screen.

TIP: Remember, you must use a $ (dollar sign) when referencing a variable with the `echo` command. The $ tells `echo` that the text which follows is a variable and that it should display the current value of the variable on the screen.

Notice that you didn't have to declare the MYNAME variable in the script. With many scripting and programming languages, you have to first declare a variable, set its size, and specify what type of information (text string, real number, integer, Boolean value, etc.) it will contain.

The Bash shell is a little more forgiving. The Bash shell will create the variable in memory dynamically from the `read` command and assign the user's input as its value. However, be aware that any value read into the variable will be formatted as text, even if numbers are placed in the variable.

If you want to mathematically manipulate numbers in variables, then you will need to first declare and type the variables you will use in the script. This is done using the `declare` command. The syntax is `declare type variable_name`. For example: `declare -i A`.

This line declares a variable named **A** and types it as **integer**. Values placed in the A variable, then, must be integers. In this situation, you can mathematically manipulate the value of A in your script. Consider the following script:

```
#!/bin/bash
#An example of declaring variables.
declare -i A
declare -i B
declare -i C
echo "Enter a number:"
read A
echo "Enter a second number:"
read B
C=$A+$B
echo "The sum of A and B is " $C
exit 0
```

In this example, the user input from each of the read commands is typed as an integer in the variables A and B. Then A and B are added together and the result is assigned to the variable C, which is also typed as an integer. The echo command is then used to display the result on the screen.

A Simple Script

In an example of a very simple script, the rsync command is used to back up files. rsync allows users to efficiently copy files from one directory to another or from one machine to another over the network. Its main advantage is that when updating a backup, only the differences between files are copied, not the entire files, speeding up the update remarkably.

rsync can be controlled with various options. Therefore, even if a script contains only one command, it can save some typing because you do not need to type the options each time rsync is invoked.

The following script is supposed to copy the user's home directory to the /tmp directory. The script needs the following elements, the she-bang line, a comment that explains what the script does, and the rsync command itself. The script could look like the following:

```
#!/bin/bash
#
# simple-backup1.sh
# Back up geeko's home directory to /tmp using rsync

rsync -a --no-whole-file /home/geeko /tmp
```

The -a (archive) option ensures the permissions are kept and directories are copied recursively. The --no-whole-file option makes sure only the changed parts of the files are updated, not the whole files copied. This does not make a difference on the initial copy, but it does speed up updates.

When you execute the script, there is no output, which is consistent with the usual behavior of Linux command line programs of "no message = success." However, if you want to see some information, you can add a message to the script:

```
#!/bin/bash
#
# simple-backup2.sh
# Backup geeko's home directory to /tmp using rsync

echo "Backing up /home/geeko to /tmp/"

rsync -a --no-whole-file /home/geeko /tmp
```

The `echo` command can be used to output text to the terminal. The `-e` option lets `echo` interpret backslash sequences. These can be used to format the output to some extent.

The following is a list of other backslash sequences that can be used with echo and what they output:

- \\ Backslash

- \a Alert (beep tone)

- \b Backspace

- \c Trailing new line

- \f Form feed

- \n New line

- \r Carriage return

- \t Horizontal tab

- \v Vertical tab

Bash scripting is not limited to listing commands in a file. In addition to features already covered, such as variables and the redirection of output to a file or as input to another program, Bash features include:

- **Command substitution**: The output of a command is used within the command line of another program. A possible use of this is to create file names that contain the current date, such as `touch file-$(date +%Y-%m-%d)`.

- **Control structures**: Bash supports the usual `if`, `while`, `until`, `for`, and `case` structures found similarly in other scripting languages.

- **Arithmetic operators**: Bash supports integer calculations (floating point calculations require the use of additional tools such as `bc`).

- **Arrays**: Arrays, which are basically variables that can hold more than one value, are available in Bash.

Control Structures

You can also add control structures to your shell scripts. The scripts presented so far execute straight through from beginning to end. You can enhance these scripts by using control structures to add decision points. You may need the script to determine a course of action based on what the user inputs.

This can be done by using the following:

- test Command

- if/then/else

- case

- Looping Structures

- seq Command

test Command

The `test` command is used to find out if a certain condition is true or false. This is most frequently used within control structures. You could, for instance, test if a file exists, and if so, do something; if not, do something else:

```
if test -f /tmp/message
  then
    echo "File /tmp/message exists, its content is as follows: "
    cat /tmp/message
  else
    echo "File /tmp/message does not exist"
fi
```

The conditions that can be tested with `test` include the following:

- test "STRING1" == "STRING2": True if strings are equal (a single = can be used as well in this comparison)

- test "STRING1" != "STRING2": True if strings are not equal

- test INTEGER1 -eq INTEGER2: True if INTEGER1 is equal to INTEGER2

- test INTEGER1 -lt INTEGER2: True if INTEGER1 is less than INTEGER2

- test INTEGER1 -gt INTEGER2: True if INTEGER1 is greater than INTEGER2

- test -e FILE. True if FILE exists

- test -f FILE. True if FILE exists and is a regular file

The above list is by no means complete. You can find more information by entering `man test` or `man bash` and searching for **test** within the Bash manual page.

if/then/else

An if/then/else structure gives your script the ability to execute different commands based on whether or not a particular condition is true or false, as shown below:

Figure 1-33   *if/then/else Structure*

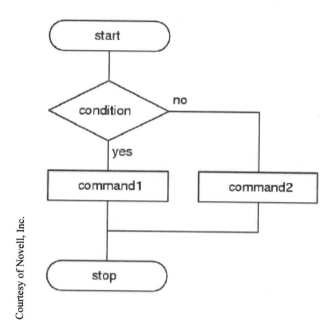

The syntax of this structure is as follows:

```
if condition; then
     commands
else
     commands
fi
```

This structure must begin with if and end with fi. The first line of the structure (if condition then) tells the shell to determine if the specified condition is true or false. If true, then the commands under the then part of the structure are run. If the condition is false, then the commands under the else part of the structure are run. For example:

```
#! /bin/bash
#An example of if/then/else
echo "Do you wish to continue? (yes/no)"
read ANSWER
if test $ANSWER = "yes"; then
     echo "The script will continue..."
else
     echo "The script will exit..."
     exit 0
fi
exit 0
```

In this example, the user is asked if he wants to continue. The user's input from the prompt is read into the **ANSWER** variable. The `if` statement then tests whether the value of ANSWER equals the text string "yes".

If true, the commands under `then` are executed. If not, then the commands under `else` are executed, which, in this example, simply exits the script.

case

The case statement is an enhanced version of the if/then/else statement. The if/then/else statement works well if your condition can be evaluated in one of two ways.

The case statement, however, allows you to use conditions that can be evaluated in many different ways. While you could use a series of multiple if/then/else statements instead of a case statement in this situation, your script could get very messy.

If you have a condition that can be evaluated to return more than two responses, you should probably use a case statement. The syntax for using a case structure is as follows:

```
case variable in
     condition_1 ) commands
       ;;
     condition_2 ) commands
       ;;
     condition_3 ) commands
       ;;
esac
```

The logical flow of the case statement is as follows:

Figure 1-34   *case Structure*

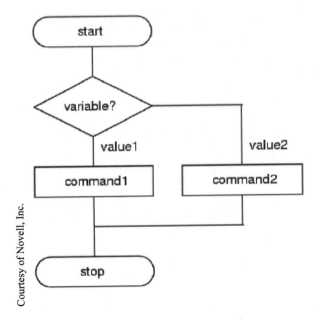

Courtesy of Novell, Inc.

A case statement compares the value of the variable listed to the list of conditions within the case statement. If a match is found, then the commands associated with that particular condition are run. Commands for all other list items are ignored. Consider the following example:

```
#! /bin/bash
#An example of using a case statement
echo "Enter the name of a month in the year:"
read MYMONTH
case $MYMONTH in
    December | January | February ) echo $MYMONTH" is in the Winter."
    ;;
    March | April | May) echo $MYMONTH" is in the Spring."
    ;;
    June | July | August) echo $MYMONTH" is in the Summer."
    ;;
    September | October | November) echo $MYMONTH" is in the Fall."
    ;;
    *) echo $MYMONTH" is not a valid month."
    ;;

esac
```

In this example, the echo command is used to ask the user to enter the name of a month. The input is read into a variable named **MYMONTH**. Then the case statement is used to evaluate the response. Based on what the user entered, the echo command is used to display text on the screen that lists the season associated with the month entered.

Notice that the last condition in the case statement is *. This condition matches everything not matched by the other conditions in the case statement and is used for error handling. If the user enters something that isn't matched by the preceding conditions, the echo command will display an error message on the screen.

Looping Structures

The if/then/else and case structures are called *branching* structures. Based on how a condition is evaluated, the script branches in one direction or another. You can also use *looping* control structures within a shell script. Looping structures are a little more complex.

Looping structures come in two varieties, the *while* loop and the *until* loop. A while loop executes over and over until a specified condition is no longer true. The structure of a while loop is as follows:

```
while condition
do
    script commands
done
```

A while loop will keep processing over and over and over until the condition evaluates to **false**.

In addition to a while loop, you can also use an until loop in your script. It works in the opposite manner. An until loop runs over and over as long as the condition is false. As soon as the condition is **true**, it stops. The structure for an until loop is as follows:

```
until condition
do
    script commands
done
```

Be aware that it is possible to get stuck in an infinite loop when using looping structures. This occurs when the condition never changes to a value that will break the loop.

In this situation, the script hangs because it keeps running the same loop structure over and over. It will continue to do so until you manually break out of it using the Ctrl+c key sequence.

seq Command

If the script will process a sequence of numbers, the `seq` command can be used to create a sequence of numbers. There are three options for using it:

- Using a single value, the sequence starts at one, increments by one, and ends at the specified value.

- Using two values, the sequence starts at the first value, increments by one, and ends at the second value.

- Using three values, the sequence starts at the first value, increments by the second value, and ends at the third value.

For example `seq 5 15` creates a sequence of numbers that starts at 5, increments by 1 and ends at 15. An example of using `seq` in a `for` loop is shown below:

```
#!/bin/sh
for i in `seq 5 15`
do
    echo "Number in sequence is $i."
done
exit 0
```

Writing Functions

As with most programming languages, you can also use functions in a shell script to group your code into logical pieces. This can be very useful for frequently used sequences of commands.

You first *declare* a function in your script and then **call** it later at the appropriate point. This allows you to reuse the same code over and over in the script without having to rewrite it each time it's used. To declare a function, enter the following at the beginning of your script:

```
function function_name { function_code }
```

For example, the following declares two functions, one named `quit` and the other named `sayhello`:

```
function quit {
                exit
        }
function sayhello {
                echo "Hello World!"
        }
```

You call a function by entering its name in the body of your script, just as you would to run a shell command. For example, the script below declares the two functions above at the beginning and then calls them later in the body:

```
#!/bin/bash
function quit {
    exit
}
function sayhello {
    echo "Hello World!"
}
sayhello
quit
```

Exercise 1-3   ***Work with the Linux Shell***

In this exercise, you use perform various tasks related to the Linux shell Bash. This includes using the history feature, getting root permission, viewing manual and info pages, creating an alias, using piping and redirections, editing a file with vi, and creating a simple shell script.

You will find this exercise at the end of the chapter.

(End of Exercise)

Objective 5   Use Command Line Tools to Work with Files and Directories

Within a terminal window, a number of tools are at your disposal for file and directory management. You can view and manipulate files, manage files and directories, perform administrative tasks, create or repair file systems, and do many other tasks.

This objective covers the more commonly used tools to

- Change Directories and List Directory Contents
- Create and View Files
- Administer Files and Directories
- Find Files on Linux
- Search File Content
- Process Text Streams Using Filters
- Use Command Line Tools to Work with Files and Directories

Change Directories and List Directory Contents

The shell prompt within a terminal contains the user name, the host name, and the current directory (such as geeko@da2:~). The tilde "~" indicates that you are in the user's home directory.

You can use the following commands to change the active directory, list the contents of a directory, and print the current working directory:

- cd Command
- pushd, popd, and dirs Commands
- ls Command
- file Command
- pwd Command

cd Command

You can use the cd (change directory) command to change between directories. Some examples include the following:

Table 1-10   *Examples of the cd Command*

Command	Meaning
cd plan	Change to the subdirectory plan
cd /etc	Change directly to the /etc directory (absolute path)
cd	Change from any directory to the home directory
cd ..	Move one directory level higher

Command	Meaning
cd ../..	Move two directory levels higher
cd -	Move to the last valid directory

pushd, popd, and dirs Commands

Using the `cd -` command, you can toggle back and forth between two directories. If you need to change directories between more than two directories, you may find the `pushd`, `popd`, and `dirs` shell built-in commands useful.

The `dirs` command is used to display the currently remembered directories. Using `pushd`, you can add directories to the list, and with `popd` remove them. Depending on the options used, you change directories at the same time.

The following will help you understand how these commands can be used:

```
geeko@da1:~> dirs
~
geeko@da1:~> pushd -n /etc
~ /etc
geeko@da1:~> pushd -n /var
~ /var /etc
geeko@da1:~> pushd /opt
/opt ~ /var /etc
geeko@da1:/opt> dirs
/opt ~ /var /etc
geeko@da1:/opt> # pushd without options toggles top two directories:
geeko@da1:/opt> pushd
~ /opt /var /etc
geeko@da1:~> pushd
/opt ~ /var /etc
geeko@da1:/opt> # pushd +1 moves through the directory stack:
geeko@da1:/opt> pushd +1
~ /var /etc /opt
geeko@da1:~> pushd +1
/var /etc /opt ~
geeko@da1:/var> pushd +1
/etc /opt ~ /var
geeko@da1:/etc> pushd +1
/opt ~ /var /etc
geeko@da1:/opt> # popd removes the top directory from the stack and
performs a cd to the new top directory
geeko@da1:/opt> popd
~ /var /etc
geeko@da2:~> # popd +n just removes that directory (counting from
left, starting with 0)
geeko@da1:~> popd +1
~ /etc
```

The following table lists the commands and their most important options:

Table 1-11 *dirs, pushd, and popd Commands*

Command	Meaning
dirs	Displays the list of currently remembered directories.
dirs -c	Clears the directory stack by deleting all of the elements.
dirs -v	Causes dirs to print the directory stack with one entry per line, prefixing each entry with its index in the stack.
pushd	With no arguments, pushd exchanges the top two directories on the stack.
pushd *dir*	Makes the current working directory be the top of the stack, and then executes the equivalent of `cd dir`, changing directory to *dir*. To only manipulate the stack without changing directory, add the −n option.
pushd +*N*	Brings the *N*th directory (counting from the left of the list printed by dirs, starting with zero) to the top of the list by rotating the stack. pushd +1 cycles through the stack.
popd	When no arguments are given, popd removes the top directory from the stack and performs a cd to the new top directory. To only manipulate the stack without changing directory, add the −n option.
popd +*N*	Removes the *N*th directory (counting from the left of the list printed by dirs), starting with zero from the stack.

For a complete list of options, enter `man bash` and search within the manual page for `popd`, `pushd`, and `dirs`.

ls Command

The `ls` command lists specified files. If a directory is included as a parameter with `ls`, the directory's contents are displayed. Without a parameter, the contents of the current directory are listed.

The following are the most important options you can use with `ls`:

Table 1-12 *Options of the ls Command*

Option	Meaning
(none)	Displays the content of the current directory in several columns (file and directory names only).
-a	Also displays hidden files (such as `.bashrc`).
-F	After each name, a character indicates the file type ("/" for directories, "*" for executable files, "|" for FIFO (first in first out) files, "@" for symbolic links).
-l	("long list") Gives a detailed list of all files. For each file name, information about permissions, modification time, and size is included.
-t	Files are sorted by date of modification. Combined with the -r option, the output is listed in reverse order (the newest file is displayed last).
-R	Output is recursive, including all subdirectories.

Option	Meaning
-u	Sorted by date of last access.

Figure 1-35   *ls Output Explained*

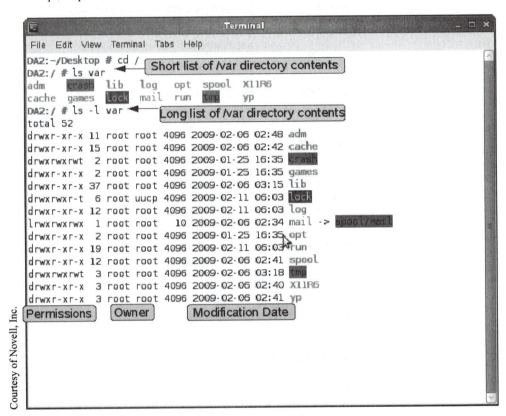

Courtesy of Novell, Inc.

The first column in the output of the `ls -l` command indicates the file type. Linux knows the following file types:

- **Regular file**. This file type contains data, scripts, or executable programs.

- **Directory**. A directory is a table listing the directories and files contained in it and their inodes. Directories are designated by the letter d in the first column of the ls output.

- **Named pipe**. A named pipe is also sometimes referred to as a FIFO (first in first out) file. It is used to transfer data from one process to another using the file system. Named pipes are designated by the letter p in the first column of the ls output.

- **Device file**. In Linux, hardware is addressed by reading from and writing to its associated device file. Depending on the type of hardware, character or block devices are used. Devices are designated by the letter c or b in the first column of the ls output.

- **Links.** A link is a directory entry that points to another file. Linux uses two kinds of links:

  - **Hard links:** Another entry in a directory that points to the inode of a file that already has a file name. Because the two entries point to the *same* inode, once the hard link is created, you can't tell which entry was first and which was added later. The number of hard links to a file is indicated in the ls output by the number that follows the file permissions.

  - **Symbolic links:** A symbolic link is a file of its own that points to another file in the file system. A symbolic link file has its own inode. Because of this, the pointer and the pointee in the file system can be easily identified. Symbolic links are designated by the letter l in the first column of the ls output.

Link Files has more information on links and explains how they are created.

file Command

Because file extensions, such as .txt, are not necessary in Linux, it is sometimes not immediately obvious from the file name what kind of file you are looking at on your system.

You can use the file command to get information about a file. The output of the file command will not only tell you the general file type (directory, named pipe, link, etc.), but based on file signatures contained in /usr/share/misc/magic, /usr/share/misc/magic.mgc, and /etc/magic, it will also give you more detailed information on regular files:

```
geeko@da2:~> file Documents/Meeting
Document/Meeting: OpenDocument Presentation
geeko@da2:~/doc> file /bin/rm
/bin/rm: ELF 32-bit LSB executable, Intel 80386, version 1 (SYSV),
for GNU/Linux 2.6.4, dynamically linked (uses shared libs), stripped
geeko@da2:~>
```

pwd Command

You can use the pwd (print working directory) command to display the path of the current directory. If you enter pwd with the -P option, pwd prints the physical directory without any symbolic links:

```
geeko@da2:~> ls -l doc/
lrwxrwxrwx  1 geeko users  15 2004-02-12 08:43 doc -> /usr/share/doc/
geeko@da2:~> cd doc/
geeko@da2:~/doc> pwd
/home/geeko/doc
geeko@da2:~/doc> pwd -P
/usr/share/doc
geeko@da2:~/doc>
```

Create and View Files

To create and view files, you need to understand how to do the following:

- Create a New File with touch
- View a File with cat
- View a File with less
- View a File with head and tail

Create a New File with touch

You can use the `touch` command to change the time stamp of a file or to create a new file with a size of 0 bytes. For instance, to create a file called example, enter `touch example`. The following are the most important options:

Table 1-13   *Options of the touch Command*

Options	Description
-a	Changes only the time of the last read access (*access time*).
-m	Changes only the time of the last modification (modification time).
-r *file*	Sets the time stamp of *file* instead of the current time.
-t *time*	Instead of the current time, sets
	time (structure: [[CC]YY]MMDDhhmm.[ss] ([Century]Year] Month Day Hour Minute [Seconds], two digits in each case)).

View a File with cat

You can use the `cat` (concatenate) command to view the contents of a file. The command must include the file name(s) of the file(s) you want to see. For instance, if you wanted to view the contents of the permissions.local file in the `/etc/` directory, you would enter `cat /etc/permissions.local`.

View a File with less

You can use the `less` command to display the contents of a file page by page. Even compressed files (such as `.gz` and `.bz2`) can be displayed. You can use the following keys within `less`:

Table 1-14   *Keys to Control less*

Keystroke	Description
Spacebar	Move one screen down.
b	Move one screen up.
Down arrow	Move one line down.
Up arrow	Move one line up.
/pattern	Search for pattern forward from current cursor position.
?pattern	Search for pattern backwards from current cursor position.
n	Move to the next instance in the search for pattern.
N	Move to the previous instance in the search for pattern.
q	Quit.

View a File with head and tail

With the `head` command, you can view the first few lines of a file only. The `tail` command shows you only the last few lines of a file.

For example, if you wanted to view the first few lines of the SUSE Linux Enterprise Server 11 Release Notes in the `/usr/share/doc` directory, you would enter

```
head /usr/share/doc/release notes/
SUSE_Linux_Enterprise_Server_11/RELEASE-NOTES.en.html
```

By default, these commands only show ten lines. To change this number, append with the *-number* option (such as `-20`).

When used with the tail command, the `-f` option displays a continuously updated view of the last lines of a file. If a line is added at the end of the file while `tail -f` is running, the line is displayed. This is a very useful feature for observing log files.

To exit `tail -f`, press Ctrl+c.

Administer Files and Directories

Creating, moving, renaming, and deleting files and directories are common administrative tasks. You need to be able to do the following:

- Copy and Move Files and Directories
- Create Directories

- Delete Files and Directories
- Link Files

Copy and Move Files and Directories

To copy and move files and directories, you need to know how to do the following:

- Move Files with mv
- Copy Files with cp

Move Files with mv

You can use the mv command (move) to move one or more files to another directory, as in the following:

```
mv *.txt /tmp
```

You can also use the mv command to rename a file, as in the following:

```
mv recipe new_recipe
```

The following are some important options you can use with **mv**:

Table 1-15 *Options of the mv Command*

Option	Description
-i	Asks for confirmation before moving or renaming a file. This prevents existing files with the same name from being overwritten.
-u	Only moves files that are newer than the target files of the same name.

Copy Files with cp

You can copy files and directories (using the $-r$ option) with the cp (copy) command. The syntax for using cp is

```
cp source destination
```

When using the cp command, you need to remember the following:

- The cp command overwrites existing files without confirmation.
- You can avoid automatic overwriting by using the $-i$ option. This option requires confirmation before overwriting occurs.
- If you want to copy just the contents of a directory (without the directory itself), the target directory must already exist. An example is making a backup copy of a directory using a different name.

For example, to copy the /tmp/quarterly-1/ directory (with all its subdirectories) to the /tmp/expenses/ directory (which already exists), you would enter the following:

```
cp -r /tmp/quarterly-1 /tmp/expenses
```

The result is a `/tmp/expenses/quarterly-1/` directory.

To copy the contents of a directory called `proposals/` (all the files contained in it, including hidden files and subdirectories) to the directory `proposals_old/` (this must already exist), do the following:

1. First, list the contents of the `proposals` directory, including the hidden files (−a switch). Enter

   ```
   ls -a proposals
   ```

   You might see output similar to this:

   ```
   .  ..  .hidden  quarterly-1  quarterly-2  quarterly-3  quarterly-4
   ```

2. Next, copy the contents of `proposals` recursively (−r, meaning including all subdirectories) to the `proposals_old` directory. Enter

   ```
   cp -r proposals/. proposals_old
   ```

3. Then, list the contents (including hidden files) of the `proposals_old` directory. Enter

   ```
   ls -a proposals_old
   ```

   ```
   .  ..  .hidden  quarterly-1  quarterly-2  quarterly-3  quarterly-4
   ```

You can use the following options with `cp`:

Table 1-16   *Options of the cp Command*

Option	Description
-a, --archive	Copies a directory and subdirectories (compare -R); symbolic links, file permissions, owners, and time stamps are not changed.
--help	Displays the options of cp.
-i, --interactive	Asks before overwriting.
-R, -r, --recursive	Copies directories recursively (the directory and any subdirectories).
-s, --symbolic-link	Makes symbolic links instead of copying.
-l, --link	Links files instead of copying them.
-u, --update	Copies a file only when the source file is newer than the destination file or when the destination file is missing.

Create Directories

You can use the `mkdir` command (make directory) to create new directories (such as `mkdir proposal`). The option −p lets you create a complete path, as in the following:

```
mkdir -p proposal/january
```

Delete Files and Directories

In this section, you learn how to do the following:

- Delete Empty Directories with rmdir
- Delete Files and Directories with rm

Delete Empty Directories with rmdir

You can use the `rmdir` (remove directory) command to remove the indicated directory or directories (for example, `rmdir proposal`). The directory or directories must be empty before you can delete them.

Delete Files and Directories with rm

You can use the `rm` command (remove) to delete files, as in the following:

```
rm part*
```

This example deletes all files in the current directory that begin with **part** without asking for confirmation. If the user does not have sufficient permissions to delete a file, that file is ignored and an error message is printed.

NOTE: Files deleted with the `rm` command cannot be restored.

The following are some important options you can use with `rm`:

Table 1-17   *Options of the rm Command*

Option	Description
-i	Asks for confirmation before deleting.
-r	(*recursively*) Allows to delete directories, including their content.
-f	(*force*) By default, **rm** asks for confirmation if the file that should be deleted is read-only. Using this option, the files are deleted without asking for confirmation.

Link Files

The `ln` command creates a link. A link is a reference to a file. Through a link you can access a file from anywhere in the file system using different names for it. This means that the file itself exists only once on the system, but it can be found under different names.

Linux recognizes two kinds of links:

- **Hard links.** A hard link is a directory reference, or pointer, to a file on a storage volume. The name associated with the file is a label stored in a directory structure that refers the operating system to the file data. As such, more than one name can be associated with the same file. When accessed through different names, any changes made will affect the same file data.

- **Symbolic links.** A symbolic link contains a text string that is interpreted and followed by the operating system as a path to another file or directory. It is a file on its own and can exist independently of its target. If a symbolic link is deleted, its target remains unaffected. If the target is moved, renamed, or deleted, any symbolic link that used to point to it continues to exist but now points to a non-existing file.

You create a *hard link* by using the `ln` command, which points to the inode of an already existing file. Inodes contain all the information about a file apart from the filename, such as permissions and time stamps. Thereafter, the file can be accessed under both names—that of the file and that of the link, and you can no longer discern which name existed first or how the original file and the link differ.

The following is an example of using the `ln` command:

```
geeko@da2:~/sell > ls -li
total 4
88658 -rw-r--r-- 1 geeko users 82 2004-04-06 14:21 old
geeko@da2:~/sell > ln old new
geeko@da2:~/sell > ls -li
total 8
88658 -rw-r--r-- 2 geeko users 82 2004-04-06 14:21 old
88658 -rw-r--r-- 2 geeko users 82 2004-04-06 14:21 new
geeko@da2:~/sell >
```

Hard links can only be used when both the file and the link are in the same file system (on the same partition), because inode numbers are only unique within the same file system.

You can create a *symbolic link* with the `ln` command and the `-s` option. A symbolic link is assigned its own inode—the link refers to a file, so a distinction can always be made between the link and the actual file.

The following is an example of creating a symbolic link:

```
geeko@da2:~/sell > ls -li
total 4
88658 -rw-r--r-- 1 geeko users 82 2004-04-06 14:21 old
geeko@da2:~/sell > ln -s old new
geeko@da2:~/sell > ls -li
total 4
88658 -rw-r--r-- 1 geeko users 82 2004-04-06 14:21 old
88659 lrwxrwxrwx 1 geeko users 3 2004-04-06 14:27 new -> old
geeko@da2:~/sell >
```

With symbolic links, the limits of the file system can be overcome, because the name of the object is shown, not the object itself. The disadvantage is that a symbolic link can point to a non-existing object if the object and its corresponding name no longer exist.

If you erase the old file in the above example, new will point to a non-existing file:

```
geeko@da2:~/sell > rm old
geeko@da2:~/sell > ls -li
total 0
88659 lrwxrwxrwx 1 geeko users 3 2004-04-06 14:27 new -> old
geeko@da2:~/sell >
```

An advantage of symbolic links is that you can create links to directories.

Find Files on Linux

If the name of the file is not completely known, you can use the two wildcards "?" (for any character) and "* "(for none, one, or several characters), for instance together with the ls command, such as ls file*.

File names are case sensitive in Linux. As a result, the file names "file1", "File1", and "FILE1" refer to three different files. Suppose the following files exist:

- File
- file
- File1
- File1a
- File1b
- File2
- File2a
- MyFile

The following table shows the results of three different search strings:

Table 1-18   *Placeholders and their Results*

Search String	Files Found
File?	File1
	File2
File*	File
	File1
	File1a
	File1b
	File2
	File2a

Search String	Files Found
?ile*	File
	file
	File1
	File1a
	File1b
	File2
	File2a

If you are searching for a file that could be located anywhere in the file system, using ls only together with the above placeholders is not very efficient, as you would have to apply them separately to each directory to find a certain file. However, in Linux there are several tools available that allow efficient searches for files based on their name.

The following tools and commands are introduced:

- Use the find Command
- Use the locate Command
- Use the whereis Command
- Use the which Command
- Use the type Command

Use the find Command

To search for files on the command line, you can use the find command. The following is the syntax for the find command:

```
find path criterion action
```

The find command has a multitude of options, a few of which are explained here. You can use the following arguments with the command:

- **path.** The section of the file system to search (the specified directory and all its subdirectories). If nothing is specified, the file system below the current directory is used.

- **criterion.** The properties the file should have. Possible criteria include the following:

Table 1-19   *Search Criteria for the find Command*

Option	Description
-ctime [+/-]*days*	Searches for files whose last change took place no later than (no earlier than) a specified number of *days* ago.
-gid *number*	Searches for files with the numeric GID (Group ID) *number*.
-group *name*	Searches for files that are owned by the group *name*. Instead of a name, the numeric GID is allowed.
-name *pattern*	Searches for files whose names contain the given *pattern*. If the pattern contains meta characters or wild cards, the name must be enclosed by quotation marks. Otherwise, the name will be interpreted by the shell and not by find.
-size [+/-]*size*	Matches files that are above or below a certain *size*. The size (in blocks of 512 bytes) is given as an argument. The suffix "c" switches to byte and "k" to blocks of 1024 bytes. A preceding "+" stands for all larger files and a "-" for all smaller files.
-type *file_type*	Searches for a *file type*. A file type can be one of the following: "d" for a directory, "f" for a file, or "l" for a symbolic link.
-uid *number*	Searches for files with the numeric UID (User ID) *number*.
-user *name*	Searches for files which are owned by user *name*. Instead of a name, the numeric UID is allowed.

- **action:** Options that influence the following conditions or control the search as a whole, such as the following:

  □ **-print** (default)

  □ **-exec command**

With the -exec option, you can call up another command. This option is frequently used to link find and grep, as in the following:

```
geeko@da2:~> find ~ -name "letter*" -type f -exec grep -H appointment
{} \;
/home/geeko/letters/letter_Smith:appointment for next meeting: 23.08.
geeko@da2:~>
```

In this example, the find command searches for files whose names begin with the word "letter", and then passes the names of the files found with -exec to the following command (in this case, grep appointment {}).

The two brackets {} stand as placeholders for the filenames which are found and passed to the grep command. The semicolon closes the -exec instruction. Because this is a special shell character, it is masked from Bash by placing a backslash in front of it.

When grep is used alone, it searches for a specific expression in a file whose exact position in the file system is known. When used in combination with find, the search is for a file that contains a certain expression, but whose location is unknown.

Use the locate Command

The `locate` command (or `slocate` on some Linux distributions) is an alternative to `find -name` (the package **findutils-locate** must be installed). The `find` command must search through the selected part of the file system, a process that can be quite slow.

On the other hand, `locate` searches through a database previously created for this purpose (`/var/lib/locatedb`), making it much faster.

The database is automatically created and updated daily by SUSE Linux Enterprise Server 11. But changes made after the update has been performed are not taken into account by `locate`, unless the database is updated manually using the `updatedb` command.

The following example shows the output of `locate`:

```
geeko@da2:~ > locate letter_Miller
/home/geeko/letters/letter_Miller
```

The following example shows that a search with `locate` returns all files whose names contain the search string:

```
geeko@da2:~> locate umount
/bin/umount
/lib/klibc/bin/umount
/opt/kde3/share/icons/crystalsvg/scalable/devices/
3floppy_umount.svgz
/opt/kde3/share/icons/crystalsvg/scalable/devices/
5floppy_umount.svgz
/opt/kde3/share/icons/crystalsvg/scalable/devices/camera_umount.svgz
/opt/kde3/share/icons/crystalsvg/scalable/devices/
cdaudio_umount.svgz
/opt/kde3/share/icons/crystalsvg/scalable/devices/cdrom_umount.svgz
geeko@da2:~>
```

NOTE: To learn more about locate, enter `man locate`.

Use the whereis Command

The `whereis` command returns the binaries (option `-b`), manual pages (option `-m`), and source code (option `-s`) of the specified command.

If no option is used, all this information is returned, provided the information is available. This command is faster than `find`, but it is less thorough.

The following is an example of using `whereis`:

```
geeko@da2:~ > whereis grep
grep: /bin/grep /usr/bin/grep
/usr/share/man/man1/grep.1.gz
/usr/share/man/man1p/grep.1p.gz
geeko@da2:~ > whereis -b grep
grep: /bin/grep /usr/bin/grep
geeko@da2:~ > whereis -m grep
grep: /usr/share/man/man1/grep.1.gz
/usr/share/man/man1p/grep.1p.gz
geeko@da2:~ > whereis -s grep
grep:
geeko@da2:~ >
```

NOTE: For more information about whereis, enter `man whereis`.

Use the which Command

The `which` command searches all paths listed in the PATH variable for the specified command and returns the full path of the command. The PATH variable specifies where the shell looks for executable files.

NOTE: To see the content of a variable, use the `echo` command and add a "$" in front of the variable's name. To see the content of the variable PATH, enter `echo $PATH`.

The `which` command is especially useful if several versions of a command exist in different directories and you want to know which version is executed when entered without specifying a path. Use the `-a` option for all occurrences of the command within the directories listed in the PATH variable.

The following is an example of using the `which` command:

```
geeko@da2:~> which find
/usr/bin/find
geeko@da2:~> which -a find
/usr/bin/find
/usr/bin/X11/find
geeko@da2:~>
```

NOTE: For more information on which, enter `man which`.

Use the type Command

The `type` command shows what kind of command is executed when you enter it:

■ A shell built-in command (an essential command that is hardcoded in the shell), for example "type" or "cd."

- An external command (called by the shell). If the command has been executed recently in the shell, the output says that the command is hashed, which means its location in the file system is stored in the shell's hash table. The next time the command is called, it is executed without searching it in the PATH directories. (Use the `hash -r` command to make the shell forget all remembered locations.)

- An alias, for example "ls". An alias defines shortcuts and synonyms for commonly used shell commands.

- A function.

The `-a` option delivers all instances of a command bearing this name in the file system.

The following is an example of using the `type` command:

```
geeko@da2:~> type type
type is a shell built in
geeko@da2:~ > type grep
grep is /usr/bin/grep
geeko@da2:~> grep file .bash_history
geeko@da2:~> type grep
grep is hashed (/usr/bin/grep)
geeko@da2:~> type -a grep
grep is /usr/bin/grep
grep is /bin/grep
grep is /usr/bin/X11/grep
geeko@da2:~>
```

Search File Content

Suppose you have dozens of text files and you need to find all files that include a particular word, phrase, or item. To scan these files without opening them in an editor, you need to know how to do the following:

- Use the grep Command
- Use Regular Expressions

Use the grep Command

The `grep` command and its variant `egrep` are used to search files for certain patterns using the syntax grep *search_pattern filename*. The command searches ***filename*** for all text that matches ***search_pattern***, and prints the lines that contain the pattern.

You can also specify several files, in which case the output will not only print the matching line, but also the corresponding file names.

Several options are available to specify that only the line number should be printed, for instance, or that the matching line should be printed together with leading and trailing context lines.

You can specify search patterns in the form of regular expressions, although the basic `grep` command is limited in this regard. The regular expressions used with `egrep` need to comply with the standard syntax of regular expressions. You can read details about this topic in the manual page of `grep`.

To search for more complex patterns, use the `egrep` command (or `grep -E`) instead, which accepts extended regular expressions. As a simple way to deal with the difference between the two commands, make sure you use `egrep` in all of your shell scripts.

To avoid having special characters in search patterns interpreted by the shell, enclose the pattern in quotation marks.

The following is an example of using egrep and grep:

```
geeko@da2:~> egrep (b|B)lurb file*
bash: syntax error near unexpected token `|'
geeko@da2:~> grep "(b|B)lurb" file*
geeko@da2:~> egrep "(b|B)lurb" file*
file1:blurb
filei2:Blurb
```

The options you can use with the **grep** command include the following:

Table 1-20   *Options of the grep Command*

Option	Description
-i	Ignores case.
-l	Shows only the names of files that contain the search string.
-r	Searches entire directory trees recursively.
-v	Gives all lines that do not contain the search string.
-n	Shows the line numbers.
-h	Shows no file names.

Use Regular Expressions

Regular expressions are strings consisting of metacharacters and regular characters and numerals (also known as "literals"). In the context of regular expressions, **metacharacters** are those characters that do not represent themselves but have special meanings. They can act as placeholders for other characters or can be used to indicate a position in a string.

Many commands (such as `egrep`) rely on regular expressions for pattern matching. It is important to remember, however, that some metacharacters used by the shell for filename expansion have a meaning different from the one discussed here.

To learn more about the structure of regular expressions, read the corresponding manual page with `man 7 regex`.

The following table presents the most important metacharacters and their meanings:

Table 1-21 *Metacharacters in Regular Expressions*

Character	Meaning	Example
^	Beginning of the line	^The: The is matched if at the beginning of the line
$	End of the line	eighty$: eighty is matched if at the end of line
\<	Beginning of the word	\<thing\>:matches the whole word thing
\>	End of the word	\<thing\>:matches the whole word thing
[abc]	One character from the set	[abc]: matches any one of "a", "b", or "c"
[0-9]	Any one from the specified range	[0-9]: matches any one number from "0" to "9" [-:+]: any one of "-", ":" and "+"
[^xyz]	None of the characters	[^xyz]: "x", "y", and "z" are not matched
.	Any single character	file.: matches file1 and file2, but not file10
+	One or more of the preceding expression	[0-9]+: matches any number
*	Any number (including none) of preceding single character	file.*: matches file, file2, and file10
{min,max}	The preceding expression min times at minimum and max times at maximum	[0-9]{1,5}: matches any one-digit to five-digit number
|	The expression before or after	file|File: matches file and File
(...)	Enclose alternatives for grouping with others	(f|F)ile: matches file and File
\?	Zero or one of the preceding	file1\?2: matches both file2 and file12
\	Escape the following character to remove its special meaning	www\.novell\.com: matches www.novell.com, literally (with the dot not being treated as a metacharacter); this is also necessary for parentheses, e.g., matching a parenthetical pattern would require the expression \([a-zA-Z]+\)

Process Text Streams Using Filters

You also need to be familiar with how to process text streams using filters. You can use several Linux commands to manipulate text read in from either a file or the standard input and then format it in a specified way. The output is sent to either a file or the standard output. The original source file is not modified in any way.

TIP: You can use piping and redirection to send the text stream from one command to another to perform complex modifications.

You can use the following tools:

- cut

- expand

- fmt

- join

- nl

- od

- paste

- pr

- sed and awk

- sort

- split

- tr

- unexpand

- uniq

- wc

cut

The `cut` command is used to print columns or fields that you specify from a file to the standard output. By default, the **Tab** character is used as a delimiter. The following options can be used with `cut`:

- `-b`*list*: Select only these bytes.

- `-c`*list*: Select only these characters.

- `-d`*delim*: Use the specified character instead of Tab for field delimiter.

- `-f`*list*: Select only the specified fields. Print any line that contains no delimiter character, unless the `-s` option is specified.

- `-s`: Do not print lines that do not contain delimiters.

For example, you can use cut to display all usernames from the `/etc/passwd` file. Usernames are contained in the first field of each line of the file. However, the file uses colons as a delimiter between fields, so you must specify a delimiter other than the default of Tab. The command to do this is shown below:

```
da1:# cut -d: -f1 /etc/passwd
at
bin
daemon
ftp
games
gdm
haldaemon
lp
mail
man
...
```

expand

The expand command is used to process a text stream and remove all instances of the Tab character and replace them with the specified number of spaces (the default is 8). You can use the -t *number* option to specify a different number of spaces. The syntax is expand -t *number filename*.

fmt

You can use the fmt command to reformat a text file. It is commonly used to change the wrapping of long lines within the file to a more manageable width. The output from the command is written to standard output; however, it can be piped to a file.

The syntax for using fmt is fmt *option file_name*. For example, suppose you have the following body of text in a file named lorem.txt:

```
Lorem ipsum dolor sit amet, consectetuer adipiscing elit. Curabitur
dignissim
venenatis pede. Quisque dui dui, ultricies ut, facilisis non, pulvinar
non,
purus. Duis quis arcu a purus volutpat iaculis. Morbi id dui in diam
ornare
dictum. Praesent consectetuer vehicula ipsum. Praesent tortor massa,
congue et,
ornare in, posuere eget, pede.
```

The text is too wide to fit this page and doesn't fit well within a standard-sized terminal window. To fix this, you could run the -w option with the fmt command to narrow the text to 40 columns, as shown below:

```
da1:~ # fmt -w 40 lorem.txt
Lorem ipsum dolor sit amet,
consectetuer adipiscing elit. Curabitur
dignissim venenatis pede. Quisque
dui dui, ultricies ut, facilisis non,
pulvinar non, purus. Duis quis arcu
a purus volutpat iaculis. Morbi id
dui in diam ornare dictum. Praesent
consectetuer vehicula ipsum. Praesent
tortor massa, congue et, ornare in,
posuere eget, pede.
```

join

The `join` command prints a line from each of two specified input files that have identical join fields. The first field is the default join field, delimited by white space. You can specify a different join field using the `-j field` option.

For example, suppose you have two files. The first file (named `firstnames`) contains the following content:

```
1 Robb
2 Kimberly
3 Mary
```

The second file (named `lastnames`) contains the following content:

```
1 Tracy
2 Sanders
3 Morgan
```

You can use the `join` command to join the corresponding lines from each file, as follows:

```
da1:~ # join -j 1 firstnames lastnames
1 Robb Tracy
2 Kimberly Sanders
3 Mary Morgan
```

nl

You can use the nl command to determine the number of lines in a file. When you run the command, the output is written to the standard output with a line number added to the beginning of each line in the file.

In the example below, the nl command is run against the `Lorem.txt` file and the output is written to the screen:

```
da1:~ # nl /home/geeko/Desktop/Lorem.txt
1  Lorem ipsum dolor sit amet, consectetuer adipiscing elit.
Curabitur dignissim
2  venenatis pede. Quisque dui dui, ultricies ut, facilisis non,
pulvinar non,
3  purus. Duis quis arcu a purus volutpat iaculis. Morbi id dui in
diam ornare
4  dictum. Praesent consectetuer vehicula ipsum. Praesent tortor
massa, congue et,
5  ornare in, posuere eget, pede.
```

You can also redirect the output of the command to a file.

od

If you need to dump a file, including binary files, you can use the od command at the shell prompt. The name od stands for *octal dump*. This utility can dump a file to standard output in several different formats, including octal, decimal, floating point, hex, and character format.

TIP: The output from od is simple text, so you can use the text manipulation tools presented above to manage it.

Performing a dump of a file can be a very effective way to locate stray characters in a file. For example, suppose you create a script file using an editor on a different operating system (such as Windows) and then tried to run it on Linux. Depending upon which editor you used, there may be hidden formatting characters within the script that aren't displayed by your Linux text editor, but are read by the Bash shell when you try to run it, causing it to error out. You could use the od command to view a dump of the script to isolate where the problem-causing characters are in the file.

The syntax for using od is od *options file_name*. Some of the more commonly used options include the following:

- **-b**: Octal dump
- **-d**: Decimal dump
- **-x**: Hex dump
- **-c**: Character dump

For example, consider the following text file named Lorem.txt:

```
da1:~ # cat /home/geeko/Desktop/Lorem.txt
Lorem ipsum dolor sit amet, consectetuer adipiscing elit. Curabitur
dignissim
venenatis pede. Quisque dui dui, ultricies ut, facilisis non,
pulvinar non,
purus. Duis quis arcu a purus volutpat iaculis. Morbi id dui in diam
ornare
dictum. Praesent consectetuer vehicula ipsum. Praesent tortor massa,
congue et,
ornare in, posuere eget, pede.
```

Using the od command to create a character dump of the file, you can see the hidden carriage return and linebreak characters at the end of each line. An example is shown below:

```
da1:~ # od -c /home/geeko/Desktop/Lorem.txt | head
0000000   L   o   r   e   m       i   p   s   u   m       d   o   l   o
0000020   r       s   i   t       a   m   e   t   ,       c   o   n   s
0000040   e   c   t   e   t   u   e   r       a   d   i   p   i   s   c
0000060   i   n   g       e   l   i   t   .       C   u   r   a   b   i
0000100   t   u   r       d   i   g   n   i   s   s   i   m  \r  \n   v
0000120   e   n   e   n   a   t   i   s       p   e   d   e   .       Q
0000140   u   i   s   q   u   e       d   u   i       d   u   i   ,
0000160   u   l   t   r   i   c   i   e   s       u   t   ,       f   a
0000200   c   i   l   i   s   i   s       n   o   n   ,       p   u   l
0000220   v   i   n   a   r       n   o   n   ,  \r  \n   p   u   r   u
da1:~ #
```

paste

The paste command works in much the same manner as the join command. It pastes together corresponding lines from one or more files into columns. By default, the Tab character is used to separate columns. You can use the -dn option to specify a different delimiter character.

Again, suppose you have two files. The firstnames file contains the following content:

```
1 Robb
2 Kimberly
3 Mary
```

The lastnames file contains the following content:

```
1 Tracy
2 Sanders
3 Morgan
```

You can use the paste command to join the corresponding lines from each file, as follows:

```
da1:~ # paste firstnames lastnames
1 Robb   1 Tracy
2 Kimberly  2 Sanders
3 Mary   3 Morgan
```

You can also use the −s option to put the contents of each file into a single line, as shown below:

```
da1:~ # paste -s firstnames lastnames
1 Robb   2 Kimberly   3 Mary
1 Tracy  2 Sanders   3 Morgan
```

pr

The pr command is used to format text files for printing. It formats the file with pagination, headers, and columns. The header contains the date and time, filename, and page number. You can use the following options with pr:

- −d: Double space the output.
- −l *page_length*: Set the page length to the specified number of lines. The default is 66.
- −o *margin*: Offset each line with the specified number of spaces. The default margin is 0.

sed and awk

Both commands are sometimes used within scripts to manipulate text strings.

sed (stream editor) manipulates text files from the command line or within scripts using regular expressions. Text manipulations that can be done with sed include searching for and replacing strings, inserting text, or deleting lines.

The syntax used can become very complex, making it a bit difficult to learn and understand. As a general rule, you need to specify where you want something done in a file and then what you want done:

sed *range action filename*

The result is written to standard out.

Examples to demonstrate the syntax and what can be done with sed include the following:

- Print the first five lines of the /etc/passwd file to standard out:

  sed -n 1,5p /etc/passwd

  By default, sed prints the lines that are not part of the range statement (1,5 above) as well. The option -n suppresses this; without this option, lines 1 to 5 appear twice in the output.

- Replace (substitute) the colons in `/etc/passwd` by space characters:

```
sed '1,$s/:/ /g' /etc/passwd
```

Within the specification of the range, $ refers to the last line. In this case the range statement 1, $ is included for illustration purposes; when working on the whole file, it could also be omitted. Without the g (for global) option, only the first occurrence within a line would be replaced.

- In each line, replace the second colon in the `/etc/passwd` file by a space character:

```
sed 's/:/ /2' /etc/passwd
```

- From line one up to the line that contains the string postfix, replace the second colon in the `/etc/passwd` file by a space character:

```
sed '1,/postfix/s/:/ /2' /etc/passwd
```

- Remove all lines starting with a comment character and all empty lines from the `/etc/postfix/main.cf` file:

```
sed -e '/#/d' -e '/^$/d' /etc/postfix/main.cf
```

An empty line is a line where the beginning of a line (^) is followed directly by the end of a line ($ in regular expression—beware of the difference in significance of the $ sign in defining the range in the second example). If you include more than one processing rule (d for delete in the example above), each statement has to be preceded by the -e (for expression) option.

For more information on sed, enter `info sed`, or visit http://sed.sourceforge.net/grabbag/ (http://sed.sourceforge.net/grabbag/).

The `awk` utility is also used to manipulate strings. (The name of the program is made up from the first letters of the programmers' names and has no further significance.) As with sed, the basic command line includes a search pattern and some action:

```
awk search_pattern program_action
```

For instance, if you wanted to create a list of user names that do not have /bin/bash as their shell and print their names and shells from `/etc/passwd`, you could use the following command:

```
awk -F: '!/\/bin\/bash/ { print $1,$7 }' /etc/passwd
```

`-F:` changes the field separator from white space to `:`. The search pattern `/bin/bash` is negated by the exclamation mark in front of it, and the slashes within the search pattern are preceded by backslashes to distinguish them from the slashes that begin and end the search pattern. The `print` statement tells `awk` to print fields one and seven.

To learn more about `awk`, look at its manual page and at awk tutorials in the Internet (search for **awk** and **tutorial** using a search engine of your choice).

sort

The `sort` command sorts the lines of a text file alphabetically. The output is written to the standard output. Some commonly used options for the `sort` command include the following:

- `-f`: Fold lowercase characters to uppercase characters.

- `-M`: Sort by month

- `-n`: Sort numerically.

- `-r`: Reverse the sort order.

For example, the following command sorts the lines in the firstnames file numerically in reverse order:

```
da1:~ # sort -n -r firstnames
3 Mary
2 Kimberly
1 Robb
```

TIP: The sort command can be used to sort the output of other commands (such as `ps`) by piping the standard output of the first command to the standard input of the sort command.

---

split

The `split` command splits an input file into a series of files (without altering the original input file). The default is to split the input file into 1,000-line segments. You can use the `-n` option to specify a different number of lines.

For example, the following command can be used to split the firstnames file into three separate files, each containing a single line:

```
da1:~ # split -1 firstnames outputfile_
da1:~ # ls -l out*
-rw-r--r-- 1 root root  7 Aug 12 10:55 outputfile_aa
-rw-r--r-- 1 root root 11 Aug 12 10:55 outputfile_ab
-rw-r--r-- 1 root root  7 Aug 12 10:55 outputfile_ac
da1:~ # cat outputfile_aa
1 Robb
da1:~ # cat outputfile_ab
2 Kimberly
da1:~ # cat outputfile_ac
3 Mary
```

tr

The `tr` command is used to translate or delete characters. This command does not work with files. To use files, you must use a command such as `cat` to send the text stream to the standard input of `tr`. The syntax is `tr` *`options SET1 SET2`*. Some commonly used options for the `tr` command include the following:

- `-c`: Use all characters *not* in SET1.

- `-d`: Delete characters in SET1; do not translate.

- `-s`: Replace each input sequence of a repeated character that is listed in SET1 with a single occurrence of that character.

- `-t`: First truncate SET1 to length of SET2.

For example, to translate all lowercase characters in the firstnames file to uppercase characters, you could use the following command:

```
da1:~ # cat firstnames | tr a-z A-Z
1 ROBB
2 KIMBERLY
3 MARY
```

unexpand

The `unexpand` command works in the opposite manner as the `expand` command. It converts spaces in a text stream into Tab characters. By default, 8 contiguous spaces are converted into tabs. You can use the `-t` option to specify a different number of spaces.

By default, `unexpand` will only convert leading spaces at the beginning of each line. To force it to convert all spaces of the correct number to tabs, you must include the `-a` option.

uniq

The `uniq` command reports or omits repeated lines. The syntax is `uniq` *`options input output`*. You can use the following options with the uniq command:

- `-d`: Only print duplicate lines.

- `-u`: Only print unique lines.

For example, suppose our firstnames file contained duplicate entries:

```
1 Robb
1 Robb
2 Kimberly
3 Mary
3 Mary
```

You can use the following command to remove the duplicate lines:

```
da1:~ # uniq firstnames
1 Robb
2 Kimberly
3 Mary
```

TIP: The `uniq` command only works if the duplicate lines are adjacent to each other. If the text stream you need to work with contains duplicate lines that are not adjacent, you can use the `sort` command to make them adjacent and then pipe the output to the standard input of `uniq`.

---

wc

The `wc` command prints the number of newlines, words, and bytes in files. The syntax is `wc` *options files*. You can use the following options:

- `-c`: Print the byte counts.

- `-m`: Print the character counts.

- `-l`: Print the newline counts.

- `-L`: Print the length of the longest line.

- `-w`: Print the word counts.

For example, to print all counts and totals for the `lastnames` file, you would use the following command:

```
da1:~ # wc lastnames
 3  6 27 lastnames
```

Exercise 1-4 **Use Command Line Tools to Work with Files and Directories**

In this exercise, you work with command line tools to administer files and directories. This includes creating and viewing files with the `touch`, `cat`, `less`, `head`, and `tail` commands, copying, moving, and deleting files and directories, and search for and within files with the find and grep commands.

You will find this exercise at the end of the chapter.

(End of Exercise)

Objective 6   Apply Locale and Time Zone Settings

In this objective, you learn how to localize a Linux system in a different language. You also learn how to configure the time zone the system is in. The following topics are addressed:

- Configuring Locale Settings
- Configuring Time Zone Settings
- Managing Time Zone Information

Configuring Locale Settings

When you install Linux, one of the settings you typically configure is the system's *locale*. The locale determines such things as

- Language and encoding of text displayed on screen
- Character classes
- Sort order
- Number format
- Currency format
- Date and time display

Your locale settings on a Linux system are configured using several environment variables:

- **LC_CTYPE**: Character types and encoding
- **LC_MESSAGES**: Natural language messages
- **LC_COLLATE**: Sorting rules
- **LC_NUMERIC**: Number format
- **LC_MONETARY**: Currency format
- **LC_TIME**: Date and time display
- **LC_PAPER**: Paper size
- **LC_NAME**: Personal name format
- **LC_ADDRESS**: Address format
- **LC_TELEPHONE**: Telephone number format
- **LC_MEASUREMENT**: Measurement units
- **LC_ALL**: Overrides all other LC environment variables
- **LANG**: Default locale value for all LC variables
- **LANGUAGE**: Override for LC_MESSAGES

Each of the above locale variables can be populated with a locale name using the following syntax:

```
language_territory.codeset @modifier
```

This syntax is described below:

- *language*: An ISO 639 language code (lower case)

- *territory*: An ISO 3166 country code (upper case)

- *codeset*: A character set

- *modifier*: Other locale attributes, such as a language dialect or currency

For example, *en_CA* is the language and territory for English in Canada while *fr_CA* is used for French Canadian. An encoding can also be specified. For example, you could use *en_US.UTF-8* to configure U.S. English with UTF-8 (Unicode).

TIP: You can also use a locale named **C**. This locale is very useful when creating scripts. It configures the system to use the following:

- ASCII encoding

- POSIX character classes

- American English time, date, number, and currency formats

To localize a Linux system, simply change the value of the appropriate environment variable. Usually, you will set all of these variables to the same value. However, it is possible to set them independently to different values, if necessary.

Not all of the above variables have the same level of precedence. The process below is used by the Linux operating system to determine which locale setting to use for a particular parameter:

1. If the LC_ALL variable is defined, its value is used and the value of the specific LC variable in question is not checked.

2. If LC_ALL is null, then the specific LC variable in question is checked. If the specific LC variable has a value, it is used.

3. If the specific LC variable is not defined, then the LANG environment variable is used.

Accordingly, if you want all variables to use the same value, you can simply set the LC_ALL variable instead of setting the value of each individual variable. If you want to use different values for different LC variables, then you need to be sure to first remove any value assigned to LC_ALL.

You can use the `locale` command at the shell prompt to view your current locale settings. An example is shown below:

```
geeko@da1:~/> locale
LANG=en_US.UTF-8
LC_CTYPE="en_US.UTF-8"
LC_NUMERIC="en_US.UTF-8"
LC_TIME="en_US.UTF-8"
LC_COLLATE="en_US.UTF-8"
LC_MONETARY="en_US.UTF-8"
LC_MESSAGES="en_US.UTF-8"
```

```
LC_PAPER="en_US.UTF-8"
LC_NAME="en_US.UTF-8"
LC_ADDRESS="en_US.UTF-8"
LC_TELEPHONE="en_US.UTF-8"
LC_MEASUREMENT="en_US.UTF-8"
LC_IDENTIFICATION="en_US.UTF-8"
LC_ALL=
```

In this example, the value of each individual LC variable is used, even though they are all identical because LC_ALL has no value assigned. As you can see in the output, the system is configured to use U.S. English and UTF-8 encoding. You can verify this using the `locale charmap` command at the shell prompt. When you do, the current encoding used by the system is displayed, as shown below:

```
geeko@da1:~/Desktop> locale charmap
UTF-8
```

If you want to change the locale or the encoding, you first need to determine what is currently available on your system. You can use the `-a` option with the `locale` command to view a list of all available locales. You can use the `-m` option to view a list of available encodings. An example is shown below:

```
geeko@da1:~/Desktop> locale -a
aa_DJ
aa_DJ.utf8
aa_ER
aa_ER@saaho
aa_ER.utf8
aa_ET
aa_ET.utf8
af_ZA
af_ZA.utf8
am_ET
am_ET.utf8
an_ES
an_ES.utf8
ar_AE
ar_AE.utf8
ar_BH
ar_BH.utf8
ar_DZ
ar_DZ.utf8
ar_EG
ar_EG.utf8
....
geeko@da1:~/> locale -m
ANSI_X3.110-1983
ANSI_X3.4-1968
ARMSCII-8
ASMO_449
BIG5
BIG5-HKSCS
BRF
BS_4730
BS_VIEWDATA
...
```

TIP: You can convert the encoding of a file from one encoding to another using the `iconv` command at the shell prompt. The syntax for using this command is shown below:

`iconv -f `**`source_encoding`**` -t `**`destination_encoding`**` -o `**`output_file_name`** **`input_file_name`**

Configuring Time Zone Settings

In addition to locale settings, you can also configure the time zone your Linux system resides in.

During the initial installation of Linux, you are prompted to specify the time zone the system will run in. The time zone you select is written to the `/etc/timezone` file. You can view your system's time zone by viewing the contents of this file with the cat command. An example is shown below:

```
bill@Ubuntu-Desktop:~$ cat /etc/timezone
America/Denver
```

NOTE: Some distributions, such as Ubuntu, use the `/etc/timezone` file. Other distributions, such as SLES, do not use this file.

You can also view the current time zone using the `date` command at the shell prompt, as shown below:

```
da1:~ # date
Thu Aug  5 12:09:57 MDT 2010
```

As you can see in the output of the `date` command, the system is set to use the U.S. Mountain Daylight Savings Time zone.

If you need to change time zones after the system has been installed, you can use the `tzselect` utility at the shell prompt. This command must be run as root, so you need to either use the `su -` command to switch to your root user or use the `sudo` command with `tzselect` to gain root-level privileges. An example is shown below:

```
da1:~ # tzselect
Please identify a location so that time zone rules can be set
correctly.
Please select a continent or ocean.
 1) Africa
 2) Americas
 3) Antarctica
 4) Arctic Ocean
 5) Asia
 6) Atlantic Ocean
 7) Australia
 8) Europe
 9) Indian Ocean
10) Pacific Ocean
11) none - I want to specify the time zone using the Posix TZ format.
#?
```

As shown in the example above, a list of continents and oceans is displayed when you run the command. Enter the appropriate *number* for the region where the time zone you want to switch to resides. When you do, a list of countries in the region is displayed. Enter the *number* for the appropriate country; then enter the *number* for time zone you want to switch to. You are prompted to confirm the time zone change, as shown below:

```
18) Mountain Time - south Idaho & east Oregon
19) Mountain Time - Navajo
20) Mountain Standard Time - Arizona
21) Pacific Time
22) Alaska Time
23) Alaska Time - Alaska panhandle
24) Alaska Time - Alaska panhandle neck
25) Alaska Time - west Alaska
26) Aleutian Islands
27) Hawaii
#? 11


The following information has been given:

  United States
  Central Time


Therefore TZ='America/Chicago' will be used.
Local time is now:  Thu Aug  5 13:10:42 CDT 2010.
Universal Time is now:  Thu Aug  5 18:10:42 UTC 2010.
Is the above information OK?
1) Yes
2) No
#?
```

Confirm the time zone change by entering **1**. Notice in the example above that the tzselect command changes time zones by setting the value of the **TZ** environment variable. In this example, the `TZ` environment variable is set to a value of **America/ Chicago**.

In fact, you can change time zones from the shell prompt without using the `tzselect` command by simply setting the value of the TZ environment variable and then exporting it. This is useful in situations where you don't have root-level access to the system or when you want to use a different time zone for your user account without changing the time zone used by other users. The syntax for doing this is shown below:

```
export TZ=time_zone
```

You can view a list of available time zones in the `/usr/share/zoneinfo/` directory, as shown below:

```
da1:~ # ls /usr/share/zoneinfo/
Africa      Canada   Factory  Iceland   MST7MDT   Portugal   Zulu
America     Chile    GB       Indian    Mexico    ROK        iso3166.tab
Antarctica  Cuba     GB-Eire  Iran      Mideast   Singapore  posix
Arctic      EET      GMT      Israel    NZ        Turkey     posixrules
Asia        EST      GMT+0    Jamaica   NZ-CHAT   UCT        right
```

```
Atlantic      EST5EDT   GMT-0       Japan       Navajo    US          zone.tab
Australia     Egypt     GMT0        Kwajalein   PRC       UTC
Brazil        Eire      Greenwich   Libya       PST8PDT   Universal
CET           Etc       HST         MET         Pacific   W-SU
CST6CDT       Europe    Hongkong    MST         Poland    WET
```

You can make this change persistent across reboots for your user account by adding the following command to the `.profile` file in your user's home directory:

```
export TZ='America/Chicago'
```

You can also change the time zone using the `/etc/localtime` file and the zone files in the `/usr/share/zoneinfo` directory. This is done by creating a symbolic link to the appropriate time zone from /etc/localtime. For example, if you wanted to use the Eastern Standard Time zone in the U.S., you would enter the following command:

```
ln -sf /usr/share/zoneinfo/EST /etc/localtime
```

Exercise 1-5   *Managing Time Zone Information*

In this exercise, you practice configuring time zone information on Linux.

You will find this exercise at the end of the chapter.

(End of Exercise)

Summary

Objective	Summary
Use the GNOME Desktop Environment	The main elements of the GNOME desktop environment are the desktop, the bottom panel, and the applications menu.
	You can customize each element according to your needs, for instance by placing icons that allow you to launch applications or access files directly.
	GNOME's file manager is called Nautilus.
Configure Accessibility Settings	Linux includes accessibility tools that address users who have physical impairments that may make it difficult for them to use a mouse or keyboard, including: ■ Using AccessX ■ Using On-Screen Keyboards ■ Using Mouse Gestures In addition to keyboard accessibility features, Linux also provides tools for the visually impaired, including: ■ Using Screen Readers and Magnifiers ■ Using Braille Devices ■ Using High-Contrast and Large-Text Desktop Themes
Access the Command Line Interface from the Desktop	SUSE Linux Enterprise Server provides the user with six virtual terminals.
	You can use the key combinations **Ctrl+Alt+F1** to **Ctrl+Alt+F6** to switch between the individual terminals.
	You can switch back to your graphical user interface by pressing **Ctrl+Alt+F7**.
	With Gnome Terminal you can access the command line interface within a window.

Objective	Summary
Work with the Linux Shell	The default shell used in SLES11 is the Bourne Again Shell (Bash). It is the interface between the user and the operating system where the user enters commands and views the result of these commands.
	Bash has many features that make its use easier, such as history function, tab completion, aliases, and variables.
	When working with the shell, many tools complement its functionality, such as the `su` command to switch user, `xargs` to extend the command line, or `sed` and `awk` used within scripts.
	Manual and info pages contain information on the purpose of commands and how to invoke them.
	Commands can be included in scripts to make complex tasks easier and facilitate automatic execution of tasks.
Use Command Line Tools to Work with Files and Directories	There are command line tools for all common tasks an administrator needs to perform with files and directories. These include
	■ cp. Copy files.
	■ mv. Move or rename files or directories
	■ touch. Create a new file.
	■ cat, head, tail. View entire files or parts of files
	■ mkdir. Create directories.
	■ rm. Remove files and directories.
	■ ln. Create links.
	■ find, locate. Search for files.
	■ grep. Search for strings within files

Objective	Summary
Apply Locale and Time Zone Settings	When you install Linux, one of the settings you typically configure is the system's **locale**. The locale determines such things as:

- Language and encoding of text displayed on screen
- Character classes
- Sort order
- Number format
- Currency format
- Date and time display

Your locale settings on a Linux system are configured using several environment variables.

In addition to locale settings, you can also configure the time zone your Linux system resides in.

During the initial installation of Linux, you are prompted to specify the time zone the system will run in. The time zone you select is written to the `/etc/timezone` file. You can view your system's time zone by viewing the contents of this file with the cat command.

You can also view the current time zone using the `date` command at the shell prompt.

If you need to change time zones after the system has been installed, you can use the `tzselect` utility at the shell prompt.

Key Terms

.command – A shortcut to the *source command*.

/dev/null – A special device file on Linux systems that represents nothing. Anything redirected to this device file is automatically deleted by the system.

/usr/share/doc directory – Stores various system and package-related documentation on a SUSE Linux system.

&& operator – Used to execute a command only if another command completed successfully.

|| operator – Used to execute a command only if another command did not complete successfully.

absolute path – A pathname to a file or directory that starts from the root (/) of the file system.

AccessX – An X Window System application that provides most keyboard-based user accessibility features within the desktop environment.

alias command – Used to create an alias within a shell.

aliases – Special variables that are used to store shortcuts to Linux commands within a shell.

apropos command – Searches the man pages by keyword. It is the same as –k option to the man command.

awk command – Formats text streams using advanced techniques.

Bash (Bourne Again Shell) –The default command line shell on Linux systems.

branching structure – A control structure that alters the actions of a shell script based on the outcome of a test condition.

cat (concatenate) command – Displays the contents of a text file.

cd (change directory) command – Used to change the current working directory on the Linux file system.

chmod command – Used to change permissions on files and directories.

Control Center – The tool within SUSE Linux that can be used to configure operating system and accessibility settings.

control structures – Components of a shell script that alter the execution of the shell script based on environmental conditions. Common control structures used in shell scripts include if/then/else, case, while, until, and for.

cp (copy) command – Used to copy files from one location to another on the file system.

cut command – Cuts a column of text from a text stream.

date command – Displays and sets the system date and time.

declare command – Used to create variables that accept a specific type of data only, such as integer data.

device file – A special file on the file system that describes a hardware device driver in the Linux kernel.

dirs command – Used to display the list of currently remembered directories.

echo command – Used to display text to the terminal screen, including the contents of environment variables such as $PATH.

egrep command – A version of the grep command that also works with extended regular expressions.

environment variables – Variables that are used to store configuration information for the shell environment.

exec command – Used to directly execute a specified command.

expand command – Replaces tab characters with spaces in a text stream.

file command – Used to determine the file type for files on the Linux file system.

filter – A command that can take stdin and produce stdout. Filter commands can exist within a long piped command as a result.

find command – Searches for files on the file system based on a variety of different criteria.

fmt command – Formats the number of characters displayed on each line in a text stream.

function – A component of a shell script that contains commands that must be run several times during script execution.

GNOME – The default graphical desktop environment within SUSE Linux. It stands for GNU Object Model Environment.

GNOME OnScreen Keyboard (GOK) – A software application within SUSE Linux that can be used to display a keyboard on the desktop that users can interact with using their mouse.

GNOME panel – The bar within the GNOME desktop environment that contains links to virtual desktops, menus, applications, files, and directories. By default, it is placed at the bottom of the GNOME desktop within SUSE Linux.

GNOME Terminal – The graphical terminal emulation program that is included within the GNOME desktop environment.

grep (global regular expression print) command – Searches for text within text files and returns the lines that contain that text.

hard link – A special file on the file system that shares the same inode with other files. When one hard link is edited, the other files that share the same inode are updated as well.

head command – Displays the beginning lines of a text file.

history command – Used to display the commands previously typed into the shell.

id command – Displays the user and group identification numbers associated with the current user.

info command – Used to access the info pages.

info pages – An alternative to the man pages that stores help information for Linux files and commands. Info pages are stored in the /usr/share/info directory within SUSE Linux.

inode – The part of a file that contains the metadata associated with the file, including ownership, permissions, modification date, size, and physical location on the file system.

join command – Joins two files together based on a common field.

Konsole – The graphical terminal emulation program that is included within the KDE desktop environment.

less command – Displays the contents of a text file in a page-by-page or line-by-line fashion.

ln command – Used to create hard and symbolic links.

locale – The geographical region that a computer system is located in. It is used to determine the default language, time, and character formatting information used within the Linux operating system.

locale command – Used to view locale information.

locate command – Finds files on the file system using a pre-indexed database.

login shell – A shell that is executed immediate after a user logs into the system. Each Bash login shell executes the commands specified in the /etc/profile, ~/.profile, /etc/bash.bashrc, /etc/bash.bashrc.local, and ~/.bashrc files.

login string – *See username*.

looping structures – Control structures that process commands within a shell script repetitively.

ls command – Used to list files and directories on a Linux file system.

man command – Used to access the man pages.

man pages – The main help system for commands and files on a Linux system. It is short for manual pages. Man pages are stored in the /usr/share/man directory within SUSE Linux.

metacharacter – A character that has special meaning to the shell.

mkdir (make directory) command – Used to create directories on the file system.

mouse gestures – An accessibility feature that can be used to perform certain actions when the mouse is moved in a specified pattern.

mv (move) command – Used to rename or move files from one location to another on the file system.

named pipe – A special file used to transfer data from one process to another via the file system.

Nautilus – The graphical file manager available within the GNOME desktop environment.

nl command – Numbers the lines in a text stream.

non-login shell – A shell that is executed from another shell. Each Bash non-login shell executes the commands specified in the /etc/bash.bashrc, /etc/bash.bashrc.local, and ~/.bashrc files.

od command – Displays a text stream or file in octal or hexadecimal format.

Orca – A screen reader and magnifier included with SUSE Linux. It also has support for Braille devices.

password – The password associated with the user account that is used to access the Linux system.

paste command – Joins two files together regardless of whether they have a common field.

PATH – An environment variable that contains a list of directories on the system that are searched for executable programs.

piping – The process whereby the stdout of a command is sent to another command as stdin.

popd command – Used to remove entries from the directory stack.

pr command – Formats a file or text stream for printing.

pushd command – Used to add entries to the directory stack.

pwd (print working directory) command – Displays the current working directory.

read command – Prompts the user for input and places that input into a variable.

redirection – The process whereby the stdout or stderr of a command is sent to a file, or the contents of a file are sent to a command as stdin.

regular expressions – Special metacharacters that can be used for matching patterns of text within a text file or command output.

relative path – A pathname to a file or directory that is relative to the current location on the file system.

return value – The value returned from a command after execution. A zero return value indicates success (true), whereas a non-zero return value indicates failure (false).

rm (remove) command – Used to remove files and directories from the file system.

rmdir (remove directory) command – Used to remove empty directories on the file system.

rsync (remote sync) command – Used to copy files to and from remote computers across a network.

screen magnifier – An application that can be used to enlarge a selected area of the desktop environment.

screen reader – An application that can be used to speak the words that are displayed on the desktop or within an application.

sed (stream editor) command – Performs search and replace operations on text streams.

seq command – Used to generate a sequence of numbers.

shell – A program that allows users to interact with the Linux system using a virtual terminal. Common Linux shells include the Bourne Again, Bourne, Korn, TC, and C shells.

sort command – Sorts the lines of a text stream.

source command – Used to read the contents of a changed configuration file into the current shell.

split command – Divides a file or text stream into chunks and saves them into different files.

standard error (stderr) – Error messages that are generated during command execution. By default, stderr is sent to the terminal screen.

standard input (stdin) – The input that commands receive during execution. By default, stdin comes from the keyboard.

standard output (stdout) – The intended output of a command during execution. By default, stdout is sent to the terminal screen.

su (switch user) command – Used to start a new shell as another user.

symbolic link – A file or directory that is merely a shortcut to another file or directory.

tail command – Displays the last lines of a text file.

tee command – Used to save stdout to a file as well as send it to stdout.

test command – Used to determine whether a condition is true or false.

text stream – A series of text characters that is received from stdin or a file.

touch command – Used to update the modification date for a file or create an empty file.

tr (transliterate) command – Replaces single characters with others in a text stream.

type command – Returns the type of command (shell function, external command, alias) for commands located in directories listed in the PATH environment variable.

tzselect command – Displays and sets the system time zone.

unalias command – Used to remove an alias from the system.

unexpand command – Replaces space characters with tab characters in a text stream.

uniq command – Reports or omits repeated lines in a text stream.

unset command – Used to remove a variable from the system.

username – The name of the user account that is used to access the Linux system.

variables – Reserved areas of memory that are used to store information that is accessed by programs.

vi editor – See *vim editor.*

vim editor – The most common text editor found on Linux systems. It stands for vi Improved.

virtual terminal – A channel that allows users the ability to interact with a Linux system. By default, there are six command line virtual terminals and one graphical virtual terminal within SUSE Linux.

wc (word count) command – Displays the number of lines, words, and characters in a file or command output.

whatis command – Displays the short description of a command from the man pages.

whereis command – Returns the binaries, manual pages, and source code for a specific command.

which command – Finds files on the file system by examining only the directories listed in the PATH environment variable.

whoami command – Prints the current username to the terminal screen.

workspaces – Areas of the GNOME desktop environment that users can work with. There are four GNOME workspaces by default in SUSE Linux.

xargs command – Converts the output of one command to command(s) that can be executed within the shell.

XTerm – The legacy graphical terminal emulation program available within any Linux graphical desktop.

YaST – The main system administration tool within SUSE Linux. It stands for Yet another Setup Tool.

Chapter Exercises

Exercise 1-1   *Work with GNOME*

In this exercise, you log in to the GNOME desktop as user **geeko** (his password is **novell**) and work with the desktop environment on da-host.

In Part I of the exercise, add the System Monitor to the bottom panel and remove it again.

In Part II of the exercise, use Nautilus to copy the /etc/DIR_COLORS file into your home directory and add the **Oh no!** emblem to the copied file. Then rename the copied file to example.txt. Finally, delete example.txt and empty the trash.

NOTE: In later exercises you will use the root account - the root password is novell.

Detailed Steps to Complete the Exercise

- Part I: Add the System Monitor to the GNOME Bottom Panel
- Part II: Use Nautilus to Work with a File

Part I: Add the System Monitor to the GNOME Bottom Panel

To add and remove an application to the bottom panel, do the following:

1. Log in to the da-host GNOME desktop as user **geeko** (password **novell**).
2. Right-click a free space in the bottom panel.
3. From the pop-up menu, select *Add to Panel*.

   An *Add to Panel* dialog appears.
4. From the list, select *System Monitor* and then click *Add*.

   A *System Monitor* icon is added to the Bottom Panel.
5. Close the *Add to Panel* dialog.
6. Double-click the System Monitor icon to view the *System Monitor* tool.
7. Close the System Monitor by selecting *Monitor > Quit*.
8. Remove the *System Monitor* applet from the Bottom Panel:
   a. Right-click the *System Monitor* applet on the Bottom Panel.
   b. From the pop-up menu, select *Remove From Panel*.

Part II: Use Nautilus to Work with a File

To become familiar with the Nautilus file manager, do the following:

1. Make sure you are logged in to da-host as geeko with a password of novell.
2. Start the Nautilus file manager by double-clicking the *geeko's Home* icon on the desktop.

3. View the file system tree in the side panel by opening the menu at the top of the side panel (labeled *Places* when Nautilus is started the first time).

4. From the menu, select **Tree**.

5. View the contents of the /etc directory by selecting the small triangle in front of the **File System** entry in the side panel.

6. In the side panel, select *etc*.

7. Copy the /etc/DIR_COLORS file onto the desktop:

    a. Scroll down to the **DIR_COLORS** file icon.

    b. While holding the Ctrl key, drag the icon onto the desktop, then release the mouse button.

8. Switch back to your home directory by selecting **Home Folder** in the side panel.

9. Move the DIR_COLORS file from the desktop into your home directory. Select the **DIR_COLORS file icon** and drag it over the right frame of the Nautilus window. Release the mouse button.

IMPORTANT: Notice there is no small plus at the mouse pointer while dragging the file, indicating that you are moving a file.

---

10. Switch to the list of emblems by opening the menu at the top of the side panel (labeled *Tree* now).

11. From the menu, select **Emblems**.

12. Scroll down to the **Important** icon.

13. Drag the **Important** icon over the **DIR_COLORS file icon** in the right frame, and release the mouse button.

14. Rename the copied file by right-clicking the **DIR_COLORS file icon**, and then selecting **Rename** from the popup menu.

15. For the new filename, type **example.txt**, then press Enter.

16. Delete the example.txt file by dragging the file icon over the **Trash** icon on the desktop and releasing the mouse button.

17. Close the **Nautilus** file manager window.

18. Right-click the **Trash** icon on the desktop, then select **Empty Trash** from the pop-up menu.

19. In the confirmation dialog, select **Empty Trash**.

(End of Exercise)

Exercise 1-2   *Access the Command Line Interface*

In this exercise, log in as user geeko at the first virtual terminal. Switch to the second virtual terminal and verify that a login prompt is shown there. Before switching back to the graphical user interface, log out from the first virtual terminal.

Detailed Steps to Complete the Exercise

Do the following:

1. Switch to the first virtual terminal by pressing Ctrl+Al+F1.

2. Type geeko as a login name, then press Enter.

3. Type novell as the password, then press Enter.

4. Switch to the second virtual terminal by pressing Alt+F2.

   Notice that you are not logged in at this terminal.

5. To switch back to the first terminal, press Alt+F1.

   You are still logged in as geeko.

6. Log out by entering exit.

7. Switch back to the graphical user interface by pressing Alt+F7.

(End of Exercise)

Exercise 1-3   *Work with the Linux Shell*

In this exercise, you practice using different shell features, learn to use vi, and create a simple shell script.

In Part I, use the history feature of the shell and get root permissions at the command line.

In Part II, use manual and info pages to get information on the man and info commands.

In Part III, create an alias labeled `hello` that prints a personal welcome message **Hello** *username* on the screen. Remove this alias again.

In Part IV, use the vi editor to write a text to a text file.

In Part V, create a simple shell script that backs up the content of your home directory to the /tmp directory.

Detailed Steps to Complete the Exercise

- Part I: Use the History Feature and Get root Permission
- Part II: Access Manual and Info Pages
- Part III: Create an Alias and Use Piping and Redirection
- Part IV: Use vi to Edit Files
- Part V: Create a Simple Shell Script

Part I: Use the History Feature and Get root Permission

Do the following:

1. Log in as geeko and open a terminal window.
2. View the history cache by entering `history`.
3. Press the Up-arrow until you see a command you would like to execute, then press Enter.
4. Type `h` and press Page Up once.

    You should see the `history` command at the command line again.
5. Press Enter to execute the `history` command.
6. Switch to root by entering

    `su -`

    Then enter a password of **novell**.
7. Check to make sure you are logged in as root by entering `id`.
8. Start YaST by entering

    `yast2`

    YaST should start in GUI mode.

9. Quit YaST by closing its window.

10. Become the user geeko again by entering

```
exit
```

Part II: Access Manual and Info Pages

1. Log in as **geeko** with the password **novell**.

2. Right-click on the GNOME desktop, and select ***open in terminal***.

3. Find the sections of the man pages for the `info` command by entering `whatis info`.

4. Read the first section (user commands) of the man pages of the `info` command by entering `man 1 info`.

5. To look for "filename," enter **/filename**.

6. Scroll through the text with the Up and Down arrow keys.

7. When you finish viewing the information, exit (quit) the man page by typing `q`.

8. From the terminal window, display the info pages for the info command by entering `info info`.

9. Move the cursor to the first reference (Getting Started) by pressing Tab.

10. Follow the reference by pressing Enter.

11. Move the cursor to the reference **Quitting Info** by pressing Tab nine times.

12. Follow the reference by pressing Enter.

13. Return to the page Getting Started by typing `l` (lowercase L).

14. Exit the info file by typing `q`.

15. Close the terminal window.

Part III: Create an Alias and Use Piping and Redirection

1. In the terminal window, view all defined aliases by entering `alias`.

2. Define a new alias by entering the following:

```
alias hello='echo Hello $USER'
```

3. Check the functionality of the alias hello by entering `hello`.

4. Check the command type of the `hello` command by entering the following:

```
type hello
```

5. Remove the alias by entering `unalias hello`.

6. In a terminal window, redirect the output of the `ls` command for the home directory ("~") to a file by entering the following:

```
ls ~ > home_directory
```

7. Display the content of the file by entering `cat home_directory`.

8. Append the output of the ls command for the root directory ("/") to the `home_directory` file by entering the following:

    `ls / >> home_directory`

9. Display the content of the file by entering `cat home_directory`.

10. Overwrite the `home_directory` file with the output of the `ls` command by entering the following:

    `ls / > home_directory`

11. Display the content of the file by entering `cat home_directory`.

12. Write the output of the ls command on the screen and into the `home_directory` file by entering the following:

    `ls ~ | tee home_directory`

13. Remove the `home_directory` file by entering `rm home_directory`.

14. Verify that the file was removed by entering `ls -l`.

15. Close the terminal window.

Part IV: Use vi to Edit Files

In this exercise, create a new `vi_test` file with the text editor vi. Then, edit the text using the command mode of vi.

To enter a text, do the following:

1. Open a terminal window.

2. Start vi by entering `vi`.

3. Switch to the insert mode by typing `i`.

4. Type the following two paragraphs of text (press Enter at the end of each line):

    Administrator training for SUSE Linux Enterprise Server 11 will be held in Training Room 4 of Building B on Tuesday of next week.

    Make sure you bring your SUSE Linux Enterprise Server 11 Administration Manual. There will be wireless Internet access available in the training room.

5. Exit the insert mode by pressing Esc.

6. Move the cursor to the middle of the second line of the first paragraph.

7. Delete text to the right of the cursor by typing `D` (uppercase d).

8. Undo the deletion by typing `u`.

9. Delete the character directly under the cursor by pressing Delete.

10. Copy the current line to the internal buffer by typing `y` twice.

11. Move the cursor to the beginning of the first line of the second paragraph.

12. Insert the contents of the internal buffer after the current line by typing `p`.

13. Save the file with filename vi_test by entering `:w vi_test`.

14. Exit vi by entering `:q`.

15. Close the terminal window.

16. Right-click the `vi_test` file on the desktop and select ***Open with gedit***.

    Notice that this is the same text as in vi.

17. Using the same conventions as you would in a Microsoft text editor, delete the word *server* and replace it with the word *desktop*.

18. Select ***File > Save***. Close the gedit window.

19. Open the command terminal.

20. Change directory to the desktop by entering `cd Desktop/`.

NOTE: Commands are case sensitive. Make sure you enter a capital "D" when typing the word Desktop.

---

21. Enter `vi vi_test`.

    The same file opens, displaying the changes you made in gedit.

22. Enter `:q` and close the terminal window.

Part V: Create a Simple Shell Script

Do the following:

1. Open a terminal window and change to the `~/bin` directory with the `cd ~/bin` command.

2. Open the backup.sh file in vi by entering `vi backup.sh`.

3. Press `i` and enter the following text:

```
#!/bin/bash
#
# backup.sh
# Backup geeko's home directory to /tmp using rsync

echo "Backing up /home/geeko to /tmp/"

rsync -a --no-whole-file /home/geeko /tmp
```

4. Save the file and close the editor by pressing Esc and entering `:wq`.

5. Change the permissions of the script by entering `chmod 744 backup.sh`.

6. Test the script by entering `backup.sh`.

(End of Exercise)

Exercise 1-4   *Use Command Line Tools to Work with Files and Directories*

In this exercise, you use different tools to administer files and directories.

In Part I, you create an empty file and view the content of a file. Use the `touch`, `cat`, `less`, `head`, and `tail` commands.

In Part II, you copy and move files with the `cp` and `mv` commands.

In Part III, you create a symbolic link to the ~/my_file file and a hardlink to the ~/my_file1 file with the `ln` command:

In Part IV, you use the `whereis`, `which`, and `find` commands.

Detailed Steps to Complete the Exercise

- Part I: Create and View Files
- Part II: Copy and Move Files and Directories
- Part III: Link Files
- Part IV: Find Files in the Linux System

Part I: Create and View Files

1. Open a GNOME terminal window from the *main menu*.
2. Create a new empty file by entering

   `touch new_file`

3. Open another terminal window and log in as root (`su -`) with a password of **novell**.
4. Display the content of the `/var/log/messages` file by entering

   `cat /var/log/messages`

5. Display the content of `/var/log/messages` page-by-page by entering

   `less /var/log/messages`

6. Find the first occurrence of the word "root" by entering

   `/root`

7. Find the next occurrence of the word "root" by typing `n`.
8. Navigate within the `/var/log/messages` file by using the cursor keys and the PageUp and the PageDown keys.
9. Quit the display and return to the command line by typing `q`.
10. Display the first 5 lines of the `/var/log/messages` file by entering

    `head -n 5 /var/log/messages`

11. View a continuously updated display of the last lines of the `/var/log/messages` file by entering

```
tail -f /var/log/messages
```

12. Arrange the terminal windows on the desktop so that you can see the content of both.

13. In the first terminal window you opened in Step 2, log in as root (`su -`), then enter an invalid password (such as *suse*).

    Notice that the failed login attempt is logged in the second terminal window.

14. In the first terminal window, log in as root (`su -`) with a password of **novell**.

    The successful login is logged in the second terminal window.

15. Log out as root in the first terminal window by entering `exit`.

16. Close the first terminal window by entering `exit`.

17. Stop the tail process in the second terminal window by pressing Ctrl+c.

18. Log out as root by entering `exit`.

Part II: Copy and Move Files and Directories

1. Open a terminal window on the GNOME desktop if none is still open.

2. Change to geeko's home directory (~) with the `cd` command.

3. Rename `new_file` to `my_file` by entering the following:

   ```
   mv new_file my_file
   ```

4. Verify that the file was renamed by entering `ls -l`.

5. Make a copy of `my_file` and name it ***my_file1*** by entering the following:

   ```
   cp my_file my_file1
   ```

6. Verify that `my_file1` was created by entering `ls -l my*`.

7. Copy the `/usr/bin/rename` and `/usr/bin/tac` files to the `/tmp/` directory by entering the following:

   ```
   cp /usr/bin/rename /usr/bin/tac /tmp
   ```

8. Verify that the files were copied by entering `ls -l /tmp`.

9. Move the `/tmp/tac` file to the home directory (~) by entering the following:

   ```
   mv /tmp/tac ~
   ```

10. Verify the move by entering `ls -l`.

11. Move and rename the `/tmp/rename` file to `~/my_file2` by entering the following:

    ```
    mv /tmp/rename ~/my_file2
    ```

12. Verify that the my_file2 file exists by entering `ls -l`.

13. Copy the complete `/bin/` directory to the home directory with the new directory named `my_dir` by entering the following:

```
cp -r /bin ~/my_dir
```

14. Verify that the files were copied by entering `ls -l ~/my_dir`.

15. Create a directory named `new_dir` inside the `my_dir` directory by entering the following:

```
mkdir ~/my_dir/new_dir
```

16. Verify that the directory was created by entering the following:

```
ls ~/my_dir
```

17. Create a directory `geeko_dir`, including a new directory `empty_dir`, by entering the following:

```
mkdir -p ~/geeko_dir/empty_dir
```

18. Verify that geeko_dir was created by entering `ls`.

19. Verify that `empty_dir` was created by entering `ls geeko_dir`.

20. Try to remove the `~/geeko_dir` directory by entering `rmdir geeko_dir`.

    A message is displayed indicating that the directory cannot be removed because the directory is not empty.

21. Remove the `~/geeko_dir/empty_dir` directory by entering the following:

```
rmdir geeko_dir/empty_dir
```

22. Verify that the `/empty_dir` directory has been removed by entering `ls geeko_dir`.

23. Remove the `~/geeko_dir` directory by entering `rmdir geeko_dir`.

24. Verify that the directory was removed by entering `ls`.

25. Remove the `~/my_dir/login` file by entering `rm ~/my_dir/login`.

26. Verify that the file has been removed by entering `ls ~/my_dir/login`.

27. Remove all files with names that begin with "a" in the `/home/geeko/my_dir/` directory by entering the following:

```
rm -i ~/my_dir/a*
```

28. Confirm every warning by entering `y`.

29. Remove the `/home/geeko/my_dir/` directory, including its content, by entering the following:

```
rm -r ~/my_dir
```

30. Confirm every warning by entering `y`.

31. Verify that the directory has been removed by entering `ls ~/my_dir`.

Part III: Link Files

1. Enter the following to create a symbolic link to the `my_file` file in your home directory:

```
ln -s ~/my_file softlink
```

2. Enter the following to create a hard link to the `my_file1` file in your home directory:

```
ln ~/my_file1 hardlink
```

3. Display the links by entering `ls -l`.

   Notice that the symbolic link identifies the file it is linked to and that the link counter is 2 on the `my-file1` and `hardlink` files.

4. Close the terminal window.

Part IV: Find Files in the Linux System

1. On the GNOME desktop, open a terminal window.

2. Find the type of the `ll` command by entering `type ll`.

3. Find the manual pages of the `find` command by entering `whereis -m find`.

4. Find the path of the program Firefox by entering `which firefox`.

   You should see this output:

```
/usr/bin/firefox
```

5. From the terminal window command line, find all files in the home directory whose names start with "my" by entering the following:

```
find ~ -name "my*"
```

6. Find all files in the `/tmp/` directory that were changed or created in the last 24 hours by entering the following:

   `find /tmp -ctime -1` (the numeral one, not the letter "l")

1. Find all HTML headings of hierarchy 2 in the `/usr/share/doc/packages/yast2-users/users.html` file by entering the following (on one line):

```
grep "<h2>" /usr/share/doc/packages/yast2-users/
users.html
```

   The output may appear similar to this:

```
<h2>Features (SL9/3)</h2>
<h2>Implementation</h2>
<h2>The files</h2>
```

2. Find all locations in the HTML files of the `/usr/share/doc/packages/yast2-users/` directory that include the word "configuration" by entering the following:

```
grep configuration /usr/share/doc/packages/yast2-
users/*.html
```

3. Find all locations in the HTML files of all "yast2" directories `/usr/share/doc/packages/yast2-*/` that include lines beginning with a number by entering the following:

    ```
    egrep "^[0-9]" /usr/share/doc/packages/yast2-*/*.html
    ```

4. Find all locations in the HTML files of all `/usr/share/doc/packages/yast2-*/` directories that include lines beginning with the letter "m" by entering the following:

    ```
    egrep "^[m]" /usr/share/doc/packages/yast2-*/*.html
    ```

5. Close the terminal window.

(End of Exercise)

Exercise 1-5   ***Managing Time Zone Information***

In this exercise, you practice configuring locale and time zone information on Linux. You use the TZ environment variable to change time zones on your da-host system.

Detailed Steps to Complete the Exercise

1. On your da-host system, log in as geeko (if necessary).

2. Right-click on the desktop and select **Open in Terminal**.

3. View the current time, date, and time zone by entering `date` at the shell prompt.

   You should see output similar to the following:

   ```
   geeko@da-host:~/> date
   Thu Aug  5 14:08:00 MDT 2010
   ```

   In this example, the system is set to the Mountain Daylight Time zone.

4. Change to the Eastern Daylight Time zone by entering `export TZ=EDT` at the shell prompt.

   TIP: If your time zone is already set to EDT, you should select a different time zone, such as **MDT**.

   ---

5. Verify that the TZ environment variable was populated by entering `env` at the shell prompt.

   You should see that TZ is set to a value of EDT, as shown below:

   ```
   geeko@da-host:~/> env
   LESSKEY=/etc/lesskey.bin
   ORBIT_SOCKETDIR=/tmp/orbit-geeko
   INFODIR=/usr/local/info:/usr/share/info:/usr/info
   NNTPSERVER=news
   MANPATH=/usr/local/man:/usr/share/man
   ...
   TZ=EDT
   ...
   QT_IM_SWITCHER=imsw-multi
   G_BROKEN_FILENAMES=1
   COLORTERM=gnome-terminal
   XAUTHORITY=/var/run/gdm/auth-for-geeko-t4AGzY/database
   _=/usr/bin/env
   ```

6. Verify that the time zone has changed by entering `date` at the shell prompt.

   You should see that the time zone has changed to the value you specified in the TZ environment variable. An example is shown below:

   ```
   geeko@da-host:~/> date
   Thu Aug  5 20:08:13 EDT 2010
   ```

7. Reset the TZ variable back to its original time zone value.

(End of Exercise)

Review Questions

1. Which of the following is not an item that you will find on the panel at the bottom of the GNOME desktop?
    a) Clock
    b) Workspaces
    c) Control Center
    d) Computer menu

2. What is the name of the GNOME File Manager?
    a) GNOMEfile
    b) Nautilus
    c) Explorer
    d) Midnight Commander

3. Which of the following AccessX keyboard accessibility settings can be used to sound an audible alert whenever Caps Lock is turned on?
    a) ToggleKeys
    b) StickyKeys
    c) BounceKeys
    d) DelayKeys

4. Which accessibility tool can be used as a screen reader and magnifier?
    a) Juptier Speech System
    b) Orca
    c) Magnifier
    d) AccessX

5. How can you switch to a graphical virtual terminal in SUSE Linux?
    a) Ctrl+Alt+F1
    b) Ctrl+Alt+F7
    c) Type GNOME at the command line
    d) Type X at the command line

6. Which file is read by all login shells?
    a) /etc/profile
    b) /etc/bashrc
    c) /etc/bash.bashrc
    d) ~/.profile

7. Which key may be used to complete file and directory names on the command line?
    a) Ctrl+c
    b) ~
    c) &
    d) Tab

8. Which command can be used to open a non-login shell as the root user and switch to the root user's home directory?
    a) su
    b) su root
    c) su -
    d) su ~

9. Which man page section refers to system calls?
    a) 1
    b) 3
    c) 8
    d) 2

10. Which command could you type at a command prompt to find out about the syntax of the "grep" command?
    a) man grep
    b) man –k grep
    c) apropos grep
    d) both b) and c)

11. Which directory contains most application and system documentation?
    a) /usr/share/doc
    b) /usr/share/man
    c) /usr/share/info
    d) /usr/share/howto

12. Which of the following is not a valid environment variable?
    a) PS1
    b) GREP
    c) HOME
    d) PATH

13. Which of the following commands can be used to set an alias?
    a) export
    b) umask
    c) alias
    d) MYALIAS=

14. Which command below is a filter command that reads the standard input and writes it to both the standard output and a specified file?
    a) trunk
    b) branch
    c) y
    d) tee

15. Which one of the following uses "proper" command syntax?
    a) Command | Command
    b) Command > Command
    c) Command < Command
    d) Command >> Command

16. Normally, redirecting is destructive on existing files, which item will append to existing files?
    a) <>
    b) ><
    c) >>
    d) none of the above

17. Which of the following will run the cd command if the ls command is successful?
    a) ls / || cd /
    b) ls / && cd /
    c) ls / &) cd /
    d) ls / |) cd /

18. What key can you press while in insert mode within the vi editor to switch to command mode?
    a) i
    b) :
    c) Esc
    d) Alt

19. Which echo backslash sequence creates a trailing new line in a shell script?
    a) \r
    b) \c
    c) \n
    d) \a

20. Which two control structures below are looping structures? (Choose two answers.)
    a) case
    b) until
    c) if
    d) while

21. Which command will determine the type of a file by examining its contents?
    a) ls
    b) dirs
    c) ls -F
    d) file

22. Which one of the following commands can be used to create a symbolic link?
    a) link
    b) symlink
    c) ln
    d) ln -s

23. Which command would we type to view the contents of the file "cert" in our present directory one page at a time?
    a) cat cert
    b) head cert
    c) less cert
    d) tail cert

24. Which option to the copy command must you use to copy a directory to another location on the file system?
    a) -d
    b) -r
    c) -c
    d) -o

25. Which command may be used to search for files in directories listed within the PATH variable?
    a) which
    b) find
    c) locate
    d) slocate

26. Which of the following commands would list all lines that contain the word "super" at the end of the line in the /etc/hosts file?
    a) grep 'super=' /etc/hosts
    b) grep '^super' /etc/hosts
    c) grep 'super$' /etc/hosts
    d) grep '[super]' /etc/hosts

27. Which text tool can be used to format a file for printing?
    a) nr
    b) expand
    c) pr
    d) split

28. Which text tool can be used to replace tab characters with space characters?
    a) tr
    b) unexpand
    c) od
    d) expand

29. Which of the following sed commands will replace all "the" strings with "the" in the /etc/
hosts file?
   a) sed s/teh/the/ /etc/hosts
   b) sed /the/teh/ /etc/hosts
   c) sed g/teh/the/ /etc/hosts
   d) sed s/teh/the/g /etc/hosts

30. Which of the following commands can be used to display your locale information?
   a) locale
   b) tzinfo
   c) tzconfig
   d) iconv

Discovery Exercises

Exploring Virtual Terminals

There are six command-line virtual terminals available in SUSE Linux by default (tty1-tty6). Use the appropriate key combination discussed in this chapter to switch to tty1. Log in as the **root** user. What prompt do you get? Type **who** and press Enter. What terminal does the **who** command indicate that you are on? Next, switch to tty2 and log in as the **geeko** user. What prompt do you get? Type **who** and press Enter. Who is logged in, and on which terminals?

All network programs use a port number to identify information that is sent to them. The X Window System that is used to display a graphic desktop environment such as GNOME is a network application that listens to information addressed to TCP/UDP port 0. Hackers can use this information to breach the security of the X Window System, and this threat is heightened when the X Window System is run as the root user, which has all rights to the Linux system. As a result, many programs will refuse to start in a graphical desktop environment while the user is logged in as root. It is best practice to log into GNOME as a regular user and only switch to the root user as necessary to perform system administration (using the **su** command).

Ensure that you have audio enabled on your PC and switch to tty7 and log in to the GNOME desktop as the **geeko** user. Do you hear the startup chime? Following this, open the GNOME Terminal application, type **who**, and press Enter. How does the **who** command indicate that you have a GUI session? Log out of the GNOME desktop and log back in to the GNOME desktop as the root user. Why don't you hear the startup chime? Log out of the GNOME desktop.

Customizing GNOME and Exploring Accessibility Tools

Log into the GNOME desktop as the **geeko** user. Spend a few moments to navigate the desktop and Computer menu. Create launchers/shortcuts on your desktop and bottom panel to programs that you may use frequently in the future (e.g., GNOME Terminal). Next, open the Control Center from your Computer menu and navigate to the various accessibility areas described in this chapter. Enable any accessibility options, such as MouseKeys, that you find enhance your own desktop experience (if any).

Obtaining Help

Log into tty1 as the **root** user. Use the manual pages to find help on the **top** and **vmstat** commands. What are these commands commonly used for? What manual page section are these commands listed in? What are some common options for each command? Use the manual pages to find help on the **free** command. Note that the man command prompts you to choose the section number if the name is in multiple sections. Choose section 1 and view the purpose and options for the **free** command.

Next, use the **apropos** command to find any utilities that have the word **who** in their name or description. How many utilities are there? What section of the manual pages are they from? Which utility may be used to see who is logged onto the system and what programs they are running? View the regular manual page for this command and note any options that can be used. Run the command to verify its purpose.

The info pages provide an alternative to the manual pages for finding command and file information, but not all commands on your system have info pages available. Use the **info** command to find help on the **top**, **free**, and **vmstat** commands. Do info pages exist for all three utilities?

Another utility that can be used to obtain information about commands on the system is the **help** utility. However, the help utility only lists **help** for commands that are built into your shell. Type **help** at a command prompt and observe the various commands for which you can obtain help. Next, type **help echo** to learn the syntax and usage of the echo command in your shell. Use the help command to learn about three more built-in shell commands of your choice.

There are many Linux help resources on the Internet. One of the most comprehensive is the Linux Documentation Project (LDP). LDP hosts a complete collection of HOWTO documents that describe how to perform most user and administrative tasks in Linux. In addition, LDP hosts online manual pages as well as longer and more in-depth guides to different Linux technologies. Search the latest HOWTO documents at the LDP (http://www.tldp.org) or for information on how to play DVDs in Linux. What is the name of the HOWTO document? How is the HOWTO document organized? Next, view the index.html document in /usr/share/doc/packages/dvd+rw-tools/ using your Firefox web browser and note the information supplied for this package.

Navigating the File System

Log into tty1 as the **root** user and perform the following actions in order. For each action, write the command(s) that you used. When finished, log out of tty1.

1. Change to the **/etc/sysconfig** directory using an absolute path and verify that it has been changed.

2. Use a relative path to change to the / directory.

3. Use a relative path to change to the **/var/lib** directory.

4. Use a relative path to change to the **/etc/sysconfig** directory.

5. Change to your home directory.

6. Without changing directories, perform a long listing of the **/dev/log** file using a relative path. What type of file is it?

Using the Filename Completion Feature

Log in to tty1 as the **geeko** user, then type **cd /e** and press the **Tab** key. What happens? Type **s** and press the **Tab** key. Press the **Tab** key again to see the possible choices. Type **ysc** and press the **Tab** key. Type **net** and press the **Tab** key. Press **Enter** to execute your command. What directory are you in? Log out of tty1.

Managing Files and Directories

Log into tty1 as the **root** user and perform the following actions in order. For each action, write the command(s) that you used. When finished, log out of tty1.

1. Copy the file **/etc/issue** to your current directory and verify that the copy was successful.

2. Copy the file **/etc/issue** to your current directory and rename it **newissue** with one command. Verify that the copy was successful.

3. Rename the file **newissue** in your current directory to **newissue2** and verify that the file was renamed successfully.

4. Make a copy of the **Desktop** directory (in your home directory) called **Desktop2** and verify that the contents of each directory are identical.

5. Rename the **Desktop2** directory **Desktop3** and verify that the rename operation was successful.

6. Remove the **newissue2** file in your home directory and verify that you were successful.

7. Remove the **Desktop3** directory in your home directory with a single command and verify that you were successful.

Locating Files

Log into tty1 as the **root** user. Use the **which** command to locate the **who**, **grep**, and **cp** executable files. What directories are the files in? Type echo $PATH and press Enter to view the PATH variable. Are these directories listed? Create a new file called **file1** with the touch command. Next, use the **which** command to find the file called **file1** in your home directory. Why were you not successful?

Use the appropriate **find** commands to perform the following actions. For each action, write the command that you used.

1. Find all files on the system called **hosts**.

2. Find all files under the **/etc** directory and subdirectories that are larger than 100K in size.

3. Find all files in the **/etc** directory and subdirectories that are less than 2K in size.

4. Find all symbolic links underneath the **/usr** directory.

5. Find all files in the **/usr** directory and subdirectories that were modified less than one day ago.

6. Find all files in the **/tmp** directory and subdirectories that are owned by the root user.

File Linking

Log in to tty1 as the **geeko** user and copy the file **/etc/issue** to your current directory. Next, perform a long listing of the **issue** file in your current directory. Is it hard linked? Is it symbolically linked? How can you tell?

Create a hard link to **issue** called **hardissue**. Next, do a long listing of both files. What are their sizes? What are their modification dates? What are their link counters? Why? Next, use the **ls —li** command to view their inode numbers. Are they the same? Remove the file **hardissue**. Was issue removed as well? What is the link count of issue now?

Create a soft link to **issue** called **symissue**. Next, do a long listing of both files. What are their sizes? What are their modification dates? What are their link counts? What is the file type of **symissue**? What does the filename of **symissue** indicate? Next, use the **ls —li** command to view their inode numbers. Are they the same?

Working with Variables and Aliases

Log in to tty1 as the **geeko** user and perform the following actions in order. For each action, write the command(s) that you used. When finished, log out of tty1.

1. Create a shell variable called **VAR1** that contains the value **test** and verify your results.

2. Run the **set** command and use the appropriate keys to view all of the contents on the terminal screen. Does **VAR1** appear in the output?

3. Remove the **VAR1** variable from memory and verify that you were successful.

4. Create an alias called **dir** which runs the commands **pwd** and **ls —l** in that order. Test your alias and then remove it from the system.

Working with Environment Files

Log into tty1 as the **geeko** user and run the **ls —a** command. How can you identify the hidden files? Next, type the command **echo "echo Welcome to your Login Shell" >> .profile** and press Enter to add a line to the bottom of your personal profile environment file. Type the command **tail .profile** to verify that it was added successfully. Next, log out of tty1 and log in again as the **geeko** user. What happened? Following this, log out of tty1 and log in again as the root user. Why didn't you see the greeting? Log out of tty1.

Log in to tty1 as the **geeko** user. Use the vi editor to open the ~/**.profile** file. Add a line to the bottom of the file that creates the **VAR1** environment variable and sets its value to **test2**. When finished, save your changes and quit the vi editor. Log out of tty1. Log in to tty1 again as the **geeko** user. Display the value of the VAR1 variable on the terminal screen to ensure that the ~/ **.profile** file was read when a login shell was created. Next, use the vi editor to open the ~/ **.bashrc** file. Add a line to the bottom of the file that creates the dir alias to run the commands **pwd** and **ls —l**, in that order. When finished, save your changes and quit the vi editor. Log out of tty1. Log in to tty1 again as the geeko user. Execute the **dir** alias to ensure that the ~/**.bashrc** file was read when a login shell was created.

Again, use the vi editor to open the ~/.bashrc file. Add a line to the bottom of the file that runs the command **echo Hi**. When finished, save your changes and quit the vi editor. Next, type the **bash** command to start another bash shell on top of your current bash shell. What was displayed and why? Use the vi editor to remove the **echo Hi** line from the bottom of the file and log out of tty1. **Note:** You will need to use the **exit** command twice, since you have two bash shells running.

Redirecting and Piping Command Output

Log in to tty1 as the **root** user and perform the following actions in order. For each action, write the command(s) that you used. When finished, log out of tty1.

1. Save the stdout of the **df** command to a file called **diskspace** in your current directory and verify that you were successful.

2. Append the output of the **date** command to the **diskspace** file in your current directory and verify that you were successful.

3. Use the **find** command to locate all files starting from the / directory called **hosts**. Save the stdout to a file called **hostfiles** in your current directory and the stderr to a file called **errors** in your current directory. When the command has completed, view the contents of each file.

4. Send the output of the **mount** command to the **wc —l** command to display only the number of mounted file systems. Describe what the **—l** option to the **wc** command is used for.

5. Send the output of the **ls —l /dev** command to the **less** command.

6. Send the output of the **ls —l /dev** command to the **grep tty** command, which should send its output to the **less** command.

7. Send the output of the **ls —l /dev** command to the **grep tty** command, which should send its output to file **ttyfile** in your current directory. View the contents of **ttyfile** to verify its contents.

Redirection Problems

Log in to tty1 as the **geeko** user. Make a copy of the **/etc/hosts** file in your home directory by typing the command **cp /etc/hosts ~** at a command prompt. Verify that you have the hosts file in your current directory. Next, use the **sort** command to sort the file by typing **sort hosts** and view the output on your terminal screen. Following this, type the command **sort hosts > hosts at** the command prompt to save the sorted output back into the file. View the contents of the hosts file. What are the contents? Explain what happened, using your knowledge of output redirection, and how it could have been remedied. When finished, log out of tty1.

Piping stderr

Only stdout is sent across a pipe to another command by default. Log in to tty1 as the **geeko** user and verify this by trying the following commands and noting the absence of stderr in file1:

ls /etc/hosts /etc/h | tee file1

cat file1

Using the information presented in this chapter, how could you send stderr across the pipe in these commands?

Working with awk and sed

Log in to tty1 as the **root** user and perform the following actions in order. For each action, write the command(s) that you used. When finished, log out of tty1.

1. Make a copy of the **/etc/passwd** file in your home directory called **passwd**.

2. Use the **sed** command to replace all occurrences of the string **bash** with **false** and save the results to a file called **passwd2** in your current directory.

3. Use the **sed** command to delete all lines in the **passwd2** file that have the string **home** in them.

4. Use the **awk** command to print the first, sixth, and seventh fields of the **passwd** file to the terminal screen. A space character should separate each field.

SECTION 2   Install SUSE Linux Enterprise Server 11

This section covers partitions, Logical Volume Manager (LVM), Redundant Array of Independent Disks (RAID), and file systems. You need these to plan and perform a successful installation of SUSE Linux Enterprise Server 11 (SLES 11). Once SLES 11 is installed, you can explore the file system layout, which is standardized in the Linux File System Hierarchy Standard.

Objectives

1. Understand Partitions, LVM, RAID, and File Systems
2. Perform a SLES 11 Installation
3. Understand the File System Hierarchy Standard (FHS)

Objective 1 Understand Partitions, LVM, RAID, and File Systems

Before you actually start installing an operating system, you need to make up your mind on how to use the available hard disk space, because later changes to the initial layout can be difficult.

The way you divide the available space should take into consideration the applications you intend to install: a file server usually needs a different layout than a web server.

To design a useful layout, you need to understand the following:

- Understand Partitions in a Linux System
- Understand Logical Volume Manager and Software RAID
- Select a Linux File System

Understand Partitions in a Linux System

On an x86 system, hard disks can be logically divided into smaller portions, called partitions. This lets you install more than one operating system on a hard drive or use different areas of the disk for programs and data.

The following partition types are available:

- **Primary partitions**. A primary partition consists of a continuous range of cylinders (physical disk areas) assigned to a particular file system.

  Due to the limitation to 64 bytes of the partition table in the master boot record (which comprises the first 512 bytes on a hard disk), only 4 primary partitions are available on x86 systems.

- **Extended partition**. An extended partition is also a continuous range of disk cylinders. However, an extended partition can be subdivided into logical partitions. Logical partitions do not require entries in the partition table.

  Only one of the primary partitions can be an extended partition.

  This partition type was created to circumvent the limitation imposed by the maximum of four primary partitions on x86 systems; it can hold several logical partitions. In other words, an extended partition is a container for logical partitions.

- **Logical partitions**. Logical partitions exist within an extended partition. With SLES 11, there can be a maximum number of 11 logical partitions.

If you need more than four partitions on a single hard disk, you should create an extended partition instead of a fourth primary partition. This extended partition should encompass the entire remaining free cylinder range. Then you can create multiple logical partitions within the extended partition.

It does not matter which type of partitions you use for your Linux system. Primary and logical partitions both work equally well.

The following will help you when planning a SLES 11 installation:

- Design Guidelines for Implementing Partitions
- Naming Conventions for Partitions

Design Guidelines for Implementing Partitions

YaST normally proposes a partitioning scheme consisting of two partitions, one swap partition (about 1.5 times the size of the RAM, but not more than 2 GB) and one partition that uses the rest of the disk space to hold the / directory.

If there is an existing partition on the hard drive, YaST attempts to maintain that partition.

If you want to implement your own partitioning scheme, consider the following recommendations (depending on the amount of space and how the computer will be used, adjust the distribution of the available disk space):

- If your hard disk has less than 4 GB of available space, you should use one partition for the swap space and one for the root partition (/). In this case, the root partition must allow for those directories that often reside on their own partitions if more space is available.

- If your hard disk has more than 4 GB of available space, you should at least create a swap partition and a root partition (4 GB). You can create separate partitions for different directories in your Linux server's file system. The following directories are good candidates for having a separate partition created:

    - **/boot/.** Depending on the hardware, it might be useful to create a boot partition (/boot) as the first partition to hold the boot mechanism and the Linux kernel. On current hardware, this is not an issue anymore, but on older hardware, a separate /boot partition is sometimes required for Linux to boot properly.

      This partition should be located at the start of the disk and should have a size of 100 – 200 MB. As a rule, always create such a partition if it was included in YaST's original proposal.

    - **/opt/.** Some third party programs install their data in /opt/. In this case, you might want to create a separate partition for /opt/ (4 GB or more). For instance, KDE and GNOME are installed in /opt/.

    - **/usr/.** The /usr/ (Unix System Resources) directory contains many of your Linux program files. Apart from directories holding user data, /usr/ is usually the biggest directory in the Linux installation. Putting it on a separate partition (at least 4GB) allows special mount options, such as read only, to prevent changes to programs. Software updates require the partition to be remounted as read-write.

    - **/var/.** The /var/ directory contains a variety of information including log files, mail spool files, and Xen virtual machine files. As such, it's usually a good idea to put /var/ on a separate partition. You should allocate at least 3 GB of space for this partition.

Situations such as excessive mail or an overly large log file would only fill the partition containing the /var/ directory, not the root file system. The administrator would still be able to administer the server and correct the issue.

❑ **/srv/.** Contains files served by Web and FTP services in a series of subdirectories such as ftp and www. The data offered by these services to users can be put on a separate partition.

❑ **/home/.** Contains users' home directories. Putting /home/ on a separate partition prevents users from using up all disk space and facilitates updates. In addition, if you have to reinstall the operating system for some reason, you can preserve data in /home/ by leaving the partition untouched.

❑ **/tmp/.** Contains temporary files. Having /tmp/ on a separate partition (1 GB or more) allows you to mount it with special options, such as noexec, and also prevents processes from filling the disk with files in /tmp/.

❑ **Additional partitions.** If the partitioning is performed by YaST and other partitions are detected in the system, these partitions are also entered in the /etc/fstab file to enable easy access to this data.

The following is an example:

```
/dev/sda8 /data2 auto noauto,user 0 0
```

Such partitions, whether they are Linux or FAT, are specified by YaST with the noauto and user options. This allows any user to mount or unmount these partitions as needed.

For security reasons, YaST does not automatically enter the exec option, which is needed for executing programs from the respective location. However, you can enter this option manually.

Entering the exec option is necessary if you encounter system messages such as Bad interpreter or Permission denied.

Naming Conventions for Partitions

The following table shows the names of the Linux devices used for hard drives:

Table 2-1   *Device Names for Hard Drives*

Device	Linux Name
First SCSI hard disk or primary master IDE hard disk	/dev/sda
Second SCSI hard disk or primary slave IDE hard disk	/dev/sdb
Third SCSI hard disk or secondary master IDE hard disk	/dev/sdc
Fourth SCSI hard disk or secondary slave IDE hard disk	/dev/sdd

NOTE: In SLES 10, as well as other past Linux distributions, the device names for IDE hard disks were `/dev/hda`, `/dev/hdb`, etc., instead of `/dev/sda`, `/dev/sdb`, etc. Device files are covered in more detail in Device Files (/dev/).

Partitions follow the naming convention of the hard drive, followed by a partition number.

For example, the first partition on the first drive would be `/dev/sda1` (`/dev/sda` + 1 as the first partition). The first logical partition defined on a hard disk will always be number 5.

The following table shows the partition names corresponding to the device the partition is defined on:

Table 2-2 *Device Names for Partitions*

Partition	Linux Name
First partition on first hard drive	/dev/sda1
Second partition on first hard drive	/dev/sda2
First partition on third hard drive	/dev/sdc1
First logical partition on primary master IDE hard drive (older systems)	/dev/hda5
Second logical partition on secondary slave IDE hard drive (older systems)	/dev/hdd6

For example, if you perform a new installation of SLES 11 on a system with two IDE drives, you might want the first drive to include a partition for swap and `/`. You also might want to put all logs, mail, and home directories on the second hard drive.

The following is an example of how you might want to partition the disks (it assumes that the DVD or CD-ROM drive is the slave on the first IDE controller):

Table 2-3 *Partitioning Example*

Partition	Linux Name
Swap partition	/dev/sda1
/ partition	/dev/sda2
Extended partition on second disk	/dev/sdc1
/var as a logical partition on second disk	/dev/sdc5
/home as a logical partition on second disk	/dev/sdc6
/app1 as a logical partition on second disk	/dev/sdc7

NOTE: On older installations you often find a small partition for `/boot/` because the LILO boot loader needs the kernel within the first 1024 cylinders of the hard disk to boot the system.

Understand Logical Volume Manager and Software RAID

The Logical Volume Manager (LVM) provides a higher-level view of the disk storage on a computer system than the traditional view of disks and partitions. This gives you much more flexibility in allocating storage space to applications and users.

After creating logical volumes with LVM, you can (within certain limits) resize and move logical volumes while they are still mounted and running.

You can also use LVM to manage logical volumes with names that make sense (such as "development" and "sales") instead of physical disk names such as "sda" and "sdb."

The Linux Kernel is capable of combining hard disks into arrays with the RAID levels 0, 1, 5, and 6.

To be able to decide when to use LVM and software RAID, you need to understand the following:

- Volume Manager Components

- Logical Volume Manager Features

- Software RAID

Both LVM and Software RAID can be managed with YaST, SLES 11's configuration and management tool, or from the command line.

Volume Manager Components

Conventional partitioning of hard disks on a Linux file system is basically inflexible. When a partition is full, you have to move the data to another medium before you can resize the partition, create a new file system, and copy the files back.

Normally, these changes cannot be implemented without changing adjacent partitions, whose contents also need to be backed up to other media and written back to their original locations after the re-partitioning.

Because it is difficult to modify partitions on a running system, LVM was developed. It provides a virtual pool of memory space (called a volume group) from which logical volumes can be generated, if needed. The operating system accesses these logical volumes like conventional physical partitions.

This approach lets you resize the physical media during operation without affecting the applications.

The basic structure of LVM includes the following components:

Figure 2-1   *LVM Components*

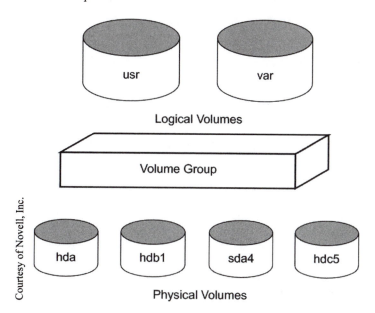

- **Physical volume.** Can be a partition or an entire hard disk.

- **Volume group.** Consists of one or several physical volumes grouped together. The physical partitions can be spread over different hard disks. You can add hard disks or partitions to the volume group during operation whenever necessary.

  The volume group can also be reduced in size by removing physical volumes (hard disks or partitions).

- **Logical volume.** Part of a volume group. A logical volume can be formatted and mounted like a physical partition.

You can think of volume groups as hard disks and logical volumes as partitions on those hard disks. The volume group can be split into several logical volumes that can be addressed with their device names (such as /dev/system/usr), just as conventional partitions can be addressed with theirs (/dev/sda1).

NOTE: Just as with other direct manipulations of the file system, a data backup should be made before configuring LVM.

Logical Volume Manager Features

LVM is useful for any computer. It is very flexible when you need to adapt to changed storage space requirements.

The following are features of LVM that help you implement storage solutions:

- You can combine several hard disks or partitions into a large volume group.

- Provided there is free space within the volume group, you can enlarge a logical volume. Resizing logical volumes is easier than resizing physical partitions.

- You can create extremely large logical volumes (terabytes).

- You can add hard disks to the volume group in a running system, provided you have hot-swappable hardware capable of such actions.

- You can add logical volumes in a running system, provided there is free space in the volume group.

- You can use several hard disks with improved performance in RAID 0 (striping) mode.

- There is no practical limit on the number of logical volumes (the limit in LVM version 1 was 256).

- The Snapshot feature enables consistent backups in the running system.

Software RAID

The purpose of RAID (Redundant Array of Independent [or Inexpensive] Disks) is to combine several hard disk partitions into one large virtual hard disk for optimizing performance and improving data security.

There are two types of RAID configurations:

- **Hardware RAID.** Hard disks are connected to a separate RAID controller. The operating system sees the combined hard disks as one device. No additional RAID configuration is necessary at the operating system level.

- **Software RAID.** Hard disks are combined by the operating system. The operating system sees every single disk and needs to be configured to use them as a RAID system.

In the past, hardware RAID provided better performance and data security than software RAID. However, with the current maturity of software RAID in the Linux kernel, it now provides comparable performance and data security.

The RAID level is determined by the method with which the hard disks are combined and by their number:

- **RAID 0.** RAID 0 improves the performance of your data access; however, there is no redundancy in RAID 0. With RAID 0, two or more hard disks are pooled together (**striping**). Disk performance is very good, but the RAID system is vulnerable to a single point of failure. If one of the disks fails, all data is lost.

- **RAID 1.** RAID 1 provides enhanced security for your data because the data is copied to one or several hard disks. This is also known as hard disk **mirroring**. If one disk is destroyed, a copy of its contents is available on the other disks. Minimum number of disks (or partitions) required for RAID 1 is two.

- **RAID 5.** RAID 5 (Redundant Striping) is an optimized compromise between RAID 0 and RAID 1 in terms of performance and redundancy. Data and a checksum are distributed across the hard disks. Minimum number of disks (or partitions) required for RAID 5 is three.

  If one hard disk fails, it must be replaced as soon as possible to avoid the risk of losing all data on the array by failure of another disk. The data on the failed disk is reconstructed on its replacement from the data on the remaining disks and the checksum. If more than one hard disk fails at the same time, the data on the RAID 5 array is lost.

- **RAID 6.** RAID 6 is comparable to RAID 5, with the difference being that two disks may fail without data loss. The minimum number of disks (or partitions) required for RAID 6 is four.

Using YaST, you can set up RAID levels 0, 1, and 5. (Other RAID levels than those described above exist, but these are not available with software RAID.)

Select a Linux File System

Before a partition or a logical volume can be used, a file system needs to be created within that partition. One of the key roles performed by the Linux operating system is to provide storage services by creating and managing a file system.

It is important to keep in mind that there is no file system best suited for every type of application. Each file system has its particular strengths and weaknesses, and they must be taken into account when making your selection.

Also keep in mind that even the most sophisticated file system cannot be a substitute for a reasonable backup strategy.

To select a file system that meets your system requirements, you need to understand the following:

- Linux File Systems
- Virtual File System Switch
- Linux File System Internals

NOTE: For additional details on specific file systems (such as ext3 and ReiserFS), see Section 18.2 in the *SLES 11 Installation and Administration* manual (`/usr/share/doc/manual/sles-admin_en/`, package `sles-admin_en`).

Linux File Systems

The type of file system you select depends on several factors, including speed and journaling. The following describes the file systems and formats available on Linux:

- Traditional File Systems
- Journaling File Systems
- Network File Systems

All of these file system types are included in the 2.6 Linux kernel (used in SLES 11).

You can enter the following command to list the file system formats the kernel currently supports:

```
cat /proc/filesystems
```

Traditional File Systems

Traditional file systems supported by Linux do not journal data or metadata (permissions, file size, timestamps, etc.). These include the following:

- **ext2.** Inode-based, designed for speed, efficient, and does not fragment easily.

  Because of these features, ext2 continues to be used by many administrators, even though it does not provide a journaling feature. The ext2 file system has been available for many years and can be easily converted to an ext3 file system.

- **MS-DOS/VFAT.** Primary file system for consumer versions of Microsoft Windows up to and including Windows Me.

  VFAT is a 32-bit virtual version of FAT (File Allocation Table) that includes long filenames.

- **minix.** Old and fairly limited, but is still sometimes used for floppy disks or RAM disks.

- **ISO9660.** The ISO9660 file system is the file system format used on CDROMs and DVDs. It is not used on hard disks.

Journaling File Systems

A journaling file system is one that logs changes to a journal before actually writing them to the main file system. Depending on the file system and how it is mounted, the journal can include metadata or also the data itself.

The following file systems available for Linux include a journaling feature:

- **ext3.** Enhanced version of the ext2 file system that supports journaling. ext3 is the default file system for SLES 11.

  The ext3 file system is a journaled file system that is most widely used in Linux today. It is quite robust and fast, although it does not scale too well to either large volumes or a great number of files.

  Recently a scalability feature called htrees was added, which significantly improves ext3's scalability. However, it is still not as scalable as some of the other file systems listed, even with htrees. With htrees, ext3's scalability is similar to NTFS. Without htrees, ext3 can't handle efficiently more than about 5,000 files in a directory.

- **ReiserFS.** Originally designed by Hans Reiser, ReiserFS organizes directories, files, and file metadata in an efficient data structure called *balanced tree*, which offers significant speed improvements for many applications, especially those which use lots of small files.

- **XFS.** High-performance journaling file system from SGI. It provides quick recovery after a crash, fast transactions, high scalability, and excellent bandwidth.

  XFS combines advanced journaling technology with full 64-bit addressing and scalable structures and algorithms.

NOTE: For details on XFS, see oss.sgi.com/projects/xfs/ (http://oss.sgi.com/projects/xfs/).

■ **NTFS.** (New Technology File System) Used by Windows NT, 2000, XP, and Vista.

Reading and writing to this system is supported under Linux. However, repair of the file system is not supported; if a repair is necessary, you have to do it from within Windows.

Network File Systems

In addition to the file systems used on local storage media, Linux can transparently include remote file systems in its file system tree. From the viewpoint of the user there is no difference whether the file system is local or remote.

The remote file systems supported include the following:

■ **NFS.** Network File System is traditionally used in UNIX/Linux environments. It is designed for sharing files and directories over a network, and it requires configuration of an NFS server (where the files and directories are located) and NFS clients (computers that access the files and directories remotely).

File systems are exported by an NFS server. With NFS, it does not matter which file system format is used on the server on individual partitions. As soon as a computer is functioning as an NFS server, it provides its file systems in a defined format NFS clients can access.

On the client, NFS appears and behaves as if the files were located on the local machine.

For example, each user's home directory can be exported by an NFS server and imported to a client, so the same home directories are accessible from every workstation on the network.

Usually NFS is used in combination with a central user management solution such as OpenLDAP.

■ **CIFS/SMBFS.** Common Internet File System (CIFS) and its forerunner, Server Message Block (SMB) file system, are used in Windows environments to provide file and print access to clients.

The Samba software package allows you to use Linux as a file and print server to provide access to files and print services to Windows and Linux clients using the SMB/CIFS protocol. Samba also allows Linux to act as a client, accessing resources hosted on Windows servers.

Virtual File System Switch

For a user or program, it does not matter which file system format is used. The same interface to the data always appears. This is implemented by the Virtual File System Switch (VFS) (also referred to as the *virtual file system*).

VFS is an abstraction level in the kernel providing defined interfaces for processes. It includes functions such as open a file, write to a file, and read from a file.

A program does not have to worry about how file access is implemented technically. The VFS forwards these requests to the corresponding driver for the file system format, as illustrated in the following:

Figure 2-2   *Virtual File System Switch*

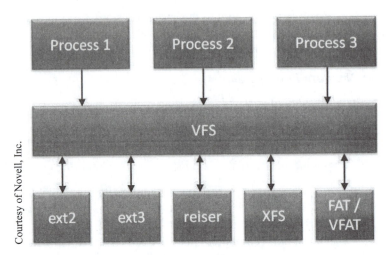

One of the features of the VFS is the display of file characteristics to the user as they are known from UNIX file system formats. This includes access permissions, even if they do not exist in the underlying file system, as is the case with FAT/VFAT.

Linux File System Internals

File systems in Linux are characterized by the fact that data and administration information are kept separate. Each file is described by an inode (index node or information node).

Each of these inodes has a size of 128 bytes and contains all the information about this file except the filename. This includes details such as the owner, access permissions, size, various time details (time of modification of data, last time of access, and time of modification of the inode), and the links to the data blocks of the file.

How data organization takes place differs from one file system format to the next. To understand the basics of file system data organization on Linux, you need to know the following:

- ext2fs File System Format
- ReiserFS Format
- Directories
- Links
- File System Journaling

ext2fs File System Format

The ext2 file system format is, in many ways, identical to traditional UNIX file system formats. The concepts of inodes, blocks, and directories are the same.

When an ext2 file system is created (the equivalent of formatting in other operating systems), the maximum number of files that can be created is specified. The inode density (together with the capacity of the partition) determines how many inodes can be created.

Remember that it is not possible to generate additional inodes later. You can specify the inode density only when creating the file system.

An inode must exist for each file or directory on the partition. The number of inodes also determines the maximum possible number of files. Typically, an inode is generated for 4096 bytes of capacity.

On average, each file should be 4 KB in size for the capacity of the partition to be used optimally. If a large number of files are smaller than 4 KB, more inodes are used compared with the capacity. This can result in the system being unable to create any more files, even if there is still space on the partition.

Therefore, for applications that create a large number of very small files, the inode density should be increased by setting the corresponding capacity to a smaller value (such as 2048 or even 1024). However, the time needed for a file system check will increase substantially.

The space on a partition is divided into blocks. These have a fixed size of 1024, 2048, or 4096 bytes. You specify the block size when the file system is created; it cannot be changed later.

The block size determines how much space is reserved for a file. The larger this value is, the more space is consumed by the file, even if the actual amount of data is smaller.

In the classic file system formats (which ext2 also belongs to), data is stored in a linear chain of blocks of equal size. A specific number of blocks is grouped together in a block group (as illustrated in the following), and each block group consists of 32768 blocks:

Figure 2-3   *ext2 File System Structure*

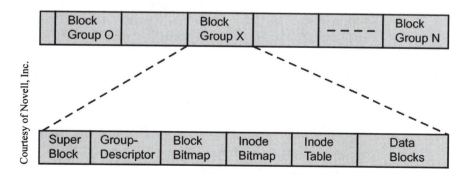

The boot sector is located at the beginning of this chain and contains static information about the file system, including where the kernel to load can be found.

Each block group contains the following components:

- **Superblock.** Read when the file system is mounted, it contains the following information about the file system:

    ❑ The number of free and occupied blocks and inodes.

    ❑ The number of blocks and inodes for each block.

    ❑ Information about file system use, such as the time of the last mount, the last write access, and the number of mounts since the last file system check.

    ❑ A valid bit, which is set to 0 when the file system is mounted and set to 1 again by umount.

       When the computer is booted, the valid bit is checked. If it is set to 0 (power failure or reset), the automatic file system check is started.

       The remains of files that can no longer be reconstructed are stored in the lost+found directory (in an ext2/ext3 file system).

    For reasons of data security, copies of the superblock are made. Because of this, the file system can be repaired, even if the first superblock has been destroyed.

- **Group Descriptor.** Information on the location of other areas (such as block bitmap and inode bitmap). This information is stored at several locations within the file system for data security.

- **Block Bitmap.** Information indicating which blocks in this group are free or occupied.

- **Inode Bitmap.** Information indicating which inodes are free or occupied.

- **Inode Table.** File information including owners, access permissions, time stamps, and links to the data blocks where the data is located.

- **Data Blocks.** Where the actual data is located.

The ext2 file system format can process filenames with a length of up to 255 characters. With the path, a name can be a maximum of 4096 characters in length (slashes included).

A file can be up to 16 GB in size for a block size of 1024 bytes or 2 TB for a block size of 4096 bytes. The maximum file system size is 2 TB (with a block size of 1024 bytes) or 16 TB (with a block size of 4096 bytes).

NOTE: The limitation on file size remains for the ext2 file system. However, the kernel can now handle files of almost any size.

ReiserFS Format

On a file system with ext2 and a block size of 1024 bytes, a file 8195 bytes in size occupies eight blocks completely and a ninth block with three bytes.

Even though only three bytes are occupied, the block is no longer available. This means that approximately 11 percent of available space is wasted.

If the file is 1025 bytes in size, two blocks are required, one of which is almost completely empty. Almost 50 percent of the space is wasted.

A worst case occurs if the file is very small: even if the file is only 50 bytes in size, a whole block is used (95 percent wasted).

A solution to this problem is provided by the ReiserFS format, which organizes data in a different way. This file system format has a fixed block size of 4096 bytes. However, small files are stored more efficiently. Only as much space is reserved as is actually required—not an entire block. Small files or the ends of files are stored together in the same block.

The inodes required are not generated when the file system is created, but only when they are actually needed. This allows a more flexible solution to storage requirements, increasing efficiency in the use of hard drive space.

Another advantage of the ReiserFS is that access to files is faster. This is done through the use of balanced binary trees in the organization of data blocks. However, balanced trees require considerably more processing power because, after every file is written, the entire tree must be rebalanced.

The current version of the ReiserFS (3.6) contained in the kernel since version 2.4.*x* allows a maximum partition size of 16 TB. A file has a maximum size of 1 EB (exabyte, one million TB).

The same limitations exist for filenames as with the ext2 file system format.

Directories

Inodes contain all the administrative information for a file except for the filename, which is stored in the directory.

Like a catalog, directories contain information on other files. This information includes the number of the inode for the file and its name.

Directories serve as a table in which inode numbers are assigned line by line to filenames. You can view the inode assigned to a filename by using the ls -i command, as in the following:

```
da1:~ # ls -i /
      2 .          104002 cdrom     80045 floppy   104081 mnt   103782 sbin
      2 ..          99068 dev       95657 home      81652 opt     80044 tmp
 104005 bin        104004 dvd      102562 lib           1 proc        4 usr
      2 boot        95722 etc       95718 media      81598 root    80046 var
```

Each filename is preceded by the inode number. On this particular Linux system, there are two partitions: one holds the / root directory and one holds the /boot directory.

Because inodes are always uniquely defined on one partition only, the same inode numbers can exist on each partition.

In the example, the two "." entries (a link to the current directory—here the root directory) and boot (the second partition is mounted on this directory) have the same inode number (2), but they are located on different partitions.

If you were to unmount the /boot partition, ls -i would show a different inode number, that of the /boot directory (the mount point) on the root partition. The same holds true for /proc.

The ".." file, which is actually a link to the previous layer in the direction of the root directory, also has an inode number of 2. Because you are already in the root directory, this link points to itself. It is another name entry for an inode number.

The table (the directory file) for the root directory can be represented as in the following example:

Table 2-4   *A Sample Directory*

Inode Number	Filename
2	.
2	..
4	usr
5	proc
18426	boot
80044	tmp
80045	floppy
80046	var
...	...

Links

A link is a special type of file that points to another file. Linux uses two kinds of links:

- **Hard links.** Another entry in a directory that points to the inode of a file that already has a file name. Because the two entries point to the *same* inode, you can't tell which entry was first and which was added later after the hard link is created. The number of hard links to a file is displayed in the output of the ls -l command in the column following the permissions.

- **Symbolic links.** A symbolic link is a file of its own that points to another file in the file system. A symbolic link file has its own inode. Because of this, the pointer and the pointee in the file system can be easily identified. Symbolic links are designated by the letter l in the first column of the ls output.

You can use the ln command at the shell prompt to create linked files. The following is an example of using the ln command to create a hard link named *new* that points to a file named *old*:

```
geeko@da1:~> ls -li
total 4
88658 -rw-r--r-- 1 geeko users 82 2004-04-06 14:21 old
geeko@da1:~> ln old new
geeko@da1:~> ls -li
total 8
88658 -rw-r--r-- 2 geeko users 82 2004-04-06 14:21 old
88658 -rw-r--r-- 2 geeko users 82 2004-04-06 14:21 new
geeko@da1:~>
```

Hard links can only be used when both the file and the link are in the same partition, because inode numbers are only unique within the same partition.

You can also create a symbolic link with the `ln -s` command. The following is an example of creating a symbolic link named *new* that points to a file named *old*:

```
geeko@da1:~> ls -li
total 4
88658 -rw-r--r-- 1 geeko users 82 2004-04-06 14:21 old
geeko@da1:~> ln -s old new
geeko@da1:~> ls -li
total 4
88658 -rw-r--r-- 1 geeko users 82 2004-04-06 14:21 old
88657 lrwxrwxrwx 1 geeko users 3 2004-04-06 14:27 new -> old
geeko@da1:~>
```

File System Journaling

File systems are basically databases that store files and use file information such as the filename and time stamp (called *metadata*) to organize and locate the files on a disk.

When you modify a file, the file system performs the following transactions:

- It updates the file (the data).
- It updates the file metadata.

Because there are two separate transactions, corruption can happen when only the file data (but not the metadata) is updated or vice versa, resulting in a difference between the data and metadata.

This can be caused, for instance, by a power outage. The data might have been written already, but the metadata might not have been updated yet.

When there is a difference between the data and metadata, the state of the file system is inconsistent and requires a file system check and possibly repair. For ext2, this includes a walk through the entire file system, which is very time consuming on today's hard disks with hundreds of GBs of capacity.

In a journal-based file system, the journal keeps a record of all current transactions and updates the record as transactions are completed. Checking the file system—

after a power outage, for example—consists mainly in replaying the journal, which is much faster than checking the entire file system.

For example, when you first start copying a file from a network server to your workstation, the journaled file system submits an entry to the journal indicating that a new file on the workstation is being created. After the file data and metadata are copied to the workstation, an entry is made indicating that the file was created successfully.

While recording entries in a journal requires extra time for creating files, it makes recovering an incomplete transaction easy because the journal can be used to repair the file system.

Objective 2   Perform a SLES 11 Installation

In this objective, you learn how to install a SLES 11 server. The installation process includes the following tasks:

- Boot from the Installation Media
- Select the System Language
- Check the Installation Media
- Select the Installation Mode
- Set the Clock and Time Zone
- Specify the Server Base Scenario
- Configure Installation Settings
- Verify Partitioning
- Select Software
- Start the Installation Process
- Set the root Password
- Set the Hostname
- Configure the Network
- Test the Internet Connection
- Configure Novell Customer Center Configuration and Online Update
- Configure Network Services
- Manage Users
- Configure Hardware
- Finalize the Installation Process
- Install SUSE Linux Enterprise Server 11

Boot from the Installation Media

To start the installation process, you need to insert the *SLES 11* installation DVD into the system's optical drive and then reboot the computer to start the installation program.

NOTE: To start the installation program, your computer needs to be configured to start from the optical drive. You may need to access the CMOS Setup program in your system's BIOS and change the boot drive order to boot from the optical drive. The keystroke required to start the CMOS Setup program varies from system to system. Consult your user manual for further information.

After your system has booted from the installation media, the following appears:

Figure 2-4   *SLES 11 Installation: Boot Menu*

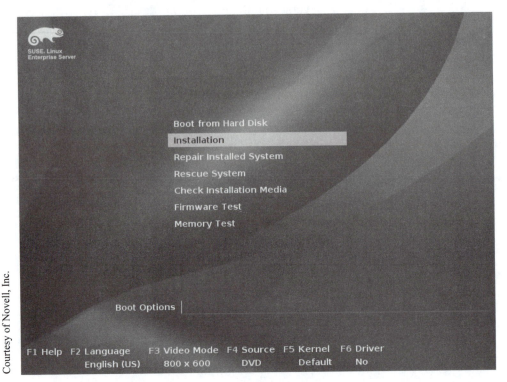

Courtesy of Novell, Inc.

You can use the arrow keys to select one of the following options:

- **Boot from Hard Disk.** Boots an operating system installed on the hard disk (if one exists). This is the default option. It allows the system to boot normally in the event you forget to remove your SLES 11 installation media from the optical drive.

- **Installation.** Starts the normal installation process. All modern hardware functions are enabled.

- **Repair Installed System.** Boots into a graphical repair utility.

- **Rescue System.** Starts the SLES 11 rescue system. If you cannot boot your installed Linux system, you can boot the computer from the installation media and select this option. This starts a minimal Linux system without a graphical user interface to allow you to access disk partitions for troubleshooting and repairing an installed system.

- **Check Installation Media.** Starts a verification routine that checks the integrity of your SLES 11 installation media.

- **Firmware Test.** Starts a BIOS checker that validates ACPI and other parts of your system BIOS.

- **Memory Test.** Starts a memory testing program that tests system RAM by using repeated read and write cycles. This is done in an endless loop, because memory corruption often shows up sporadically, and many read and write cycles might be necessary to detect it.

If you suspect that your RAM might be defective, start this test and let it run for several hours. If no errors are detected, you can assume that the memory is intact. Terminate the test by rebooting the system.

Notice that at the bottom of this screen are a series of function keys. You can use these function keys to change a variety of installation settings:

- **F1 Help.** Open context-sensitive help for the currently selected option of the boot screen.

- **F2 Language.** Select the display language and a corresponding keyboard layout for the installation. The default language is English (US).

- **F3 Video Mode.** Select a graphical display mode (such as *640x480* or *1024x768*) for the installation process. You can also select *Text Mode*, which can be used if the graphical modes cause display problems.

- **F4 Source.** Select an installation media type. Normally, you install from the inserted installation disc.

  In some cases you might want to select another source, such as an *FTP*, *HTTP*, or *NFS* server. Using an installation server is especially useful if you have to install several computers, not just one.

  You would need to select the appropriate protocol to connect to your installation server. A dialog will appear where you can enter the name or IP address of the server and the path to the installation repository on that server.

- **F5 Kernel.** Use the options provided by this function key if you encounter problems with the regular installation. This menu allows you to disable potentially problematic hardware features.

  If your hardware does not support Advanced Configuration and Power Interface (ACPI) select *No ACPI* to install without ACPI support. The *No Local APIC* option disables support for Advanced Programmable Interrupt Controller (APIC), which may cause problems with some hardware.

  The *Safe Settings* option boots the system with Direct Memory Access (DMA) for optical drives and power management functions disabled.

  If you are not sure, try the options provided in this menu in the following order:
  - **Default**
  - **ACPI Disabled**
  - **Safe Settings**

- **F6.** Specify an optional driver update for SLES 11. You can select from the following:
  - **Yes.** You will be prompted to insert the update disk at the appropriate point in the installation process.
  - **File or URL.** Drivers will be loaded directly before the installation starts.

After you select an installation option, a minimal Linux system loads and runs the YaST installation module.

Select the System Language

After YaST starts, the system language and license agreement dialog appears, as shown below:

Figure 2-5   *SLES 11 Installation: License Agreement*

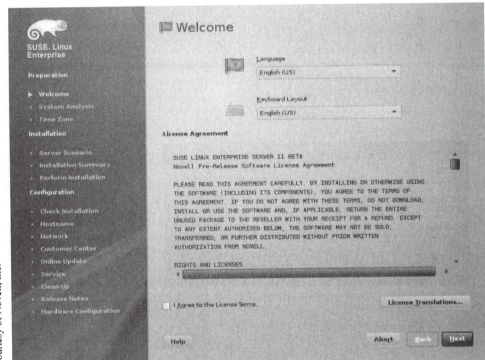

Courtesy of Novell, Inc.

Most YaST installation dialogs use the same user interface:

- The left panel displays an overview of the installation status.

- The right panel displays the current installation step.

- In the lower-left corner of the right panel, you can click the *Help* button to get information about the current installation step.

- The lower-right side provides buttons used to navigate to the previous or next installation steps or to abort the installation.

NOTE: If the installation program does not detect your mouse, you can use the Tab key to navigate through the dialog elements, the arrow keys to scroll in lists, and Enter to select buttons. Don't be alarmed if this occurs. You can change the mouse settings later on in the installation process.

From the Language dialog, select your *language* and your *keyboard layout*. Review the license agreement and select *I Agree to the License Agreement*, then click *Next* to continue.

Check the Installation Media

You can verify that your installation media is valid. This recommended step is done in the *Media Check* screen, shown below:

Figure 2-6   *SLES 11 Installation: Media Check*

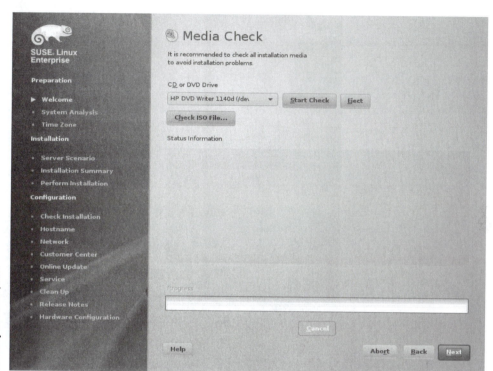

From the **CD or DVD Drive** drop-down list, select the optical drive where your SLES 11 installation media resides, then click **Start Check**.

NOTE: If you're installing from an ISO image, you can click **Check ISO File** instead.

The verification process may take several minutes to complete. If the verification fails, you should not continue the installation because you will probably encounter problems during the installation process or with the server itself afterwards. In this situation, you should obtain a replacement copy of the installation media and restart the install.

NOTE: If you burn the installation media yourself from an ISO file, be sure to use the Pad option in your DVD burning software. This prevents read errors at the end of the media during the verification process.

If the media passes the check, click **Next**. After doing so, the hardware in your system is probed and a corresponding basic set of kernel modules (drivers) are loaded.

Select the Installation Mode

You next need to select your installation mode in the *Installation Mode* screen, shown below:

Figure 2-7   *SLES 11 Installation: Installation Mode*

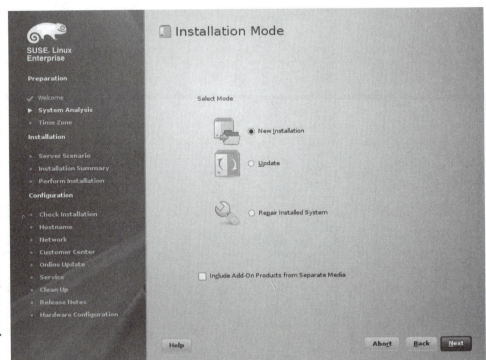

You can select from the following options in this screen:

■ **New installation.** Performs a normal new installation of SLES 11. This is the default option.

■ **Update.** Updates a previously installed SLES 10 installation to SLES 11.

■ **Repair Installed System.** Repairs an existing system that has been damaged.

For a standard installation, select *New Installation* and then click *Next* to proceed to the next step.

Set the Clock and Time Zone

Next, you need to configure your clock and time zone in the *Clock and Time Zone* screen, shown below:

Figure 2-8   *SLES11 Installation: Clock and Time Zone*

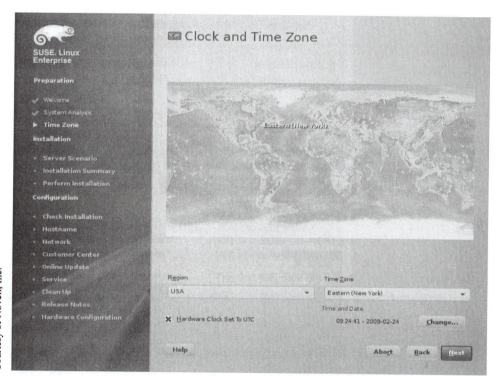

Courtesy of Novell, Inc.

By default, YaST selects the time zone based on your language selection. If necessary, you can change the time zone.

If your hardware clock is set to UTC (Universal Time Coordinated), the system time is set according to your time zone and automatically adjusted to daylight saving time. If your hardware clock is set to local time, deselect *Hardware Clock Set to UTC*.

NOTE: If necessary, you can also adjust the date and time by selecting *Change*.

When done, click *Next*.

Specify the Server Base Scenario

Next, you need to specify your server's base scenario in the *Server Base Scenario* screen, shown below:

Figure 2-9   *SLES 11 Installation: Server Base Scenario*

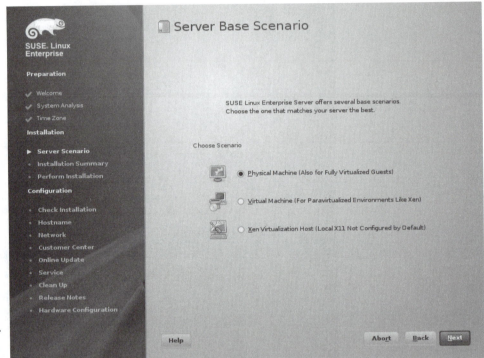

Courtesy of Novell, Inc.

In SLES 11, you can choose from three base scenarios. The scenario you select determines the default package selection in the next screen. Select one of the following:

- **Physical Machine.** Select if installing on physical hardware without XEN. You should also use this option when creating a VMware 5.*x* or earlier virtual machine that uses full virtualization.

- **Virtual Machine.** Select if installing in a para-virtualized virtual machine environment, such as XEN or VMware 6 (and later).

- **XEN Virtualization Host.** Select if installing on a machine that will function as a host for XEN virtual machines.

NOTE: For information about the difference between full virtualization and paravirtualization, VMware_paravirtualization.pdf (http://www.vmware.com/files/pdf/ VMware_paravirtualization.pdf) is a useful resource.

Click *Next*.

Configure Installation Settings

Next you need to configure the installation settings for your SLES 11 server in the *Installation Settings* screen, shown below:

Figure 2-10   *SLES 11 Installation: Installation Settings, Overview*

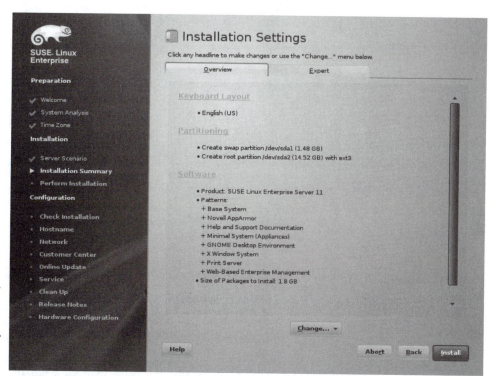

Courtesy of Novell, Inc.

YaST analyzes your system and creates an installation proposal, shown in the figure above. The proposed settings are displayed on two tabs. The ***Overview*** tab shows the main categories that are necessary for a base installation. You can change these settings by selecting the following options:

- **Keyboard layout.** Changes the keyboard layout. YaST selects the default keyboard layout based on your previous settings. Change the keyboard settings if you prefer a different layout.

- **Partitioning.** Changes the hard drive partitioning. If the automatically generated partitioning scheme does not fit your needs, you can change it by selecting this option.

- **Software.** Changes the software packages that will be automatically installed during the server installation. You can select or deselect software as needed.

- **Language.** Changes the default language.

You can further customize the installation proposal by selecting the *Expert* tab, shown below:

Figure 2-11   *SLES 11 Installation: Expert Installation Settings*

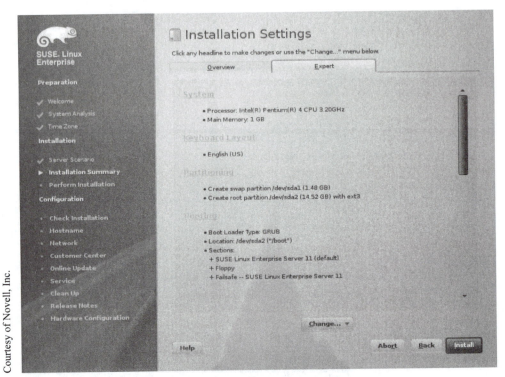

Courtesy of Novell, Inc.

This tab displays the same options as the Overview tab, but also includes the following options:

- **System.** Restarts the hardware detection process and displays a list of all available hardware components. You can change the PCI-ID setup, select single components, view details, or save the list to a file.

- **Booting.** Allows you to change your Grand Unified Bootloader (GRUB) boot loader settings. You can also configure the system to use the Lilo (**L**inux **Lo**ader) bootloader instead of GRUB.

- **Add-on Products.** Allows you to include any add-on products.

- **Time zone.** Opens the Clock and Time Zone dialog described earlier.

- **Default Runlevel.** Changes the runlevel. If a graphical environment is installed, the default is runlevel 5; otherwise, it is 3.

- **Kdump.** Saves a dump of the kernel in the event of a system crash, allowing you to analyze what went wrong. Use this option to enable and configure kdump.

Verify Partitioning

In most cases, YaST proposes a reasonable partitioning scheme that you can use without modification. However, you might need to manually change the partitioning scheme if any of the following applies:

- You want to optimize the partitioning scheme for a special-purpose server (such as a file server)

- You want to configure LVM

- You have more than one hard drive and want to configure software RAID

- You want to delete existing operating systems on the hard drive to free up space for your SLES 11 installation

The basics of hard drive partitioning are covered in Understand Partitions in a Linux System.

To partition the hard drive manually, you need to be familiar with the following:

- The Basic Linux Partitioning Scheme

- Changing the Default Partitioning Proposal

The Basic Linux Partitioning Scheme

The optimal partitioning scheme for a server depends on the purpose of the server. A SLES 11 installation needs at least two partitions:

- **Swap partition.** Extends the physically available system RAM. This makes it possible to use more memory than the amount of physical ram installed. The Linux operating system moves unused data from RAM to the swap partition on the hard dive, thus freeing system RAM for active processes.

    NOTE: Prior to version 2.4.10 of the Linux kernel, the swap partition needed to be at least twice the size of your installed system RAM. For example, if you had 1 GB of RAM in your system, the swap partition had to be at least 2 GB in size. If the swap partition was smaller than this, the overall performance of the system suffered. With the latest version of the Linux kernel, however, this is no longer the case.

- **Root partition.** Holds the root directory (/) of the file system. The root directory is the top directory in the Linux file system hierarchy.

No matter what partitioning scheme you choose, you must have at least one swap partition and a root partition. Partitions and partitioning schemes will be covered more extensively in the objective Manage Partitions, File Systems, Quotas, and NFS.

Changing the Default Partitioning Proposal

You can also change the default partitioning proposal to create separate partitions for various directories in the Linux file system. Doing so adds a degree of stability to the system. Problems encountered in one partition are isolated from other partitions in the system. This is covered in detail in Design Guidelines for Implementing Partitions.

To change the default partition scheme, select **Partitioning** in the installation proposal. The following is displayed:

Figure 2-12   *SLES 11 Installation: Preparing Hard Disk, Step 1*

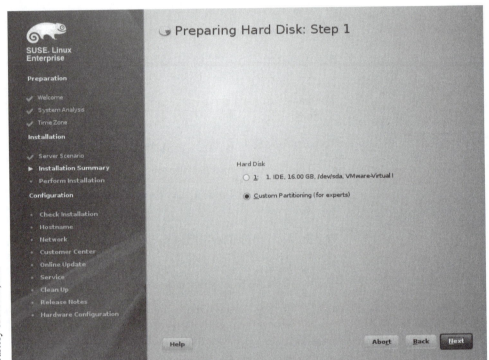

Courtesy of Novell, Inc.

In this screen, you can select from the following options:

- **A hard disk.** Mark this option and click *Next* to open a dialog where you can choose to use the entire hard disk or some of the existing partitions for the installation of SLES 11.

- **Custom Partitioning.** Mark this option and click *Next* to open the YaST Expert Partitioner and display the existing partition layout.

When you start the YaST Expert Partitioner, the following is displayed:

Figure 2-13 *SLES 11 Installation: Expert Partitioner*

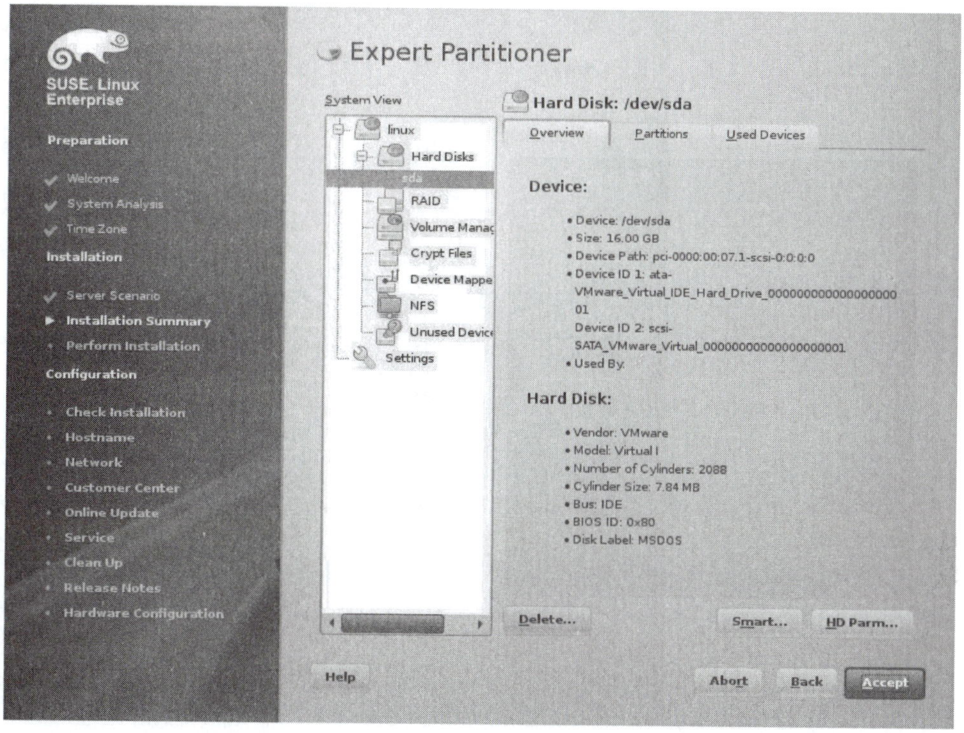

Courtesy of Novell, Inc.

In the right side of the dialog, YaST lists the details of the current partition setup. Depending on your previous choice, the list may contain the partitioning proposal created by YaST or the partitions that currently reside on the hard disk.

The Expert Partitioner allows you to create, edit, delete, and resize partitions. You can also administer LVM or RAID.

IMPORTANT: The changes made with the YaST Expert Partitioner are not written to disk until the installation process is started. You can always discard your changes by clicking ***Back*** or ***Abort***.

An entry for each hard disk is displayed in the left column of the Expert Partitioner. Expand ***Hard Disks***, then select the hard disk entry. Overview information about the device is displayed on the ***Overview*** tab, as shown below:

Figure 2-14   *SLES 11 Installation: Expert Partitioner*

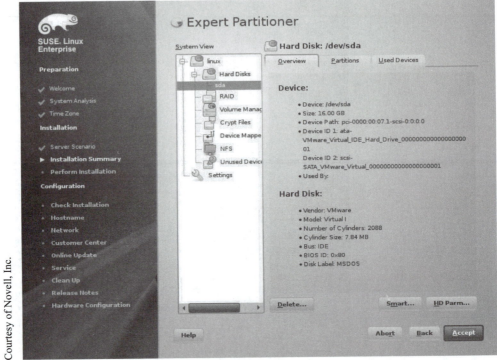

To view a list of partitions on the hard drive, select the ***Partitions*** tab, as shown below:

Figure 2-15 *SLES 11 Installation: Expert Partitioner*

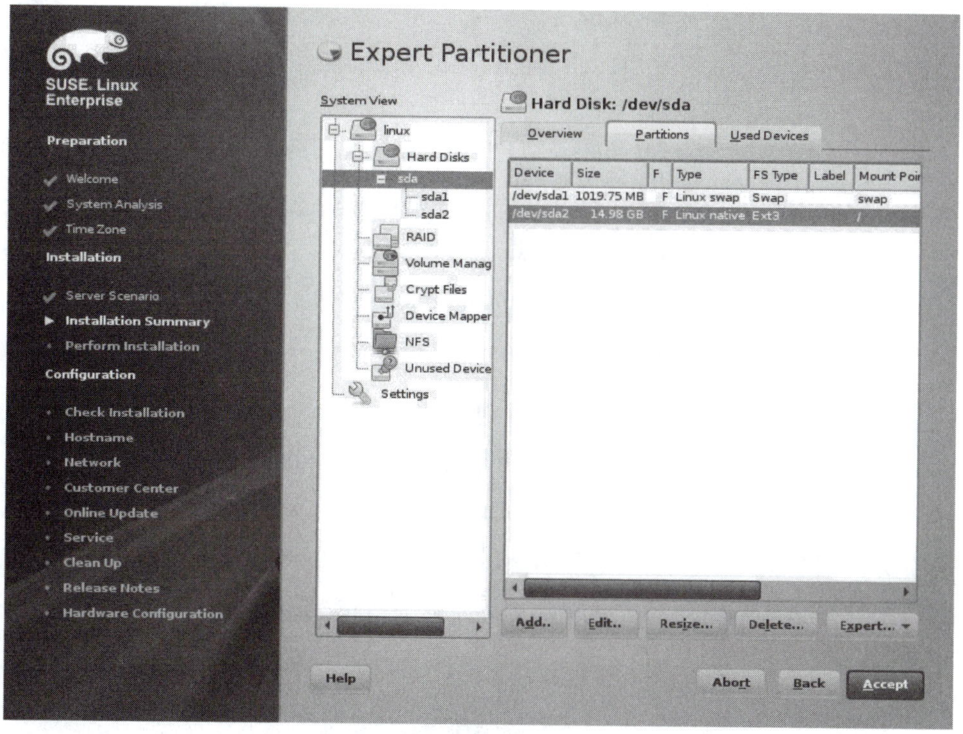

Courtesy of Novell, Inc.

One entry is listed for every partition on the hard disk. Each entry includes information about the partition in the following columns:

- **Device.** Device name of the partition.
- **Size.** Size of the hard disk or partition.
- **F.** Indicates the partition will be formatted during the installation process.
- **Type.** Partition type. Depending upon the operating system and the architecture, partitions can have various types, including Linux native, Linux swap, Win95, FAT 32, or NTFS.
- **FS Type.** Type of file system that will be installed on the partition, such as ext2, ext3, or Reiser. The default is **ext3**.
- **Label.** Label that will be applied to the file system.
- **Mount Point.** Mount point of a partition. For swap partitions, the keyword **swap** is used instead of a directory.
- **Mount By.** Indicates how the file system is mounted:
    - K. Kernel Name
    - L. Label
    - U. UUID (Universally Unique Identifier)
    - I. Device ID
    - P. Device Path

■ **Start Cylinder.** Start cylinder of the partition.

■ **End Cylinder.** End cylinder of the partition.

■ **Used By.** Information about the system using the partition, such as LVM or RAID.

The buttons in the lower part of the dialog let you do the following:

■ Create New Partitions

■ Edit Existing Partitions

■ Delete Existing Partitions

■ Resize Existing Partitions

Create New Partitions

To create a new primary partition, do the following:

1. Click *Add*.

   A dialog similar to the following is displayed:

Figure 2-16   *SLES 11 Installation: Add Partition*

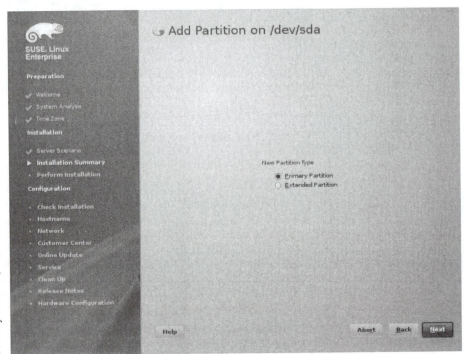

One of the following is displayed in this dialog. What you actually see depends on your hard disk setup.

■ If you have more than one disk in your system, you are asked to select a disk for the new partition first.

- If you do not have an extended partition, you are asked if you want to create a primary or an extended partition.

- If you have an extended partition and you have space on the hard drive outside the extended partition for additional primary partitions, you are asked if you want to create a primary or a logical partition.

- If you have three primary partitions and an extended partition, you are told you can create only logical partitions.

NOTE: You need enough space on your hard disk to create a new partition. You learn later in this section how to delete existing partitions to free used disk space.

---

2. Mark the appropriate option, then click *Next*.

If you choose to create either a primary or a logical partition, the following is displayed:

Figure 2-17   *SLES 11 Installation: Add Partition*

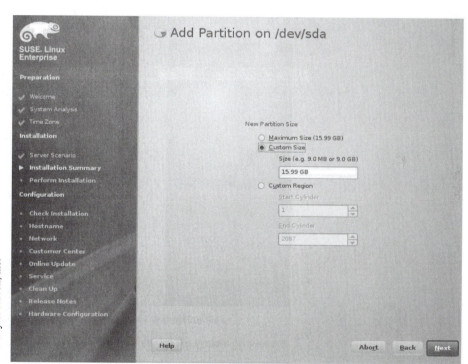

Courtesy of Novell, Inc.

3. Specify the size of the new partition by selecting one of the following:

   ■ **Maximum Size.** Allocates the remaining free contiguous space on the drive to the partition.

   ■ **Custom Size.** Allows you to specify the size of the partition. You have two options:

      ❑ Enter a *size* for the partition (in MB or GB) in the Size field. For example: **20 GB**.

      ❑ Mark ***Custom Region***, then specify the ***start*** and ***ending cylinders***. The start cylinder determines the first cylinder of the new partition. YaST normally preselects the first available free cylinder of the hard disk. The end cylinder specifies the last cylinder allocated to the partition, which determines the total size of the new partition. YaST preselects the last available free cylinder.

4. Click ***Next***.

   The Add Partition screen is displayed:

Figure 2-18   *SLES 11 Installation: Add Partition*

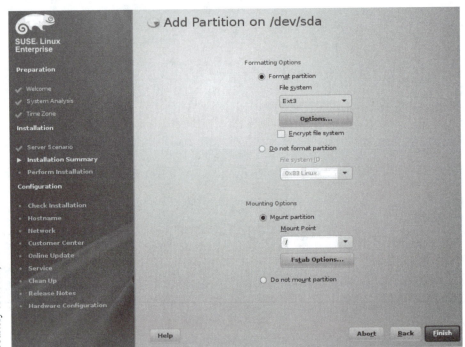

5. Specify how the partition will be formatted by selecting one of the following:

   ■ **Format Partition.** Formats the partition. Select one of the following file systems for the partition from the File System drop-down list:

      ❑ **Ext2.** Formats the partition with the Ext2 file system. Ext2 is an old and proven file system, but it does not use journaling.

- ❑ **Ext3.** Formats the partition with the Ext3 file system. Ext3 is an improved version of Ext2 and offers journaling. (This is the default option.)

- ❑ **JFS.** Formats the partition using the JFS file system. JFS is a 64-bit journaling file system created by IBM.

- ❑ **Reiser.** Formats the partition with ReiserFS, a modern journaling file system.

- ❑ **FAT.** Formats the partition with the FAT file system. FAT is an older file system used in DOS and Windows. You can use this option to create a data partition that can be accessed from both Windows and Linux.

NOTE: You must not create a root partition using the FAT file system.

- ❑ **XFS.** Formats the partition with XFS, a journaling file system developed by SGI.

- ❑ **Swap.** Formats the partition as a swap partition.

If you select *Format Partition*, you can also select the *Encrypt File System* option. Encrypting a file system prevents unauthorized mounting of the partition. However, once mounted, the files in the partition are accessible like files on an unencrypted file system.

NOTE: You should use this option only for non-system partitions such as user home directories.

- ■ **Do Not Format Partition.** Leaves the newly created partition unformatted. No file system will be created on the new partition. You can select a partition type in the *File System ID* drop-down list.

6. Configure your mount options for the new partition. You can select one of the following:

- ■ **Mount Partition.** Mounts the partition after it is created. You can select the mount point of the new partition from the *Mount Point* drop-down list. You can also specify a mount point manually if it is not available in the list. If you do, the mount point directory will be automatically created during the installation process.

    You can also, optionally, select *Fstab Options* to edit the entry in the /etc/ fstab file for this partition. The default settings should work in most cases.

- ■ **Do Not Mount Partition.** Creates the partition but leaves it unmounted in the file system.

7. Click *Finish* to add the new partition to the partition list.

If you need to create an extended partition instead of a primary partition, do the following:

1. Click *Add*.

2. Mark *Extended Partition*, then click *Next*.

The following is displayed:

Figure 2-19   SLES 11 Installation: Add Partition

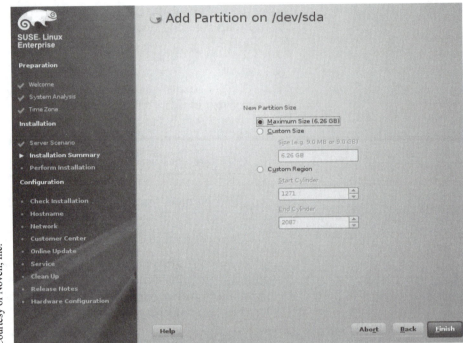

Courtesy of Novell, Inc.

3. Specify the size of the new partition by selecting one of the following:

    ■ **Maximum Size.** Allocates the remaining free contiguous space on the drive to the partition.

    ■ **Custom Size.** Allows you to specify the size of the partition. You have two options:

        ❑ Enter a *size* for the partition (in MB or GB) in the Size field. For example: 20 GB.

        ❑ Mark ***Custom Region***, then specify the ***start*** and ***end cylinders***. The start cylinder determines the first cylinder of the new partition. YaST normally preselects the first available free cylinder of the hard disk. The end cylinder specifies the last cylinder allocated to the partition, which determines the total size of the new partition. YaST preselects the last available free cylinder.

4. Click *Finish*.

The extended partition is added to the list of partitions on the drive:

Figure 2-20   *SLES 11 Installation: Expert Partitioner*

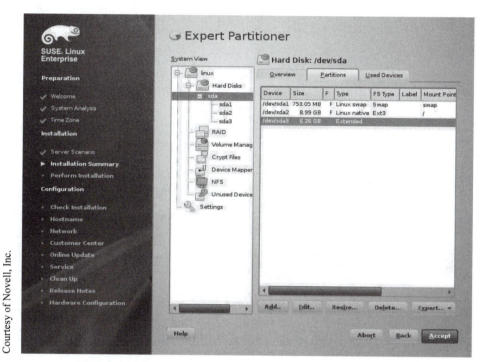

Courtesy of Novell, Inc.

At this point, you can complete the steps in Create New Partitions to create logical partitions within the extended partition.

Edit Existing Partitions

If you need to edit an existing partition, select it from the list and then select *Edit*. You can edit only primary and logical partitions with the Expert Partitioner. You cannot edit extended partitions.

If you edit a primary or logical partition, a dialog similar to the following is displayed:

Figure 2-21   *SLES 11 Installation: Edit Partitions*

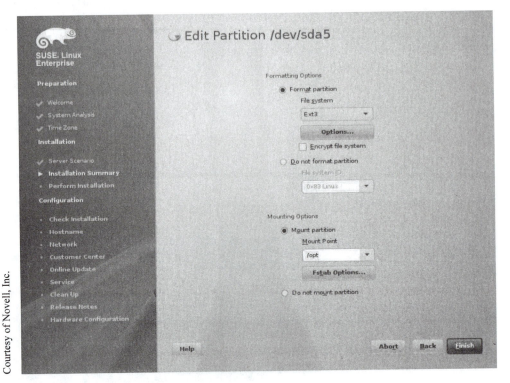

Courtesy of Novell, Inc.

You can change all options for the partition except its size. After changing the partition parameters, click *Finish* to save your changes to the partition and return to the partition list.

Delete Existing Partitions

You can also delete a partition using the Expert Partitioner. To do this, complete the following:

1. Select a *partition* from the list.

2. Click *Delete*, then click *Yes* in the confirmation dialog.

    The partition is deleted from the partition list.

IMPORTANT: Remember that you delete all logical partitions if you delete an extended partition.

Resize Existing Partitions

The Expert Partitioner can also be used to resize an existing partition. To do so, select a *partition* from the list and then click *Resize*.

NOTE: Although you can reduce a partition's size without deleting it, you should always back up the data on the partition before resizing it.

NOTE: If the selected partitions are FAT or NTFS partitions with a Windows operating system installed, you should first reboot the system into Windows and scan the partitions for errors and defragment them before resizing. See the installation section in the *SLES 11 Administration Manual* for details.

After you click ***Resize***, the following is displayed:

Figure 2-22   *SLES 11 Installation: Resize Partition*

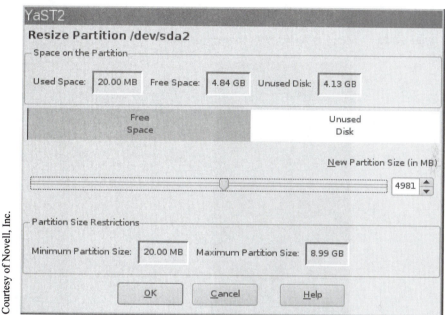

This dialog includes the following elements:

- Bars representing free and used space in the partition. Used space is designated by dark blue and available space by light blue. Space that is not assigned to a partition is designated by white.

- A slider to change the size of the partition.

- Fields that display the amount of free and used space on the partition being resized and the space available for a new partition after the resizing process.

To resize the partition, move the slider until enough unused disk space is available for a new partition. When you click ***OK***, the partition size changes in the partition list.

When you finish configuring settings in the Expert Partitioner, return to the installation proposal by clicking ***Accept***.

Select Software

SLES 11 includes a wide variety of software packages that you can include in your installation. These packages provide various applications and services for your server system.

191

Instead of selecting packages to be included in the installation one at a time, YaST allows you to select categories (called patterns) of software based on function. For example, if you want your server to function as a DNS and DHCP server on your network, you could include the DHCP and DNS Server pattern in your SLES 11 installation. All the packages needed to provide these two services would be installed automatically.

Depending on the available disk space, YaST preselects several of the software patterns for you by default. To view these, select **Software** in the installation overview. The the following is displayed:

Figure 2-23   *SLES 11 Installation: Software Selection*

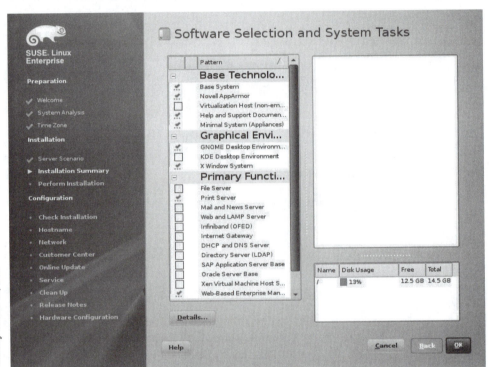

Courtesy of Novell, Inc.

This screen shows the default patterns for your server installation. A brief description appears on the right when you highlight a pattern in the left column.

To find out which packages are contained in a pattern, click **Details**. The following is displayed:

Figure 2-24   *SLES 11 Installation: Software Patterns*

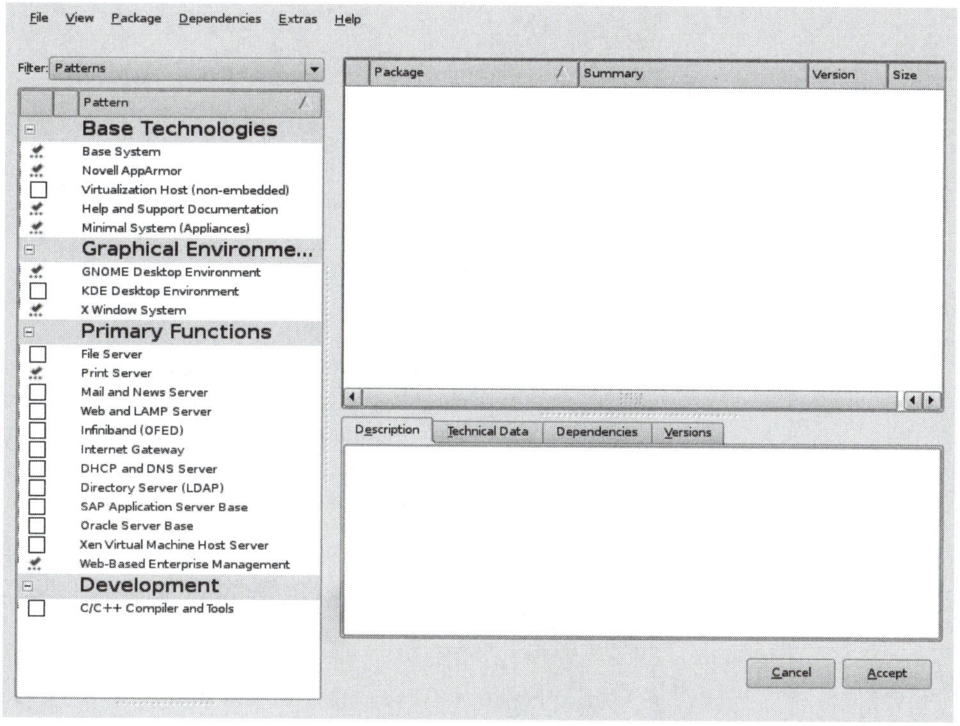

Courtesy of Novell, Inc.

Selecting a pattern on the left causes the software packages contained in that pattern to be displayed on the right. Marking a pattern selects it for installation. Unmarking a pattern deselects it.

A package typically contains an application and all supporting files required to use the software. Sometimes larger applications are split into multiple packages. Sometimes several small applications are bundled into a single package.

NOTE: SLES 11 uses the RPM Package Manager (rpm) for software management.

Frequently one software package needs another one to already be installed for it to run. These are called dependent packages (or dependencies). Dependency information is stored within each RPM package. If YaST encounters a package with dependencies, it automatically adds the additional dependent software packages to the installation proposal.

You can install a package by marking it in the package list on the right. The details for the selected package are displayed below the package list.

The *Filter* drop-down list offers different views for the software packages:

Figure 2-25 *Filter Drop-Down Menu*

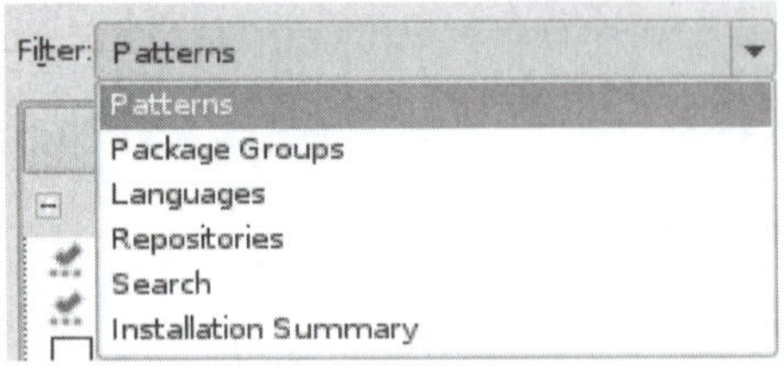

You can select from the following:

- **Patterns.** Displays the dialog shown in Figure 2-24.

- **Package Groups.** Displays the packages in a hierarchical tree view. There are several main categories, such as Productivity, Programming, System, and Hardware. Within the main categories are subcategories, such as File Utilities, Filesystems, and Modem. Selecting a category on the left displays the software packages belonging to that category on the right.

- **Languages.** Lets you select support for additional languages.

- **Repositories.** Displays the configured installation sources.

- **Search.** Lets you search for packages.

- **Installation Summary.** Displays a summary of the packages selected for installation.

From the top menu, you can select *Dependencies > Check* to identify the dependencies of the selected packages. This check is also done when you confirm the package selection. You can also select *Dependencies > Autocheck* to have dependencies checked every time you select or deselect a package.

NOTE: This option is enabled by default.

Confirm your package selection and return to the installation proposal by clicking *Accept*.

Start the Installation Process

After customizing the installation proposal, click *Install*. A dialog appears asking you to confirm the proposal. Start the installation process by clicking *Install* in the confirmation dialog. You can always return to the installation proposal by clicking *Back*.

NOTE: When you click *Install*, YaST implements the partitions contained in your partitioning proposal. Existing data on the disk may be lost.

Before installing software packages, YaST changes the hard disk partitioning. Based on your installation proposal, YaST creates your new partitions, installs the specified files systems on them, and then mounts them. Once done, YaST installs the software you specified in your installation proposal, as shown below:

Figure 2-26   *SLES 11 Installation*

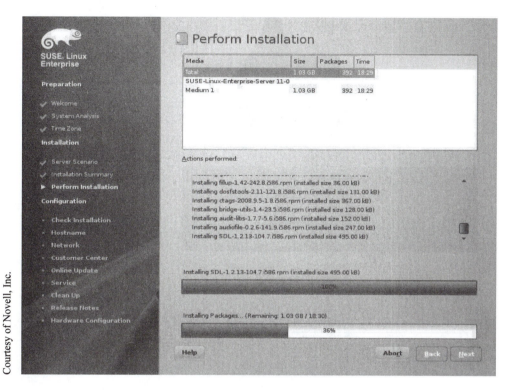

Courtesy of Novell, Inc.

Depending on your software selection and the performance of your system, the installation process takes about 15–45 minutes to complete.

After all software packages are installed, YaST reboots the computer and prompts you for the hostname, root password, network configuration details, and so on, to further customize your installation.

Set the root Password

After the system reboots, you need to set the password for the root user on your server. root is the name of the Linux system administrator. Unlike regular users, who might not have permission to do certain things on the system, root has unlimited access to do anything. As root user, you can:

- Access every file and device in the system

- Change the system configuration

- Install software

- Set up hardware

The root account should be used only for system administration, maintenance, and repair. Logging in as root for daily work is risky—a single mistake can lead to irretrievable loss of many system files.

You need to set the root password during the installation process. YaST displays the following screen:

Figure 2-27   *SLES 11 Installation: Root Password*

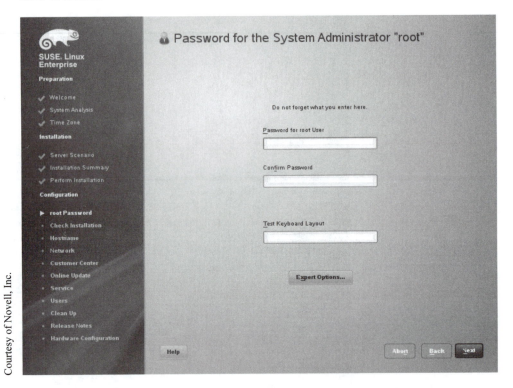

Enter the same password in both text fields of the dialog.

You should use a password that cannot be easily guessed. We recommend that you use numbers and lowercase and uppercase characters to avoid dictionary attacks. If desired, you can select *Expert Options* to customize the password encryption algorithm. In most cases, you can just use the default setting of *Blowfish*.

After entering the root password, continue by clicking *Next*. If your password is too simple or weak, a warning is displayed. You can either go back and specify a stronger password or accept the weaker password and continue.

Set the Hostname

Next, you need to set the hostname for the server. YaST suggests a default hostname of *linux-xxxx*, with *xxxx* being composed of random characters. The domain name defaults to *site*. Change the hostname and the domain name to the correct values for your network.

If the computers on your network get their hostname and domain name via a DHCP option, you can leave *Change Hostname via DHCP* selected. Otherwise, you should deselect this option and also select *Write Hostname to /etc/hosts*.

When done, click *Next*.

Configure the Network

Next, you need to set up your network configuration on the server. YaST displays the *Network Configuration* screen, as shown below:

Figure 2-28   *SLES 11 Installation: Network Configuration*

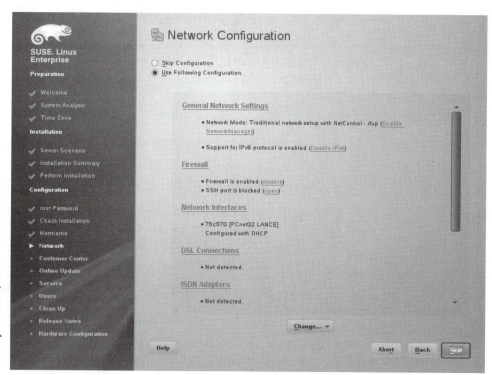

Courtesy of Novell, Inc.

In the top part of this screen, you can select one of the following options:

- **Skip Configuration.** Skip the network configuration for now. You can configure your network settings after the system has been installed.

- **Use Following Configuration.** Use the network configuration proposal that is currently displayed.

The network configuration proposal is similar to the installation proposal at the beginning of the base installation. The headings can be selected to view and configure specific parameters. The proposal includes the following entries:

- **General Network Settings.** Lets you switch between the traditional method of managing network connections and using the NetworkManager utility. On a server, you should use the traditional method. The NetworkManager utility is more suitable for a notebook system, enabling users to switch between wired and wireless interfaces.

- **Firewall.** Lets you customize your firewall settings. If you want to be able to administer your server remotely using SSH, toggle ***SSH port is blocked*** to ***SSH port is open*** by selecting ***open***.

In addition, you can disable the firewall entirely by selecting ***Disable***. Selecting the ***Firewall*** heading itself opens a dialog that allows you to configure detailed firewall settings.

- **Network Interfaces.** Displays network interfaces detected in the system and their configuration settings.

- **DSL Connections.** Displays DSL devices detected in the system and their configuration settings.

- **ISDN Adapters.** Displays ISDN devices detected in the system and their configuration settings.

- **Modems.** Displays analog modems detected in the system and their configuration settings.

- **VNC Remote Administration.** Lets you configure remote administration using VNC.

- **Proxy.** Displays the HTTP and FTP proxy settings.

You can change a configuration by selecting the headline of the entry or by selecting the entry from the ***Change*** drop-down list. This menu also lets you reset all settings to the defaults generated by YaST. If you are not sure which settings to use, use the defaults generated by YaST.

By default, your network interfaces are configured to use DHCP. Because you are configuring a server system, you should configure the network interface to use a static IP address. Select the ***Network Interfaces*** heading to do this.

YaST displays the ***Network Settings Overview***. It lists all configured and unconfigured network cards:

Figure 2-29   *SLES 11 Installation: Network Settings*

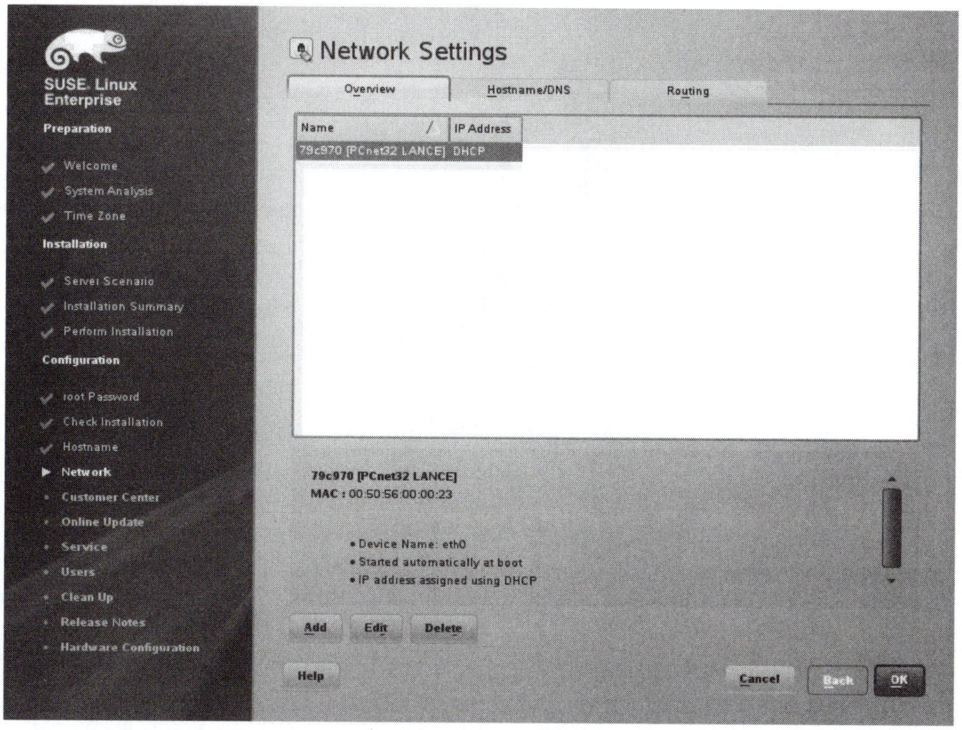

The upper part of this screen displays a list of all network cards detected. The lower part displays configuration details for the selected network card.

At this point, you can do one of the following:

- Add a Network Card Manually
- Edit an Existing Configuration
- Delete an Existing Configuration

Add a Network Card Manually

If you want to configure a network card that was not automatically detected, do the following:

1. Click *Add*.

   The *Hardware* Dialog is displayed:

Figure 2-30   *SLES 11 Installation: Network Hardware Dialog*

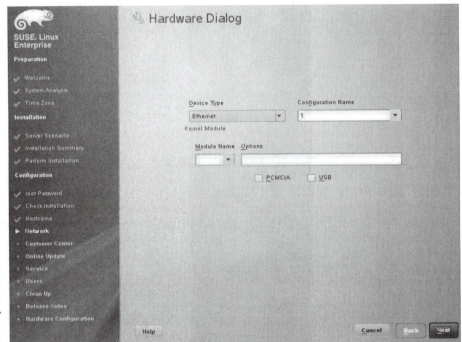

In this screen, you can configure the following settings:

- **Device Type.** Network device type (such as Ethernet, Bluetooth, Wireless, etc.)

- **Configuration Name.** Interface's device number

- **Module Name.** If your network card is a PCMCIA or USB device, select the corresponding check boxes. Otherwise, select your network card from the Module Name list. YaST automatically loads the appropriate driver for the selected card.

2. Click *Next*.

If you selected *Wireless* as the device type for a WLAN card, the *Network Card Setup* dialog is displayed:

Figure 2-31   *SLES 11 Installation: Network Card Setup*

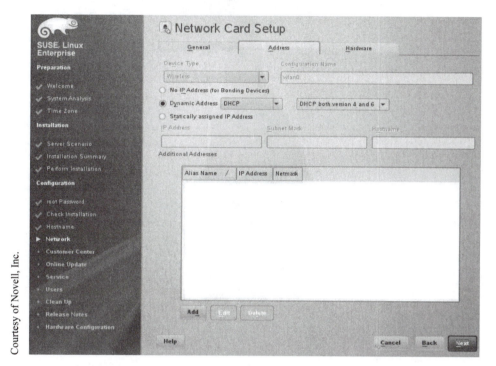

Courtesy of Novell, Inc.

3. Configure the interface to use DHCP or a static IP address, then click *Next* again.

A dialog is opened where you can specify WLAN specific configuration parameters, such as *Operating Mode*, *Network Name (ESSID)*, *Authentication Mode*, and the *Encryption Key*:

Figure 2-32   *SLES 11 Installation: Wireless Network Card Configuration*

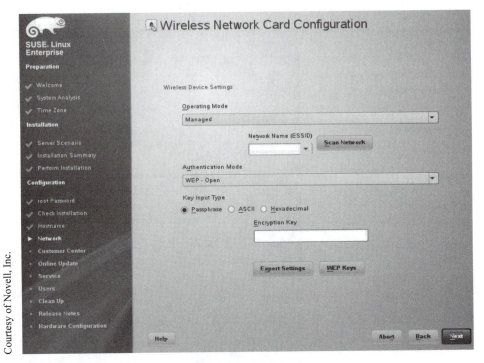

Courtesy of Novell, Inc.

4. Configure your settings, then select *WEP Keys* to enter your key information. You can also select *Expert Settings* to configure additional parameters such as the bit rate.

5. When you are finished, click *Next* to return to the *Network Settings Overview*.

Edit an Existing Configuration

In addition to adding a new network interface, you can also edit an existing network interface configuration. To edit a network card, do the following:

1. Select the *network card* from the list in the Network Settings dialog, then click *Edit*.

The following is displayed:

Figure 2-33   *SLES 11 Installation: Network Card Setup*

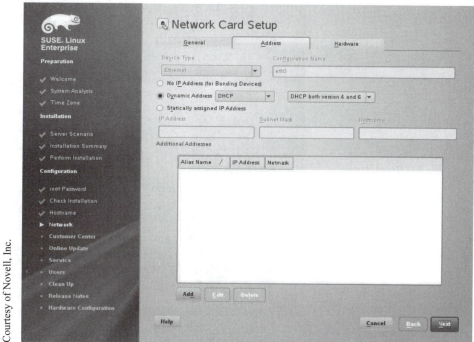

2. Configure your interface on the *Address* tab using the following options:

   ■ **Dynamic Address.** If your network uses a DHCP server, you can set up your system's network address automatically by selecting this option.

   You can choose from one of several dynamic address assignment methods in the drop-down list provided. Select ***DHCP*** if you have a DHCP server running on your local network. If you want to search for an IP address and assign it statically, select ***Zeroconf*** from the drop-down list. To use DHCP, but fall back to Zeroconf if it fails, select ***DHCP + Zeroconf***.

   ■ **Statically Assigned IP Address.** If you want to use a static address, select this option. Then type an appropriate ***IP address*** and ***subnet mask*** for your network. You should also type your server's ***hostname*** in the ***Hostname*** field.

   ■ **Hostname and Name Server.** Lets you set the hostname and name server manually.

3. When done, click *Next*.

4. Select the ***Hostname/DNS*** tab.

   The following is displayed:

Figure 2-34   *SLES 11 Installation: Network Settings*

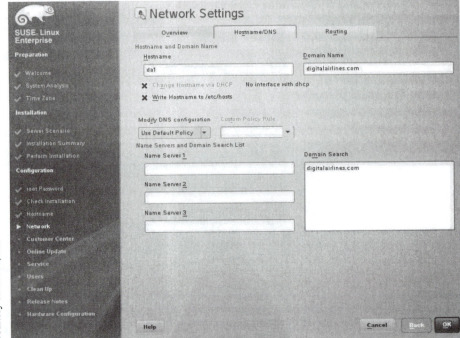

Courtesy of Novell, Inc.

5. Enter the following:

    ■ *Hostname*

    ■ *Domain name*

    ■ *Name servers*

6. Select the *Routing* tab.

    The following is displayed:

Figure 2-35   *SLES 11 Installation: Network Settings*

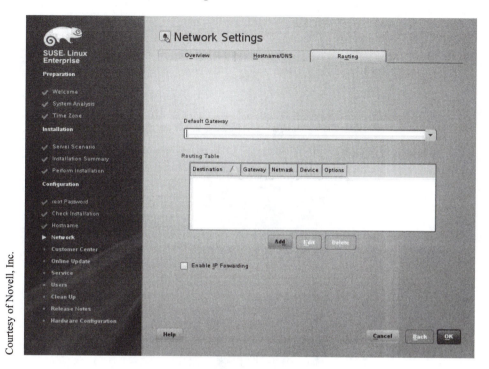

7. Type your default gateway router's *IP address* in the Default Gateway field.

8. Click *OK*.

Delete an Existing Configuration

To delete an existing network card configuration, highlight it in the upper part of the Network Settings screen, then click *Delete*.

When finished with adding, editing, or deleting network card configurations, save the network device configuration and return to the Network Configuration proposal by clicking *OK*.

When you're done configuring your network interfaces, click *Next*.

Test the Internet Connection

Next, YaST asks you to test your connection to the Internet:

Figure 2-36   *SLES 11 Installation: Internet Connection Test*

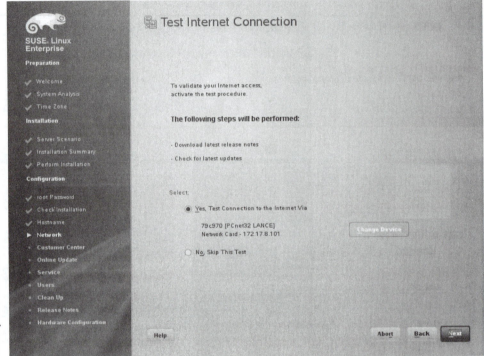

Courtesy of Novell, Inc.

Select one of the following options:

■ **Yes, Test Connection to the Internet.** YaST tries to test the Internet connection by downloading the latest release notes and checking for available updates. The results are displayed in the next screen.

■ **No, Skip This Test.** YaST skips the connection test. If you do this, you can't update the system during installation.

Select one of the above options and click *Next*.

NOTE: If the test fails, you can view the log files to determine why the test failed.

Configure Novell Customer Center Configuration and Online Update

Next, you can configure the Novell Customer Center, which is required to perform online updates:

Figure 2-37 *SLES 11 Installation: Novell Customer Center Configuration*

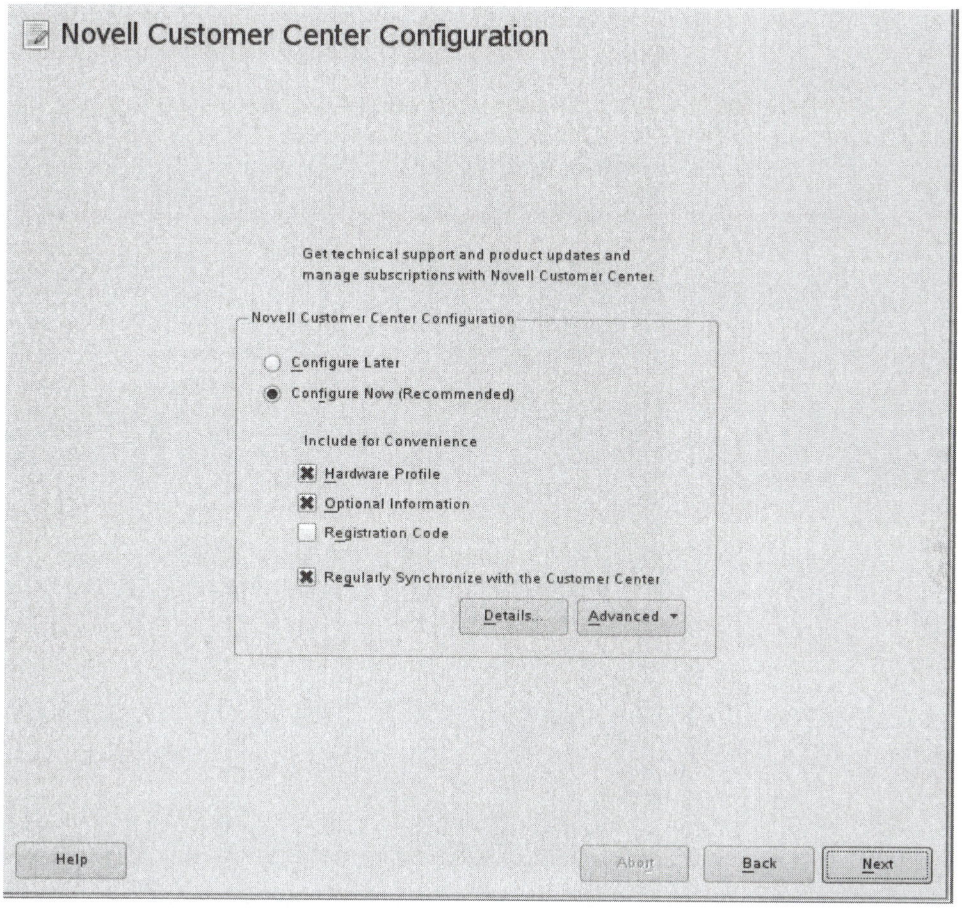

Courtesy of Novell, Inc.

Update packages available on the SUSE update servers can be downloaded and installed to fix known bugs or security issues.

Clicking ***Next*** starts a browser and connects to the Novell Web site, where you enter your e-mail address and activation code, if available.

After successful registration, the ***Online Update*** dialog opens. You can start the online update by selecting ***Run Update***. You can also select ***Skip Update*** to perform the update later after the system has been installed.

If you choose to run the update, a list of available patches appears. Select the patches you want to install, and then start the update process by clicking ***Accept***.

Once the installation is complete, you can visit the Novell Customer Center at http://www.novell.com/center/ (http://www.novell.com/center/) to manage your Novell products and subscriptions.

Configure Network Services

In the next installation step, you configure your certificate authority (CA) and OpenLDAP server. YaST displays the following dialog:

Figure 2-38   SLES 11 Installation: CA Management and Open LDAP Server

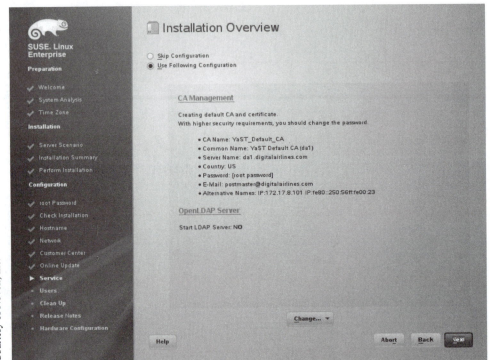

In the top part of the dialog, you can select one of the following options:

■ **Skip Configuration.** Skip this configuration step. You can enable the services later in the installed system.

■ **Use Following Configuration.** Use the automatically generated configuration displayed. You can select the following options to change the configuration:

   ❑ **CA Management.** The purpose of a CA (certification authority or certificate authority) is to guarantee a trust relationship among all network services that communicate with each other.

   If you decide that you do not want to establish a local CA, you must secure server communications using SSL (Secure Sockets Layer) and TLS (Transport Layer Security) with certificates from another CA.

   By default, a CA is created and enabled during the installation.

NOTE: To create proper certificates, the hostname has to be set correctly earlier in the Network Interface Configuration; otherwise, the generated certificate will contain an incorrect hostname.

❑ **OpenLDAP Server.** You can optionally run an Lightweight Directory Access Protocol (LDAP) server. Typically, an LDAP server stores user and group account data. But starting with SLES 9, you can also use LDAP for mail, DHCP, and DNS configuration data. By default, the LDAP server is not installed and configured during installation.

If you are not sure about the correct settings, use the defaults generated by YaST. You can change the configuration later in the installed system. When you are finished, select *Next*.

Manage Users

Next, you need to configure your user authentication method. YaST displays the following:

Figure 2-39   *SLES 11 Installation: User Authentication Method*

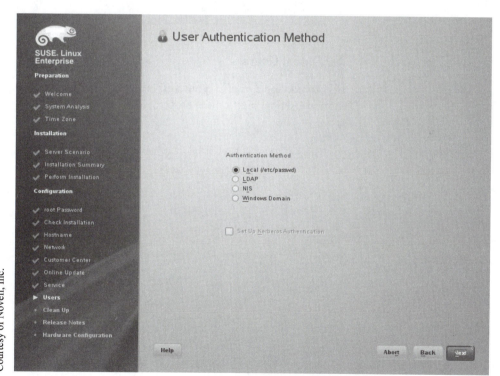

The *User Authentication Method* dialog offers four different authentication methods that you can use on your server:

■ **Local (/etc/passwd).** Configures the system to use the traditional file-based authentication method. This is the default option.

- **LDAP.** If you have an LDAP directory server installed on your server or on another server in your network, configures your system as an LDAP client. In this configuration, the user and group accounts in the LDAP directory will be used for authentication.

- **NIS.** If you have a NIS server in your network, configures your system as a NIS client.

- **Windows Domain.** If you have a Windows server in your network, configures the server to use the user and group accounts in the domain for authentication.

If you are not sure which method to select, select *Local*. After selecting an authentication method, click *Next*.

The next dialog differs, depending on which authentication method you selected. We will cover the following here:

- Add Local Users

- Configure the System as an LDAP Client

NOTE: The dialogs for NIS and Windows Domain are used in a similar manner to enable each respective authentication method.

Add Local Users

If you selected *Local* as your authentication method, you need to create at least one regular user account on the system. YaST displays the following:

Figure 2-40   *SLES 11 Installation: New Local User*

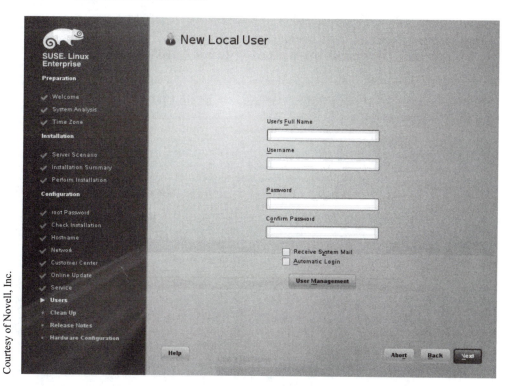

Courtesy of Novell, Inc.

Type the following information in this dialog to add local users to the system. The account information is stored in the `/etc/passwd` and `/etc/shadow` files.

- **User's full name.** User's full name.

- **Login name.** Username the user will use to log in.

- **Password.** Password for the user.

    To provide effective security, a password should be eight or more characters long. The maximum length for a password ranges from 8 to 128 characters, depending on the algorithm used to hash the password. While the Crypt algorithm commonly used in the past used only the first eight characters of the password, more recent algorithms allow longer passwords.

    Passwords are case sensitive. Special characters are allowed, but they might be hard to enter depending on the keyboard layout.

- **Receive System Mail.** All e-mails addressed to the root account are forwarded to this user.

- **Automatic Login.** Enables automatic login for this user. This option logs in the user automatically (without requesting a password) when the system starts.

NOTE: You should not enable this feature on a production system.

- **User Management.** Lets you add more users with the YaST User Management module.

NOTE: You can add other users later (after installation), but you have to create at least one user during installation so you don't have to work as the user root after the system has been set up.

After you have entered all required information, select *Next*.

Configure the System as an LDAP Client

If you selected LDAP for your authentication method, the following appears:

Figure 2-41   *SLES 11 Installation: LDAP Client Configuration*

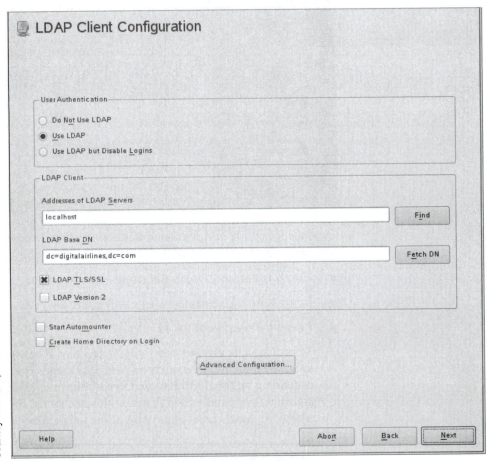

In this dialog, you can configure your system as an LDAP client. The default configuration points to a locally installed LDAP server. You can change the configuration with the following options:

- **LDAP client.** You can configure the following:

    - **Addresses of LDAP Servers.** IP address or DNS name of the LDAP server.

    - **LDAP base DN.** Search base context on the server.

❑ **LDAP TSL/SSL.** Encrypts communications with the LDAP server.

❑ **LDAP Version2.** Select if your LDAP server supports only LDAP version 2. By default, LDAP version 3 is used.

■ **Start Automounter.** If your LDAP server provides information about the automatic mounting of file systems (such as home directories), you can start the automounter and use the automount information from the LDAP server.

■ **Advanced Configuration.** Lets you change advanced LDAP settings.

When finished with the LDAP configuration, click *Next*. You are next prompted to create a new LDAP user:

Figure 2-42   *SLES 11 Installation: New LDAP User*

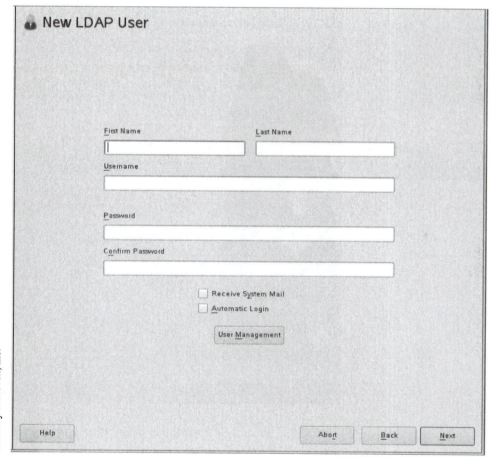

Courtesy of Novell, Inc.

Enter the following information:

■ **First Name / Last Name.** User's full name.

■ **Username.** Username the user will use to log in.

■ **Password.** Password for the user.

■ **Receive System Mail.** All e-mails addressed to the root account are forwarded to this user.

- **Automatic Login.** Enables automatic login for this user. This option logs in the user automatically (without requesting a password) when the system starts.

- **User Management.** Lets you add more users with the YaST User Management module.

After you have entered all required information, click *Next*.

The Release notes are displayed. You should read them to make sure you are informed about the latest changes. When done, click *Next*.

Configure Hardware

Next, you need to configure your server hardware. YaST displays the *Hardware Configuration* dialog:

Figure 2-43   *SLES 11 Installation: Hardware Configuration*

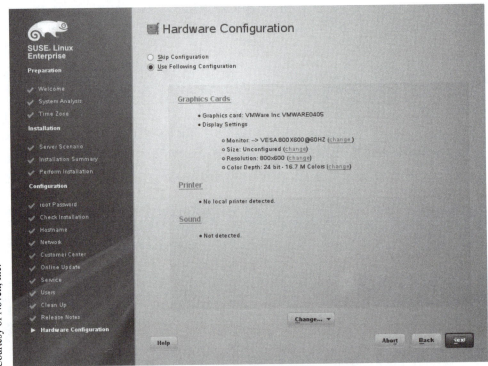

This dialog contains a hardware configuration proposal for your server, which is composed of the following:

- **Graphics Cards.** Graphic card and monitor setup.

- **Printers.** Printer and printer server settings.

- **Sound.** Sound card configuration.

To change the automatically generated configuration, select the headline of the item you want to change, or select the corresponding entry from the *Change* drop-down list. You can also use the *Change* drop-down list to reset all settings to the automatically generated configuration proposal.

You can skip the hardware configuration at this time and configure your devices later in the installed system. However, if the settings of the graphics card in the configuration proposal are not correct, you should change them now to avoid problems during the first system start.

When done making changes, click *Next*.

Finalize the Installation Process

At this point, your installation is complete. YaST displays the following:

Figure 2-44   *SLES 11 Installation: Installation Completed*

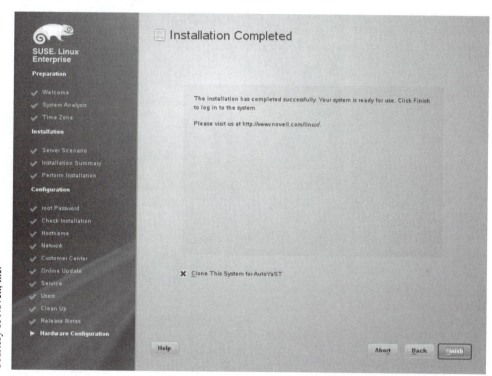

Click *Finish* to complete the install. Notice that the ***Clone This System for Autoyast*** option is selected by default. When selected, this option causes an AutoYaST file to be generated and saved as `/root/autoinst.xml`. This file can then be used to set up identical systems.

The system starts and the graphical login screen is displayed, allowing you to log in using the user account you created during the installation:

Figure 2-45   *Login Screen*

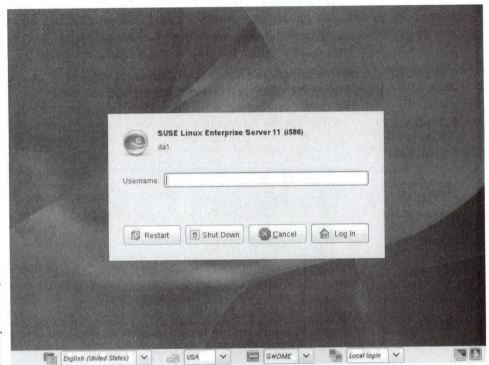

Courtesy of Novell, Inc.

Exercise 2-1 *Install SUSE Linux Enterprise Server 11*

In this exercise, you install SUSE Linux Enterprise Server 11 in a VMware virtual machine.

You will find this exercise at the end of the chapter.

(End of Exercise)

Objective 3   Understand the File System Hierarchy Standard (FHS)

The file system concept of Linux (and, in general, of all UNIX systems) is considerably different than that of other operating systems:

- Files in the file systems can be spread out over several devices. Each file system can be "mounted" any place in the directory hierarchy. With other file systems, each file system is placed on the same level, at the top. With Linux, the file systems can be placed at lower levels of the directory structure.

- A filename in Linux can be up to 255 characters long. It can contain special characters ("_" or "%", for example).

- Certain characters (the dollar sign "$", the semicolon ";", or the space, for example) have a special significance for shells, such as Bash. If you want to use one of these characters without the associated special meaning, the character must be preceded by a "\" (backslash) to mask (switch off) its special meaning.

- You can use umlauts, letters with diacritical marks, or other language-specific characters.

NOTE: Using language-specific characters can lead to problems if you exchange data with people in other countries using other settings, because these characters are not present on their keyboards.

- Linux differentiates between upper-case and lower-case letters. For example, the file names Invoice, invoice, and INVOICE refer to three different files.

To understand the concept of the Linux file system, you need to understand the following:

- The Hierarchical Structure of the File System

- File System Hierarchy Standard

The Hierarchical Structure of the File System

The file system concept of Linux involves a hierarchical file system that can be shown in the form of a tree.

This tree is not limited to a local partition. It can stretch over several partitions, which can be located on different computers in a network. It begins at the **root** directory (/), from which the name for the system administrator comes, and branches out like the branches of a tree.

The following shows part of a typical file system tree:

Figure 2-46   *The Content of the Root Directory*

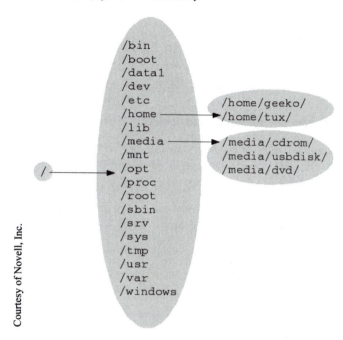

A file in this directory tree is uniquely defined by its path. A path refers to the directory names which lead to this file.

The separation character between individual directory names is the slash ("/"). The path can be specified in two ways:

■   As an **absolute path** starting from the root of the entire file system tree.

    The absolute path always begins with a slash ("/"), the symbol for the root directory.

■   As a **relative path** starting from the current directory.

Figure 2-47   *Absolute and Relative Path*

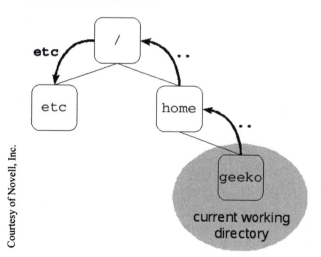

In this example, the current position in the file system is geeko's home directory. To change to the /etc directory, you can use either one of the following commands:

- absolute path: cd /etc

- relative path: cd ../../etc

The length of the path cannot exceed 4096 characters, including the slashes.

File System Hierarchy Standard

The structure of the file system is described in the File System Hierarchy Standard (FHS). The FHS specifies which directories must be located on the first level after the root directory and what they contain.

The FHS does not dictate all details. In some areas it allows for your own definitions. The FHS defines a two-layered hierarchy:

- The directories in the top layer (immediately below the root directory "/").

- As a second layer, the directories under /usr/ and /var/.

Figure 2-48   *File System Hierarchy Standard*

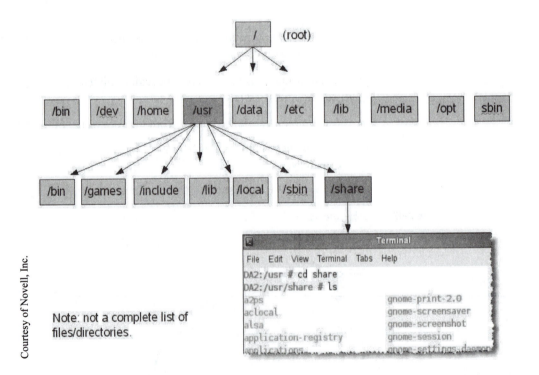

Root Directory (/)

Similar to the root of the C: drive (C:\) in Windows, the root directory refers to the highest layer of the file system tree. Normally only directories (not files) are located here. When the system is booted, the partition on which this directory is located is the first one mounted.

As the kernel cannot fulfill all the tasks of the operating system, all programs that are run at system start must be available on this partition (they cannot be located on another partition).

The following directories always have to be on the same partition as the root directory: `/bin/`, `/dev/`, `/etc/`, `/lib/`, and `/sbin/`.

Essential Binaries for Use by All Users (`/bin/`)

Similar to the `C:\Program Files` directory in Windows, the `/bin/` directory contains important binaries (executable programs) that are required when no other file systems are mounted, such as all programs necessary for the system start.

These include the various shells, the most important commands for working with files, and several commands for system analysis and configuration.

The following table provides an overview of the contents of the `/bin/` directory:

Table 2-5   *Important Executables in the /bin/ Directory*

File	Description
/bin/bash	The Bourne Again SHell
/bin/cat	Display files
/bin/cp	Copy files
/bin/dd	Copy files byte-wise
/bin/gzip	Compress files
/bin/mount	Mount file systems
/bin/rm	Delet files
/bin/vi	vi editor

Boot Directory (`/boot/`)

Similar to the `C:\Windows\System` directory in Windows, the `/boot/` directory contains system files. Specifically, it contains

- Static files related to the boot loader GRUB. These files (with the exception of configuration files) are required for the boot process.

- The backed-up information for the Master Boot Record (MBR) and the system map files.

- The kernel, which has the file name `vmlinuz`. According to the FHS, however, the kernel can also be located directly in the root directory.

Other Partitions (/data/)

If YaST, the graphical administration tool, finds other (non-Windows) partitions or another hard disk during the installation, it creates mount points for each partition labeled data*x* (/data1/, /data2/, and so on).

Device Files (/dev/)

Each hardware component in the system (such as hard drive partitions, CD drives, printer, and mouse) is represented as a file in the /dev/ directory.

The hardware components are addressed via these files by writing to or reading from one of these files. Two kinds of device files are included:

- Character-oriented device files (for devices working sequentially, such as printer, mouse, or tape drive)
- Block-oriented device files (such as floppy disks and hard drives).

The connection to device drivers in the kernel is implemented via numbered channels, which correspond to the number of the device driver in question. These are referred to as major device numbers.

A driver might be responsible for several devices of the same type. To distinguish between these devices, the minor device number is used.

Instead of the size of the files, these two numbers are displayed in the output of ls (the files do not occupy any space on the hard drive anyway). In the following example, you want a long list of all hard drives in the /dev/ directory. You enter ls -l /dev/sda*:

```
DA2:/dev # ls -l /dev/sda*
brw-rw---- 1 root disk 8, 0 2009-02-11 06:02 /dev/sda
brw-rw---- 1 root disk 8, 1 2009-02-11 06:02 /dev/sda1
brw-rw---- 1 root disk 8, 2 2009-02-11 06:02 /dev/sda2
```

- The major device number 8 is listed for all files. This refers to the driver for hard drives.
- The minor device numbers are 0, 1, and 2.

If special device files are required for specific devices, you can generate these with the mknod command. The necessary parameters must be provided by the hardware manufacturer.

The null device /dev/null is also located in this directory. The null device is a special file that discards all data written to it (but reports that the write operation succeeded), and provides no data to any process that reads from it. Program output that would normally be sent to the screen can be redirected to this device (for example, using redirects). The redirected data will be discarded.

The following are some important device files:

Table 2-6   *Important Device Files in the /dev/ Directory*

Device	Device File	Description
Terminals	/dev/console	The system console.
	/dev/tty1	The first virtual console, reachable with Ctrl+Alt+F1.
Serial ports	/dev/ttyS0 /dev/ttyS*	The first serial port.
Parallel ports	/dev/lp0 /dev/lp*	The first parallel port.
Floppy disk drives	/dev/fd0 /dev/fd*	The first floppy disk drive. If the drives are addressed via the device files fd0 and fd1, the kernel tries to recognize the floppy disk format itself.
hard drives	/dev/sda /dev/sda*	The first hard drive (first SCSI or SATA drive or master on the IDE controller). The device names are given numbers to label the various partitions. For example, /dev/sda1 is the first primary partition on the first hard drive.
CD-ROM drives	/dev/sr0 /dev/sr*	The first SCSI CD-ROM drive. /dev/scd0 is a link that points to /dev/sr0.
IDE hard drives (older systems)	/dev/hda	The first IDE hard drive on the first IDE controller.
	/dev/hdc	The first IDE hard drive on the second IDE controller.
	/dev/hd*	To label the partitions, the device names are given numbers. Numbers 1 to 4 refer to the primary partitions, higher numbers to logical partitions. Example: /dev/hda1 is the first primary partition (1) on the first IDE hard drive (a).
IDE CD-ROM drives (older systems)	/dev/hd*	The drives are named in the same way as the IDE hard drives. This means that the CD-ROM drive /dev/hdd is the second drive on the second IDE controller.
Pseudo-Random number device	/dev/random	High quality random numbers.
	/dev/urandom	Lower quality random numbers.
Null device	/dev/null	Anything written to this device is ignored.
Zero device	/dev/zero	A source of zero bytes.

Configuration Files (/etc/)

Similar to C:\Windows, this directory and its subdirectories contain system configuration files. Almost all these files are ASCII files, which can be processed with any editor.

Normal users can read nearly all of these files, but only root can edit them. According to the FHS, no executable programs can be located here.

However, the subdirectories contain many shell scripts. Some important configuration files are listed in the following table:

Table 2-7   *Configuration Files in the /etc/ Directory*

File	Description
/etc/SuSE-release	Version number of the installed SUSE Linux Enterprise Server
/etc/inittab	Configuration file for the init process
/etc/init.d/*	Scripts for starting services
/etc/modprobe.conf	Configuration file of the kernel modules
/etc/DIR_COLORS	Specifies the colors for directory listings (ls)
/etc/X11/xorg.conf	Configuration file of the X Window System
/etc/fstab	Table of the file systems automatically mounted at the system start
/etc/profile	Login script of the shell
/etc/passwd	User database
/etc/shadow	Encrypted passwords of users
/etc/group	Database of user groups
/etc/cups/*	Files for the CUPS printing system
/etc/hosts	Mapping of computer names to IP addresses
/etc/motd	Welcome message after a user logs in (message of the day)
/etc/issue	Linux welcome message before the login prompt
/etc/sysconfig/*	Central configuration files of the system

Nearly every installed service has at least one configuration file in the /etc/ directory or a subdirectory.

User Directories (/home/)

Every user on a Linux system has his own area in which to work with files (this is similar to the C:\Documents and Settings*username* directory in Microsoft Windows). This area is called the home directory of the user. When a user logs in, he is in his own home directory.

Individual configuration files can be found in the user's home directory. These configuration files are hidden files, because they are normally not displayed by the ls command (use the -a option to display them). All of these files have names that begin with a dot.

The following are the most important files in a user's home directory:

Table 2-8   *Configuration Files in a User's Home Directory*

File	Description
.profile	Private login script of the user
.bashrc	Configuration file for bash
.bash_history	List of commands previously run in bash

If there are no special settings, the home directories of all users are located beneath the /home/ directory. The home directory of a user can also be addressed via the shortcut "~", so ~/.bashrc refers to the .bashrc file in the user's home directory.

In many cases, the /home/ directory is located on a different partition or can even be located on a different computer (with central administration of home directories).

Libraries (/lib/)

Many programs use specific functions that are also used by other programs. Such standard functions are removed from the actual program, stored in the system, and only called up when the program runs. They are called shared libraries.

The /lib/ directory contains the libraries that are used by programs in the /bin/ and /sbin/ directories. The kernel modules (hardware drivers not compiled into the kernel) are located in the /lib/modules/ directory.

You can find additional libraries below the /usr/ directory.

Mount Point for Removable Media (/media/*)

All files accessible in a Linux system are arranged in one big tree, the file hierarchy, rooted at /. These files can be spread out over several devices. The mount command attaches a device's file system to the big file tree.

SLES 11 creates directories in the /media/ directory for mounting removable media when detecting media:

- /media/floppy/. Created for a floppy disk drive.
- /media/cdrom/. Created for a CD-Rom drive.
- /media/cdrecorder/. Created for a CD burner.
- /media/dvd/. Created for a DVD drive.
- /media/usbdisk/. Created for a USB stick.
- /media/*media_name/*. Created after inserting a labeled removable media.

Application Directory (/opt/)

Installed programs can store their static files in the /opt/ directory. First, a directory with the name of the application or vendor is created. The files are then stored in that directory.

Examples include KDE (/opt/kde3/) and applications from Novell (/opt/novell/).

Administrator's Home Directory (/root/)

The home directory of the system administrator is not located beneath /home/ as are the home directories of normal users. Preferably, it should be on the same partition as the root directory (/) so that it is separate from other users, whose home directories should be on a different partition. Only then is it guaranteed that the user named root can always log in without a problem and have his or her own configured environment available.

System Binaries

The /sbin/ directory contains important programs for system administration. By contrast, programs that are run by normal users are located in /bin/.

Programs in the /sbin/ directory can also, as a rule, be run by normal users but only to display the configured values. Changes to the configuration can only be made by the user root.

The following is an overview of important files in the /sbin/ directory:

Table 2-9   *Important Executables in the /sbin/ Directory*

File	Description
/sbin/SuSEconfig	Starts the SuSEconfig modules in the /sbin/conf.d/ directory.
/sbin/conf.d/*	Contains the scripts from the SuSEconfig family that are called up by /sbin/SuSEconfig.
	They are used to configure the overall system, evaluate entries in the configuration files in the /etc/sysconfig/ directory, and write further configuration files.
/sbin/yast	Administration tool for SLES 11.
/sbin/fdisk	Modifies partitions.
/sbin/fsck*	Checks file systems (file system check).
/sbin/init	Initializes the system.
/sbin/mkfs*	Creates a file system (formatting).
/sbin/shutdown	Shuts down the system.

Data Directories for Services (/srv/)

The /srv/ directory contains subdirectories designed for containing data of various services. For example, the files of the Apache web server are located in the /srv/ www/ directory and the FTP server files are located in the /srv/ftp/ directory.

Temporary Area (/tmp/)

Various programs create temporary files that are stored in the /tmp/ directory until they are deleted.

The Hierarchy Below /usr/

The /usr/ directory, in accordance with the FHS, represents a second hierarchical layer (/usr/ stands for *UNIX-Specific Resources* or *UNIX System Resources*).

This is the location for all application programs, graphical interface files, additional libraries, locally installed programs, and commonly shared directories containing documentation.

These include the following:

Table 2-10   *Subdirectories of the /usr/ Directory*

Directory	Description
/usr/X11R6/	Files of the X Window System
/usr/bin/	Almost all executable programs
/usr/lib/	Libraries
/usr/lib64/	64-bit libraries
/usr/local/	Locally installed programs, now frequently found in the /opt/ directory
/usr/sbin/	Programs for system administration
/usr/share/doc/	Documentation
/usr/share/man/	The manual pages (command descriptions)
/usr/src/	Source files of all programs and the kernel (if installed)

Variable Files (/var/)

This directory and its subdirectories contain files that can be modified while the system is running.

The following table provides an overview of the most important directories beneath /var/:

Table 2-11   *Subdirectories of the /var/ Directory*

Directory	Description
/var/lib/	Variable libraries (such as databases for the `locate` and `rpm` commands)
/var/log/	Log files for most services
/var/run/	Files with information on running processes
/var/spool/	Directory for queues (printers, e-mail)
/var/lock/	Lock files that are used to protect devices from multiple use

Windows Partitions (`/windows/`)

If YaST finds a partition with a Microsoft file system, it creates a `/windows/` directory automatically. Inside this directory are subdirectories labeled with Windows drive characters (e.g., C, D).

Process Files (`/proc/`)

Linux handles process information that is made available to users via the `/proc/` directory. This directory does not contain any real files and, therefore, does not occupy any space on the hard disk.

`/proc/` is generated dynamically when it is accessed (for example, with `ls /proc`). Each process has its own directory. The values in these directories can be read as if they were in a file, like a "virtual" file. Some values can also be set by writing to the corresponding "files." Changes to this virtual file system only have an effect as long as the system is running.

For example, the `init` process always has the process number "1". Information about it is, therefore, found in the `/proc/1/` directory. Each numbered directory corresponds to a running process.

You can view the contents of the files with the `cat` command, which shows the status of the process, as in the following example:

```
DA-SLED:/proc/1 # cat status
Name:    init
State:   S (sleeping)
Tgid:    1
Pid:     1
PPid:    0
TracerPid:      0
Uid:     0       0       0       0
Gid:     0       0       0       0
FDSize: 256
```

In this example, a list is displayed of what the process is called (**init**), what state it is in (**sleeping**), and to which user it belongs (**Uid: 0** for root).

In addition to directories for each individual process, /proc/ also includes directories and files containing information about the state of the system.

The following are the most important of these:

Table 2-12   *Important Files and Directories in the /proc/ Directory*

File	Description
/proc/cpuinfo	Information about the processor
/proc/dma	Use of the Direct Memory Access (DMA) ports
/proc/interrupts	Use of the interrupt
/proc/ioports	Use of the intrasystem I/O ports
/proc/filesystems	File system formats that the kernel understands
/proc/modules	Active modules
/proc/mounts	Mounted file systems
/proc/net/*	Network-specific information and statistics in human-readable form
/proc/partitions	Existing partitions
/proc/bus/pci	Existing PCI devices
/proc/bus/scsi/	Connected SCSI devices
/proc/sys/*	System and kernel information
/proc/version	Kernel version

System Information Directory (/sys/)

The /sys/ directory provides information in the form of a tree structure on various hardware buses, hardware devices, active devices, and their drivers. As the /proc/ directory, this directory does not contain any real files and, therefore, does not occupy any space on the hard disk.

Mount Point for Temporarily Mounted File Systems (/mnt/)

Unlike in Windows, where you can access file systems (partitions and devices) by simply going to *My Computer*, in the Linux world, you have to integrate or "mount" them before you can access them. You can mount file systems anywhere, but the standard directory for mounting is /mnt/. It should only be used for temporary purposes. For permanent mounts, you should create an appropriately named directory.

In the following example, the hard drive partition /dev/sda7 is mounted at the position /mnt/ in the directory tree using the mount command:

```
mount /dev/sda7 /mnt
```

All files on this partition can now be reached via the /mnt/ directory. To remove this partition again, you use the umount command:

```
umount /mnt
```

If you do not include any options with the mount command, the mount program tries out several file system formats. If you want to specify a specific file system, use the -t option.

If the file system format is not supported by the kernel, the command is aborted and you receive an error message. In this case, you must compile a new kernel that supports the file system format.

Directories for Mounting Other File Systems

Other file systems, such as other hard drive partitions, directories from other computers via the network, or removable media (floppy disk, CD-ROM, or removable hard drive) can be mounted to the file system at any point.

A directory must exist at the point where you intend to mount the file system. This directory is referred to as the mount point. The complete directory structure of the mounted file system can be found beneath this directory.

In most cases, only the user root can mount and unmount directories. Removable media, such as floppy disks and CDs, can be mounted by a normal user.

To mount a file system, enter the mount command, specifying the device file and the directory to which the file system should be mounted.

A file system can be removed again with the umount command. (Note that the command is NOT called unmount, but umount.) The /etc/mtab file, which is updated by the mount command, shows which file systems are currently mounted. It is possible to mount one file system at different positions.

You can mount file systems in directories that contain files and subdirectories. The existing contents of these directories, however, will no longer be accessible. After the file system is unmounted, the data becomes available again.

You can also share certain directories with many computers. This approach is often used for the home directories of users, which are then located centrally on one machine and exported to other computers in the network.

The directories that can be shared include the following:

Table 2-13   *Directories that May Exist on a Remote Computer*

Directory	Description
/home/	Home directories
/opt/	Applications
/usr/	The hierarchy below /usr

The following directories cannot be imported from other computers. They must always be present locally on each computer:

Table 2-14   *Directories that Must Exist on the Local Machine*

Directory	Description
/bin/	Important programs
/boot/	Kernel and boot files
/dev/	Device files
/etc/	Configuration files
/lib/	Libraries needed by programs in /bin/ and /sbin/.
/sbin/	Important programs for system administration

Summary

Objective	Summary
Understand Partitions, LVM, RAID, and File Systems	The storage space on hard drives can be divided into smaller pieces called partitions. On x86-type hardware, a hard disk can hold 4 primary partitions. If one of these is an extended partition, 11 logical partitions can be created within this extended partition.
	Before a partition can be used to store files and directories, a file system has to be created on it.
	Logical volume management (LVM) provides a higher-level view of the disk storage on a computer system than the traditional view of disks and partitions. Several hard disks and partitions can be combined into a volume group. Several logical volumes can be created within a volume group.
	Logical volumes behave much like partitions but are more flexible.
	Software RAID allows you to combine several disks to provide increased performance and redundancy.
	Linux supports various file systems. Each file system has its particular strengths and weaknesses, which must be taken into account.
	File systems that keep a journal of transactions recover faster after a system crash or a power failure.
Perform a SLES 11 Installation	SLES 11 can be installed using the installation DVD, or using a boot medium (such as the installation DVD) and an installation repository located in the network.
	Installation consists of configuring hardware-related parameters, such as partitioning, selecting the software to be installed, and configuring user-related aspects such as root password, usernames, and users' passwords.
Understand the File System Hierarchy Standard (FHS)	The layout of a Linux file system follows the File System Hierarchy Standard. This standard defines the directory structure and the purpose of directories within the root (/) directory and the directories that exist in the /usr/ and /var/ directories.
	The /bin/, /sbin/, /lib/, /etc/, and /dev/ directories have to exist on the same partition as the / directory on the local machine. Other directories, such as /home/ and /usr/ can reside on different partitions or even on different machines in the network.

Key Terms

AutoYaST file – An XML file that contains SUSE Linux installation settings that can be imported into future SUSE Linux installations.

block-oriented device file – A device file that describes devices that transfer information block-by-block to a formatted file system.

certification authority (CA) – A software service that digitally signs encryption keys for other entities to prove their authenticity.

character-oriented device file – A device file that describes devices that transfer information in a character-by-character format.

extended partition – A section of the physical hard disk that serves to contain logical partitions.

File System Hierarchy Standard (FHS) – The widely adopted standard that details the names and function of files and directories on a Linux or UNIX system.

file system journaling – The process whereby disk operations are first written to a journal file before they are performed. Following a power outage, the system does not need to check the entire file system for errors, as it can simply consult the journal file.

hardware RAID – A form of RAID in which the read and write operations are performed by a specific hardware-based disk controller.

journaling file system – A file system that logs disk operations to a journal file prior to performing them. Common journaling file systems include ext3, ReiserFS, XFS, and NTFS.

logical partition – A section of an extended partition that can be formatted with a file system and mounted by the operating system.

logical volume – A section of an LVM volume group that can contain a file system and be mounted by the operating system for use.

Logical Volume Manager (LVM) – A set of software components that can be used to create and manage logical volumes across several hard disks on a Linux system.

major number – The number stored within a device file that indicates the associated device driver in the Linux kernel.

minor number – The number stored within a device file that indicates the instance of the physical hardware device.

mirroring – A type of RAID in which a single copy of data is written to two hard disks simultaneously to allow for redundancy in the event that a single hard drive fails. It is also called RAID level 1.

mknod command – Used to create device files.

mount command – Used to mount a file system on a device to a directory in the Linux file system hierarchy.

network file system – A file system that allows remote access to files from computers across a network. Common network file systems include NFS and CIFS/SMBFS.

partition – A section of a physical hard disk that can be formatted with a file system and mounted by the operating system.

physical volume – A partition or hard disk that is used by the LVM.

primary partition – The default partition type used to subdivide a hard disk. They can be formatted with a file system and mounted by the operating system.

Red Hat Package Manager (RPM) – The default package management system used by SUSE Linux.

Redundant Array of Independent Disks (RAID) – A technology that writes data to multiple hard disks from a single volume. It is sometimes referred to as Redundant Array of Inexpensive Disks.

redundant striping – A type of RAID in which data is written across several disks alongside parity information that can be used to regenerate data if a hard disk fails. It is implemented by RAID level 5 and 6.

root partition – A partition that is mounted to the root (/) of the file system hierarchy on a Linux system. It is one of the two partitions that need to be specified during the Linux installation process.

software RAID – A form of RAID in which the read and write operations are performed by an operating system component.

striping – A type of RAID in which data is written across several disks. It is a form of RAID level 0.

swap partition – A partition that can be used to store virtual memory by the Linux operating system. It is one of the two partitions that need to be specified during the Linux installation process.

traditional file system – A file system that does not support journaling. Common traditional file systems include ext2, MS-DOS/VFAT, minix, and ISO9660.

umount command – Used to dismount a file system on a device from a directory in the Linux file system hierarchy.

Virtual File System Switch (VFS) – A Linux kernel component that allows multiple file systems to be used on the same computer.

volume group – A group of physical volumes used by the LVM.

Chapter Exercises

Exercise 2-1 *Install SUSE Linux Enterprise Server 11*

In this exercise, you install a SUSE Linux Enterprise Server 11 system as a virtual VMware machine. A virtual machine with no operating system installed is provided on your Course DVD. Use the following specifications as a guideline for the installation:

- Create the following partitions:
  - ❑ 1 GB swap partition.
  - ❑ 6 GB for / (you should leave unpartitioned space on the hard disk to add partitions in later exercises).
- Use default software patterns, but add the *C/C++ Compiler and Tools* pattern.
- root password: novell

NOTE: This password is not appropriate for a production environment.

- Use a static IP address:
  - ❑ IP address: 172.17.8.101
  - ❑ Network mask: 255.255.0.0
  - ❑ Hostname: da1
  - ❑ Domain name: digitalairlines.com
  - ❑ Name server: none
  - ❑ Default gateway: 172.17.8.1
- Use local authentication. Create a geeko user account with a password of novell.
- Skip the online update.

Detailed Steps to Complete the Exercise

Do the following:

1. Insert your *SUSE Linux Enterprise Server 11* installation DVD into your host workstation's DVD drive.
2. On your host workstation, start VMware Player.
3. In VMware Player, select *Open an existing Virtual Machine*.
4. Browse to and select the `/vmware/da1-3112/da1.vmx` file.
5. If prompted to create a new identifier for the virtual machine, select *Keep*, then click *OK*.
6. When the GRUB installation screen appears, select *Installation* with the arrow keys and then press Enter.

   Wait while Linux is loaded and the YaST Installation module starts.
7. In the Language Selection dialog, select *your language* and your *keyboard layout*.

NOTE: Although you can select any available language, the exercises in this manual are written for English US.

---

8. In the License Agreement field, select *I Agree to the License Terms*, then click *Next*.

9. In the Media Check screen, click *Next*.

   Wait while the system hardware is probed.

10. In the *Installation Mode* dialog, select *New Installation*, then click *Next*.

11. In the Clock and Time Zone dialog, select your *time zone*.

12. Deselect *Hardware Clock Set To UTC*.

13. Adjust the date and time to the correct parameters, if needed.

14. When done, click *Next*.

15. In the Server Base Scenario screen, select *Physical Machine*, then click *Next*.

    The Installation Settings proposal dialog appears.

16. Change the partitioning settings by selecting *Partitioning*.

17. Select *Custom Partitioning (for experts)*, then click *Next*.

18. Create a swap partition by doing the following:

    a. Under System View, select *Hard Disks > sda*.

    b. Select *Add*.

    c. Select *Primary Partition*, then click *Next*.

    d. Select *Custom Size*, then enter a size of **1 GB**.

    e. Click *Next*.

    f. From the File System drop-down list, select *Swap*.

    g. Add the swap partition by clicking *Finish*.

19. Create the root partition by doing the following:

    a. Select *Add*.

    b. Select *Primary Partition*, then click *Next*.

    c. Select *Custom Size*, then enter a size of **6 GB**.

    d. Click *Next*.

    e. Configure the following options:

       ■ Select *Ext3* from the File System drop-down list.

       ■ Select / from the *Mount Point* drop-down list.

    f. Add the root partition by clicking *Finish*.

20. Confirm the partitioning setup and return to the installation proposal by clicking *Accept*.

21. In the *Installation Settings Overview*, select *Software*.

22. Under Patterns, scroll down to and select *C/C++ Compiler and Tools*.

23. Click *OK*.

24. If prompted to accept license agreements for packages to be installed, select *Accept*.

25. In the Installation Settings dialog, click *Install*.

26. In the confirmation dialog, click *Install*.

    Wait while the disk is partitioned and the packages are installed. This may take up to 30 minutes to complete.

27. In the Password for the System Administrator "root" screen, enter novell in the password fields.

28. Click *Next*.

29. When warned that the password is too simple, click *Yes*.

30. When warned that the password uses only lowercase letters, click *Yes*.

31. In the Hostname and Domain Name dialog, enter da1 in the Hostname field and digitalairlines.com in the Domain Name field.

32. **Deselect** *Change Hostname via DHCP*.

33. Select *Write Hostname to /etc/hosts*, then click *Next*.

34. In the Network Configuration screen under Firewall, click *disable* next to *Firewall is enabled*.

    The entry will change to *Firewall is disabled*.

    NOTE: Turning off the firewall is not generally recommended. Within this course, however, having SuSE Firewall enabled would interfere with a later exercise involving the `iptables` command.

    ---

35. Select *Network Interfaces*.

36. Select the first detected network card, then click *Edit*.

37. Select *Statically Assigned IP Address*.

38. In the IP Address field, enter 172.17.8.101.

39. In the Subnet Mask field, enter 255.255.0.0.

40. In the Hostname field, enter da1.

41. Click *Next*.

42. Select the *Hostname/DNS* tab.

    Your hostname and domain name should already be filled. If not, enter a hostname of da1 and the domain name digitalairlines.com.

NOTE: Because this virtual machine runs in host-only mode, it is isolated from the rest of your network. In a production environment, you would configure one or more DNS server addresses and a gateway router address.

43. Return to the Network Configuration dialog by selecting *OK*.

44. Continue with the installation by clicking *Next*.

45. In the Test Internet Connection dialog, select *No, Skip This Test*, then click *Next*.

46. In the Installation Overview dialog, accept the default settings by clicking *Next*.

47. In the User Authentication Method screen, select *Local (/etc/passwd)*, then click *Next*.

48. In the New Local User screen, add a user named geeko by entering the following:

    ■   User's Full Name: Geeko Novell

    ■   User Login: geeko

    ■   Password: novell

49. Create the user by clicking *Next*.

50. Confirm the password warnings by clicking *Yes* twice.

51. In the Release Notes screen, review the release notes, then click *Next*.

52. In the Hardware Configuration dialog, review the settings suggested under *Graphics Cards*, then click *Next*.

53. Uncheck *Clone this System for AutoYaST* and complete the installation process by clicking *Finish*.

    Wait while the graphical login is loaded.

54. In the lower right corner of the VMware Player window, click the Network Adapter icon and make sure the *Host Only* entry is selected.

55. To make sure that da-host and da1 can access each other over the network, do the following on da-host:

    a.   Select *Yast > Security and Users > Firewall*.

    b.   In the tree on the left select *Interfaces*. In the *Firewall Interfaces* frame, select *vmnet1* and click *Change*. From the *Interface Zone* drop down menu select *Internal Zone*, then click *OK*.

    c.   In the tree on the left select *Masquerading*. In the *Masquerading* frame on the right, make sure *Masquerade Networks* is selected, then click *OK*. In the *Firewall Configuration: Summary* dialog, click *Finish*.

(End of Exercise)

Review Questions

1. How many primary partitions can be created on a hard disk for an x86 system?
   a) 1
   b) 4
   c) 256
   d) 1022

2. Which two partitions are required for a SUSE Linux installation at minimum? (Choose two answers.)
   a) A swap partition
   b) A /boot partition
   c) A root (/) partition
   d) A /usr partition

3. Which file is used to the list of partitions and file systems that are mounted at boot time?
   a) /etc/mtab
   b) /tmp/filesystems
   c) /dev/sda
   d) /etc/fstab

4. Which device file refers to the second partition on the third SCSI hard disk in SUSE Linux?
   a) /dev/sdb2
   b) /dev/sdc2
   c) /dev/sdb3
   d) /dev/sdc3

5. Which of the following statements are true regarding the LVM?
   a) Physical volumes are created from the available space within a volume group that is comprised of one or more logical volumes
   b) Volume groups contain logical volumes that are created from the available space within a physical volume
   c) Logical volumes are grouped into volume groups and store information in a specific physical volume
   d) Logical volumes are created from the available space within a volume group that is comprised of one or more physical volumes

6. Which RAID level provides redundant striping for three or more hard disks?
   a) 0
   b) 1
   c) 5
   d) 6

7. Hardware RAID is implemented directly by the SUSE Linux operating system.
   a) True
   b) False

8. Which of the following files systems is a journaling file system?
   a) ext2
   b) VFAT
   c) ReiserFS
   d) NFS

9. Which of the following statements is not true regarding file systems?
   a) Each file and directory on a file system has a unique inode number
   b) Journaling file systems are less robust than their counterparts
   c) The Linux kernel uses the VFS to allow processes to access different file systems on the same computer seamlessly
   d) Hard links share the same inode number

10. Which of the following options are available when you boot your computer from a SUSE Linux installation DVD? (Choose all that apply.)
   a) Boot from Hard disk
   b) Rescue System
   c) Check Installation Media
   d) Firmware Test

11. What function key could you press during a SUSE Linux installation to perform an installation from source files hosted on an FTP server across the network?
   a) F1
   b) F3
   c) F4
   d) F5

12. What Default Runlevel is selected by default on the Installation Settings page during a SUSE Linux installation if a graphical environment is installed?
   a) 2
   b) 3
   c) 4
   d) 5

13. What partitioning and file system options can be configured during a SUSE Linux installation? (Choose all that apply.)
   a) Software RAID
   b) Partition creation, deletion and resizing
   c) LVM
   d) File system selection

14. What can you select during the software selection phase of a SUSE Linux installation to determine whether there are any prerequisite software packages for the software that you have selected?
   a) Dependencies > Check
   b) Patterns > Repositories
   c) Patterns > Installation Summary
   d) Dependencies > Package Groups

15. Which of the following are configured on the first boot following a SUSE Linux installation? (Choose all that apply.)
   a) The root password
   b) System packages
   c) Host name
   d) Network configuration

16. If you select the Clone This System for Autoyast option at the end of the installation process, what file will contain the installation settings?
   a) /root/autoyast.txt
   b) /root/autoinst.xml
   c) /autoyast.txt
   d) /autoinst.xml

17. How long can a file name be on a Linux system?
   a) 8 characters
   b) 255 characters
   c) 1023 characters
   d) unlimited

18. Which of the following is an absolute pathname?
   a) ../../etc
   b) var
   c) var/spool/..
   d) /

19. Which directory in the FHS stores system configuration files?
    a) /usr
    b) /var
    c) /sbin
    d) /etc

20. Which directory in the FHS stores programs that can only be executed by the root user?
    a) /sbin
    b) /usr
    c) /bin
    d) /var

Discovery Exercises

Using AutoYaST to Perform an Unattended Installation

During the workbook exercise *Install SUSE Linux Enterprise Server 11,* you installed SLES 11 in a VMWare virtual machine using your SLES 11 DVD.

Repeat this exercise again (you can reuse the existing partitions created during the installation process) but do not unselect Clone this System for AutoYaST at the end of the installation. Next, log into tty1 as the root user and view the autoinst.xml file in your home directory using the **less autoinst.xml** command. Note that your installation choices and settings are present.

Next, type the **mount** command to view the mounted file systems and note the device file that is used for your root (/) file system (e.g. sda2). Shut down your VMWare virtual machine.

Now, you can perform an unattended installation using the information in your autoinst.xml file. Ensure that your SLES 11 DVD is inserted into your DVD drive and start your VMWare virtual machine. Highlight **Installation** at the startup screen and type **autoyast=device://device_file/root/autoinst.xml** in the Boot Options dialog box, where device_file is the device file for your root file system (seen earlier with the **mount** command). For example, if your root file system uses the device file sda2, you could type **autoyast=device://sda2/root/autoinst.xml** in the Boot Options dialog box. Press Enter and watch your unattended installation! When finished, shut down your VMWare virtual machine.

Checking for Memory Errors

During the interactive and non-interactive sections of an SLES installation, your computer may suddenly reboot, hang, or display a Fatal Signal 11 (Segmentation Fault) error. Although these problems may be the result of incompatible or malfunctioning hardware devices, they are most often the result of defective RAM. The SLES installation program can use all of the available locations in your RAM during the installation process. Hence, even if your system worked well before you started the SLES installation, the installation program may still detect bad locations in your RAM. As a result, it is best practice to use the memtest86 utility that is included on your SLES DVD to check your RAM before starting the installation. Ensure that your SLES 11 DVD is inserted into your DVD drive and start your VMWare virtual machine. At the boot screen, select **Memory Test** to run the memtest86 utility on your computer. Were any errors found? When one full series of tests has been performed, press **Esc** to stop the utility and reboot your system.

Text-Based Installation

Some video adapter cards (especially newer high-end video cards) are incompatible with the SLES installation program. In this case, you can install SLES using a text-based menu interface (called ncurses) rather than a graphical interface; on the first boot following installation, SLES will then detect and install your video card. Some administrators choose to perform a text-based installation because it is faster than a graphical installation since the graphical subsystem does not need to be loaded. Perform the workbook exercise *Install SUSE Linux Enterprise Server 11* again, but instead of selecting Installation after booting your VMWare virtual machine, press the F3 key and choose Text Mode. Next, select **Installation** to begin the text mode installation. You will need to use the Tab key to navigate through screen options during the installation, and certain installation options will be in a different location.

SECTION 3 Administer SUSE Linux Enterprise Server 11 with YaST

YaST is a powerful tool for configuring your SUSE Linux Enterprise Server 11. Many modules are available for important configuration tasks. In this section you will get an overview of YaST's capabilities.

YaST is not a topic that is part of the LPI Level One objectives, but is covered here because it is the main tool for many administrative tasks on SLES 11.

Objectives

1. Get to Know YaST

2. Manage Software with YaST

3. Manage User and Group Accounts with YaST

4. The X Window System

Objective 1   Get to Know YaST

YaST stands for **Yet another Setup Tool**. You can use YaST to complete many configuration tasks as a SLES 11 administrator.

User Interfaces

The YaST user interface can appear in two modes:

- **ncurses** (Text mode)

- **QT** (Fully graphical mode)

Because YaST can be used in both modes, it is available on systems that have a graphical user interface installed as well as systems that do not. The following table lists the available options:

Table 3-1   *YaST User Interface in Different Environments*

Command	Terminal in X Window	Command Line
yast2	Qt	ncurses
yast	ncurses	ncurses

The appearance of the user interface depends on which command you use to start YaST and on whether you use the graphical system or the command line.

Navigating the Text Interface (ncurses)

You control the ncurses interface with the keyboard. To start the ncurses interface of YaST, start a terminal emulation from your GNOME desktop by selecting *Gnome Terminal* from the main menu (application group: *System*). Enter su – to get root permissions. After entering the root password, start YaST by entering yast.

Figure 3-1   *YaST ncurses Interface*

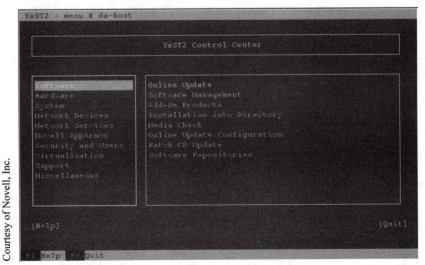

Courtesy of Novell, Inc.

Press Tab to move from one box to another or to the text buttons. To go back to the previous box, press Shift+Tab. Use the arrow keys to navigate within the box. Select highlighted menu items by pressing the Spacebar.

To select a menu item, press Enter. You can often press the Alt key and the highlighted letter to access an item directly.

Except for the controls and the appearance, the graphical mode and the text mode of YaST are identical.

You can list the available YaST modules with the `yast -l` or `yast --list` command. To start an individual module, specify its name. For example, you can enter the following to start the software installation module:

`yast sw_single`

You can enter the software module name with the `yast` or `yast2` command, as in the following:

- `yast sw_single` (text mode)

- `yast2 sw_single` (graphical mode)

To display a list of YaST options, enter one of the following:

- `yast --help`

- `yast -h`

The main dialog of YaST is called the *YaST Control Center*.

From the YaST Control Center you can select a category on the left (such as ***Software*** or ***System***) and a module on the right (such as ***Online Update***) to configure and manage your system.

When you finish making changes with a YaST module, YaST writes the configuration into the proper configuration files to implement the changes in the system. (In rare cases, such as the Postfix configuration, the additional step of running the `SuSEconfig` script is executed by YaST to write the actual configuration.)

Navigating the Graphical Interface (QT)

In the graphical interface, you can control YaST with the mouse. To start it, select ***YaST*** from the main menu (application group: ***System***). You are asked to enter the root password.

Figure 3-2   *Root Password Dialog*

Courtesy of Novell, Inc.

The *YaST Control Center* dialog appears.

Figure 3-3   *The YaST Control Center*

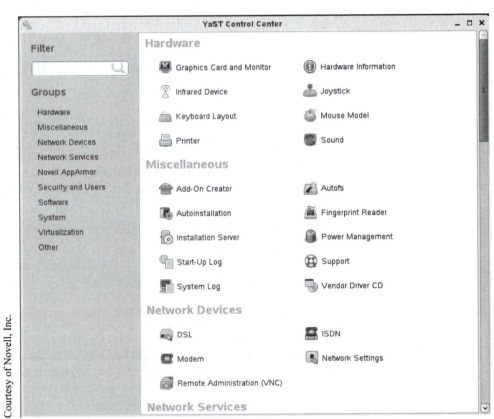

Courtesy of Novell, Inc.

YaST Groups

YaST includes many modules for various administrative tasks. YaST groups consist of modules that are used to perform related administrative tasks. The following table lists the groups available and some of the functions that are covered by the modules included in the respective group:

Table 3-2   *YaST Groups*

YaST Group	Function of Modules in Group
Hardware	■ Add, configure, and remove printers. ■ Configure keyboard settings. ■ Manage external devices such as Web cams, joysticks, and mice.
Miscellaneous	■ View start-up and system logs. ■ Connect with Novell Support Center. ■ Configure Autoinstallation settings.
Network Devices	■ Configure network settings. ■ Assign IP addresses and domain names. ■ Manage network cards, modems, fax machines, and so on. ■ Configure remote administration with Virtual Network Computing (VNC).
Network Services	■ Configure hostnames. ■ Manage various network clients. ■ Create Windows domains and workgroups. ■ Configure additional server settings.
Novell AppArmor	Novell AppArmor is a security framework that comes installed with SLES 11. It gives you network application security via mandatory access control for programs, protecting against the exploitation of software flaws and compromised systems. AppArmor offers an advanced toolset that largely automates the development of per-program application security so that no new expertise is required. Tasks you can perform in the Novell AppArmor category include: ■ Enable or disable AppArmor. ■ Run security reports and event notification warnings. ■ Create and modify AppArmor profiles. NOTE: More information on this topic can be found in Course 3102 *SUSE Linux Enterprise 11 Adminstration*.
Security and Users	■ Add/delete users. ■ Change password settings. ■ Manage firewall settings.
Software	■ Install and manage software. ■ Check for online updates. ■ Check the integrity of installation media.

YaST Group	Function of Modules in Group
System	Some tasks you can perform in the System category are: ■ Adjust date and time settings. ■ Back up, archive, and restore the system. ■ Change language settings. ■ Manage disk partitions.
Virtualization	■ Install and manage Xen Hypervisor. ■ Access libvirt and other utilities.
Other	■ Review release notes with updates to the latest version of SLES 11. ■ Manage Novell Customer Center settings.

Exercise 3-1   **Get to Know YaST**

In this exercise, you learn how to use the different user interfaces of YaST and how to start some YaST modules.

You will find this exercise at the end of the chapter.

(End of Exercise)

Objective 2   Manage Software with YaST

YaST Software Management is a GUI front end for managing RPM packages.

As a root-level administrative tool, the YaST software management module serves as the default software management interface for SUSE Linux Enterprise Server 11. YaST Software Management supports the GNOME, KDE, and Ncurses interfaces - this course focuses on GNOME.

YaST Software Manager allows administrators to

- Access YaST Software Manager on the Server
- Search for Packages Using Filters
- View Information About a Package on the Server
- Install Software on the Server with YaST
- View and Resolve Package Dependencies
- Manage Software with YaST

Access YaST Software Manager on the Server

1. Go the main menu (*Computer*).

2. From the *System* panel on the right, select *YaST*.

3. Go to *Software > Software Management*.

   The search dialog is displayed.

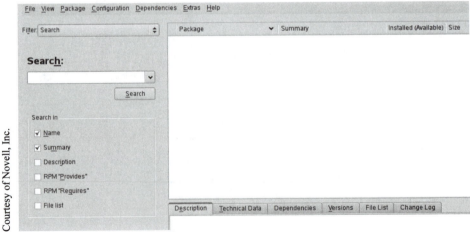

Search for Packages Using Filters

You can view and search for packages using different filters. Just select the filter from the *Filter* drop-down list:

- **Pattern.** A pattern is an installable list of packages, e.g., the *Base System*. Here is a list of patterns as shown in the YaST interface. The patterns with a check mark next to them are installed patterns.

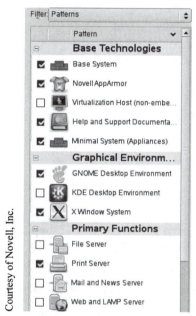

Courtesy of Novell, Inc.

- **Package Group.** Package groups show packages by functional category; for example, all security-related packages will be grouped together. Here is an excerpt from the list as it appears in YaST:

Courtesy of Novell, Inc.

- **Language.** Packages that are needed to add support of specific languages to applications such as Firefox, YaST, or KDE.

- **Repository.** A repository is a local or remote directory containing packages, plus additional information (metadata) about these packages.

- **Search.** The search dialog that first appears when you open the *Software Manager* contains a search box. It lets you search for packages that meet various criteria, such as name, summary, description, etc. If you know the name of the package, this is usually the easiest way to find it.

- **Installation summary.**

  You can show an installation summary of packages with a certain status:

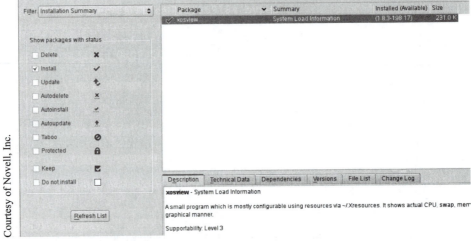

Courtesy of Novell, Inc.

For example, to show all packages that have the **Install** status (i.e., that are to be installed), do the following:

1. Check the box next to *Install*. Notice that the installation state is shown by a small symbol in front of the package name. The most commonly displayed symbols include the following:

Figure 3-4   *Installation Symbols Used in YaST*

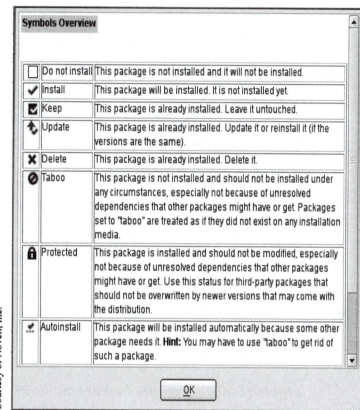

Courtesy of Novell, Inc.

2. Click *Refresh List*.

NOTE: It is good general practice to check dependencies and perform an installation summary before clicking *Accept*. This way you can see all the changes that will be made to your system.

---

3. Click *Accept*.

View Information About a Package on the Server

YaST allows the system administrator to view a lot of information about a package, including

- A summary and description
- Technical data such as version, size, build, and architecture

- Dependencies on other packages

- File list (only for installed packages)

- Change log (when and what changes were made)

To view information about a package, do the following:

1. Filter on a pattern or a package group. For example, filter on the *Print Server* pattern:

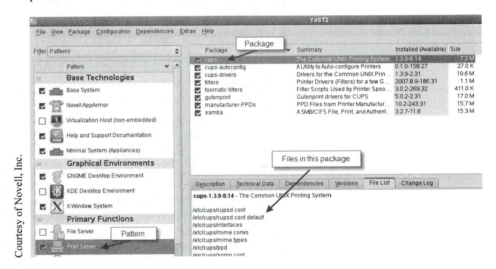

2. Click the pattern.

3. Select a Package to display its information.

4. Move from tab to tab to display description, technical data, dependencies, versions, file list, and change log.

Install Software on the Server with YaST

1. Go to the main menu (*Computer*) and open *YaST* from the *System* panel on the right side.

2. Click the *Software* group in the left panel.

3. Double-click *Software Management*.

4. In the search box, type the package name or a part of it and click *Search*.

5. From the results, select the package you want to install.

6. Look at some of the detailed descriptions and dependencies for this package.

7. Double-click the square in front of the package until a green check mark appears.

8. Click *Accept*.

   YaST now automatically resolves dependencies. If other packages need to be changed/installed as a result of your choice, review the suggested changes and click *Continue*.

View and Resolve Package Dependencies

You have just seen how *YaST Software Manager* resolves dependencies automatically. You can manage package dependencies in different ways:

- View a package's dependencies. To do so, select a package and select the ***Dependencies*** tab below the list of packages.

- Resolve package dependencies automatically (***Dependencies > Autocheck***). This is the default setting in the Dependencies menu:

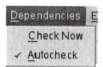

- Perform an ad hoc check anytime (***Dependencies > Check Now***). You should always check dependencies before performing an installation to be aware of the consequences of the installation for your system.

- Reset ignored dependency conflicts (***Extras > Reset Ignored Dependency Conflicts***).

- Generate a dependency resolver test case (***Extras > Generate Dependency Resolver Test Case***).

Exercise 3-2   *Manage Software with YaST*

In this exercise, you practice installing and uninstalling software packages with the YaST Software Management module.

You will find this exercise at the end of the chapter.

(End of Exercise)

Objective 3 Manage User and Group Accounts with YaST

With YaST, you can manage users and groups. To do this, you need to understand the following:

- Basics About Users and Groups
- User and Group Administration with YaST
- Manage User Accounts with YaST

Basics About Users and Groups

One of the main characteristics of a Linux operating system is its ability to handle several users at the same time (multiuser) and to allow these users to perform several tasks on the same computer simultaneously (multitasking).

For this reason the system must be able to uniquely identify all users. To achieve this, every user must log in with the following:

- A user name
- A password

Because the operating system can handle numbers much better than strings, users are handled internally as numbers, the UID (User ID).

Every Linux system has a privileged user, the user root. This user always has the UID 0. This is the administrator of the system.

Users can be grouped together based on shared characteristics or activities. For example:

- Normal users are usually members of the group users.
- All users who intend to create web pages can be placed in the group *webedit*.

Of course, file permissions for the directory in which the web pages are located must be set so that the group webedit is able to write (save) files.

As with users, each group is also allocated a number internally called the GID (Group ID), and can be one of the following:

- Normal group (GID from 1000 on up)
- Group used by the system
- The root group (GID = 0)

User and Group Administration with YaST

You can access YaST user and group account administration in the following ways:

- From the YaST Control Center, select *Security and Users > User and Group Management*.

  or

- From a terminal window, enter `yast2 users` or `yast2 groups`.

If you have selected LDAP for authentication during the installation of the SLES 11, you are prompted for the LDAP server administrator password.

You can switch back and forth between administering users and administering groups by selecting the *Users* and *Groups* tabs at the top of the module window.

User Administration

The user account management window lists the existing user accounts (as in the following):

Figure 3-5   *YaST: User and Group Administration*

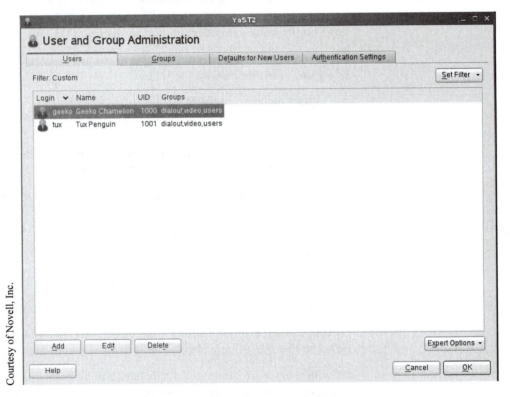

Courtesy of Novell, Inc.

A list of users (accounts on your server) appears with information such as login name, full name, UID, and associated groups included for each user.

Select *Set Filter*, then select one of the following to change the users listed:

- **Local Users.** User accounts you have created on your local server for logging into the server.

- **System Users.** User accounts created by the system for use with services and applications.

- **Custom.** A customized view of users based on the settings configured with *Customize Filter*.

- **Customize Filter.** This option lets you combine listed user sets (such as *Local Users* and *System Users*) to display a customized view (with *Custom*) of the users list.

Additional sets of users (such as *LDAP users*) are added to the *Set Filter* drop-down list as you configure and start services on your server.

To create a new user account (or edit an existing account), do the following:

1. Click *Add* or *Edit*.

   The following appears:

Figure 3-6   *YaST: New Local User*

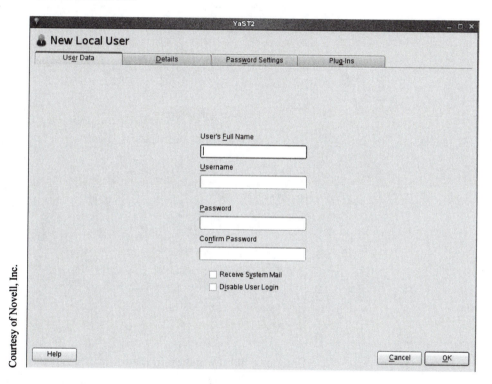

Courtesy of Novell, Inc.

2. Enter or edit information in the following fields:

   - **User's Full Name.** Enter a real user name (such as *Geeko Chameleon*).

   - **Username.** Enter a user name that is used to log in to the system (such as *geeko*).

   - **Password and Confirm Password.** Enter and re-enter a password for the user account.

     When entering a password, distinguish between uppercase and lowercase letters.

     Valid password characters include letters, digits, blanks, and #*,.;:._-+!$%&/ |?{[()]}=.

However, use special characters (those listed above and foreign language characters) with caution, because you might find it difficult to type these characters on a different keyboard layout when logging in from another country.

With the current password encryption (Blowfish), the password length should be between 8 and 72 characters.

To set the properties of the user (such as the UID, the home directory, the login shell, group affiliation, and additional user account comments), do the following:

1. Select the *Details* tab. The following dialog appears:

Figure 3-7   *YaST: Local User Details*

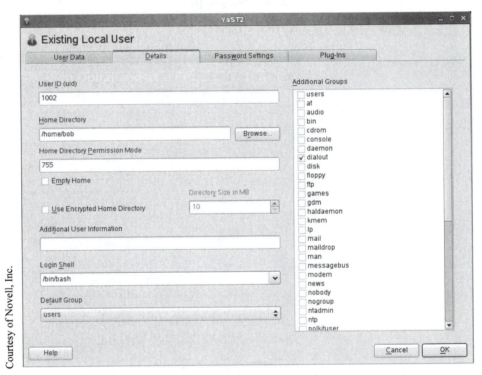

Courtesy of Novell, Inc.

2. Enter or edit information in the following fields:

    ■   **User ID (uid).** For normal users, this defaults to a UID greater than 999 because the lower UIDs are used by the system for special purposes and pseudo logins. The default UID ranges for system and normal users are defined in the `/etc/login.defs` file.

        If you change the UID of an existing user, the permissions of the files this user owns must be changed as well. This is done automatically for the files in the user's home directory, but not for files located elsewhere.

        NOTE: If this does not happen automatically, you (as root) can change the permissions of the user files in the home directory by entering
        `chown -R username /home/username`.

- **Home Directory.** The home directory of the user. On a default installation of SLES 11, this is `/home/`**username**.

  You can select an existing directory by selecting **Browse**.

- **Additional User Information.** This field can contain up to three parts separated by commas. It is often used to enter *office,work phone,home phone*.

  This information is displayed when you use the `finger` command on this user.

- **Login Shell.** From the drop-down list, select the default login shell for this user from the shells installed on your system.

- **Default Group.** This is the group to which the user belongs. Select a group from the list of all groups configured on your system.

- **Groups.** From the list, select all additional memberships you want to assign to the user.

To set various password parameters (such as duration of a password), do the following:

1. Select the **Password Settings** tab. The following appears:

Figure 3-8   *YaST: Local User Password Settings*

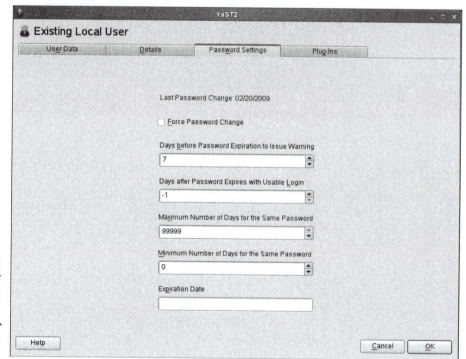

Courtesy of Novell, Inc.

2. Enter or edit information in the following fields:

- **Days before Password Expiration to Issue Warning.** Enter the number of days before password expiration that a warning is issued to users.

Enter -1 to disable the warning.

- **Days after Password Expires with Usable Login.** Enter the number of days after the password expires that users can continue to log in.

  Enter -1 for unlimited access.

- **Maximum Number of Days for the Same Password.** Enter the number of days a user can use the same password before it expires.

- **Minimum Number of Days for the Same Password.** Enter the minimum age of a password before a user can change it.

- **Expiration Date.** Enter the date when the account expires. The date must be in the format YYYY-MM-DD.

  Leave the field empty if the account never expires.

Group Administration

To administer groups, do the following:

1. Select the *Groups* tab.

Figure 3-9   *YaST: Group Administration*

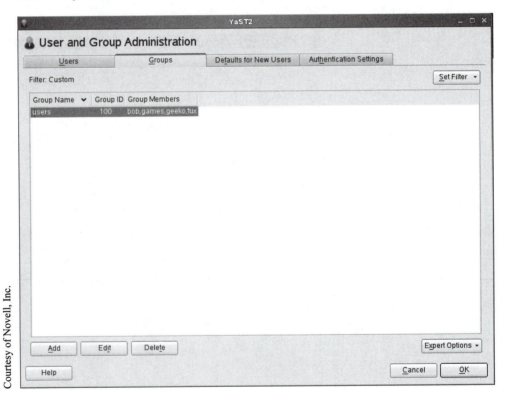

Courtesy of Novell, Inc.

A list of groups appears with information such as group name, Group ID (GID), and group members.

Select **Set Filter**, then select one of the following to change the groups listed:

- **Local Groups.** Groups created on your local server to provide permissions for members assigned to the group.

- **System Groups.** Groups created by the system for use with services and applications.

- **Custom.** A customized view of groups based on the settings configured with **Customize Filter**.

- **Customize Filter.** This option lets you combine listed group sets (such as **Local Groups** and **System Groups**) to display a customized view (with **Custom**) of the groups list.

Additional sets of groups (such as LDAP) are added to the **Set Filter** drop-down list as you configure and start services on your server.

To create a new group or edit an existing group, do the following:

1. Click **Add** or **Edit**.

   The following appears when you select **Edit**:

Figure 3-10   *YaST: Local Group Data*

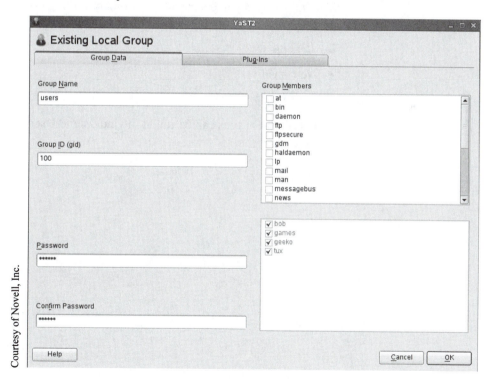

2. Enter or edit information in the following fields:

   - **Group Name.** The name of the group. Avoid long names. Normal name lengths are between two and eight characters.

- **Group ID (gid).** The GID number assigned to the group. The number must be a value between 0 and 60000. GIDs up to 499 represent system groups. GIDs beyond 999 are used for normal groups. YaST warns you if you try to use a GID that is already in use. The default GID ranges for system and normal groups are defined in the `/etc/login.defs` file.

- **Password** (optional). Require the members of the group to identify themselves when switching to this group (see `man newgrp`). To do this, assign a password.

  For security reasons, the password is represented by asterisks ("*").

- **Confirm Password.** Enter the password a second time to avoid typing errors.

- **Group Members.** Select which users should be members of this group.

  A second list appears (when you select ***Edit***) that shows users for which this group is the default group. This list cannot be edited from YaST.

3. When you finish entering or editing the group information, click ***OK***. You are returned to the *Group Administration* dialog.

4. Save the configuration settings by selecting ***OK***.

The information you enter when creating or editing users and groups with YaST is saved to the following user administration files:

- /etc/passwd

- /etc/shadow

- /etc/group

Details on these files can be found in Understand User and Group Configuration Files.

Exercise 3-3   *Manage User Accounts with YaST*

In this exercise, you create and remove a user account with the YaST User Management module.

You will find this exercise at the end of the chapter.

(End of Exercise)

Objective 4   The X Window System

X Window is a system that runs on UNIX and Linux operating systems. X Window is also called X or X11 and is the system and protocol that provides a GUI for computer networks for both client and server machines. This Graphical User Interface that we use today for many of our environments was developed by the Massachusetts Institute of Technology (MIT).

In this objective, the following will be discussed:

- Basics of the X Window System

- Advantages and Disadvantages of Installing the GUI

- X11 Installation, Video Card, and Monitor Requirements

- Understanding the X Font Configuration File

- Configuring the X Window Configuration File

- Window Managers - GNOME and KDE

Basics of the X Window System

The X Window system was created in 1984 at Massachusetts Institute of Technology (MIT). The goal was to be able to use graphical applications across a network, independent of hardware.

The X Window System allows graphical applications to be displayed and operated on any monitor, without running the applications on the machines to which these monitors are connected.

To be able to administer the X Window system, you need to understand:

- X Window Architecture

- Configuration of the X Window System

- Remote Access

X Window Architecture

The basis for this is the separation into a server component (X server) and the application itself (client application). The X server and client application communicate with each other by way of various communication channels.

- **X server.** The X server controls the graphical screen. This corresponds roughly to a graphics driver on other systems. In addition, it manages the input devices, such as keyboard and mouse, and transmits their actions to the X client.

  The X server, however, has nothing to do with the appearance of the window and the desktop; this is the task of the window manager. XFree86 and XOrg are free implementations of the X server. SLES 11 defaults to using XOrg.

- **Client application.** The client application is a graphical application that uses the services of the X server to receive keyboard and mouse actions and to have its own output displayed on the screen.

NOTE: The communication between X server and X client uses the network protocol TCP/IP—even if the server and client run on the same computer.

As can be seen in the following figure, the X server is running on computer da5, while the X applications are running on computers da1 and da2:

Figure 3-11   *X Server and X Client*

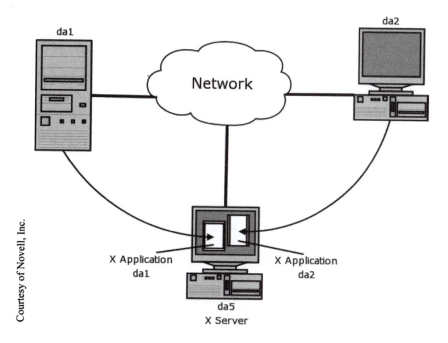

The applications are displayed, however, on the monitor attached to da5. All of these computers can be running different operating systems.

Configuration of the X Window System

The graphical system is automatically configured during SLES 11 installation and, in most cases, you can just accept the suggested values. If you want to change the configuration of graphics card and monitor, there are several options:

- **YaST**. Start YaST and select *Hardware > Graphics Card and Monitor*. YaST starts the SaX2 tool which checks the hardware resources and displays the suggested configuration values in the *Card and Monitor Properties* dialog:

Figure 3-12   *YaST: Card and Monitor Properties*

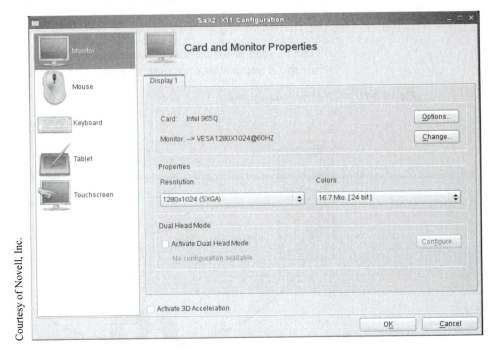

You can choose different values than those suggested by selecting the applicable buttons or drop-down menus.

- **SaX2**. SaX2 can also be started directly. Switch to a virtual terminal using the Ctrl+Alt+F1 keys, log in as root, and enter `sax2`. You can either accept the configuration directly, or select ***Change Configuration***, which opens the same dialog as the one offered from within YaST.

- **xorgconfig**. `xorgconfig` is a command line tool that guides you through the different aspects of the X11 configuration, asking you to enter the hardware parameters manually. It requires detailed knowledge of your hardware and the parameters involved in the graphical configuration.

The X11 configuration created by one of the above tools is written to the `/etc/X11/xorg.conf` file.

If X11 is configured on SLES11, it is usually started automatically and you see a graphical log in screen when the boot process is finished or when you log out from the graphical environment. However, the system can also be started without offering a graphical login, as covered in Understand System Initialization and Manage Runlevels. In this case you can log in on one of the virtual terminals and start the X Window system with the `startx` command.

Using the `startx -- :1` command, you can even start a second X server and toggle between the two with the Ctrl+Alt+F7 and Ctrl+Alt+F8 key combinations.

Remote Access

The X11 protocol allows the display on a local machine to access applications on remote computers. You do this by logging in to the remote machine, using Telnet (deprecated) or Secure Shell (ssh, recommended) and starting the application, such as a word processor like OpenOffice.org.

If you want to access the whole desktop, not just a single application, a different approach is needed. The solution that is included with SLES 11 is the Virtual Network Computing (VNC) protocol.

You need a VNC server that exports a desktop on the remote machine, and a VNC client that shows the remote desktop in a window on the local machine.

On the VNC server, you log in as the user whose desktop you want to export, and enter the vncserver command at a command line:

```
geeko@da-host:~> vncserver

You will require a password to access your desktops.

Password:
Verify:
Would you like to enter a view-only password (y/n)? n

New 'X' desktop is da-host:1

Creating default startup script /home/geeko/.vnc/xstartup
Starting applications specified in /home/geeko/.vnc/xstartup
Log file is /home/geeko/.vnc/da-host:1.log

geeko@da-host:~>
```

The default ~/.vnc/xstartup file is a shell script with the following content:

```
#!/bin/sh
xrdb $HOME/.Xresources
xsetroot -solid grey
xterm -geometry 80x24+10+10 -ls -title "$VNCDESKTOP Desktop" &
twm &
```

On the client, log in to the graphical environment, open a terminal window, and enter vncviewer. You are prompted for the password set on the server. Inside a window, a desktop using the twm window manager opens up:

Figure 3-13   *Tab Window Manager*

Courtesy of Novell, Inc.

To disconnect, simply close the TightVNC window.

To end the vncserver process, on the server enter `vncserver -kill :1`, with `:1` referring to the display number that appeared in the output of `vncserver` when it was started.

If you want to use the GNOME desktop instead of TWM, replace `twm &` in the `~.vnc/xstartup` file by the following:

```
metacity &
gnome &
```

When working locally at your GNOME desktop, you can allow others to view your desktop using the *Remote Desktop* application that can be accessed by selecting ***Computer > More Applications > System > Remote Desktop***. The *Remote Desktop Preferences* dialog appears:

Figure 3-14   *Remote Desktop Preferences*

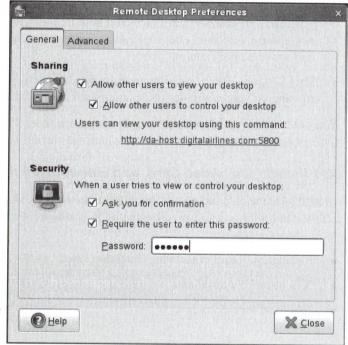

Set the preferences and select *Close*.

On the remote side, enter `vncviewer hostname:1` to open a window containing the shared desktop.

In addition to opening a new desktop or sharing a desktop, it is also possible to show the login dialog in VNC. This is covered in the section on `xinetd` later in the course.

WARNING: Because the VNC protocol is not encrypted, you should use it only within trusted environments.

Advantages and Disadvantages of Installing the GUI

Installing a graphical user interface has the following advantages:

- **Ease of use.** Like any GUI, the Linux Desktop makes it easier to find and access functionality, especially for beginning users and for those who would prefer not to use the command line interface. Other users may find it easier to use the command line after they have learned to navigate it.

- **Functionality.** Desktop programs like OpenOffice.org or GIMP require a GUI. Multiple desktops (or workspaces) can help to better organize the work environment.

- **Familiarity.** The SUSE Linux desktop is full-featured and similar to other desktop environments such as Microsoft Windows or Mac OS.

Not installing a graphical user interface has the following advantages:

- **Stability.** Every program contains errors that can make your system unstable. The fewer programs are installed on a system, the more stable the system will be. A graphical user front end is a large program that may contain a number of undiscovered programming errors.

- **Performance.** Every running program needs system resources. Fewer programs running on your computer means increased performance.

You need to distinguish between graphical applications, which run in their own windows, and text-based applications, which are carried out in a terminal window.

X11 Installation, Video Card, and Monitor Requirements

In SLES 11, the X Window configuration is easily done with YaST and the sax2 utility. The following topics will help you to configure Linux systems where these tools are not available:

- Installation Requirements vs. Hardware Used

- X11 Video Requirements

- X11 Monitor Requirements

Installation Requirements vs. Hardware Used

Always make sure that the machine hardware is supported by the X system. The X server program that comes with most Linux distributions is XFree86. XFree86 is a free open-source distribution of the X Window System. The Xfree86 version of XFree86 4.8.0 binary distribution should only be used if you are sure you know what you are doing; hence, those unsure should avoid the binary distribution. It is possible to download and install XFree86 in the common .rpm or .deb package format, but they should not be used by administrators with little knowledge of installing binaries.

Another open-source implementation of X window is the X.Org project release of X11R7.5, with X11R7.6 to be released soon.

Remember that hardware requirements differ among hardware platforms. When using Intel-based systems, most distributions of X Window suggest a minimum of a 486 processor, with a minimum of 16 MB RAM, making it all the easier for the system to function smoothly without utilizing swap space, which will slow down a hard disk. XFree86 says that a minimum of 60-80 MB of disk space is required. The resources of current systems by far exceed these minimum requirements.

When calculating space, remember to include not only the X server but also libraries, fonts, and other utilities so the requirement may rise to 200+ MB very swiftly. Remember also to refer to the documentation for X Window before trying to install it. There are numerous files that you must download and install in the proper order to ensure a successful installation.

If you have determined you will install over an existing installation, perform a backup, ensuring any pre-existing configuration files are backed up, before beginning.

When installing over an existing installation, the install process should prompt for input before each new set of configuration files is installed into your system. If you have modified and customized configuration files, you may want to answer **no** to prompts, instead of **yes** to overwriting the files.

Being sure of the installation requirements will also help you verify that the video card and monitor requirements are met.

If your decision is to install the binaries, you will find using the XFree86 Xinstall.sh script to be beneficial. There are numerous steps to manual installations, and depending on the hardware and platform being used, the steps may differ for each. Also you should carefully follow the guidelines which you can review at the XFree86 website.

When running the installer from within an X session the installation process will warn you about continuing. Exit the X session, stop X from running, and then continue.

During installation, the setup should automatically configure your mouse, keyboard, video card, and monitor. With XFree86 you should be able to interact with the configuration options at the top of the screen.

If runlevel 5 (runlevels are discussed later in this course) is not used, then start X Windows with the startx terminal session command. You may need to specify any environment variables or options such as in startx -- -display or startx -- -dpi 100.

The startx syntax is:

```
startx [[client] options] [-- [server] options]
```

Using -- will signify the end of the client options used and the start of the server options to be used.

When determining the client that it is to run, the startx command looks for the file .xinitrc, a hidden file in the user's home directory. It specifies any customizations for that user. If not found, it then finds the xinitrc file in the xinit library directory, usually found in a path similar to /usr/X11R*x*/lib/X11/xinit (where *x* is the version).

When determining the server that it is to run, the startx command looks for the file named .xserverrc, a hidden file in the user's home directory. This also contains any customizations unique to the user. If not found, then it will use the system xserverrc file in the xinit library directory structure.

Because .xinitrc is normally run from a shell script, it can start multiple clients, depending upon the configuration. When the script exits, startx will kill the server session and then complete other session shutdown activities as is needed. For this reason users usually prefer to use a session manager, a window manager, or an xterm application or program.

X11 Video Requirements

The video drivers supported by X11 are available at the XFree86 website. Whether you need ATI, Ark Logic, Cirrus Logic, NeoMagic, VESA, or VMware guest OS drivers, you will most likely find the driver you need. Be aware of which driver you download. You may find them to be a preliminary release and not yet stable enough for use in a production environment.

Check with the video card manufacturer or documentation for information concerning the chipset and the necessary amount of RAM needed. It is best to check these requirements before purchasing a video card.

You can determine chipset support using a utility called `SuperProbe`. The usage is as follows:

```
SuperProbe [-verbose] [-no16] [-excl list] [-mask10] [-order list]
[-noprobe list] [-bios base] [-no_bios] [-no_dac] [-no_mem] [-info]
```

The syntax is explained below:

Table 3-3   *SuperProbe Syntax*

-verbose	Verbose output of information.
-no16	No port requiring 16 bit I/O address decoding will be used.
-excl list	Any port on the specified exclusion list will not be accessed.
-mask10	Compared I/O port tested against exclusion list masked to 10 bits.
-order list	Comma-separated list of chipsets to test and what order. Overrides default test order.
-noprobe list	List of chipsets not to test and what order, comma-separated. To find list of acceptable names use -info option below.
-bios base	Specifies base address for graphics-hardware BIOS. If failure to locate BIOS then use this option.
-no_bios	Assume that EGA or later board is primary video hardware. Does not allow reading of the video BIOS.
-no_dac	Skip probing for RAMDAC type when SVGA or VGA is determined.
-no_mem	Do not probe for the amount of installed video memory.
-info	Print out listing of all known video hardware able to identify.

X11 Monitor Requirements

As with the video driver, make sure you understand the requirements for your monitor ahead of installation time. As a general rule of thumb, a monitor uses the compatibility given to it by the video card. In other words, if the video card can drive the monitor, it should work well.

As with the video card, always check the manufacturer's website for its hardware compatibility guidelines and follow it. When having X11 monitor issues, use the `xvidtune` application to fine tune the X server's video modes and its monitor-related settings. If `xvidtune` cannot be used, it will display a message in the terminal window.

A simple adjustment may be made using the `sax2` terminal command to let it self-adjust the monitor resolution for you; alternatively it may run your video configuration utility for you to adjust and test the settings. As with any utility, always read ahead to find out the options, settings, configurations, etc., that will best fit your needs.

Some administrators feel it is unlikely a monitor can be damaged by experimenting with it. Many others feel it is better to be cautious and be prepared by reading documentation on the monitor, or reading the man or info pages that cover the commands to be used. While most monitors now have built-in safety settings and precautions, remember, it is yours or your company's money that purchased the monitor. When X is not configured for its optimal prime settings, try running the vendor's configuration utilities once again and see if the resulting display is better.

If you overdo it, X may not be able to start. For this reason, some prefer to use the `startx` option for starting X while experimenting. This way, if X crashes, the display manager (GUI login) will not loop and cause you severe headaches; `startx` just gracefully returns to a text console screen, where an error message may be visible.

X11 uses the monitor's configuration specifications to determine what will be the resolution and refresh rate to run at. Specifications such as these can usually be ascertained from the documentation that was included with the monitor at purchase or directly from the manufacturer's website. The numbers that are needed indicate a range and refer to the horizontal scan rate and the vertical synchronization rate.

When testing your monitor's display, some tests can produce a black screen which often makes it difficult to determine whether X11 is working properly. You can kill the X server by pressing Ctrl+Alt+Backspace twice.

During the initial setup, Xorg uses a configuration file called `xorg.conf`. The `xorg.conf` file is normally found in `/etc/X11/` and can be generated by the root user or edited by the root user if it already exists. The `xorg.conf` file is discussed in the X Window configuration file section in more detail.

Understanding the X Font Configuration File

The X Window system display requires that it be supplied with fonts. Under normal conditions, the X font server is started by boot files such as the `/etc/rc.local` file.

The process of using fonts with X can sometimes be daunting to understand for new Linux administrators. Usually the installed fonts are sufficient for everyday tasks that you may perform.

Configuration of XFree86 will support TrueType fonts, PostScript fonts, and bitmap fonts. XFree86 can support one or more X font servers.

A font server is a background process that makes your installed set of fonts available to XFree86 and other machines running X.

xfs and xfstt are the most widely used X Window system font servers.

The main configuration file that the font server will use is the default file of `/etc/X11/fs/config`.

You can use the following options with xfs:

- **-config** *configuration_file*: Specifies the file the font server will be using. The default file `/etc/X11/fs/config` will be used.

- **-ls** *listen_socket*: Used by the font server itself when auto spawning a copy to care for any additional connections.

- **-port** *tcp_port*: Defines the TCP port number on which the server will listen for connections. Default port number is **7100**.

- **-daemon**: Directs xfs to fork and then goes into the background at startup. If the option is not specified, xfs will run as a regular process (the exception is if xfs was built to daemonize as the default).

- **-nodaemon**: Prevents xfs from running as a daemon and starts xfs up as a regular process.

- **-droppriv**: Causes xfs to try to run as user and group **xfs**, unless the **-user** option is used. If you use this option, you may also want to use **no-listen = tcp** in the config file. This ensures that xfs will not use a TCP port.

- **-user** *username*: Causes xfs to run with the privileges of the specified user.

X Font Server Setup

Setting up an X font server requires careful planning. The following gives a high-level overview of those steps:

1. Install the font server if necessary.

2. Edit the `xfs.conf` file that comes with it.

3. Set up a font directory such as `/home/fonts/lib/ttfonts`.

4. Have X use the font server after all other fonts by specifying `xset fp+ tcp/localhost:7100`.

5. Test the font server.

To use outline fonts on X, you need a version of X that will support their use. This will include all versions of OpenWindows, X11R5, some newer versions of XFree86, as well as others.

There are three ways to use outline fonts:

- Use the X server itself.

- Use an external font server.

- Use X modules that can be loaded, such as those with OpenWindows.

The following is a sample of a configuration file:

```
#This is a sample X Font server configuration file
#Only a maximum of 10 clients may connect to this server
client-limit = 10
#X font server will reach its limit, then start up a new one
clone-self = on
# an alternate font server that clients may use
alternate-servers = cannon:7101,cannon:7102
#look for fonts in this path
#catalogue = /usr/X11R7/lib/X11/fonts/fonttype
/usr/X11R7/lib/X11/fonts/100dpi/
#use 12 points, decimal points
default-point-size = 120
#Resolutions to use,100 x 100 and 75 x 75
default-resolutions = 100,100,75,75
use-syslog = off
```

Configuring the X Window Configuration File

The **sysutils/hal** and **devel/dbus** ports are installed as dependencies of **x11/xorg**; however, they must be enabled by making the following entries in the `/etc/rc.conf` file:

`hald_enable="YES"`

`dbus_enable="YES"`

Start these services either manually or by a reboot before any further configuration of Xorg is carried out.

If the automatic configuration does not work with your hardware, manual configuration will be required.

Configuration of X11 is a multiple-step process. The first step you need to perform is to build an initial configuration file. As the super user root, simply run `Xorg -configure`.

A skeleton or template file for X11 configuration is generated in the `/root` directory named `xorg.conf.new`.

X11 will attempt to probe the machine's graphics hardware on the system and then create a configuration file to load the proper drivers for the hardware detected on the target system.

Testing is the next step for the configuration. This is to verify that Xorg will work with the installed graphics hardware on the target system.

In Xorg versions up to 7.3, enter `Xorg -config xorg.conf.new`.

As of Xorg 7.4 and later, the test produces a black screen which makes it somewhat difficult to diagnose whether X11 is working properly.

Older behavior is still available by using a `retro` option:

`Xorg -config xorg.conf.new -retro`

The configuration file consists of numerous sections, including the following:

```
Files              File pathnames
FlagServer         Flags
ModuleDynamic      Module Loading
Modes              Description of the Video Modes
Screen             Screen Configuration
InputDevice        Description of the Input Device
Device             Description of the Graphics Device
VideoAdapter       Description of the Xv Video Adaptor
Monitor            Description of the Monitor
ServerLayout       The Overall Layout
DRI                Configuration specific to DRI
Vendor             Vendor-specific Configuration
```

In the configuration file, arguments may follow keywords. The arguments are

```
Integer    A number that is in hex, octal, or decimal format
Real       A floating point number is used
String     A string that is enclosed in "" double quote marks
```

The setup utilities may vary depending on the flavor of Linux you are running.

For example, in Fedora Linux you can run `system-config-display` (as root) to create a configuration file for you. If it is not installed, you will need to first download the package and install it. By default, the command runs interactively. However, it can run non-interactively using the `--noui` option.

```
system-config-display --noui
```

You may need to run it if you cannot run X at all.

Window Managers - GNOME and KDE

Window managers are specialized client applications. A window manager works together with the X server and provides additional functionality. The window manager

- Provides control elements

- Manages virtual desktops

- Provides functionality of window frames (for example, changing their size)

The X Window System is not linked to any specific window manager and thus it is not linked to any particular look and feel.

SLES 11 is currently released with several window managers, including Metacity (the GNOME window manager) and Tab Window Manager (twm).

Desktop environments go far beyond the look and feel window managers provide for desktops and manipulating windows. The aim is to provide clients with a unified look and feel:

- GNOME (originally an acronym for GNU Network Object Model Environment) is the standard graphical desktop for SLES 11.

- You can install another open-source desktop, the KDE (Kool Desktop Environment) desktop, instead.

In this part of this objective, you learn how to complete the following tasks:

- Enabling or Disabling the Display Manager

- Configuring the Display Manager

- Configure the Display Manager for Use by X Terminals

Enabling or Disabling the Display Manager

You can enable or disable the display manager. On SUSE Linux Enterprise systems, the X display manager is managed by the **xdm** init script located in the /etc/init.d directory.

NOTE: Other Linux distributions may use the GNOME display manger (**GDM**) or the KDE display manager (**KDM**). KDM is based on XDM and usually uses its configuration files. However, some distributions will store the KDM settings separately in /etc/kde/kdm or /etc/X11/kdm. If this is the case, then most of your configuration changes will be made in the kdmrc file in one of these directories.

GDM configuration files are stored in /etc/X11/gdm/. Most of your configuration changes are made in the gdm.conf file in this directory.

To manually stop the display manager, do the following:

1. Open a terminal session.

2. Switch to root using the su – command.

3. At the shell prompt, enter /etc/init.d/xdm stop.

TIP: On SLES 11, you can also enter rcxdm stop to accomplish the same task.

When you do, the display manager is unloaded and the text-based interface is displayed. This is shown below:

Figure 3-15   *Unloading the Display Manager*

To restart the display manager after it has been unloaded, do the following:

1. If necessary, log in to the system.

2. Use the `su -` command to switch to root.

3. At the shell prompt, enter `/etc/init.d/xdm start`.

TIP: On SLES 11, you can also enter `rcxdm start` to accomplish the same task.

When you do, the display manager is loaded and the graphical login screen is displayed:

Figure 3-16   *Loading the Display Manager*

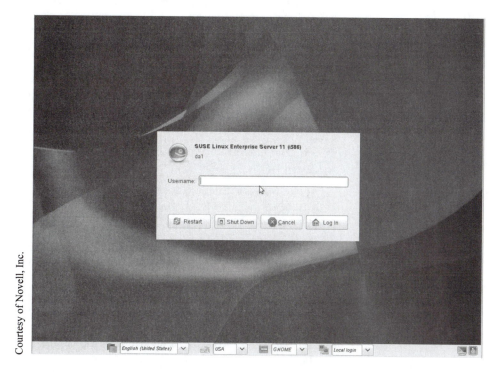

Courtesy of Novell, Inc.

You can control whether or not the display manager is loaded when the system boots using the chkconfig command at the shell prompt. To configure whether or not the display manager loads at system boot, do the following:

1.   Open a terminal session.

2.   Use the su - command to switch to root.

3.   Do one of the following:

▪   To configure the display to not load at boot, enter chkconfig xdm off; then enter chkconfig xdm -l.

Verify that the display manager is disabled on all runlevels, as shown below:

```
da1:~ # chkconfig xdm off
da1:~ # chkconfig xdm -l
xdm              0:off  1:off  2:off  3:off  4:off  5:off  6:off
```

▪   To configure the display to load at boot, enter chkconfig xdm on; then enter chkconfig xdm -l.

Verify that the display manager is enabled on runlevel 5, as shown below:

```
da1:~ # chkconfig xdm on
da1:~ # chkconfig xdm -l
xdm              0:off  1:off  2:off  3:off  4:off  5:on   6:off
```

NOTE: When you configure your system to boot into runlevel 5, the display manager is automatically loaded by default.

Configuring the Display Manager

The files in the /etc/X11/xdm/ directory control the behavior of the display manager on your system. These files are shown below:

```
da1:/etc/X11/xdm # ls
GiveDevices       SuSEconfig.xdm    Xresources     Xsetup      sys.xsession
README.SuSE       TakeDevices       Xservers       Xstartup    xdm-config
README.security   Xaccess           Xservers.fs    Xwilling
RunChooser        Xreset            Xsession       authdir
```

You can use the Xresources file to customize the display manager login interface as well as other xdm widgets. This file is read each time xdm starts. Some of the more useful parameters in this file include the following:

- xlogin*Foreground: Configures the default foreground color for the login box.

- xlogin*Background: Configures the default background color for the login box.

- xlogin*greetColor: Configures the color of the greeting in the login box.

- xlogin*failColor: Configures the color used when the user name or password entered is invalid.

- xlogin*login.Font: Configures the font used for the user name.

- xlogin*login.greetFont: Configures the font used for the greeting.

- xlogin*login.promptFont: Configures the font used for the username and password prompts.

- xlogin*loginfailFont: Configures the font used for failed logins.

- xlogin*greeting: Displays a welcome greeting in the login box. You can include CLIENTHOST in the greeting to display the host name of the system in the greeting.

- xlogin*namePrompt: Configures the prompt displayed for the username.

- xlogin*fail: Configures the text displayed when an unsuccessful login occurs.

To change the appearance of the login box, open the Xresources file in a text editor (as root) and make the appropriate changes to the values of the parameters shown above. After saving your changes, you must restart xdm using the /etc/init.d/xdm script to apply them.

You can use the Xservers file in this directory to change the default color depth for the display manager. To do this, open the file in a text editor as root and locate the following line:

```
:0 local /usr/bin/X -nolisten tcp -br vt7
```

To set the default color depth for the xdm display manager, add `-bpp` `color_depth` to the end of the line where color_depth is the desired depth (8, 16, 24, or 32). For example, to set the default color depth to 24 bits, you would use the following:

```
:0 local /usr/bin/X -nolisten tcp -br vt7 -bpp 24
```

Again, xdm must be restarted after saving your changes to the file.

Configure the Display Manager for Use by X Terminals

It is possible to utilize X terminal systems for end users. Instead of implementing a full computer system, they use a simple diskless device that uses X server software (usually embedded in the hardware) to run a display manager from a remote system over the network. The output from the display manager is displayed on the device's local monitor.

Essentially, this allows organizations to provide a full graphical desktop environment to all of its users using only a limited number of expensive, high-powered xdm host systems and a larger number of inexpensive X terminals.

To configure this implementation, do the following:

1. Identify which system will function as your host and verify that a display manger is running on it.

    This host will listen on the network for inbound connection requests from X terminals. This is done using the *xdm Control Protocol* (XDMCP) on port **177**.

2. Do one of the following:

    -   If your system is running XDM or KDM, open the `/etc/X11/xdm/Xservers` file in a text editor. Locate the line that begins with `:0` and verify that this line does not contain the `-nolisten tcp` option. If it does, remove it, save your changes to the file, and restart the system.

    -   If your system is running GDM, open the `/etc/X11/gdm/gdm.conf` file in a text editor and look for the line that reads `DisallowTCP=`. If it is set to `true`, then change it to `false`.

    -   If you are running SUSE Linux Enterprise, open the `/etc/sysconfig/displaymanager` file in a text editor and make the following changes:

        -   Set `DISPLAYMANAGER_REMOTE_ACCESS="no"` to `"yes"`.
        -   Set `DISPLAYMANAGER_XSERVER_TCP_PORT_6000_OPEN="no"` to `"yes"`.

3. If necessary, open port 177 in the firewall on the xdm host system.

4. Enable remote access to the host system's xdm daemon.

    This is done by editing the `/etc/X11/xdm/Xaccess` file and adding entries for the systems that will be allowed access to the xdm service on the host. You can add each system's hostname individually, or you can specify an entire domain.

For example, to allow all systems from the digitalairlines.com domain to access the xdm service on the host, you could add the following entry to the file:

```
*.digitalairlines.com
```

If you want to forbid systems from accessing the xdm service on the host, you also add their hostnames to the file, but put an exclamation point before it. For example, if you wanted to forbid a host named fs1.digitalairlines.com, you would add the following entry to the file:

```
!fs1.digitalairlines.com
```

Summary

Objective	Summary
Get to Know YaST	YaST can be used as a graphical application as well as in a terminal window:
	■ In the graphical interface, YaST can be controlled intuitively with the mouse.
	■ The ncurses interface is controlled exclusively with the keyboard.
	Individual modules can be started directly. Available modules can be listed with the `yast -l` or `yast --list` command.
Manage Software with YaST	To install new software packages, use the YaST module **Software > Software Management**.
	The installation status of a package is indicated by a symbol. An overview about all possible symbols can be reached via the **Help > Symbols** menu.
	There are dependencies between the packages. In most cases these dependencies can be resolved automatically. Otherwise, they must be resolved manually.
Manage User and Group Accounts with YaST	Linux is a multiuser system. For this reason, the system must be able to uniquely identify all users. This is done by assigning each user account a unique internal number: the UID (UserID).
	Every Linux system has a privileged user, the user root. This user always has the UID 0.
	As with users, the groups are also allocated a number internally: the GID (GroupID).
	You can administer user and group accounts from the YaST Control Center by selecting **Security and Users > User and Group Management**.
	The entered information is saved by YaST to the following configuration files:
	■ `/etc/passwd`
	■ `/etc/shadow`
	■ `/etc/group`
The X Window System	The X Window System consists of a server component (X server) and client applications.
	Server and Client can run on different machines. You can run a graphical program, the X client, such as a spreadsheet application, on another machine and interact with it on your local machine.
	The X11 configuration is contained in the `/etc/X11/xorg.conf` file.
	Using a VNC server and a VNC client, you can work on the desktop remotely.

Key Terms

/etc/group – A file that stores group information on a Linux system.

/etc/init.d/xdm – A script that can be used to control the display manger on a SUSE Linux system.

/etc/login.defs – A file that contains default user parameters used by the SUSE Linux system.

/etc/passwd – A file that stores user account information on a Linux system.

/etc/shadow – A file that stores password and expiry information associated with the user accounts on a Linux system.

/etc/X11/fs/config – The configuration file used by the X Font Server.

/etc/X11/xorg.conf – The XOrg configuration file.

chkconfig command – Used to configure the software services and components that are started during system initialization on a SUSE Linux system.

chown command – Used to change the current owner of a file or directory on the file system.

desktop environment – A software subsystem that provides a specific set of standard applications that can be used alongside a window manager and the X Window System.

display manager – A graphical screen that allows a user to log into the system and start a desktop environment.

finger command – Used to obtain information about user accounts on a Linux system.

GNOME – The default desktop environment used in SUSE Linux. It stands for GNU Network Object Model Environment.

Group ID (UID) – A unique number that is given to groups on a Linux system.

KDE – A common desktop environment used by Linux systems. It stands for Kool Desktop Environment.

ncurses – A text-based interface that is used by some Linux utilities such as YaST.

newgrp command – Used to change the primary group used by a Linux user within the current shell session.

package – A group of software programs that provide a certain functionality on an SUSE Linux system.

QT – A graphical interface that is used by Linux utilities such as YaST.

sax2 – A command that can be used to start the SaX2 utility.

SaX2 – The main configuration utility for the X Window System in SUSE Linux.

Secure Shell – A software system that allows Linux computers to access remote Linux computers in a secure manner by encrypting any data sent across the network.

ssh command – Used to connect to a remote system using Secure Shell.

startx command – Used to start the X Window System.

SuperProbe – A utility that can be used to determine the chipset information for your video card.

User ID (UID) – A unique number that is given to user accounts on a Linux system.

Virtual Network Computing (VNC) – A software system that allows Linux, UNIX, Macintosh and Windows systems to gain access to the graphical user interface of other systems across the network.

vncserver command – Used to share a graphical user interface on a SUSE Linux system.

vncviewer command – Used to connect to a remote graphical user interface from a SUSE Linux system.

window manager – A software subsystem that provides the look and feel of windows within the X Window System.

X client application – The component of the X Window System that interacts with the X server and allows information to be sent to and from the graphical user interface.

xdm Control Protocol (XDMCP) – A display manager component that allows remote computers and X terminals to access the X Windows System on a SUSE Linux computer.

XFree86 – A common X server used on Linux systems.

XOrg – The default X server used on SUSE Linux systems.

xorgconfig command – A command-line utility that can be used to configure the XOrg X server on a SUSE Linux system.

X server – The component of the X Window System that draws the graphical user interface on the screen. XOrg and XFree86 are the two common X servers available for Linux systems.

xvidtune command – Used to perform low-level adjustment of a video card's mode settings including horizontal and vertical refresh rates.

X Window System – The set of software on a Linux system that provides the graphical user interface.

yast command – Used to start the ncurses YaST utility.

yast2 command – Used to start the QT YaST utility.

Chapter Exercises

Exercise 3-1   *Get to Know YaST*

In this exercise, you learn how to use the different user interfaces of YaST and how to start some YaST modules.

Start the graphical user interface of YaST. View the `/proc/version` file with the YaST System Log module and set the time with the Date and Time module. Repeat the first tasks with the ncurses user interface of YaST.

This exercise is performed on the da-host server.

Detailed Steps to Complete the Exercise

- Part I: Use the Graphical User Interface of YaST
- Part II: Use the ncurses Interface of YaST

Part I: Use the Graphical User Interface of YaST

To use the graphical user interface of YaST, do the following:

1. Log in to da-host as geeko.
2. From the **Computer** menu under the System heading, select **YaST**.
3. Enter the root password **novell**, then select **Continue** or press Enter.

    The YaST *Control Center* appears.
4. Select **Miscellaneous > System Log**.
5. From the top drop-down list, select **/proc/version**.
6. Close the log window by selecting **OK**.
7. Select **System > Date and Time**.
8. Select **Change**.
9. Enter the current time (such as **08:00:00**) and the current date (such as **07/04/2009**).
10. Select **Accept**.
11. Select **OK**.
12. Close the YaST window.

Part II: Use the ncurses Interface of YaST

To use the ncurses interface of YaST, do the following:

1. Switch to the first virtual terminal by pressing Crtl+Alt+F1.
2. Log in as root with a password of **novell**.
3. View a list of the available YaST modules by entering `yast -l`.
4. Enter `yast` to start the ncurses interface of YaST.

5. Press the Down-arrow until *Miscellaneous* is highlighted in the left frame and press Enter.

6. Press the Down-arrow until *System Log* is highlighted in the right frame and press Enter.

7. Press the Down-arrow until */proc/version* is highlighted and press Enter.

8. Press Tab twice to highlight *OK* and press Enter.

9. Press Alt+Q to select *Quit*.

10. Log out by entering `exit`.

11. Switch back to the graphical interface by pressing Crtl+Alt+F7.

(End of Exercise)

Exercise 3-2   ***Manage Software with YaST***

In this exercise, you practice installing and uninstalling software packages with the YaST Software Management module.

Install the xosview package, and uninstall the 3ddiag and xosview packages.

This exercise is performed on da-host.

Detailed Steps to Complete the Exercise

■   Part I: Install Software with YaST

■   Part II: Uninstall Software with YaST

Part I: Install Software with YaST

1. Make sure you are logged in as geeko on da-host.

2. Insert the *SUSE Linux Enterprise Server 11 Product DVD*.

3. Open *YaST*.

4. From the *Groups* panel on the left, select *Software*.

5. From the applications under *Software*, select *Software Repositories*.

    The *Configured Software Repositories* dialog opens.

6. Verify that there is an DVD entry. If not, do the following:

    a. Select any existing entry and click *Delete*, then click *Yes* in the confirmation dialog.

    b. In the *Configured Software Repositories* dialog, select *Add*.

    c. In the Media Type dialog, select *DVD*, then click *Next*.

    d. If a license agreement is displayed, accept it.

    e. Close the *Configured Software Repositories* dialog by clicking OK.

7. In the *YaST Control Center*, from the applications under *Software*, select *Software Management*.

    This starts the *YaST Software Manager*.

8. In the search field at the top left, enter xosview.

NOTE: Notice that the icon shows an empty box. This indicates that the package is not yet installed.

---

9. From the list on the right, select *xosview*.

10. Click *Accept* to install the xosview package.

Part II: Uninstall Software with YaST

1. In YaST, select *Software > Software Management*.

2. In the search field at the top left, enter 3ddiag.

NOTE: Notice that the list shows a box already checked. This means that the package is installed.

---

3. In the list on the right, click *3ddiag* until a red X appears to the left.

4. Click *Accept* at the bottom right.

   You are returned to the YaST Control Center.

5. Repeat steps 1-4 to uninstall xosview.

6. Close any open windows.

(End of Exercise)

Exercise 3-3   ***Manage User Accounts with YaST***

In this exercise, create and remove a user account with the YaST User Management module by doing the following:

- Create a new account labeled **tux** for the user **Tux Penguin** with the password of **novell**.

- Log in as user **tux**.

- Open the /etc/passwd file and look for the entries for **geeko** and **tux**.

- Log in as **geeko** and remove **tux's** account.

This exercise is performed on the da-host server.

Detailed Steps to Complete the Exercise

- Part I: Create a New User Account with YaST

- Part II: Log In as a New User

- Part III: View the passwd File

- Part IV: Log In as User geeko and Remove the New User Account

Part I: Create a New User Account with YaST

To create a new user account with YaST, do the following:

1. Log in to da-host as root and open the ***YaST Control Center***.

2. Select ***Security and Users > User and Group Management***.

3. On the ***Users*** tab, add a new user by selecting ***Add***.

4. Enter the following information:

   - User's Full Name: **Tux Penguin**

   - Username: **tux**

   - Password: **novell**

   - Confirm Password: **novell**

5. When you finish, click ***OK***.

6. Confirm the password warnings by clicking ***Yes***.

7. Save the new settings by clicking ***OK***.

8. Close the ***YaST*** window.

Part II: Log In as a New User

To log in as the new user, do the following:

1. From the main menu, select ***Logout***.

2. In the *logout* dialog, select ***Log Out***.

X Window is restarted and the GUI login screen appears.

3. In the Username field, enter **tux** and press Enter.

4. In the Password field, enter **novell** and press Enter.

5. Close or cancel any displayed dialogs.

Part III: View the passwd File

To view the passwd file, do the following:

1. Start the Nautilus file manager by double-clicking *tux's Home* icon on the desktop.

   The content of tux's home directory is displayed.

2. Browse the File System to the /home directory.

   Notice there are directories for users tux and geeko.

3. Browse the File System to the /etc directory.

4. Open the passwd file by double-clicking it.

   Notice the entries for users tux and geeko at the end of the file.

5. Close all windows.

6. From the bottom panel, log out by selecting *Computer > Log Out*.

7. In the logout dialog, select *Log Out*.

   X Window is restarted and the GUI login screen appears.

Part IV: Log In as User geeko and Remove the New User Account

To log in as user geeko and remove the new user account, do the following:

1. Log in as geeko with a password of **novell**.

2. From the GNOME desktop, select *Computer > More Applications > System > YaST*, then enter a password of **novell** and select *Continue*.

3. From the YaST Control Center, select *Security and Users > User and Group Management*.

4. From the list of users, select *tux*, then click *Delete*.

5. Select *Delete Home Directory /home/tux*, then click *Yes*.

6. Click *OK*.

7. Confirm that the user tux has been removed by doing the following:

   a. Start the Nautilus file manager by double-clicking the *geeko's Home* icon on the desktop.

      The content of Geeko's home directory is displayed.

   b. Browse the File System to the /home directory.

Notice there is only one entry for user geeko.

c. Browse to the /etc directory.

d. Open the passwd file by double-clicking it.

The entry for tux has been removed from the end of the file.

8. Close the Nautilus window and YaST Control Center.

(End of Exercise)

Review Questions

1. What keys can you use in the menu-based (ncurses) YaST interface to navigate between selections? (Choose two answers.)
   a. Tab
   b. Spacebar
   c. Alt
   d. Shift+Tab

2. Which command could you execute at a command prompt to start a particular management module?
   a. yast module_name
   b. yast /module_name
   c. yast sw_module_name
   d. yast -u module_name

3. What option to the yast command could you use to display a list of YaST modules?

4. You wish to install another software package using YaST from your SLES installation media. How can you verify that your system has the appropriate prerequisite packages?
   a. Start the YaST program using the --dependencies option.
   b. Click the Check Dependencies button within YaST.
   c. View the Description tab within YaST.
   d. Right-click the package in YaST and select Verify.

5. What UID is used by the root user account?

6. What is the lowest GID used by normal groups?

7. What file stores the default UID and GID ranges used YaST when creating normal users and groups?
   a. /bin/login
   b. /etc/login.defs
   c. /home/.login
   d. /var/spool/useradd

8. What is the default home directory path used for a new user created using YaST?
   a. /users/*username*
   b. /var/*username*
   c. /home/users/*username*
   d. /home/*username*

9. What two files are modified when you add a new user using YaST?

10. What file is modified when you add a new group using YaST?

11. Which of the following are desktop environments that can be used in SUSE Linux? (Choose all that apply.)
    a. Metacity
    b. TWM
    c. GNOME
    d. KDE

12. Which of the following commands can be used to start the X server, window manager, and desktop environment from a command-line interface?
    a. X
    b. startx
    c. Xinitialize
    d. X --start

13. What command may be used to start a second X server on tty8?

14. Which command would you use to connect to a computer across a network in order to perform systems administration using an encrypted session?
    a. rlogin hostname
    b. rsh −X hostname
    c. rcp hostname
    d. ssh hostname

15. VNC consists of two components. What are they? (Choose two answers.)
    a. a VNC server component
    b. a VNC proxy
    c. a VNC client program
    d. a VNC router

16. What are the two X servers that are available for Linux systems? (Choose two answers.)
    a. XFree86
    b. XServer86
    c. X11
    d. XOrg

17. What files contains the main configuration for XOrg?
    a. /etc/X11/xorg.conf
    b. /etc/X11/fs/config
    c. /etc/X11/xorg/config
    d. /etc/X11/fs/xorg.conf

18. What key combination can you press twice to kill an X Window session?

19. What could you type at a command prompt to start the X display manager (xdm) if it is not already started?

20. Which of the following configuration utilities may be used to configure your XOrg server settings using a text-based interface?
    a. SaX2
    b. xvidtune
    c. SuperProbe
    d. xorgconfig

Discovery Exercises

Configuring the X Server

Log in to the GNOME desktop as the geeko user. Use Nautilus to navigate to the /etc/X11/xorg.conf file. What is this file used for? Examine the different sections of this file and close Nautilus when finished.

Open a GNOME terminal, type **su** –and supply the root user password to obtain a root user shell. Type **sax2** and navigate the different areas of the SaX2 utility to see the different X components can be configured. Make a change to your display Resolution and Colors that is supported by your video card and monitor. Apply your settings and exit the SaX2 utility.

Press **Ctrl+Alt+Backspace** twice to exit your X session and reload the display manager. Log in as the geeko user and note your new resolution and color depth. Use Nautilus again to navigate to the /etc/X11/xorg file again. Can you tell that SaX2 modified this file? Log out of the GNOME desktop.

Modifying Screen Options

Log in to the GNOME desktop as the geeko user. Open a GNOME terminal and type **xvidtune**. Click **OK** when you see the warning message. Use the appropriate buttons to fine-tune the position of the X server on your screen. What other X server options can you change using xvidtune? Optionally make a change that is supported by your video card and monitor and exit the utility. To test your change, press **Ctrl+Alt+Backspace** twice and log in again as the geeko user. When finished, log out of the GNOME desktop.

Using SSH to Run Remote Programs

Log in to the GNOME desktop as the geeko user and open a GNOME terminal. At the command prompt, type **ssh root@localhost** and press Enter to connect to your own computer across the network using the encrypted Secure Shell utility as the root user. When prompted to accept the RSA key fingerprint, type **yes** and press Enter. Supply the password for your root user account when prompted. You now have a remote shell across the network to your own computer.

At the command prompt, type **who** and press Enter. Can you tell that you are connected remotely to your own computer? Type **yast2 users** and press Enter. Notice that you get an ncurses interface instead of a QT interface. This is because **ssh** does not tunnel X Window graphics across the Secure Shell connection by default so you are limited to commands and ncurses interfaces. Exit YaST and then type **exit** at the command prompt and press Enter to close your remote Secure Shell connection.

Now, type **ssh –X root@localhost** and press Enter to connect to your own computer in much the same way that you did earlier, but with the ability to send X Windows graphics across the Secure Shell connection. Supply the password for your root user account when prompted. Type **yast2 users** and press Enter. Note that you get a graphical QT interface. Close YaST when finished and log out of your GNOME desktop.

Using VNC to Run Remote Programs

Log in to the GNOME desktop as the geeko user and open a GNOME terminal. At the command prompt, type **vncserver** and press Enter. When prompted, enter the password **secret** to secure access to your VNC server for the geeko user. When prompted to set a view-only password, press **n** and note that the VNC server created a .vnc/xstartup file in geeko's home directory.

Type **cat .vnc/xstartup** and view the last line of the file. This line loads the Tab Window Manager (TWM) for remote VNC connections.

Type **vncviewer localhost:1** to connect to your own computer across the network using the VNC protocol. Supply the password **secret** when prompted and note the TWM desktop started as the geeko user. What file would you need to change in order to use the GNOME desktop instead? Close the VNC client window (TightVNC) and log out of the GNOME desktop.

SECTION 4 Administer SLES 11 with the Command Line Interface

In this section, you learn how to administer different components of your SLES 11 system using command line tools. The areas covered include the management of software, users and groups, file systems including Network File System (NFS), backup, and hardware.

Objectives

1. Manage Software

2. Manage Shared Libraries

3. Manage User and Group Accounts

4. Manage File Permissions and Ownership

5. Manage Partitions, File Systems, Quotas, and NFS

6. Manage Backup and Restore

7. Manage Hardware

Objective 1   Manage Software

Software management is a central task of a system administrator. A software program today usually consists of more than a single executable. Additional files include configuration and help files. Furthermore, software often needs other software to function properly that is not part of the software itself, such as software libraries.

Package management software keeps track of the files installed by software packages and their dependency on other software. It allows you to install and uninstall software easily. SLES 11 and RedHat-based systems use the RPM Package Management (RPM) software, whereas Debian-based systems use Debian Package Management (DPKG).

Using package management software to install software is the preferred method because it warns you during installation if dependencies are not met, allows you to remove software completely when uninstalling it, and warns you if you try to uninstall software that is needed by other packages.

If there is no software package available for your system, you can compile the software from its sources.

To manage software, you need to be able to

- Manage Software with RPM
- Understand Debian Package Management
- Install Software from Source
- Manage Software with RPM

Manage Software with RPM

When using RPM package management with SLES 11, you will use packages prepared by Novell or other vendors for SLES 11. This course does not cover how to create such packages.

To manage software with RPM, you need to understand the following:

- RPM Components and Features
- RPM Basics
- Manage Software Packages with RPM
- Use the yum Command as a Front End to RPM

RPM Components and Features

Package management consists of several parts. The basic components of RPM are

- **RPM Package Manager.** This utility handles installing and uninstalling RPM packages.
- **RPM database.** The RPM database works in the background of the package manager and contains a list of all information on all installed RPM packages.

The database keeps track of all files that are changed and created when a user installs a program. This helps the Package Manager to easily remove the same files that were originally installed.

- **RPM package.** RPM lets you take software source code and package it into source and binary packages for users. These are called RPM packages or RPM archives.

- **Package label.** Every RPM package includes a package label that contains information such as the software name, version, and package release number.

  This information helps the Package Manager track the installed versions of software to make it easier to manage software installations on a Linux computer.

Some of the advantages of using RPM Package Manager and RPM packages include the following:

- Administrators have a consistent method for installing programs in Linux.

- Programs are easily uninstalled (because of the RPM database).

- Original source archives (such as tar.gz or .tar.bz2) are included as needed and easy to verify.

- RPM tools can be used to enable software installations using non-interactive scripts.

- RPM tools can be used to verify that software was installed correctly.

- RPM tracks dependent software, preventing deinstallation of packages needed by other packages. It also informs the administrator if required software is missing when he or she tries to install a software package.

NOTE: RPM packages of source code are not included in the RPM database and thus are not tracked.

- Digital signatures are supported to verify integrity of RPM archives.

RPM Basics

To manage software packages with RPM, you need to understand the following:

- RPM Package File-Naming Convention
- RPM Configuration File
- RPM Database

RPM Package File-Naming Convention

RPM package files use the following naming format:

software_name-software_version-release_number.architecture.rpm

Example: apache2-2.2.10-2.18.i586.rpm

The following describes each component of the naming format:

- **software_name**. This is the name of the software being installed.

- **software_version**. This is the version number of the software in the RPM package.

- **release_number**. This is the number of times the package has been rebuilt using the same version of the software.

- **architecture**. This indicates the architecture the package was built under (such as i586, i686, or ppc) or the type of package content.

  For example, if the package has an i586 architecture, you can install it on 32-bit Intel-compatible machines that are Pentium class or higher.

  The package does not include any binary code if the package architecture is indicated as **noarch**.

- **rpm**. RPM archives normally have the extension `.rpm`. The distribution also includes source packages, called source RPMs, which have the filename extension `.src.rpm` (`.spm` or `.srpm` are also possible).

RPM Configuration File

The global RPM configuration file of the `rpm` command is `/usr/lib/rpm/rpmrc`. However, when the **rpm** software package itself is updated, all changes to this file are lost.

To prevent this from happening, write any changes to the `/etc/rpmrc` file (for the system configuration) or to the `~/.rpmrc` file (for the user configuration).

RPM Database

The RPM database files are stored in `/var/lib/rpm/`. If the `/usr/` partition is 1 GB in size, this database can occupy nearly 30 MB, especially after a complete update.

If the database is much larger than expected, it is useful to rebuild the database by entering `rpm --rebuilddb`. Before doing this, make a backup of the old database.

The cron script `suse.de-backup-rpmdb`, which is stored in `/etc/cron.daily/`, checks daily to see if there are any changes. If so, a copy of the database is made (compressed with gzip) and stored in `/var/adm/backup/rpmdb/`.

The number of copies is controlled by the variable `MAX_RPMDB_BACKUPS` (default is 5) in `/etc/sysconfig/backup`.

The size of a single backup is approximately 5 MB for 1 GB in `/usr/`.

Manage Software Packages with RPM

You can use the `rpm` command to manage software packages. This includes querying the RPM database for detailed information about the installed software.

The command provides the following modes for managing software packages:

- Installing, uninstalling, or updating software packages
- Querying the RPM database or individual RPM archives
- Checking the integrity of packages
- Rebuilding the RPM database

You can use the `rpmbuild` command to build installable RPM packages from pristine sources (`rpmbuild` is not covered in this course).

RPM packages contain program, configuration, and documentation files to install, and certain meta information used during installation by RPM to configure the software package. This same information is stored in the RPM database after installation for documentation purposes.

To manage software packages with RPM, you need to know how to do the following:

- Verify Package Authenticity
- Install, Update, and Uninstall Packages
- Query the RPM Database and RPM Archives
- Use the Yast CLI Command as a Front End to RPM

Verify Package Authenticity

All SLES 11 RPM packages are signed with the following GnuPG key:

Figure 4-1   *SUSE Build GnuPG Key*

```
DA2:/ # gpg --list-keys -v --fingerprint "build@suse.de"
gpg: using PGP trust model
pub   1024R/307E3D54 2006-03-21 [expires: 2010-05-05]
      Key fingerprint = 4E98 E675 19D9 8DC7 362A  5990 E3A5 C360 307E 3D54
uid                  SuSE Package Signing Key <build@suse.de>

pub   1024D/9C800ACA 2000-10-19 [expires: 2010-05-05]
      Key fingerprint = 79C1 79B2 E1C8 20C1 890F  9994 A84E DAE8 9C80 0ACA
uid                  SuSE Package Signing Key <build@suse.de>
sub   2048g/8495160C 2000-10-19 [expires: 2010-05-05]
```

Courtesy of Novell, Inc.

Verifying the signature of an RPM package lets you determine whether the package originated from SUSE or from another trustworthy facility. To verify the signature of an RPM package, enter the following command:

```
rpm --checksig package_name
```

Example:

```
rpm --checksig apache2-2.2.10-2.18.i586.rpm
```

Verifying the package signature is especially recommended for update packages from the Internet.

The SUSE package signature public key is stored in the `/root/.gnupg/` and `/usr/lib/rpm/gnupg/` directories. Storing the key in `/usr/lib/rpm/gnupg/` lets normal users verify the signature of RPM packages.

Install, Update, and Uninstall Packages

To manage RPM software packages, you need to know how to do the following:

- Install an RPM Package
- Update an RPM Package
- Uninstall an RPM Package

Install an RPM Package

For most RPM packages, you use the following command to install the software:

```
rpm -i package_name.rpm
```

When you install an RPM package, the executable programs, documentation files, configuration files, and start scripts are copied to the appropriate directories in the file system.

During installation, the RPM database ensures that no conflicts arise (such as a file belonging to more than one package). The package is installed only if its dependencies are fulfilled and there are no conflicts with other packages.

If dependencies are not fulfilled, RPM lists those packages that need to be installed to meet dependency requirements. Packages that conflict with the packages to be installed are also listed.

You could use other options to ignore these errors (such as `--nodeps` to ignore dependencies or `--force` to overwrite existing files), but this is only for experts. If you force the installation despite dependency requirements not being met, the installed software most likely will not work properly.

With the `-v` option (verbose), more information is displayed; the `-h` option (hash) produces a progress bar consisting of # signs during package installation.

NOTE: For a number of packages, the components needed for software development (libraries, headers, include files, etc.) have been put into separate packages. These development packages are only needed if you want to compile software (such as the most recent GNOME packages) yourself.

Such packages can be identified by the name extension -devel, such as the packages alsa-devel or gimp-devel.

Update an RPM Package

You can use the `-U` (or `--upgrade`) and `-F` (or `--freshen`) options to update a package by using the following syntax:

```
rpm -Fvh package_name.rpm
```

This command removes the files of the old version and immediately installs the new files. If no previous version is installed, the package is not installed. The -vh options create more output and hash marks.

If an old version is installed, the -U option does the same as -F. However, if no previous version is installed, -U installs the new version.

NOTE: The -U option is *not* equivalent to uninstalling with the -e option and installing with the -i option. Use -U whenever possible for updating packages.

RPM updates configuration files carefully using the following guidelines:

- If a configuration file was not changed by the system administrator, RPM installs the new version of the appropriate file. No action by the system administrator is required.

- If a configuration file was changed by the system administrator before the update, RPM saves the changed file with the extension .rpmorig or .rpmsave (backup file). It then installs the version from the new package but only if the originally installed file and the newer version are different.

  If this is the case, compare the backup file (.rpmorig or .rpmsave) with the newly installed file and make your changes again in the new file. Be sure to delete all .rpmorig and .rpmsave files afterwards to avoid problems with future updates.

  The .rpmorig extension is assigned if the file has not previously been recognized by the RPM database; otherwise, .rpmsave is used.

  In other words, .rpmorig results from updating from a foreign format to RPM; .rpmsave results from updating from an older RPM to a newer RPM.

- A set of .rpmnew files is created if the configuration file already exists and if the noreplace label was specified in the file controlling the package creation (the so-called .spec-file).

  This is used to not overwrite certain configuration files (such as /etc/httpd/httpd.conf) and to ensure continued operation.

  .rpmnew does not disclose any information as to whether the system administrator has made any changes to the configuration file.

  The /etc/init.d/rpmconfigcheck script searches for such files and writes a list of these files to /var/adm/rpmconfigcheck.

Uninstall an RPM Package

To uninstall (remove) an RPM package, enter the following:

```
rpm -e package_name
```

When you uninstall a package, all files except modified configuration files are removed from the system with the help of the RPM database. This ensures a clean uninstall.

RPM will delete the package only if this does not break dependencies. If other packages depend on the package you want to delete, these are listed in the error message.

You could force deletion of the package with the --nodeps parameter. However, this is not advisable because the dependent software will most likely not work anymore.

Query the RPM Database and RPM Archives

With the -q option, you can query the RPM database of installed packages and, by adding the -p option, inspect RPM archives that are not yet installed.

The following are the most commonly used RPM query options:

Table 4-1   *RPM Query Options, Used Together With the -q Option*

Option	Results
-a	List all installed packages.
-i	List package information.
-l	Display a file list.
-f *file*	Find out to which package *file* belongs (the full path must be specified with *file*).
-d	List only documentation files (implies -l).
-c	List only configuration files (implies -l).
--dump	Display a file list with complete details (to be used with -l, -c, or -d).
--provides	List features of the package that another package can request with --requires.
--requires, -R	List the capabilities the package requires.
--scripts	List installation scripts (preinstall, postinstall, uninstall).
--changelog	Displays a detailed list of information (updates, configuration, modifications, etc.) about a specific package.

For example, entering the rpm -qi wget command displays the following information about the wget package:

```
DA2:/ # rpm -qi wget
Name        : wget                    Relocations: (not relocatable)
Version     : 1.11.4                      Vendor: SUSE LINUX Products GmbH
, Nuernberg, Germany
Release     : 1.9                     Build Date: Fri 23 Jan 2009 09:57:01
 PM MST
Install Date: Fri 06 Feb 2009 02:36:26 AM MST     Build Host: albeniz
Group       : Productivity/Networking/Web/Utilities   Source RPM: wget-1.11.4-1.
9.src.rpm
Size        : 1530350                    License: GPL v3 or later
Signature   : RSA/8, Fri 23 Jan 2009 09:57:12 PM MST, Key ID e3a5c360307e3d54
URL         : http://www.gnu.org/software/wget/
Summary     : A Tool for Mirroring FTP and HTTP Servers
Description :
Wget enables you to retrieve WWW documents or FTP files from a server.
This can be done in script files or via the command line.


Authors:
--------
    Hrvoje Niksic <hniksic@srce.hr>
Distribution: SUSE:SLE-11:GA
```

The -f option works only if you specify the complete filename with a full path. You can enter several filenames, as in the following:

```
DA2:/ # rpm -qf /bin/rpm /usr/bin/wget
rpm-4.4.2.3-23.58
wget-1.11.4-1.9
```

This returns information for both /bin/rpm and /usr/bin/wget.

With the help of the RPM database, you can perform verification checks with the -V or --verify option. If any files in a package have been changed since installation, they will be displayed.

RPM uses the following character symbols to provide hints about the changes:

Table 4-2   *RPM --verify Output*

Character	Description
5	MD5 check sum
S	File size
L	Symbolic link
T	Modification time
D	Major and minor device numbers
U	Owner
G	Group
M	Mode (permissions and file type)

Use the Yast CLI Command as a Front End to RPM

One of the major functions of YaST is software installation. If you know the name of a software package, the `-i` option (install) is very useful. Example:

```
yast -i wireshark
```

This example installs the Wireshark package plus any software package that is needed by Wireshark from the installation media. The advantage of using `yast -i` is that any dependencies are automatically resolved.

You can also install any RPM package with the `-i` option, specifying the RPM package file name, not just the name of the software package. Example:

```
yast -i apache2-2.2.10-2.18.i586.rpm
```

However, dependencies are not resolved in this case.

Use the yum Command as a Front End to RPM

yum or the Yellowdog Updater Modified is used for Linux systems that are rpm-compatible. yum evolved (from YUP) in order to update and manage RHL systems. Since that time, it has been used in other Linux distributions, such as Fedora, RHEL, and CentOS.

In this part of this objective, you learn how to do the following with yum:

- Using the yum Command
- Managing yum Configuration Files
- Using yumdownloader

Using the yum Command

`yum` is a command line front end to RPM. It takes care of such things as dependencies when installing a package. The basic syntax is as follows:

```
yum option command package_name
```

yum defines a layout for package repositories. A repository based on this standard can also be used with YaST.

yum has a command line interface and it has a plugin interface for the addition of other features. yum-utils extends and acts as a supplement to yum. It is a collection of different utilities and plugins which can perform queries, manage package cleanup, and perform repository synchronization.

Common yum commands include the following:

Table 4-3   *yum Commands*

Command	Description
`yum list` or `yum list all`	List all packages in a repository and packages installed on your system

Command	Description
`yum list installed`	List all packages installed on your system
`yum list installed packagename`	Displays if named package is installed
	`yum list installed samba_1.2.3-2_i386.rpm`
`yum install packagename`	Install the named package, for example
	`yum install samba_1.2.3-2_i386.rpm`
`yum list updates`	List of updates for all installed packages
`yum list update packagename`	Check for and update named package
	`yum list update samba_1.2.3-2_i386.rpm`
`yum list available`	List of packages available to be installed
`yum info packagename`	Displays detailed package information, such as version, status, dependencies, signatures
	`yum info samba_1.2.3-2_i386.rpm`
`yum whatprovides path_to_file`	Display which package provides a file
	`yum whatprovides /etc/motd`
`yum list packagename`	Search repository for the named package
	`yum list samba_1.2.3-2_i386.rpm`
`yum remove packagename`	Removes the specific named package
	`yum remove samba_1.2.3-2_i386.rpm`
`createrepo /pathtorepodirectory`	Used to create a repository

Managing yum Configuration Files

The following yum configuration files are located in `/etc/yum.conf` and `/etc/yum.repos.d/`:

- **yum.conf.** `yum.conf` is the configuration file for the yum package. This file lists software sites with one or more URLs and their names. For example, the following uses the fictitious site SUSE Linux rpms and its URL:

```
[SUSE Linux rpms]
name=SUSE Linux $releasever - $basearch - suserpms
baseurl=http://suselinux.novell.com/suse/linux/$releasever/
$basearch/suserpms
```

  `yum.conf` can be populated by editing the file and uncommenting a line in the file or adding your own lines. Best practices when editing `yum.conf` is to add your entries to the end of the file. If you find that any are marked as unstable or as a test, it is better to avoid those.

An example `yum.conf` configuration file is shown below:

```
# This is the suselinuxrpms yum.conf file for my repository.
# You can also add, delete or edit the settings, URLs, sections, or
sites as needed.
#
[main]
cachedir=/var/cache/yum
keepcache=0
debuglevel=2
logfile=/var/log/yum.log
pkgpolicy=newest
distroverpkg=suselinux-release
tolerant=1
exactarch=1
# Don't check keys for localinstall
gpgcheck=0
plugins=1
metadata_expire=1500
# Change timeout depending on stability of mirrors contacted.
timeout=7


# PUT YOUR REPOS INFO HERE OR IN separate files named file.repo
```

Another sample of a `yum.conf` configuration file is shown below:

```
#Main settings for my yum.conf file
#Last edited on January 21, 2010 5:18:29pm
[main]
cachedir=/var/cache/yum
debuglevel=3
logfile=/var/log/yum.log
pkgpolicy=newest
distroverpkg=suselinux-release
gpgcheck=1
tolerant=1
retries=1
exactarch=1

[base]
name=SUSE Linux Base $releasever - $basearch - Base
baseurl=http://suserpm.novell.com/linux/suse/core/$releasever/
$basearch/os
http://mirrors.backupstore.org/pub/linux/suse/sle11/base/
$releasever/$basearch/yum/os
http://suse.novell.com/releases/suse-linux-core-$releasever

[released-updates]
name=SUSE Linux Core $releasever - $basearch - Released Updates
baseurl=http://suserpm.novell.com/linux/suse/core/updates/
$releasever/$basearch/updates
http://mirrors.backupstore.org/pub/linux/suse/sle11/base/
$releasever/$basearch/yum/updates
http://suse.novell.com/releases/suse-linux-core -$releasever
```

```
[suselinux-extras]
name=SUSE Linux Extras $releasever - $basearch - Extra Packages
baseurl=http://mirrors.backupstore.org/pub/linux/suse/sle11/base/
$releasever/$basearch/os
failovermethod=priority

[core]
name=SUSE Linux Core $releasever - $basearch - core
baseurl=http://suserpm.novell.com/linux/suse/core/$releasever/
$basearch/core

[SUSE Linux Enterprise 11 stable]
name=SUSE Linux Core $releasever Stable
baseurl=suselinux.novell.com/suse/linux/$releasever/$basearch/yum/
stable
http://suselinuxde.linux.de/suse/linux/$releasever/$basearch/yum/
stable
http://mirrors.backupstore.org/pub/suse/linux/enterprise11/
$releasever/$basearch/yum/stable

[updates]
name=SUSE Linux Updates $releasever - $basearch - updates
baseurl=http://suserpm.novell.com/suse/linux/$releasever/
$basearch/updates
```

Notice in the above examples that each section is named according to its purpose. You can add sections according to your need, such as *development*, *updates*, or *kernel*.

NOTE: Additional information for yum.conf and its options may be found at linux.die.net (http://linux.die.net/man/5/yum.conf) and www.linuxquestions.org (http://www.linuxquestions.org).

■ **yum.repos.d.** yum.repos.d is the directory you use to hold the .repo files you create when specifying a repository location. This method can be used instead of entering the locations in the yum.conf file. Remember to run the createrepo command after adding new packages; current versions of yum require its usage. Using the createrepo command generates the XML metadata necessary for your repository.

Using a local repository for your network installations and updates can save time for you and also save demand on your internet bandwidth because all of the packages you need are now local to you. You may also set up a yum repository to install or update a package using an ISO image that you create.

You may need to modify the yum.conf file to reflect the location of the local yum repository. Notice that the last lines of the first example shown above mentions either placing the repository URLs there or in separate files which you should name *filename*.repo in the /etc/yum.repos.d directory.

For example, the entries contained in a .repo file might look like the following:

```
# filename /etc/yum.repos.d/install.repo
#
# Specify the path to the directory following baseurl= as shown
here
#
[MyInstallRepository]
name=Install
baseurl=file:///myrepos/myinstallrepo
enabled=1
```

The above is an example of a .repo file located in the `/etc/yum.repos.d` directory. It contains the path to the repository directory; for example, you created a root directory named `/myrepos`, with repository sub-directories below it holding your files for each repository you want, such as a `/myinstallrepo` directory for installations. Enter any comments you wish to make about the file, and enter the `baseurl= location` path. Enable it using the `enabled=1` entry.

For ease of viewing and recognizing your .repo files, it is often best to have a `.repo` file for each repository you create.

You may need to import all the gpg keys for the packages if you did not sign the rpm packages, or you can use `gpgcheck=0` in the .repo file.

Using yumdownloader

`yumdownloader` is a tool used to download RPMs from yum repositories. Repositories can exist in numerous locations; having to manually search and download packages would be time-consuming. Using `yumdownloader` along with its many options can prove to be beneficial to you. For example, instead of downloading RPMs, you can use a list of URLs to get package downloads.

Using the `--resolve` option allows downloading of an RPM package to resolve any dependencies and also downloading of the packages that are required to fulfill that dependency.

`yumdownloader` uses the yum libraries for retrieving all information. For yumdownloader to know which repositories to use for downloads, it must rely on the yum configuration. That configuration information is passed to yumdownloader to use for its default values.

When the yum-utils package is installed, the yumdownloader tool is installed with it. You must be root or have root privileges to install yum-utils and yumdownloader.

The command to install yum-utils as root user is as follows:

Table 4-4   *Installing yum*

Command	Purpose
`yum install yum-utils`	yumdownloader is in the package.
`yumdownloader -source RPMsourcepackage`	Installs the named RPM source package.

Command	Purpose
`yumdownloader --source kernel`	Installs the latest kernel source package.

If you are not root, you may be able to use the `sudo` command if you have been granted the permissions.

The default configuration for yumdownloader is to put the downloaded package under the current working directory. You can, however, use the `--destdir` option to use another destination directory of your choice. For example, you could enter `yumdownloader --source --destdir /tmp/`*`directory`*.

Understand Debian Package Management

Debian-based systems use the Debian Package Manager (dpkg) instead of RPM. The Advanced Package Tool (apt) is a higher-level software on top of dpkg that resolves dependencies automatically and facilitates administration.

This section presents the basic features of using the Debian package management tools. Tasks discussed focus on installing, upgrading, and removing the Debian `.deb` packages. Using the `apt-get` and `dpkg` tools will assist you in finding file or package information such as content, installation status, version of package, dependencies, and package integrity.

To manage Debian packages, you need to be familiar with the following topics:

- Debian Linux Basics

- Manage Software Packages Using apt

- Managing Software Packages Using dpkg

Debian Linux Basics

Debian is an operating system that uses the Linux kernel for its core. Yet most of the tools used come from the GNU project; thus it is called Debian GNU/Linux. Debian states that it comes with over 25,000 packages. As of this writing, the latest stable release is Debian 5.0.

NOTE: See http://www.debian.org for more information.

Debian packages use the following naming syntax:

*`<packagename>`*_*`<versionnumber>`*_*`<architecture>`*.deb

For example: `apache_2.2.17-5_i386.deb`

The following describes each component of the naming format:

- *package_name.* This is the name of the software being installed.

- ***versionnumber.*** This is the version number of the software.

- ***architecture.*** This indicates the architecture the package was built under, such as i386, i586, i686, or ppc.

  For example, if it is a i386 architecture, you can install it on 32-bit systems.

  Debian can be installed on different architectures; hence, there is a need to make sure that the package you want to install is supported on the architecture you have.

Packages normally have the extension `.deb`.

Finding Debian Software Packages on the Internet can be accomplished by searching for Debian packages using the following urls:

- **http://packages.debian.org/***name* (where ***name*** is a package name)

- **http://package.debian.org/src:***name* (where ***name*** is a source package name)

Manage Software Packages Using apt

Like RPM package management, Debian package management also has tools that can be used at the command line or with a gui.

When installing `.deb` packages, remember to always back up your existing data, documents, or even the whole system, just in case an issue arises.

Always make sure you verify any package you want to install on your Debian system. `.deb` files come from a variety of sources; those coming directly from Debian are considered trustworthy; however, a good habit to have is to verify before you install.

You can use `apt-get` to find, download, and install `.deb` packages over the Internet using either ftp or http.

TIP: *apt* is an acronym that stands for Advanced Package Tool.

You can also use apt-get to perform upgrades. You need to be familiar with the following apt commands:

- apt-get

- apt-cache

- aptitude

apt-get

To install a new package, use the syntax `apt-get install` ***packagename***. For example: `apt-get install ldap_2.5.3_i686.deb`

To upgrade a package, use the syntax `apt-get upgrade` ***packagename***. For example: `apt-get upgrade nfs_3.1.5-3_i586.deb`

To remove a package from the system, use `apt-get remove` ***packagename***. For example: `apt-get remove samba_2.1.7-2_i383.deb`

To upgrade all packages on your system, use `apt-get dist-upgrade`.

Using `dist-upgrade` also will install extra packages such as dependencies. Using `upgrade` alone will keep an installed package at its older version, even if the upgrade requires extra packages or the removal of packages.

apt-cache

The apt suite of tools also includes `apt-cache`, which queries packages. Using apt-cache, you can find packages, get dependencies listed, and receive detailed information about available package versions.

The apt-cache syntax is as follow:

To get information about a package, use `apt-cache show packagename`. For example: `apt-cache show ldap_3.1.5-3_i586.deb`

For available package versions, use `apt-cache showpkg packagename`. For example: `apt-cache showpkg samba_2.5.1-2.deb`

To list dependencies for a package, use `apt-cache depends packagename`. For example: `apt-cache depends nfs_2.4-2-i383.deb`

To search for packages with a specific word in its description, use `apt-cache search searchword`. For example: `apt-cache search language`

aptitude

The apt suite of tools includes an Ncurses-based frontend for the apt utility. Aptitude is text-based and runs from a command line interface. It includes a number of features including the ability to mark packages as manually installed or automatically installed. This feature allows packages to be auto-removed when they are not required any longer. It also has the ability to retrieve and display Debian change logs for many packages.

Among its features are a dependency resolver, a color preview of actions to be taken, and a command line mode.

The command line interface syntax is shown in the table below:

Table 4-5   *aptitude CLI Commands*

Command	Description
`aptitude`	Enter at terminal to run aptitude
`aptitude upgrade`	Upgrade packages
`aptitude update`	Update packages list
`aptitude install samba`	Install samba package
`aptitude remove samba`	Remove samba package
`aptitude purge samba`	Purge samba package

Command	Description
`aptitude dist-upgrade`	Use to upgrade current distribution use with `cat /etc/debian_version`
`aptitude ~D samba`	List samba dependencies in reverse
`aptitude search samba`	Search samba

Within the text user interface, use the following syntax:

Table 4-6 *aptitude TUI Syntax*

u	Update list of available packages.
U	Mark packages which are upgradable.
g	View pending actions (modify pending actions). Press g a second time to start the download.

Actions (menu) > Cancel pending action

Managing Software Packages Using dpkg

You can use dpkg to find, download, and install `.deb` packages. Using dpkg, you can retrieve package information and description as well as the version of the package.

To list information and verify (installed or not) a single package, use `dpkg -l` *packagename* or `dpkg -s` *packagename* `| grep Status`.

- Example: `dpkg -l samba_3.2.2-1_i686.deb`
- Example: `dpkg -s ldap | grep Status`

To list information on all installed packages, type `dpkg -l`.

For package description, version, etc., type `dpkg -info` *packagename*.

- Example: `dpkg -info apache_2.4.5-1_i386.deb`

To list files provided by an installed package, use `dpkg -L` *packagename*.

- Example: `dpkg -L ldap_2.2.5-7_i383.deb`

To list files provided by a package, use `dpkg -contents` *packagename*.

- Example: `dpkg -contents samba_1.2.3-2_i386.deb`

To find out which package owns a file, type `dpkg -S` *path to filename*.

- Example: `dpkg -S /etc/exports`

Other options that can be used include

- `-L` or `-list`
- `-s` or `-status`
- `-split` or also use `--join`

- `--control` (file control information)
- `--help` (options list)
- `--install` (installs packages)
- `--extract` (packages unpacked using this will be incorrectly installed)

Install Software from Source

If there is no RPM package for the software you want to install, but the source code is available to you, you can compile the software yourself.

NOTE: A more elegant way would be to create an RPM package yourself and install that RPM package, as it would make removing the software much easier. The creation of RPM packages is not part of this course, though.

In most cases programs use more than one source code file. In order to structure the source, developers tend to spread the code over multiple files.

It would be very difficult to compile a program with multiple source code files manually on the command line. Fortunately, some tools are available to manage the compilation process.

You need to know how to do the following to perform a standard build process:

- Install the Required Packages for a Build Environment
- Prepare the Source Code
- Use configure to Prepare the Build Process
- Use make to Compile the Source Code
- Use make install to Install the Compiled Program

Install the Required Packages for a Build Environment

A lot of different software packages are required to compile software from its source code. The easiest way to install all required packages is to select the *C/C++ Compiler and Tools* pattern in the YaST package manager.

This pattern includes the necessary tools and files to compile software, including the following:

- **Compilers.** The pattern includes gcc (Gnu C Compiler) and gcc++ (Gnu C++ Compiler).
- **Development Packages.** These packages usually have -devel in their name. They contain include/header files that are needed when compiling software. This pattern contains packages such as glibc-devel and libstdc++-devel.

Depending on what kind of software you are going to install, additional -devel files might be needed. These are contained in the SUSE Linux Enterprise 11 SDK that can be downloaded from www.novell.com/ (http://www.novell.com/).

- **Tools for Programmers.** These include autoconf, a tool used to configure source code and makefiles, or cvs (concurrent version system), software used to manage file versions and facilitate collaboration between programmers.

Prepare the Source Code

Source code is simple ASCII text. Using a programming language, the source code provides the information needed to build the binary executable file using a software compiler.

The various files needed to compile the software are contained in archives. On Linux/UNIX, these are most often tar archives (.tar, .tgz, .tar.gz, .tar.bz2 extensions), but zip archives (.zip extensions) are used as well sometimes. After obtaining the source code from a Web site or a CDROM, tar archives need to be unpacked using a tar command similar to the following in a terminal window:

```
tar -xzf source-code-package.tgz
```

Lots of options can be used with tar, but the following are usually sufficient to unpack an archive:

Table 4-7   *tar Options*

option	Description
x	Extract files from the archive.
z	Use the zip algorithm (gzip) to uncompress the archive.
f *file*	Process the archive contained in *file*. The file name has to follow after the f option, with no other options between the f and the file name.
t	Test the archive. The content of the archive is listed, but no files are extracted.
I	Use the bzip2 algorithm to uncompress the archive.

After having unpacked the archive, you should look for files named INSTALL or README in the top-level directory or the source code tree, as these often contain valuable information on how to compile and install the source code.

Use configure to Prepare the Build Process

Before the actual compilation process can be started, you must prepare the compilation with the `configure` script that is usually provided with the source code. This needs to be done for the following reasons:

- Many applications can be compiled on different UNIX systems, Linux distributions, and hardware platforms. To make this possible, the build process needs to be prepared for the actual environment.

  The configure script examines the environment and informs you if some components are missing, such as certain compilers or header files. If this is the case, install the missing packages, such as development packages, and run the configure script again.

- The build process itself is controlled by a program called `make`. The instructions for how to compile the different source files are read from makefiles. The configure script generates these makefiles depending on the system environment.

- You can use `configure` to enable or disable certain features of an application.

To run the configure script, use the following command at the top of the source directory:

```
./configure
```

To enable or disable certain features of an application, configure takes additional arguments. The available arguments depend on the application that will be compiled. You can use the following command to list all available configure options:

```
./configure  --help
```

Use make to Compile the Source Code

You use the tool `make` to compile multiple source files in the correct order. `make` is controlled by makefiles. Normally, these makefiles are generated by the configure script, but you can also create them manually.

You can also use make to install the program to and uninstall the program from the right location on the hard disk.

Every makefile consists of targets, dependencies, and commands for the targets. Targets and dependencies are separated by a colon. The commands must be placed under the target, indented with **one tab** character. A # introduces comments.

The following is an example of a very simple makefile:

```
# Makefile for my_name

all: my_name

my_name: my_name.c
  gcc my_name.c -o my_name

install: my_name
  install -m 755 my_name /usr/local/bin/my_name
```

```
uninstall: /usr/local/bin/my_name
  rm -f /usr/local/bin/my_name

clean:
  rm -f my_name
```

This makefile can perform the following tasks:

- Compile the program from source (my_name target)

- Install the program (install target)

- Uninstall the program (uninstall target)

- Clean up the directory where the compilation is performed (clean target)

If you execute the make command while you are in the respective directory, the make program will search this directory for the GNUMakefile, Makefile, or makefile files.

If make is executed without any parameters, the first target of a makefile is used. In the example above, this is all. This target is associated with the target my_name, which specifies the step to take: compile the file my_name.c with gcc.

The make command can also be used with individual targets. For example, the make install command (as root) installs the binary file at the specified location and make uninstall removes the binary file. Some make files include a test target that you use before make install to check if the compiled program works as expected.

Large software projects are created in the same way, but the makefiles are much more extensive and complex. If the software will be compiled to a functional program on multiple architectures, things are even more complicated.

For this reason, the makefile is usually generated by the configure script.

Use make install to Install the Compiled Program

The last step when installing a program from source is to install the binary file and additional files belonging to the application. This step is usually done with make and an install target in the corresponding makefile.

To perform the installation, enter make install. You must enter this command as root at the top level of the source directory.

Exercise 4-1   Manage Software with RPM

In this exercise, you practice gathering information on installed software and installing software packages.

You will find this exercise at the end of the chapter.

(End of Exercise)

Objective 2   Manage Shared Libraries

In addition to checking for software package dependencies, you might also need to verify that the system is configured properly to access the dynamic libraries an application uses.

Normally this is handled by the software installation, but occasionally you might need to verify software library access after installation.

For example, if an application that has been installed fails to start, try starting it from a terminal window. If the application reports that a library could not be found, then you might need to verify access to the dynamic libraries.

To verify the libraries needed for an application, you need to be familiar with the following:

- Software Library Basics
- View Shared Library Dependencies
- Modify the Software Library Configuration File
- Update the Library Cache
- Manage Shared Libraries

Software Library Basics

To understand the role of software libraries in SUSE Linux, you need to know the following:

- Dynamic Software Libraries
- Static Software Libraries
- Library Naming Syntax

Dynamic Software Libraries

In a Linux environment, most programs share some code through the use of shared libraries. This provides advantages from a development and a system management standpoint.

For developers, it means their programs include only the code that is unique to the program itself, sharing functions that other programs have in common with it.

This reduces the size of the program executable, thus reducing the amount of disk space required for the application (an advantage for system administrators).

Unlike some other operating systems, a Linux system locates its dynamic libraries through a configuration file that points to the locations, eliminating confusion about which version of which dynamic library is used by each piece of software.

NOTE: Developers still have the ability to link everything into their executable. This can be important if the program will be used on a system that might not include all of the necessary libraries, such as an emergency rescue disk or minimal Linux installation.

Static Software Libraries

In contrast to dynamic program linking, you can link the needed libraries statically when a program is compiled.

Although static linking increases the program size, it provides independence from libraries at runtime and is especially useful for system maintenance purposes.

An example of a program with statically linked libraries is `sash` (stand-alone shell); `sash` is useful for recovering from certain types of system failures. It was created to cope with the problem of missing shared libraries or important executables. Built-in commands include `-mount`, `-mknod`, `-kill`, `-ln`, `-gzip`, `-gunzip`, and others.

Library Naming Syntax

Library file names normally use the following syntax:

lib*name*.so.*version*

The letters "so" indicate a shared dynamic library; the letter "a" (as in `/usr/lib/libc.a`) is used for static libraries. The version indicates a major version number of the library (such as 1, 2, or 6).

For example, the library used for the ncurses screen library (version 4.2) might be named:

libncurses.so.4.2

View Shared Library Dependencies

You can view the shared libraries required by a specific program or shared library by using the `ldd` command. The following is the syntax of the command:

ldd *option filename*

For example, if you enter `ldd -v /usr/bin/nautilus`, information similar to the following appears:

```
da1:~ # ldd -v /usr/bin/nautilus
  linux-gate.so.1 =>  (0xffffe000)
  libbeagle.so.1 => /usr/lib/libbeagle.so.1 (0xb7ecd000)
  libnautilus-extension.so.1 => /usr/lib/libnautilus-extension.so.1
(0xb7ec3000)
  libeel-2.so.2 => /usr/lib/libeel-2.so.2 (0xb7e53000)
  libglade-2.0.so.0 => /usr/lib/libglade-2.0.so.0 (0xb7e3a000)
  librsvg-2.so.2 => /usr/lib/librsvg-2.so.2 (0xb7e02000)
  libgnome-desktop-2.so.7 => /usr/lib/libgnome-desktop-2.so.7
(0xb7dd8000)
```

```
libgnomeui-2.so.0 => /usr/lib/libgnomeui-2.so.0 (0xb7d41000)
libbonoboui-2.so.0 => /usr/lib/libbonoboui-2.so.0 (0xb7cd6000)
libgnomecanvas-2.so.0 => /usr/lib/libgnomecanvas-2.so.0 (0xb7ca1000)
```

...

By using the `ldd` command, you can also find out if all required libraries are installed on a system for a specific program. The output of `ldd` would indicate "not found" for the missing library.

NOTE: For additional information on the `ldd` command, enter `man ldd` from a terminal window.

Modify the Software Library Configuration File

The software library configuration file is `/etc/ld.so.conf`. It contains a list of paths the Linux system uses to search for libraries, as in the following:

```
da1:~ # cat /etc/ld.so.conf
/usr/X11R6/lib/Xaw3d
/usr/X11R6/lib
/usr/lib/Xaw3d
/usr/i386-suse-linux/lib
/usr/local/lib
/opt/kde3/lib
include /etc/ld.so.conf.d/*.conf
```

To modify the `/etc/ld.so.conf` file, you need to be authenticated as the root user. The file format for this file is simply a list of system directories containing dynamic libraries.

Typical library directories include the following:

- `/lib/`
- `/usr/lib/`
- `/usr/local/lib/`
- `/usr/X11R6/lib/`

Because the `/lib/` and `/usr/lib/` directories are taken into account in all cases, they are not listed in this file. You can enter the `/sbin/ldconfig -p` command to list all libraries available in the cache that will be found by the system.

If a library is located in a directory not listed above, you can set the variable `LD_LIBRARY_PATH=path` to make sure that it is loaded using the following command:

```
export LD_LIBRARY_PATH=path
```

NOTE: For a listing of variables that can be used, enter `man 8 ld.so`.

Update the Library Cache

The file that contains the library cache is `/etc/ld.so.cache`. The `/lib/ld-linux.so.2` program (this is a link to `/lib/ld-2.4.so`), referred to as the runtime linker, makes sure that the needed libraries are found and loaded when a program is started.

If you modify the `/etc/ld.so.conf` file to reflect any new dynamic library paths, you need to enter the `ldconfig` command to update the library cache. If new libraries are installed during operation, you also need to run `ldconfig` manually.

This is the same command used to update the library cache when rebooting the system.

The command sets the required links to the current shared libraries that are located in directories listed in the `/etc/ld.so.conf` file or in the `/usr/lib/` and `/lib/` directories.

The library cache file is `/etc/ld.so.cache` and is read by the runtime linker. The cache file contains a list of all the system libraries stored in a binary format to speed the location of the libraries on the system.

Running `ldconfig` with the `-v` option displays detailed information about the libraries `ldconfig` has found.

Exercise 4-2   Manage Shared Libraries

In this exercise, you use some common utilities to manage the shared libraries on your SUSE Linux Enterprise Server 11.

You will find this exercise at the end of the chapter.

(End of Exercise)

Objective 3   Manage User and Group Accounts

You can use command line tools to perform the same user and group management tasks available with YaST. In this objective you learn how to

- Manage User Accounts

- Manage Groups

- Understand User and Group Configuration Files

- Monitor Login Activity

- Create and Manage Users and Groups from the Command Line

Manage User Accounts

The user root can use the following commands to perform user management tasks:

- useradd Command

- userdel Command

- usermod Command

- passwd Command

While the above commands exist on all Linux systems, they do not behave identically on all systems. The main difference is how users are added to groups:

- **All users are member of the same group.** This is the system used on SLES 11. By default, each user has the group users as his primary group.

- **Each user is a member of a group of his own.** This system, also sometimes referred to as user private groups, is used on Debian and RedHat systems. For every user a group with the same name is created, and the user is the only member of this group.

As the commands to manage users and groups automatically take this into consideration, their functionality differs depending on the system.

useradd Command

You can create a new user account with the useradd command. If no option is specified, the useradd command creates a user without a home directory and without a valid password.

The following are the most important options of the useradd command:

- -m. This option automatically generates the home directory for the user. Without further arguments, the directory is created under /home/.

    In addition, several files and directories are copied to this directory. The /etc/ skel/ directory (from skeleton) is used as a template for the user home directory.

- -c. When creating a new user, you can enter text for the comment field by using the -c (comment) option.

- **-u**. This option specifies the UID of the new account. If this option is not given, the next free UID is used (at maximum 60000).

- **-g**. This option defines the primary group of the user. You can specify either the GID or the name of the group.

- **-e**. The $-e$ (expire date) option lets you set an expiration date for the user account, in the form of YYYY-MM-DD, as in the following:

```
useradd -m -e 2009-09-15 geeko
```

You can display a description of additional options by entering man 8 useradd.

After adding a new user, you need to assign a password. To do so, you use the passwd command. Enter the following:

```
passwd geeko
```

You will be prompted for a new password and will be asked to confirm it.

When creating a user account, the necessary standard configuration information (primary group, location of the home directory, default shell, etc.) is derived from the /etc/default/useradd and /etc/login.defs files.

The following is an example of the /etc/default/useradd file:

```
GROUP=100
HOME=/home
INACTIVE=-1
EXPIRE=
SHELL=/bin/bash
SKEL=/etc/skel
GROUPS=video,dialout
CREATE_MAIL_SPOOL=no
```

The variables mean

- **GROUP**. The primary group the user belongs to.

- **HOME**. Path where the home directories are stored.

- **INACTIVE**. Number of days of inactivity after a password has expired before the account is locked (-1 disables this feature).

- **EXPIRE**. Date (days since January 1, 1970) when an account will expire.

- **SHELL**. Path of the login shell.

- **SKEL**. Path of the home directory skeleton.

- **GROUPS**. Other groups the user belongs to.

- **CREATE_MAIL_SPOOL**. Specifies whether a mail spool directory is created automatically.

NOTE: In addition to the useradd command, some systems also have an adduser command that acts as an interactive frontend to useradd, asking for account information and password.

---

userdel Command

This command lets you delete an existing user account. It provides a single option, -r, which deletes the user's home directory when the user's account is deleted.

Before using `userdel -r`, it is important that you determine the user's UID (`id user`). The UID enables you to locate files outside the user's home directory that are assigned to the user (such as `/var/mail/$USER`).

To delete these files, enter

```
find / -uid user_ID -exec rm {} \;
```

NOTE: In addition to the `userdel` command, some systems also have a `deluser` command that acts as a frontend to `userdel`.

---

usermod Command

This command lets you modify settings (such as UID, standard shell, home directory, and primary group) for an existing user account.

The `usermod` options are basically the same as those for the `useradd` command.

The following are examples:

- Change the home directory:

  ```
  usermod -d /data/geeko -m geeko
  ```

- Change the UID:

  ```
  usermod -u 1001 geeko
  ```

passwd Command

You can change a user's password with the `passwd` command. If users enter `passwd` without a username as an argument, they can change their own password.

Besides allowing for password changes, the `passwd` command provides the following features:

- **Locking a user account:** With the -l (lock) option, a user can be locked out. Notice that after the account is locked, the password hash in `/etc/shadow` begins with an exclamation mark "!". With the -u (unlock) option, the user's account can be reactivated:

Figure 4-2   *Locking and Unlocking a User Account*

```
DA2:/ # grep geeko /etc/shadow
geeko:$2a$05$6lVmYIOLOB7IHD9cZPx9cewuPD.zUQKT6wauuxDMtGmWe9NiTOVk6:14281:0:99999
:7:::
DA2:/ # passwd -l geeko
Password changed.
DA2:/ # grep geeko /etc/shadow
geeko:!$2a$05$6lVmYIOLOB7IHD9cZPx9cewuPD.zUQKT6wauuxDMtGmWe9NiTOVk6:14281:0:9999
9:7:::
DA2:/ # passwd -u geeko
Password changed.
DA2:/ # grep geeko /etc/shadow
geeko:$2a$05$6lVmYIOLOB7IHD9cZPx9cewuPD.zUQKT6wauuxDMtGmWe9NiTOVk6:14281:0:99999
:7:::
```

Courtesy of Novell, Inc.

- **Listing the status of a user account:** The -S option lists the status of a user account:

Figure 4-3   *Status of a User Account*

```
DA2:/ # passwd -S geeko
geeko PS_02/06/2009 0 99999 7 -1
```

Courtesy of Novell, Inc.

The status follows directly after the username. In the above example,

- PS means that this is a valid password
- 02/06/2009 is the date of the last password change
- 0 is the minimum length of validity
- 99999 is the maximum length of validity in days
- 7 signifies the warning periods
- -1 signifies the inactivity periods when a password expires

Other options: **LK** (locked) means that the user is unable to log in and **NP** means there is no password.

- **Changing password times:** You can change password times by using the following options:

Table 4-8   *Options for Changing Password Times*

Option	Description
-i *number*	Disable an account after the password has been expired for *number* of days.
-n *number*	Sets the minimum number of days before a password can be changed.
-w *number*	Warns the user that in *number* of days his password will expire.
-x *number*	Sets the maximum number of days a password remains valid. After *number* of days, the password must be changed.

The following is an example:

```
passwd -x 30 -w 5 geeko
```

In this example, the password of the user geeko remains valid for 30 days. After this time, user geeko needs to change his password. Geeko receives a warning five days before password expiration.

/etc/default/passwd File

When you use the `passwd` command to establish or change the password of a user account, the `/etc/default/passwd` file is checked for the encryption method to be used:

Figure 4-4   *The /etc/default/passwd File*

```
DA2:/ # cat /etc/default/passwd
# This file contains some information for
# the passwd (1) command and other tools
# creating or modifying passwords.

# Define default crypt hash. This hash will be
# used, if there is no hash for a special service
# the user is stored in.
# CRYPT={des,md5,blowfish}
CRYPT=md5

# Use another crypt hash for group passwords.
# This is used by gpasswd, fallback is the CRYPT entry.
# GROUP_CRYPT=des

# We can override the default for a special service
# by appending the service name (FILES, YP, NISPLUS, LDAP)

# for local files, use a more secure hash. We
# don't need to be portable here:
CRYPT_FILES=blowfish
```

Courtesy of Novell, Inc.

The encryption method is set in the CRYPT variable (set to md5 in the above example taken from SLES 11; des is the Linux default). For local files (such as `/etc/shadow`), the method is changed to blowfish later in the `/etc/default/passwd` file using the CRYPT_FILES variable. YaST also uses the `/etc/default/passwd` file.

Manage Groups

You can use the following commands to perform group management tasks:

NOTE: You need to be logged in as root (or switch to root by entering `su -`) to use these commands.

- **groupadd.** You can create a new group by entering `groupadd group_name`. In this case, the next free GID is used.

  Use the `-g` option (such as `groupadd -g 1200 sports`) to specify a GID.

  Use the `-p` option to specify an encrypted password. You can use the `mkpasswd` command to create the encrypted password.

  NOTE: In addition to the `groupadd` command, some systems also have an `addgroup` command that acts as a frontend to `groupadd`.

- **groupdel.** You can delete a group by entering `groupdel group_name`. There are no options for this command.

  You can only delete a group if no user has this group assigned as a primary group.

  NOTE: In addition to the `groupdel` command, some systems also have a `delgroup` command that acts as a frontend to `groupdel`.

- **groupmod.** You can modify the settings (such as GID, group name, and users) for an existing group.

  The following are examples:

  □ Change the GID:

  ```
  groupmod -g 1201  sports
  ```

  □ Change the group name from sports to water:

  ```
  groupmod -n water  sports
  ```

  □ Add the user geeko to the group:

  ```
  groupmod -A geeko water
  ```

- **gpasswd.** Change passwords for group accounts. Only the administrator may change the password for any group. The group password can be removed with the `-r` option.

  NOTE: You can learn more about these commands by referring to the manual pages (such as `man groupadd`) or help page (such as `groupadd --help`).

- **newgrp.** Change the effective group of the executing user.

Figure 4-5   *The newgrp Command*

```
geeko@DA2:/> id
uid=1000(geeko) gid=100(users) groups=16(dialout),33(video),100(users)
geeko@DA2:/> newgrp video
geeko@DA2:/> id
uid=1000(geeko) gid=33(video) groups=16(dialout),33(video),100(users)
```
Courtesy of Novell, Inc.

In this example you can see that the current group (users) is replaced with a new group (video). To return to the previous group, enter exit.

A password is requested if the group has a password and the user is not listed in the group file as being a member of that group.

NOTE: Instead of the newgrp command, the sg command can be used, which is a link to newgrp.

Understand User and Group Configuration Files

The Linux system stores all user and group configuration data in plain text files. These include the following:

- The /etc/passwd File
- The /etc/shadow File
- The /etc/group File

WARNING: Whenever possible, you should not modify these files with an editor. Instead use the *Security and Users* modules provided in YaST or the command line tools described on previous pages in this section.

Modifying these files with an editor can lead to errors (especially in /etc/shadow), such as a user—including the user root—no longer being able to log in.

The /etc/passwd File

The /etc/passwd file stores user information such as the user name, the UID, the home directory, and the login shell.

In the past, /etc/passwd also contained the password hash. However, because the file needs to be readable by all (for instance, to show user and group names when using ls -l), the hashed password is now stored in /etc/shadow, which is only readable by root and members of the shadow group.

The following is an example of an /etc/password file:

```
at:x:25:25:Batch jobs daemon:/var/spool/atjobs:/bin/bash
bin:x:1:1:bin:/bin:/bin/bash
daemon:x:2:2:Daemon:/sbin:/bin/bash
ftp:x:40:49:FTP account:/srv/ftp:/bin/bash
...
root:x:0:0:root:/root:/bin/bash
...
geeko:x:1000:100:Geeko Novell:/home/geeko:/bin/bash
student:x:1001:100:Student:/home/student:/bin/bash
```

Each line consists of fields separated by colons. The fields contain from left to right:

- User name.

- Password hash. As the password hash is now moved to the /etc/shadow file, this field just contains the letter x.

- User ID.

- Group ID of primary group.

- Comment. Can contain full name, room number, telephone number, separated by commas. This field is sometimes also referred to as the General Electric Comprehensive Operating System (GECOS) field. This field was introduced in the early Unix days.

- Home directory of the user.

- Login shell of the user.

The /etc/shadow File

The /etc/shadow file stores encrypted user passwords and password expiration information. Most Linux systems use shadow passwords. The file can only be changed and read by the user root and members of the shadow group. The following is an excerpt from a sample /etc/shadow file:

```
at:*:14356:0:99999:7:::
bin:*:14312::::::
daemon:*:14312::::::
ftp:*:14312::::::
...
root:$2a$05$r1/wVV24XQZ5fyRMniinsOTLp787/mrm4mEwfUvMGRhPuqqnNBjA6
:14356:0:99999:7:::
...
geeko:$2a$05$Eso3tbJJXTVAjUdRk0L9DODn/pgleIwhwsjIhmN0hoT5dYGVOfIxq
:14356:0:99999:7:::
student:$2a$05$cV6gN3HrI9s7sWU0wIutre3qVzs/KryduxOescwIyNjRZOV1RI06u
:14356:0:99999:7:::
```

Each line in the /etc/shadow file belongs to one user and contains the following fields, separated by colons:

- User name.

- Password hash.

On SLES 11, the encrypted password is coded with the Blowfish function. The encrypted word consists of letters, digits, and some special characters. If an invalid character occurs in the password field (such as "*" or "!"), that user has an invalid password.

Many users, such as bin or wwwrun (Apache Web server), have an asterisk ("*") in the password field. This means that these users cannot log in to the system but are needed for special applications.

If the password field is empty, then the user can log in to the system without entering a password. A password should always be set in a Linux system.

- **Last Change.** Date of last password change. The number represents the number of days since January 1, 1970.

- **Next Possible Change.** Minimum age of a password before a user can change it.

- **Next Obligatory Change.** Number of days a user can use the same password before it expires.

- **Warning.** Number of days before password expiration that a warning is issued to users.

  Enter -1 to disable the warning.

- **Limit.** Number of days after the password expires that the user can continue to log in.

  Enter -1 for unlimited access. (This does not make sense, of course.)

- **Lock.** Date when the account expires. The number represents the number of days since January 1, 1970.

  Leave the field empty if the account never expires.

The /etc/group File

The /etc/group file stores group information. The following is an excerpt from the file:

```
at:!:25:
audio:x:17:pulse
bin:x:1:daemon
cdrom:x:20:
console:x:21:
daemon:x:2:
dialout:x:16:geeko,student
```

Each line in the file represents a single group record and contains the group name, the GID (Group ID), and the members of the group. For example

dialout:x:15:geeko,student

- dialout - Group name

- x - password hash or placeholder if no password is set

- 16 - Group ID

- geeko,student - Group members

The `/etc/group` file shows secondary group memberships but does not identify the primary group for a user.

Monitor Login Activity

There are different tools to monitor your server, many of which are covered in the next section of this course. In the context of user accounts, there are several tools to specifically monitor login activity. These include:

- **who:** Shows who is currently logged in to the system and information such as the time of the last login.

  You can use options such as `-H` (display column headings), `-r` (current runlevel), and `-a` (display information provided by most options).

  For example, entering `who -H` returns information similar to the following:

```
da1:~ # who -H
NAME       LINE          TIME             COMMENT
root       pts/0         2009-05-24 10:33 (da2.digitalairlines.com)
geeko      :0            2009-05-24 13:54
...
```

- **w:** Displays information about the users currently on the machine and their processes.

  The first line includes information on the current time, how long the system has been running, how many users are currently logged on, and the system load averages for the past 1, 5, and 15 minutes.

  Below the first line is an entry for each user that displays the login name, the TTY name, the remote host, login time, idle time, JCPU, PCPU, and the command line of the user's current process.

  The JCPU time is the time used by all processes attached to the tty. It does not include past background jobs, but it does include currently running background jobs. The PCPU time is the time used by the current process, which is named in the What field.

  You can use options such as `-h` (don't display the header), `-s` (don't display the login time, JCPU, and PCPU), and `-V` (display version information).

  For example, entering `w` returns information similar to the following:

```
da1:~ # w
 05:18:45 up  1:02,  2 users,  load average: 0.05, 0.07, 0.02
USER       TTY          LOGIN@   IDLE   JCPU   PCPU WHAT
root       pts/1        04:28    0.00s  0.06s  0.00s w
geeko      :0           05:16    ?xdm?  10.16s 0.02s /usr/lib/gdm/gdm-
simple-slave --display-id /org/gnome/DisplayManager/Display1
...
```

- **finger:** Displays information about local and remote system users. By default, the following information is displayed about each user currently logged in to the local host:

  - User's login name

  - User's full name

  - Associated terminal name

  - Idle time

  - Login time (and from where)

  You can use options such as -l (long format) and -s (short format).

  For example, entering `finger -s` returns information similar to the following:

  ```
  da1:~ # finger -s
  Login       Name                     Tty      Idle   Login Time    Where
  geeko       Geeko Novell             *:0       -     Tue 05:16
  root        root                     pts/1     -     Tue 04:28  da1.dig
  ```

- **last:** Displays a list of users who logged in and out since the `/var/log/wtmp` file was created.

  Last searches back through the `/var/log/wtmp` file (or the file designated by the `-f` option) and displays a list of all users who have logged in (and out) since the file was created. You can specify names of users and TTY's to show only information for those entries.

  You can use options such as **-n** (where *n* is the number of lines to display), `-a` (display the host name in the last column), and `-x` (display system shutdown entries and runlevel changes).

  For example, entering `last -ax` returns information similar to the following:

  ```
  da1:~ # last -ax
  geeko     :0             Tue Jul 28 05:16    still logged in
  geeko     tty7           Tue Jul 28 05:16    still logged in      :0
  root      pts/1          Tue Jul 28 04:28    still logged in
  da2.digitalairlines.com
  runlevel (to lvl 5)      Tue Jul 28 04:17 - 05:21   (01:04)
  2.6.27.19-5-pae
  reboot    system boot    Tue Jul 28 04:13            (01:08)
  2.6.27.19-5-pae
  ...
  ```

Exercise 4-3   *Create and Manage Users and Groups from the Command Line*

In this exercise, you add and remove a user using command line tools.

You will find this exercise at the end of the chapter.

(End of Exercise)

Objective 4   Manage File Permissions and Ownership

Each file in a Linux system is owned by a user and belongs to a group. Access permissions can be set separately for the owning user, the owning group, and all others. The available permissions are read, write, and execute. In addition to these three, special file permissions can be set, such as disallowing the deletion of a file.

You can change the current values associated with ownership and permissions by knowing how to do the following:

- Understand File Permissions
- Change File Permissions with chmod
- Change File Ownership with chown and chgrp
- Modify Default Access Permissions with umask
- Configure Special File Attributes
- Manage File Permissions and Ownership

Understand File Permissions

You can use the `ls -l` command to display the contents of the current directory with the assigned permissions for each file or subdirectory.

For example, to display the permissions for the `quarterly-1` file, you would enter

```
ls -l quarterly-1
```

The output might look like this:

```
geeko@da-host:~> ls -l quarterly-1
-rw-r--r-- 1 geeko users 0 2009-07-28 06:42 quarterly-1
```

Look at the first ten characters of the output ("-rw-r--r--"). The first character ("-") is not of interest regarding permissions, because it indicates the type of the file:

- **-.** Normal file
- **d.** Directory
- **l.** Link

The remaining nine characters show the file permissions.

You can assign the following permissions to a file or directory:

- **Read (r).** This permission allows the file to be read or the contents of a directory to be listed.
- **Write (w).** This permission allows a file to be modified. It allows files to be created or deleted within a directory.
- **Execute (x).** This permission allows a file to be executed. When set on directories, it allows you to change into that directory with the `cd` command.

If a permission is set, the character is shown. Otherwise a "-" appears.

The permission characters are grouped ("**rwx rwx rwx**"):

- **Characters 1 to 3.** These represent the permissions of the file owner.

- **Characters 4 to 6.** These represent the permissions of the owning group.

- **Characters 7 to 9.** These represent the permissions of all other users.

The number to the right of the permissions indicates the number of hard links to the file.

Each file (and directory) can belong to only one user and one group. The name of the file owner (geeko) is shown in the `ls` output next to the link counter. The name of the owning group (users) is shown next to the file owner.

NOTE: The file permissions are evaluated from left to right, and the check ends when a match is found. This means that if the owning user is denied read access due to the permissions for the owning user, he is denied access even if members of his group are allowed to read the file.

root can read any file no matter what permissions are set for it.

View Permissions with Nautilus

You can also view permissions, owner, and group from the Nautilus file manager.

1. Right-click the icon of the file you want to look at.

2. Select *Properties* from the pop-up menu.

3. Select the *Permissions* tab.

Figure 4-6   *File Permissions in Nautilus*

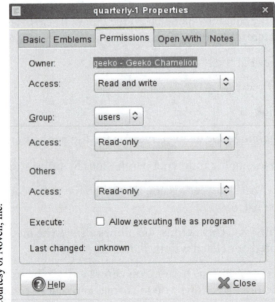

Courtesy of Novell, Inc.

From this dialog, you can change the Read and Write permissions for Owner, Group, and Others by selecting the appropriate option.

As root, you can modify the user and group ownership of the file or directory by selecting a user or group in the appropriate field. As normal user, you can only change the group ownership to a group you are a member of.

Change File Permissions with chmod

You can use the chmod command to add ("+") or remove ("−") permissions. Both the owner of a file and root can use this command.

There are options to change the permissions for the owning user ("u"), group ("g"), other ("o"), or all ("a").

The following table lists chmod command examples:

Table 4-9   *chmod Command Examples*

Example	Result
chmod u+x file	The owner (user) is given permission to execute the file.
chmod g=rw file	All group members can read and write.
chmod u=rwx file	The owner receives all permissions.
chmod u=rwx,g=rw,o=r file	All permissions for the owner (user), read and write for the group, read for all others.
chmod +x file	All users (owner, group, others) receive executable permission (depending on umask).
chmod a+x file	All users (owner, group, others) receive executable permission (**a** for **all**).

In the following example, the user geeko allows the other members of the group **users** (g) to write (w) to the hello.txt file by entering the following command:

```
chmod g+w hello.txt
```

The output might look something like the following:

```
geeko@da-host:~> ls -l hello.txt
-rw-r--r-- 1 geeko users 0 2009-07-28 07:01 hello.txt
geeko@da-host:~> chmod g+w hello.txt
geeko@da-host:~> ls -l
total 1324
-rw-rw-r-- 1 geeko users 0 2009-07-28 07:01 hello.txt
```

With the option −R (recursive) and a specified directory, you can change the access permissions of all files and subdirectories under the specified directory. This option should be used with due care, as it can be quite lengthy to undo an error, having to correct the permissions on lots of files.

Besides using letters (rwx), you can also use the octal way of representing the permission letters with groups of numbers. Three digits are required to define the permissions for the user, group, and others.

The first digit represents the permissions assigned to the file or directory owner. The second digit represents the permissions assigned to the group associated with the file or directory. The third digit represents the permissions assigned to others.

Each digit is the sum of the following three values assigned to it:

■ Read: 4

■ Write: 2

■ Execute: 1

For example, suppose a file named myfile.txt has 754 permissions assigned to it.

This means the owner of the file has read, write, and execute permissions (4+2+1), the group associated with the file has read and execute permissions (4+1), and others have read permissions (4).

By using number equivalents, you can add the numbers together, as in the following:

Table 4-10   *Octal Permission Values*

Owner	Group	Others
rwx	r-x	r--
421 (4+2+1=7)	4-1 (4+1=5)	4-- (4)

The following are examples of using numbers instead of letters:

Table 4-11   *chmod and Octal Permission Values*

Example	Result
chmod 754 hello.txt	All permissions for the owner, read and execute for the group, read for all other users (rwx r-x r--).
chmod 777 hello.txt	All users (user, group, others) receive all permissions (rwx rwx rwx).

Change File Ownership with chown and chgrp

The user root can use the chown command to change the user and group affiliation of a file by using the following syntax:

chown *new_user.new_group* file

To change only the owner, not the group, you can use the following command syntax:

chown *new_user* file

To change the owner and the group to the primary group of the new owner, you can use the following syntax:

```
chown new_user. file
```

To change only the group, not the user, you can use the following command syntax:

```
chown .new_group file
```

You can also change the group affiliation of a file with the chgrp command using the following syntax:

```
chgrp new_group file
```

While root can assign the file to any group using the chgrp or chown commands, a normal user can only assign the file to groups he is a member of. A normal user cannot change the owner of a file.

In the following example, root changes the ownership of the hello.txt file from geeko to the user tux by entering chown tux.users hello.txt

Figure 4-7   *Use of the chown Command*

```
DA2:/tmp # ls -la hello.txt
-rw-rw-r-- 1 geeko users 0 2009-02-20 09:45 hello.txt
DA2:/tmp # chown tux.users hello.txt
DA2:/tmp # ls -la hello.txt
-rw-rw-r-- 1 tux users 0 2009-02-20 09:45 hello.txt
```
Courtesy of Novell, Inc.

In the following example, chown is used to change access to the list.txt file from members of the advanced group to members of the users group:

Figure 4-8   *Use of the chown Command*

```
geeko@DA2:/tmp> ls -la list.txt
-rw-r--r-- 1 geeko advanced 0 2009-02-20 10:08 list.txt
geeko@DA2:/tmp> chown .users list.txt
geeko@DA2:/tmp> ls -la list.txt
-rw-r--r-- 1 geeko users 0 2009-02-20 10:08 list.txt
```
Courtesy of Novell, Inc.

Of course, root and the file owner continue to have rights to access the file.

Although the group has changed, the owner permissions remain the same.

Modify Default Access Permissions with umask

The umask command is used to change the permissions for newly created files and directories. Without a specific umask setting, files are created with the access mode **666** and directories with **777**.

To modify (restrict) these default access mode settings, you can use the umask command. You use this command with a 3-digit numerical value such as **022**.

The permissions set in the umask are subtracted from the default permissions. (In actual fact it's a bit more complicated, as you will see when setting the umask to 011 and creating a file—but for most practical purposes it's good enough. See man umask for the exact algorithm.)

For example, entering umask 022 has the following result:

Table 4-12   *umask Effects*

	Directories			Files		
Default Permissions	rwx	rwx	rwx	rw-	rw-	rw-
	7	7	7	6	6	6
umask	---	-w-	-w-	---	-w-	-w-
	0	2	2	0	2	2
Result	rwx	r-x	r-x	rw-	r--	r--
	7	5	5	6	4	4

By entering umask 077 you restrict access to the owner and root only; the group and others do not have any access permissions.

Enter umask without any parameter to show the current value of the umask. The output shows 4 digits, but the first digit is always 0 and cannot be changed with the umask command.

To make the umask setting permanent, you can change the value of umask in the system-wide /etc/profile.local configuration file. In SLES 11, changing the UMASK value in the /etc/login.defs file has the same effect, as there is a PAM module that sets the umask value accordingly. If you want the setting to be user-specific, enter the value of umask in the .bashrc file in the home directory of the respective user.

Configure Special File Attributes

The following attributes are used for special circumstances:

Table 4-13   *Special File Permissions*

Letter	Number	Name	Files	Directories
t	1	Sticky bit	No effect.	A user can only delete files within this directory if the user is the owner of the file or the owner of the directory, or he is the root user. This is usually applied to the /tmp/ directory.

Letter	Number	Name	Files	Directories
s	2	SGID (set GroupID)	When a program is run, this sets the group ID of the process to that of the group of the file.	Files created in this directory belong to the group to which the directory belongs and not to the group of the user. New directories created in this directory inherit the SGID bit.
s	4	SUID (set UserID)	Sets the user ID of the process to that of the owner of the file when the program is run.	No effect.

You set the SUID bit with chmod, using one of the following:

- Permissions of the owning user (such as chmod u+s /usr/bin/passwd)

- Numerically (such as chmod 4755 /usr/bin/passwd)

The following is an example for SUID:

```
DA2:/ # ls -l /usr/bin/passwd
-rwsr-xr-x 1 root shadow 80268 2009-01-23 22:08 /usr/bin/passwd
```

Each user is allowed to change his password, but root permissions are needed to write it into the /etc/shadow file.

You set the SGID bit with chmod, using one of the following:

- Permissions of the group (such as chmod g+s /tmp)

- Numerically (such as chmod 2777 /directory)

The following is an example for SGID:

```
DA2:/ # ls -l /usr/bin/wall
-rwxr-sr-x 1 root tty 14040 2009-01-23 21:49 /usr/bin/wall
```

With wall, you can send messages to all virtual terminals. If you use wall, this command is executed with the permissions of the group **tty**.

If the SUID or SGID attributes are set, the programs are carried out with the privileges the owner (in the example for SUID above: root) or the group (in the example for SGID above: tty) have.

If root is the owner of the program, the program is carried out with the permissions of root. Unfortunately, there is a security risk in doing this.

For example, it could be possible for a user to take advantage of an error in the program, retaining root privileges after the process has been ended.

You set the sticky bit with chmod, using one of the following:

- Permissions of others (such as chmod o+t /tmp)

- Numerically (such as chmod 1777 /tmp)

NOTE: The sticky bit on older UNIX systems enabled the keeping of an executable program in memory after it had been terminated, so it could be quickly restarted. However, with modern UNIX and Linux systems, this bit only affects directories.

The sticky bit is listed in the permissions for Others (t), as in the following:

```
DA2:/ # ls -ld /tmp
drwxrwxrwt 32 root root 4096 2009-02-20 10:30 /tmp
```

On ext2/ext3 file systems, a view additional attributes can be set with the chattr command and viewed with the lsattr command. (Other file systems may or may not support these attributes.)

Attributes are set with + and removed with − in front of the attribute, such as chattr +i file and chattr -i file. The attributes that can be set include the following:

Table 4-14   *chattr Options*

option	Description
i	Immutable. The file cannot be deleted or written to. Can be set and cleared by root only.
a	Append only. Data can be appended to the file, but it cannot be deleted or changed. Can be set and cleared by root only.
A	When a file with the 'A' attribute set is accessed, its atime record is not modified. This avoids a certain amount of disk I/O for laptop systems.
j	A file with the `j' attribute has all of its data written to the ext3 journal before being written to the file itself, if the file system is mounted with the "data=ordered" or "data=writeback" options.

See man chattr for the complete list.

The following is an example of setting and viewing these attributes:

```
da-host:/var/log # lsattr messages
--------------- messages
da-host:/var/log # chattr +a messages
da-host:/var/log # lsattr messages
-----a--------- messages
geeko@da-host:~>
```

NOTE: While the above can make it more difficult for an attacker to manipulate the log file, it also prevents the regular rotation of this logfile by logrotate.

Exercise 4-4   *Manage File Permissions and Ownership*

In this exercise, you create directories with different permissions.

You will find this exercise at the end of the chapter.

(End of Exercise)

Objective 5   Manage Partitions, File Systems, Quotas, and NFS

A basic task of all system administrators is providing users with access to the files they need. This includes the management of local file systems, the administration of quotas, as well as access to files that reside on file servers within the corporate network.

The general Linux file system layout is covered in Understand the File System Hierarchy Standard (FHS), and the use of YaST to administer file systems is covered in Verify Partitioning as part of the SLES 11 installation process. The YaST interface used during installation is exactly the same as the one you use on the installed system.

To administer partitions, file systems, quotas, and Network File System (NFS) on SLES 11, you need to

- Manage Partitions with fdisk
- Manage Linux File Systems
- Set Up and Configure Disk Quotas
- Manage Partitions and File Systems
- Configure the Network File System
- Set Up and Manage Network File System (NFS)

NOTE: You should always back up your data before working with tools that change the partition table or the file systems.

Manage Partitions with fdisk

The `fdisk` program is used for partitioning hard disks from the command line.

To view the current partitioning scheme, use the `-l` option with fdisk, as shown below:

```
da1:~ # fdisk -l
Disk /dev/sda: 17.1 GB, 17179869184 bytes
255 heads, 63 sectors/track, 2088 cylinders
Units = cylinders of 16065 * 512 = 8225280 bytes
Disk identifier: 0x0000683e

Device     Boot   Start    End      Blocks     Id   System
/dev/sda1          1       97       779121     82   Linux swap / Solaris
/dev/sda2   *      98      620      4200997+   83   Linux
/dev/sda3          621     1111     3943957+   f    W95 Ext'd (LBA)
/dev/sda5          621     751      1052226    83   Linux
```

To change the partition scheme, enter the device of the hard disk as a parameter, as shown below:

```
da1:~ # fdisk /dev/sda

The number of cylinders for this disk is set to 1111.
There is nothing wrong with that, but this is larger than 1024,
and could in certain setups cause problems with:
1) software that runs at boot time (e.g., old versions of LILO)
2) booting and partitioning software from other OSs
   (e.g., DOS FDISK, OS/2 FDISK)

Command (m for help):
```

To use fdisk, enter a letter to carry out an action. The following table lists the most frequently used commands:

Table 4-15   *Commands Used Within fdisk*

Letter	Action
d	Deletes a partition.
m	Gives a short summary of the fdisk commands.
n	Creates a new partition.
p	Shows a list of partitions that are currently available on the specified hard disk.
q	Ends the fdisk program without saving changes.
t	Changes a partition's system ID.
w	Saves the changes made to the hard disk and ends fdisk.

The following shows the partitioning using fdisk. The example starts with a hard disk with no partitions configured so far.

Begin by entering fdisk *hard_disk* (for example, fdisk /dev/sdb). You can always enter m (help) to view the available commands. Enter p (print) to view the current partition table:

```
Disk /dev/sdb: 80.0 GB, 80026361856 bytes
255 heads, 63 sectors/track, 9729 cylinders
Units = cylinders of 16065 * 512 = 8225280 bytes
Disk identifier: 0x2c746b9c

  Device Boot      Start         End      Blocks   Id  System

Command (m for help):
```

To create a primary partition, enter n (new), then enter p (primary) as shown in the following:

```
Command (m for help): n
Command action
   e   extended
   p   primary partition (1-4)
p
Partition number (1-4): 1
First cylinder (1-9729, default 1): 1
Last cylinder, +cylinders or +size{K,M,G} (1-9729, default 9729):
+20G

Command (m for help):
```

To display the partition table with the current settings, enter p (print). The following is displayed:

```
Command (m for help): p

Disk /dev/sdb: 80.0 GB, 80026361856 bytes
255 heads, 63 sectors/track, 9729 cylinders
Units = cylinders of 16065 * 512 = 8225280 bytes
Disk identifier: 0x2c746b9c

   Device Boot      Start         End      Blocks   Id  System
/dev/sdb1               1        2612    20980858+  83  Linux

Command (m for help):
```

This partition table contains all the relevant information on the partition created:

- /dev/sdb1 is the first partition of the hard disk (Device).

- It begins at cylinder 1 (Start) and ends at cylinder 2612 (End).

- It consists of 20980858 blocks (Blocks; Information on the + character can be found in /usr/share/doc/packages/util-linux/README.fdisk).

- Its Hex code is 83 (Id).

- Its type is Linux (System).

To set up an extended partition, enter n (new), then enter e (extended) as shown in the following:

```
Command (m for help): n
Command action
   e    extended
   p    primary partition (1-4)
e
Partition number (1-4): 2
First cylinder (2613-9729, default 2613):
Using default value 2613
Last cylinder, +cylinders or +size{K,M,G} (2613-9729, default 9729):
Using default value 9729

Command (m for help):
```

To display the partition table with the current settings, again enter p. The following is displayed:

```
Command (m for help): p

Disk /dev/sdb: 80.0 GB, 80026361856 bytes
255 heads, 63 sectors/track, 9729 cylinders
Units = cylinders of 16065 * 512 = 8225280 bytes
Disk identifier: 0x2c746b9c

   Device Boot      Start         End      Blocks   Id  System
/dev/sdb1               1        2612    20980858+  83  Linux
/dev/sdb2            2613        9729    57167302+   5  Extended

Command (m for help):
```

After an extended partition has been created, you can now set up logical partitions by entering n (new) and then entering l (logical) as shown in the following:

```
Command (m for help): n
Command action
   l    logical (5 or over)
   p    primary partition (1-4)
l
First cylinder (2613-9729, default 2613):
Using default value 2613
Last cylinder, +cylinders or +size{K,M,G} (2613-9729, default 9729):
+1G

Command (m for help):
```

The current settings now look like this:

```
Command (m for help): p

Disk /dev/sdb: 80.0 GB, 80026361856 bytes
255 heads, 63 sectors/track, 9729 cylinders
Units = cylinders of 16065 * 512 = 8225280 bytes
Disk identifier: 0x2c746b9c

   Device Boot      Start         End      Blocks   Id  System
/dev/sdb1               1        2612    20980858+  83  Linux
/dev/sdb2            2613        9729    57167302+   5  Extended
/dev/sdb5            2613        2744     1060258+  83  Linux
Command (m for help):
```

The standard type for these partitions is Linux. To view the available types, enter l:

```
Command (m for help): l

0  Empty          1e Hidden W95 FAT1 80 Old Minix        bf Solaris
1  FAT12          24 NEC DOS         81 Minix / old Lin c1 DRDOS/sec (FAT-
2  XENIX root     39 Plan 9          82 Linux swap / So c4 DRDOS/sec (FAT-
3  XENIX usr      3c PartitionMagic  83 Linux           c6 DRDOS/sec (FAT-
...
```

To change the partition type (for instance, to create a swap partition), do the following:

1. Enter t.

2. Enter the partition number.

3. Enter the hex code.

The following shows this procedure:

```
Command (m for help): t
Partition number (1-5): 5
Hex code (type L to list codes): 82
Changed system type of partition 5 to 82 (Linux swap / Solaris)

Command (m for help):
```

The partition table now looks like this:

```
Command (m for help): p

Disk /dev/sdb: 80.0 GB, 80026361856 bytes
255 heads, 63 sectors/track, 9729 cylinders
Units = cylinders of 16065 * 512 = 8225280 bytes
Disk identifier: 0x2c746b9c

   Device Boot      Start         End      Blocks   Id  System
/dev/sdb1              1        2612    20980858+  83  Linux
/dev/sdb2           2613        9729    57167302+   5  Extended
/dev/sdb5           2613        2744     1060258+  82  Linux swap /
Solaris

Command (m for help):
```

So far, nothing has been written to disk. If you want to discard your changes, enter q (quit). To actually write your changes to the partition table on the disk, enter w (write).

```
Command (m for help): w
The partition table has been altered!

Calling ioctl() to re-read partition table.

WARNING: Re-reading the partition table failed with error 16: Device
or resource busy.
The kernel still uses the old table.
The new table will be used at the next reboot.
Syncing disks.
da1:~ #
```

NOTE: When the new table is written, you are **not** asked to confirm if you really want to write the changes to disk. Therefore, use caution when using the write option.

As the output of fdisk says, you cannot directly use the new partition to create a file system on a new partition. You could now reboot as suggested, but you can also use the partprobe command to get the kernel to use the new partition table.

NOTE: In addition to the fdisk utility, you can also use the cfdisk utility from the shell prompt to create and manage disk partitions.

Manage Linux File Systems

To perform basic Linux file system management tasks in SLES 11, you need to know how to do the following:

- Create a File System with Command Line Tools
- Mount File Systems
- Monitor and Check a File System

Create a File System with Command Line Tools

There are several commands that you can use to create file systems, including `mke2fs`, `mkfs.ext3`, and `mkreiserfs`. These are used to create file systems such as ext2, ext3, and ReiserFS.

An alternative is to simply use the `mkfs` command, which is a front-end for the actual commands that create file systems (such as `mkfs.ext2`, `mkfs.ext3`, or `mkfs.msdos`).

When using `mkfs`, you need to use the `-t` option to indicate the file system type you want to create. If you do not indicate a file system type, `mkfs` automatically creates an ext2 file system.

You need to know how to do the following:

- Create an ext2 or ext3 File System

- Create a Reiser File System

Create an ext2 or ext3 File System

When you create an ext2 or ext3 file system with `mkfs`, you can use the following options:

Table 4-16   *mkfs Options for ext2/ext3 File Systems*

Option	Description
-b *blocksize*	Specifies the size of the data blocks in the file system. Values of 1024, 2048, and 4096 are allowed for the block size.
-i *bytes_per_inode*	Specifies how many inodes are created on the file system.
	For *bytes_per_inode*, you can use the same values available for the block size.
-j	Creates an ext3 journal on the file system.

If you do not include `-b` and `-i` options, the data block sizes and the number of inodes are set by `mkfs`, depending on the size of the partition.

The following is an example of creating an ext3 file system on a partition. Be aware that no confirmation is required—the partition is formatted immediately after pressing Enter:

```
da1:~ # mkfs -t ext3 /dev/sdb1
mke2fs 1.41.1 (01-Sep-2008)
Filesystem label=
OS type: Linux
Block size=4096 (log=2)
Fragment size=4096 (log=2)
1313760 inodes, 5245214 blocks
262260 blocks (5.00%) reserved for the super user
First data block=0
Maximum filesystem blocks=0
161 block groups
32768 blocks per group, 32768 fragments per group
8160 inodes per group
Superblock backups stored on blocks:
        32768, 98304, 163840, 229376, 294912, 819200, 884736, 1605632,
        2654208, 4096000

Writing inode tables: done
Creating journal (32768 blocks): done
Writing superblocks and filesystem accounting information: done

This filesystem will be automatically checked every 38 mounts or
180 days, whichever comes first.  Use tune2fs -c or -i to override.
```

This `mkfs` example creates ext3 file system on an existing partition with the following values:

- **Block size=4096 (log=2)**. Block size is 4 KB.

- **1313760 inodes, 5245214 blocks.** Maximum number of files and directories is 1313760. The total number of blocks is 5245214.

- **262260 blocks (5.00%) reserved for the super user.** 5% of the entire space is reserved for the system administrator. If the hard disk is 95% full, then a normal user cannot use any more space.

NOTE: You can also use the `mke2fs` command (`mkfs.ext2` and `mkfs.ext3` are hardlinks to the same file) to create an ext2 or ext3 file system (see `man mke2fs`).

Create a Reiser File System

You can create a Reiser file system by using the `mkreiserfs` or `mkfs -t reiserfs` command:

```
da1:~ # mkreiserfs /dev/sdb6
mkreiserfs 3.6.21 (2009 www.namesys.com)

A pair of credits:
Joshua Macdonald wrote the first draft of the transaction manager.
...

Guessing about desired format.. Kernel 2.6.27.19-5-pae is running.
Format 3.6 with standard journal
Count of blocks on the device: 4889776
Number of blocks consumed by mkreiserfs formatting process: 8361
Blocksize: 4096
Hash function used to sort names: "r5"
Journal Size 8193 blocks (first block 18)
Journal Max transaction length 1024
inode generation number: 0
UUID: 94b3ad1a-ec19-4260-962c-efd734be7059
ATTENTION: YOU SHOULD REBOOT AFTER FDISK!
        ALL DATA WILL BE LOST ON '/dev/sdb6'!
Continue (y/n):y
Initializing journal - 0%....20%....40%....60%....80%....100%
Syncing..ok
ReiserFS is successfully created on /dev/sdb6.
da1:~ #
```

To find out about the available options, enter `man mkreiserfs` at the shell prompt. Usually there is no need to use values different than those used by default.

NOTE: `parted` is a tool that can be used to administer partitions as well as various file systems. You can create new partitions and file systems or change existing ones. For more information, enter `parted --help`, `man parted`, or `info parted`.

Mount File Systems

In Windows systems, drive letters represent different partitions. Linux does not use letters to designate partitions; instead, it mounts partitions to a directory in the file system. Directories used for mounting are called mount points.

For example, to add a new hard disk to a Linux system, first you partition and format the drive. You then use a directory (such as `/data/`) in the file system and mount the drive to that directory using the `mount` command.

To unmount (detach) a file system, you use the `umount` command (notice that the command is umount, not unmount; for details, enter `man umount` at the shell prompt).

NOTE: You can also mount remote file systems, shared via the Network File System (NFS), to directories you create in your file system.

To manage mounting (and unmounting) file systems, you need to know the following:

- Configuration File for Mounting File Systems

- Mount a File System

- View Currently Mounted File Systems

- Unmount a File System

- Manage Swap Partitions

Configuration File for Mounting File Systems

The file systems and their mount points in the directory tree are configured in the /etc/fstab file. This file contains one line with six fields for each mounted file system.

The lines look similar to the following:

Field 1	Field 2	Field 3	Field 4	Field 5	Field 6
/dev/sda2	/	ext3	acl,user_xattr	1	1
/dev/sda1	swap	swap	defaults	0	0
proc	/proc	proc	defaults	0	0
sysfs	/sys	sysfs	noauto	0	0
debugfs	/sys/kernel/debug	debugfs	noauto	0	0
usbfs	/proc/bus/usb	usbfs	noauto	0	0
devpts	/dev/pts	devpts	mode=0620,gid=5	0	0
/dev/fd0	/media/floppy	auto	noauto,user,sync	0	0

Each field provides the following information for mounting the file system:

- **Field 1:** Lists the name of the device file, the file system label, or the UUID (Universally Unique Identifier). Using LABEL=*label* or UUID=*uuid* ensures the partition is mounted correctly even if the device file used changes (for instance, because you swapped hard disks on the SATA controller).

- **Field 2:** Lists the mount point—the directory the file system should be mounted to. The directory specified here must already exist. You can access the content on the media by changing to the respective directory.

- **Field 3:** Lists the file system type (such as ext2, reiserfs).

- **Field 4:** Shows the mount options. Multiple mount options are separated by commas (such as noauto,user,sync).

- **Field 5:** Indicates whether the dump backup utility will back up the file system. 0 indicates no backup.

- **Field 6:** Indicates the sequence of the file system checks (using the fsck utility) when the system is booted:

    - **0:** File systems that are not to be checked

- ❑ **1**: root directory
- ❑ **2**: All other modifiable file systems (file systems on different drives are checked in parallel)

Although /etc/fstab lists the file systems and where they should be mounted in the directory tree during startup, it does not contain information on any file systems mounted at a later point in time.

The /etc/mtab file lists the currently mounted file systems and their mount points. The mount and umount commands affect the state of mounted file systems and modify the /etc/mtab file.

The kernel also keeps information for /proc/mounts, which lists all currently mounted partitions.

For troubleshooting purposes, if there is a conflict between /proc/mounts and /etc/mtab information, the /proc/mounts data is always more current and reliable than /etc/mtab.

Mount a File System

You can use the mount command to manually mount a file system. The syntax is:

```
mount [-t file_system_type] [-o mount_options] device
mount_point_directory
```

Using mount, you can override the default settings in /etc/fstab. For example, entering the following mounts the partition /dev/sda9 to the /space directory:

```
mount /dev/sda9 /space
```

You do not usually specify the file system type because it is recognized automatically using magic numbers in the superblock, or simply by trying different file system types. (See man mount for details.)

The /mnt/ directory is used by default for temporarily mounting local and remote file systems. All removable devices are mounted by default to /media/, such as the following:

- A CD-ROM on /dev/cdrom is mounted by default to /media/cdrom
- A floppy disk on /dev/floppy is mounted by default to /media/floppy

When using SLES 11 from a desktop environment such as Gnome or KDE, media such DVDs and CDROMs are automatically mounted and unmounted. If the media has a label, it is mounted to /media/*label*.

The following are some of the options you can use when mounting a file system with the mount command or by entering them in /etc/fstab:

- **remount.** Causes file systems that are already mounted to be mounted again.

  When you make a change to the options in /etc/fstab, you can use remount to incorporate the changes.

- **rw, ro.** Indicates whether a file system should be writable (rw) or only readable (ro).

- **sync, async.** Sets synchronous (sync) or asynchronous (async) input and output in a file system. The default setting is async.

- **atime, noatime.** Determines whether the access time of a file is updated in the inode (atime) or not (noatime). The noatime option should improve the performance.

- **nodev, dev.** The nodev option prevents device files from being interpreted as such in the file system.

- **noexec, exec.** You can prohibit the execution of programs on a file system with the noexec option.

- **nosuid, suid.** The nosuid option ensures that the suid and sgid bits in the file system are ignored.

- **loop.** This option is used when mounting image files containing file systems, such as ISO9660 CDROM or DVD images, using a loopback device. To mount an ISO image, use a command similar to the following:

```
mount -o loop image.iso /mnt
```

Some options make sense only in the `/etc/fstab` file, including the following:

- **auto, noauto:** File systems set with the noauto option in the `/etc/fstab` file are not mounted automatically when the system is booted.

- **user, nouser:** The user option lets users mount the file system. Normally, this is a privilege of the user root.

- **defaults:** Causes the default options rw, suid, dev, exec, auto, nouser, and async to be used.

The `noauto` and `user` options are usually combined for removable media such as floppy disk or CD-ROM drives.

View Currently Mounted File Systems

You can view the file systems currently mounted by entering `mount`. Information similar to the following appears:

```
da1:~ # mount
/dev/sda2 on / type ext3 (rw,acl,user_xattr)
/proc on /proc type proc (rw)
sysfs on /sys type sysfs (rw)
debugfs on /sys/kernel/debug type debugfs (rw)
udev on /dev type tmpfs (rw)
devpts on /dev/pts type devpts (rw,mode=0620,gid=5)
fusectl on /sys/fs/fuse/connections type fusectl (rw)
securityfs on /sys/kernel/security type securityfs (rw)
none on /proc/sys/fs/binfmt_misc type binfmt_misc (rw)
nfsd on /proc/fs/nfsd type nfsd (rw)
gvfs-fuse-daemon on /home/geeko/.gvfs type fuse.gvfs-fuse-daemon
 (rw,nosuid,nodev,user=geeko)
/dev/sdb1 on /media/disk type ext3 (rw,nosuid,nodev)
da1:~ #
```

You can also view this information in the /proc/mounts file.

Unmount a File System

Once a file system is mounted, you can use the umount command (without an "n") to unmount the file system. You can use umount with the device name or the mount point. For example, to unmount a CD file system mounted at /media/cdrecorder, you could enter one of the following:

umount /media/cdrecorder

umount /dev/sr0

To unmount the file system, no application or user may be using the file system. If it is being used, Linux sees the file system as being "busy" and will refuse to unmount the file system.

NOTE: To help determine the processes that are acting on a file or directory, you can use the fuser utility. For details, see Identify Processes Using Files (fuser).

One way to make sure the file system is not busy is to enter cd / at the shell prompt before using the umount command. This command takes you to the root of the file system.

However, there might be times when the system (kernel) still sees the file system as busy, no matter what you try to do. In these cases, you can enter umount -f to force the file system to unmount. However, we recommend using this only as a last resort, as there is probably a reason why the kernel thinks the file system is still busy.

Manage Swap Partitions

The memory available consists of physical RAM and virtual memory on the hard disk. In Linux systems, usually at least one swap partition is available to provide virtual memory.

The partition used for swapping has to be prepared with the mkswap command. Its syntax is `mkswap` *`device`*, such as `mkswap /dev/sdb5`.

The swapon command enables the swap partition in the system. The syntax is `swapon` *`device`*, such as `swapon /dev/sdb5`. To activate all swap partitions listed in the `/etc/fstab` file, enter `swapon -a`.

Swap partitions are deactivated with the `swapoff` command, such as `swapoff /dev/sdb5`. To deactivate all known swap devices, use the `swapoff -a` command.

Monitor and Check a File System

Once you set up and begin using your Linux file system, you can monitor the status and health of the system by doing the following from the command line:

- Check Partition and File Usage (df and du)
- Check Open Files (lsof)
- Identify Processes Using Files (fuser)
- Check and Repair File Systems (fsck)
- Use Additional Tools to Manage File Systems

Check Partition and File Usage (df and du)

The following commands help you monitor usage by partitions, files, and directories:

- **df.** Provides information on where hard drives and their partitions or other drives are mounted in the file system, and how much space they occupy.

  If you use the `df` command without parameters, the space available on all currently mounted file systems is displayed. If you provide a filename, `df` displays the space available on the file system this file resides in.

  Some useful options include `-h` (human readable format—in MB or GB), `-i` (list inode information instead of block usage), and `-l` (limit listing to local file systems).

  For example, to list information for all local file systems in human-readable format, you would enter `df -lh`.

- **du.** Provides information on the space occupied by files and directories.

  Some useful options include `-c` (display a grand total), `-h` (human-readable format), `-s` (display only a total for each argument), and `--exclude=`*`pattern`* (exclude files that match *pattern*).

  For example, to display information for files in human-readable format except for files that end in ".o", you would enter the following:

  ```
  du -h --exclude='*.o'
  ```

Check Open Files (lsof)

The `lsof` command lists open files. Entering `lsof` without any options lists all open files belonging to all active processes. An open file can be a regular file, directory, device file, library, stream, or network file (Internet socket, NFS file, or UNIX domain socket).

In addition to producing a single output list, lsof can run in repeat mode using the `-r` option. In this mode it outputs, delays, and then repeats the output operation until stopped with an interrupt or quit signal.

Some useful options include `-c` *x* (list only files starting with *x*), `-s` (display file sizes), and `-u` *x* (list only files for users who are *x*).

For example, to list open files for the users root and geeko only and include the file sizes, you would enter `lsof -s -u root,geeko`.

Identify Processes Using Files (fuser)

The `fuser` command displays the PIDs of processes using the specified files or file systems. In the default display mode, each filename is followed by a letter that describes the type of access:

- **c:** Current directory
- **e:** Executable being run
- **f:** Open file (omitted in default display mode)
- **r:** root directory
- **m:** Memory mapped file or shared library

A non-zero return code is displayed if none of the specified files is accessed or in the case of a fatal error. If at least one access has been found, fuser returns zero.

Some useful options include `-a` (return information for all files, even if they are not accessed by a process), `-v` (verbose mode), and `-u` (append the username of the process owner to each PID).

Another useful option is `-m`. To check the PID information for processes accessing files on the partition that holds `/home`, you would enter `fuser -m /home`.

Check and Repair File Systems (fsck)

Switching off the Linux system without unmounting partitions (for example, when a power outage occurs) can lead to errors in the file system.

The next time you boot the system, the fact that the computer was not shut down correctly is detected and a file system check is performed. If errors are found in the file system, they are corrected, if possible. If not, the computer does not start up properly and you are prompted to enter the root password, together with a hint on how to correct the issue. In cases of severe file system damage, you may even have to resort to the rescue system to repair the system.

The `fsck` command lets you check and optionally repair one or more Linux file systems. `fsck` is a front-end for the various file system checkers (`fsck.fstype`) available on the system. Depending on the file system type, these tools check the file system for a correct superblock (the block at the beginning of the partition containing information on the structure of the file system), faulty data blocks, or faulty allocation of data blocks.

If you do not specify a file system on the command line and do not specify the -A option, fsck defaults to checking file systems in /etc/fstab serially. Normally, fsck tries to run file systems on different physical disk drives in parallel to reduce the total amount of time to check all file systems.

To check a specific file system, use the following syntax:

```
fsck device
```

For example, if you wanted to check the file system on /dev/sda2, you would enter fsck /dev/sda2.

Some options that are available with fsck include -A (walk through the /etc/fstab file and try to check all the file systems in one pass), -N (don't execute, just show what would be done), and -V (verbose output). The fsck utility looks for the system-specific checker in /sbin/ first, then in /etc/fs/ and /etc/, and finally in the directories listed in the PATH environment variable.

The tool to repair ext2/3 file systems is fsck.ext2 (fsck.ext3 and e2fsck are hardlinks to this file). A possible problem in the ext2 (or ext3) file system is damage to the superblock. You can first view the location of all copies of the superblock in the file system using dumpe2fs. Then, with e2fsck, you can use one of the backup copies, as in the following:

```
e2fsck -f -b 32768 /dev/sda1
```

In this example, the superblock located at data block 32768 in the ext2 file system of the partition /dev/sda1 is used, and the primary superblock is updated appropriately upon completion of the file system check.

NOTE: With a block size of 4 KB, a backup copy of the superblock is stored every 32768 blocks.

The lost+found directory is a special feature of the ext2 and ext3 file system formats. After a system crash, Linux automatically carries out a check of the complete file system. Files or file fragments which a name can no longer be allocated to are not simply deleted but are stored in this directory.

By reviewing the contents of this directory, you can try to reconstruct the original name and purpose of a file.

With reiserfsck (or fsck.reiserfs, a hardlink to this file), the file system is subjected to a consistency check. The journal is checked to see if certain transactions need to be repeated. With the --fix-fixable option, errors such as wrong file sizes are fixed as soon as the file system is checked.

With an error in the binary tree, it is possible to have this rebuilt by entering reiserfsck --rebuild-tree.

Use Additional Tools to Manage File Systems

There are additional tools to administer various aspects of file systems:

- **tune2fs.** Used to adjust tunable file system parameters on ext2/ext3 file systems. Among these is how often (number of days or number of mounts) a file system check is done. It is also used to add a label to the file system or to add a journal to an ext2 file system, turning it into an ext3 file system.

- **reiserfstune.** Corresponding tool for ReiserFS. See the reiserfstune manual page for options and uses for this tool.

- **resize2fs** and **resize_reiserfs.** Used to shrink or enlarge an ext2/3 and ReiserFS, respectively. `resize_reiserfs` can enlarge ReiserFS online. Shrinking file systems as well as enlarging ext2/3 can be done only while the file system is unmounted.

NOTE: As stated before, when planning to manipulate partitions and file systems, back up your data first!

Set Up and Configure Disk Quotas

For system administrators, ensuring there is enough available drive space is a regular responsibility. When no limits are imposed, a user can easily fill up hard drive space with all kinds of data.

Linux includes a quota system that allows you to specify a specific amount of storage space each user or group may use and how many files users or groups may create. In SLES 11, you can use the quota package to enforce these limitations.

The following illustrates the quota architecture:

Figure 4-9   *Quotas*

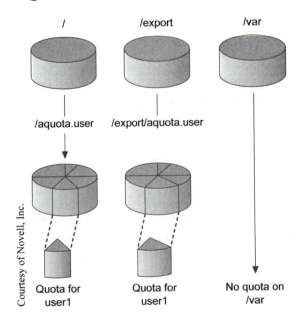

You can implement disk quotas for partitions configured with the ext2, ext3, Reiser, or XFS file systems.

Setting up and configuring the disk quota service on your system includes installing the package quota and the following tasks:

- Prepare the File System
- Initialize the Quota System
- Start and Activate the Quota Service
- Configure and Manage User and Group Quotas

Prepare the File System

When the system is started, the quotas for the file system must be activated. You can indicate for which file systems quotas are to be activated by configuring entries in the /etc/fstab file.

You enter the keyword **usrquota** for quotas on the user level and the keyword **grpquota** for group quotas, as in the following:

```
/dev/sda2   /           ext3    acl,user_xattr,usrquota,grpquota 1 1
/dev/sda1   swap        swap    defaults                    0 0
proc        /proc       proc    defaults                    0 0
...
```

In this example, quotas are configured for the file system / (root). Quotas are always defined for file systems (partitions).

If you have configured /etc/fstab without rebooting your system, you need to remount the file systems for which quotas have been defined. In the case of quotas for the partition holding the root file system, you do this by using the remount (-o) mount option as shown in the following:

```
mount -o remount /
```

Initialize the Quota System

After remounting, you need to initialize the quota system. You can do this by using the quotacheck command. This command checks the partitions with quota keywords in /etc/fstab to determine the already occupied data blocks and inodes, and stores the determined values in the aquota.user file (for user quotas) and aquota.group file (for group quotas).

NOTE: Up to kernel version 2.4, these files were called quota.user and quota.group and had to be created before quotacheck was run.

If you enter the quotacheck -avug command, all file systems with the usrquota or grpquota option in /etc/fstab (-a) are checked for data blocks and inodes that are occupied by users (-u) and groups (-g). The -v option provides a detailed output.

When checking mounted file systems, you might need to use the -m option to force the check.

Assuming the quota entries exist for /, after running quotacheck the following files are created:

```
da1:~ # ls -l /aquota* /export/aquota*
-rw-------  1 root root 9216 Aug 27 10:06 /aquota.group
-rw-------  1 root root 9216 Aug 27 10:06 /aquota.user
```

Start and Activate the Quota Service

In order for the quota system to be initialized when the system is booted, the appropriate links must be created in the runlevel directories by entering insserv boot.quota (insserv quotad for NFS). Runlevels and the insserv command are explained in detail in Understand System Initialization and Manage Runlevels.

You can then start the quota system by entering /etc/init.d/boot.quota start at the shell prompt. You can also start or stop the quota system by entering one of the following:

/sbin/quotaon *filesystem*
/sbin/quotaoff *filesystem*

You can use the -a option to activate and deactivate all automatically mounted file systems (except NFS) with quotas.

NOTE: For additional information on quotaon options, enter man quotaon at the shell prompt.

Configure and Manage User and Group Quotas

To configure quotas for users and groups, you need to know how to do the following:

■ Configure Soft and Hard Limits for Blocks and Inodes

■ Configure Grace Periods for Blocks and Inodes

■ Copy User Quotas

■ Generate a Quota Report

Configure Soft and Hard Limits for Blocks and Inodes

With the `edquota` command and the following options, you can edit the current quota settings for a user or group:

- `edquota -u` *user*: Sets up user quotas.

- `edquota -g` *group*: Sets up group quotas. All members of the group together share this quota.

The current settings are displayed in the vi editor for you to edit. You can edit the soft and hard limits. The values under blocks and inodes show the currently used blocks and inodes and are for information only; changing them has no effect.

For example, you can enter the following to configure quotas for the user geeko:

```
edquota -u geeko
```

After entering the command, the following quota information appears in vi:

```
Disk quotas for user geeko (uid 1001):
  Filesystem        blocks    soft     hard      inodes    soft     hard
  /dev/sda2           7820   10000    20000         145       0        0
```

The following describes the settings:

- **blocks:** How much hard disk space is currently used, with soft and hard limits listed.

    The values for blocks are given in blocks of 1 KB (independent of the block size of the file system).

    For example, the value 7820 indicates that the user geeko is currently using about 8 MB of hard drive space.

    Notice that the soft limit is set to 10 MB and the hard limit is set to 20 MB.

- **inodes:** How many files belong to the user on the file system, with soft and hard limits listed.

    Notice that the soft and hard limits for geeko are set to 0, which means that the user can create an unlimited number of files.

The soft limits indicate a quota that the user cannot permanently exceed. The hard limits indicate a boundary beyond which no more space or inodes can be used.

If users move beyond the soft limit, they have a fixed time available (a grace period) to free up space by deleting files or blocks.

If users exceed the grace period, they cannot create any new files until they delete enough files to get below the soft limit.

Configure Grace Periods for Blocks and Inodes

You can edit the grace periods in vi for blocks and inodes by entering `edquota -t`. A screen similar to the following appears:

```
Grace period before enforcing soft limits for users:
Time units may be: days, hours, minutes, or seconds
   Filesystem                 Block grace period     Inode grace period
   /dev/sda2                        7days                  7days
```

You can set the grace periods in days, hours, minutes, or seconds for a listed file system. However, you cannot specify a grace period for a specific user or group.

Copy User Quotas

You can copy user quotas from one user to another by using `edquota -p`. For example, by entering `edquota -p tux geeko`, you can copy the user quotas for the user tux to the user geeko.

Generate a Quota Report

The quota system files contain information in binary format about the space occupied by users and groups, and about which quotas are set up. You can display this information using the `repquota` command.

For example, entering `repquota -aug` displays a report similar to the following for all users and groups:

```
*** Report for user quotas on device /dev/sda2
Block grace time: 7days; Inode grace time: 7days
                        Block limits              File limits
User            used    soft    hard  grace    used  soft  hard  grace
--------------------------------------------------------------------------
root        -- 2646650     0       0           140161    0     0
geeko       +-   20000 10000   20000 7days        146    0     0
```

For additional details on using repquota, enter `man 8 repquota` at the shell prompt.

Exercise 4-5   *Manage Partitions and File Systems*

In this exercise, you practice creating partitions using `fdisk`. You also use command line tools to create and administer file systems and user quotas.

You will find this exercise at the end of the chapter.

(End of Exercise)

Configure the Network File System

Network File System (NFS) is used in Linux/UNIX environments to access files over the network. To provide access to files, you need to configure the NFS file server that gives users transparent access to data and programs files on the server. The client needs to be configured to mount the directories exported by the server.

To administer NFS successfully, you need to know the following:

- NFS Background

- NFS Server Configuration

- NFS Client Configuration

- NFS System Monitoring

NFS Background

In Linux and UNIX environments, NFS is a very reliable way to provide users with file access over the network. As a background to NFS, you need to understand the following:

- Network File System Basics

- How NFS Works

- NFSv4 Features

- NFS Configuration Overview

Network File System Basics

NFS is designed for sharing files and directories over a network, and it requires configuration of an NFS server (where the files and directories are located) and NFS clients (computers that access the files and directories remotely).

File systems are exported by an NFS server, and they appear and behave on an NFS client as if they were located on a local machine.

For example, each user's home directory can be exported by an NFS server and imported to a client, so the same home directories are accessible from every workstation on the network.

Directories like `/home/`, `/opt/`, and `/usr/` are good candidates for export via NFS. However, others—including `/bin/`, `/boot/`, `/dev/`, `/etc/`, `/lib/`, `/root/`, `/sbin/`, `/tmp/`, and `/var/`—should be available on the local disk only.

Using NFS for home directories makes sense only with central user management (for instance, OpenLDAP).

The following is an example of mounting the directory /home/ (exported by the NFS Server sun) on the computer earth:

Figure 4-10   *NFS*

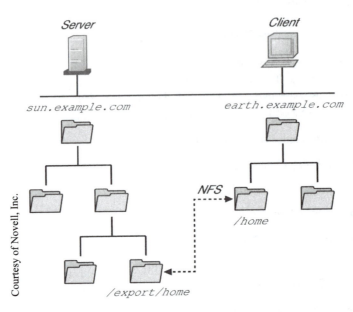

A computer can be both an NFS server and an NFS client. It can supply file systems over the network (export) and mount file systems from other hosts (import).

The NFS daemon is part of the kernel and only needs to be configured and then activated. The start script is /etc/init.d/nfsserver. The kernel NFS daemon includes file locking, which means that only one user at a time has write access to files.

How NFS Works

NFS is a Remote Procedure Call (RPC) service. An essential component for RPC services is rpcbind (previously called portmapper), which manages these services and needs to be started first. The rpcbind utility is activated by default on SLES 11.

When an RPC service starts up, it binds to a port in the system (as any other network service), but it also communicates this port and the service it offers (such as NFS) to rpcbind.

Because every RPC program must be registered by rpcbind when it is started, RPC programs must be restarted each time you restart rpcbind.

The following lists the services required on an NFS server:

Table 4-17   *Services Required by an NFS Server*

Service	Program (daemon)	Start Script
rpcbind utility	/sbin/rpcbind	/etc/init.d/rpcbind
NFS server v3	/usr/sbin/rpc.nfsd	/etc/init.d/nfsserver
	/usr/sbin/rpc.mountd	
	/usr/sbin/rpc.statd	
NFS server v4	Same as version 3 plus:	/etc/init.d/nfsserver
	NFSv4 ID <-> name mapping daemon, /usr/sbin/rpc.idmapd	
	If encryption is used, /usr/sbin/rpc.svcgssd (requires Kerberos)	

In SLES 11, the NFS lock manager is started automatically by the kernel. The /sbin/rpc.lockd program starts the NFS lock manager on kernels that do not start it automatically.

The manual pages for the respective programs contain additional information on their functionality.

You can use the /etc/init.d/nfsserver command to start the NFS server. The nfsserver script passes the list of exported directories to the kernel, and then starts or stops the daemon rpc.mountd and, using rpc.nfsd, the nfsd kernel threads.

The mount daemon (/usr/sbin/rpc.mountd) accepts each mount request and compares it with the entries in the configuration file /etc/exports. If access is allowed, the data is delivered to the client.

Because rpc.nfsd can start several kernel threads, the start script interprets the variable USE_KERNEL_NFSD_NUMBER in the file /etc/sysconfig/nfs. This variable determines the number of threads to start. By default, four server threads are started.

NFSv4 support is activated by setting the variable NFS4_SUPPORT to yes in /etc/sysconfig/nfs.

NFSv4 Features

NFS version 4 comes with several improvements compared to version 3. These include:

- The mount and lock protocol are now part of the NFS protocol, simplifying firewall rules for NFS. NFS uses TCP port 2049; UDP is no longer supported.

- Using Kerberos, it is possible to allow access on a per-user basis (version 3 was based only on IP addresses or DNS names).

- Encryption is part of the specification. While Secure-RPC allowed encryption with version 3, it was hardly ever used.

- Additional improvements concern the use of user@computername instead of numeric IDs to identify users, ACLs, and changes in the way files are locked.

NFS Configuration Overview

The /etc/exports file on the NFS server contains all settings regarding which directories are exported, how they are exported, and to which clients. Client-side configuration is written to the /etc/fstab file. Both files will be covered in detail later.

Some configuration parameters for the NFS server (for instance, if version 4 and encryption should be used) are specified in the /etc/sysconfig/nfs file.

Both the NFS server and the clients can be configured with YaST modules. You can also modify the configuration files directly.

For the NFS server to start automatically when the computer is booted, the corresponding symbolic links in the runlevel directories must be created. If you configure the NFS server with YaST, this is done automatically; otherwise, you need to create them with insserv nfsserver.

NFS Server Configuration

To provide file access with NFS, you need to be able to

- Configure an NFS Server

- Export a Directory Temporarily

Configure an NFS Server

SLES 11 provides a YaST module to configure an NFS server. The YaST NFS module is not covered in this course, but once you understand the manual NFS configuration as explained below, you won't have trouble figuring out how the YaST module works.

You can configure the server from the command line by doing the following:

- **Check for service (daemon) availability.** Make sure the nfs-kernel-server rpm package is installed on your NFS server.

- **Configure the services to start at bootup.** For services to be started by the /etc/init.d/rpcbind and /etc/init.d/nfsserver scripts when the system is booted, enter the following commands:

  insserv rpcbind (activated by default)

  insserv nfsserver

- **Define exported directories in /etc/exports.** One line is needed to define which computers using what permissions can access each directory that will be exported. All subdirectories of this directory are automatically exported as well.

The following is the general syntax of the /etc/exports file:

directory [*host*[(*option1*,*option2*,*option3*,...)]] ...

Do not put any spaces between the hostname, the parentheses enclosing the options, and the option strings themselves.

A host can be one of the following:

❑ A standalone computer with its name in short form (it must be possible to resolve this with name resolution), with its Fully Qualified Domain Name (FQDN) or its IP address.

❑ A network, specified by an address with a netmask, or by the domain name with a prefixed placeholder (such as ***.digitalairlines.com**).

Authorized computers are usually specified with their full names (including domain name), but you can use wildcards like * or ?.

If you do not specify a host or use *, any computer can import the file system with the given permissions.

■ **Set permissions for exported directories in /etc/exports.** You need to set permission options for the file system to export in parenthesis after the computer name. The most commonly used options include the following:

Table 4-18   *NFS Export Options*

Option	Meaning
bind=/path/directory	This is an NFS Version 4 option. On the server, this directory is mounted with the exported directory as mount point using the bind mount option. On the client, the content of the directory specified after bind= appears in the exported directory within the pseudo-root directory tree.
crossmnt	This is an NFS Version 4 option. If you use the bind=/path/directory option, the option crossmnt needs to be added to the line that contains the fsid=0 option. Without it, NFSv4 does not cross file systems.
fsid=0	This is an NFS Version 4 option. In version 4, the client is presented with one seamless directory tree. The option fsid=0 (or fsid=root, which is equivalent) indicates that this exported directory is the pseudo-root of that directory tree.
no_root_squash	Does not assign user ID 65534 to user ID 0, keeping the root permissions valid.
no_subtree_check	(Default since version 1.1.0 of nfs-utils) No subtree_check is performed. If you do not specify either subtree_check or no_subtree_check, a message informs you when starting the NFS server that no_subtree_check is used.
ro	File system is exported with read-only permission (default).

Option	Meaning
root_squash	(Default) This ensures that the root user of the client machine does not have root permissions on this file system. This is achieved by assigning user ID 65534 to users with user ID 0 (root). This user ID should be set to nobody (which is the default).
rw	File system is exported with read-write permission. The local file permissions are not overridden.
subtree_check	If a subdirectory of a file system is exported, but the whole file system is not, then whenever an NFS request arrives, the server must check not only that the accessed file is in the appropriate file system but also that it is in the exported tree. This check is called subtree check.
sync	Reply to requests only after the changes have been committed to stable storage (this is the default, but if neither sync nor async are specified, a warning appears when starting the NFS server).

The following is an example of an edited /etc/exports file for NFS version 3 that includes permissions:

```
#
# /etc/exports
#
/home          da10(rw,sync,no_subtree_check) \
                              da20(rw,sync,no_subtree_check)
/srv/ftp       *(ro,sync,no_subtree_check)
```

Whenever you want to specify different permissions for a subdirectory (such as /home/geeko/pictures/) from an already exported directory (such as /home/geeko/), the additional directory needs its own separate entry in /etc/exports.

The following is an example of an edited /etc/exports file for NFS version 4 that includes permissions:

```
#
# /etc/exports
#
/export    *(fsid=0,crossmnt,rw,sync,no_subtree_check)
/export/data *(ro,sync,no_subtree_check,bind=/data)
```

The /export and /data directories are separate on the server, whereas on the client, the content of both directories appears within one directory structure. If, for example, the client mounts the pseudo-root directory on /imports, the content of /data from the server appears in /imports/data on the client.

- **Reload the configuration.** The /etc/exports is read by mountd and nfsd. If you change anything in this file, you need to reload the configuration for your changes to take effect. You can do this by entering rcnfsserver reload (rcnfsserver restart works as well).

Export a Directory Temporarily

You can export a directory temporarily (without editing the file /etc/exports) by using the exportfs command:

For example, to read-only export the /software directory to all hosts in the network 192.168.0.0/24, you would enter the following command:

```
exportfs -o ro,root_squash,sync 192.168.0.0/24:/software
```

To restore the original state, all you need to do is enter the command exportfs -r. The /etc/exports file is reloaded and any directories not listed in the /etc/exports file are no longer exported.

After adding directories to export in the /etc/exports file, exportfs -a exports the additional directories.

The directories that are currently exported are listed in the /var/lib/nfs/etab file. The content of this file is updated when you use the command exportfs.

NFS Client Configuration

To configure and mount NFS directories, you need to know how to do the following:

- Import Directories Manually from an NFS Server
- Mount NFS Directories Automatically

Import Directories Manually from an NFS Server

You can import a directory manually from an NFS server by using the mount command. The only prerequisite is a running rpcbind (portmapper), which you can start by entering (as root) rcrpcbind start.

The mount command automatically tries to recognize the file system (such as ext2, ext3, or ReiserFS). However, you can also use the mount option -t to indicate the file system type. For NFS version 3 and earlier, the file system type is **nfs**; for NFS version 4, it is **nfs4**.

In the following example, the file system type nfs is specified:

```
mount -t nfs -o options host:/directory /mountpoint
```

Instead of a device file, the name of the NFS server together with the directory to import is used within the command.

The following are the most important mount options (-o) used with NFS:

- **soft (opposite: hard).** If the attempt to access the NFS server extends beyond the default number of tries (or the value set with the `retrans=` option), the mount attempt will be aborted.

  If the hard option (or neither soft nor hard) is specified, the client attempts to mount the exported directory until it receives feedback from the server that the attempt was successful.

  If a system tries to mount an NFS file system at boot time, the hard option can cause the boot process to hang because the process will stop at this point when it attempts to mount the NFS directory.

  For directories that are not essential for the system to function, you can use the soft option. For directories that must be mounted (such as home directories), you can use the hard option.

- **bg (default: fg).** If you use the bg option and the first attempt is unsuccessful, all further mount attempts are run in the background.

  This prevents the boot process from hanging when NFS exports are automatically mounted, with attempts to mount the directories continuing in the background.

- **rsize=***n*. Lets you set the number of bytes (*n*, positive integral multiple of 1024, maximum 1,048,576) that NFS reads from the NFS server at one time.

  If this value is not set, the client and server negotiate the highest possible value that they both support.

  The negotiated value is shown in /proc/mounts.

- **wsize=***n*. Lets you set the number of bytes (*n*, positive integral multiple of 1024, maximum 1,048,576) that can be written to the NFS server.

  If this value is not set, the client and server negotiate the highest possible value that they both support.

  The negotiated value is shown in /proc/mounts.

- **retry=***n*. Lets you set the number of minutes (*n*) an attempt can take to mount a directory through NFS. The default value for foreground mounts is two minutes; for background mounts, it is 10,000 minutes (approximately one week).

- **nosuid.** Lets you disable any interpretation of the SUID and SGID bits on the corresponding file system.

  For security reasons, always use this option for any file system that might be susceptible to tampering.

  If you do not use this option, a user could obtain root access to the local file system by putting a SUID root executable on the imported file system.

- **nodev.** Lets you disable any interpretation of device files in the imported file system. We recommend that you use this option for security reasons.

Without setting this option, someone could create a device such as /dev/sda on the NFS export and then use it to obtain write permissions for the hard disk as soon as the file can be accessed from the client side.

- **exec (opposite: noexec).** Lets you permit or disallow the execution of binaries on the mounted file system.

You can use the `umount` command to unmount a file system. However, you can do this only if the file system is currently not being accessed.

NOTE: For additional information on **nfs**, mount options, and the `/etc/fstab` file enter `man 5 nfs`, `man 8 mount`, or `man 5 fstab` in a terminal window.

Mount NFS Directories Automatically

To automatically mount directories (such as the home directories from a file server) when booting, you need to make corresponding entries in the `/etc/fstab` file.

When the system is booted, the `/etc/init.d/nfs` start script loads the `/etc/fstab` file, which indicates which file systems are mounted, where they are mounted, and with which options.

The following is an example of an entry for an NFS mount point in the `/etc/fstab` file:

```
da1:/training/home /home nfs soft,noexec 0 0
```

In this entry, the first value indicates the hostname of the NFS server (`da1`) and the directory it exports (`/training/home/`).

The second value indicates the mount point, which is the directory in the local file system where the exported directory should be attached (`/home/`).

The third value indicates the file system type (`nfs`). The comma-separated values following the file system type provide NFS-specific and general mounting options.

At the end of the line, there are two numbers (0 0). The first indicates whether to back up the file system with the help of dump (1) or not (0). The second number configures whether the file system check is disabled (0), done on this file system with no parallel checks (1), or parallelized when multiple disks are available on the computer (2).

In the example, the system does neither because both options are set to 0.

After modifying an entry of a currently mounted file system in the `/etc/fstab` file, you can have the system read the changes by entering `mount -o remount / mountpoint`. To mount all file systems that are not currently mounted and do not contain the option noauto, enter `mount -a`. (noauto is used with devices that are not automatically mounted, like floppy disks.)

NFS System Monitoring

Some tools are available to help you monitor the NFS system.

Enter `rpcinfo -p` to display information about rpcbind (portmapper). The option `-p` displays all the programs registered with the portmapper, similar to the following:

```
da10:~ # rpcinfo -p
program vers proto   port   service
    100000    4   tcp    111   portmapper
    100000    3   tcp    111   portmapper
    100000    2   tcp    111   portmapper
    100000    4   udp    111   portmapper
    100000    3   udp    111   portmapper
    100000    2   udp    111   portmapper
    100005    1   udp  42763   mountd
    100005    1   tcp  49450   mountd
    100005    2   udp  42763   mountd
    100005    2   tcp  49450   mountd
    100005    3   udp  42763   mountd
    100005    3   tcp  49450   mountd
    100024    1   udp  41731   status
    100024    1   tcp  53770   status
    100003    2   udp   2049   nfs
    100003    3   udp   2049   nfs
    100003    4   udp   2049   nfs
    100021    1   udp  46880   nlockmgr
    100021    3   udp  46880   nlockmgr
    100021    4   udp  46880   nlockmgr
    100003    2   tcp   2049   nfs
    100003    3   tcp   2049   nfs
    100003    4   tcp   2049   nfs
    100021    1   tcp  53206   nlockmgr
    100021    3   tcp  53206   nlockmgr
    100021    4   tcp  53206   nlockmgr
```

The NFS server daemon registers itself to the portmapper with the name nfs. The NFS mount daemon uses the name mountd.

You can use the `showmount` command to display information about the exported directories of an NFS server.

`showmount -e da1` displays the directories exported on the machine da1. The option `-a` shows which computers have mounted which directories.

Exercise 4-6 **Set Up and Manage Network File System (NFS)**

In this exercise, you set up an NFS server, and connect to the server with an NFS client.

You will find this exercise at the end of the chapter.

(End of Exercise)

Objective 6   Manage Backup and Restore

One of the key tasks that you must perform as a SLES 11 administrator is to ensure that the data on the systems you are responsible for is protected. One of the best ways that you can do this is to back up the data on a regular basis. Having a backup creates a redundant copy of important system data so that if a disaster occurs, the information can be restored.

To back up and restore data successfully, you need to

- Develop a Backup Strategy
- Create Backups with tar
- Copy Data with dd
- Mirror Directories with rsync
- Use cpio to Copy Files
- Use dump and restore for Backups
- Copy Files to Removable Media
- Create Backup Files with tar
- Create Drive Images with dd
- Back Up a Home Directory with rsync

Develop a Backup Strategy

Remember that the data on your Linux system is usually stored on hard drives, which are mechanical devices. Hard drives use electrical motors, spinning platters, and other moving parts that gradually wear out over time.

All hard drives have a Mean Time Before Failure (MTBF) value assigned to them by the manufacturer. This value provides an estimate of how long a given drive will last before it fails. Remember, with hard drives, it's not a matter of *if* a hard drive will fail, but a matter of *when*.

In addition to hard drive failures, there is always the possibility that one or more of the following will occur:

- Users delete files by accident.
- A virus deletes important files.
- A notebook system gets lost or destroyed.
- An attacker deletes data on a server.
- Natural disasters, such as thunderstorms, generate electrical spikes that destroy storage systems.

Because of these factors, it is very important that you regularly back up important data. In this section, you learn how to do this. Before you can actually back up data, you first need to develop a backup strategy by doing the following:

- Choosing a Backup Method

- Choosing a Backup Media
- Defining a Backup Schedule
- Determining What to Back Up

Choosing a Backup Method

The first step in developing a backup strategy is to select the type of backups you will use. The following options are available:

- Full Backup
- Incremental Backup
- Differential Backup

Full Backup

The first option is to run a full backup. In a full backup, all specified files are backed up to your backup media, regardless of whether they have been modified since the last backup. After being backed up, each file is flagged as having been backed up.

This strategy is thorough and exhaustive. It's also the fastest option when you need to restore data from a backup.

The disadvantage, however, is that full backups can take a very long time to complete because every single file is backed up, whether it has been changed or not.

Incremental Backup

Because of the amount of time require to complete full backups, many administrators mix full backups with incremental backups. During an incremental backup, only the files that have been modified since the last backup (full *or* incremental) are backed up. After being backed up, each file is flagged as having been backed up.

If you use a full/incremental strategy, you normally run a full backup only once a week. This is usually done when the system load is lightest, such as Friday night. Then you run incremental backups each of the other six days in the week. Using this strategy, you end up with one full backup and six incremental backups for each week.

The advantage of this strategy is primarily speed. Because incrementals back up only files that have changed since the last full or incremental backup, they generally run much faster than full backups.

However, incremental backups do have a drawback. If you need to restore data from the backup set, you must restore up to six backups in exactly the correct order. The full backup is restored first, followed by the first incremental, then the second incremental, and so on. This can be a relatively slow process.

Differential Backup

As an alternative to incremental backups, you can also combine *differential* backups with your full backup. During a differential backup, only the files that have been modified since the last full backup are backed up. Even though they have been backed up during a previous differential backup, the files involved are *not* flagged as having been backed up.

You must use differential backups in conjunction with full backups. Again, you usually run a full backup once a week when the system load is lightest. Then you run a differential backup each of the other nights of the week. Remember that a differential backup backs up only files that have changed since the last full backup, not since the last differential. Therefore, each day's backup gets progressively bigger.

The main advantage to this strategy is that restores are really fast. Instead of the up to seven backups required to restore from a full/incremental backup, you have to restore only two backups when using full/differential backups: the last full backup followed by the last differential backup.

The disadvantage to this method is that the differential backups start out running very fast, but can become almost as long as a full backup by the time you reach the last day in the cycle.

NOTE: Do not mix incremental and differential backups together! Your backups will lose data.

The following illustrates the difference between incremental and differential backups:

Figure 4-11   *Sizes of a Full Backup and Incremental or Differential Backups*

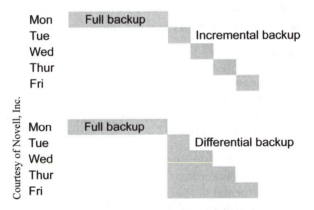

Choosing a Backup Media

Once you have selected your backup strategy, you next need to select your backup media type. You must choose an appropriate backup media for the amount of data to be backed up.

Tape drives are commonly used by Linux administrators because they have the best price-to-capacity ratio. Most tape drives are SCSI devices. This allows multiple types of tape drives (such as DAT, EXABYTE, and DLT) to be accessed in the same way. In addition, tapes can be easily rotated and reused.

Other options for data backup include writable DVDs, removable hard drives, and magneto-optical (MO) drives.

Another option is a Storage Area Network (SAN). With a SAN, a storage network is set up to back up data exclusively from different computers on a central backup server. But even a SAN often uses magnetic tapes to store the data.

Backup media should always be stored separately from the backed-up systems. This prevents the backups from being lost in case of a fire or other natural disaster in the server room. We recommend that you keep a copy of your sensitive backup media stored safely offsite.

Defining a Backup Schedule

Next, you need to define when you will run your backups. You can select whatever backup schedule works best for your organization. However, many Linux admins work on a weekly rotation, as discussed previously. Identify one day for your full backup and then designate the remaining days of the week for your incremental or differential backups.

As stated earlier, you should schedule your backups to occur when the load on the system is at its lightest. Late at night or in the early morning is usually best, depending on your organization's work schedule.

You should also be sure to keep a rotation of backups. We recommend that you rotate your backup media such that you have three to four weeks of past backups on hand. That way, if a file that was deleted two weeks ago is suddenly needed again, you can restore it from one of your rotated media sets.

Determining What to Back Up

Finally, you need to determine what data you will include in your backups. One option is to back up the entire system. This is a safe, thorough option. However, it is also somewhat slow due to the sheer amount of data involved.

Another option is to back up only critical data on the system, such as users' files and the system configuration information. In the event of a disaster, you can simply reinstall a new system and then restore the critical data to it from your backups.

If you choose this strategy, then you should consider backing up the following directories in the Linux file system:

- /etc
- /root
- /home
- /var
- /opt
- /srv

Create Backups with tar

The tar (tape archiver) tool is the most commonly used application for data backup on Linux systems. It archives files in a special format, either directly on a backup medium (such as magnetic tape or floppy disk) or to an archive file in the file system.

To use tar, you need to be familiar with the following tasks:

- Creating tar Archives
- Unpacking tar Archives
- Excluding Files from Backup
- Performing Incremental and Differential Backups
- Using tar Command Line Options

Creating tar Archives

The tar format is a container format for files and directory structures. By convention, the extension of the archive files end in `.tar`. tar archives can be saved to a file and stored in a file system. They can also be written directly to a backup tape.

Normally the data in the archive files is not compressed, but you can enable compression with additional compression commands. If archive files are compressed (usually with the gzip command), then the extension of the filename is either `.tar.gz` or `.tgz`.

The syntax for using tar is as follows:

```
tar options archive_file_name directory_to_be_backed_up
```

You can also use

```
tar options tape_device_file_name
directory_to_be_backed_up
```

All directories and files under the specified directory are included in the archive. For example:

```
tar -cvf /backup/etc.tar /etc
```

In this example, the tar command backs up the complete contents of the `/etc` directory to the `/backup/etc.tar` file.

The `-c` option (create) creates the archive. The `-v` option (verbose) displays a more detailed output of the backup process. The name of the archive to be created is entered after the `-f` option (file).

This can be either a normal file or a device file (such as a tape drive), as in the following:

```
tar -cvf /dev/st0 /home
```

In this example, the `/home` directory is backed up to the tape drive `/dev/st0`.

When an archive is created, absolute paths are made relative by default. This means that the leading / is removed, as shown in the following output:

```
tar: Removing leading  /  from member names
```

You can view the contents of an archive by entering the following:

```
tar -tvf /backup/etc.tar
```

Unpacking tar Archives

Once you've created your archives, you can then use tar to also extract (unpack) files from the archive. To do this, use the following syntax:

```
tar -xvf device_or_file_name
```

For example:

```
tar -xvf /dev/st0
```

This writes all files in the archive to the current directory. Due to the relative path specifications in the tar archive, the directory structure of the archive is created here.

If you want to extract to another directory, use the -C option followed by the directory name. If you want to extract a specific file, list the file in the command as in the following example:

```
tar -xvf /test1/backup.tar home/user1/.bashrc
```

To restore the file to its original location, either run this command with / as current directory, or add the -C / option to the above command.

Excluding Files from Backup

If you want to exclude certain files from the backup, you can create a list of these files in an exclude file. Each excluded file is listed on its own line, as shown in the following:

```
/home/user1/.bashrc
/home/user2/Text*
```

In this example, the /home/user1/.bashrc file from user1 and all files that begin with Text in the home directory of user2 will be excluded from the backup. This list is then passed to tar with the -X option, as in the following:

```
tar -cv -X excluded_files -f /dev/st0 /home
```

Performing Incremental and Differential Backups

With `tar`, you can approximate an incremental or differential backup by backing up only files that have been changed or newly created since a specific date. This can be done using either of the following options:

- Use a Snapshot File for Incremental Backups
- Use find to Create a Differential Backup

Use a Snapshot File for Incremental Backups

`tar` lets you use a snapshot file that contains information about the last backup process. This file needs to be specified with the `-g` option.

First, you need to make a full backup with a tar command, as in the following:

```
tar -cz -g /backup/snapshot_file -f /backup/
backup_full.tar.gz /home
```

In this example, the `/home` directory is backed up to the `/backup/backup_full.tar.gz` file. The snapshot `/backup/snapshot_file` file does not exist and is created.

You can then perform an incremental backup the next day using the following command:

```
tar -cz -g /backup/snapshot_file -f /backup/
backup_mon.tar.gz /home
```

In this example, tar uses the snapshot file to determine which files or directories have changed since the last backup. Only changed files are included in the new backup `/backup/backup_mon.tar.gz`.

Use find to Create a Differential Backup

You can also use the `find` command to identify files that need to be backed up as a differential backup. First, you use the following command to make a full backup:

```
tar -czf /backup/backup_full.tar.gz /home
```

In this example, the /home directory is backed up into the `/backup/backup_full.tar.gz` file. Then you can use the following command (all on one line) to back up all files that are newer than the full backup:

```
find /home -type f -newer /backup/backup_full.tar.gz
-print0 | tar --null -cvf /backup/backup_mon.tar.gz -T -
```

In this example, all files (`-type f`) in the `/home` directory that are newer than the `/backup/backup_mon.tar.gz` file are archived.

The `-print0` and `--null` options ensure that files with spaces in their names are also archived. The `-T` option determines that file names piped to stdin are included in the archive.

One problem with the previous command line might be caused by its long execution time when you have to back up a lot of data. If a file is created or changed after the backup command is started but before the backup is completed, this file is older than the reference backup archive but at the same time is not included in this archive.

This could lead to a situation where the file is not backed up in the next differential backup, because only the files which are newer than the reference archive are included. Instead of the previous backup archive, you can also create a file with the touch command and use this file as reference in the find/tar command line.

Using tar Command Line Options

The following are several useful tar command line options:

Table 4-19 *tar Options*

Options	Description
-c	Creates an archive.
-C	Changes to the specified directory.
-d	Compares files in the archive with those in the file system.
-f	Uses the specified archive file or device.
-j	Directly compresses or decompresses the tar archive using bzip2, a modern, efficient compression program.
-r	Appends files to an archive.
-u	Includes only those files in an archive that are newer than the version in the archive (update).
-v	Displays the files which are being processed (verbose mode).
-x	Extracts files from an archive.
-X *file*	Excludes files listed in a file.
-z	Directly compresses or decompresses the tar archive using gzip.

NOTE: For more information about tar, enter man tar at the shell prompt.

Copy Data with dd

The dd command is a special file management command that you can use at the command line with SLES 11.

You can use the dd command to convert and copy files byte-wise. Normally dd reads from the standard input and writes the result to the standard output. But with the appropriate parameters, regular files can be addressed as well.

You can copy all kinds of Linux data with this command, including entire hard disk partitions. You can even copy an entire installed system (or just parts of it).

A file can be copied with the dd utility using the following command:

```
dd if=/etc/protocols of=protocols.orig
```

The output of dd during the copying process is shown below:

```
12+1 records in
12+1 records out
```

Use the if= (input file) option to specify the file to be copied, and the of= (output file) option to specify the name of the copy.

The dd utility copies files in this way using records. The default size for a record is 512 bytes. The output shown above indicates that 12 complete records of the standard size and an incomplete record (that is, less than 512 bytes) were copied.

If the record size is modified by the bs=*block_size* option, then the output will also be modified. An example is shown below:

```
da1:~ # dd if=/etc/protocols of=protocols.old bs=1
6561+0 records in
6561+0 records out
```

A file listing shows that their sizes are identical:

```
da1:~ # ls -l protocols*
-rw-r--r-- 1 root root 6561 Apr 30 11:28 protocols
-rw-r--r-- 1 root root 6561 Apr 30 11:30 protocols.old
```

If you want to copy a complete partition, then the corresponding device file of the partition should be given as the input, as in the following:

```
dd if=/dev/sda1 of=boot.partition
```

In this example, the entire /dev/sda1 partition is written to the boot.partition file.

You can also use dd to create a backup copy of the master boot record (MBR) and the partition table. For example:

```
dd if=/dev/sda of=/tmp/mbr_copy bs=512 count=1
```

In this example, a copy of the MBR is created from the hard disk /dev/sda and is written to the /tmp/mbr_copy file.

Mirror Directories with rsync

In addition to the utilities discussed previously in this section, you can also use the rsync (remote synchronization) utility to back up data from your SLES 11 system.

The rsync utility is actually designed to create copies of entire directories across a network to a different computer. As such, rsync is an ideal tool to back up data across the network to the file system of a remote computer or to a locally connected USB drive.

It is important to note that rsync works in a very different manner than the other backup utilities we have been discussing. Instead of creating an archive file, rsync creates a mirror copy of the data being backed up in the file system of the destination device.

A key benefit of using rsync is that, when coping data, rsync compares the source and the target directory and transfers only data that has changed or has been created. Therefore, the first time rsync is run, all of the data is copied. Thereafter, only files that have been changed or newly created in the source directory are copied to the target directory.

In this objective, you learn how to use rsync in two different ways:

- Using rsync to Create a Local Backup

- Using rsync to Create a Remote Backup

Using rsync to Create a Local Backup

The `rsync` utility can be used to create a local backup. The mirrored target directory could reside in the same file system as the source directory, or it could reside on a removable device such as a USB or Firewire hard drive.

For example, you could mirror all home directories by entering the following at the shell prompt:

```
rsync -a /home /shadow
```

In this example, the `/home` directory is mirrored to the `/shadow` directory.

The `/home` directory is first created in the `/shadow` directory, and then the actual home directories of the users are created under `/shadow/home`.

If you want to mirror the content of a directory and not the directory itself, you can use a command such as the following:

```
rsync -a /home/ /shadow
```

By adding a `/` to the end of the source directory, only the data under `/home` is copied. If you run the same command again, only files that have changed or are new since the last time rsync was run will be transferred.

The `-a` option used in the examples above puts rsync into archive mode. Archive mode is a combination of various other options (namely `rlptgoD`) and ensures that the characteristics of the copied files are identical to the originals.

The `-a` option ensures the following are preserved in the mirrored copy of the directory:

- Symbolic links (`l` option)

- Access permissions (`p` option)

- Owners (`o` option)

- Group membership (`g` option)

- Time stamp (`t` option)

In addition, the -a option incorporates the -r option, which ensures that subdirectories are copied recursively.

The following are some other useful rsync options:

Table 4-20 *rsync Options*

Option	Description
-a	Puts rsync into the archive mode.
-x	Saves files on one file system only, which means that rsync does not follow symbolic links to other file systems.
-v	Enables the verbose mode. Use this mode to output information about the transferred files and the progress of the copying process.
-z	Compresses the data during the transfer. This is especially useful for remote synchronization.
--delete	Deletes files from the mirrored directory that no longer exist in the original directory.
--exclude-from	Does not back up files listed in an exclude file.

The last option can be used as follows:

```
rsync -a --exclude-from=/home/exclude /home/ /shadow/home
```

In this example, all files listed in the /home/exclude file are not backed up. Empty lines in this file or lines beginning with ; or # are ignored.

Using rsync to Create a Remote Backup

Using rsync and SSH, you can log in to other systems over the network and perform data synchronization remotely. For example, the following command copies the home directory of the tux user to a backup server:

```
rsync -ave ssh root@da1:/home/tux /backup/home/
```

In this example, the -e option specifies the remote shell (ssh) that should be used for the transmission (as ssh is the default used, you would only have to specify the -e option if you wanted to use some other shell). The source directory is specified by the expression root@da1:/home/tux. This means that rsync should log in to da1 as root and transfer the /home/tux directory.

Of course, this also works in the other direction. In the following example, the backup of the home directory is copied back to the da1 system:

```
rsync -ave ssh /backup/home/tux root@da1:/home/
```

NOTE: rsync must be installed on both the source and the target computer for this to work.

Another way to perform remote synchronization with rsync is to employ an rsync server. This allows you to use remote synchronization without allowing an SSH login.

NOTE: For more information, consult the rsync documentation at http://samba.anu.edu.au/rsync/ (http://samba.anu.edu.au/rsync/).

Use cpio to Copy Files

`cpio` stores files in archives, similar to `tar`. To copy files into an archive, a list of filenames is read from standard input (which can be redirected to a file). The output is written to standard output.

```
cpio -o < filelist > archive
```

The option `-o` (or `--create`) copies the files to the archive.

To extract the files from the archive, use

```
cpio -i < archive
```

If you only want to list the files in the archive, use the options `-it`.

An example for the use of `cpio` is the initial ramdisk which may be used during startup of the system (see Initial RAM File System).

Use dump and restore for Backups

`dump` and `restore` are not part of SLES 11. The commands are included in the manual as dump is mentioned in Configuration File for Mounting File Systems regarding the fifth field of the `/etc/fstab` file.

The `dump` command is used to back up ext2/ext3 file systems automatically and with different backup levels (full backup or incremental backups). A dump that is larger than the output medium is broken into multiple volumes. The syntax of the `dump` command is

```
dump options files-to-dump
```

files-to-dump is either a mountpoint of a file system or a list of files and directories to be backed up. More often used options are

- **-level.** The dump level (any integer). A level 0 (`-0`, full backup) guarantees the entire file system is copied. A level number above 0 (incremental backup) tells dump to copy all files new or modified since the last dump of a lower level. The default level is 9.

- **-D** *file.* Set the path name of the file storing the information about the previous full and incremental dumps. The default location is `/var/lib/dumpdates`.

- **-f** *file.* Write the backup to *file*; *file* may be a special device file like `/dev/st0` (a tape drive), an ordinary file, or `-` (the standard output).

For automatic backups, `dump` checks the `/etc/fstab` file to determine which file systems should be included in the backup. All file systems whose fifth field in /

etc/fstab contains a 1 will be backed up. Those containing a 0 in the fifth field will not be backed up.

The restore command is used to work with backups created with the dump command. Important options are

- **-C.** Compare the files in the backup with the files on the disk.

- **-i.** Do an interactive restoration of the files from the dump. This starts a shell-like interface and prompts for information.

- **-r.** Restore (rebuild) the file system, starting with the original level 0 backup. This will overwrite everything on the file system!

- **-t.** List the named files if they are in the backup. This can be used with the -X *filelist* option.

- **-x.** Extract the listed files from the backup. This can be used with the -X *filelist* option.

- **-f** *file*. Use the given filename to read the backup from.

Copy Files to Removable Media

Although backups are normally done using either hard disks or tapes, it is also possible to write files to removable media like recordable CDs or DVDs. The best way to do so is by using graphical applications, such as *k3b* or the *Nautilus* file manager.

To write data to optical media, you first have to create an ISO9660 image. To do so, use the genisoimage command (which is a fork of the mkisofs command). You have to specify the name of the ISO file to be created and the path to the directory containing all files and subdirectories which will be copied into the ISO file:

```
genisoimage -R -o /tmp/home-backup.iso /home
```

This will create an ISO image with Rock Ridge extensions.

To write this image to a CD (or DVD), the wodim command (which is based on a source code fork from the cdrecord sources) is used:

```
wodim dev=/dev/dvd /tmp/home-backup.iso
```

The dev= option defines which device to use. This can be either the name (as in this example) or the number of the device (e.g., for a device with SCSI ID 2 on the primary SCSI bus, it would be dev=2, 0).

Exercise 4-7   ***Create Backup Files with tar***

In this exercise, you use tar to create a full backup and an incremental backup.

You will find this exercise at the end of the chapter.

(End of Exercise)

Exercise 4-8   ***Create Drive Images with dd***

In this exercise, you use dd to create a drive image from an optical disk.

You will find this exercise at the end of the chapter.

(End of Exercise)

Exercise 4-9   ***Back Up a Home Directory with rsync***

In this exercise, you use rsync to back up a user's home directory.

You will find this exercise at the end of the chapter.

(End of Exercise)

Objective 7   Manage Hardware

Although most hardware devices can be configured with YaST and are automatically detected when plugged into the system, you should understand how devices are managed in background, and know the command line tools related to hardware management.

In this objective, you learn how SLES 11 handles hardware and device drivers. You also learn how to add and replace certain types of hardware.

- Describe How Device Drivers Work in Linux
- Gather Hardware Information
- Manage Kernel Modules
- Describe How udev Works
- Coldplug vs. Hotplug Hardware
- Manage Linux Kernel Modules and udev Rules

Describe How Device Drivers Work in Linux

To manage hardware in Linux, you first must understand how device drivers work. You need to understand

- The Difference Between Devices and Interfaces
- How Device Drivers Work
- How Device Drivers Are Loaded

The Difference Between Devices and Interfaces

To understand how Linux handles hardware, you must first understand the difference between the terms **device** and **interface**. These terms are often confused by users, administrators, and even software developers. This course uses the following definitions:

- **Device:** A device is a physical piece of hardware, such as a PCI network card, an AGP graphic adapter, or a USB printer.
- **Interface:** An interface is a software component associated with a device. To be used, a physical piece of hardware must be accessed by a software interface. A device can have more than one interface.

How Device Drivers Work

Interfaces are usually created by a driver. In Linux, a driver is usually a software module that can be loaded into the Linux kernel. A driver can be thought of as the "glue" between a device and its interfaces. Device drivers access and use a device.

There are two basic kinds of device drivers:

- **Kernel modules:** The functionality of the Linux kernel can be extended by adding kernel modules. They allow the kernel to provide access to hardware and can be loaded or removed at runtime.

- **User space drivers:** Some hardware needs additional drivers that work in user space. Examples of this kind of hardware include printers or scanners.

The following figure illustrates the roles of kernel and user space drivers:

Figure 4-12   *Kernel Module and User Space Driver*

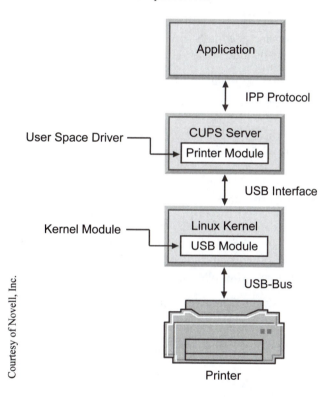

How Device Drivers Are Loaded

There are several methods used to load kernel modules automatically. The following is an overview of how device drivers are loaded in SLES 11:

- **initrd.** Important device drivers that are necessary to access the root partition are loaded from initrd, which is a special file that is loaded into memory by the boot loader. Examples of such modules are SCSI host controller and file system drivers.

- **Init scripts.** Some of the init scripts in /etc/init.d/ are used to load and set up hardware devices. For example, the ALSA sound script is used to load drivers for sound cards.

- **udev.** Used to load kernel modules.

- **X Server.** Although graphics card drivers are not kernel modules, the X Server loads special drivers to enable hardware 3D support.

- **Manually.** You can load kernel modules from the command line or in scripts using the `modprobe` command.

Gather Hardware Information

To find out what hardware is built into a computer, you can take a screwdriver, open the case, and have a look. In practice this is not always feasible (when the machine is hosted in a data center, for instance) and even if it is, you might not get all the information you need, because you can't look inside the chips.

Using the tools included in SLES 11 to gather hardware information is much more efficient. These include

- The hwinfo Command

- The lspci Command

- The lsusb Command

- The sysfs and procfs File Systems

The hwinfo Command

The `hwinfo` command gives a very comprehensive overview on the hardware built into a system. It probes the system hardware and generates a system overview report. Without options, hwinfo produces a very long report, but you can limit the report to single subsystems. The following options can be used with the hwinfo command:

- **--help.** Lists the available options.

- **--hwitem.** Probes for a specific item of hardware. Replace ***hwitem*** with one of the items listed in the output of `hwinfo --help`, such as `hwinfo --usb`:

```
da1:~ # hwinfo --usb
03: SCSI 600.0: 10600 Disk
  [Created at block.243]
  UDI: /org/freedesktop/Hal/devices/
storage_serial_WDC_WD80_0BEVS_00RST0_WDC_WD800B_WD_WXEY07V88988_0
_0
  Unique ID: R_O4.3K897PTdhjB
  SysFS ID: /class/block/sdb
  SysFS BusID: 6:0:0:0
...
```

- **--short:** Displays a summary listing:

```
da1:~ # hwinfo --short
cpu:
                        Intel(R) Core(TM)2 CPU 6600  @ 2.40GHz, 1596 MHz
                        Intel(R) Core(TM)2 CPU 6600  @ 2.40GHz, 1596 MHz
keyboard:
  /dev/input/event0    AT Translated Set 2 keyboard
mouse:
  /dev/input/mice      ImPS/2 Logitech Wheel Mouse
monitor:
                        Generic Monitor
graphics card:
                        Intel 965Q
...
```

- --log *file_name*. Writes the output from hwinfo to the specified log file.

The lspci Command

The output of the `lspci` command lists all Peripheral Component Interconnect (PCI) devices. The `-k` option lists the kernel modules associated with the device:

```
da-host:~ # lspci -k
00:00.0 Host bridge: Intel Corporation 82Q963/Q965 Memory Controller
Hub (rev 02)
        Kernel driver in use: agpgart-intel
        Kernel modules: intel-agp
00:02.0 VGA compatible controller: Intel Corporation 82Q963/Q965
Integrated Graphics Controller (rev 02)
00:03.0 Communication controller: Intel Corporation 82Q963/Q965 HECI
Controller (rev 02)
00:03.2 IDE interface: Intel Corporation 82Q963/Q965 PT IDER
Controller (rev 02)
00:03.3 Serial controller: Intel Corporation 82Q963/Q965 KT
Controller (rev 02)
        Kernel driver in use: serial
00:19.0 Ethernet controller: Intel Corporation 82566DM Gigabit
Network Connection (rev 02)
        Kernel driver in use: e1000e
        Kernel modules: e1000e
...
```

With the `-v` option the output for each device is more verbose. Use the `--help` option to get an overview on the options available or `man hwinfo` for a more detailed description of the command.

The lsusb Command

The `lsusb` command lists the USB devices. Use the `-v` option to obtain more detailed information on each device:

```
da1:~ # lsusb -v

Bus 007 Device 001: ID 1d6b:0001 Linux Foundation 1.1 root hub
Device Descriptor:
  bLength                 18
  bDescriptorType          1
  bcdUSB                1.10
  bDeviceClass             9 Hub
  bDeviceSubClass          0 Unused
  bDeviceProtocol          0 Full speed (or root) hub
  bMaxPacketSize0         64
  idVendor            0x1d6b Linux Foundation
  idProduct           0x0001 1.1 root hub
  bcdDevice             2.06
  iManufacturer            3 Linux 2.6.27.19-5-pae uhci_hcd
  iProduct                 2 UHCI Host Controller
  iSerial                  1 0000:00:1d.2
  bNumConfigurations       1
...
```

Use the `--help` option to view the options available or `man lsusb` for a more detailed description of the command.

The sysfs and procfs File Systems

Both the sysfs and the procfs file systems are virtual file systems mounted under `/sys/` and `/proc/`, respectively. In a virtual file system there is no physical device that holds the information. Instead, the file system is generated virtually by the kernel. However, you can view the contents of the files within `/proc/` using standard Linux shell commands such as `cat`, `more`, and `less`.

To get information from sysfs and procfs, you need to understand

- The /sys/ Directory
- The /proc/ Directory

The /sys/ Directory

sysfs is a mechanism to export information from the kernel to user processes. Kernel objects, their attributes, and their relationships are represented by directories, files and symbolic links, respectively. In fact, the tools introduced above take most of the information they display from files in the sysfs.

The top level of the `/sys` directory contains a number of directories. The most important of these are described below:

- **/sys/block**. This directory contains an entry for each block device that has been discovered in the system. In SLES 11, these entries are all symbolic links to entries in the `/sys/devices/` directory. Each partition of the block device is represented as a subdirectory.

- **/sys/bus**. Each physical bus type is represented by a subdirectory in this directory. Examples include isa, pci, scsi, and usb. Each bus type has two subdirectories: devices and drivers. The devices subdirectory contains entries for every device discovered on that type of bus. These entries are actually symbolic links pointing to entries in the /sys/devices/ directory. The drivers directory contains subdirectories for each driver for this bus type (such as usb, usb-storage, and usbfs for the usb bus).

- **/sys/class**. This directory contains all device classes that are available. A device class describes a functional type of device, such as graphics, net, or pci_bus. Again, all entries in these subdirectories are symbolic links to entries in the /sys/devices directory.

- **/sys/devices**. The global device hierarchy is contained in this directory—every physical device that has been discovered is represented here. Each device is shown as a subordinate device of the device that it is physically (electrically) connected to.

- **/sys/module**. This directory contains subdirectories for each module that is loaded into the kernel. The name of each directory is the name of the module. Depending on the module, there are different numbers of files located in the directory.

You could use sysfs, for instance, to establish the size of the partition /dev/sda2 using the following command:

```
da1:~ # cat /sys/block/sda/sda2/size
83891430
```

This partition has a size of 83891430 512-byte blocks (about 40 GB). To find out where this information is actually located, you could proceed as follows:

```
da1:~ # cd /sys/block/sda/sda2/
da1:/sys/block/sda/sda2 # ls
dev  holders  power  size  start  stat  subsystem  uevent
da1:/sys/block/sda/sda2 # /bin/pwd
/sys/devices/pci0000:00/0000:00:1f.2/host2/target2:0:0/2:0:0:0/
block/sda/sda2
da1:/sys/block/sda/sda2 #
```

The /bin/pwd command prints the fully resolved name of the current directory, without symbolic links (pwd -P would do the same).

The /proc/ Directory

The /proc/ directory contains a great deal of information about the running SLES 11 system, including hardware information stored in the kernel memory space.

For example, if you enter cat /proc/cpuinfo, output is generated from data stored in kernel memory that displays information such as the CPU model name and cache size. An example is shown below:

```
da1:~ # cat /proc/cpuinfo
processor       : 0
vendor_id       : GenuineIntel
cpu family      : 6
model           : 15
model name      : Intel(R) Core(TM)2 CPU       6600  @ 2.40GHz
stepping        : 6
cpu MHz         : 1596.000
cache size      : 4096 KB
physical id     : 0
siblings        : 2
core id         : 0
cpu cores       : 2
apicid          : 0
initial apicid  : 0
fdiv_bug        : no
hlt_bug         : no
f00f_bug        : no
coma_bug        : no
fpu             : yes
fpu_exception   : yes
cpuid level     : 10
wp              : yes
flags           : fpu vme de pse tsc msr pae mce cx8 apic sep mtrr pge
mca cmov pat pse36 clflush dts acpi mmx fxsr sse sse2 ss ht tm pbe nx
lm constant_tsc arch_perfmon pebs bts pni monitor ds_cpl vmx est tm2
ssse3 cx16 xtpr lahf_lm
bogomips        : 4795.20
clflush size    : 64
power management:

processor       : 1
...
```

Some of the more commonly used files in /proc/ include the following:

- **/proc/bus/pci/devices.** Displays information about the PCI devices in your Linux system.

- **/proc/cpuinfo.** Displays processor information.

- **/proc/devices.** Displays information about the devices installed in your Linux system.

- **/proc/dma.** Displays information about the Direct Memory Access (DMA) channels used in your Linux system.

- **/proc/ioports.** Displays information about the input/output ports in your server.

- **/proc/interrupts.** Displays information about the Interrupt Requests (IRQ) assignments in your Linux system.

- **/proc/partitions.** Displays information about the disk partitions on your system.

- **/proc/scsi/scsi.** Displays summary information about the SCSI devices installed in your Linux system.

- **/proc/sys.** Contains a series of subdirectories and files that contain kernel variables. These directories are listed below:

  - **debug.** Contains debugging information.

  - **dev.** Contains information and parameters for specific devices on your system.

  - **fs.** Contains file system information and parameters.

  - **kernel.** Contains kernel information and configuration parameters.

  - **net.** Contains network-related information and parameters.

  - **vm.** Contains information and variables for memory management tuning, and buffer and cache management.

Some of the files in these directories are read-only. However, some of the files are writable and contain variables that can be used to configure a particular kernel parameter. In fact, you can change kernel parameters while the system is running and have the changes applied without rebooting by simply modifying the appropriate file.

NOTE: Any changes you make to these files are not persistent. If you reboot the system, your modifications will be lost.

To determine whether a file is configurable or not, use the cd command to change to the appropriate directory and enter `ls -l`. If a file has the write (w) attribute assigned, you can modify it. An example of the files in the `/proc/sys/dev/cdrom` directory is shown below:

```
da1:/proc/sys/dev/cdrom # ls -l
total 0
-rw-r--r-- 1 root root 0 Apr 22 15:37 autoclose
-rw-r--r-- 1 root root 0 Apr 22 15:37 autoeject
-rw-r--r-- 1 root root 0 Apr 22 15:37 check_media
-rw-r--r-- 1 root root 0 Apr 22 15:37 debug
-r--r--r-- 1 root root 0 Apr 16 14:35 info
-rw-r--r-- 1 root root 0 Apr 22 15:37 lock
da1:/proc/sys/dev/cdrom #
```

Notice that the autoclose, `autoeject`, `check_media`, debug, and `lock` files are writable by root, but the `info` file is not.

To change the value of a file in `/proc/sys/`, use the `echo` command to write the desired value to the file. For example, `/proc/sys/vm/` contains a file named `swappiness`. This file determines how aggressively the Linux kernel swaps unused data out of physical RAM into the swap partition on disk. As you can see below, this file contains a single number as its value. The default is **60**.

```
da1:/proc/sys/vm # cat ./swappiness
60
da1:/proc/sys/vm #
```

This variable can be set to any value between 0 and 100. The higher the value, the more aggressively the system will swap data into the swap partition.

NOTE: There are far too many variables in `/proc/sys/` to cover in this objective. A fairly detailed listing of variables and their possible values can be viewed by entering `man proc` at the shell prompt.

If you wanted to set the value of the swappiness variable to a higher value, you would use the echo command at the shell prompt (as root) to write a new value to the file. For example, if you wanted to set the variable to a value of 75, you would enter the following:

```
echo 75 >/proc/sys/vm/swappiness
```

The `echo` command normally just writes its output to the screen. However, by adding `>/proc/sys/vm/swappiness` to the end of the command, the output from the echo command is redirected to the `/proc/sys/vm/swappiness` file, overwriting the original content in the file.

- **/proc/version.** This file contains the kernel version. The content of the file is very similar to the output of the `uname -a` command.

Manage Kernel Modules

Although SUSE Linux initializes most hardware devices automatically, it is helpful to know how to manage kernel modules manually. To manage kernel modules, you need to understand the following:

- Kernel Module Basics
- Managing Modules from the Command Line
- The modprobe Configuration File (/etc/modprobe.conf)

NOTE: For the latest kernel documentation, see `/usr/src/linux/Documentation/`.

Kernel Module Basics

The kernel that is installed in the `/boot/` directory is configured to support a wide range of hardware. Drivers can either be compiled into the kernel or be loaded as kernel modules.

It is not necessary to compile a driver into a custom kernel. These modules can be loaded later while the system is running without having to reboot the computer. This is especially true of kernel modules that are not required to boot the system. By loading them as components after the system boots, the kernel can be kept relatively small.

Kernel modules are stored as files in sub-directories of the `/lib/modules/`*kernel-version*`/` directory. Hardware modules are stored in the `/lib/modules/`*kernel-version*`/kernel/drivers` directory. Modules normally work only with the kernel version they are built for; therefore, a new directory is created for every kernel update you install.

Modules are stored in several subdirectories with a filename extension of .ko (kernel object). However, when loading a module with modprobe, you omit the extension and just use the module name.

Managing Modules from the Command Line

To manage modules from the command line, you use the following commands:

- **lsmod.** Lists the currently loaded modules in the kernel, for example:

```
da1:~ # lsmod

Module                   Size     Used by
quota_v2                 12928    2
edd                      13720    0
joydev                   14528    0
sg                       41632    0
st                       44956    0
sr_mod                   21028    0
ide_cd                   42628    0
cdrom                    42780    2 sr_mod,ide_cd
nvram                    13448    0
usbserial                35952    0
parport_pc               41024    1
lp                       15364    0
parport                  44232    2 parport_pc,lp
ipv6                     276348   44
uhci_hcd                 35728    0
intel_agp                22812    1
agpgart                  36140    1 intel_agp
evdev                    13952    0
usbcore                  116572   4 usbserial,uhci_hcd
```

The list includes information on the module name, size of the module, how often the module is used, and which other modules use it.

- **insmod.** Loads the indicated module into the kernel. The module must be located in the /lib/modules/**version_number**/ directory. However, we recommend that you use modprobe to load modules instead of insmod because insmod does not resolve dependencies automatically.

- **modprobe.** Loads the indicated module into the kernel or removes it (if you use the -r option). Dependencies of other modules are taken into account when using modprobe. modprobe also reads the /etc/modprobe.conf file and uses any customized configuration settings you may have added. For example, the following command:

```
modprobe usb-storage
```

loads the usb-storage module which is needed to access storage devices connected with the USB bus. Because this module requires other USB modules, modprobe also loads these modules automatically.

This command can only be used if the /lib/modules/***version_number***/ modules.dep file (created by the depmod command) exists. This file is used to determine module dependencies.

Additional configuration files for modprobe are located in the /etc/ modprobe.d/ directory. All files in this directory are automatically evaluated by modprobe.

For more detailed information, enter man modprobe at the shell prompt.

- **rmmod.** Removes the indicated module from the kernel. A module can only be removed if no processes are accessing hardware connected to it or corresponding services. However, we recommend that you use modprobe -r for removing modules instead of rmmod.

- **depmod:** Creates the /lib/modules/***version_number***/modules.dep file. This file contains the dependencies of individual modules. When a module is loaded with modprobe, the modules.dep file ensures that all modules it depends on are also loaded.

  On SLES 11, depmod also creates the modules.aliases file, which is used by modprobe to determine which driver needs to be loaded for which device.

- **modinfo.** Displays information (such as license, author, and description) about the indicated module. For example:

```
da1:/lib/modules/2.6.27.19-5-pae # modinfo isdn
filename:        /lib/modules/2.6.27.19-5-pae/kernel/drivers/isdn/
i4l/isdn.ko
license:         GPL
author:          Fritz Elfert
description:     ISDN4 Linux: link layer
srcversion:      D9D0DB16D10916739E8D916
depends:         slhc
supported:       yes
vermagic:        2.6.27.19-5-pae SMP mod_unload modversions 586
```

For more detailed information, enter man modinfo at the shell prompt.

The modprobe Configuration File (/etc/modprobe.conf)

The /etc/modprobe.conf file is the configuration file used to configure kernel modules for 2.6-series kernels (/etc/modules.conf is the equivalent on 2.4-series kernels). Commands that can be found in the file include the following:

- **install.** Lets modprobe execute commands when loading a specific module into the kernel. For example:

```
install    eth0    /bin/true
```

- **alias.** Determines which kernel module will be loaded for a specific device file. For example:

```
alias    parport_lowlevel    parport_pc
```

- **options.** Options for loading a module. For example:

```
options    ne    io=0x300 irq=5
```

NOTE: For more detailed information, enter `man 5 modprobe.conf` at the shell prompt.

Describe How udev Works

Before you can use a hardware device, the appropriate driver module has to be loaded and the corresponding interface has to be set up. For most devices in SLES 11 this is done by udev.

You learn the following regarding udev:

- The Purpose of udev

- How udev Works

- Persistent Interface Names

The Purpose of udev

udev has three main purposes:

- **Create device files:** The main task of udev is to create device files under `/dev` automatically when a device is connected to the system.

  In earlier versions of Linux, the `/dev` directory was populated with every device that could possibly appear in the system, even though most of the device files were actually not used. This led to the `/dev` directory being very large, complex, and confusing.

- **Persistent device names:** udev provides a mechanism for persistent device names.

- **Hotplug replacement:** In SLES 11, udev replaces the hotplug system, which was responsible for the initialization of hardware devices in previous versions. udev is now the central point for hardware initialization.

How udev Works

udev is implemented as a daemon (`udevd`), which is started at boot time through the `/etc/init.d/boot.udev` script. udev communicates with the Linux kernel through the **uevent** interface. When the kernel sends out a uevent message that a device has been added or removed, udevd does the following, based on the udev rules:

- Initializes devices

- Creates device files in `/dev`

- Sets up network interfaces with `ifup`, if necessary

- Renames network interfaces, if necessary

- Mounts storage devices which are identified as hotplug in `/etc/fstab`

- Informs other applications about the new device

To handle uevent messages which have been issued before udevd was started, the udev start script triggers these missed events by parsing the sysfs file system. In previous SLES versions, this part of the system initialization was done by the `coldplug` script.

Everything that udev does depends on rules defined in configuration files located in one of the following directories:

- **/lib/udev/rules.d/**: Files in this directory contain the default rules.

- **/etc/udev/rules.d/**: Files in this directory contain custom rules.

- **/dev/.udev/rules.d/**: Files in this directory contain temporary rules.

Rule files are sorted and processed in lexical order, no matter in which of these directories they are located. Files in `/etc/udev/rules.d/` have precedence over files with the same name in `/lib/udev/rules.d/`. This can be used to ignore a default rules file if needed.

A detailed description of udev rules is beyond the scope of this course. We will limit our discussion to the following:

- udev rules are spread over several files, which are processed in alphabetical order. Each line in these files is a rule. Comments can be added with the # character.

- Each rule consists of multiple key value pairs. An example of a key value pair is

  kernel=="sda"

- There are two different key types:

  - **Match keys:** Determine if a rule should be used to process an event.

  - **Assignment keys:** Determine what to do if an event is processed.

    There always has to be at least one match and one assignment key in a rule.

- For every uevent, all rules are processed. Processing does not stop when a matching rule is found.

Persistent Interface Names

The interface files in the `/dev` directory are created and assigned to the corresponding hardware device when the device is recognized and initialized by a driver. Therefore, the assignment between device and interface file depends on

- The order in which device drivers are loaded.

- The order in which devices are connected to a computer.

This can lead to situations where it is not clear which device file is assigned to a device. For example, suppose you have two USB devices: a digital camera and a flash card reader. These devices are accessed as storage devices through the `/dev/sdb` and `/dev/sdc` device files (assuming that `/dev/sda` is assigned to the hard disk).

Which device is assigned to which device file usually depends on the order in which they are plugged in. The first device becomes `sdb`, the second becomes `sdc`, and so on. Therefore, in one session, the camera may be `/dev/sdb` and the card reader `/dev/sdc`. In another session, however, the camera may be `/dev/sdc` and the card reader `/dev/sdb`.

udev can help make this process more predictable. With the help of sysfs, udev can find out which device is connected to which interface file. The easiest solution for persistent device names would be to rename the interface files, for example from `/dev/sdb1` to `/dev/camera`.

Unfortunately, interface files cannot be renamed under Linux. The only exception to this rule are network interfaces, which traditionally have no interface files under `/dev`.

Therefore, udev uses a different approach. Instead of renaming an interface file, a link with a unique and persistent name is created to the assigned interface file. By default, udev is configured to create these links for all storage devices. For each device, a link is created in each of the following subdirectories under `/dev/disk/`:

- `by-id`. The name of the link is based on the vendor and on the name of a device.

- `by-path`. The name of the link is based on the bus position of a device.

- `by-uuid`. The name of the link is based on a UUID (Universally Unique ID) of a device.

- `by-label`. The name of the link is based on the media label.

This means that the association between devices and interface files still depends on the order in which the drivers are loaded or in which order devices are connected with the system. With udev, however, persistent links are created and adjusted every time the device configuration changes.

As mentioned above, network interfaces are treated differently. They do not have interface files and they can be directly renamed by udev. Persistent network interface names are configured as udev rules in the `/etc/udev/rules.d/70-persistent-net.rules` file. The following is an example:

```
SUBSYSTEM=="net", ACTION=="add", DRIVERS=="?*",
ATTR{address}=="00:50:56:00:00:37", ATTR{type}=="1", KERNEL=="eth*",
NAME="eth0"
```

The matching key in the rule is used to identify a network device by its MAC address. At the end of the rule, the name of the interface is given—in this example, **eth0**.

NOTE: In SUSE Linux Enterprise 9 it was possible to configure persistent network interface names in the interface configuration files in `/etc/sysconfig/network`. Since SUSE Linux Enterprise 10, this is no longer supported because interface names began to be configured in a udev rule.

Coldplug vs. Hotplug Hardware

When working with hardware devices in a Linux system, you should be aware of two different types:

- **Hotplug**: Hotplug devices can be connected to the computer system after the system has been turned on. Examples of hotplug devices include USB storage devices, FireWire (IEEE 1394) cameras and storage devices, and some Ethernet interfaces. A limited number of hotplug PCI hardware devices and SATA storage devices have been developed for servers as well.

- **Coldplug**: Coldplug devices must be connected to the computer system *before* the system is powered on. Examples of coldplug hardware include:

  - RAM

  - CPUs

  - Standard PCI, AGP, and PCI Express devices

  - Older PATA storage devices

Coldplug devices typically rely on the `/dev` file system to provide an interface between the hardware and applications running in the user space. To support hotplug devices, however, Linux relies on the following utilities:

- **hald**: The Hardware Abstraction Layer Daemon (hald) runs in the user space and provides applications with information about available hardware in the system.

- **sysfs**: sysfs is a virtual file system mounted in the `/sys` directory that provides information about the hardware devices in the system.

- **D-Bus**: The Desktop Bus (D-Bus) daemon allows processes running on the Linux system to communicate with each other. This allows processes to be notified when hotplug hardware is connected to the system.

- **udev**: udev dynamically creates device files when hot plug devices are connected to the system and their drivers are loaded.

Exercise 4-10   *Manage Linux Kernel Modules and udev Rules*

In this exercise, you load and unload kernel modules and you modify udev rules.

You will find this exercise at the end of the chapter.

(End of Exercise)

Summary

Objective	Summary
Manage Software	Linux supports various file systems. Each file system has its particular strengths and weaknesses, which must be taken into account.
	File systems that keep a journal of transactions recover faster after a system crash or a power failure.
Manage Shared Libraries	In a Linux environment, most programs share some code through the use of shared libraries. This provides advantages from a development and a system management standpoint.
	For developers, it means their programs include only the code that is unique to the program itself, sharing functions that other programs have in common with it.
	This reduces the size of the program executable, thus reducing the amount of disk space required for the application (an advantage for system administrators).
	Unlike some other operating systems, a Linux system locates its dynamic libraries through a configuration file that points to the locations, eliminating confusion about which version of which dynamic library is used by each piece of software.
	In contrast to dynamic program linking, you can link the needed libraries statically when a program is compiled.
	Although static linking increases the program size, it provides independence from libraries at runtime and is especially useful for system maintenance purposes.
Manage User and Group Accounts	A basic task of all system administrators is maintaining file system layouts. Under Linux, new partitions can be transparently grafted into existing file system structures using the `mount` command.
	In most cases, YaST proposes a reasonable partitioning scheme during installation. However, you can use YaST to customize partitioning during and after installation.
	You learned about design guidelines for implementing partitions and how to administer partitions using YaST or command line tools.
Manage File Permissions and Ownership	To perform basic Linux file system management tasks in SLES 11, you learned how to use YaST and command line tools to create file systems on partitions.

Objective	Summary
Manage Partitions, File Systems, Quotas, and NFS	`/etc/fstab` is the configuration file that holds information about where each partition is to be mounted.
	`mount` is the command used to attach file systems on partitions to the file system tree; `umount` detaches them.
	Various tools exist to monitor, repair, and tune file systems.
	Linux includes a quota system that lets you specify a specific amount of storage space for each user or group and how many files that individual user or members of the group can create.
	The Network File System is used to export directories on a server and to import them on a client.
Manage Backup and Restore	Backing up and restoring files in case of accidental deletion or catastrophic loss is an important part of a system administrator's work.
	A suitable backup strategy ensures that files can be restored with relative ease.
	The tools you can use for backup and restore on SLES 11 include `tar`, `rsync`, and `dd`.
Manage Hardware	Tools such as `hwinfo`, `lspci`, `lsscsi`, and `lsusb` allow you to establish the hardware used within your computer without having to open the physical machine to look at its components.
	Kernel modules are used to control hardware components such as network cards or hard disks.
	The udev system allows you to change hardware components, such as USB drives, during runtime.

Key Terms

/etc/default/useradd – A file that contains the default parameters used by the useradd command.

/etc/exports – The file that lists exported directories on an NFS server.

/etc/modprobe.conf – A file that lists the modules that are inserted into the Linux kernel at system initialization using the modprobe command.

/etc/skel – A directory whose contents are copied to all new users' home directories when they are created.

/etc/yum.conf – The main configuration file for the yum command.

/etc/yum.repos.d – A directory that contains files that list the location of software repositories on the Internet.

/proc – A directory that is mounted to a special procfs file system and used to store hardware and process information.

/sys – A directory that is mounted to a special sysfs file system and used to store information exported by the Linux kernel. It is commonly used by processes on the system.

apt-cache command – Used to find information about Debian software packages.

apt-get command – Used to obtain and install Debian packages from software repositories on the Internet.

aptitude command – A fully featured utility that can be used to manage the Debian Package Manager and related packages on a Linux system.

chattr command – Used to modify file and directory attributes.

chgrp command – Used to change the group owner for a file or directory.

coldplug device – A hardware device that can only be safely inserted and removed from the system while the system is powered off.

configure script – The script included with source code that analyzes a system for prerequisites and stores its results in a Makefile.

cpio command – Used to create backups of files and directories. It stands for copy in and out, and supports advanced file processing options.

createrepo command – Used to re-create software repository metadata for yum repositories listed within files under the /etc/yum.repos.d directory.

dd command – Used to create byte-wise copies of files on a system. It is commonly used to create backups of file systems.

Debian Package Manager (dpkg) – The package manger software used on Debian-based Linux distributions.

depmod command – Used to generate a list of dependent kernel modules.

device – A physical hardware device.

df command – Displays disk free space by mounted file system.

differential backup – A backup of any files on a particular system, file system, or directory that have been changed since the previous full backup.

dpkg command – Used to install, remove, view, and manage software on the system using the Debian Package Manager.

du command – Displays disk usage for a particular directory.

dump command – Used to create backups of files, directories, and file systems. It can also be used to create incremental backups.

dumpe2fs command – Used to obtain file system information from ext2 and ext3 file systems.

dynamic software libraries – Sets of functions that are shared by several different programs. They are loaded dynamically by the program as needed.

e2fsck command – Used to check and repair ext2 and ext3 file systems.

edquota command – Used to specify quota limits for users and groups.

exportfs command – Used to temporarily export directories on an NFS server.

fdisk command – Used to create, delete, and modify hard disk partitions.

fsck command – Used to check and repair file systems.

full backup – A backup of all specified files on a particular system, file system, or directory.

fuser command – Lists the users that are using a particular file or directory on the system.

genisoimage command – Used to create an ISO 9660 image.

GnuPG – A technology that is used to generate and digitally sign asymmetric encryption keys. It stands for Gnu Privacy Guard.

gpasswd command – Used to set or change a password for a group account.

groupadd command – Used to add a group to the system.

groupdel command – Used to delete a group from the system.

groupmod command – Used to modify the name, membership, or GID of a group on the system.

hard limit – A quota limit that cannot be exceeded.

hotplug device – A hardware device that can be safely inserted and removed from the system while the system is powered on.

incremental backup – A backup of any files on a particular system, file system, or directory that have been changed since the previous incremental or full backup.

insmod command – Used to insert a kernel module into the Linux kernel.

insserv command – Used to update the system initialization files to include additional items.

interface – Software components that are used to directly access hardware devices.

kernel module – A compiled object file that can be inserted into the Linux kernel to provide additional support for features and hardware devices.

last command – Displays the users that have recently logged into the system by examining the /var/log/wtmp log file.

ldconfig command – Used to view and update the library cache that lists shared dynamic libraries on the system.

ldd command – Lists the shared dynamic software libraries that are used by a specific Linux program.

lsattr command – Used to view file and directory attributes.

lsmod command – Used to list kernel modules currently inserted into the Linux kernel.

lsof command – Lists open files on the system.

lspci command – Used to list the details regarding the PCI devices in a system.

lsusb command – Used to list the details regarding the USB devices currently attached to a system.

make command – Used to compile software from source code files using the settings stored in the Makefile generated by the configure script.

make install command – Used to copy compiled program files to the correct directory within the file system hierarchy.

Mean Time Before Failure (MTBF) – The estimated lifespan of a hard disk drive assigned by the manufacturer.

mkfs command – Used to create most file systems in Linux.

mkisofs command – Used to create an ISO 9660 image.

mkreiserfs command – Used to create ReiserFS file systems.

mkswap command – Used to prepare a swap partition for use in Linux.

modinfo command – Used to obtain information about a specific kernel module.

modprobe command – Used to insert a kernel module and the associated dependent kernel modules into the Linux kernel.

Network File System (NFS) – A file-sharing protocol used by UNIX and Linux systems.

NFS client – A computer that accesses exported files on an NFS server using the NFS protocol.

NFS server – A computer that hosts (exports) files using the NFS protocol.

package management software – Software that is used to manage the installation, maintenance and removal of software packages on a system. The RPM and Debian package mangers are the two most commonly used package managers on Linux systems.

partprobe command – Used to reload the partition table into the Linux kernel.

passwd command – Used to change the password for a user account on the system. It can also be used to lock a user account on the system.

quotacheck command – Used to update the quota database files.

quotaoff command – Used to deactivate disk quotas.

quotaon command – Used to activate disk quotas.

quotas – File system usage limits that may be imposed upon users and groups.

reiserfsck command – Used to check and repair ReiserFS file systems.

Remote Procedure Call (RPC) – A routine that is executed on a remote computer.

repquota command – Used to produce a report on quotas for a particular file system.

restore command – Used to view or restore a backup created using the dump command.

rmmod command – Used to remove a kernel module from the Linux kernel.

rpcinfo command – Displays information regarding the RPM portmapper daemon.

rpm command – Used to install, remove, view, and manage software on the system using the RPM package manger.

rsync command – Used to create mirror copies of directories on local and remote systems.

Set Group ID (SGID) – A special per mission set on executable files and directories. When you run an executable program that has the SUID permission set, you become the group owner of the executable file for the duration of the program. On a directory, the SGID sets the group that gets attached to newly created files.

Set User ID (SUID) – A special per mission set on executable files. When you run an executable program that has the SUID permission set, you become the owner of the executable file for the duration of the program.

showmount command – Displays exported director ies on an NFS server.

soft limit – A quota limit that can be exceeded for a certain period of time.

static software libraries – Sets of functions that are compiled into a specific program and not available to other programs.

sticky bit – A special per mission that is set on directories that prevents users from removing files that they do not own.

Storage Area Network (SAN) – A technology used to store files from multiple computers on devices across a network using a fast interconnect.

sudo command – Used by non-root users to run commands as another user via the permissions granted in the /etc/sudoers file.

swapoff command – Used to deactivate a swap partition from being used by the Linux kernel.

swapon command – Used to activate a swap partition for use by the Linux kernel.

tar command – Used to create archives of files. Source code for many Linux programs are distributed in a compressed tar archive. It stands for tape archive.

udev – A special file system that is used to manage the creation and use of device files within the /dev directory.

umask command – Used to view and modify the permissions for files and directories that are created in the future.

user space driver – A software component separate from the Linux kernel that is used to directly access hardware devices.

useradd command – Used to add a user account to the system.

userdel command – Used to remove a user account from the system.

usermod command – Used to modify the properties of a user account on the system.

w command – Displays the users that are logged onto the system and their active processes.

wall (warn all) command – Used to send a message to all system users.

who command – Displays the users that are logged onto the system.

wodim command – Used to write an ISO 9660 image to optical media.

yum command – Used to obtain and install RPM packages from software repositories on the Internet. It stands for Yellowdog Updater Modified.

yumdownloader command – Used to download RPM package files from RPM software repositories on the Internet without installing them afterwards.

Chapter Exercises

Exercise 4-1   *Manage Software with RPM*

In this exercise, you practice gathering information on installed software and installing software packages. The exercise has two parts.

In the first part, you learn how to get information on RPMs by looking for information on the `/usr/bin/wget` file. Find out what package contains the `/usr/bin/wget` file, get information on that package, list the files contained in that package, and verify the integrity of the files. List the files in that package containing documentation.

In the second part, install the gvim package from the *SUSE Linux Enterprise Server 11 Product DVD*, run the gvim program, and uninstall gvim again.

This exercise is performed on da-host.

Detailed Steps to Complete the Exercise

- Task I: Get Information on Software Packages
- Task II: Install and Remove Software with RPM

Task I: Get Information on Software Packages

To get information on a software package, do the following:

1. Log in to the da-host as **geeko** (password **novell**), open a terminal window, and switch to the root (password **novell**) user using the `su –` command.

2. Use RPM to find out information on the wget package:

    a. From a terminal window, determine which package installed the `/usr/bin/wget` file by entering

    ```
    rpm -qf /usr/bin/wget
    ```

    Notice that the wget package installed the wget file.

    b. Find out information on the wget package by entering

    ```
    rpm -qi wget
    ```

    Notice that the information includes the install date and a description.

    c. Show all the files installed by the wget package by entering

    ```
    rpm -ql wget
    ```

    Where can you find information on the wget package? (Notice the location of the README files.)

3. Enter the following:

    ```
    vi /etc/wgetrc
    ```

4. Activate the edit mode of vi by pressing Insert on your keyboard.

5. Using the arrow keys, move the cursor to the first line and the first space after the three comment marks (###).

6. Type the following:

```
# This is a test.
```

7. Save the file and close the editor by pressing Esc and entering

```
:wq
```

You are returned to the command prompt.

8. See what has changed in the files on your hard drive since the wget RPM was originally installed by entering

```
rpm -V wget
```

9. The following is displayed:

```
S.5....T c /etc/wgetrc
```

Refer to the student manual (Section 4, first objective) to interpret what has changed.

10. View the documentation files for the wget by entering

```
rpm -qd wget
```

Notice that some of the files are still compressed (*.gz).

Task II: Install and Remove Software with RPM

To install and remove software with RPM, do the following:

1. Insert the *SUSE Linux Enterprise Server 11 DVD* into your DVD drive.

2. List all files included in the not-yet-installed gvim package by entering

```
rpm -qpl /media/SUSE_SLES-11-0-0.001/suse/i586/gvim-
7*.i586.rpm
```

3. Install the gvim package by entering

```
rpm -ihv /media/SUSE_SLES-11-0-0.001/suse/i586/gvim-
7*.i586.rpm
```

4. Conditional: If you see an error message: Failed dependencies: libruby.so.1.8 is needed by gvim-7.2-8.8.i586, use the following command (in one line) instead of the above:

```
rpm -ihv /media/SUSE_SLES-11-0-0.001/suse/i586/ruby-
1*rpm /media/SUSE_SLES-11-0-0.001/suse/i586/gvim-
7*.i586.rpm
```

5. Remove the DVD from your drive.

6. (Conditional) If the DVD drive does not open, enter `eject`, then remove the DVD.

7. Test the installation of the software package by entering `gvim`.

A VIM window opens.

8. Close the VIM window by selecting *File > Exit*.

9. List all files included in the installed gvim package by entering the following:

   ```
   rpm -ql gvim
   ```

10. Remove the gvim package by entering `rpm -e gvim`.

11. Verify that the package is no longer installed by entering the following:

    ```
    rpm -ql gvim
    ```

12. Log out as root and close the terminal window by entering `exit`.

(End of Exercise)

Exercise 4-2   Manage Shared Libraries

In this exercise, you use common utilities to manage the shared libraries on your SUSE Linux Enterprise Server 11.

You use `ldd` to view the shared libraries needed by slpd (Service Location Protocol Daemon). Change the name of one of the libraries used `/lib/libnsl.so.1` and view again the shared libraries needed by slpd. View the content of the library cache.

View the content of and rebuild the library cache.

Do the following:

1. From the DA-OES-A virtual machine, log in as geeko with a password of novell.

2. Open a terminal window; then su - to root (password n0v3ll).

3. View the shared libraries by doing the following:

    a. View all of the libraries linked to the SLP daemon (slpd) by entering `ldd /usr/sbin/slpd`.

    Several libraries are listed, including the `/lib/libnsl.so.1` file.

    b. Rename the `/lib/libnsl.so.1` file to `/lib/libnsl.so.1.bak` by entering `mv /lib/libnsl.so.1  /lib/libnsl.so.1.bak`.

    c. Enter `ldd /usr/sbin/slpd` again.

    Notice that the output indicates that the `libnsl.so.1` library is not found.

    d. Rename the `/lib/libnsl.so.1.bak` file back to `/lib/libnsl.so.1` by entering `mv /lib/libnsl.so.1.bak /lib/libnsl.so.1`.

    e. Verify that the file can be found again by entering `ldd /usr/sbin/slpd`.

4. Rebuild the library cache by doing the following:

    a. View the library cache by entering `ldconfig -p`.

    b. Rebuild the system library cache by entering `ldconfig -v`.

5. View the contents of the /etc/ld.so.conf file by entering `cat /etc/ld.so.conf`.

6. Close the terminal window.

(End of Exercise)

Exercise 4-3   **_Create and Manage Users and Groups from the Command Line_**

In this exercise, you add and remove a user using command line tools.

Create, change, and delete a user account, using the following information:

- Use the `useradd` command to add a new user account labeled **tux** for user **Tux Penguin**.
- Look for the new entries in the `/etc/passwd` and `/etc/shadow` files.
- Use the `passwd` command to set the password for tux to **novell**.
- Use the `su` command to switch to user tux.
- Use the `passwd` command to change the password to **d1g1t@l**.
- Use the `userdel` command to remove the account of user **tux**.

This exercise is performed on the da-host server.

Detailed Steps to Complete the Exercise

- Part I: Add a New User
- Part II: Create a Password for the New User
- Part III: Log In as the New User and Change Your Password
- Part IV: Remove the New User Account

Part I: Add a New User

To add a new user, complete these steps:

1. Open a terminal windowand use the `su` – command to switch to root (password novell).

2. Create a new local user by entering the following:

   `useradd -c "Tux Penguin" -m tux`

3. Verify that a home directory for tux was created by entering

   `ls /home`

4. Verify that there is an entry for the tux user in `/etc/passwd` by entering

   `cat /etc/passwd`

   The "x" in the second field indicates that the password for tux is stored in `/etc/shadow`.

5. Look at the password in `/etc/shadow` by entering

   `cat /etc/shadow`

   The "!" in the second field indicates that there is no valid password for tux.

Part II: Create a Password for the New User

To create a password for the new user, do the following:

1. Create a password for the user tux by entering `passwd tux`.
2. Enter the password **novell** twice.
3. Log out as root by entering `exit`.

Part III: Log In as the New User and Change Your Password

To log in as the new user and change your password, do the following:

1. Log in as tux by entering `su - tux`. Enter the password **novell** when prompted.
2. Change the password of the user tux by entering `passwd`.
3. Enter the old password of the user tux: **novell**
4. Try to change the password to novell by entering **novell**.

    You receive a warning that you must choose a new password.
5. Enter **d1g1t@l** as the new password (enter twice).
6. Log out as user tux by entering `exit`.

Part IV: Remove the New User Account

To remove the new user account, do the following:

1. Switch to user root using the `su -` command (password **novell**).
2. Delete the user tux by entering

    `userdel -r tux`
3. Verify that the home directory for tux has been removed by entering

    `ls /home`
4. Verify that there is no entry for tux in `/etc/passwd` by entering

    `cat /etc/passwd`
5. Close the terminal window.

(End of Exercise)

Exercise 4-4   *Manage File Permissions and Ownership*

In this exercise, manage directories with different permissions by

- Creating a /files/ directory with two subdirectories: private/ and public/
- Changing the permissions for the private/ directory so that only root has read, write, and execute permissions, and changing the permissions of public/ so that everyone has rights to the directory
- Switching to user geeko
- Trying to create a geeko file inside each of these directories
- Changing the permissions of the geeko file so that members of the users group may write to it, but others may not

This exercise is performed on the da-host server.

Detailed Steps to Complete the Exercise

- Part I: Create a Private and a Public Directory
- Part II: Try to Create a File as a Normal User in Both Directories

Part I: Create a Private and a Public Directory

To create a private and a public directory, do the following:

1. Open a terminal window and switch to root (su -) with a password of **novell**.

2. Create the /files/ directory by entering

    mkdir /files

3. Change to the /files/ directory by entering

    cd /files

4. To create the private and public subdirectories under /files/, enter

    mkdir private public

5. Change the permissions on the private directory so that only root has read, write, and execute permissions by entering

    chmod 700 private

6. Change permissions on the public directory so that everyone has rights to the directory by entering

    chmod 777 public

7. Verify the changes by entering

    ls -l

Part II: Try to Create a File as a Normal User in Both Directories

To try to create a file as a normal user in both directories, do the following:

1. Switch to virtual terminal 3 by pressing Ctrl+Alt+F3.

2. Log in as geeko with a **novell** password.

3. Switch to the /files directory by entering

   cd /files

4. Try to create a file named geeko in the private directory by entering

   touch private/geeko

   Permission is denied.

5. Try to create a file named geeko in the public directory by entering

   touch public/geeko

6. Verify that the file is created by entering

   ls public

7. Change to the public directory by entering

   cd public

8. List the permissions of the geeko file by entering

   ls -l geeko

   Notice that the groups *users* and *other* have only read permission for the file.

9. Change permissions so that the group *users* has write permissions and *other* does not have any permissions by entering the following

   chmod g+w,o-r geeko

10. Verify the change by entering

    ls -l

11. Log out as geeko by pressing Ctrl+d or by entering

    exit

12. Return to the GNOME desktop by pressing Ctrl+Alt+F7.

13. Close the terminal window.

(End of Exercise)

Exercise 4-5   Manage Partitions and File Systems

In this exercise, you practice creating partitions using `fdisk`. You also use command line tools to create and administer file systems and user quotas.

In the first part of this exercise, you use fdisk to create the following partitions:

- An extended partition using the remaining disk space.

- Tow logical partitions with a size of 1 GB each.

In the second part of this exercise, you create file systems on the partitions you created in the first part using the applicable options for mkfs:

- Create an ext3 file system on `/dev/sda5`.

- Create an ext2 file system on `/dev/sda6`.

- Create the mountpoints `/export/data1` and `/export/data2` and edit the `/etc/fstab` file to mount the partitions you just created automatically.

In the third part of this exercise, you run e2fsck on the ext3 file system you created on `/dev/sda5`, which is mounted in `/export/data1`.

In the fourth part of the exercise, you convert the `/dev/sda6` partition to an ext3 file system by adding a journal. You also add a label to it.

In the fifth part of this exercise, you administer user quotas. You install the quota package and then configure quotas for `/dev/sda6`, which is mounted at `/export/data2`.

This exercise is done on the da-host server.

Detailed Steps to Complete the Exercise

- Part I: Partition Manually with fdisk

- Part II: Manage File Systems from the Command Line

- Part III: Run e2fsck

- Part IV: Customize the File Systems

- Part V: Set Up and Configure Disk Quotas

Part I: Partition Manually with fdisk

To partition manually from the command line with fdisk, do the following:

1. Open a terminal window and `su` - to root (password **novell**) and start the fdisk utility on the first hard disk on your server by entering

    ```
    fdisk /dev/sda
    ```

    A message is displayed, indicating that the number of cylinders is above 1024, which might cause problems under certain circumstances.

2. View the current partition table in fdisk by entering `p`.

3. Create an extended partition that uses the entire free space of the hard disk by doing the following:

    a. Create a new partition by entering n.

    b. Enter e for extended.

    c. Conditional: When asked for a partition number, enter 3.

    d. Accept the suggested first cylinder by pressing Enter.

    e. Accept the suggested last cylinder by pressing Enter.

4. Create two logical partitions with a partition type of Linux (the default) by doing the following:

    a. Create a new partition by entering n.

    b. Enter l (lower case L) to create a logical partition.

    c. Accept the default first cylinder by pressing Enter.

    d. Specify a partition size of 1 GB by entering +1G.

    e. Create another new partition by entering n.

    f. Enter l (lower case L) to create a logical partition.

    g. Accept the default first cylinder by pressing Enter.

    h. Indicate the partition size by entering +1G.

    i. Verify the new partition configuration by entering p.

5. Write the new partition table to your hard drive and exit fdisk by entering w.

    You will see a warning message that the kernel is still using the old partition table and that the new table will be used at the next reboot.

6. View the current partition table used by the kernel by entering

    ```
    cat /proc/partitions
    ```

    Notice that the three new partitions you just created are not listed.

7. To access the new partitions, you must update the kernel's partition table which is stored in memory. Do one of the following:

    ■ Have the kernel update its partition table by entering partprobe.

    ■ Reboot the system by entering reboot.

8. View the partition table again by entering

    ```
    cat /proc/partitions
    ```

Part II: Manage File Systems from the Command Line

To manage file systems from the command line, do the following:

1. In the terminal window where you are logged in as root, create the following file systems:

    a. On `/dev/sda5`, create a new ext3 file system with verbose output by entering the following:

    ```
    mkfs -t ext3 -v /dev/sda5
    ```

    Notice that by adding the option `-v`, extensive information about the new file system is displayed.

    b. On `/dev/sda6`, create a new ext3 file system by entering

    ```
    mkfs -t ext2 /dev/sda6
    ```

2. Create the directories named `data1` and `data2` under `/export/` by entering

    ```
    mkdir  -p  /export/data{1,2}
    ```

3. Verify that the directories were created by entering

    ```
    ls  -l  /export
    ```

4. As root, add entries to the `/etc/fstab` file for the new file systems:

    a. Open the `/etc/fstab` file in the vi editor by entering `vi /etc/fstab` at the shell prompt.

    b. Press Ins.

    c. At the end of the `/etc/fstab` file, add the following new lines:

    ```
    /dev/sda5      /export/data1      ext3      defaults      1 2
    /dev/sda6      /export/data2      ext2      defaults      1 2
    ```

    NOTE: You should add an empty line after the last new entry at the end of the file to make sure the mount command can interpret the file properly.

    These new entries ensure the sda5 and sda6 partitions are mounted when starting or rebooting the system.

    d. Save the changes to `/etc/fstab` by pressing Esc and then entering `:wq`.

5. In the terminal window, reread the `/etc/fstab` file and mount all of the new file systems by entering

    ```
    mount -a
    ```

6. View the information on the mounted file systems by entering the following two commands:

    ```
    mount
    cat /proc/mounts
    ```

    You should see entries for the two new partitions you created.

Part III: Run e2fsck

To run `e2fsck`, do the following:

1. Open a terminal session and, at the shell prompt, switch to your root user account by entering `su` – followed by a password of **novell**.

2. Unmount the file system on `/dev/sda5` by entering

    `umount /export/data1`

3. Verify that the file system is no longer mounted by entering

    `mount`

    The `/dev/sda5` partition should not be listed in the output of the mount command.

4. Start a file system check on sda5 running in verbose mode with an automatic response of **yes** to all prompts by entering

    `e2fsck -f -y -v /dev/sda5`

5. Mount the `/export/data1` file system again by entering

    `mount /export/data1`

6. Verify that the file system on `/dev/sda5` is mounted by entering

    `mount`

Part IV: Customize the File Systems

In this part of the exercise, you add a journal to an ext2 file system, effectively making it an ext3 file system. Complete the following:

1. Modify the `/dev/sda6` partition:

    a. In the terminal window, umount the `/dev/sda6` partition and view details about the ext2 file system on it by entering

    `umount /dev/sda6 ; dumpe2fs /dev/sda6 | more`

    Notice the block size and the file system state.

    b. Give the ext2 file system a volume name of */export/data2* while the file system is unmounted by entering

    `tune2fs -L /export/data2 /dev/sda6`

    NOTE: It is common practice to use this naming convention. Naming a file system after its mount point can be useful in system rescue situations when the `/etc/fstab` file is not available.

    ---

    c. Verify that the file system now has a volume name by entering

    `dumpe2fs /dev/sda6 | less`

    You should see that the volume name has been set to the partition's mount point.

d. Add a journal to the file system (making it an ext3 file system) by entering

```
tune2fs -j /dev/sda6
```

e. Verify that the file system now contains a journal by entering

```
dumpe2fs /dev/sda6 | less
```

f. Mount /dev/sda6 again by entering

```
mount /dev/sda6
```

g. View information on the mounted file systems by entering

```
mount
```

Notice that the file system is still mounted as an ext2 file system.

h. Unmount the partition /dev/sda6 again by entering

```
umount /dev/sda6
```

i. Verify that the file system state is clean by entering

```
dumpe2fs /dev/sda6 | less
```

j. Edit the /etc/fstab file to change the file system type from ext2 to ext3 by entering vi /etc/fstab at the shell prompt.

k. Locate the entry for /dev/sda6 and change the file system type from ext2 to ext3. Save the file and close the editor.

l. At the command line, reread /etc/fstab and mount the partition as an ext3 file system by entering

```
mount -a
```

m. Verify the change by entering

```
mount
```

You should see that /dev/sda6 has been mounted as an ext3 file system.

n. Unmount the partition /dev/sda6 again by entering

```
umount /export/data2
```

o. Mount the partition as an ext2 file system manually by entering

```
mount -t ext2 /dev/sda6 /export/data2
```

p. Verify that the file system is mounted without a journal (as an ext2 file system) by entering

```
mount
```

As you can see, ext3 is backward compatible with ext2.

q. Remount /dev/sda6 as an ext3 file system and verify the change by entering the following commands:

```
umount /export/data2
mount -a
mount
```

Part V: Set Up and Configure Disk Quotas

Complete the following:

1. Open a terminal window, then switch to root using the `su` - command and a password of **novell**.

2. Install the quota package by entering `yast -i quota`.

3. (Conditional) Insert the *SUSE Linux Enterprise Server 11* installation DVD, if prompted.

4. View the disk quota configuration for user geeko by entering

   ```
   quota  -vu  geeko
   ```

   The lack of any output indicates there are no quotas currently configured for geeko.

5. Add quota mount options to the `/dev/sda6` partition by doing the following:

   a. Open the `/etc/fstab` file in the vi editor by entering

      ```
      vi /etc/fstab
      ```

   b. Change the `/dev/sda6` entry in `/etc/fstab` so it looks like the following (in one line):

      ```
      /dev/sda6   /export/data2   ext3
      defaults,usrquota,grpquota  1 2
      ```

   c. Save the file and exit vi.

6. Remount the file system so that the changes in the `/etc/fstab` file are read by the system by entering

   ```
   mount -o remount /dev/sda6
   ```

   NOTE: If you receive the error message "/export/data2 mounted already, or bad option," check the contents of the `/etc/fstab` file. You might have misspelled the **usrquota** or **grpquota** option.

   ---

7. Run quotacheck to initialize the quota database by entering

   ```
   quotacheck  -mavug
   ```

   NOTE: You will receive several status messages about old quota files. These indicate that this is a new quota database with no previous quota database files on the system.

   ---

8. Verify that the `aquota.user` and `aquota.groups` files exist in the `/export/data2` directory by entering

   ```
   ls  -l  /export/data2
   ```

9. Turn quotas on for all file systems that are mounted with these options by entering

   ```
   quotaon -av
   ```

10. Make the quota system persistent after reboot by entering

    ```
    insserv  boot.quota
    ```

11. Set a quota for geeko with a soft block limit of about 20 MB and a hard block limit of about 30 MB on /dev/sda6 by entering

    ```
    edquota  -u  geeko
    ```

    The quota editor appears in the vi editor.

12. Under soft, remove the 0 and enter **20000**.

13. Under hard, remove the 0 and enter **30000**.

14. When you're finished, press Esc, then enter :wq.

15. View the quota information about all configured users by entering

    ```
    repquota  -av
    ```

16. (Optional) If you finish early, set a quota for the users group of 100 MB for the soft limit and 150 MB for the hard limit.

17. Test the quotas by doing the following:

    a. As root, create a directory named /export/data2/geeko and change the owner to geeko by doing the following:

    ```
    mkdir  /export/data2/geeko
    chown  geeko.users  /export/data2/geeko
    ```

    b. Change to the user account geeko and create a file by entering

    ```
    su - geeko
    dd if=/dev/zero  of=/export/data2/geeko/bigfile
    ```

    After a short time, you should see a message indicating the quota was exceeded.

18. Close all open windows.

(End of Exercise)

Exercise 4-6   ***Set Up and Manage Network File System (NFS)***

In this exercise, you set up an NFS server, and connect to the server with an NFS client.

In the first part of this exercise, you create an `/export/documentation` directory on da-host, copy documents from `/usr/share/doc/manual/` into it, and export it to others using NFS.

In the second part, you create the `/import/docs` directory on da1 and use it as mountpoint to import the `/export/documentation` directory using NFS. Create an `/etc/fstab` entry to mount the directory automatically at boot time.

Detailed Steps to Complete the Exercise

- Part I: Set Up an NFS Server
- Part II: Add a Remote File System to the NFS Client

Part I: Set Up an NFS Server

On da-host, do the following:

1. Open a terminal window and `su` – to root (password: **novell**).

2. Create the `/export/documentation` directory by entering

   `mkdir -p /export/documentation`

3. Copy some files into that directory using the following commands:

   `cd /export/documentation`

   `cp /usr/share/doc/manual/sles-admin_en-pdf/* .`

4. Install the kernel-nfsserver package using the `yast -i nfs-kernel-server` command.

5. Open the `/etc/exports` file in vi and add the following line to it:

   `/export/documentation *(ro,root_squash,sync,no_subtree_check)`

6. Start the NFS server with the `rcnfsserver start` command.

7. Make sure the NFS server is started when the system boots by entering

   `chkconfig nfsserver on`

8. At the terminal window, verify that the file system was exported by entering the following:

   `showmount -e localhost`

Part II: Add a Remote File System to the NFS Client

This exercise uses the da1 virtual machine as the NFS client.

1. (Conditional) If your virtual machine is not running, start VMware player and boot the da1 virtual machine.

2. Log in to da1 as geeko, open a terminal window, and `su` – to root (password **novell**).

3. Create a mountpoint named `/import/docs` for the remote file system to be mounted by entering the following:

   ```
   mkdir -p /import/docs
   ```

4. Open the `/etc/fstab` file in vi and add the following line to it:

   ```
   172.17.8.1:/export/documentation /import/docs nfs defaults 0 0
   ```

   Save the file and close the editor.

5. At the terminal window, mount the file system by entering

   ```
   mount -a
   ```

6. Verify that the file system is mounted by entering `mount`.

   You see the remote host's directory mounted on `/import/docs`.

7. List the files in the mounted file system by entering

   ```
   ls -l /import/docs
   ```

(End of Exercise)

Exercise 4-7   *Create Backup Files with tar*

In this exercise, you use tar to create a full backup and an incremental backup.

In the first part of the exercise, back up the /srv/www/htdocs directory and its content to a tar archive located in the /tmp directory.

In the second part of the exercise, create a full backup of the /srv/www/htdocs directory but this time include the -g **snapshotfile** option of tar in your command. Then add a file to the /srv/www/htdocs directory and create an incremental backup.

NOTE: In this exercise, you copy backup files to the /tmp directory. This is done for demonstration purposes only. You should *never* store an actual backup in the /tmp directory.

This exercise is done on the da-host server.

Detailed Steps to Complete the Exercise

- Part I: Create a Full Backup
- Part II: Create an Incremental Backup

Part I: Create a Full Backup

To create a full backup, do the following:

1. Open a terminal window and su – to root using a password of novell.

2. Change to the /srv/www directory by entering

   cd /srv/www/

3. Create a tar archive of the htdocs directory by entering

   tar czf /tmp/htdocs.tar.gz htdocs

4. Delete the htdocs directory by entering

   rm -r htdocs

5. Copy the backup archive to the /srv/www/ directory by entering

   cp /tmp/htdocs.tar.gz /srv/www

6. Restore the htdocs directory by entering

   tar xzf htdocs.tar.gz

7. View the content of the restored directory by entering

   ls htdocs

Part II: Create an Incremental Backup

To create an incremental backup, do the following:

1. Create a full backup of the htdocs directory by entering

    ```
    cd /srv/www

    tar czv -g /tmp/snapshot_file -f /tmp/
    htdocs_full.tar.gz htdocs
    ```

2. Create a new file in the htdocs directory by entering

    ```
    touch htdocs/incremental.html
    ```

3. Perform an incremental backup by entering

    ```
    tar czv -g /tmp/snapshot_file -f /tmp/
    htdocs_incremental.tar.gz  htdocs
    ```

    Note that tar backs up the file incrementally.

4. View the content of the incremental backup file by entering

    ```
    tar  -tzf  /tmp/htdocs_incremental.tar.gz
    ```

5. View the content of the snapshot_file by entering

    ```
    cat /tmp/snapshot_file
    ```

6. Remove the htdocs directory by entering

    ```
    rm -r htdocs
    ```

7. Unpack the full backup by entering

    ```
    tar xzf /tmp/htdocs_full.tar.gz
    ```

8. Unpack the incremental backup by entering

    ```
    tar xzf /tmp/htdocs_incremental.tar.gz
    ```

9. Close all open windows.

(End of Exercise)

Exercise 4-8   *Create Drive Images with dd (Optional)*

In this exercise, you use dd to create a drive image from an optical disc.

Detailed Steps to Complete the Exercise

Complete the following on da-host:

1. If necessary, insert your *Novell's Guide to the LPIC-1 Certification Using SUSE Linux Enterprise Server 11* Course CD into your host workstation's optical drive.

2. Open a terminal window and `su -` to root using a password of **novell**.

3. At the shell prompt, enter `mount`.

4. In the output, look for an entry similar to the following

   `/dev/sr0 on /media/...`

5. Note the corresponding device name (listed in the first column of the output):

6. Copy an image of the CD to the hard disk by entering the following at the shell prompt:

   `dd if=/dev/device_name of=/tmp/course_cd.iso`

   Copying the DVD can take some time.

7. When the copy process is complete, mount the image file by entering

   `mount -o loop /tmp/course_cd.iso /mnt/`

8. Change to the `/mnt/` directory by entering `cd /mnt` at the shell prompt.

9. Display the content of the image file by entering `ls` at the shell prompt.

   You should see the files from the CD.

10. Enter `cd /media/3112*`, then enter `ls`.

    Note that the content of the image file is identical to the original CD.

11. Change to your home directory and unmount the image file by entering the following command:

    `cd ; umount /mnt`

12. Delete the image file by entering

    `rm /tmp/course_cd.iso`

(End of Exercise)

Exercise 4-9   Back Up a Home Directory with rsync

In this exercise, you use rsync to back up a user's home directory.

This exercise has two parts:

In the first part, use rsync to copy geeko's home directory to the /tmp directory.

In the second part, use rsync to backup the /home/geeko directory on da-host to the /tmp/rsync_test directory on da1.

Detailed Steps to Complete the Exercise

- Part I: Perform a Local Backup with rsync

- Part II: Perform a Remote Backup with rsync

Part I: Perform a Local Backup with rsync

To perform a local backup with rsync, do the following on da-host:

1. Open a terminal window and switch to root using the su – command along with a password of **novell**.

2. Create a test backup directory by entering mkdir /tmp/rsync_test at the shell prompt.

3. Copy geeko's home directory to the backup directory by entering the following command at the shell prompt:

   rsync -av /home/geeko /tmp/rsync_test

4. At the shell prompt, enter cd /tmp/rsync_test/geeko.

5. Enter ls to view the files copied by rsync.

   You should see all of the files in geeko's home directory.

6. Open a second terminal window.

7. As the geeko user, create a new file by entering touch new_file at the shell prompt.

8. Switch to the root terminal window and enter the same rsync command again:

   rsync -av /home/geeko /tmp/rsync_test

   Notice that rsync transfers only the new file and the corresponding directory.

Part II: Perform a Remote Backup with rsync

In this part of the exercise, you perform a a remote backup from da-host to your da1 virtual server. Do the following:

1. If necessary, power on your da1 virtual workstation and wait for it to boot.

2. Log in to da1 as geeko, open a terminal window, and enter su – to switch to the root account (password *novell*).

3. From the root terminal window on da1, perform a remote backup of the geeko user's home directory on da-host by entering the following at the shell prompt (all on one line):

```
rsync -ave ssh root@172.17.8.1:/home/geeko /tmp/
rsync_test
```

4. When prompted to accept the security certificate, enter yes.

5. When prompted, enter a password of novell.

   You should see the geeko user's files on da-host being synchronized to your da1 server.

6. Switch to your da-host workstation and do the following:

   a. Open a terminal session on da-host.

   b. As geeko, create a new file in the geeko home directory by entering echo "A new file" > ~/new_file2 at the shell prompt.

7. Switch back to your da1 server.

8. Enter the rsync command again at the shell prompt:

```
rsync -ave ssh root@172.17.8.1:/home/geeko /tmp/
rsync_test
```

9. When prompted, enter a password of novell.

   Notice that only new files created since the last time rsync was run are copied.

10. Close all terminal windows.

(End of Exercise)

Exercise 4-10   *Manage Linux Kernel Modules and udev Rules*

In this exercise, you load and unload kernel modules and you modify udev rules.

In the first part of this exercise, find out if the joydev kernel module is loaded. If it is loaded, unload the module, then load and unload the module again.

In the second part of this exercise, modify a udev rule to rename your eth0 interface to eth1.

This exercise is done on your da-host server.

Detailed Steps to Complete the Exercise

- Part I: Load and Unload Kernel Modules
- Part II: Modify udev Rules

Part I: Load and Unload Kernel Modules

1. Open a terminal window, then switch to the root user by entering `su -` followed by a password of **novell**.

2. View the currently loaded kernel modules by entering `lsmod` at the shell prompt.

3. Scroll through the modules to see if the joystick module (**joydev**) is loaded. If it's difficult to locate in the output, you can enter `lsmod | grep joydev` at the shell prompt.

   The **0** in the Used column indicates that the module is not in use.

   NOTE: If the joydev module is not listed, skip to step Step 6.

   ---

4. Remove the joystick module from the kernel memory by entering

   `rmmod joydev`

5. Verify that the joydev kernel module was removed from memory by entering `lsmod | grep joydev` at the shell prompt.

   Notice that the joydev module is no longer listed.

6. Load the joystick kernel module by entering

   `modprobe joydev`

7. Verify that the joydev kernel module is loaded in memory by entering `lsmod | grep joydev` at the shell prompt.

8. View the kernel module configuration by entering `modprobe -c | less` at the shell prompt.

9. Scroll through the module configuration information by pressing the Space bar.

10. When you have finished, return to the command line by typing `q`.

11. Create a list of kernel module dependencies by entering

```
depmod -v | less
```

Wait a few minutes for the information to be generated.

12. Scroll through the dependency information by pressing the Space bar.

13. When you have finished, return to the command line by typing `q`.

14. Close the terminal window by entering `exit` twice.

Part II: Modify udev Rules

Complete the following:

1. Open a terminal window and switch to the root user account by entering `su -` followed by a password of **novell**.

2. At the shell prompt, enter `cd /etc/udev/rules.d`.

3. Open the 70-persistent-net.rules file in the vi editor by entering `vi 70-persistent-net.rules` at the shell prompt.

4. Locate and scroll down to the line that sets the name of your network interface to eth0.

5. Change the `NAME=eth0` parameter to **NAME=eth1**.

   (If there is an eth1 entry already because your machine has two network interfaces, change `NAME=eth0` to `NAME=eth2`.)

6. Save your changes and exit the editor by pressing Esc and entering `:exit`.

7. (Conditional) If your da1 virtual server is running, shut it down.

8. Reboot your da-host server by entering `init 6` at the shell prompt.

9. Wait for your default GRUB menu item to be selected to start the boot process.

10. When the system starts to boot, press Esc so you can view your system's boot messages.

    You should see a message indicating eth0 is being renamed to eth1 by udev.

    You should also see a message indicating the eth1 interface has not been configured.

    This happens because there is no configuration for eth1 in `/etc/sysconfig/network/`.

11. When the system has rebooted, log in as geeko with a password of **novell**.

12. Open a terminal session and switch to root with the `su -` command and a password of **novell**.

13. At the shell prompt, enter `cd /etc/udev/rules.d`.

14. Open the 70-persistent-net.rules file in the vi editor by entering `vi 70-persistent-net.rules` at the shell prompt.

15. Change the NAME=eth1 parameter back to **NAME=eth0**.

16. Save your changes and exit the editor by entering `:exit`.

17. Reboot your da-host server by entering `init 6` at the shell prompt.

18. Wait for your default GRUB menu item to be selected to start the boot process.

19. When the system starts to boot, press Esc so you can view your system's boot messages.

20. Verify that your network interface is now named **eth0** and that the appropriate network configuration parameters are applied.

(End of Exercise)

Review Questions

1. What command can you use to list the package in the RPM database that the /etc/hosts file belongs to?

2. Which of the following can be used to automatically obtain software packages from Internet software repositories? (Choose all that apply.)
   a) yum
   b) get
   c) apt-get
   d) yast -i

3. What command can you use to rebuild the RPM database?

4. You have downloaded the source code for a program that you wish to compile. Which command must you first run in the source code directory?
   a) ./configure
   b) make
   c) make file
   d) make install

5. Which of the following commands can be used to list the shared libraries used by the Bash shell (/bin/bash)?
   a) ldconfig –v /bin/bash
   b) ldd –v /bin/bash
   c) rpm –ivh /bin/bash
   d) rpm –ql /bin/bash

6. Which of the following are always stored in the /etc/passwd file? (Choose all that apply.)
   a) encrypted user passwords
   b) user home directory locations
   c) the default shell that each user uses
   d) primary groups for each user

7. When you check the /etc/shadow file on your system, you notice that the date of the last password change is 12904. What does this number represent?
   a) The number of days since installation of the operating system
   b) December 9th 2004
   c) The number of days since January 1st 1970
   d) February 29th 2001

8. Which of the following files are used to obtain default user account settings when you create a user with the useradd command? (Choose all that apply.)
   a) /etc/login.defs
   b) /etc/useradd.default
   c) /etc/default/useradd
   d) /etc/skel

9. You have a file called "Policies&Procedures.txt" that you wish to place in the home directories of all newly created users. What directory should you place this file in?

10. After creating a new user account, what must you do to allow the user to log in to the system?

11. What two commands below can be used to create the group acctg and add the user bob to it?
    a) groupadd —p acctg
    b) groupadd acctg
    c) groupmod —A bob acctg
    d) groupmod —A acctg bob

12. What command can be used to list the users who have logged into the system recently but who are not currently logged in?
    a) last
    b) who
    c) w
    d) btmp

13. Which of the following file permissions gives the group owner the ability to edit the file contents? (Choose all that apply).
    a) rw-rw-r-x
    b) rw-r-x-r-x
    c) rw-r--r-x
    d) r--rw-r-x

14. What single command could you use to change the owner to bob and the group owner to acctg for the file /etc/yearend?

15. What command could you use change the permissions on the file /etc/yearend to rw-rw-r-- using octal notation?

16. What per missions does the system give to new files and directories by default prior to applying the umask?
    a) Files receive 666 and directories receive 666.
    b) Files receive 666 and directories receive 777.
    c) Files receive 777 and directories receive 666.
    d) Files receive 777 and directories receive 777.

17. What will the permission be on a new directory if the umask is set to 027?

18. Which of the following commands will set the Sticky bit special per mission on the directory /public? (Choose all that apply.)
    a) chmod 1777 /public
    b) chmod 2777 /public
    c) chmod 4777 /public
    d) chmod 7777 /public

19. Which of the following commands can be used to set the immutable attribute on a file called file1?
    a) chattr –i file1
    b) lsattr –i file1
    c) lsattr +i file1
    d) chattr +i file1

20. What key within fdisk can be used to change the partition type?

21. Which of the following commands can be used to create an ext2 file system? (Choose all that apply.)
    a) mkfs
    b) mke2fs
    c) mkfs.ext2
    d) mkreiserfs –ext2

22. You have just created a swap partition (/dev/sda3) using fdisk. What commands must you now run to ensure that the swap partition is usable by the system? (Choose all that apply.)
    a) mkfs –swapfs /dev/sda5
    b) mkswap /dev/sda5
    c) swapon /dev/sda5
    d) mount /dev/sda5 swap

23. What file must you edit to ensure that your new swap partition in Question 22 is available by the system after each boot?

24. What command can be used to show disk usage by file system?
    a) du
    b) df
    c) mount
    d) repquota

25. You have enabled user and group quotas on the file system that is mounted to the /var directory. Which files contain the quota limits? (Choose two answers.)
    a) /var/aquota.group
    b) /var/aquota.user
    c) /aquota.group
    d) /aquota.user

26. What command can you use to modify the grace period for quota soft limits?

27. What command would you use to check a ReiserFS file system for errors?
    a) fsckreiser
    b) reiserfsck
    c) reiserfs -check
    d) reiserfs --check

28. You cannot unmount a file system that you had previously mounted to the /mnt directory. What command can show you which users are still using the /mnt directory?

29. You need to add another shared directory on your NFS server for /data. What steps must you perform? (Choose all that apply.)
    a) Add the /data directory to the /etc/exports file
    b) Run the **exportfs –a** command
    c) Restart the NFS daemons
    d) Restart the RPC daemon

30. Which of the following utilities can be used to monitor NFS? (Choose all that apply.)
    a) mount
    b) exportfs
    c) showmount
    d) rpcinfo

31. Which backup type only includes files that were modified since the last full backup?
    a) full
    b) incremental
    c) differential
    d) copy

32. Which of the following archive utilities must be given a list of files to archive via stdin?
    a) cpio
    b) dump
    c) tar
    d) dd

33. What tar command would you use to create a gzip-compressed archive file called /root/myfile.tar.gz that contains the entire contents of the /opt directory?

34. What command can be used to obtain a hardware report for your system?

35. What file in the /proc directory can be used to list the features supported by your system's CPU?

36. Which of the following commands can be used to insert a kernel module into the Linux kernel? (Choose all that apply.)
    a) insmod
    b) modprobe
    c) lsmod
    d) depmod

Discovery Exercises

Installing RPM Software Packages

Use the Internet to find an RPM package that has been compiled for use on SLES 11 (Some common Internet resources include http://rpmfind.net and http://rpm.pbone.com). As the **root** user, use the appropriate command to verify that the package has not already been installed. Then download the RPM package, install it on your system, and use the appropriate commands to view the files installed and version information. When finished, use the appropriate command to remove the software package from your system. Finally, use the **yum** command to obtain and install the package automatically from a software repository on the Internet.

Installing Software Packages from Source

Use the Internet to find the source code for a program that you do not have installed on your system. (The best Internet resource for source code is http://sourceforge.net.) Next, download the source code tar archive, extract it, and use the appropriate commands within the source code directory to compile and install the program as the **root** user. How can you determine which directory the program was installed in? How can you remove the software from your system?

Managing User Accounts

Log in to tty1 as the **root** user and create a user account called **bozo** that has a home directory of /home/bozo and a UID of 600. Next, perform a long listing of all files in /etc/skel (including hidden files). Then perform a long listing of all files in the /home/bozo directory. Why are the lists identical? Who is the owner of the files in /home/bozo?

Next, delete the user bozo from the system without removing the home directory. Then perform another long listing of the files in the /home/bozo directory. Who is the owner?

Create a new user called bozoette that has a home directory of /home/bozoette and a UID of 600. Perform long listings of all files in the /home/bozoette and /home/bozo directories. Who is the owner and why? How could the steps in this Discovery Exercise be useful in a real world environment? When finished, log out of tty1.

Changing Primary Groups

Log in to tty1 as the **root** user and type the **id** command to list the groups that the root user is a member of. How many groups are there? Which one is the primary group? Next, create a new file using the **touch** command and perform a long listing of the file. Who is the group owner of the file? Then run the **newgrp sys** command to temporarily change your primary group for this session to the sys group. Create another new file using the **touch** command and perform a long listing of the file. Who is the group owner of the file now? When finished, log out of tty1.

Setting File Ownership and Permissions

Log in to tty1 as the root user and perform the following actions in order. For each action, write the command(s) that you used. When finished, log out of tty1.

1. Create a new file in the root directory called **permtest** and perform a long listing of the file. What are the default permissions assigned to this file and why?

2. Change your umask to 157, create a new file in the root directory called permtest2, and perform a long listing of the file. What are the default per missions assigned to this file and why?

3. Change the owner of the /permtest file to geeko and group owner to sys.

4. Change the permissions on the /permtest file such that the geeko user can open and edit it, members of the group sys can read and execute it, and everyone else can read it.

5. Change the permissions on the /permtest2 file such that the user, group, and other have no per missions.

6. Try to open the /permtest2 file using the vi editor, then add a line and save your changes using **:w!** in the vi editor. Were you successful? Why?</NL>

Creating Partitions and Filesystems

Provided that you have free space on your hard disk that is not used by a Linux partition, log in to tty1 as the **root** user and use **fdisk** to create an additional partition and **mkfs** to place the ext2 file system on it. Next, use the **tune2fs** command to convert the ext2 file system to ext3 (use the manual pages to identify the appropriate option required). Then reformat the partition to use the ReiserFS file system, create a /data directory, and add a line to /etc/fstab that will mount the file system automatically at boot time to the /data directory. Reboot your computer, log into tty1 as the root user, and verify that the mount was successful. Finally, unmount and check the /data file system for errors. When finished, remount the /data file system and log out of tty1.

Creating, Viewing, and Extracting Archives

Log in to tty1 as the **geeko** user and perform the following actions in order. For each action, write the command(s) that you used. When finished, log out of tty1.

1. Use the tar utility to create a gzip-compressed tar archive (also known as a tarball) called sample.tar.gz in your current directory that contains the entire contents of the Desktop directory.

2. View the contents of your tarball.

3. Extract the contents of your tarball to the /tmp directory and verify that the action was successful.

4. Insert a USB flash drive into your computer and use the cpio utility to create an archive on it that contains the entire contents of the Desktop directory. (Instead of using a filename, specify the /dev/sdb1 device file if your system has a single SATA or SCSI hard disk – check the output of the mount command when you insert your USB drive to confirm the device file used by your USB flash drive.)

5. View the contents of the cpio archive on your USB flash drive.

6. Extract the contents of your cpio archive to the /tmp directory and verify that the action was successful.

SECTION 5 Manage Processes, Jobs, and Runlevels

In this section, you learn how to manage Linux processes, jobs, and runlevels. You also learn how to configure system logging and how to monitor your SLES 11 system.

Objectives

1. Understand and Manage Linux Processes

2. Manage Jobs with cron and at

3. Understand System Initialization and Manage Runlevels

4. Use Monitoring and Troubleshooting Tools

Objective 1   Understand and Manage Linux Processes

To manage processes on your SLES 11 system, you need to be familiar with the following concepts:

- Process-Related Terms and Definitions
- Jobs and Processes
- Manage Linux Processes

Process-Related Terms and Definitions

Before discussing process management, you need to understand the terminology associated with Linux processes. The following terms are commonly used when discussing Linux processes:

- **Program.** A structured set of commands stored in an executable file in the Linux file system. When a program is executed, a process is created.

- **Process.** A program that is loaded into memory and executed by the CPU.

- **User Process.** A process launched by a user that is started from a terminal or within the graphical environment.

- **Daemon Process.** A system process that is not associated with a terminal or a graphical environment. It is a process or collection of processes that wait for an event to trigger an action.

  For network-based services, this event is usually a network connection. Other services, such as cron and atd, are time-based and perform certain tasks at certain points in time.

  The following illustrates the relationship between daemon processes and user processes:

Figure 5-1   *Daemon and User Processes*

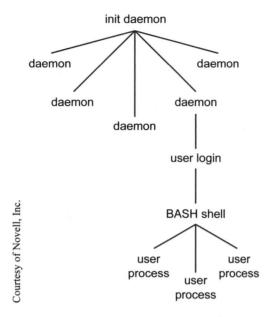

Courtesy of Novell, Inc.

In this example, the init process launches several daemons (**daemon processes**) during the bootup of a Linux system, including a daemon for user login.

After users log in from a text console, a shell is started that lets them start processes manually (**user processes**). Within a graphical environment, users can open a terminal window from which to start user processes. They can also start processes by clicking icons or choosing shortcuts in menus.

- **Process ID (PID).** A unique identifier assigned to every process as it begins.

- **Child Process.** A process that is started by another process (the parent process).

- **Parent Process.** A process that starts one or more other processes (child processes).

- **Parent Process ID (PPID).** The PID of the parent process that created the current process.

The following illustrates the relationship between parent and child process ID numbers:

Figure 5-2   *Relationship between Parent and Child Processes*

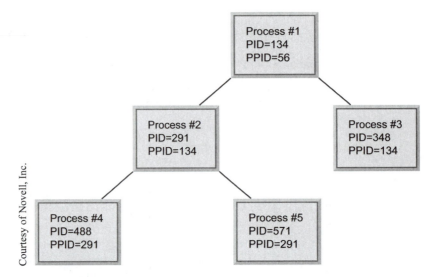

Courtesy of Novell, Inc.

For example, Process #1 is assigned a PID of 134. This process launches Process #2 with a PID of 291 and Process #3 with a PID of 348.

Because Process #1 launched Process #2 and Process #3, the second and third processes are considered child processes of Process #1 (the parent process). The PPID of Processes #2 and #3 is the PID of process #1—134.

Jobs and Processes

You also need to understand the difference between jobs and processes. In Linux, you use a job identifier (commonly called a **job ID**) to refer to processes when launching processes from the command line. The job identifier is a shell-specific numeric value that uniquely identifies the running program.

Independent of the shell, each process is identified using a **process ID** (commonly called a PID) that is unique across the entire system. All jobs have a PID, but not all processes have a usable job ID.

PID 1 always belongs to the init process. This is the first process started on the system and it creates a number of other processes which, in turn, can generate additional processes.

If the highest possible PID within a system has been reached, the next process is allocated the lowest available number (such as PID 17494). Processes run for different lengths of time. After a process has ended, its number becomes available again to be assigned to a new process.

When performing tasks such as changing the priority level of a running program, you use the PID instead of the job ID. When you want to switch a process from the background to the foreground (and the process was started from a terminal), you use the job ID.

Manage Linux Processes

Now that you understand how Linux processes work, you are ready to learn how to manage them. In this objective, the following topics are addressed:

- Managing Foreground and Background Processes
- Viewing and Prioritizing Processes
- Ending a Process
- How Services (Daemons) Work
- Managing a Daemon Process

Managing Foreground and Background Processes

First, you need to understand how to move processes between the foreground and the background. The Linux shell environment allows processes to run in either manner.

Processes executed in the foreground are started in a terminal window and run until the process completes. During the time the process is running, the terminal window does not return to a prompt until the program execution is complete.

Background process execution occurs when a process is started from the shell prompt but the terminal window returns to the prompt before the process finishes executing.

Existing processes can be switched from foreground to background execution under the following circumstances:

- The process must be started in a terminal window or console shell
- The process must not require input from the terminal window

If the process meets these criteria, it can be moved to the background. Processes that require input within the terminal can be moved to the background as well—but when input is requested, the process will be suspended until it is brought to the foreground and the requested input is provided.

Commands in a shell can be started in either the foreground or background. Processes in the foreground directly receive signals.

For example, if you enter `xeyes` to start the xeyes program, it is running in the foreground. If you press Ctrl+z, the process stops:

```
geeko@da1:~> xeyes
[1]+  Stopped                 xeyes
geeko@da1:~>
```

You can continue running a stopped process in the background by entering `bg`, as in the following:

```
geeko@da1:~> bg
[1]+ xeyes &
geeko@da1:~>
```

The ampersand (&) displayed in the output indicates the process is now running in the background. Appending an ampersand to a command starts the process in the background instead of the foreground, as shown in the following:

```
geeko@da1:~> xeyes &
[2] 4351
geeko@da1:~>
```

With this, the shell that you started the program from is available again for user input.

In the above example, both the job ID ([2]) and the process ID of the program (4351) are returned.

Each process started from the shell is assigned a job ID by the job control of the shell. The `jobs` command lists the contents of the job control, as in the following:

```
geeko@da1:~> jobs
[1]+  Stopped                 xeyes
[2]   Running                 xeyes &
[4]-  Running                 sleep 99 &
geeko@da1:~>
```

In this example, the process with job ID 3 has already been terminated. Processes 2 and 4 are running in the background (notice the &), and process 1 is stopped.

The plus sign (+) indicates the process that will respond to `fg` without options, while the minus sign (-) indicates the process that will inherit the + sign once the process currently with the + sign ends.

In this example, the next process will be assigned the job ID of 5 (highest number + 1).

Not only can you continue running a stopped process in the background by using the `bg` command, you can also switch a process to the foreground by entering `fg` *job_ID*, as in the following:

```
geeko@da1:~> fg 1
xeyes
```

The shell also informs you about the termination of a process running in the background:

```
[4]-  Done                    sleep 99
```

The job ID is displayed in square brackets. "Done" indicates the process terminated properly. If you see "Terminated" instead, it indicates the process received a request to terminate. "Killed" indicates a forceful termination of the process.

Viewing and Prioritizing Processes

You can view information about the processes running on your Linux system and assign priorities to them using the following command line tools:

- ps
- pstree
- nice and renice
- top

ps

You can view running processes on your Linux system with the ps (**process status**) command:

```
geeko@da1:~> ps
  PID TTY          TIME CMD
 3103 pts/0    00:00:00 bash
 3129 pts/0    00:00:00 sleep
 3130 pts/0    00:00:00 ps
```

Using the x option, you can also view terminal-independent processes, as shown in the following:

```
geeko@da1:~> ps x
  PID TTY      STAT   TIME COMMAND
 3102 ?        S      0:00 sshd: geeko@pts/0
 3103 pts/0    Ss     0:00 -bash \
 3129 pts/0    S      0:00 sleep 99
 3133 pts/0    R+     0:00 ps x
```

In the above example, the process with PID 3102 is a terminal-independent process.

Some of the more commonly used ps command options are shown in the table below:

Table 5-1   *ps Options*

Option	Description
a	Show all processes that have controlling terminals, including those of other users.
x	Show processes with and without controlling terminals.
-w, w	Provide detailed, wide output.
u	Display user-oriented format.
f	List processes hierarchically (in a tree format).
-l, l	Long format.
U *userlist*	Select by effective user ID (EUID) or name.

For example, the output of entering `ps axl` is similar to the following:

```
geeko@da1:~> ps axl
F  UID   PID  PPID  PRI NI  VSZ   RSS  WCHAN  STAT  TTY    TIME COMMAND
...
0  1013  4170  4169  15  0  3840 1760  wait4  Ss    pts/0  0:00 -bash
0  1013  4332  4170  15  0  4452 1812  finish T     pts/0  0:00 xeyes
0  1013  4351  4170  15  0  4452 1812  schedu S     pts/0  0:01 xeyes
0  1013  4356  4170  17  0  2156  652  -      R+    pts/0  0:00 ps axl
```

If you enter `ps aux`, the output is formatted differently, as shown in the following:

```
geeko@da10:~> ps aux
USER    PID  %CPU %MEM   VSZ   RSS TTY     STAT START   TIME COMMAND
geeko  4170  0.0  0.3   3840 1760 pts/0   Ss   12:10   0:00 -bash
geeko  4332  0.0  0.3   4452 1812 pts/0   T    12:59   0:00 xeyes
geeko  4351  0.3  0.3   4452 1812 pts/0   S    13:01   0:03 xeyes
geeko  4375  0.0  0.1   2156  680 pts/0   R+   13:19   0:00 ps aux
```

With the `l` option, you see the process ID of the parent process (PPID), the process priority (PRI), and the nice (NI) value of the individual processes. With the `u` option, the load percentage is shown (%CPU, %MEM).

The following is a description of some of the fields (columns) displayed in the output of the `ps` command:

Table 5-2   *ps Output Fields*

Field	Description
UID	User ID.
PID	Process ID.
PPID	Parent process ID.
TTY	Number of the controlling terminal.
PRI	Priority number (the lower it is, the more computer time is allocated to the process).
NI (nice)	Influences the dynamic priority adjustment.
STAT	Current process status (see Table 5-3).
TIME	CPU time used.
COMMAND	Name of the command.

NOTE: These and other fields are explained in the manual page of `ps`. Enter `man ps` at the shell prompt to learn more about `ps`.

In the preceding table, one of the fields in the output of PS is the STAT field. The STAT process state can be one of the following values:

Table 5-3   *Process State Codes*

Code	Description
R (Runnable)	Process can be run.
S (Sleeping)	Process is waiting for an external event (such as data arriving).
D (Uninterruptable sleep)	Process cannot be terminated at the moment.
T (Traced or Stopped)	Process is suspended.
X	Process is dead.
Z (Zombie)	Process has terminated itself, but its return value has not yet been requested.

You can also use the `--format` option with ps to specify exactly which fields you want included in the output of the command. This allows you to format the output of `ps` to present exactly the information you need:

```
geeko@da3:~ > ps ax --format 'cputime %C, nice %n, name %c'
cputime %CPU, nice  NI, name COMMAND
cputime  0.0, nice   0, name bash
cputime  0.0, nice   0, name xeyes
cputime  0.3, nice   0, name xeyes
cputime  0.0, nice   0, name ps
```

pstree

In addition to ps, you can also use the `pstree` command to view information about the processes running on your Linux system. This command displays a list of processes in the form of a tree structure, which provides an overview of the hierarchy of a process.

This can be very useful. For example, if you need to end multiple processes, you can use pstree to identify the appropriate parent process and end that process instead. The `-p` option displays the PID of the processes. The `-u` option displays the user ID if the owner has changed.

Because the list of processes is often long, you can enter the following command to pause the output one page at a time:

```
pstree -up | less
```

nice and renice

In addition to viewing processes, you can also use command line tools to configure the priority of processes running on the Linux system.

Linux always tries to distribute the available computing time equitably to all running processes. However, there may be times when you need to assign a process more or less computing time. You can do this with the `nice` command, as shown in the following:

```
geeko@da1:~ > nice -n +5 xeyes
```

This command runs a program and assigns the corresponding process a specific nice value that affects the calculation of the process priority (which can be either increased or decreased). If you do not specify a nice value with this command, the process is started with a default value of +10. In the example above, the xeyes program is started with nice and assigned a nice value of +5.

The NI column in the top list (see Figure 5-3) contains the nice values assigned to the process. The default value 0 is regarded as neutral. You can assign the nice level using a numeric value of -20 to 19.

The lower the value of the nice level, the higher the priority of the process. A process with a nice level of -20 runs at the highest priority; a process with a nice level of 19 runs at the lowest priority. The nice level is used by the scheduler to determine how frequently to service a running process.

Only root is permitted to start a process with a negative nice value (such as `nice -n -3 xeyes`). If a normal user attempts to do this, an error message is returned.

In addition to nice, you can also use the `renice` command to change the nice value of a running process without restarting it. An example is shown in the following:

```
geeko@da1:~ > renice 5 1712
```

In this example, the command assigns the process with the PID 1712 a new nice value of 5.

Only root can reduce the nice value of a running process (such as from 10 to 9 or from 3 to -2). All other users can only increase the nice value (such as from 10 to 11). For example, if the user geeko attempts to assign the process 28056 that currently has a nice value of 3 to a nice value of 1, a "Permission denied" message is returned.

top

The `top` command allows you to view process information in a continuously updated list. The list of processes is updated in short intervals, thus providing a real-time view of what's happening in the running system. This command can also be used to assign a new nice value to running processes or to end processes.

The information displayed by `top` can be filtered by a specific user and can be sorted on any displayed field. If you have sufficient privileges, you can type `r` to adjust the priority of a process.

NOTE: The same restrictions apply when changing process nice levels using `top`. Non-root users can increase the nice level, but they cannot lower it.

When you enter `top`, a list similar to the following is displayed:

Figure 5-3   *The top Command*

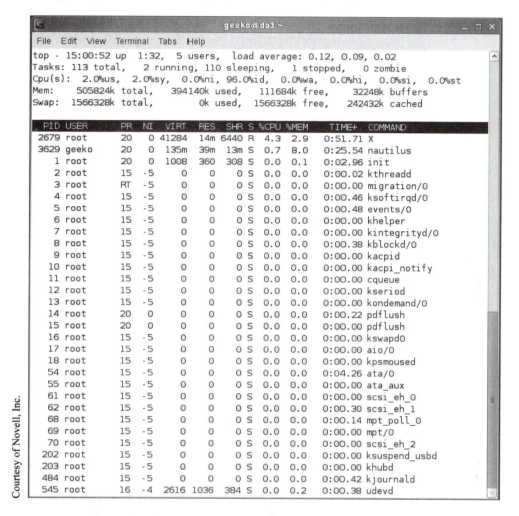

The list displayed is sorted by computing time and is updated every three seconds. You can terminate top by typing q.

The following table describes the default columns seen in the output of the `top` command:

Table 5-4   *top Columns*

Column	Description
PID	Process ID.
USER	User name.
PR	Priority.
NI	Nice value.
VIRT	Virtual image (in KB).

Column	Description
RES	Resident memory size (in KB).
SHR	Shared memory size (in KB).
S	Process status.
%CPU	CPU usage.
%MEM	Memory usage (RES).
TIME+	CPU time.
COMMAND	Command name/line.

You can view the process management commands available in top by entering ? or h. The following are some of the more commonly used commands:

Table 5-5   *Commands Within top*

Command	Description
r	Assign a new nice value to a running process.
k	Send the termination signal (same as kill or killall) to a running process. The user is asked for the signal to send.
N	Sort by process ID.
P	Sort by CPU load.
i	Show non-idle processes only.

Command line options can be used to change the default behavior of top. For example, top -d 5 (delay) changes the default delay (three seconds) before refresh to five seconds. Use top -b (batch mode) when you want to write the output of top to a file or pass it to another process. Use top -n 3 (iterations) to cause top to quit after the third refresh. This is especially useful in combination with -b (e.g., top -b -n 1).

Ending a Process

A key part of managing processes is knowing how to manually end a process from the shell prompt. From time to time, you may encounter hung processes that won't exit normally. In this situation, you can do the following to end the process:

- Use kill and killall
- Use the GNOME System Monitor

NOTE: You can also send a signal to end the process in top using the k command.

Use kill and killall

You can use the `kill` and `killall` commands from the shell prompt to terminate a process (to be more exact: to send a signal to a process). The `killall` command sends the signal to all processes with an indicated command name; the `kill` command sends the signal only to the specified process.

The `kill` command requires the PID of the process. You can use `ps` or `top` to find the PID of the process. The `killall` command requires the command name of the process instead of the PID.

For example, suppose you enter `xeyes` at the command line to start the xeyes program. The process is assigned a PID of 18734. To end this process, you could enter either of the following commands:

```
kill 18734
```

```
killall xeyes
```

A process may respond in one of the following ways when receiving a kill signal:

- Captures the signal and reacts to it (if it has a corresponding function available). For example, an editor may close an open file properly before it terminates.

- Ignores the signal if no function exists for handling that signal.

However, the process does not have control over how the following signals are handled by the kernel:

```
kill -SIGKILL or kill -9
```

```
kill -STOP or kill -19
```

These signals cause the process to be ended immediately (SIGKILL) or to be stopped (STOP).

You should use SIGKILL with caution. Although the operating system closes all files that are still open, the process's data buffered in memory is no longer processed and data can get lost.

NOTE: For a complete list of signals generated by kill and what their numbers stand for, enter `kill -l` or `man 7 signal` at the shell prompt.

The following are some of the more commonly used signals:

Table 5-6   *Signals that Can Be Sent to Processes*

Number	Name	Description
1	SIGHUP	Reload configuration file.
2	SIGINT	Interrupt from keyboard (Ctrl+c).
9	SIGKILL	Kill process.

Number	Name	Description
15	SIGTERM	End process immediately. (Terminate process in a controlled manner so cleanup is possible.)
18	SIGCONT	Continue process stopped with STOP.
19	STOP	Stop process.

For the kernel to forward the signal to the process, the signal must be sent by the owner of the process or by root. By default (without options), `kill` and `killall` send signal 15 (SIGTERM).

The following is the recommended procedure for ending a misbehaving process:

1. Send SIGTERM by entering the following:

    `kill PID`

    This is equivalent to `kill -SIGTERM PID` or `kill -15 PID`. You can use `killall` instead of `kill` and the command name of the process instead of the PID.

    If a process has been started from the Bash, you can also use the job ID (such as `kill %4`) instead of the process number.

2. Wait a few moments for the process to be cleaned up.

3. If the process is still hung, send a SIGKILL signal by entering one of the following:

    `kill -SIGKILL PID`

    `kill -9 PID`

    You can use `killall` instead of `kill` and the command name of the process instead of the PID.

Use the GNOME System Monitor

In addition to using the `kill` and `killall` commands, you can also use the GNOME System Monitor to end a process on your Linux system.

Start the System Monitor by selecting *Computer > More Applications > System > GNOME System Monitor*. Within System Monitor, click the *Processes* tab. When you do, the following is displayed:

Figure 5-4   *GNOME System Monitor*

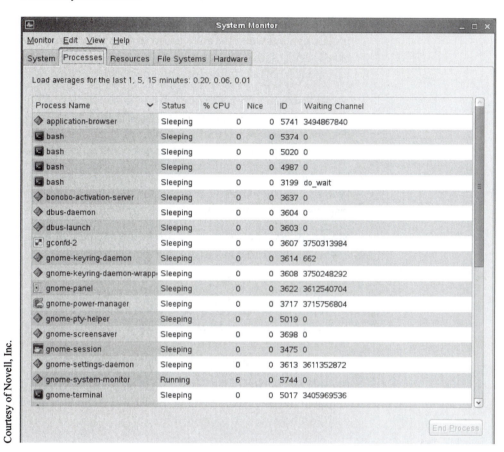

Courtesy of Novell, Inc.

You can kill a misbehaving or hung process by selecting it from the list of processes and then selecting ***End Process***.

The following information is displayed by default in columns in the Processes tab:

Table 5-7   *System Monitor Columns*

Column	Description
Process Name	Name of the process.
Status	Status of the process (running, sleeping, etc.).
CPU%	Processor load caused by the process.
Nice	Nice value, determines the priority of the process when allocated computer time by the kernel.
ID	Number of the process (Process ID).

You can customize what information is displayed by editing the preferences (***Edit > Preferences***).

How Services (Daemons) Work

On Linux, a service is also called a **daemon**. It is a process (or collection of processes) that waits for an event to trigger an action of the program. In network-based services, this event is usually a network connection. Other services, such as cron and atd, are time-based and perform specified tasks at certain points in time.

Network-based services create a listener on a TCP or UDP port when they start up, usually during system boot. This listener waits for network traffic to appear on the designated port. When traffic is detected, the program processes the traffic as input and generates output that is sent back to the requester.

For example, when a Web browser connects to a Web server, it sends a request to the Web server. The Web server processes the request and sends back its response. This response is then handled by the Web browser, which renders the page on the screen.

Most network-based services work in this manner, although the information is not always clear text data as in the Web server example.

Managing a Daemon Process

To manage Linux processes, you must understand how to manage daemon processes. Daemons run in the background and are usually started when the system is booted. Daemons provide a number of services on the system.

For this reason, daemons are terminal-independent processes and are identified in the output of the ps x command in the TTY column by a question mark (?). An example is shown below:

```
da3:~ # ps x
PID  TTY        STAT    TIME COMMAND
...
2767 ?          Ssl     0:00 /usr/sbin/nscd
...
```

In most cases, the name of a daemon on Linux ends with the letter d, such as syslogd or sshd. However, this is not a hard-and-fast rule. There are a number of Linux services whose name does not end with the letter d, such as cron or rpcbind (not rpcbindd).

Two types of daemons are used on Linux:

- **Signal-controlled daemons.** Activated when a corresponding task exists (cupsd, for example).

- **Interval-controlled daemons.** Activated at specified time intervals (cron or atd, for example).

Each daemon has a corresponding script in /etc/init.d/. Each script can be managed with at least the following parameters:

Table 5-8   *Init-Script Parameters*

Parameter	Description
start	Starts the service.
stop	Stops the service.
reload (or restart)	Reloads the configuration file of the service, or stops the service and starts it again.

Many scripts have an **rc** symbolic link, either in the `/usr/sbin/` directory or the `/sbin/` directory, as in the following:

```
da1:~ # ls -l /usr/sbin/rcsshd
lrwxrwxrwx  1 root root 16 Jul 16 17:26 /usr/sbin/rcsshd -> /etc/
init.d/sshd
```

You can start the service from the `/etc/init.d/` directory (such as `/etc/init.d/sshd start`). If a link exists in `/usr/sbin/` or `/sbin/`, you can also use `rcservice` (such as `rcsshd start`).

You can find configuration files for daemons in the `/etc/` directory or one of its subdirectories. The executables (the actual daemons) are located either in the `/sbin/` directory or the `/usr/sbin/` directory.

NOTE: For documentation on most daemons, see the respective directory in `/usr/share/doc/packages/`.

Some important Linux daemons that you should become familiar with include the following:

- **cron.** Starts other processes at specified times.

- **cupsd.** Manages printers and print queues.

- **httpd.** Provides Web pages.

- **sshd.** Enables secure communication by way of insecure networks (secure shell).

- **syslog-ng.** Logs system messages in the `/var/log/` directory.

Exercise 5-1   *Manage Linux Processes*

In this exercise, you start and stop processes and change their priorities.

You will find this exercise at the end of the chapter.

(End of Exercise)

Objective 2   Manage Jobs with cron and at

As a SLES 11 administrator, you will find that there are many tasks that need to be carried out on a regular basis on your Linux system. For example, you may need to update a database or back up users' data in the /home directory. While you could run these tasks manually, it would be more efficient (and more reliable) if you were to configure the Linux system to run them automatically for you.

You need to know how to

- Schedule Jobs with cron
- Schedule Jobs with at
- Use anacron
- Schedule Jobs with cron and at

Schedule Jobs with cron

One option for doing this is to use cron. The cron daemon allows you to schedule jobs that will be carried out for you on a regular schedule.

In this objective, the following topics are addressed:

- crontab File Syntax
- Defining System Jobs
- Defining User Jobs

crontab File Syntax

The cron daemon is activated by default on SLES 11. Once a minute, it checks to see if any jobs have been defined for the current time.

The cron daemon uses files called crontabs. These files list jobs and when they are to be run. Several crontab files exist on a Linux system. They are used to run system jobs. Users on the system can also define their own crontab files.

Each line in a crontab file defines a single cron job. There are six or seven fields in each line, separated by whitespace characters (spaces or tabs). The first five fields define when the cron job should be run. The sixth field in the line specifies the command to be run. If system jobs are defined, the sixth field contains the name of user to be used to run the job, and the seventh field specifies the command to be run.

The cron daemon can run any command or shell script. However, no user interaction is available when the command or shell script is run.

The first five fields in the crontab file use the following syntax:

Table 5-9   *Crontab Time Fields*

Field Number	Field Label	Range
1	Minutes	0–59
2	Hours	0–23
3	Day of the Month	1–31
4	Month	1–12
5	Weekday	0–7 (0 and 7 represent Sunday)

The following are guidelines for configuring these fields:

- If you want a job to run every minute, hour, day, or month, type an asterisk (*) in the corresponding field.

- You can include several entries in a field in a list separated by commas.

- You can specify a range with start and end values separated by a hyphen.

- You can configure time steps with /*n* (where *n* represents the size of the step).

- You can specify months and weekdays using the first three letters of their names (for example, MON, TUE, JAN, FEB). The letters are not case sensitive. However, when you use letters, you cannot use ranges or lists.

- Numbers representing the weekdays start at **0** for Sunday and run through the entire week consecutively, with **7** representing Sunday again.

  For example, **3** is Wednesday and **6** is Saturday.

- If the first field starts with a - character and the job belongs to root, no log entry is written to the /var/log/messages file.

The following is an example of a cron job entry:

```
*/10 8-17 * * 1-5 fetchmail mailserver
```

In this example, every 10 minutes (***/10**) between 8:00 AM and 5:50 PM (**8-17**), from Monday to Friday (**1-5**) the fetchmail command is run to fetch incoming emails from the **mailserver** server.

For system jobs, the user who has the permissions to run the command must also be specified. Enter the username between the time definition (the first five fields) and the name of the command (which now becomes the seventh field).

Defining System Jobs

The cron daemon can be configured to run scheduled system jobs. You can define system jobs in the /etc/crontab file. This file is shown below:

```
SHELL=/bin/sh
PATH=/usr/bin:/usr/sbin:/sbin:/bin:/usr/lib/news/bin
MAILTO=root
#
# check scripts in cron.hourly, cron.daily, cron.weekly, and
cron.monthly
#
-*/15 * * * *   root  test -x /usr/lib/cron/run-crons && /usr/lib/
cron/run-crons >/dev/null 2>&1
```

The job pre-defined in /etc/crontab runs the scripts contained in the following directories at the intervals indicated:

Table 5-10   *The /etc/cron.**time-interval** Directories*

Directory	Interval
/etc/cron.hourly	Jobs that run on an hourly basis.
/etc/cron.daily	Jobs that run on a daily basis.
/etc/cron.weekly	Jobs that run on a weekly basis.
/etc/cron.monthly	Jobs that run on a monthly basis.

NOTE: While you can add lines to /etc/crontab, you should not delete the default lines.

NOTE: For a detailed description of the syntax for /etc/crontab, enter man 5 crontab at the shell prompt.

In the default configuration, only the /etc/cron.daily/ directory contains scripts, as shown below:

```
da1:~ # ls -l /etc/cron.*ly
/etc/cron.daily:
total 32
-rwxr-xr-x 1 root root  587 Feb 20 19:50 logrotate
-rwxr--r-- 1 root root  948 Feb 20 23:01 suse-clean_catman
-rwxr--r-- 1 root root 1693 Feb 20 23:01 suse-do_mandb
-rwxr-xr-x 1 root root 1875 Sep  1  2003 suse.de-backup-rc.config
-rwxr-xr-x 1 root root 2059 Sep  8  2003 suse.de-backup-rpmdb
-rwxr-xr-x 1 root root  566 Jul 23  2004 suse.de-check-battery
-rwxr-xr-x 1 root root 1314 Jul 27  2005 suse.de-clean-tmp
-rwxr-xr-x 1 root root  371 Sep  1  2003 suse.de-cron-local

/etc/cron.hourly:
total 0

/etc/cron.monthly:
total 0

/etc/cron.weekly:
total 0
```

These shell scripts may get overwritten if you update your system. Any modifications you made to these files will be lost if these files are updated. Therefore, we recommend that you add your own customized scripts to `/root/bin/cron.daily.local` (which is sourced by `/etc/cron.daily/suse.de-cron.local`) because this file is not overwritten when you update your system.

The `/usr/lib/cron/cron-runs` script called from the `/etc/crontab` file not only ensures that the scripts in the `/etc/cron.`*time-interval* directories are run at the prescribed intervals, but also that jobs are run later if they cannot be run at the specified time.

For example, if a script could not be run because the computer was turned off at the scheduled time, the script is automatically run later using the settings in `/etc/crontab`. This is true only for jobs defined in `cron.hourly`, `cron.daily`, `cron.weekly`, or `cron.monthly`.

The information about the last time jobs were run is provided by the existence of the corresponding file in the `/var/spool/cron/lastrun/` directory. The time stamp of the empty files (e.g., `cron.daily`) in this directory is the time the script was run.

To add a system cron job, complete the following:

1. Open a terminal session and switch to your root user account.

2. Open `/etc/crontab` in a text editor.

3. Scroll to the bottom of the file and insert your cron job.

    For example, suppose you wanted to regularly update a database on your system using a script in `/usr/local/bin/` named updb. You need this script to be run every hour from 8:00 AM to 6:00 PM, Monday through Friday. You would add the following line to the file:

```
0 8-18 * * 1-5 root /usr/local/bin/updb
```

4. Save your changes to the file and exit the text editor.

In addition to putting cron jobs directly in /etc/crontab, you can also create individual crontab files for system jobs in the /etc/cron.d/ directory. These files must use the same syntax format as /etc/crontab. However, be aware that jobs defined in files in /etc/cron.d are *not* run automatically at a later time if they can't be run at their scheduled time.

Defining User Jobs

In addition to system jobs, the cron daemon can also run jobs for individual users. Users can define their own crontab files in the /var/spool/cron/tabs/ directory. These crontab files contain a schedule of jobs each user wants run. These files always belong to the root user.

Users create and maintain their own crontab files using the crontab command. The following options can be used with the crontab command:

Table 5-11   *crontab Command Options*

Option	Description
crontab -e	Creates or edits jobs. The vi editor is used.
crontab *file*	Replaces any existing crontab file for the current user with the specified *file*.
crontab -l	Displays current jobs.
crontab -r	Deletes all jobs.

For example, suppose you want to define a cron job that copies the contents of your user's home directory to an external USB drive mounted in /media/USB.001 every night at 5:05 PM Monday to Friday. You would need to do the following:

1. Open a terminal session.

2. At the shell prompt, enter crontab -e.

    The existing crontab file is opened in the vi editor, or, if no crontab file exists yet, a blank crontab file is created for your user using the vi editor.

3. Press i, then enter the following:

    ```
    5 17 * * 1-5 cp -r ~/* /media/USB.001
    ```

4. Press Esc, then enter :wq.

You can specify which users are allowed to create cron jobs and which aren't by creating the following two files:

■   **/etc/cron.allow.** Users listed in this file can create cron jobs.

■   **/etc/cron.deny.** Users who are *not* listed in this file can create cron jobs.

By default, the `/etc/cron.deny` file already exists with its own entries, including the following:

- guest

- gast

If the `/etc/cron.allow` file exists, it is the only file evaluated; `/etc/cron.deny` will be ignored in this situation. If neither of these files exists, only the root user is allowed to define user cron jobs.

Schedule Jobs with at

If you want to schedule a job to run *one* time only in the future (instead of scheduling it on a regular basis with cron) you can use the `at` command. To use `at`, you must first verify that the at package has been installed and that the atd service has been started.

You define an at job at the command prompt by entering `at launch_time`, where `launch_time` is the time (12:34, for example) when you want the job to begin.

Then you enter the commands you want at to run one line at a time at the **at>** prompt. When you finish entering commands, you save the job by pressing Ctrl+d.

The following is an example of creating a job with the `at` command:

```
geeko@da1:~> at 21:00
warning: commands will be executed using /bin/sh
at> /home/geeko/bin/doit
at> mail -s "Results file of geeko" geeko@da1 < /home/geeko/results
at> <EOT>
job 4 at 2009-08-27 21:00
```

You can also enter the commands you want to be executed by `at` in a text file. If you do this, then you need to enter `at -f file launch_time` at the shell prompt, where `file` is the path and file name of the file.

The following table lists some other commonly used at commands and options:

Table 5-12   *The atq and atrm Commands*

Command	Description
atq	Displays day, time, and username for scheduled jobs (including job numbers, which are needed to delete a job)
atrm *job_number*	Deletes a job (using the job number)

As with cron, you can restrict access to the atd daemon. Two files determine which users can run the at command:

- **/etc/at.allow.** Users entered in this file can define jobs.

- **/etc/at.deny.** Users who are **not** listed in this file can define jobs.

These files are text files you can modify or create. By default, the /etc/at.deny file already exists with its own entries, as shown below:

```
da1:~ # cat /etc/at.deny

alias
backup
bin
daemon
ftp
games

...
```

If the /etc/at.allow file exists, only this file is evaluated. If neither of these files exists, only the user root can define at jobs.

Use anacron

The cron daemon works well, but it has one weakness. If you schedule a job to run, but the system ends up being shut off at the time you configured, cron won't run the job when the system comes back up. Instead, it waits until the next time the job is scheduled to run.

This can be a problem if cron jobs are scheduled to run late at night, but the system is typically shut off at night.

To fix this problem, you can install anacron on your system.

NOTE: You can download anacron from anacron.sourceforge.net (http://anacron.sourceforge.net).

Anacron is designed to ensure that jobs are run at intervals. When anacron runs, it checks to see if any jobs have not been run yet. If so, it will run them automatically. This ensures the appropriate jobs are run even if the system has been down for some time.

Typically, you reconfigure your standard system cron jobs as anacron jobs, which are stored in the /etc/anacrontab file. The anacron job definitions in this file use the following syntax:

period   delay   job_identifier   command

As you can see, four fields are used to define each anacron job. These fields are defined below:

- **period.** Frequency (in days) when the command specified in the job should be run.

- **delay.** Delay (in minutes) between the time when anacron starts and when the command specified in the job should run.

  This is a very useful feature. If a system has been down for some time, you probably don't want anacron to run multiple jobs all at once when it comes back up. Using the delay parameter, you can space out the time when each job runs.

- **job_identifier.** Identifies the job with a unique identifier.

- **command.** Specifies the actual command to be run by the job.

It's important to note that anacron is not a service and is not started automatically when the system starts. It can be run by a startup script, such as `.bashrc` or `.bash_profile`. It can also be run automatically as a cron job. When you run anacron, you can specify the `-t` option if you want to use a configuration file other than the default.

Exercise 5-2   **Schedule Jobs with cron and at**

In this exercise, you practice scheduling jobs with cron and at.

You will find this exercise at the end of the chapter.

(End of Exercise)

Objective 3 Understand System Initialization and Manage Runlevels

In order to manage the Linux boot process, you need to understand how the operating system is loaded. You need to understand the following:

- Describe the Linux Load Procedure
- Manage the Grand Unified Bootloader (GRUB)
- Use the LILO Boot Manager
- Manage Runlevels
- Manage the Boot Loader
- Manage Runlevels

Describe the Linux Load Procedure

The following represents the basic steps of booting a computer with the Linux operating system installed:

Figure 5-5   *The Linux Boot Process*

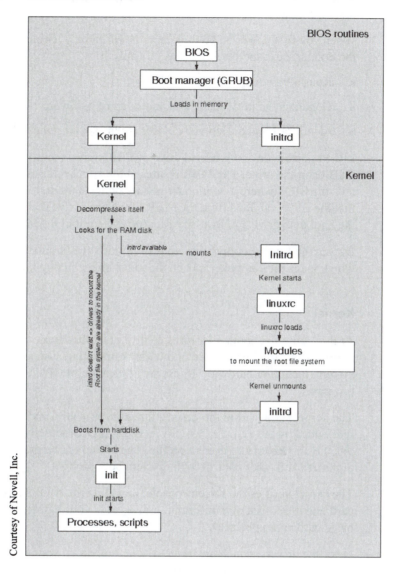

Courtesy of Novell, Inc.

The Linux boot process can be categorized into the following phases:

- BIOS and Boot Manager
- Kernel
- Initial RAM File System
- init

BIOS and Boot Manager

The first phase involves the Basic Input Output System (BIOS) and the bootloader. The BIOS is a a series of small programs and drivers contained in a chip integrated in the system motherboard that allow the CPU to communicate with basic system devices, such as keyboards, I/O ports, the system speaker, system RAM, floppy drives, and hard drives.

When you first power on your system, the BIOS on your motherboard takes charge of the boot process and performs several tasks. It

- Runs a Power-On Self Test (POST)

- Conducts the initial detection and setup of hardware

- Identifies bootable storage devices (such as your optical drive or hard disk drive).

If the bootable device is a hard drive, the BIOS also reads the *master boot record* (MBR) on the drive. The MBR resides in the boot sector of your hard drive and it tells the BIOS where a *bootloader* resides on the hard drive. A bootloader is software that the BIOS can load from the MBR of the hard drive that allows the CPU to access the hard disk drive and load an operating system into RAM.

During the Linux boot process, the BIOS starts the bootloader (such as GRUB), which loads the Linux kernel and the initrd image into memory.

Kernel

At this point, the bootloader turns control of the boot process over to the Linux kernel. The kernel is the core of the Linux operating system. It controls the entire system, including hardware access and allocation of CPU time and memory to programs.

The kernel is located in the /boot directory of your Linux file system. It is referenced by the /boot/vmlinuz file, which is actually a link to the /boot/vmlinuz-*kernel_version* file. The kernel uncompresses itself and then organizes and takes control of the system boot process.

The kernel verifies the screen console, including the BIOS registers for your graphics card and the screen output format. It also reads your BIOS settings and initializes basic hardware interfaces.

Next, the drivers, which are part of the kernel, probe your system's hardware and initialize each device accordingly.

Initial RAM File System

The Initial RAM File System (initramfs) is a cpio archive that the kernel can load into a ramdisk.

The initramfs image is used because Linux systems can use a wide variety of storage devices for the root (/) file system. Some devices may be created from a software RAID array; some devices may even reside on a different computer and be accessed through NFS or Samba. These types of file systems can't be mounted by the kernel until other software, which resides on those unmounted file systems, is loaded.

To make the system boot correctly in these situations, the bootloader creates a small, virtual hard drive in memory called a ramdisk and transfers a temporary root file system from the image into it. The Linux kernel then uses this temporary file system to load the software and complete the tasks required for it to mount the real file systems on your storage devices.

The initramfs must always provide an executable named `init` that should execute the actual init program on the root file system for the boot process to proceed.

NOTE: Earlier SUSE Linux versions used an initial ramdisk named **initrd**. Despite the fact that the format changed, the file is still `/boot/initrd`. This file is actually just a link to `/boot/initrd-`***kernel_version***, which is the file that holds the gzipped cpio archive.

The kernel starts the `init` program contained in the initramfs. The init program is a shell script that, among other things, loads the kernel modules needed to mount the actual root file system, mounts the root file system, and then finally starts `/sbin/init` from the root file system.

To view the init script in initramfs, you can unpack the cpio archive. An example is shown below:

```
da1:~ # mkdir /tmp/initramfs
da1:~ # cd /tmp/initramfs/
da1:/tmp/initramfs # gunzip -c /boot/initrd-2.6.27.11-1-pae | cpio -i
25061 blocks
da1:/tmp/initramfs # ls
bin    boot  bootsplash  config  dev  etc  init  lib  mkinitrd.config
proc   root  run_all.sh  sbin    sys  tmp  usr  var
da1:/tmp/initramfs # less init
```

The initramfs is created with the proper modules included, such as those needed to access the file system, during installation. The modules to include are listed in the `INITRD_MODULES` variable in `/etc/sysconfig/kernel`. If additional or different modules are needed (because of a hardware change, for example), you would edit the list of modules, and then rebuild the initramfs. The command is the same as the one to build an initrd: `mkinitrd`. This is shown below:

```
da1:~ # mkinitrd
Kernel image:   /boot/vmlinuz-2.6.27.11-1-pae
Initrd image:   /boot/initrd-2.6.27.11-1-pae
Root device:    /dev/disk/by-id/ata-VMware_Virtual_IDE_Hard_Drive_
00000000000000000001-part2 (/dev/sda2) (mounted on / as ext3)
Resume device:  /dev/disk/by-id/ata-VMware_Virtual_IDE_Hard_Drive_
00000000000000000001-part1 (/dev/sda1)
Kernel Modules: hwmon thermal_sys processor thermal dock scsi_mod
libata ata_piix scsi_transport_spi mptbase mptscsih mptspi
ata_generic ide-core piix ide-pci-generic fan jbd mbcache ext3 edd
crc-t10dif sd_mod usbcore ohci-hcd ehci-hcd uhci-hcd ff-memless hid
usbhid
Features:       block usb resume.userspace resume.kernel
Bootsplash:     SLES (800x600)25065 blocks
```

NOTE: The man page for `mkinitrd` lists the parameters that can be passed to the init program in the initramfs via the kernel command line.

init

After checking the partitions and mounting the root file system, the `init` program (located in the initramfs image) starts `/sbin/init`, which boots the system and loads all of the services and programs configured for the system.

The init process is always assigned a process ID number of 1. It uses the configuration information in the `/etc/inittab` file to determine how to run the initialization process.

Once the init process starts, it runs the `/etc/init.d/boot` script. This script completes initialization tasks such as creating device files in `/dev` and executing scripts in the `/etc/init.d/boot.d/` directory (e.g., mounting local file systems and setting disk quotas).

After the boot script has been completed, init starts the `/etc/init.d/rc` script. This script uses your runlevel configuration to start services and daemons. Each runlevel has its own set of services configured that are initiated. For example, runlevel 5 includes the X Window components that run the Linux desktop.

NOTE: For additional details on init, see The init Program and Linux Runlevels.

Manage the Grand Unified Bootloader (GRUB)

To manage the Linux boot process, you need to understand how to manage the Grand Unified Bootloader (GRUB), as covered in the following:

- How a Boot Manager Works
- Boot Managers in SLES 11
- Start the GRUB Shell
- Modify the GRUB Configuration File
- Configure GRUB with YaST
- Boot a System Directly into a Shell
- Use Rescue Media to Boot the System

How a Boot Manager Works

To boot a Linux system, the computer's BIOS needs to run a program that can load the operating system into memory. This program is called the boot loader. Its job is to load the operating system kernel, which then initializes the Linux system.

After running the Power-On Self Test (POST), the BIOS searches the various storage devices configured in the BIOS for a boot loader. If it finds one, it turns control of the boot process over to the boot loader. The boot loader then locates the operating system files on the hard drive and starts the operating system kernel.

A boot manager is a boot loader that can handle the booting of multiple operating systems. If more than one operating system is present on the system hard drive, the boot manager presents a menu that allows you to select which operating system to load.

For example, Linux boot managers can be used to load the Linux operating system or other operating systems, such as Microsoft Windows.

One of the most commonly used Linux boot managers today is GRUB. The GRUB boot manager is designed with a two-stage architecture:

- **Stage 1.** Usually installed in the MBR of the hard disk (first-stage boot loader). It can also be installed in the boot sectors of disk partitions or even on a floppy disk.

  Because the space allocated to the MBR is limited to 446 bytes, the first stage program code contains only the information required to load the GRUB file system drivers (e.g., `/boot/grub/e2fs_stage1_5`) and the next stage.

- **Stage 2.** Usually contains the actual boot loader. The files of the second-stage boot loader are located in the `/boot/grub/` directory.

Boot Managers in SLES 11

SLES 11 uses GRUB as the default boot manager. Some of its features are

- **File system support.** GRUB includes file system drivers for ReiserFS, ext2, ext3, Minix, JFS, XFS, FAT, and FFS (BSD). Because of this, it can actually access files in the file system by filename before the operating system is loaded. This can be useful in situations when the boot manager configuration is faulty and you need to manually search for and load the kernel.

- **Interactive control.** GRUB includes its own shell, which enables interactive control of the boot manager.

NOTE: More information on GRUB can be found in `/usr/share/doc/packages/grub/`.

Start the GRUB Shell

Because GRUB has its own shell, you can boot the system manually if the Linux system does not start due to an error in the boot manager. There are two ways to start the GRUB shell:

- Start the GRUB Shell in the Running System
- Start the GRUB Shell at the Boot Prompt

Start the GRUB Shell in the Running System

To start the GRUB shell during operation, enter the `grub` command as root at the shell prompt. The following is displayed:

```
da1:/boot/grub # grub
GNU GRUB  version 0.97  (640K lower / 3072K upper memory)

 [ Minimal BASH-like line editing is supported.  For the first word,
   TAB lists possible command completions.  Anywhere else TAB lists
   the possible completions of a device/filename. ]
grub>
```

NOTE: As in a Bash, you can use Tab-complete with GRUB shell commands.

To find out which partition contains the kernel, enter the `find` command, as in the following:

```
grub> find /boot/vmlinuz
find /boot/vmlinuz
   (hd0,1)
grub>
```

In this example, the kernel (`/boot/vmlinuz`) is located in the second partition of the first hard disk (hd0,1). You can close the GRUB shell by entering `quit`.

Start the GRUB Shell at the Boot Prompt

Start the GRUB shell at the boot prompt by doing the following:

1. From the graphical boot selection menu, press Esc.

2. When prompted that you are leaving the graphical boot menu, select *OK*.

   A text-based menu is displayed:

Figure 5-6   *GRUB Boot Menu*

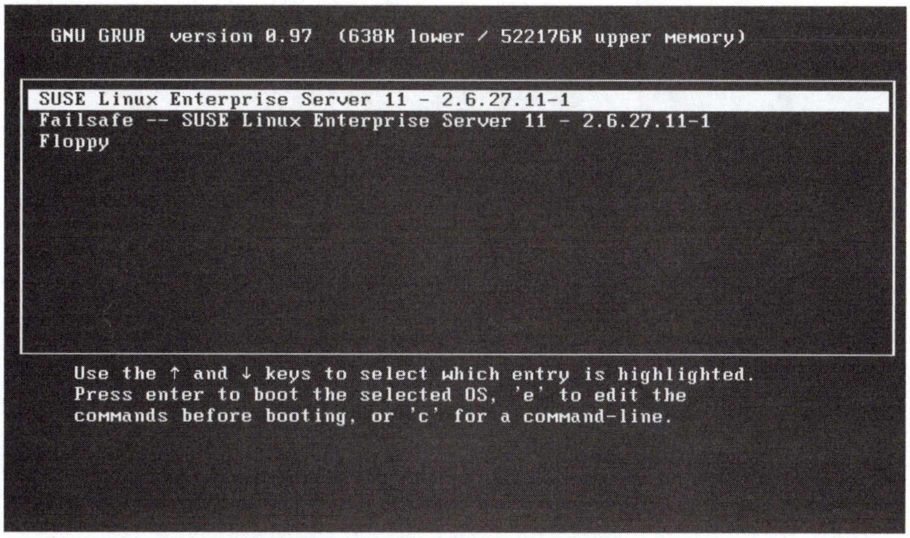

GNU GRUB   version 0.97   (638K lower / 522176K upper memory)

```
SUSE Linux Enterprise Server 11 - 2.6.27.11-1
Failsafe -- SUSE Linux Enterprise Server 11 - 2.6.27.11-1
Floppy
```

```
Use the ↑ and ↓ keys to select which entry is highlighted.
Press enter to boot the selected OS, 'e' to edit the
commands before booting, or 'c' for a command-line.
```

Courtesy of Novell, Inc.

3. Start the GRUB shell by typing c (US keyboard layout).

    The GRUB shell prompt is displayed:

Figure 5-7   *The Grub Shell*

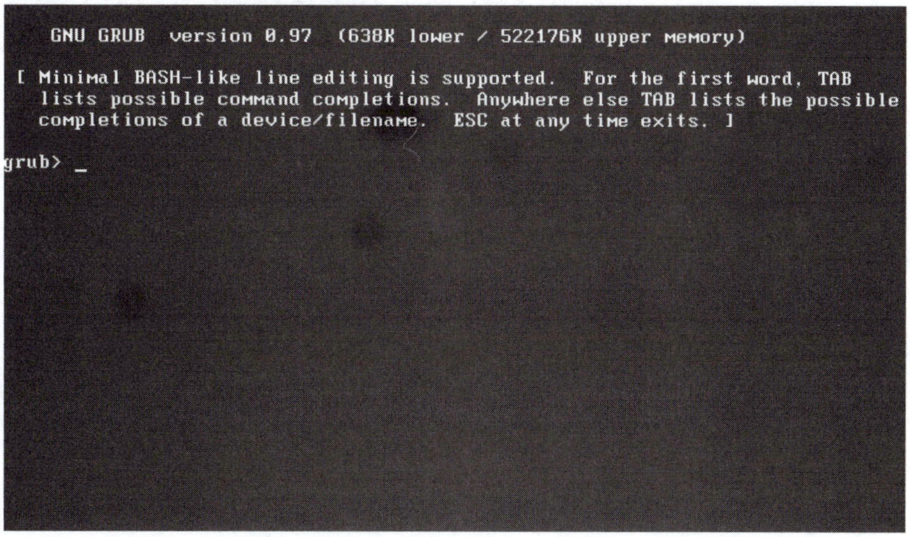

GNU GRUB   version 0.97   (638K lower / 522176K upper memory)

```
[ Minimal BASH-like line editing is supported.  For the first word, TAB
  lists possible command completions.  Anywhere else TAB lists the possible
  completions of a device/filename.  ESC at any time exits. ]

grub> _
```

Courtesy of Novell, Inc.

Modify the GRUB Configuration File

You can customize the behavior of the GRUB boot manager by editing the /boot/grub/menu.1st configuration file.

The following is an example of the /boot/grub/menu.1st configuration file:

```
# Modified by YaST2. Last modification on Tue Feb 10 00:08:12 UTC 2009
default 0
timeout 8
##YaST - generic_mbr
gfxmenu (hd0,1)/boot/message
##YaST - activate

###Don't change this comment - YaST2 identifier: Original name: linux
###
title SUSE Linux Enterprise Server 11 - 2.6.27.11-1
    root (hd0,1)
    kernel /boot/vmlinuz-2.6.27.11-1-pae root=/dev/disk/by-id/ata-
    VMware_Virtual_IDE_Hard_Drive_00000000000000000001-part2
    resume=/dev/disk/by-id/ata-VMware_Virtual_IDE_Hard_Drive_000000
    00000000000001-part1 splash=silent showopts vga=0x332
    initrd /boot/initrd-2.6.27.11-1-pae

###Don't change this comment - YaST2 identifier: Original name:
### failsafe
title Failsafe -- SUSE Linux Enterprise Server 11 - 2.6.27.11-1
    root (hd0,1)
    kernel /boot/vmlinuz-2.6.27.11-1-pae root=/dev/disk/by-id/ata-
    VMware_Virtual_IDE_Hard_Drive_00000000000000000001-part2
    showopts ide=nodma apm=off noresume nosmp maxcpus=0 edd=off
    powersaved=off nohz=off highres=off processor.max_cstate=1
    x11failsafe vga=0x332
    initrd /boot/initrd-2.6.27.11-1-pae

###Don't change this comment - YaST2 identifier: Original name:
floppy###
title Floppy
    rootnoverify (fd0)
    chainloader +1
```

The following is the general structure of the file:

- First, there are general options:

    - **default 0.** Default boot entry that starts automatically if no other entry is selected with the keyboard. In this example, the first menu entry (entry 0) is loaded by default.

    - **timeout 8.** Specifies that the default boot entry will be started automatically after eight seconds.

    - **gfxmenu (hd0,1)/boot/message.** Where the graphical menu is stored on the hard drive.

- The general options are followed by options for the various operating systems that can be booted by GRUB:

    - **title** *title.* Title for a menu entry. Each entry for an operating system begins with this.

    - **root (hd0,1).** Hard disk partition where the operating system resides (in this example, the second partition [1] on the first hard disk [0]). By defining the root, you don't need to specify a partition for the entries that follow it, such as kernel.

GRUB does not distinguish between IDE and SCSI hard disks. The hard disk that is recognized by the BIOS as the first hard disk is designated as hd0, the second hard disk as hd1, and so on. The first partition on the first hard disk is called hd0,0, the second partition hd0,1, and so on.

- **kernel /boot/vmlinuz.** Kernel location, relative to the partition specified by the root option. It is followed by kernel parameters, such as `root=/dev/hda1` and `vga=normal`. Instead of the device file name, partitions can also be named using their id (as in the example above).

- **initrd /boot/initrd.** Location of the initial ramdisk (initramfs in SLES 10 and later), relative to the root partition specified above. The initrd contains hardware drivers (such as a driver for the IDE or SCSI controller) that are needed before the kernel can access the hard disk.

Configure GRUB with YaST

GRUB can be configured using the `grub-install` command. On SLES 11, this is not supported. The binary has been renamed to `/usr/sbin/grub-install.unsupported`. Instead of using this command, YaST should be used which simplifies the configuration of the boot manager. You should not modify your GRUB configuration unless you fully understand how the boot manager works.

To start the YaST Boot Loader module, start YaST, enter the root password, and then select **System > Boot Loader**. You can also start the Boot Loader module directly from a terminal window by logging in as root and entering `yast2 bootloader`.

The following is displayed:

Figure 5-8 *YaST Boot Loader Setting*

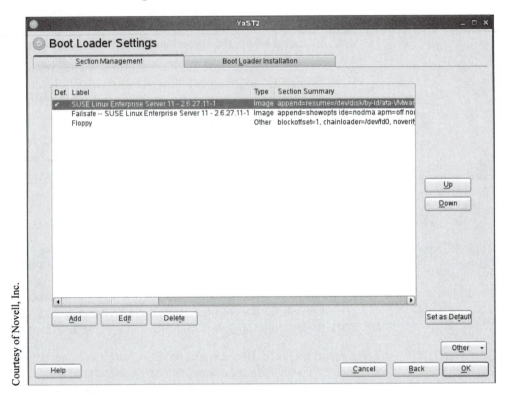

Courtesy of Novell, Inc.

Click the *Section Management* tab to view the current GRUB settings for your system. The Def (Default) column indicates which entry is selected as the default when booting the system.

To add a new section, click *Add*. You are offered several choices:

Figure 5-9   *YaST Boot Loader Settings: Section Management*

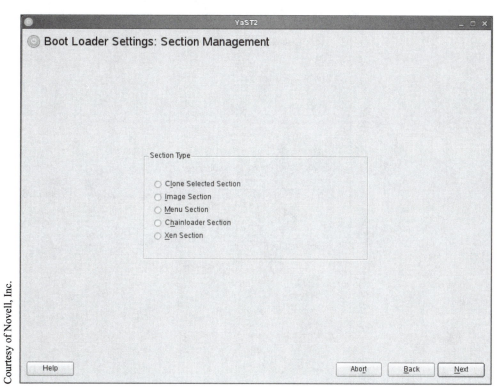

NOTE: Each of the section types is explained in the help text. You can access help by clicking the ***Help*** button on the left.

When you click ***Clone Selected Section > Next***, the dialog is automatically filled with the values from the existing selected section:

Figure 5-10 *YaST Boot Loader Settings: Section Management*

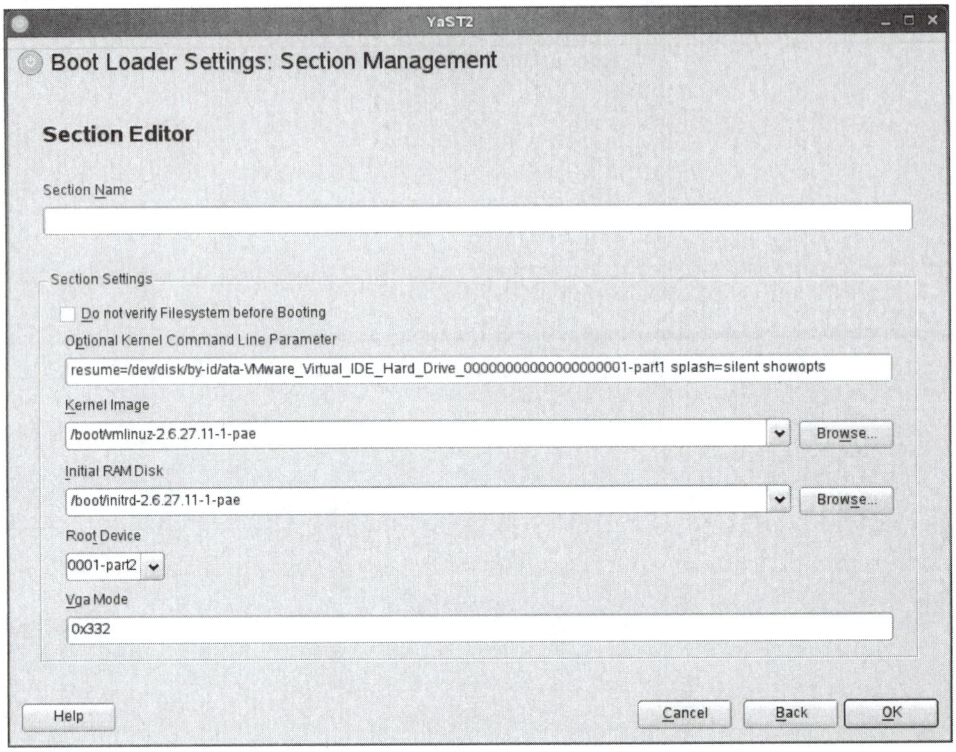

Courtesy of Novell, Inc.

The dialogs displayed for the other section types shown in Figure 5-9 are similar to that shown in Figure 5-10, but the lines are empty. The dialog for the ***Chainloader Section*** offers a line for a section name and a device to load another boot loader (such as the Windows bootloader) from.

If you want to modify an existing section, select it in the ***Section Management*** tab (Figure 5-8), then select ***Edit***. When you do, the same dialog opens up and allows you to change the existing settings. To delete an entry, select it and then click ***Delete***.

You can use the ***Boot Loader Installation*** tab to specify which bootloader you want your SLES 11 system to use, as shown below:

Figure 5-11   *YaST Boot Loader Settings: Boot Loader Installation*

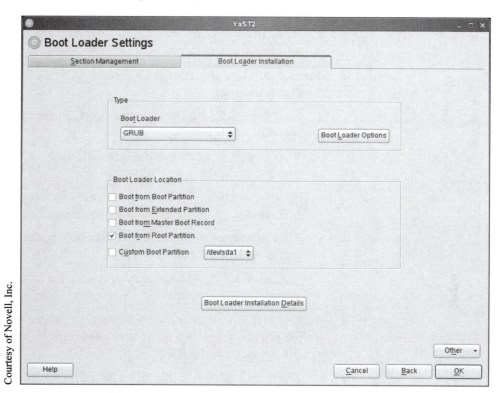

Courtesy of Novell, Inc.

You can configure the following settings in this tab:

- **Boot Loader.** Switch between the GRUB and LILO boot managers.

- **Boot Loader Options.** Configure advanced boot loader settings.

NOTE: The default boot loader settings work best in most situations. We recommend that you don't change these settings unless you have a specific reason for doing so.

You can configure the following:

- **Set Active Flag in Partition Table for Boot Partition.** Activates the partition that contains the boot loader. Some legacy operating systems, such as Windows 98, can boot only from an active partition.

- **Debugging Flag.** Sets GRUB in debug mode where it displays messages to show disk activity.

- **Write Generic Boot Code to MBR.** Replaces the current MBR with generic, operating system-independent code.

- **Hide Boot Menu.** Hides the boot menu and boots the default entry.

- ❑ **Use Trusted GRUB.** Starts Trusted GRUB, which supports trusted computing functionality.

- ❑ **Password for the Menu Interface.** Defines a password that will be required to access the boot menu.

- ■ **Boot Loader Location.** Defines where to install the boot loader. You can select from the following:

  - ❑ **Boot from Boot Partition.** Installs GRUB in the boot sector of the `/boot` partition.

  - ❑ **Boot from Extended Partition.** Installs the boot loader in the extended partition container.

  - ❑ **Boot from Master Boot Record.** Installs the boot loader in the MBR of the first disk (according to the boot sequence preset in the BIOS).

  - ❑ **Boot from Root Partition.** Installs the boot loader in the boot sector of the `/` partition (default).

  - ❑ **Custom Boot Partition.** Lets you specify the location of the boot loader manually.

- ■ **Boot Loader Installation Details.** Offers specialized configuration options, such as activating a certain partition or changing the order of disks to correspond with the sequence in the BIOS.

- ■ **Other.** Offers a menu with the following additional choices:

  - ❑ **Edit Configuration Files.** Lets you display and edit the configuration files (`/boot/grub/device.map`, `/boot/grub/menu.lst`, or `/etc/grub.conf`).

  - ❑ **Propose New Configuration.** Generates a new configuration suggestion. Older Linux versions or other operating systems found on other partitions are included in the boot menu, enabling you to boot Linux or its old boot loader. The latter takes you to a second boot menu.

  - ❑ **Start from Scratch.** Lets you create the entire configuration from scratch. No suggestions are generated.

  - ❑ **Reread Configuration from Disk.** If you configured changes and are not satisfied with the result, this option lets you reload your current configuration.

  - ❑ **Propose and Merge with Existing GRUB Menus.** If another operating system and an older Linux version are installed in other partitions, the menu is generated from an entry for the new SUSE Linux, an entry for the other system, and all entries of the old boot loader menu.

    This procedure might take some time and is available only with GRUB.

- ■ **Restore MBR from Hard Disk.** This option restores the MBR that was saved on the hard disk.

When done making changes to your boot loader configuration, save the changes by clicking *OK*.

Boot a System Directly into a Shell

The boot screen of the GRUB boot loader lets you specify parameters that modify the behavior of the Linux kernel. At the bottom of the GRUB boot screen is the **Boot Options** field, where you can specify other kernel options than those defined in the GRUB configuration:

Figure 5-12   *Boot Menu*

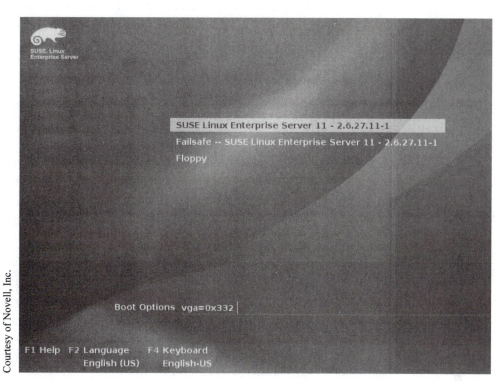

To add a boot option, select a GRUB menu entry, then type the additional boot option in the **Boot Options** field. An example is shown in the figure above.

This can be a very useful feature. For example, one way to access a system that is not booting anymore is to set a different program for the init process. Normally, the Linux kernel tries to find a program named `init` and start it as the first process. All other processes are then started by `init`.

By entering init=**new_init_program** as a boot option, you can change the first program loaded by the kernel. For example, if you enter `init=/bin/bash` as a boot option, the system is started directly into Bash. You are directly logged in as root without being asked for a password. Booting into a Bash can also be used to regain access as root when the password has been lost.

You can then use this shell to access the file system and fix whatever misconfiguration is causing the system not to boot.

NOTE: On some Linux systems, the root file system is mounted as read-only after booting into a shell. To modify configuration files, you need to remount the file system with the following command:

```
mount -o remount,rw,sync -t filesystem_type device_name mountpoint
```

Entering `exec /sbin/init` at the bash prompt replaces the shell with the init program and continues the boot process until the default runlevel is reached.

If you want to prevent access to the machine as described above, you can change the boot configuration to require a password before boot options can be modified.

The following line in the `/boot/grub/menu.lst` file (within the general options) ensures that the choices defined further below in the file can be selected only in unmodified form:

`password` **password**

The use of additional kernel parameters requires you to enter the specified password. In this case the **password** would be in clear text.

Because the graphical boot menu could be used to circumvent the password feature, it is automatically disabled when the `password` entry appears in the configuration file.

GRUB can also handle MD5-encrypted passwords that are generated as follows:

```
da1:~ # grub-md5-crypt
Password:
Retype password:
$1$T11Pw$35mkaMRciD3Uv70CHPEY00
da1:~ #
```

This string can then be copied into the `/boot/grub/menu.lst` file using the following syntax:

`password --md5 $1$T11Pw$35mkaMRciD3Uv70CHPEY00`

The `lock` parameter within a title section can be used to force the password query before these title entries can be selected.

```
title Floppy
     lock
     chainloader (fd0)+1
```

Selecting **Floppy** in the boot menu is now possible only after entering the password.

The `password` parameter can also be used in individual title entries to define a special password for those title entries.

Be aware, however, that the password feature enhances security only to an extent. It does not prevent booting the computer from another medium, such as the SLES 11 rescue system and then accessing the files on the hard disk.

NOTE: You can also use the `confirm` parameter at the boot prompt if you want to manually specify whether each service (postfix, sshd, etc.) should or should not start during system boot.

Use Rescue Media to Boot the System

If the system does not boot at all (e.g., due to a misconfigured `/etc/fstab` file or a damaged boot manager), rescue media (CDs, DVDs or USB keys) can be used to recover the system. Normally, these media boot a Linux system which you can log into as the root user without specifying a password. You should then be able to mount the file systems and have write access to all files to correct the configuration errors.

Use the LILO Boot Manager

In addition to GRUB, you can also use the LILO boot loader on a Linux system. LILO stands for *LInux LOader*. LILO is a very flexible bootloader that can be used to launch just about any operating system from your computer's hard drive, including Linux, Windows, or DOS.

NOTE: At one time, LILO was the default bootload used by most distributions. However, most distributions now use GRUB instead.

When LILO is used as the default bootloader, the LILO boot menu is displayed to end-users, allowing them to select which operating system kernel they want to boot. A sample LILO boot menu is shown below:

Figure 5-13   *LILO Boot Menu*

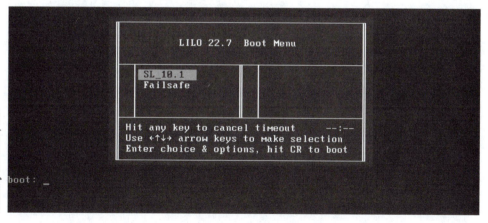

Courtesy of Novell, Inc.

There are two different ways you can install the LILO bootloader. First, with most Linux distributions, you can specify that the LILO bootloader be used for the system during the installation of the operating system.

TIP: The LILO bootloader is no longer supported on SLE 11.

In addition, you can also install the LILO bootloader on a system that's already configured with the GRUB bootloader by entering `lilo` at the shell prompt. This overwrites the existing bootloader and installs the LILO bootloader.

However, before you do this, you need to configure LILO. The LILO bootloader is configured using `/etc/lilo.conf`. A sample `lilo.conf` file from a SLES 10 system is shown below:

Notice that there are three sections of information within this file. The first section contains global options that apply to all other sections in the file. The last two sections contain options specific to each menu item. The information in these lines is described below:

```
DA1:/etc # cat ./lilo.conf
# Modified by YaST2. Last modification on Tue Aug 10 17:04:14 MDT 2010
menu-scheme = Wb:kw:Wb:Wb
timeout = 80
lba32
change-rules
reset
read-only
prompt
default = SLES_10_SP3
message = /boot/message
boot = /dev/sda2

image = /boot/vmlinuz-2.6.16.60-0.54.5-default
###Don't change this comment - YaST2 identifier: Original name:
linux###
    label = SLES_10_SP3
    append = "   resume=/dev/sda1 splash=silent showopts"
    vga = 0x317
    initrd = /boot/initrd-2.6.16.60-0.54.5-default
    root = /dev/sda2

image = /boot/vmlinuz-2.6.16.60-0.54.5-default
###Don't change this comment - YaST2 identifier: Original name:
failsafe###
    label = Failsafe
   append = "showopts ide=nodma apm=off acpi=off noresume nosmp noapic
maxcpus=0 edd=off   3"
    vga = 0x317
    initrd = /boot/initrd-2.6.16.60-0.54.5-default
    root = /dev/sda2
```

Table 5-13   *lilo.conf Configuration Options*

Section	Option	Description
Global Options	menu-scheme	Describes the colors used in the LILO boot menu. The syntax is: *text_color:highlight_color:border_color: title_color* Two characters are used for each value. The first character is the foreground color while the second is the background color. See the `lilo.conf` man page for a listing of all the colors and their associated characters that can be used with this option.
	timeout	Sets the timeout period in 1/10th seconds before the default menu item is automatically run. In the sample configuration file presented above, this option is set to 80, which gives the user 8 seconds to select a menu item.
	lba32	Tells lilo to ignore the hard drive's physical geometry and use logical block addressing. This allows LILO to work with disks that have more than 1023 cylinders, which all modern hard drives do.
	change-rules	Defines boot-time changes to partition type numbers.
	reset	Specifies that all default change-rules are removed.
	read-only	Specifies that the root (/) file system be mounted read-only at first. After checking the integrity of the file system, the kernel will usually remount the file system in read-write mode.
	prompt	Specifies that the boot: prompt be displayed.
	default	Specifies the default image that will be used if the user doesn't make a selection.
	message	Specifies the location of the image file that LILO will display.
	boot	Specifies the device that contains the boot sector.
Image Options	image	Specifies the path to the boot image of a Linux kernel.
	label	Specifies a name for the image.
	append	Appends the specified options to the parameters that are passed to the kernel by LILO. This is usually only used if the system uses hardware that the kernel is having a difficult time auto-detecting.
	vga	Specifies the VGA text mode that should be used while the system is booting.
	initrd	Specifies the initial ramdisk image to be loaded with the kernel.
	root	Specifies the device that should be mounted as root.

After modifying the file, you must run `lilo` from the shell prompt. If you don't, your changes to the configuration file won't be applied.

Manage Runlevels

Managing runlevels is an essential part of Linux system administration. In this objective, you learn what runlevels are, the role of the init program, and how to configure runlevels. The following topics are addressed:

- The init Program and Linux Runlevels

- init Scripts and Runlevel Directories

- Change the Runlevel

The init Program and Linux Runlevels

To understand how the init program works in conjunction with Linux runlevels, you need to be familiar with the following:

- The init Program

- Runlevels

- init Configuration File (`/etc/inittab`)

The init Program

As discussed earlier in this section, Linux is initialized by `/sbin/init`, which is started by the kernel as the first process of the system. This process, or one of its child processes, starts all additional processes.

In addition, because init is the last process running when Linux is shut down, it ensures that all other processes are ended correctly. Essentially, init controls the entire booting up and shutting down of the system. Because of its priority, signal 9 (SIGKILL), which can normally end all processes, has no effect on the init process.

The configuration file for init is `/etc/inittab`. A sample `inittab` file is shown below:

```
# The default runlevel is defined here
id:5:initdefault:

# First script to be executed, if not booting in emergency (-b) mode
si::bootwait:/etc/init.d/boot

# /etc/init.d/rc takes care of runlevel handling
#
# runlevel 0 is System halt   (Do not use this for initdefault!)
# runlevel 1 is Single user mode
# runlevel 2 is Local multiuser without network (e.g. NFS)
# runlevel 3 is Full multiuser with network
...
```

```
l0:0:wait:/etc/init.d/rc 0
l1:1:wait:/etc/init.d/rc 1
l2:2:wait:/etc/init.d/rc 2
l3:3:wait:/etc/init.d/rc 3
...
```

This file defines the various scripts that will be started by init. All of these scripts are located in the /etc/init.d/ directory. This configuration file also defines the default runlevel the system will boot into when it's powered on.

Runlevels

In Linux, runlevels define the state of the system. The following runlevels are defined:

Table 5-14 *Linux Runlevels*

Runlevel	Description
0	Halt
S	Single-user mode, when switched from boot phase to single-user mode (only one console available)
1	Single-user mode, when switched from any normal runlevel to single-user
2	Multiuser mode without network server services
3	Multiuser mode with network
4	Not used
5	Multiuser mode with network and display manager
6	Reboot

The runlevel command displays the runlevel you are currently in (second number) and the previous runlevel (first number), as in the following:

```
da1:~ # runlevel
N 5
da1:~ #
```

A previous runlevel N means that the system booted directly into the current runlevel.

init Configuration File (/etc/inittab)

To effectively manage the init process on your Linux system, you need to be familiar with the contents and syntax of the /etc/inittab file. The following topics are addressed here:

- inittab File Syntax
- inittab Standard Entries

inittab File Syntax

Each line in the `/etc/inittab` file uses the following syntax:

id:rl:action:process

The parameters are explained below:

- **id.** Defines a unique name for the entry in `/etc/inittab`. It can be up to four characters long.

- **rl.** Refers to one or more runlevels where this entry should be evaluated.

- **action.** Describes what init is to do.

- **process.** Identifies the process connected to this entry.

inittab Standard Entries

The first entry in the `/etc/inittab` file contains the following parameters:

```
id:5:initdefault:
```

The `initdefault` parameter signals to the init process which level it should bring the system to. The default runlevel is normally 3 or 5.

The next entry in `/etc/inittab` looks like this:

```
si::bootwait:/etc/init.d/boot
```

The `bootwait` parameter tells init to carry out this command while booting and wait until it has finished before proceeding.

The next few entries describe the actions for runlevels 0 to 6:

```
l0:0:wait:/etc/init.d/rc 0
l1:1:wait:/etc/init.d/rc 1
l2:2:wait:/etc/init.d/rc 2
l3:3:wait:/etc/init.d/rc 3
#l4:4:wait:/etc/init.d/rc 4
l5:5:wait:/etc/init.d/rc 5
l6:6:wait:/etc/init.d/rc 6

# what to do in single-user mode
ls:S:wait:/etc/init.d/rc S
~~:S:respawn:/sbin/sulogin
```

The `wait` parameter tells `init` to wait until the appropriate command has been carried out when the system changes to the indicated level. This parameter also indicates that further entries for the level are to be performed only after this process is completed.

The single user mode S is a special case; it works even if the `/etc/inittab` file is missing. In such a case, enter S at the boot prompt when the computer starts. The `sulogin` command is started, which allows only the system administrator to log in. The `respawn` parameter tells `init` to wait for the end of the process and to then restart it. This runlevel is used to repair a system which does not boot correctly.

The `/etc/inittab` file also defines what should happen when the Ctrl+Alt+Del key combination is pressed. By default, this causes the system to restart, as shown below:

```
ca::ctrlaltdel:/sbin/shutdown -r -t 4 now
```

The `ctrlaltdel` action is carried out by the init process only if these keys are pressed at the same time. If you want to disable this keystroke combination, comment out (#) or remove the line from the file. You may also set the command `/bin/false` to be executed.

The final large block of entries describes which runlevels **getty** processes (login processes) are started in:

```
1:2345:respawn:/sbin/mingetty --noclear tty1
2:2345:respawn:/sbin/mingetty tty2
3:2345:respawn:/sbin/mingetty tty3
4:2345:respawn:/sbin/mingetty tty4
5:2345:respawn:/sbin/mingetty tty5
6:2345:respawn:/sbin/mingetty tty6
```

The getty processes provide the login prompt and in return expect a username as input. They are started in runlevels 2, 3, and 5.

NOTE: Runlevel 4 in the above example is ignored because the line that defines the actions for the runlevel is commented out earlier in the file (`#14:4:wait:/etc/init.d/rc 4`).

If a session ends, the processes are started again by init. If a line is disabled here, no further login is possible at the corresponding virtual console.

NOTE: You should take great care when making changes to the `/etc/inittab` file. If the file is corrupted, the system will no longer boot correctly.

If an error does occur, first try entering S at the Boot Options prompt in the GRUB boot menu. If this does not work, it is still possible to boot the system by entering `init=/bin/bash` at the **Boot Options** prompt in the GRUB boot menu.

This causes the init process to be replaced by a Bash, which causes inittab to not be read. You can then repair the system.

If you change your `/etc/inittab` file, you need to run `init q` at the shell prompt to cause `init` to reload its configuration information.

init Scripts and Runlevel Directories

The `/etc/inittab` file defines the default runlevel the system uses after the boot process is complete. The services that need to be started in a certain runlevel are not defined in `/etc/inittab` itself. These are configured by symbolic links in `/etc/init.d/rc`**x**`.d/` directories that point to scripts in `/etc/init.d/`.

To be able to manage runlevels, you need to understand the following:

- init Scripts
- Runlevel Symbolic Links
- How init Determines Which Services to Start and Stop
- Activate and Deactivate Services for a Runlevel

init Scripts

The `/etc/init.d/` directory contains shell scripts that are used to perform certain tasks at bootup and to start and stop services in the running system. The following shows some of the files in `/etc/init.d/`:

```
da1:~ # ls -al /etc/init.d/
total 684
drwxr-xr-x  11 root root  4096 Feb 26  2009 .
drwxr-xr-x 100 root root 12288 Feb 25 18:47 ..
-rw-r--r--   1 root root  1046 Feb 26  2009 .depend.boot
-rw-r--r--   1 root root   527 Feb 26  2009 .depend.halt
-rw-r--r--   1 root root   918 Feb 26  2009 .depend.start
-rw-r--r--   1 root root   714 Feb 26  2009 .depend.stop
-rw-r--r--   1 root root  8924 Jan 10 21:02 README
-rwxr-xr-x   1 root root  1468 Jan 10 19:19 SuSEfirewall2_init
-rwxr-xr-x   1 root root  1576 Jan 10 19:19 SuSEfirewall2_setup
-rwxr-xr-x   1 root root  3412 Jan 13 19:08 aaeventd
-rwxr--r--   1 root root  3755 Jan 10 14:09 acpid
-rwxr-xr-x   1 root root  5509 Jan 11 02:50 alsasound
-rwxr-xr-x   1 root root  3955 Jan 11 02:58 atd
-rwxr-xr-x   1 root root  6933 Jan 11 02:45 auditd
-rwxr-xr-x   1 root root  5778 Jan 11 03:22 autofs
-rwxr-xr-x   1 root root  2989 Dec 16 07:15 autoyast
-rwxr-xr-x   1 root root  7678 Dec 18 17:02 boot
-rwxr-xr-x   1 root root  2880 Jan 13 19:08 boot.apparmor
...
```

The `.depend.{boot,start,stop}` files are created by `insserv` and contain dependencies that are used to determine which services can be started in parallel. See `/etc/init.d/README` for details on this functionality.

The shell scripts can be called up in the following ways:

- Directly by `init` when you boot the system, when the system is shut down, or when you reboot the system with Ctrl+Alt+Del. Examples for these scripts are `/etc/init.d/boot` or `/etc/init.d/rc`.

- Indirectly by init when you change the runlevel. In this case, the `/etc/init.d/rc` script calls the necessary scripts in the correct order and with the correct parameter during the runlevel change.

- Directly when you enter `/etc/init.d/script parameter` at the shell prompt.

NOTE: You can also enter **rc*script parameter*** if corresponding links are set in `/sbin/` or `/usr/sbin/`.

The following parameters may be used when running an init script:

Table 5-15   *Init Script Parameters*

Parameter	Description
start	Starts a service that is not running.
restart	Stops a running service and restarts it.
stop	Stops a running service.
reload	Rereads the configuration of the service without stopping and restarting the service itself.
force-reload	Reloads the configuration if the service supports this. Otherwise, it does the same thing as restart.
status	Displays the current status of the service.

When a script is called without parameters, a message informs you about the possible parameters.

Some of the more important scripts stored in `/etc/init.d/` include the following:

- **boot.** Started directly by init when the system starts. It is run only once. It evaluates the `/etc/init.d/boot.d/` directory and starts all the scripts linked by filenames with an "S" at the beginning of their names (see Runlevel Symbolic Links).

  Some of the tasks these scripts perform include the following:

  ❏ Check the file systems.

  ❏ Set up LVM.

  ❏ Delete unnecessary files in `/var/lock/`.

  ❏ Set the system time.

- **boot.local.** Includes additional commands to be executed at boot before changing into a runlevel. You can add your own system extensions to this script.

- **halt.** Run if runlevels 0 or 6 are entered. It is called with either the `halt` command (which completely shuts the system down) or the `reboot` command (which shuts the system down and then reboots it).

- **rc.** This script is responsible for changing from one runlevel to another. It runs the stop scripts for the current runlevel and then runs the start scripts for the new runlevel.

- *service.* Each service on your Linux system (such as cron, apache2, or cups) comes with a script that allows you to start or stop the service, reload its configuration, or view its status.

NOTE: If you want to create your own scripts, you can use the `/etc/init.d/skeleton` file as a template.

Runlevel Symbolic Links

To enter a runlevel, init calls the `/etc/init.d/rc` script with the runlevel as parameter. This script examines the respective runlevel `/etc/init.d/rc**x**.d/` directory and starts and stops services depending upon the links present in this directory.

Each runlevel has a corresponding subdirectory in `/etc/init.d/`. For runlevel 1, this is `/etc/init.d/rc1.d/`; for runlevel 2, this is `/etc/init.d/rc2.d/`; and so on.

When you view the files in one of these directories (such as `/etc/init.d/rc3.d/`), you will see two kinds of files—those that start with a "K" and those that start with an "S", as shown below:

```
da1:~ # ls /etc/init.d/rc3.d/
K01auditd          K02alsasound      S01acpid          S05nfs
K01cron            K02cups           S01dbus           S05smbfs
K01irq_balancer    K02fbset          S01earlysyslog    S06kbd
K01microcode.ctl   K02haldaemon      S01fbset          S08alsasound
...
```

The first letter is always followed by two digits and then the name of a service. Whether a service is started in a specific runlevel depends on whether there are S*xxservice* and K*xxservice* files in the `/etc/init.d/rc**x**.d/` directory.

Entering `ls -l` in an `/etc/init.d/rc**x**.d/` directory indicates that these files are actually symbolic links pointing to service scripts in `/etc/init.d/` (as in the following):

```
da1:~ # ls -l /etc/init.d/rc3.d/
total 0
lrwxrwxrwx 1 root root  9 Feb  9 16:48 K01auditd -> ../auditd
lrwxrwxrwx 1 root root  7 Feb  9 16:54 K01cron -> ../cron
lrwxrwxrwx 1 root root 15 Feb  9 16:50 K01irq_balancer -> ../
irq_balancer
lrwxrwxrwx 1 root root 16 Feb  9 16:46 K01microcode.ctl -> ../
microcode.ctl
lrwxrwxrwx 1 root root  7 Feb  9 16:46 K01nscd -> ../nscd
lrwxrwxrwx 1 root root  9 Feb  9 16:50 K01random -> ../random
...
```

By using symbolic links in subdirectories, only the script in `/etc/init.d/` needs to be modified when changes are necessary. Because the links in the various runlevel directories simply point to the script in `/etc/init.d/`, they are all automatically updated.

Usually, two links within a runlevel directory point to the same script. For example, if you enter `ls -l *network` in the `/etc/init.d/rc3.d/` directory, you see that two network links both point to the `/etc/init.d/network` script:

```
da1:/etc/init.d/rc3.d # ls -l *network
lrwxrwxrwx 1 root root 10 Feb  9 16:58 K07network -> ../network
lrwxrwxrwx 1 root root 10 Feb  9 16:57 S02network -> ../network
```

Sometimes K*xx* links are referred to as kill scripts, while S*xx* links are referred to as start scripts. In fact, there are no separate scripts for starting and stopping services, but the script is either called with the `stop` parameter or with the `start` parameter.

How init Determines Which Services to Start and Stop

You already know that a service is started with the `start` parameter, and stopped with the `stop` parameter. These same two parameters are used when changing from one runlevel to another.

When the runlevel is changed, `init` calls the rc script with the new runlevel as parameter (such as `/etc/init.d/rc 3`). The `/etc/init.d/rc` script examines the `/etc/init.d/rc` ***currentrl***`.d/` and `/etc/init.d/rc` ***newrl***`.d/` directories and determines what to do.

For example, suppose you change from runlevel 5 to runlevel 3. There are three possible scenarios that could occur as a result:

- There is a K*xx* link for a certain service in `/etc/init.d/rc5.d/` and there is an S*xx* link in `/etc/init.d/rc3.d/` for the same service.

  In this case, the service is neither started nor stopped because the service should run in both runlevels. Therefore, the service's script in `/etc/init.d/` is not called at all.

- There is a K*xx* link for a certain service in `/etc/init.d/rc5.d/`, but there is no corresponding S*xx* link in `/etc/init.d/rc3.d/`.

  In this case, the script `/etc/init.d/`***service*** is called with the `stop` parameter and the service is stopped.

- There is an S*xx* link in `/etc/init.d/rc3.d/` and there is no corresponding K*xx* link for the service in `/etc/init.d/rc5.d/`.

  In this case, the script `/etc/init.d/`***service*** is called with the `start` parameter and the service is started.

The number after K or S determines the sequence in which the scripts are called. For example, the `K10cron` script is called before the `K20haldaemon` script, which means that cron is shut down before haldaemon.

The S05network script is called before S11postfix, which means that the network service starts before postfix. This is important if one service requires another service to be running in order for it to start.

Consider what happens when you change from runlevel 3 to runlevel 5:

1. As root, you tell init to change to a different runlevel by entering init 5.

2. init checks its configuration file (/etc/inittab) and determines it should start /etc/init.d/rc with the new runlevel (5) as a parameter.

3. rc calls the stop scripts (Kxx) of the current runlevel for those services which should not be running in the new runlevel.

4. The start scripts (Sxx) in the new runlevel for those services which are not running in the current runlevel are launched.

When changing to the same runlevel as the current runlevel, init checks only /etc/inittab for changes and takes the appropriate steps (such as starting a getty).

Activate and Deactivate Services for a Runlevel

Services are activated or deactivated in a runlevel by adding or removing the respective K*xx*service and S*xx*service links in the /etc/init.d/rc**x**.d/ runlevel directories.

You can use any of the following utilities to set these links properly:

- insserv
- chkconfig
- YaST Runlevel Editor

NOTE: It is possible to manually create the symbolic links in the runlevel subdirectories using the ln command. However, using the above tools is the far better choice because they not only set the links, but they also make sure that the sequence in which services are started is correct by renumbering existing links as needed.

---

insserv

You can use the insserv utility to configure a service to run in a specific runlevel. insserv uses the information in the INIT INFO block of a start script to determine the default runlevels for a service. With this information, it determines in which runlevel subdirectories the links need to be created. It also determines what numbers need to be added after K and S.

The INIT INFO block at the beginning of the script for a service describes which runlevel the service should start or stop in and what services should run as a prerequisite:

```
### BEGIN INIT INFO
# Provides:       syslog
# Required-Start: network
# Should-Start:   earlysyslog
# Required-Stop:  network
# Should-Stop:    earlysyslog
# Default-Start:  2 3 5
# Default-Stop:
# Description:    Start the system logging daemons
### END INIT INFO
```

The entry Default-Start determines which runlevel directories the links are to be placed in. The entry Required-Start determines which services have to be started before this service can be started.

To change the default runlevels, edit the Default-Start entry of the script and then enter insserv -d *service* (default) to create the needed links and to renumber the existing ones as needed.

To remove all links for a service (disabling the service), stop the service (if it is running) by entering /etc/init.d/*service* stop, and then enter insserv -r *service* (remove).

It is possible to override the information in the INIT INFO block on the command line. To do this, first remove all existing links for the service with insserv -r service, then set the new links with insserv *service*,start=*x*, with *x* being the runlevel you want the service to run in. You can list multiple runlevels, as in the following example:

insserv *service*,start=2,3,5

NOTE: For details on the insserv program, enter man 8 insserv at the shell prompt.

Within the INIT INFO block, the use of certain variables is possible. These are explained and defined in /etc/insserv.conf.

chkconfig

The chkconfig utility works in a similar manner. It can be used to disable or enable services and also to list which services are enabled in which runlevel. The following example gives a brief overview on how to use chkconfig:

```
da1:~ # chkconfig cron
cron   on
da1:~ # chkconfig cron -l
cron                    0:off  1:off  2:on   3:on   4:off  5:on   6:off
da1:~ # chkconfig cron off
da1:~ # chkconfig cron -l
cron                    0:off  1:off  2:off  3:off  4:off  5:off  6:off
da1:~ # chkconfig cron on
da1:~ # chkconfig -l
SuSEfirewall2_init      0:off  1:off  2:off  3:off  4:off  5:off  6:off
SuSEfirewall2_setup     0:off  1:off  2:off  3:off  4:off  5:off  6:off
aaeventd                0:off  1:off  2:off  3:off  4:off  5:off  6:off
acpid                   0:off  1:off  2:on   3:on   4:off  5:on   6:off
alsasound               0:off  1:off  2:on   3:on   4:off  5:on   6:off
atd                     0:off  1:off  2:off  3:off  4:off  5:off  6:off
auditd                  0:off  1:off  2:off  3:on   4:off  5:on   6:off
...
```

YaST Runlevel Editor

In addition to the `insserv` and `chkconfig` command line utilities, you can also configure runlevels using the YaST Runlevel Editor module.

Start YaST and select **System > System Services (Runlevel)**. (You can also open a terminal window and as root enter `yast2 runlevel`.)

The following is displayed:

Figure 5-14 *YaST Runlevel Editor*

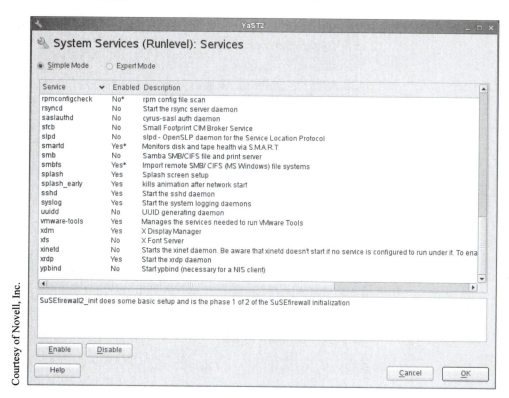

Courtesy of Novell, Inc.

In this screen, you can select from the following modes:

■ **Simple Mode.** Displays a list of all available services and the current status of each service.

You can select a service and then click **Enable** or **Disable**.

Clicking **Enable** starts the service (and services it depends on) and enables them to start at system boot time. Clicking **Disable** stops dependent services and the service itself and disables their start at system boot time.

■ **Expert Mode.** Gives you control over the runlevels which a service is started or stopped in and lets you change the default runlevel.

The **Expert Mode** interface is shown below:

Figure 5-15   *YaST Runlevel Editor: Expert Mode*

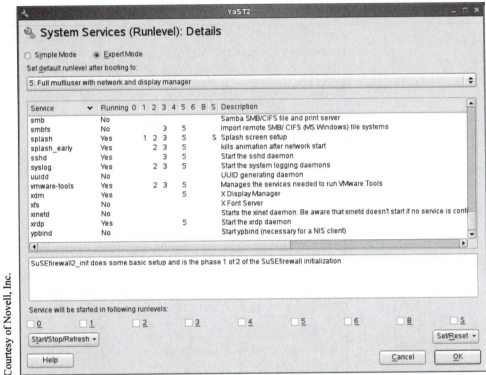

Courtesy of Novell, Inc.

In this mode, the dialog displays the current default runlevel at the top. You can select a new default runlevel from the drop-down menu.

Normally, the default runlevel of a SUSE Linux system is runlevel 5 (full multiuser with network and graphical environment). A suitable alternative might be runlevel 3 (full multiuser with network).

NOTE: Runlevel 4 is initially undefined to allow you to create your own custom runlevel.

Changes to the default runlevel take effect the next time you boot your computer.

To configure a service, select a service from the list, then, from the options below the list, select the runlevels you want associated with the service. The list includes the available services and daemons, indicates whether they are currently enabled on your system, and lists the runlevels currently assigned.

If you want a service activated after editing the runlevels, select **Start now**, **Stop now**, or **Refresh status** from the drop-down list.

You can use **Refresh status** to check the current status (if this has not been done automatically).

From the **Set/Reset** drop-down list, select one of the following:

- **Enable the Service.** Activates the service in the standard runlevels.

- **Disable the Service.** Deactivates the service.
- **Enable All Services.** Activates all services in their standard runlevels.

Remember that faulty runlevel settings can make a system unusable. Before applying your changes, make absolutely sure you know the impact of the changes you are making.

When you finish configuring the runlevels, save the configuration by clicking *OK*.

Change the Runlevel

When starting the system, you can choose a runlevel different from the default runlevel defined in /etc/inittab. The runlevel can also be changed in the running system.

Consider the following:

- Changing the Runlevel at Boot
- Managing Runlevels from the Command Line

Changing the Runlevel at Boot

The standard runlevel is usually 3 or 5, as defined in the /etc/inittab file by the initdefault entry. However, it is also possible to boot to another runlevel by specifying the runlevel on the *Boot Options* line of the GRUB boot menu.

Any parameters that are not evaluated by the kernel itself are passed to init as parameters. The desired runlevel, such as 1, is simply appended to the boot options already specified in GRUB configuration file (/boot/grub/menu.lst).

Managing Runlevels from the Command Line

You can also change to another runlevel after the system is already running. This is done using the init or telinit commands. For example, you can change to runlevel 1 by entering init 1 at the shell prompt.

NOTE: The init and telinit commands can be used interchangeably. telinit is simply a link to the init command.

In the same way, you can change back to the standard runlevel where all programs needed for operation are run and where individual users can log in to the system. For example, you can return to a full GUI desktop and network interface (runlevel 5) by entering init 5 at the shell prompt.

Like most modern operating systems, Linux reacts sensitively to being switched off without warning. If this happens, the file systems need to be checked and corrected before the system can be used again.

For this reason, the system should always be shut down properly. With the appropriate hardware, Linux can also switch off the computer itself in the last stage of the shutdown process.

You can stop the system by entering `init 0` at the shell prompt. You can restart the system by entering `init 6` at the shell prompt. The `halt` and `poweroff` commands are equivalent to `init 0`; the `reboot` command is equivalent to `init 6`.

The `shutdown` command shuts down the system after a specified amount of time:

- **+m.** Minutes from now.

- **hh:mm.** Time in hours:minutes when Linux should shut down.

- **now.** System is stopped immediately.

The `-h` option causes a system halt; if you use the `-r` option instead, the system is rebooted. Without options, it changes to runlevel 1 (single user mode).

The `shutdown` command controls the shutdown of the system in a special way, compared with the other stop commands. The command informs all users that the system will be shut down and does not allow other users to log in before it shuts down.

The shutdown command can also be supplied with a warning message, such as the following:

```
shutdown +5 The new hard drive has arrived
```

If a shutdown planned for a later time should not be carried out after all, you can revoke the shutdown by entering `shutdown -c`.

Exercise 5-3   Manage the Boot Loader

In this exercise, you practice booting into a shell and modifying `/boot/grub/menu.lst`.

You will find this exercise at the end of the chapter.

(End of Exercise)

Exercise 5-4   Manage Runlevels

In this exercise, you practice configuring runlevels.

You will find this exercise at the end of the chapter.

(End of Exercise)

Objective 4   Use Monitoring and Troubleshooting Tools

As a system administrator, you are probably responsible for documenting and monitoring your systems. In addition to system log files, various tools are at your disposal to monitor your SLES 11 system.

To monitor your system effectively, you need to

- Use System Logging Services with syslog
- Use System Logging Services with syslog-ng
- Archive Log Files with logrotate
- Monitor the SLES 11 System
- Manage System Logging
- Monitor Your SLES 11 Server

Use System Logging Services with syslog

In a Linux system, there are many logs that track various aspects of system operation. Many services log their activities to their own log files, and the level of detail can be set on a per-service basis. In addition, system logs in /var/log/ track system-level events.

The information logged in these log files is typically used to assist in troubleshooting and security auditing. However, you will probably want to review the logs from time to time as a preventative measure.

To use system logging services, you need to understand the following:

- The syslog Daemon
- Setting Up a syslog Server

The syslog Daemon

The syslog daemon syslogd is used by many services to log system events. The advantage in using a single service for logging is that all logging can be managed from one configuration file.

TIP: The daemon syslogd in Linux is based on the BSD syslogd service. While it conforms to standard behavior, it has been extended for use in Linux. This means that syslogd is compatible with non-Linux systems that conform to the documented BSD interfaces.

The syslog daemon accepts messages from system services and logs them based on settings in the configuration file /etc/syslog.conf.

TIP: For details on the syslog.conf file, enter man syslog.conf.

The following is an example of the syslogd configuration file:

```
# /etc/syslog.conf - Configuration file for syslogd(8)
#
# For info about the format of this file, see "man syslog.conf".
#
#
# print most on tty10 and on the xconsole pipe
#
kern.warning;*.err;authpriv.none /dev/tty10
kern.warning;*.err;authpriv.none |/dev/xconsole
*.emerg *
# enable this, if you want that root is informed
# immediately, e.g. of logins
#*.alert root
...
```

The /etc/syslog.conf file contains one rule per line. Each rule consists of two fields separated by spaces or tabs. The **category** is given in the first field, which is always allocated a **priority**, separated by a dot (such as kern.warn). The second field specifies what should be done with the corresponding system messages (such as / dev/xconsole).

To understand how syslog.conf works, you need to know about the following components:

- Categories

- Priorities

- Second Field Options

- Additional Priority Parameters

Categories

The category (also called a facility) refers to the subsystem that provides the corresponding message. Each program that uses syslog for logging is assigned such a category. The following describes these categories:

- **authpriv.** Used by all services that have anything to do with system security or authorization. All PAM messages use this category. The ssh daemon uses the auth category.

- **cron.** Accepts messages from the cron and at daemons.

- **daemon.** Used by various daemons, such as the ppp daemon, that do not have their own category.

- **kern.** A category for all kernel messages.

- **lpr.** This category handles messages from the printer system.

- **news.** This category is for messages from the news system. As with the mail system, many messages might need to be logged in a short time.

- **mail.** This category is for messages from the mail system. This is important because many messages can arrive very quickly.

- **syslog.** This category is for internal messages of the syslog daemon.

- **user.** This is a general category for messages on a user level. For example, it is used by login to log failed login attempts.

- **uucp.** This category handles messages from the uucp system.

- **local0 – local7.** These categories are available for your own configuration. All of the local categories can be used in your own programs. By configuring one of these categories, messages from your own programs can be administered individually through entries in the /etc/syslog.conf file.

Priorities

The priority gives details about the urgency of the message. The following priorities are available (listed in increasing degree of urgency):

- **debug.** This priority should only be used for debugging purposes, since all messages of this category and higher are logged.

- **info.** This priority is for messages that are purely informative.

- **notice.** This priority is for messages that describe normal system states that should be noted.

- **warning.** This priority is for messages displaying deviations from the normal state.

- **err.** This priority displays the occurrence of an error.

- **crit.** This priority informs you of critical conditions for the specified program.

- **alert.** This priority level informs the system administrator that immediate action is needed to keep the system functioning.

- **emerg.** This priority warns you that the system is no longer usable.

Second Field Options

As already mentioned, the second field for each entry determines what will be done with the corresponding message. The following options are available:

- **Output of a file.** Adding a - before the filename specifies that the file is not synchronized for each entry. The following is an example:

```
mail.*          -/var/log/mail
```

- **Specifying the device file for a text console.** All corresponding messages are sent to the specified console. The following is an example:

```
kern.warn;*.err;authpriv.none /dev/tty10
```

- **Specifying a FIFO file (named pipe)** by putting the pipe character (|) in front of the file name. All corresponding messages are written into the FIFO file. The following is an example:

```
kern.warn;*.err;authpriv.none |/dev/xconsole
```

- **Specifying a user list.** All mentioned users who are also logged in receive a message on their text terminals (this does not work on all terminal types). The following is an example:

```
*.alert      root,geeko
```

- **Specifying a computer name with a prefixed @.** Messages are forwarded to the computer specified and logged there by syslog, depending on the configuration on that computer. The following is an example:

```
*.*          @mars.example.com
```

- **Using an asterisk (*).** All users logged in receive a message through the wall (write all) command. The following is an example:

```
*.crit       *
```

Additional Priority Parameters

The rules configured are always valid for the specified priority and all higher priorities. The following are additional parameters you can use for defining the priority in a rule:

- **An equal sign (=) before the priority.** By entering an equal sign, the rule is set only for messages of this priority. The following is an example:

```
*.=warn;*.=err -/var/log/warn
```

- **An exclamation mark (!) before the priority.** By entering an exclamation mark, this and all higher priorities are excluded from logging. The following is an example:

```
mail.*;mail.!=info    /var/adm/mail
```

- **Add an asterisk (*).** If you enter an asterisk, it stands for "all categories" or "all priorities."

- **Set none as the priority.** You can exclude a category from logging by setting none as the priority. The following is an example:

```
*.*;mail.none;news.none     -/var/log/messages
```

You can specify parameters for the syslog daemon in the /etc/sysconfig/syslog file. The KERNEL_LOGLEVEL variable determines the logging level for the kernel log daemon (klogd). You can use the SYSLOGD_PARAMS variable to pass start parameters to the daemon.

Setting Up a syslog Server

The syslogd daemon can be configured to communicate over the network. This allows you to configure multiple systems to send all of their logging information to a single log server. Doing this can be very beneficial on a large network. Instead of having to visit each system to review log messages, you can access all of your log messages on a single syslog server.

The first thing you need to do is to configure the syslog daemon on your syslog server to listen on the network for logging requests from syslog clients. Complete the following:

1. Open the /etc/sysconfig/syslog file in a text editor.

2. Add the `-r` parameter to `SYSLOGD_PARAMS=`. For example:

```
## Type: string
## Default: ""
## Config: ""
## ServiceRestart: syslog
#
# if not empty: parameters for syslogd
# for example SYSLOGD_PARAMS="-r -s my.dom.ain"
#
SYSLOGD_PARAMS="-r"
```

This enables logging from remote machines and disables DNS lookups on incoming syslog messages.

3. Save your changes to the file and exit the editor.

4. Restart the syslogd daemon.

5. Open port 514 (UDP) in the firewall.

Next, you need to configure the syslog client systems to send the log messages you specify to the syslog server. Do the following:

1. Open the `/etc/syslog.conf` file in a text editor.

2. Configure your facilities and priorities and send them to the syslog server using the following syntax:

    facility.priority   ***@hostname_of_syslog_server***

    For example:

    ```
    auth.*          @da1.digitalairlines.com
    ```

3. Restart the syslogd daemon.

4. Test the configuration by generating a test log message using the `logger` command at the shell prompt of the client system.

    Use the following syntax:

    `logger -p` ***priority message***

5. Verify the log message was received on the syslog server.

Use System Logging Services with syslog-ng

A Linux system maintains many log files that track various aspects of system operation. Many individual services running on the system maintain their own log files. All log files are located in the `/var/log/` directory (or in subdirectories).

The information saved in these log files can be an invaluable resource for troubleshooting problems and verifying security. As such, you should review these log files regularly.

In this objective, you learn how to use system logging services. The following topics are addressed:

- Configure the Syslog Daemon (syslog-ng)
- View Commonly Used Linux Log Files

Configure the Syslog Daemon (syslog-ng)

The syslog-ng daemon is used by many Linux services to log system events. The advantage in using a single service for logging is that all configuration settings can be managed from one file.

In SLES 9 and earlier versions, syslogd was used to log system events. Beginning with SLES 10, these events are logged by syslog-ng. The main advantage of syslog-ng over syslogd is its ability to filter messages based on the content of each message.

The syslog daemon accepts messages from services and logs them based on settings in its configuration files.

NOTE: The syslog daemon can also accept log messages from other Linux hosts. Many system administrators set up a single logging host in their networks and configure all other systems to send their log messages to it. This allows you to view log messages from your entire network in one single location.

The configuration of syslog-ng is distributed across the following files:

- /etc/sysconfig/syslog
- /etc/syslog-ng/syslog-ng.conf

/etc/sysconfig/syslog

The /etc/sysconfig/syslog file contains general parameters applicable to syslog-ng as well as syslogd. Parameters set in this file include the following:

- Options passed to syslogd or syslog-ng when the service starts
- Kernel log level
- Parameters for klogd
- Parameters that determine which syslog daemon is to be used

A sample file is shown below:

```
...
## Type:            string
## Default:         ""
## Config:          ""
## ServiceRestart:  syslog
## if not empty: parameters for syslogd
# for example SYSLOGD_PARAMS="-r -s my.dom.ain"
#
SYSLOGD_PARAMS=""
```

```
## Type:              string
## Default:           -x
## Config:            ""
## ServiceRestart:    syslog
## if not empty: parameters for klogd
# for example KLOGD_PARAMS="-x" to avoid (duplicate) symbol resolution
#
KLOGD_PARAMS="-x"

## Type:              list(syslogd,syslog-ng,"")
## Default:           ""
## Config:            "
## ServiceRestart:    syslog
## The name of the syslog daemon used as
# syslog service: "syslogd", "syslog-ng" or "" for autodetect
#
SYSLOG_DAEMON="syslog-ng"
...
```

Parameters set in `/etc/sysconfig/syslog` are evaluated by the `/etc/init.d/syslog` script when the daemon is started.

/etc/syslog-ng/syslog-ng.conf

The log system uses two configuration elements that you must understand:

- Facilities

- Priorities

In addition, the configuration of syslog-ng consists of the following parts, which are then combined to configure what information is logged where. These are

- Sources

- Filters

- Destinations

- Log Paths

Facilities

The **facility** refers to the subsystem that provides the corresponding message. Each program that uses syslog for logging is assigned such a facility, usually by the developer. The following describes these facilities:

Table 5-16   *Syslog Facilities*

Facility	Description
authpriv	Used by all services that have anything to do with system security or authorization. All PAM messages use this facility.
cron	Used by the cron and at daemons.

Facility	Description
daemon	Used by various daemons that do not have their own facility, such as the ppp daemon.
kern	All kernel messages.
lpr	Printer system messages.
mail	Mail system messages.
news	News system messages.
syslog	syslog daemon internal messages.
user	General facility for messages generated at a user level. For example, It is used by login to log failed login attempts.
uucp	uucp system messages.
local0 – local7	Eight facilities available for your own custom configuration. You can use all of the local categories in your own programs.
	By configuring one of these facilities, messages from your own programs can be administered individually through entries in the `/etc/syslog-ng/syslog-ng.conf` file.

Priorities

The **priority** provides details about the urgency of the message. The following priorities are available (listed in increasing degree of urgency):

Table 5-17 *Syslog Priorities*

Priority	Description
debug	Should be used only for debugging purposes, since all messages of this category and higher are logged.
info	Messages that are purely informative.
notice	Messages that describe normal system states that should be noted.
warning	Messages displaying deviations from the normal state.
err	Messages displaying errors.
crit	Messages on critical conditions for the specified program.
alert	Messages that inform you that immediate action is required to keep the system functioning.
emerg	Messages that warn you that the system is no longer usable.

Sources

A **source** is a collection of source drivers which collect messages using a given method. These sources are used to gather log messages. The general syntax used in the `/etc/syslog-ng/syslog-ng.conf` file is as follows:

```
source <identifier> { source-driver(params); source-driver(params);
... };
```

The respective section in `/etc/syslog-ng/syslog-ng.conf` looks like this:

```
source src {
        # include internal syslog-ng messages
        # note: the internal() source is required!
        internal();

        # the following line will be replaced by the
        # socket list generated by SuSEconfig using
        # variables from /etc/sysconfig/syslog:
        unix-dgram("/dev/log");

        # uncomment to process log messages from network:
        #udp(ip("0.0.0.0") port(514));
};
```

In this example, one source for internal messages of syslog-ng and the `/dev/log` socket are defined.

Filters

A **filter** is a boolean expression that is applied to messages and is evaluated as either true or false. The general syntax is as follows:

```
filter <identifier> { expression; };
```

The identifier has to be unique within the configuration and is used later to configure the actual logging.

The following excerpt of `/etc/syslog-ng/syslog-ng.conf` shows some filters used in SLES 11:

```
#
# Filter definitions
#
filter f_iptables   { facility(kern) and match("IN=") and
match("OUT="); };

filter f_console    { level(warn) and facility(kern) and not
       filter(f_iptables) or level(err) and not facility(authpriv); };

filter f_newsnotice { level(notice) and facility(news); };
filter f_newscrit   { level(crit)   and facility(news); };
filter f_newserr    { level(err)    and facility(news); };
filter f_news       { facility(news); };
...
filter f_messages   { not facility(news, mail)
       and not filter(f_iptables); };
...
```

As you can see, facility and priority (level) can be used within filters. However, it is also possible to filter according to the content of a line being logged, as in the f_iptables filter above. Combining the expressions with and, or, or and not allows you to create very specific filters.

Destinations

A **destination** defines where messages will be logged. The general syntax is as follows:

```
destination <identifier> { destination-driver(params);
destination-driver(params); ... };
```

Possible destinations are files, fifos, sockets, ttys of certain users, programs, or other hosts. A sample from /etc/syslog-ng/syslog-ng.conf looks like this:

```
destination console  { file("/dev/tty10"  group(tty) perm(0620)); };
destination messages { file("/var/log/messages"); };
```

Log Paths

A **log path** is the point where it all comes together. It defines which messages are logged where, depending upon the source, filter, and destination. The general syntax is as follows:

```
log { source(s1); source(s2); ...
      filter(f1); filter(f2); ...
      destination(d1); destination(d2); ...
      flags(flag1[, flag2...]); };
```

The following entries in /etc/syslog-ng/sylog-ng.conf, for instance, are responsible for logging to /dev/tty10 and /var/log/messages:

```
log { source(src); filter(f_console); destination(console); };
log { source(src); filter(f_messages); destination(messages); };
```

In the first line, log messages that come in through sources defined in source src are logged to tty10 if they match the f_console filter. In line two, messages that come in through sources defined in source src are logged to /var/log/messages if they match the f_messages filter.

View Commonly Used Linux Log Files

On SLES 11, most messages are written to the /var/log/messages log file. This file is extremely useful for troubleshooting problems. You can often find hints about system problems, such as why a service does not start properly.

If you can't find useful information in /var/log/messages, you should also check the /var/log/audit/audit.log file. This is the log file for AppArmor messages and might provide more information. Firewall messages are logged in /var/log/firewall.

To monitor new messages written to a log file, you can use the tail -f command. To end the command, press Ctrl+c.

The following are important log files and directories:

Table 5-18   *Important Log Files and Directories*

Log File	Description
`/var/log/audit/`	Stores the Novell AppArmor logfile `audit.log`.
`/var/log/cups/`	Stores the log files for the CUPS printing system.
`/var/log/news/`	Stores messages for the news system.
`/var/log/YaST2/`	Stores log files for YaST.
`/var/log/boot.msg`	When the system boots, all boot script messages are displayed on the first virtual console. You can later read the boot messages in this file.
`/var/log/mail`	Messages from the mail system are written to this file. Because this system often generates a lot of messages, there are additional log files: ■ `/var/log/mail.err` ■ `/var/log/mail.info` ■ `/var/log/mail.warn`
`/var/log/wtmp`	Contains information about which user was logged in, where the user logged in, and how long the user was logged in (since the file was created). The file contents are in binary form and can be displayed only with the `last` command.
`/var/log/lastlog`	Contains information about which user was last logged in, where the user logged in, and how long the user was logged in. You can view the contents only with the `lastlog` command.

Almost any name can be used for log files, and systems other than SLES 11 might use different names. Other filenames to be looked for include `/var/log/syslog`, `/var/log/maillog` or `/var/log/secure`.

Archive Log Files with logrotate

You need to pay attention to the size of your log files on Linux to ensure that they do not get too large. In this case, they may consume all of the available space in the partition, causing the system to cease to work properly.

For this reason, the size and age of log files are monitored automatically by the `logrotate` program. The program is run daily by the cron daemon via `/etc/cron.daily/logrotate`. The program checks all log files listed in its configuration files and takes any action required by the configuration for the respective file.

The configuration file of logrotate is `/etc/logrotate.conf`, which contains general configuration settings. The following is an example:

```
# see "man logrotate" for details
# rotate log files weekly
weekly
# keep 4 weeks worth of backlogs
rotate 4
# add the date to the filename after rotating
dateext
# create new (empty) log files after rotating old ones
create
# uncomment these to switch compression to bzip2
compresscmd /usr/bin/bzip2
uncompresscmd /usr/bin/bunzip2
# RPM packages drop log rotation information into this directory
include /etc/logrotate.d
```

The following table describes the settings in the file:

Table 5-19   *logrotate Settings*

Option	Description
weekly	Log files are rotated once a week.
rotate 4	Keep 4 versions of the log file.
create	Old file is saved under a new name and a new empty log file is created.
compress	Copies are stored in a compressed form.

Many RPM packages contain preconfigured files for evaluation by logrotate. These files are stored in /etc/logrotate.d/ and are read by logrotate through the include /etc/logrotate.d entry in /etc/logrotate.conf. Settings in these files supersede the general settings in /etc/logrotate.conf.

You must list the files that you want to be monitored by logrotate in the /etc/logrotate.conf file or in separate configuration files. The following is an example of the /etc/logrotate.d/syslog file:

```
#
# Please note, that changing of log file permissions in this
# file is not sufficient if syslog-ng is used as log daemon.
# It is required to specify the permissions in the syslog-ng
# configuration /etc/syslog-ng/syslog-ng.conf.in as well.
#
/var/log/warn /var/log/messages /var/log/allmessages
 /var/log/localmessages /var/log/firewall {
    compress
    dateext
    maxage 365
    rotate 99
    missingok
    notifempty
    size +4096k
    create 640 root root
    sharedscripts
```

```
postrotate
    /etc/init.d/syslog reload
endscript
}
...
```

The `/etc/logrotate.d/syslog` file contains settings for how the log files written by syslog-ng will be treated. The following table describes the settings in the file:

Table 5-20   *Logrotate Settings*

Option	Description
size +4096k	Files are not rotated until they reach a size of 4096 KB.
rotate 99	Ninety-nine versions of each file are kept.
compress	Old log files are stored in compressed form, using the compression command defined in `/etc/logrotate.conf`.
maxage 365	As soon as a compressed file is older than 365 days, it is deleted.
notifempty	If a log file is empty, no rotation takes place.
create 640 root root	New log files are created after the rotation, and owner, group, and permissions for the new file are specified.
postrotate . . . endscript	Scripts can be called after the rotation. For example, some services have to be restarted after log files have been changed.
	In the example above, the syslog daemon rereads its configuration files after the rotation (`/etc/init.d/syslog reload`).

Most of the services whose log files should be monitored come with preconfigured files. Usually only minor adjustments are needed.

Monitor the SLES 11 System

As a system administrator, you are probably responsible for documenting and monitoring your systems. Most administrators use a variety of utilities to develop an initial baseline when the system is deployed. This provides a snapshot of how the system was performing at the point right after it was initially installed.

Then you create subsequent baselines at regular intervals over time. You compare these baselines against your initial baseline to evaluate performance trends. Analyzing your baselines against your system documentation and your change log can help you identify issues that may be impacting performance.

To develop your system documentation and baselines, you need to evaluate the following questions:

■   Does the system boot normally?

■   What is the version number of the kernel?

- What services are running on the system?

- What is the average system load?

In this objective, you are introduced to SLES 11 tools that you can use to answer these questions. The following topics are addressed:

- Gather Boot Log Information

- View Hardware Information in /proc/

- Gather Hardware Information Using Command Line Utilities

- Gathering System and Process Information from the Command Line

- Monitor Hard Drive Space Usage

Gather Boot Log Information

When SLES 11 initially starts, you can press Esc to view system boot messages. A sample is shown below:

Figure 5-16   *Boot Messages*

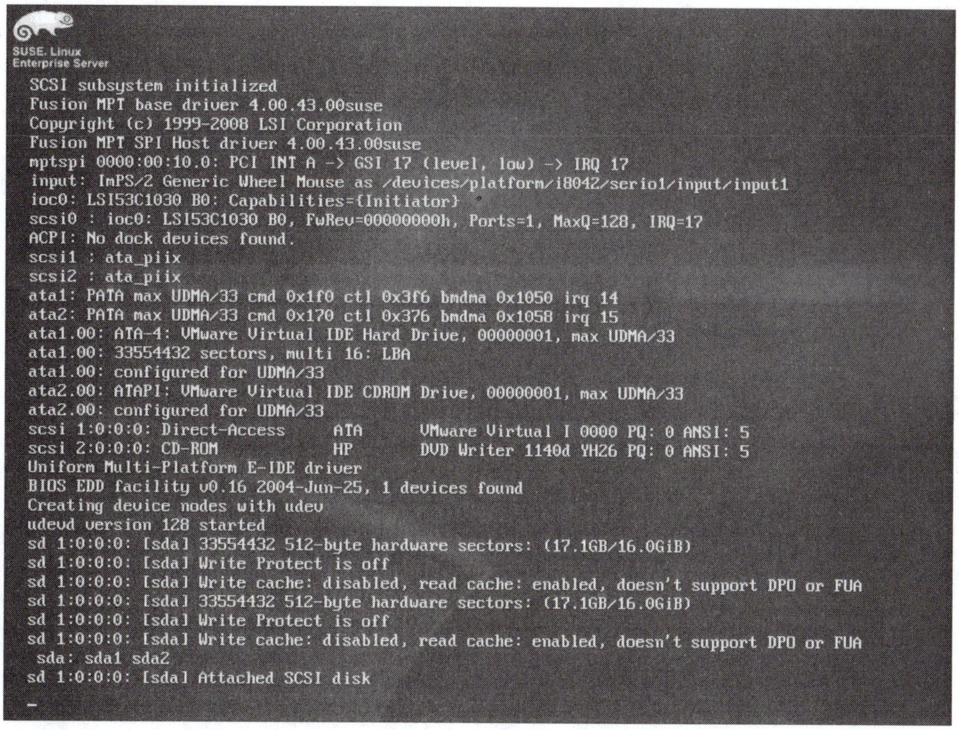

Courtesy of Novell, Inc.

```
SCSI subsystem initialized
Fusion MPT base driver 4.00.43.00suse
Copyright (c) 1999-2008 LSI Corporation
Fusion MPT SPI Host driver 4.00.43.00suse
mptspi 0000:00:10.0: PCI INT A -> GSI 17 (level, low) -> IRQ 17
input: ImPS/2 Generic Wheel Mouse as /devices/platform/i8042/serio1/input/input1
ioc0: LSI53C1030 B0: Capabilities={Initiator}
scsi0 : ioc0: LSI53C1030 B0, FwRev=00000000h, Ports=1, MaxQ=128, IRQ=17
ACPI: No dock devices found.
scsi1 : ata_piix
scsi2 : ata_piix
ata1: PATA max UDMA/33 cmd 0x1f0 ctl 0x3f6 bmdma 0x1050 irq 14
ata2: PATA max UDMA/33 cmd 0x170 ctl 0x376 bmdma 0x1058 irq 15
ata1.00: ATA-4: VMware Virtual IDE Hard Drive, 00000001, max UDMA/33
ata1.00: 33554432 sectors, multi 16: LBA
ata1.00: configured for UDMA/33
ata2.00: ATAPI: VMware Virtual IDE CDROM Drive, 00000001, max UDMA/33
ata2.00: configured for UDMA/33
scsi 1:0:0:0: Direct-Access     ATA      VMware Virtual I 0000 PQ: 0 ANSI: 5
scsi 2:0:0:0: CD-ROM            HP       DVD Writer 1140d YH26 PQ: 0 ANSI: 5
Uniform Multi-Platform E-IDE driver
BIOS EDD facility v0.16 2004-Jun-25, 1 devices found
Creating device nodes with udev
udevd version 128 started
sd 1:0:0:0: [sda] 33554432 512-byte hardware sectors: (17.1GB/16.0GiB)
sd 1:0:0:0: [sda] Write Protect is off
sd 1:0:0:0: [sda] Write cache: disabled, read cache: enabled, doesn't support DPO or FUA
sd 1:0:0:0: [sda] 33554432 512-byte hardware sectors: (17.1GB/16.0GiB)
sd 1:0:0:0: [sda] Write Protect is off
sd 1:0:0:0: [sda] Write cache: disabled, read cache: enabled, doesn't support DPO or FUA
 sda: sda1 sda2
sd 1:0:0:0: [sda] Attached SCSI disk
_
```

These boot messages contain a wealth of valuable system information. However, most of the messages scroll by so quickly that they are difficult to read. If an error message were to be displayed, it's unlikely that you would be able to read it before it scrolled off the screen.

Fortunately, the boot messages are stored in the *kernel ring buffer*. But the capacity of the kernel ring buffer is quite limited. Therefore, the oldest entries in the kernel ring buffer are deleted when new entries are added to it. To preserve the boot messages, they are written to the `/var/log/boot.msg` file before they are deleted from the buffer.

You can use the `dmesg` command to view the current contents of the kernel ring buffer:

```
da1:~ # dmesg
Initializing cgroup subsys cpuset
Initializing cgroup subsys cpu
Linux version 2.6.27.11-1-pae (geeko@buildhost) (gcc version 4.3.2
[gcc-4_3-branch revision 141291] (SUSE Linux) ) #1 SMP 2009-01-14
23:28:13 +0100BIOS-provided physical RAM map:
BIOS-e820: 0000000000000000 - 000000000009f800 (usable)
BIOS-e820: 000000000009f800 - 00000000000a0000 (reserved)
BIOS-e820: 00000000000dc000 - 0000000000100000 (reserved)
BIOS-e820: 0000000000100000 - 000000001fef0000 (usable)
BIOS-e820: 000000001fef0000 - 000000001feff000 (ACPI data)
...
```

The output of dmesg shows messages generated during the initialization of the hardware by the kernel or kernel modules.

The `/var/log/boot.msg` file contains additional information beyond what can be displayed with `dmesg`, including the messages generated by the various init scripts at boot time as well as exit status codes. An example is shown in the following:

```
da1:~ # cat /var/log/boot.msg
...
INIT: Entering runlevel: 5

Boot logging started on /dev/tty1(/dev/console) at Thu Apr 16
09:16:55 2009

Master Resource Control: previous runlevel: N, switching to runlevel:
5
<notice>startproc: execve (/sbin/syslog-ng) [ /sbin/syslog-ng ], [
CONSOLE=/dev/console ROOTFS_FSTYPE=ext3 TERM=linux SHELL=/bin/sh
ROOTFS_FSCK=0 crashkernel=128M-:64M@16M LC_ALL=POSIX
INIT_VERSION=sysvinit-2.86 REDIRECT=/dev/tty1 COLUMNS=96 PATH=/bin:/
sbin:/usr/bin:/usr/sbin DO_CONFIRM= vga=0x332 RUNLEVEL=5 SPLASHCFG=/
etc/bootsplash/themes/SLES/config/bootsplash-800x600.cfg PWD=/
PREVLEVEL=N LINES=33 SHLVL=2 HOME=/ SPLASH=yes splash=silent
ROOTFS_BLKDEV=/dev/disk/by-id/ata-VMware_Virtual_IDE_Hard_Drive_
00000000000000000001-part2 _=/sbin/startproc DAEMON=/sbin/syslog-ng ]
<notice>startproc: execve (/sbin/klogd) [ /sbin/klogd -c 1 -x ], [
CONSOLE=/dev/console ROOTFS_FSTYPE=ext3 TERM=linux SHELL=/bin/sh
ROOTFS_FSCK=0 crashkernel=128M-:64M@16M LC_ALL=POSIX
INIT_VERSION=sysvinit-2.86 REDIRECT=/dev/tty1 COLUMNS=96 PATH=/bin:/
sbin:/usr/bin:/usr/sbin DO_CONFIRM= vga=0x332 RUNLEVEL=5 SPLASHCFG=
Starting syslog servicesdone
...
```

The contents of the /var/log/boot.msg file can be extremely useful when creating system baselines and troubleshooting problems.

You can use YaST to view the file contents by starting YaST and then selecting *Miscellaneous > Start-up Log*. You can also start the module directly by entering yast2 view_anymsg in a terminal window as root. In either case, the contents of the /var/log/boot.msg file is displayed, as shown below:

Figure 5-17   *The /var/log/boot.msg File Viewed With YaST*

Courtesy of Novell, Inc.

NOTE: You can use the drop-down list in this screen to also view the system log file.

View Hardware Information in /proc/

The /proc/ directory contains information about the running SLES 11 system, including the hardware information stored in the kernel memory space. The /proc/ directory and all of its subdirectories and files are not "real" files. Instead, they are dynamically generated when you access them.

However, you can view the contents of the files within /proc/ using standard Linux shell commands such as cat and less.

For example, if you enter cat /proc/cpuinfo, output is generated from data stored in kernel memory that displays information such as the CPU model name and cache size. An example is shown below:

```
da1:~ # cat /proc/cpuinfo
processor       : 0
vendor_id       : GenuineIntel
cpu family      : 15
model           : 4
model name      : Intel(R) Pentium(R) 4 CPU 3.20GHz
stepping        : 8
cpu MHz         : 3200.116
cache size      : 1024 KB
fdiv_bug        : no
hlt_bug         : no
f00f_bug        : no
coma_bug        : no
fpu             : yes
fpu_exception   : yes
cpuid level     : 5
wp              : yes
flags           : fpu vme de pse tsc msr pae mce cx8 apic sep mtrr pge
mca cmov pat pse36 clflush dts acpi mmx fxsr sse sse2 ss nx
constant_tsc up pebs bts pni ds_cpl
bogomips        : 6400.23
clflush size    : 64
power management:
```

Some of the more commonly used files in /proc include the following:

- **/proc/devices.** Displays information about the devices installed in your Linux system.

- **/proc/cpuinfo.** Displays processor information.

- **/proc/ioports.** Displays information about the I/O ports in your server.

- **/proc/interrupts.** Displays information about the IRQ assignments in your Linux system.

- **/proc/dma.** Displays information about the Direct Memory Access channels used in your Linux system.

- **/proc/bus/pci/devices.** Displays information about the Peripheral Component Interconnect (PCI) devices in your Linux system.

- **/proc/scsi/scsi.** Displays summary information about the SCSI devices installed in your Linux system.

- **/proc/partitions.** Displays information about the disk partitions on your system.

- **/proc/sys.** Contains a series of subdirectories and files that contain kernel variables. These directories are listed below:

  - **debug.** Contains debugging information.

  - **dev.** Contains information and parameters for specific devices on your system.

  - **fs.** Contains file system information and parameters.

  - **kernel.** Contains kernel information and configuration parameters.

   ❑   **net.** Contains network-related information and parameters.

   ❑   **vm.** Contains information and variables for the virtual memory subsystem.

Some of the files in these directories are read-only. However, some of the files are writable and contain variables that can be used to configure a particular kernel parameter. In fact, you can change kernel parameters while the system is running and have the changes applied without rebooting by simply modifying the appropriate file.

NOTE: Any changes you make to these files are not persistent. If you reboot the system, your modifications will be lost.

To determine whether a file is configurable or not, look at the permissions. If a file has the write (w) attribute assigned, you can modify it. As an example, the files in the `/proc/sys/dev/cdrom` directory are shown below:

```
da1:/proc/sys/dev/cdrom # ls -l
total 0
-rw-r--r-- 1 root root 0 Apr 22 15:37 autoclose
-rw-r--r-- 1 root root 0 Apr 22 15:37 autoeject
-rw-r--r-- 1 root root 0 Apr 22 15:37 check_media
-rw-r--r-- 1 root root 0 Apr 22 15:37 debug
-r--r--r-- 1 root root 0 Apr 16 14:35 info
-rw-r--r-- 1 root root 0 Apr 22 15:37 lock
```

Notice that the `autoclose`, `autoeject`, `check_media`, `debug`, and `lock` files are writable by root, but the `info` file is not.

To change the contents of a file in `/proc/sys`, use the `echo` command to write the desired value to the file. For example, `/proc/sys/vm/` contains a file named `swappiness`. This file determines how aggressively the Linux kernel swaps unused data out of physical RAM into the swap partition on disk. As you can see below, this file contains a single number as its value. The default is 60.

```
da1:/proc/sys/vm # cat swappiness
60
```

This variable can be set to any value between 0 and 100. The higher the value, the more aggressively the system will swap data into the swap partition. To set the value of the variable to 75, you would enter

```
da1:/proc/sys/vm # echo 75 > swappiness
```

NOTE: There are far too many variables in `/proc/sys/` to cover in this objective. A fairly detailed listing of variables and their possible values can be viewed by entering `man 5 proc` at the shell prompt.

As mentioned above, all changes to the `/proc/` file system are non-persistent. To set the values permanently when booting the system, put them into the `/etc/`

`sysctl.conf` file. The `sysctl` command is called during boot and sets all parameters defined in the configuration. If a parameter is not defined, a default value is set.

The `sysctl` command can set parameters in directories below `/proc/sys/`, so all files are accessed via their relative path from this directory. To have a look at the currently set values, use the `-a` option:

```
da1:~ # sysctl -a
...
vm.swappiness = 75
...
```

To set the value of a parameter, the `-w` option is used:

```
da1:~ # sysctl -w vm.swappiness=80
```

To set values via the configuration file `/etc/sysctl.conf`, the same syntax as for using `sysctl -w` is used:

```
# /etc/sysctl.conf
...
vm.swappiness=75
```

You can now set the values manually via `sysctl -p` (if no filename is given, `/etc/sysctl.conf` is used). During the next reboot, the values will be set automatically.

Gather Hardware Information Using Command Line Utilities

In addition to viewing the contents of the files in /proc/, you can also use the following utilities to gather information about the hardware in your Linux system:

■ **hwinfo.** Displays specific information about the devices installed in your Linux system. Sample output from hwinfo about the network card installed in a SLES 11 system is shown below:

```
da1:~ # hwinfo
...
45: None 01.0: 10701 Ethernet
  [Created at net.124]
  Unique ID: L2Ua.ndpeucax6V1
  Parent ID: JNkJ.weGuQ9ywYPF
  SysFS ID: /class/net/eth1
  SysFS Device Link: /devices/pci0000:00/0000:00:11.0
  Hardware Class: network interface
  Model: "Ethernet network interface"
  Driver: "pcnet32"
  Driver Modules: "pcnet32"
  Device File: eth1
  HW Address: 00:50:56:00:00:47
  Link detected: yes
  Config Status: cfg=new, avail=yes, need=no, active=unknown
  Attached to: #21 (Ethernet controller)
```

If you are only interested in information about certain hardware components, you can add options to hwinfo. To display only information about network cards, use hwinfo --network. For a summary listing, enter hwinfo --short.

You can also enter hwinfo --log *filename* to write the information to a log file.

■ **hdparm.** Displays information about your hard drive and lets you manage certain hard drive parameters.

For example, the -i option displays hard drive identification information available at boot time. An example is shown below:

```
da1:~ # hdparm -i /dev/sda
/dev/sda:

Model=VMware Virtual IDE Hard Drive, FwRev=00000001,
SerialNo=00000000000000000001
Config={ HardSect NotMFM HdSw>15uSec SpinMotCtl Fixed DTR>5Mbs
FmtGapReq }
RawCHS=16383/15/63, TrkSize=0, SectSize=0, ECCbytes=0
BuffType=unknown, BuffSize=32kB, MaxMultSect=64, MultSect=?16?
CurCHS=17475/15/63, CurSects=15530835, LBA=yes, LBAsects=33554432
IORDY=on/off, tPIO={min:160,w/IORDY:120}, tDMA={min:120,rec:120}
PIO modes:  pio0 pio1 pio2 pio3 pio4
DMA modes:  mdma0 mdma1 mdma2
UDMA modes: udma0 udma1 *udma2
AdvancedPM=yes: disabled (255)
Drive conforms to: ATA/ATAPI-4 T13 1153D revision 17:  ATA/ATAPI-
1,2,3,4
 * signifies the current active mode
```

You can also use the -I option to request information directly from the hard drive. For a summary list of available options, enter hdparm or hdparm -h.

■   **fdisk.** Used primarily to manage the partition table on a Linux system. You can also use options such as -l (list partition tables) or -s (size of partition) to view hard drive information. This is shown below:

```
da1:~ # fdisk -l /dev/sda
Disk /dev/sda: 17.1 GB, 17179869184 bytes
255 heads, 63 sectors/track, 2088 cylinders
Units = cylinders of 16065 * 512 = 8225280 bytes
Disk identifier: 0x000d1cd1

Device    Boot  Start    End   Blocks    Id   System
/dev/sda1          2      98   779152+   82   Linux swap / Solaris
/dev/sda2    *    99    1142  8385930    83   Linux
```

■   **iostat.** Displays CPU and input/output (I/O) statistics for devices and partitions.

NOTE: You must install the sysstat package to use iostat.

This command generates reports that can be used to change system configuration to better balance the input/output load between physical disks.

The first generated line provides statistics concerning the time since the system was booted. Each subsequent line covers the time since the previous line. You can generate two types of reports with the command:

❑   CPU usage report

❑   Device usage report

The -c option generates only the CPU usage report; the -d option generates only the device usage report. Using the -x option displays extended statistics for the device usage report. An example is shown below:

```
da1:~ # iostat
Linux 2.6.27.19-5-pae (da1)          14.08.2009        _i686_

avg-cpu:   %user    %nice %system %iowait   %steal    %idle
           0,46     0,03    0,10    0,30     0,00    99,11

Device:           tps    Blk_read/s    Blk_wrtn/s    Blk_read    Blk_wrtn
sda              1,86         33,68         20,97       617448      384496
sda1             0,00          0,10          0,00         1874           0
sda2             0,00          0,04          0,00          698           0
sda3             1,85         33,52         20,97       614572      384496
```

iostat can be used to continuously monitor the usage. To do so, add two numbers to the command. The first number defines the interval in seconds when the output will be updated. The second number defines how many intervals the command should use. If you omit the second number, you need to stop the command by using Ctrl+c.

■ **lspci.** Displays information about all PCI buses in your Linux system and all devices connected to them. An example is shown below:

```
da1:~ # lspci
00:00.0 Host bridge: Intel Corporation 440BX/ZX/DX - 82443BX/ZX/
DX Host bridge (rev 01)
00:01.0 PCI bridge: Intel Corporation 440BX/ZX/DX - 82443BX/ZX/DX
AGP bridge (rev 01)
00:07.0 ISA bridge: Intel Corporation 82371AB/EB/MB PIIX4 ISA
(rev 08)
00:07.1 IDE interface: Intel Corporation 82371AB/EB/MB PIIX4 IDE
(rev 01)
00:07.3 Bridge: Intel Corporation 82371AB/EB/MB PIIX4 ACPI
(rev 08)
00:0f.0 VGA compatible controller: VMware Inc Abstract SVGA II
Adapter
00:10.0 SCSI storage controller: LSI Logic / Symbios Logic 53c1030
PCI-X Fusion-MPT Dual Ultra320 SCSI (rev 01)
00:11.0 Ethernet controller: Advanced Micro Devices [AMD] 79c970
[PCnet32 LANCE] (rev 10)
```

You can use the -v and -vv options to generate verbose reports. The -b option can be used to display a bus-centric view of all the IRQ numbers and addresses as seen by the cards (instead of the kernel) on the PCI bus.

Gathering System and Process Information from the Command Line

Besides `ps` and `top`, which were covered in Manage Processes, Jobs, and Runlevels, you can use the following utilities to gather system and process information on your SLES 11 system:

- uptime
- netstat
- uname
- xosview
- vmstat
- sar

uptime

You can use the `uptime` command at the shell prompt to display the current time, the length of time the system has been running, the number of users on the system, and the average number of jobs in the run queue over the last 1, 5, and 15 minutes.

The following is an example of the information that is displayed when you enter the `uptime` command:

```
da1:~ # uptime
  8:50am   up    0:25,   3 users,   load average: 0.00, 0.02, 0.08
```

netstat

You can use the `netstat` command at the shell prompt to find out which network ports are open on your system. You can also view a list of connections that have been established through these ports. The netstat command is covered in more detail in View Connection Information with netstat.

uname

You can use the `uname` command to view information about the current kernel version, as shown in the following:

```
da1:~ # uname -a
Linux da1 2.6.27.19-5-pae #1 SMP 2009-02-28 04:40:21 +0100 i686 i686
i386 GNU/Linux
```

Information about the kernel version is also available by reading the contents of the `/proc/version` file.

xosview

You can use the `xosview` utility to display the status of several system-based parameters such as CPU usage, load average, memory usage, swap space usage, network usage, interrupts, and serial port status.

To use xosview, you must first install the xosview package. To start xosview, open a terminal window and enter xosview &.

A window similar to the following is displayed:

Figure 5-18   *xosview*

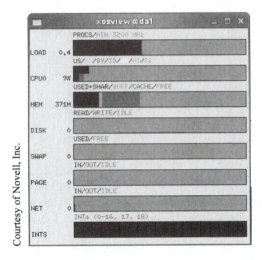

Courtesy of Novell, Inc.

Each parameter status is displayed as a horizontal bar separated into color-coded regions. Each region represents a percentage of the resource that is being put to a particular use.

When you finish viewing the information, you can quit by closing the window.

vmstat

Using vmstat, you can get reports on virtual memory statistics. If you add a number to the command, this defines the interval in seconds for getting updated information. If you add a second number, this defines the number of intervals for which information is collected and displayed.

A simple usage of the command is shown below:

```
da1:~ # vmstat
procs ----------memory-------- -swap- --io-- -system- ----cpu-----
 r  b  swpd    free  buff  cache  si so  bi  bo   in   cs us sy id wa st
 1  0     0 3332232 35324 327692  0  0   8   5   18   55  0  0 99  0  0
```

The output from the command is organized in several sections.

The first section (**procs**) contains information about processes. The column named **r** contains the number of processes waiting for run time. The second column named **b** contains the number of processes in uninterruptable sleep.

The second section (**memory**) contains information about the memory usage. The first column (**swpd**) shows the amount of virtual memory used. The next column (**free**) contains the amount of free memory. The third column (**buff**) shows the amount of memory used as buffers and the fourth column (**cache**) shows the amount of memory used as cache.

The third section (**swap**) provides information about swapping: swap in (**si**) and swap out (**so**).

The next section (**io**) shows input/output operations on the hard disk: **bi** (blocks in) shows how many blocks are read per second and **bo** (blocks out) shows how many blocks are written per second.

The final two sections (**system** and **cpu**) show information about the system.

The next example shows how the information changes when some I/O-intensive tasks are performed. In this case, the `find` command has been run (the lines have been shortened for better readability):

```
da1:~ # vmstat 2 8
procs -----------memory---------- ---swap-- -----io---- -system--
 r  b   swpd    free   buff  cache   si   so    bi    bo   in    cs
 0  0      0 3329836  35392 327736    0    0     8     5   18    55
 0  1      0 3318584  35972 338268    0    0   298     0  154   675
 0  1      0 3315360  38420 338752    0    0  1224   146  458  2227
 0  1      0 3310752  42272 339316    0    0  1922   912  620  2947
 1  0      0 3306536  45864 339936    0    0  1796     0  566  2985
 0  1      0 3302332  49448 340468    0    0  1792     0  579  2447
 0  1      0 3300224  51356 340812    0    0   950   972  311  1482
 0  1      0 3298804  52468 341008    0    0   556     0  184   999
```

If you are only interested in disk-related information, use the `-d` option:

```
da1:~ # vmstat -d
disk- ------------reads------------ ------------writes---------- ---
--IO------
        total merged sectors      ms  total merged  sectors       ms
cur     sec
sda    26853   7059 678816  160372  15852  36722   429984 1478200
0      140
sda1      34   1154   1874     612      0      0        0       0  0 0
sda2      18    133    698     400      0      0        0       0  0 0
sda3   26577   5752 675940  157772  15852  36722   429984 1478200
0      139
sr0        0      0      0       0      0      0        0       0  0 0
loop0      0      0      0       0      0      0        0       0  0 0
loop1      0      0      0       0      0      0        0       0  0 0
loop2      0      0      0       0      0      0        0       0  0 0
loop3      0      0      0       0      0      0        0       0  0 0
loop4      0      0      0       0      0      0        0       0  0 0
loop5      0      0      0       0      0      0        0       0  0 0
loop6      0      0      0       0      0      0        0       0  0 0
loop7      0      0      0       0      0      0        0       0  0 0
```

A summary of different memory-related information is shown by using the `-s` option:

```
da1:~ # vmstat -s
    3898824  total memory
     615612  used memory
     315552  active memory
     227616  inactive memory
    3283212  free memory
      66144  buffer memory
     342968  swap cache
    1044216  total swap
          0  used swap
    1044216  free swap
      17122 non-nice user cpu ticks
       1183 nice user cpu ticks
       3802 system cpu ticks
    3738679 idle cpu ticks
      13854 IO-wait cpu ticks
         16 IRQ cpu ticks
         33 softirq cpu ticks
          0 stolen cpu ticks
     339408 pages paged in
     210856 pages paged out
          0 pages swapped in
          0 pages swapped out
     697276 interrupts
    2107864 CPU context switches
 1250231620 boot time
       6319 forks
```

sar

As part of the **sysstat** package, two monitoring tools are installed: sar and sadc. Both tools are scheduled via a cron job in /etc/cron.d/sysstat. This is a symbolic link pointing to /etc/sysstat/sysstat.cron, which is created when the /etc/init.d/sysstat script is started. Via cron, two scripts are started:

- **/usr/lib/sa/sa1.** This script runs the sadc (System Activity Data Collector) command every 10 minutes. The information collected is appended to the file /var/log/sa/sa*dd* where *dd* stands for the current day (e.g., /var/log/sa/sa17). The data is stored in binary format in this file.

- **/usr/lib/sa/sa2.** This script runs the sar (System Activity Report) command every 6 hours. It converts the information from the sa*dd* file to a human-readable format and stores this in the /var/log/sa/sar*dd* file.

sar can, of course, also be run interactively from the command line. For all options possible, refer to the man page. If sar is run interactively, you normally provide the interval for collecting information and the number of intervals to run the command.

The following example shows information about the CPU utilization:

```
da1:~ # sar -u 2 5
Linux 2.6.27.19-5-pae (da1)          08/17/09        _i686_

12:56:41  CPU   %user   %nice   %system   %iowait   %steal   %idle
12:56:43  all   0.49    0.00    2.44      46.21     0.00     50.86
12:56:45  all   0.73    0.00    1.95      47.20     0.00     50.12
12:56:47  all   0.74    0.00    1.96      46.81     0.00     50.49
12:56:49  all   1.44    0.00    2.39      44.98     0.00     51.20
12:56:51  all   0.25    0.00    0.76      49.87     0.00     49.11
Average:  all   0.73    0.00    1.91      46.99     0.00     50.37
```

Monitoring the disk I/O is shown in the following example:

```
da1:~ # sar -b 2 5
Linux 2.6.27.19-5-pae (da1)          08/17/09        _i686_

12:58:27          tps     rtps     wtps     bread/s   bwrtn/s
12:58:29          0.00    0.00     0.00     0.00      0.00
12:58:31          0.00    0.00     0.00     0.00      0.00
12:58:33          14.00   1.50     12.50    12.00     9076.00
12:58:35          0.00    0.00     0.00     0.00      0.00
12:58:37          0.00    0.00     0.00     0.00      0.00
Average:          2.80    0.30     2.50     2.40      1813.39
```

If you do not provide any interval length and number of intervals, sar displays a summary of the activity of the current day (taken from the /var/log/sa/sa**dd** file), as shown in the following example:

```
da1:~ # sar
Linux 2.6.27.19-5-pae (da1)          08/24/09        _i686_

08:12:38          LINUX RESTART

08:20:01  CPU   %user   %nice   %system   %iowait   %steal   %idle
08:30:01  all   0.37    0.00    0.04      0.07      0.00     99.52
08:40:01  all   0.40    0.00    0.04      0.07      0.00     99.49
08:50:01  all   0.37    0.00    0.04      0.07      0.00     99.53
09:00:01  all   0.37    0.00    0.03      0.07      0.00     99.53
09:10:01  all   0.46    0.00    0.04      0.06      0.00     99.45
Average:  all   0.45    0.00    0.06      0.26      0.00     99.23
```

Monitor Hard Drive Space Usage

Next, you need to monitor your hard drive space usage. This can be done from the command line with the df and du utilities.

NOTE: We talked about df and du earlier in Check Partition and File Usage (df and du).

You can also use the Gnome System Monitor as a graphical equivalent to df. Select *Computer* > *More Applications* > *System* > *GNOME System Monitor*. When you select the *File Systems* tab, the following is displayed:

Figure 5-19   *GNOME System Monitor: File Systems Tab*

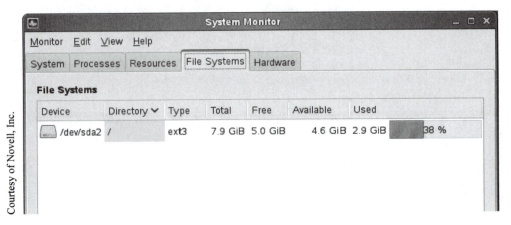

Courtesy of Novell, Inc.

Exercise 5-5   Manage System Logging

In this exercise, you practice configuring syslog-ng and logrotate.

You will find this exercise at the end of the chapter.

(End of Exercise)

Exercise 5-6   Monitor Your SLES 11 Server

In this exercise, you practice using the tools to get information on the computer you are using and to monitor system performance.

You will find this exercise at the end of the chapter.

(End of Exercise)

Summary

Objective	Summary
Understand and Manage Linux Processes	The following terms are commonly used when discussing Linux processes:

■ **Program.** A structured set of commands stored in an executable file in the Linux file system. A program can be executed to create a process.

■ **Process.** A program that is loaded into memory and executed by the CPU.

■ **User Process.** A process launched by a user that is started from a terminal or within the graphical environment.

■ **Daemon Process.** A system process that is not associated with a terminal or a graphical environment. It is a process or collection of processes that waits for an event to trigger an action on the part of the program.

In network-based services, this event is usually a network connection. Other services, such as cron and atd, are time-based and perform certain tasks at certain points in time.

■ **Process ID.** A unique identifier assigned to every process as it begins.

To manage Linux processes, you need to be familiar with the following:

■ Manage foreground and background processes

■ View and prioritize processes

■ End a process

■ Manage daemon processes

| Manage Jobs with cron and at | The cron daemon (`/usr/sbin/cron`) allows you to create jobs that will be carried out for you on a regular schedule. |

The cron daemon is activated by default on SLES 11. Once a minute it checks to see if any jobs have been defined for the current time.

The cron daemon uses a file called a crontab that contains a list of jobs and when they are to be run.

A crontab file exists for the entire Linux system. Each user on the system can also define their own crontab file.

If you want to schedule a job to run one time only in the future (instead of scheduling it on a regular basis with cron), you can use the `at` command.

Objective	Summary
Understand System Initialization and Manage Runlevels	The elements involved when the Linux operating system boots include
	■ BIOS and Boot Manager
	■ Kernel
	■ initramfs (initial RAM File System)
	■ init process
	The default boot manager in SLES 11 is GRUB. GRUB is responsible for loading the operating system. Its configuration file is `/boot/grub/menu.lst`.
	The GRUB shell allows you to access files in the file system before the operating system itself is running.
	The initialization of the system is done by `/sbin/init`, which is the first process started by the kernel during boot. The configuration file of init is `/etc/inittab`.
	Various scripts are started by init. These scripts are located in the `/etc/init.d/` directory.
	In Linux, runlevels define the state of the system.
	The system administrator can change from one runlevel to another with the `init` command. The `runlevel` command displays the previous and the current runlevels.
Use Monitoring and Troubleshooting Tools	In a Linux system, there are many logs that track various aspects of system operation. Many services log their activities to their own log files, and the level of detail can be set on a per-service basis. In addition, system logs in `/var/log/` track system-level events.
	The logrotate utility archives log files.
	Tools such as `dmesg`, `hwinfo`, `hdparm`, `iostat`, `vmstat`, `uptime`, `uname`, and others help you gather information needed to monitor and troubleshoot SLES 11. Files in `/proc` and its subdirectories are also a source of valuable information.

Key Terms

boot/grub/menu.lst – The main GRUB boot configuration file.

etc/anacrontab – A file that lists cron jobs executed by the anacron daemon.

etc/at.allow – A file that lists users who can use the at command.

etc/at.deny – A file that lists users who cannot use the at command.

etc/cron.allow – A file that lists users who can use the crontab command.

etc/cron.d – A directory that contains additional system cron tables.

etc/cron.deny – A file that lists users who cannot use the crontab command.

etc/crontab – The system cron table.

etc/init.d – The directory that contains the scripts used to start most daemons.

etc/inittab – The configuration file for the init daemon.

etc/lilo.conf – The main configuration file for LILO.

etc/logrotate.conf – The configuration file for the logrotate command. Additional configuration files for logrotate may be in the /etc/logrotate.d directory.

etc/logrotate.d – A directory that contains additional configuration files for the logrotate command.

etc/rc.d/rc – The script that executes files in the /etc/rc.d/rc*.d directories.

etc/rc.d/rc*.d – The directories used by the init daemon to start and kill daemons in each runlevel.

etc/sysconfig/syslog – A file that contains parameters for the syslogd and syslog-ng daemons.

etc/syslog-ng/syslog-ng.conf – The main configuration file for the syslog-ng daemon.

etc/syslog.conf – The main configuration file for the syslogd daemon.

usr/lib/sa/sa1 – A script that monitors system activity using the sar command every 10 minutes and writes a report to the /var/log/sa directory in binary format.

usr/lib/sa/sa2 – A script that monitors system activity using the sar command every 6 hours and writes a report to the /var/log/sa directory in text format.

var/log – The directory that stores most log files on a Linux system.

var/log/boot.msg – A text file that lists system initialization messages.

var/log/boot.msg – The log file that stores information about daemon startup at system initialization.

var/log/messages – A log file used on Linux systems to store most system-related messages.

var/log/sa – A directory used to store reports generated by sar scripts.

var/spool/cron/tabs – The directory used to store user crontabs.

& – A special character used to start a program in the background.

anacron – An optional replacement for the cron daemon that allows jobs to execute after the system has been down for some time.

at command – Used to schedule commands to run at a certain time in the future.

atq command – Used to view scheduled at jobs.

atrm command – Used to remove a scheduled at job.

background process – A process that runs unnoticed in your terminal and does not interfere with your command line interface.

Basic Input Output System (BIOS) – The firmware on a PC that locates and loads the boot manager from media such as the active partition of a hard disk.

bg command – Used to start a process in the background.

boot manager – See bootloader.

bootloader – The program used to load and start the operating system kernel at system startup.

child process – A process that is started by another process.

chkconfig – Used to configure the daemons that start in a runlevel.

cron – The system service that executes commands regularly in the future based on information in crontabs.

crontab (cron table) – A file specifying the commands to be run by the cron daemon and the schedule to run them.

crontab command – Used to view and edit user cron tables.

daemon process – A system process that is not associated with a terminal.

dmesg command – Used to view the contents of /var/log/boot.msg.

fg command – Used to force a background process to run in the foreground.

foreground process – A process that runs in your terminal and must finish execution before you receive your shell prompt.

getty – A program used to display a login prompt on a character-based terminal.

GNOME System Monitor – A graphical utility that displays system information as well as allows users to view and manage processes.

Grand Unified Bootloader (GRUB) – The default bootloader in SLES.

grub command – Used to start the interactive GRUB shell.

grub-install command – Used to install or reinstall GRUB.

halt command – Used to quickly bring a system to runlevel 0.

hdparm command – Used to display physical hard disk information as well as tune hard disk parameters.

init – The first daemon started by the Linux kernel; it is responsible for starting and stopping other daemons.

init command – Used to change the system runlevel.

Initial RAM File System (initramfs) – A small ramdisk image that stores device drivers for the kernel required for system initialization.

insserv command – Used to enable scripts that are used to start and stop daemons.

interval-controlled daemon – A daemon that is started at a certain time on a regular basis.

iostat command – Used to display input and output statistics for system devices.

job – See background process.

job ID – The ID given to a background process that may be used in commands that manipulate the process during execution.

jobs command – Used to view background processes in your terminal.

kernel ring buffer – An area of memory that stores messages from the Linux kernel.

kill command – Used to send a signal to a process by PID or job ID.

killall command – Used to send a signal to a process by name.

lilo command – Used to install or update the LILO configuration on the MBR or partition boot sector.

LInux LOader (LILO) – The legacy bootloader used on Linux systems.

logrotate command – Used to archive log files using the parameters stored in the /etc/logrotate.conf file and other configuration files that may exist in the /etc/logrotate.d directory.

Master Boot Record (MBR) – The section of a hard disk that stores the partition table and location of the active (bootable) partition.

mkinitrd command – Used to create an Initial RAM File System image.

netstat command – Displays network interface and port statistics.

nice command – Used to change the priority of a process as it is started.

nice value – Represents the priority of a process. A higher nice value reduces the priority of the process.

parent process – A process that has started another process.

Parent Process ID (PPID) – The PID of the parent process.

poweroff command – Used to quickly bring a system to runlevel 0 and power off the system.

process – A program currently loaded into memory and running on the CPU.

Process ID (PID) – A unique identifier assigned to every process.

program – A file that may be executed to create a process.

ps (process status) command – Used to list processes that are running on the system.

pstree command – Used to list processes that are running on the system as well as their parent and child relationships.

reboot command – Used to quickly bring a system to runlevel 6.

renice command – Used to change the priority of a running process.

runlevel – A category that describes the number and type of daemons on a Linux system.

runlevel command – Used to display the current and most recent runlevel.

sar (system activity reporter) command – Displays performance statistics from different areas of the system.

shutdown command – Used to change to runlevel 0 at a certain time.

signal – A termination request that is sent to a process.

signal-controlled daemon – A daemon that is started when an event occurs on the system.

sulogin – A program used to display a login prompt on a character-based terminal for the root user only in runlevel 1.

sysctl command – Used to view and configure parameters in the /proc directory.

syslog-ng – A replacement for the syslogd daemon that has better message filtering abilities and daemon support. It stands for System Log Daemon – New Generation.

syslogd – The daemon responsible for most logging on Linux systems. It stands for System Log Daemon.

telinit command – A shortcut to the init command.

top command – Used to view, renice, and kill the processes on the system that are using the most CPU time.

uname command – Displays system architecture and name information.

uptime command – Displays system uptime and load statistics.

user process – A process that is begun by a user and runs on a terminal.

vmstat command – Displays system usage and virtual memory statistics.

xosview command – Displays key system usage statistics in a graphical desktop environment.

Chapter Exercises

Exercise 5-1   ***Manage Linux Processes***

In this exercise, you practice starting and stopping processes and changing their priorities.

In the first part of the exercise, you start and suspend gcalctool, move it to the background and foreground, and then stop it.

In the second part, you start gcalctool and set the priority of the running program to a nice value of -5. Then you start xeyes with a nice value of 10.

Detailed Steps to Complete the Exercise

- Part I: Move Processes to the Background
- Part II: Modify Process Priorities

Part I: Move Processes to the Background

To move processes to the background and to the foreground, do the following:

1. If necessary, log in to your da-host workstation as geeko with a password of **novell**.

2. Open a terminal window and `su -` to root using a password of **novell**.

3. At the command line, display the processes that are currently owned by geeko by entering

   `ps -lU geeko` (with a lowercase L)

4. Display the processes that are currently owned by root by entering

   `ps -lU root` (with a lowercase L)

5. Start the GNOME Calculator program by entering `gcalctool` at the shell prompt.

   Notice that the terminal is not available to receive new commands because no command line is displayed. This is because the calculator program is running in the foreground.

6. Arrange the calculator window and the terminal window so that you can see them both, then select the terminal window to activate it.

7. Suspend the calculator program by pressing Ctl+z.

8. Try using the calculator tool to calculate several numbers.

   Because its process was suspended, the calculator does not respond.

9. View the job in the background by entering

   `jobs`

   You should see that the gcalctool job is stopped.

10. View the gcalctool process running from the current terminal by entering

    `ps -l` (with a lower case L)

The process shows a status of **T**, which indicates that it is being traced or stopped.

11. Resume the calculator program running in the background by entering

    `bg 1`

    Notice that the calculator program is running again. Because it's running in the background, you can now use the terminal window to enter other commands.

12. Verify that the job status is running by entering

    `jobs`

    You should see that the gcalctool job is now running.

13. View the gcalctool branch in the process tree by entering

    `pstree -p | grep gcalctool`

    Notice that the gcalctool process is listed at the end of the tree.

14. Bring the gcalctool process into the foreground by entering

    `fg 1`

15. Close the calculator program.

16. Start the calculator in the background by entering

    `nohup gcalctool&`

    NOTE: The nohup command runs a command such that it ignores any hangup kill signals sent to it.

    ---

17. Close the terminal window.

    The calculator program remains running.

18. Open a new terminal window.

19. Start the top program by entering

    `top`

20. View only the processes started by root by typing `u` and then entering **root**.

21. Check for the calculator program (gcalctool) listed in top.

22. (Conditional) If you cannot find the gcalctool program, try maximizing the terminal window. You can also activate the Calculator window and use it to calculate several numbers. This should cause the gcalctool process to be moved near the top of the output in top.

    You can also enter `F` in top and select PID as the sort column. If needed, you can also reverse the sort order by pressing `R`.

23. Record the PID of the gcalctool process:

24. Exit top by typing `q`.

25. View information about the gcalctool process by entering

```
ps PID_of_gcalctool_process
```

26. Switch to your root user account using the `su -` command and a password of **novell**.

27. Stop the calculator program and check the status by entering the following commands:

```
kill PID_of_gcalctool_process

ps aux | grep gcalctool
```

28. Start the xeyes program in the background by entering

```
xeyes&
```

29. Kill the xeyes program by entering

```
killall xeyes
```

Part II: Modify Process Priorities

To modify process priorities, do the following:

1. Switch back to your geeko user by entering `exit` at the shell prompt.

2. Start the gcalctool program in the background by entering

```
gcalctool&
```

3. Record the PID for gcalctool (displayed in the terminal window):

4. View the running process by entering

```
ps  lf
```

Notice that the nice value (NI) is currently at 0.

5. Increase the priority of the process to a nice value of -5 by entering

```
renice -5 -p PID_of_gcalctool_process
```

Notice that a regular user cannot change the nice value to a value below 0, only 0-20.

6. Switch to root (`su -`) with a password of **novell**.

7. Try setting the nice value to -5 again by entering

```
renice -5 -p PID_of_gcalctool_process
```

8. Check that the setting is effective by entering

```
ps  lf
```
(lowercase L)

Notice that the process is not displayed, because `ps lf` only displays processes started by the current user. The calculator program was started by geeko (not root).

9. View all processes by entering

   `ps alf`

   The gcalctools process is now displayed.

10. Change the nice value for the gcalctools process to a higher priority by entering

    `renice -10 -p PID_of_gcalctools_process`

11. Verify that the gcalctools process nice value is set to -10 by entering

    `ps alf` (with a lowercase L)

12. Exit the shell running as root by entering

    `exit`

    You should now be user geeko again.

13. Start the xeyes program in the background with the nice value of +10 by entering

    `nice xeyes&`

14. Verify that the xeyes process nice value is set to +10 by entering

    `ps lf` (with a lowercase L)

15. Kill the gcalctools and xeyes processes by entering the following commands:

    `kill PID_of_gcalctools_process`

    `killall xeyes`

16. Close your terminal window.

(End of Exercise)

Exercise 5-2   *Schedule Jobs with cron and at*

In this exercise, you practice scheduling jobs with cron and at.

In the first part of the exercise, you create a cron job as a normal user that logs the output of finger to ~/users.log every minute and another cron job as root that backs up /etc/ to /export/data2/etc.tgz using tar and the options czvf every Tuesday at 2 a.m.

In the second part of the exercise, you redirect the output of the finger command to /var/log/messages three minutes from the current time. Then you schedule the same job for tomorrow at noon. Finally, you schedule a program to run tomorrow at 2 p.m. and afterwards remove the job.

Detailed Steps to Complete the Exercise

- Part I: Schedule Jobs with cron

- Part II: Schedule Jobs with at

Part I: Schedule Jobs with cron

To schedule jobs with cron, do the following:

1. Open a terminal window and schedule a cron job as geeko by doing the following:

    a. Enter crontab -e at the shell prompt.

    The vi editor is displayed with geeko's crontab file loaded.

    b. Schedule finger to run every minute and write the output to the ~/users.log file by entering the following:

    ```
    * * * * *  finger  >>  ~/users.log
    ```

    c. Save the file and exit vi.

    d. Watch the users.log file for a few minutes and validate that it is being updated by entering tail -F ~/users.log at the shell prompt.

    NOTE: The -F option is a shortcut for -f --retry, which keeps trying to open a file even if it is inaccessible when tail starts.

    ---

    e. When finished, press Ctrl+c to break out of tail.

2. Remove geeko's crontab file by entering crontab -r at the shell prompt.

3. Verify that the crontab file no longer exists by entering crontab -l at the shell prompt.

4. Verify that the cron job you defined in Step 1 is no longer active by entering tail -f ~/users.log at the shell prompt.

    Notice that entries to users.log are no longer being added.

5. Press Ctrl+c.

6. Close all open windows.

Part II: Schedule Jobs with at

To schedule jobs with at, do the following:

1. Open a terminal window and switch to root using the `su  -` command and a password of **novell**.

2. Check to see if the at service is running by entering `rcatd  status` at the shell prompt.

3. If the command returns a status of *unused*, start the at service by entering `rcatd start` at the shell prompt.

4. Display the current date and time by entering `date` at the shell prompt.

5. Three minutes from now, log who is currently logged in to the `/var/log/messages` file by entering the following commands:

   `at hh:mm`

   `finger >> /var/log/messages`

   NOTE: Make sure you enter *two* > characters in the above command. If you have only one > character, all existing entries in `/var/log/messages` will be overwritten.

   ---

6. Exit the at editor by pressing Ctrl+d.

7. View the scheduled at jobs by entering `atq` (or `at  -l`).

   Note the job number listed.

8. Enter `tail  -f  /var/log/messages` at the shell prompt and wait for the three minuts to pass.

   Login information for geeko is listed at the end of the file.

   Press Ctrl+c to quit tail.

9. Schedule the same job to run tomorrow at noon by entering the following commands:

   `at noon tomorrow`

   `finger >> /var/log/messages`

10. Exit the at editor by pressing Ctrl+d.

11. Schedule the date to be logged tomorrow at 2:00 p.m. to the `/var/log/messages` file by entering the following:

    `at 14:00 tomorrow`

    `date >> /var/log/messages`

12. Exit the at editor by pressing Ctrl+d.

13. View the scheduled at jobs by entering `atq` (or `at -l`).

    Notice that the two jobs are listed, each with an individual job number.

14. Remove the job scheduled for tomorrow at 2:00 p.m. by entering

    `atrm job_number`

15. View the scheduled at jobs by entering `atq` (or `at -l`).

    Only the job scheduled for 12:00 p.m. should still be listed.

(End of Exercise)

Exercise 5-3 *Manage the Boot Loader*

In this exercise, you practice booting into a shell and modifying /boot/grub/menu.lst.

You enter **init=/bin/bash** at the boot prompt and modify /boot/grub/menu.lst to require a password before kernel parameters can be modified. You then test the new GRUB configuration.

Detailed Steps to Complete the Exercise

Do the following:

1. If your da1 virtual server is running, shut it down.

2. Open a terminal window and enter su - followed by a password of **novell**.

3. Reboot the system by entering init 6 at the shell prompt.

4. When the GRUB boot menu is displayed, press the Space bar to stop the timer.

5. In the Boot Options field, enter **init=/bin/bash**.

   After a few moments, the bash prompt is displayed.

6. Remount the root partition read-writable by entering

   mount -o remount,rw,sync /

7. At the shell prompt, enter vi /boot/grub/menu.lst.

8. Comment out the line starting with "gfxmenu" by inserting a pound sign (#) in front of the line.

9. To avoid having the password displayed in clear-text in the configuration file, create an MD5-Hash encrypted password by doing the following within vi:

   a. Add a new, blank line after the "gfxmenu" line you just commented out.

   b. Press Esc.

   c. Enter

      :r! echo -e "secret\nsecret" | grub-md5-crypt

      This runs an external command from within the vi editor. The echo command sends the secret and secret text strings to the standard input of the grub-md5-crypt command.

      The grub-md5-crypt command uses these strings as input for its Password: and Retype Password: prompts. It then encrypts the password.

      The output from the grub-md5-crypt command, including the encrypted password; is inserted into the file.

   d. Arrow up to the line that reads stty: standard input: Invalid argument.

   e. Type dd to delete the line.

   f. Repeat this process to delete the following lines:

```
Password:
Retype Password:
stty: standard input: Invalid argument
```

   g. Press **Ins**.

   h. At the beginning of the line with the encrypted password, enter

   ```
   password --md5
   ```

   The line should look similar to the following:

   ```
   password --md5 $1$/5bSD....
   ```

   i. Save the file by pressing Esc and then entering `:wq`.

10. Reset the computer by entering `reboot` at the shell prompt.

You will notice that the start screen looks different now, because you turned off the graphical menu.

11. If you want to edit the kernel command line, press `p` and then enter a password of **secret**.

12. Select the *SUSE Linux Enterprise Server 11* menu option and press Enter.

Wait while the system boots.

13. Undo the changes in `/boot/grub/menu.lst`:

   a. Log in as geeko with a password of **novell**.

   b. Open a terminal window and `su` – to root using a password of **novell**.

   c. At the shell prompt, enter `vi /boot/grub/menu.lst`.

   d. Put a comment sign (#) at the beginning of the line beginning with `password`.

   e. Remove the comment sign in front of the line starting with `gfxmenu`.

   f. Save the file and close vi.

   g. At the shell prompt, enter `exit` twice.

(End of Exercise)

Exercise 5-4   *Manage Runlevels*

In this exercise, you practice configuring runlevels. This exercise has three parts.

In the first part, you use the runlevel command to determine the current runlevel. You also use the init command to change to runlevel 3 and then back to 5.

In the second part, you activate the at service atd.

In the third part, you reboot your computer and boot into runlevel 3 instead of the default runlevel 5. You then log in and switch back to runlevel 5.

In the fourth part, you activate the rsync daemon using the YaST runlevel editor.

This exercise is done on da-host.

Detailed Steps to Complete the Exercise

- Part I: View and Change the Current Runlevel
- Part II: Activate the atd Service
- Part III: Set a Runlevel at Boot Time
- Part IV: Enable rsyncd with YaST

Part I: View and Change the Current Runlevel

To view and change the current runlevel, do the following:

1. If your da1 virtual server is running, shut it down.

2. Open a terminal window and `su` – to root using a password of **novell**.

3. Check the previous and current runlevels by entering `runlevel` at the shell prompt.

   List the runlevels in the table below:

Previous	Current

   Notice that the previous runlevel is listed as **N**, which means that there was no previous runlevel set.

4. Change to runlevel 3 by entering `init 3` in the terminal window.

   The graphical environment is terminated and you are left at a terminal login prompt.

5. Log in as root with a password of **novell**.

6. Check the previous and current runlevel by entering `runlevel`.

   List the runlevels in the table below:

Previous	Current

7. Switch to runlevel 5 by entering `init 5`.

   The GUI login screen appears.

8. Log in as geeko with a password of **novell**.

Part II: Activate the atd Service

To activate the atd service, do the following:

1. Open a terminal window.

2. At the shell prompt, `su` – to root with a password of **novell**.

3. View the current runlevel configuration for atd by entering `chkconfig atd -l` at the shell prompt.

   Notice that the atd service is turned off for all runlevels.

4. Install the service to its predefined runlevels by entering

   `insserv -d atd`

5. Check the modified runlevel configuration for atd by entering `chkconfig atd -l` again.

   Notice that the default configuration for atd sets runlevels 2, 3, and 5 to **on**.

6. Change to the `/etc/rc.d/rc3.d` directory by entering `cd /etc/rc.d/rc3.d` at the shell prompt.

7. List the atd files in the directory by entering `ls -l *atd` at the shell prompt.

   Notice that there are two atd links—one is used to start the atd service and one is used to kill it.

8. Start the at service by entering `rcatd start` at the shell prompt.

9. Verify that the service is running by entering `rcatd status` at the shell prompt.

10. Switch to virtual terminal 1 by pressing Ctrl+Alt+F1.

11. Press Ctrl+c to bring up the shell prompt.

12. You should be still be logged in as root. Verify this by entering `whoami` at the shell prompt.

13. Switch to runlevel 1 by entering `init 1` at the shell prompt.

14. When prompted, enter a root password of **novell**.

15. Determine if the atd service is running by entering `rcatd status` at the shell prompt.

The service is listed as unused because it is not configured to start at runlevel 1.

16. Switch back to your previous runlevel (5) by entering `init 5` at the shell prompt.

    The GUI login screen appears.

17. Log in as geeko with a password of *novell*.

18. Open a terminal session and enter `su -` to switch to root using a password of *novell*.

19. From the command line, remove the atd service from system startup runlevels by entering `chkconfig atd off`.

20. View the current runlevel configuration for at by entering `chkconfig atd -l` at the shell prompt.

    Notice that the service is off for all runlevels.

21. Re-enable the service to start at the default runlevels by entering `chkconfig atd on` at the shell prompt.

Part III: Set a Runlevel at Boot Time

To set a runlevel at boot time, do the following:

1. Reboot by entering `init 6` at the shell prompt.

2. When the GRUB boot menu is displayed, press the Space bar to stop the timer.

3. In the Boot Options field, add the number 3 at the end of the line.

4. Press Enter to boot the Linux system to runlevel 3.

5. When the login prompt appears, log in as root with a password of *novell*.

6. Display the current runlevel by entering `runlevel` at the shell prompt.

7. Switch to runlevel 5 by entering `init 5` at the shell prompt.

8. Switch back to the virtual terminal by pressing Ctrl+Alt+F1.

9. Log out as root by entering `exit`.

10. Switch back to the graphical user interface by pressing Ctrl+Alt+F7.

11. Log in as geeko with a password of *novell*.

Part IV: Enable rsyncd with YaST

To enable rsyncd with YaST, do the following:

1. In the graphical desktop, select *Computer > YaST*.

2. Enter a password of *novell*.

    The YaST Control Center appears.

3. Select *System > System Services (Runlevel)*.

The Runlevel Editor: Services dialog appears.

4. Switch to a more detailed view (with additional options) by selecting *Expert Mode*.

5. Scroll to and select *rsyncd*.

6. Below the list, configure this service to start at runlevels 3 and 5 by selecting *3* and *5*.

7. From the Set/Reset drop-down list, select *Enable the Service*.

8. Start the rsyncd service by selecting *Start Now* from the *Start/Stop/Refresh* drop-down list.

   A status message appears indicating that the service started successfully.

9. Close the status message by selecting *OK*.

10. Stop the rsyncd service by selecting *Stop Now* from the *Start/Stop/Refresh* drop-down list.

    A status message appears indicating that the service stopped successfully.

11. Close the status message by selecting *OK*.

12. Save the changes by selecting *OK* > *Yes*.

13. Close the YaST Control Center.

(End of Exercise)

Exercise 5-5   Manage System Logging

In this exercise, you practice configuring syslog-ng and logrotate.

First, you configure syslog-ng to log messages of the local4 facility. The /var/log/local4 file is used for messages of the local4 facility regardless of the priority. The /var/log/local4.debug file logs only messages with the debug priority. A third file, /var/log/local4.info, logs only messages with the info priority.

Then you configure logrotate to manage these log files. You create an /etc/logrotate.d/local4 file that does the following with these three files:

- Compresses the old logs

- Saves the old logs with a date extension

- Limits the oldest log to one day

- Limits the rotated logs saved to five

- Limits the maximum size of the file to 20 bytes

- Proceeds without error if a log file is missing

- Logs the date in the local4.info file each time a new log file is generated

---

NOTE: The above values (one day, five logs, 20 bytes) are used for demonstration purposes only. In a production environment, these values should be much higher.

This exercise is done on da-host.

Detailed Steps to Complete the Exercise

- Part I: Modify the syslog-ng Configuration

- Part II: Configure logrotate

Part I: Modify the syslog-ng Configuration

To modify the syslog-ng configuration, do the following:

1. Open a terminal window and switch to root using the su – command and a password of **novell**.

2. At the shell prompt, enter vi /etc/syslog-ng/syslog-ng.conf.

3. Add the following lines at the bottom of the file to create filters for the messages you want to log:

```
filter f_local4debug  { level(debug)   and facility(local4); };
filter f_local4info   { level(info)    and facility(local4); };
filter f_local4        { facility(local4); };
```

4. Specify the destinations and log paths by adding the following lines:

```
destination local4debug { file("/var/log/local4.debug"); };
log { source(src); filter(f_local4debug);
                    destination(local4debug); };

destination local4info { file("/var/log/local4.info"); };
log { source(src); filter(f_local4info);
                    destination(local4info); };

destination local4 { file("/var/log/local4"); };
log { source(src); filter(f_local4); destination(local4); };
```

NOTE: Check your syntax carefully. If you make a mistake in this file, syslog won't start.

NOTE: You can find the syslog-ng.conf file in the Exercises/Section_05 directory on the Course DVD.

---

5. Save the changes and close the editor.

6. Restart the syslog daemon by entering `rcsyslog restart` at the shell prompt.

7. Open a new terminal window and enter `su` – followed by a password of **novell**.

8. To check the configuration, log an entry to the info level in the local4 facility by doing the following:

    a. Enter the following in one of your terminal sessions to monitor the activity of the log file:

```
tail -f --retry /var/log/local4.info
```

NOTE: You will see warnings regarding the `--retry` option and the fact that the file does not yet exist. You can disregard this error because the file will be created when you complete the next step.

---

    b. In the other terminal window, log an entry to the info level in the local4 facility by entering

```
logger -p local4.info "Info message 1"
```

    c. Check the results in the second terminal window. The message is logged in the `/var/log/local4.info` file.

        The message should also be logged in the `/var/log/local4` file and, because of other entries in `/etc/syslog-ng/syslog-ng.conf`, in `/var/log/localmessages`.

NOTE: If no messages appear, there might be something wrong with your syslog configuration, for instance a typo or a missing ";". To diagnose what is wrong, enter `rcsyslog restart` at the shell prompt and see if syslog starts properly. If there is an issue with the configuration, an error message will say so. Look for the line number shown in the output for the error, correct it, and restart syslog.

d. In the terminal window where the log activity is being monitored with tail, stop the monitoring by pressing Ctrl+c.

9. Repeat this process for the debug log level. Use the following command in the first terminal window:

```
tail -f --retry /var/log/local4.debug
```

Use the following command in the second terminal window:

```
logger -p local4.debug "Info message 2"
```

NOTE: Only those `level4` log files with entries will be compressed during log rotation in Part II of this exercise.

10. In the terminal window where the log activity is being monitored with tail, stop the monitoring by pressing Ctrl+c.

Part II: Configure logrotate

To configure logrotate, do the following:

1. At the shell prompt, enter `vi /etc/logrotate.d/local4`.

2. Add the following content to the file:

```
/var/log/local4.debug /var/log/local4.info /var/log/local4
{
    compress
    dateext
    maxage 1
    rotate 5
    size 20
    postrotate
        date >> /var/log/local4.info
    endscript
}
```

NOTE: Make sure the directories in the first line are separated with spaces.

3. Save the changes and close the editor.

4. Switch to virtual terminal 1 by pressing Ctrl+Alt+F1.

5. Log in as root with a password of **novell**.

6. Rotate the logs manually by entering

```
logrotate  /etc/logrotate.conf
```

7. Check the directory `/var/log` for the zipped `local4` log files by entering

   ```
   ls -l /var/log | less
   ```

   You see the following files:

   - local4.debug-*current_date*.bz2

   - local4.info-*current_date*.bz2

   For example, if the current date is July 15, 2009, then the zipped file for local4.info will be `local4.info-20090715.bz2`.

   The `.bz2` extension is used because the command to compress files is set to `bzip2` in `/etc/logrotate.conf`.

   NOTE: Only those log files with entries are zipped.

   ---

8. Exit the list by entering `q`.

9. Check the contents of the `local4.info` zipped archive by entering

   ```
   less /var/log/local4.info-current_date.bz2
   ```

   You should see the entries you added to the log file.

10. Press `q` to exit.

11. Log out as root by entering

    ```
    exit
    ```

12. Return to the GNOME desktop by pressing Ctrl+Alt+F7.

13. Close all open windows.

(End of Exercise)

Exercise 5-6   Monitor Your SLES 11 Server

In this exercise, you practice using the tools to get information on the computer you are using and to monitor system performance. This exercise has three parts.

In the first part, you gather system information, such as CPU type, amount of RAM, and kernel version.

In the second part, you install the **sysstat** package from the installation media. You use the `iostat` and `vmstat` commands.

In the third part, you use the `sar` command to perform long-term monitoring of the system.

This exercise is done on the da-host system.

Detailed Steps to Complete the Exercise

- Part I: Gather Information on Your SLES 11 Server
- Part II: Use iostat and vmstat
- Part III: Use sar

Part I: Gather Information on Your SLES 11 Server

As you work through this exercise, write down the appropriate value in the right-hand column of the following table:

System Parameter	Value
OS	
Hardware Architecture	
Processor Type	
Hostname	
Kernel Release	
Kernel Version (include date and time)	
System Up Time	
Load Averages	
SLES 11 Version	
System Date and Time	
Model Name of Processor	
Free Memory	
Patch Level	

Complete the following:

1. Open a terminal window and switch to root using the `su` – command and a password of **novell**.

2. View the kernel release of the Linux distribution you are running by entering

   `uname -r`

3. View the computer's hardware architecture by entering

   `uname -m`

4. View the processor type for this Linux build by entering

   `uname -p`

5. View all information, including hostname, kernel release, and kernel version, by entering

   `uname -a`

6. View the system uptime and the load averages by entering

   `uptime`

7. View the version of the SUSE Linux Enterprise Server distribution by entering

   `cat /etc/SuSE-release`

8. View the system date and time by entering

   `date`

9. View information on the processor by entering

   `cat /proc/cpuinfo`

10. View the current memory statistics by entering

    `cat /proc/meminfo`

Part II: Use iostat and vmstat

To use the `iostat` and `vmstat` commands, do the following:

1. Open a terminal window on da-host and switch to root using the `su` – command and a password of **novell**.

2. At the shell prompt, enter `yast -i sysstat` to install the sysstat package. When prompted for the installation media, insert the *SUSE Linux Enterpirse Server 11* installation DVD.

3. Run the `iostat` command and have the information updated every second by entering `iostat 1`.

4. Open a new terminal window and enter `su` – followed by a password of **novell**.

5. Run the vmstat command and have the information updated every second by entering `vmstat 1`.

6. Open a new terminal window and enter `su` – followed by a password of **novell**.

7. Run the find command to generate system activity by entering

   `find / -iname *pdf`

8. View the output of the iostat and vmstat commands.

9. Terminate the iostat and vmstat commands by pressing `Ctrl-C`.

Part III: Use sar

To monitor system activity using `sar`, do the following:

1. To create some data in a short amount of time, modify the crontab definition for the sa1 script. To do so, edit the `/etc/sysstat/sysstat.cron` file and modify the definition for the sa1 script to look like this:

   `*/1 * * * * root [ -x /usr/lib/sa/sa1 ] && exec /usr/lib/sa/sa1 -S ALL 1 1`

2. To copy the above crontab file to the `/etc/cron.d/` directory, enter

   `/etc/init.d/boot.sysstat start`

3. At the shell prompt, enter `sar 1`.

4. In another terminal window, generate some system activity by entering

   `ls -lR > /dev/null 2> /dev/null`.

5. View the output of the `sar` command.

6. Press Ctrl+c to terminate the `sar` command.

7. To have `sar` report the data from the `/var/log/sa/sa`***dd*** file, enter

   `sar`

   You should see information for a couple of points in time with an interval of 1 minute. If you do not see this information, wait 5 minutes and try again.

8. Close all open windows.

(End of Exercise)

Review Questions

1. Which of the following terms refers to a system service that does not run on a terminal?
   a) Program
   b) User Process
   c) Daemon Process
   d) Child Process

2. What is the PID of init?

3. Which of the following statements are true? (Choose all that apply.)
   a) A parent process may only have one child process.
   b) Each process is given a PPID that is used to uniquely identify it on the system.
   c) A child process may only have one parent process.
   d) All background processes have a PID and a job ID.

4. Which of the following commands can quickly identify the child processes started by a particular daemon?
   a) top
   b) lsof
   c) ps
   d) pstree

5. To what processes are regular users allowed to send kill signals?

6. You have just run the ps aux command and notice that most daemons have an S in the STAT column. What does this mean?

7. What key can you press in the top command to send the process a signal?
   a) s
   b) k
   c) R
   d) N

8. What can you type at a command prompt to run the updatedb command in the background?

9. Which of the following key combinations can you use to pause a foreground process, such that it may be send to the background with the bg command?
   a) Ctrl+c
   b) Ctrl+p
   c) Ctrl+z
   d) Ctrl+r

10. Which of the following kill commands may be used to send the second background job a SIGINT?
    a) kill -2 %2
    b) kill -1 −b 2
    c) kill -9 %2
    d) kill -15 2

11. If you do not specify the type of signal when using the kill or killall commands, which signal is used by default?
    a) SIGHUP
    b) SIGINT
    c) SIGKILL
    d) SIGTERM

12. What command could you use to change the priority of a process (PID=592) to run with the highest priority?

13. You have a script that is used to remove temporary files and would like this script to run on a daily basis. What directory could you place this script in to have the cron daemon execute it each day?

14. What command could a regular user use to edit their crontab?

15. What lines would you add to your crontab to schedule the /bin/false command to run at 2:50 p.m. from Monday to Friday?

16. What command can you use to run the contents of the file cleanup at noon?

17. Which command can you use to view at jobs that have been scheduled on your system?
    a) at --view
    b) atq
    c) atrm
    d) cron --view

18. What is the config file used by GRUB?
    a) /boot/grub-install
    b) /etc/grub.config
    c) /boot/grub.config
    d) /boot/grub/menu.lst

19. You notice the line root(hd0, 2) in your GRUB configuration file. What does this line indicate?
    a) The root file system for the operating system resides on the third partition on the second hard disk in the computer
    b) The root file system for the operating system resides on the third partition on the first hard disk in the computer
    c) The root file system for the operating system resides on the first partition on the second hard disk in the computer
    d) The root file system for the operating system resides on the first partition on the third hard disk in the computer

20. You have just modified the /etc/lilo.conf file but your changes have not taken effect. What command must you run to rewrite the LILO boot loader to the MBR?

21. What action in the /etc/inittab file is used to determine the default runlevel at system initialization?

22. What is the default runlevel in SLES?

23. What runlevel loads all networking daemons (including NFS) but does not start a display manager?
    a) 1
    b) 2
    c) 3
    d) 5

24. What command(s) could you type at a command prompt as the root user to change your runlevel to Single User Mode?

25. Which of the following commands will force your system to reboot? (Choose all that apply.)
    a) init 0
    b) reboot
    c) powerwait
    d) init 6

26. Which of the following commands may be used to stop the SSH daemon (sshd)? (Choose all that apply.)
    a) rcsshd stop
    b) kstopsys sshd
    c) /etc/init.d/sshd stop
    d) /etc/rc/stopsshd

27. Which of the following methods can you use to start the SSH daemon (sshd) upon entering runlevel 3? (Choose all that apply.)
    a) Create a shortcut to the /etc/init.d/sshd script called /etc/init.d/rc3.d/S88sshd
    b) Create a shortcut to the /etc/init.d/sshd script called /etc/init.d/rc3.d/K88sshd
    c) Change the INIT INFO section of the /etc/init.d/sshd script and run the insserv command
    d) Run the YaST Runlevel Editor

28. What line can you add to the /etc/syslog.conf file to log messages of priority crit from the Linux kernel to /var/log/ker nlog?
    a) kern.crit /var/log/kernlog
    b) kern.=crit /var/log/kernlog
    c) kern.crit -/var/log/kernlog
    d) kern.crit |/var/log/kernlog

29. Which of the following commands may be used to display boot error messages? (Choose all that apply.)
    a) dmesg | less
    b) less /var/log/boot
    c) less /var/log/wtmp
    d) less /var/log/boot.log

30. You have added the following lines to the /etc/logrotate.d/mylog file:
    /var/log/mylog {
    maxage 44
    rotate 5
    notifempty
    compress
    }
    Which of the following statements are true about the rotation of the /var/log/mylog file? (Choose all that apply.)
    a) A maximum of five archive logs will be kept.
    b) A maximum of 44 archive logs will be kept.
    c) The log file will be rotated if the file is empty.
    d) The log file will be compressed after being rotated.

31. Which of the following can be used to obtain detailed performance statistics regarding virtual memory usage? (Choose all that apply.)
    a) Files stored within the /proc directory.
    b) The iostat command.
    c) The vmstat command.
    d) The sar command.

32. Which of the following commands can be used to tune system parameters that are stored within the /proc directory?
    a) sysctl
    b) iostat
    c) sar
    d) hdparm

Discovery Exercises

Using Kill Signals

Log in to tty1 as the **root** user and perform the following actions in order. For each action, write the command(s) that you used.

1. Run the **ps** command to view processes in your current shell. Record the PID for your bash shell.

2. Send the PID of your bash shell as SIGINT. What happened?

3. Send the PID of your bash shell as SIGTERM. What happened?

4. Send the PID of your bash shell as SIGKILL. What happened and why?

Process Priorities

Log in to tty1 as the **root** user and perform the following actions in order. For each action, write the command(s) that you used. When finished, log out of tty1.

1. Start the **ps -l** command with the default nice value. What nice value is shown in the output?

2. Start the **ps -l** command with a nice value of **-20** and verify the correct nice value in the output. Did this command run with high or low priority? Which users can run this command?

3. Start the **ps -l** command with a nice value of **-19** and verify the correct nice value in the output. Did this command run with high or low priority? Which users can run this command?

Manipulating Background Processes

Log in to tty1 as the root user and perform the following actions in order. For each action, write the command(s) that you used. When finished, log out of tty1.

1. Start the **sleep 50000** command in the background (this command simply waits for 50000 seconds). Repeat this command four more times.

2. View the background jobs.

3. Run the third background process in the foreground. Press **Ctrl+z** to stop the foreground process and view the background jobs. What is the status of the third background job?

4. Start the third background process in the background again. Verify that is it running in the background.

5. Send the fifth background process a SIGTERM and verify that it has stopped.

6. Kill all other sleep processes using a SIGINT.

Testing Daemon Startup Files

Log in to tty1 as the **root** user and create a file called /etc/init.d/sampledaemon that has the permissions 755. Next, edit this file with the vi editor and add a line that reads **echo My daemon has started**. Then create a symbolic link to this file called /etc/init.d/rc3.d/S90sampledaemon. In which runlevel will this script be run? Finally, change to runlevel 3 (press Enter to receive your prompt). Did your daemon start in this runlevel? Press Enter to return to your prompt and log out of tty1.

Scheduling Processes Using the at Daemon

The at command is versatile in that it can understand nearly any time for mat. Log in to tty1 as the **root** user, ensure that the at daemon is running (and start it if necessary), and schedule the **date** and **who** commands to run **at teatime** (use the at teatime command). When you have finished scheduling the at job, note the time that the two commands will be scheduled. Next, remove your at job and use the manual or info pages to research other time for mats that may be used with the at command. When finished, log out of tty1.

Cron Tables

Write the lines that you could use in your crontab to schedule the /bin/sample command to run at the following times (use the man pages if necessary):

1. Every Friday at 1:30 a.m.

2. At 4:30 p.m. on May 15th only

3. At 4:00 p.m. and 4:30 p.m. on the first Sunday of every month

4. Every 10 minutes from 9:00 a.m. to 5:00 p.m. on Monday

5. At 8:15 a.m. and 6:30 p.m. Monday to Friday

Using the GRUB Shell

One of the most useful features of the GRUB boot loader over other boot loaders is its interactive shell, which can run several functions and search files on the file system. The GRUB shell can also be run after the Linux kernel has been executed and your system is in full functional mode. Log in to tty1 as the **root** user and type **grub** to start the GRUB shell. Next, run the **help** command to see a list of commands that are available to you in this shell. Which command can display memory statistics? Execute this command. Next, type **find /boot/vmlinuz** to determine which drive and partition your kernel resides on. Explain the results. Then type **cat hd(0,0)/boot/ grub/menu.lst** to list the contents of the GRUB configuration file. (If your kernel is not on hd(0,0), supply the appropriate hard disk and partition instead.) Finally, run the quit command to exit the GRUB shell and log out of tty1.

Using sar to Troubleshoot Problems

The **sar** command is a powerful command that can be used to obtain detailed system statistics and narrow down the cause of a performance problem.

Run the **sar –u 1 5** command to take CPU usage statistics once per second for 5 seconds. %user is the percentage of time the system is running user programs, and %sys is the percentage of time the operating system is maintaining itself in order to execute the user programs. On a production system (that is running several tasks), %user should always be larger than %sys if the system is healthy and can handle the amount of processes running. %idle is the amount of time the CPU is not used and should always be larger than 25% on average over a long period of time. If %sys is larger than %user and %idle is less than 25%, then your system is running too many processes, and you could look at moving some processes to another system. Alternatively, you could upgrade or add an additional CPU to handle requests from applications.

Explore some additional options and their available performance statistics using the manual pages for the sar command. Briefly summarize those that you feel may be beneficial in the future.

SECTION 6 Configure the Network

Although almost every step of a network configuration is done for you when you use YaST, it is sometimes useful to configure the network settings manually. For testing and troubleshooting, it can be much faster to change the network setup from the command line.

In this section, you learn how to configure network devices and how to perform other network-related tasks.

Objectives

1. Understand TCP/IP and Linux Network Terms
2. Manage the Network Configuration Information from YaST
3. Manage the Network Configuration with Command Line Tools
4. Troubleshoot Networking Issues
5. Configure DHCP
6. Understand the iptables Command

Objective 1   Understand TCP/IP and Linux Network Terms

A fundamental understanding of the basics of TCP/IP and the networking terms used in Linux is required to be able to configure networking on a Linux machine. You need to

- Understand the Fundamentals of TCP/IP
- Understand Linux Network Terms

Understand the Fundamentals of TCP/IP

In today's world, computers are connected to each other, locally within an office or company, and to computers anywhere in the world. To communicate with each other, computers need a common language, or protocol. The Internet Protocol Suite (commonly known as TCP/IP - Transmission Control Protocol/Internet Protocol) is the protocol used in the Internet and most Local Area Networks (LANs).

To understand TCP/IP, you need to be familiar with the following:

- Elements of a Network
- TCP/IP Layers

Elements of a Network

Networks consist of several elements, including the following:

- Network Nodes
- Transmission Media
- Network Protocols
- Network Connections (Sockets)
- Network Services

Network Nodes

Network nodes are processing locations on a network. A node can be a computer or a device, such as a printer. Every node on a network has a unique address, distinguishing it from other nodes.

Transmission Media

Transmission media are the paths used by network components to access data or resources. Transmission media provide a transmission path for data.

Transmission media include bounded and unbounded technologies. Bounded technologies use cables for transmission purposes; unbounded technologies use radio waves for transmission.

The following are commonly used transmission media:

- Copper wire cabling (bounded)

- Radio waves or microwave (unbounded)
- Fiber optic cable (bounded)

Network Protocols

Network protocols enable network elements to communicate with each other.

To understand the basics of protocols, consider this example. Suppose two people are trying to communicate with each other without knowing each other's language. They would require an interpreter to facilitate communication. Similarly, protocols ensure communication between different network nodes. Protocols are sets of rules that enable different network nodes to communicate.

Protocols can have different capabilities, depending on the purpose for which they are designed, and can be classified into the following types:

- **Routable protocols**. These enable communication between networks connected to each other through a device known as a router.

  Routable protocols are like phone services that allow you to make local and long-distance phone calls. Routable protocols can communicate across routers.

- **Nonroutable protocols**. These are limited to networks composed of a small number of computers.

  Nonroutable protocols are like phone services that allow you to make only local phone calls. Nonroutable protocols cannot communicate across routers.

Protocols can be further classified as follows:

- **Connection-oriented**. These inform the sender that the delivery of data was successfully delivered by sending an acknowledgment when data is received at the destination.

  Connection-oriented protocols act like courier services that send packages. When you send a package by a courier service, you receive a delivery receipt after the package is delivered.

  Consider an example of using a connection-oriented protocol. During an online stock transaction, it is important to have all the data packets required for a complete transaction. If any data packet is lost, the stock transaction does not occur.

  In this example, you can use a connection-oriented protocol to make sure all data packets reach the destination.

  TCP (Transmission Control Protocol) is a connection-oriented protocol.

- **Connectionless**. These send data across networks but do not provide feedback about the successful data delivery.

  Connectionless protocols function like a postal service. When you mail a letter at the post office, you do not get feedback about its arrival at the destination.

  For example, connectionless protocols are used when sending streaming video files. Even if a packet is lost during transmission, the loss creates only a small blip in the video image. The video image can still be viewed and understood.

Connectionless protocols involve smaller overhead and are faster than connection-oriented protocols.

UDP (User Datagram Protocol) is a connectionless protocol.

Network Connections (Sockets)

In UNIX and some other operating systems, a software object that connects an application to a network protocol is called a socket. This enables two-way communication between programs on a network.

For example, a program can send and receive TCP/IP messages by opening a socket and reading data from and writing data to the socket.

This simplifies program development because the programmer only needs to worry about working with the socket and can rely on the operating system to actually transport messages across the network correctly.

Each socket gets bound to a given port, which lets the transport layer protocol (such as TCP or UDP) identify which application to send data to.

For TCP and UDP protocols, a socket on a host is defined as the combination of an IP address and a port number (such as http://192.168.1.1:5801).

Network Services

Network services are programs that let users share network resources. On a network, nodes use network services to communicate using transmission media, such as cables.

Network services require resources and processing capabilities to accomplish a task, such as data processing.

Some examples of network services are Common Unix Printing System (CUPS), Domain Name Service (DNS), and Network File System (NFS).

TCP/IP Layers

TCP/IP communication consists of different elements, with one element depending on the next. The lowest level is the actual hardware, followed by the IP protocol, which in turn is needed for the next level, the TCP or UDP protocols, followed by the top level, the application, such as a Web server or a Web browser.

To understand TCP/IP layers, you need to be familiar with the following:

- The Network Access Layer
- The Internet Layer
- The Transport Layer
- The Application Layer

The Network Access Layer

The network access layer consists of the actual hardware and the pertinent driver.

One reason TCP/IP is so popular is that it runs on different network architectures for Wide Area Networks (WAN) and LANs, such as the following:

- Ethernet

- Token ring

- ATM (Asynchronous Transfer Mode)

- FDDI (Fiber Distributed Data Interface)

- Telephone, solutions include PPP (Point to Point Protocol) or SLIP (Serial Line Interface Protocol)

The Internet Layer

The Internet layer of the TCP/IP model ensures the connection between individual hosts in the network beyond the limits of local networks in the Internet.

The main tasks of the Internet layer are providing an address space for the Internet, routing, and data transfer between end systems (host computers).

The protocols that are part of this layer include the following:

- **Internet Protocol.** IP provides the underlying services for transferring data between end systems in TCP/IP networks and is specified in RFC 791.

  Data is transported through the network in packet form (also called datagrams). The main characteristics of this protocol are that it is connectionless and unreliable.

  The fact that IP is a connectionless protocol means that no end-to-end connection of communication partners is set up for data transfer. In addition, IP is an unreliable protocol because it has no mechanisms for error detection or error correction. In other words, unreliable means that IP cannot guarantee delivery of data.

  However, if data arrives at the destination host, the data is correct. This is guaranteed by the Network Access layer.

  The following are basic characteristics of IP:

  - Specifies datagrams that form the basic units for transferring data in the Internet.

  - Defines the addressing scheme.

  - Routes, exchanges, and transfers datagrams through the network.

  - Fragments and assembles datagrams.

  - IP header included with every packet or datagram transmitted over the TCP/IP network.

    The IP header includes the IP address (such as 192.168.1.10) of the sending and the receiving host.

- **Address Resolution Protocol (ARP).** ARP (RFC 826) resolves IP addresses to hardware addresses (MAC addresses, Medium Access Control). ARP could be considered the link between the network access layer and the IP layer.

The MAC address is always composed of 6 bytes (in hexadecimal notation, such as 00:11:11:23:45:67). The first 3 bytes indicate the manufacturer, and the last 3 bytes are the serial number of the network card.

To send an IP packet to a host, the sending host has to establish the MAC address of the receiving host with the destination IP address. It does this by sending an ARP broadcast package (address ff:ff:ff:ff:ff:ff) asking for the MAC address of the host with the IP address of the destination host. The host with that IP address answers with its MAC address included in the answer. The sending host then sends the IP packet to that MAC address.

Because the sending and the receiving hosts keep a table of MAC address – IP address associations in a cache, the ARP broadcast doesn't need to be repeated for every IP packet. You can view this table with the `arp -a` command.

ARP broadcasts work only within a local network; they do not cross routers.

- **Internet Control Message Protocol (ICMP).** In the event of a communication problem during the transmission of an IP datagram, the sender of the datagram receives a corresponding error report through ICMP.

  However, this error report can only be transmitted to the sender of the IP datagram if a gateway or the recipient of the IP datagram can analyze the error that occurred.

  Because of this, ICMP (as defined in RFC 792) is a protocol that is usually used for transmitting error reports to the senders of IP datagrams.

  For example, an IP datagram should be sent to a specific destination network through a specific router. However, the router in question is not able to reach the destination, so a destination unreachable message is sent.

  Or, if the router notices that the received packet can reach the destination quicker using another path (another gateway), a redirect message is sent.

  The analysis tool `ping` uses the ICMP protocol for transmitting control messages (echo request and echo reply).

  In turn, ICMP uses IP for transmitting the control messages and packs the control messages into the data section of the IP header.

  ICMP places the type ID of the control message in the first octet of the data section in the IP header. The type ID classifies the control message and defines which and how much data is contained in the subsequent bytes of the datagram.

The following are additional IP topics you should be familiar with:

- **Routing.** The main characteristic of IP is its connectionless data transfer (packet exchange) between two computers. This means that a new path through the network is sought for each packet.

  The advantage of this approach lies in its robustness. If a cable fails for any reason, packets can take a different route (if there is one).

  The task of routing is to find a path through the Internet for each packet to send from machine A to machine B. To do this, routing protocols and algorithms are used.

- **IP addresses.** In IP-based networks, each computer (or each network interface of a computer) has a unique, 32-bit IP address.

  For the sake of readability, these 32 bits are not shown as a sequence of 32 zeros and ones, but are divided into 4 bytes.

  These four bytes, called octets, are separated by dots (32-bit/4-byte dot notation, or dotted quad notation) and are recorded either as decimal or binary numbers.

  For example, 32 bits "in sequence" from the machine's point of view looks like the following:

  11000000 10000001 00110010 00000001

  Readable IP representation in decimal format looks like the following:

  192.129.50.1

  An IP address consists of the network prefix (the front part of the IP address) and a host number (the end part of the IP address).

  The network prefix helps to determine the network class in which the host is located. By means of the IP address, data is delivered to the required host in the destination network.

NOTE: The above pertains to IP protocol version 4. IP protocol version 6 (IPv6) addresses are 128 bits long. For more information on IPv6, visit www.ipv6.org/ (http://www.ipv6.org/).

The Transport Layer

The third layer in the TCP/IP architecture is the transport layer. While IP allows you to address different hosts based on IP address, the protocols on this layer allow you to address different applications on the host, based on port number.

The protocols in this layer include the following:

- **Transmission Control Protocol (TCP).** The Transmission Control Protocol (TCP) is a reliable, connection-oriented, bytestream protocol.

  The protocol was originally defined in RFC 793. Over the course of time, these definitions were improved by removing errors and inconsistencies (RFC 1122) and expanded with a number of requirements (RFC 1323).

  The main task of TCP is to provide secure transport of data through the network. TCP provides reliability of the data transfer with a mechanism referred to as Positive Acknowledgement with Retransmission (PAR). The sending system repeats the transfer of data until it receives positive confirmation from the receiver that the data has been received.

  The data units exchanged between the sending and receiving TCP units are called packets. A TCP packet consists of a protocol header, at least 20 bytes in size, and the data to transmit.

  Each of these packets includes a checksum by means of which the receiver can check to see if the data is error-free.

  In the case of an error-free transmission, the receiver sends a confirmation of receipt to the sender. Otherwise, the packet is discarded and no confirmation of receipt is sent. If, after a specific length of time (timeout period) no receipt has arrived, the sender resends the packet in question.

  Because TCP is a connection-oriented byte-stream protocol, a client-server dialog connection is required before data can be transmitted. The process of setting up this connection is referred to as the TCP handshake or three-way handshake.

- **User Datagram Protocol (UDP).** UDP is an unreliable, connectionless datagram protocol. The main task of UDP is to make a simple and fast transport of data available through the network.

  In this case, "unreliable" means that UDP has no mechanism to guarantee the delivery of a datagram. Applications that use UDP must implement their own routines on the application layer for guaranteeing the correct transmission of data.

  "Connectionless" means that no computer-to-computer connection is established for transmitting UDP datagrams. Instead, UDP datagrams are sent by the sender without the destination machine making any further checks.

Ports and Port Numbers

To allow applications, such as browsers, to address specific services, such as Web servers, the transport layer uses numbers that are referred to as ports. Because port numbers are 16 bits in length, there is a maximum of 65536 different ports.

To simplify communication and to avoid collisions, fixed port numbers (well-known ports) are assigned by the Internet Assigned Numbers Authority (IANA) for widely used services.

All important network services run on privileged ports (ports from 0 to 1023). They are referred to as "privileged" because the associated services must be started with root permissions. The upper ports (from 1024 to 65535) are non-privileged ports.

The following lists some well-known ports registered with IANA:

- **20 and 21.** File Transfer Protocol (FTP)
- **22.** Secure Shell (SSH)
- **23.** Telnet
- **25.** Simple Mail Transfer Protocol (SMTP)
- **53.** Domain Name Service (DNS)
- **80.** Hypertext Transfer Protocol (HTTP, used for Web services)
- **110.** Post Office Protocol version 3 (POP3)
- **123.** Network Time Protocol (NTP)
- **143.** Internet Message Access Protocol (IMAP)
- **443.** HTTP over Transport Layer Security/Secure Sockets Layer TLS/SSL (HTTPS)
- **631.** Internet Printing Protocol (IPP)
- **3306.** MySQL

The `/etc/services` file contains a complete listing of assigned ports.

For TCP and UDP, the port numbers are assigned separately. For example, port 4912 for UDP can specify a different service from the same port number for TCP.

The Application Layer

The application layer comprises the application-specific protocols, such as

- FTP (file transfer)
- SMTP (e-mail)
- DNS (Domain Name System)
- HTTP (Hypertext Transfer Protocol)
- SMB (Server Message Block)

Understand Linux Network Terms

Before you can configure the network manually with the `ip` utility, you need to understand the following Linux networking terms:

Table 6-1 *Linux Networking Terms*

Term	Description
Device	Network adapter built into the system.

Term	Description
Interface	To use a physical device, a software component creates an interface to the device. This interface can be used by other software applications.

The software component which creates the interface is also called a *driver*.

In Linux, network interfaces use a standard naming scheme. Interfaces to Ethernet adapters follow the naming scheme **eth0, eth1, eth2**, and so on. For every adapter installed in the system, an interface is created when the appropriate driver is loaded.

The command line tools for the network configuration use the term *device* when they actually mean an interface. The term *device* is used in this section for both physical devices and software interfaces. |
| Link | Connection of a device to the network. |
| Address | IP address assigned to a device. The address can be either an IPv4 or an IPv6 address.

To use a device in a network, you have to assign at least one address to it. You can assign more than one address to a device. |
| Broadcast | Broadcast address of a network. By sending a network packet to the broadcast address, you can reach all hosts in the locally connected network at the same time. When you assign an IP address to a device, you can also set this broadcast address. |
| Route | Path an IP packet takes from the source to the destination host. The term *route* also refers to an entry in the routing table of the Linux kernel. |

Objective 2   Manage the Network Configuration Information from YaST

The YaST module for configuring network cards and the network connection can be accessed from the YaST Control Center. To activate the network configuration module, select *Network Devices > Network Settings*. The following appears:

Figure 6-1   *YaST Network Settings: Overview*

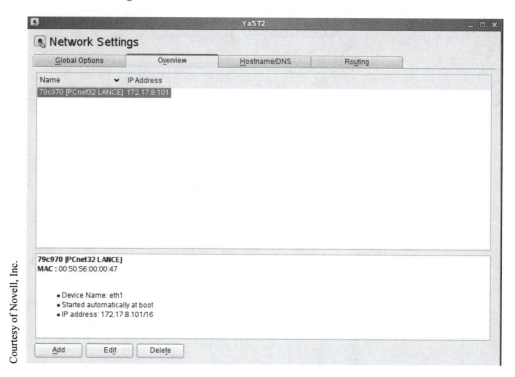

Courtesy of Novell, Inc.

You can set up and modify your configuration information using the following:

- Global Options Tab
- Overview Tab
- Hostname/DNS Tab
- Routing Tab
- General Tab
- Configure the Network Connection Using YaST

Global Options Tab

When you select the *Global Options* tab, the following appears:

Figure 6-2   *YaST Network Settings: Global Options*

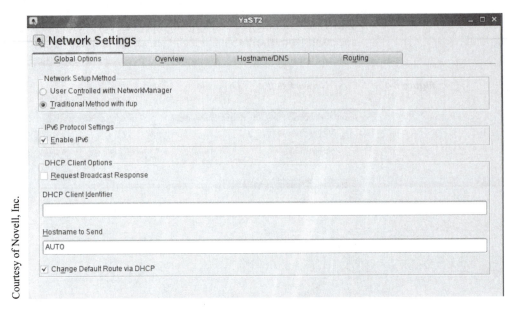

Courtesy of Novell, Inc.

Select one of the following network setup methods:

- **User Controlled with NetworkManager.** Uses a desktop applet to manage the connections for all network interfaces.

- **Traditional Method with ifup.** Uses the `ifup` command. This is the recommended setup method for SLES 11.

You can also enable IPv6 and your DHCP Client options in this tab.

Overview Tab

Using the traditional method, select the *Overview* tab to view the detected network cards, as shown in the following:

Figure 6-3   *YaST Network Settings: Overview*

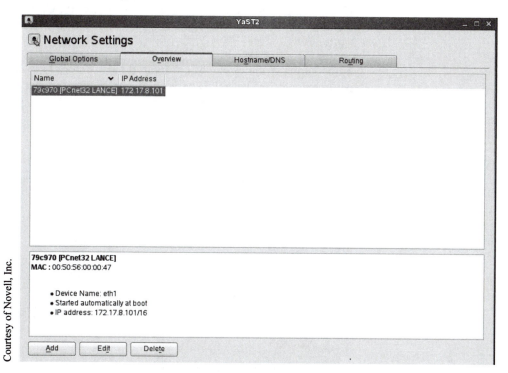

Courtesy of Novell, Inc.

Select the ***card*** you want to configure, then click ***Edit***.

Usually the cards are auto-detected by YaST, and the correct kernel module is used. If the card is not recognized by YaST, the required module must be entered manually in YaST. Do this by clicking ***Add*** in the *Overview* tab. The following dialog appears:

Figure 6-4   *YaST Network Settings: Hardware Dialog*

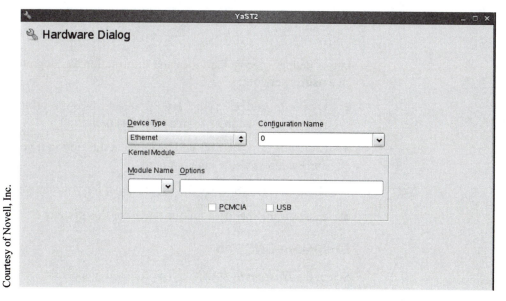

Courtesy of Novell, Inc.

In this dialog, you specify the details of the interface to configure, such as *Network Device Type* (Ethernet) and *Configuration Name* (0). Under **Kernel Module**, specify the name of the module to load. You can select the card model from a list of network cards.

Some kernel modules can be configured more precisely by adding options or parameters for the kernel. Details about parameters for specific modules can be found in the kernel documentation.

After clicking *Next*, the following dialog appears:

Figure 6-5   *YaST Network Card Setup: Access*

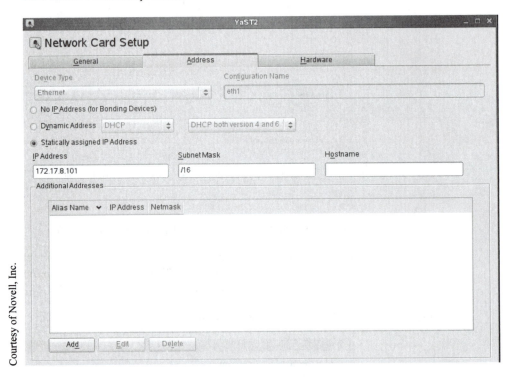

Courtesy of Novell, Inc.

In this dialog, specify the following information to integrate the network device into an existing network:

■ **Dynamic Address (via DHCP).** Select this option if the network card should receive an IP address from a DHCP server.

■ **Statically assigned IP Address.** Select this option if you want to statically assign an IP address to the network card.

■ **Subnet Mask.** Specify the subnet mask for your network.

■ **Hostname.** Specify a unique name for this system.

Hostname/DNS Tab

Select the **Hostname/DNS** tab. The following appears:

Figure 6-6   *YaST Network Settings: Hostname/DNS*

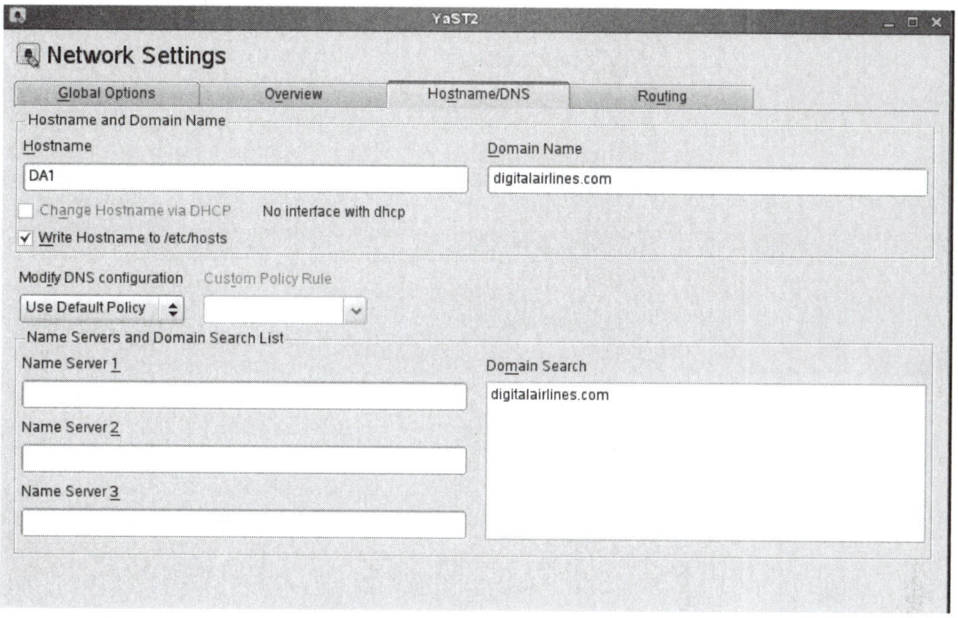

Courtesy of Novell, Inc.

This dialog lets you enter the following:

- **Hostname.** Enter a name for the computer. This name should be unique within the network.

- **Domain Name.** Enter the DNS domain the computer belongs to.

  A computer can be addressed uniquely using its FQDN (Fully Qualified Domain Name). This consists of the host name and the name of the domain. For example: **da51.digitalairlines.com**.

- **List of name servers.** Enter the IP address of your organization's DNS server(s). You can specify a maximum of three name servers.

- **Domain search list.** Enter your DNS domain.

  In the local network, it is usually more appropriate to address other hosts with their host names. not with their FQDN. The domain search list specifies the domains that the system can append to the host name to create the FQDN.

  For example, **da51** is expanded with the search list **digitalairlines.com** to the FQDN **da51.digitalairlines.com**. This name is then passed to the name server to be resolved.

  If the search list contains several domains, the completion takes place one after the other, and the resulting FQDN is passed to the name server until an entry returns an associated IP address. Separate the domains with commas or white space.

Routing Tab

To modify routing, select the ***Routing*** tab. The following appears:

Figure 6-7   *YaST Network Settings: Routing*

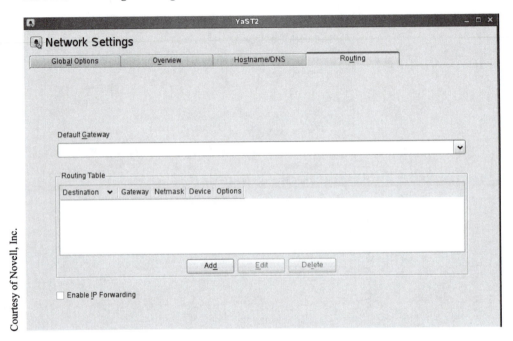

On the Routing tab, you can define the following:

■ **Default Gateway.** If the network has a gateway (a computer that forwards information from a network to other networks), its address can be specified in the network configuration.

  All data not addressed to the local network is forwarded directly to the gateway.

■ **Routing Table.** You can create entries in the routing table of the system by selecting *Expert Configuration*.

■ **Enable IP Forwarding.** If you select this option, IP packages that are not dedicated for your computer are routed.

All the necessary information is now available to activate the network card.

General Tab

On the *General* tab of the Network Card Setup dialog, you can set up additional network card options, as shown in the following:

Figure 6-8   *YaST Network Card Setup: General Tab*

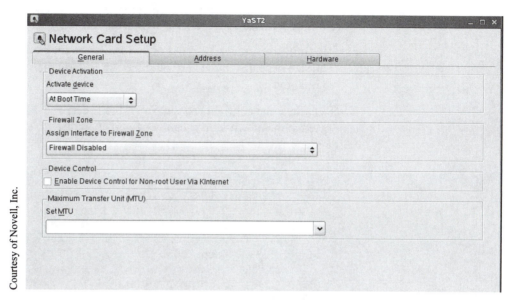

Courtesy of Novell, Inc.

You can configure the following:

- **Device Activation.** Specify when the interface should be set up. Possible values include the following:

    □ **At Boot Time.** During system start.

    □ **On Cable Connection.** If there is a physical network connection.

    □ **On Hotplug.** When the hardware is plugged in.

    □ **Manually.** The interface must be manually started.

    □ **Never.** The interface is never started.

    □ **On NFSroot.** The interface is automatically started, but can't be shut down using the `rcnetwork stop` command. The `ifdown` command, however, can still be used to bring the interface down. This is useful when the root file system resides on an NFS server.

- **Firewall Zone.** Use to activate/deactivate the firewall for the interface. If activated, you can specify which firewall zone to put the interface in:

    □ **Firewall Disabled**

    □ **Internal Zone (Unprotected)**

    □ **Demilitarized Zone**

    □ **External Zone**

- **Device Control.** Normally only root is allowed to activate and deactivate a network interface. To allow normal users to do this, activate the ***Enable Device Control for Non-root User via KInternet*** option.

- **Maximum Transfer Unit (MTU).** Specify the maximum size of an IP package. The size depends on the hardware. For an Ethernet interface, the maximum size is 1500 bytes.

After you save the configuration in YaST, the Ethernet card should be activated and connected to the network. You can verify this with the `ip` command, as shown in the following:

```
geeko@da1:~> ip address show
1: lo: <LOOPBACK,UP,LOWER_UP> mtu 16436 qdisc noqueue state UNKNOWN
    link/loopback 00:00:00:00:00:00 brd 00:00:00:00:00:00
    inet 127.0.0.1/8 brd 127.255.255.255 scope host lo
    inet 127.0.0.2/8 brd 127.255.255.255 scope host secondary lo
    inet6 ::1/128 scope host
       valid_lft forever preferred_lft forever
2: eth0: <BROADCAST,MULTICAST,UP,LOWER_UP> mtu 1500 qdisc pfifo_fast
state UNKNOWN qlen 1000
    link/ether 00:0c:29:7f:82:69 brd ff:ff:ff:ff:ff:ff
    inet 172.17.8.101/16 brd 172.16.255.255 scope global eth0
    inet6 fe80::20c:29ff:fe7f:8269/64 scope link
       valid_lft forever preferred_lft forever
```

In this example, the eth0 interface was configured. Additionally, the loopback device (lo) is always set up. On some Linux distributions you also see a sit0 (Simple Internet Transition) device; it is needed to connect to IPv6 networks.

YaST writes the network configuration information for eth0 the `/etc/sysconfig/network/ifcfg-eth0` file. The content of this file looks similar to the following:

```
BOOTPROTO='static'
STARTMODE='auto'
NAME='nForce2 Ethernet Controller'
BROADCAST=''
ETHTOOL_OPTIONS=''
IPADDR='172.17.8.101/16'
MTU=''
NETWORK=''
REMOTE_IPADDR=''
USERCONTROL='no'
```

Exercise 6-1   Configure the Network Connection Using YaST

In this exercise, you learn how to configure the network settings using YaST.

You will find this exercise at the end of the chapter.

(End of Exercise)

Objective 3   Manage the Network Configuration with Command Line Tools

The advantage of YaST is that it not only changes the network configuration, but also takes care of all network configuration files in a consistent manner.

To change the current network configuration, YaST uses commands in the background that you should be familiar with. This will help you to better understand what YaST actually does, and also help you to make quick changes, for instance to test a certain setup without making permanent configuration changes.

To work effectively with command line tools to configure network settings, you need to be able to do the following:

- Use the ip Tool to Configure Network Settings
- Use Additional Tools to Configure Network Settings
- Configure the Hostname and Name Resolution
- Configure the Network Connection Manually

Use the ip Tool to Configure Network Settings

You can use the ip command to change the network interface configuration quickly from the command line. You can use the ip command as a normal user to display the current network setup. To change the network setup, you have to be logged in as root.

NOTE: Changes made with the ip tool are not persistent. If you reboot the system, all changes will be lost. To make them persistent, you must edit the appropriate configuration files.

Changing the network interface configuration at the command line is especially useful for testing purposes, but if you want a configuration to be permanent, you must save it in a configuration file. These configuration files are generated automatically when you set up a network card with YaST, but you can also create and edit them with a text editor.

When using the ip command, you need to be able to do the following:

- Display the Current Network Configuration
- Change the Current Network Configuration
- Set Up Routing with the ip Tool
- Save Device Settings to a Configuration File

Display the Current Network Configuration

With the ip tool, you can display the following information:

- IP Address Setup
- Device Attributes
- Device Statistics

IP Address Setup

To display the IP address setup of all interfaces, enter `ip address show` at the shell prompt. Depending on your network setup, you see information similar to the following:

```
da1:~ # ip address show
1: lo: <LOOPBACK,UP,LOWER_UP> mtu 16436 qdisc noqueue state UNKNOWN
    link/loopback 00:00:00:00:00:00 brd 00:00:00:00:00:00
    inet 127.0.0.1/8 brd 127.255.255.255 scope host lo
    inet 127.0.0.2/8 brd 127.255.255.255 scope host secondary lo
    inet6 ::1/128 scope host
       valid_lft forever preferred_lft forever
2: eth0: <BROADCAST,MULTICAST,UP,LOWER_UP> mtu 1500 qdisc pfifo_fast
state UNKNOWN qlen 1000
    link/ether 00:0c:29:7f:82:69 brd ff:ff:ff:ff:ff:ff
    inet 172.17.8.101/16 brd 172.16.255.255 scope global eth0
    inet6 fe80::20c:29ff:fe7f:8269/64 scope link
       valid_lft forever preferred_lft forever
```

The information is grouped by network interfaces. Every interface entry starts with a digit, called the interface index; the interface name is displayed after the interface index.

In the above example, there are two interfaces:

- **lo.** The loopback device, which is available on every Linux system, even when no network adapter is installed. (As stated above, *device* and *interface* are often used synonymously in the context of network configuration.) Using this virtual device, applications on the same machine can use the network to communicate with each other.

  For example, you can use the IP address of the loopback device to access a locally installed Web server by typing **http://127.0.0.1** in the address bar of your Web browser.

- **eth0.** The first Ethernet adapter of the computer in this example. Ethernet devices are normally called eth0, eth1, eth2, and so on.

You always have the entries for the loopback device, and on some systems there is also by default a sit0 device. sit stands for Simple Internet Transition. sit0 is a special virtual device which can be used to encapsulate IPv6 packets into IPv4 packets. It is not used in a normal IPv4 network. Depending on your hardware setup, you might have more Ethernet devices in the `ip` output.

Several lines of information are displayed for every network interface, such as eth0 in the preceding example:

```
2: eth0: <BROADCAST,MULTICAST,UP,LOWER_UP> mtu 1500 qdisc pfifo_fast
state UNKNOWN qlen 1000
```

The most important information of the line in this example is the interface index (2) and the interface name (eth0).

The other information shows additional attributes set for this device, such as the hardware address of the Ethernet adapter (00:0c:29:7f:82:69):

```
link/ether 00:0c:29:7f:82:69 brd ff:ff:ff:ff:ff:ff
```

In the following line, the IPv4 setup of the device is displayed:

```
inet 172.17.8.101/16 brd 172.16.255.255 scope global eth0
```

inet is followed by the IP address (172.17.8.101), and brd follows the broadcast address (172.17.255.255). The length of the network mask in bits (16) is displayed after the IP address and separated from it by a /.

The following lines show the IPv6 configuration of the device:

```
inet6 fe80::20c:29ff:fe7f:8269/64 scope link
      valid_lft forever preferred_lft forever
```

The IPv6 address shown here is the automatically assigned link local address. The address is generated from the hardware address of the device. The link local IPv6 address allows you to contact other computers in the same network segment only and has limited functionality. IPv6 is not covered in this course.

Depending on the device type, the information can differ. However, the most important information (such as assigned IP addresses) is always shown.

NOTE: IPv6 is covered in the *SUSE Linux Enterprise Server Administration* (3103) course.

Device Attributes

If you are interested only in the device attributes and not in the IP address setup, you can enter ip link show:

```
da2:~ # ip link show
1: lo: <LOOPBACK,UP,LOWER_UP> mtu 16436 qdisc noqueue state UNKNOWN
    link/loopback 00:00:00:00:00:00 brd 00:00:00:00:00:00
2: eth0: <BROADCAST,MULTICAST,UP,LOWER_UP> mtu 1500 qdisc pfifo_fast
state UNKNOWN qlen 1000
    link/ether 00:0c:29:7f:82:69 brd ff:ff:ff:ff:ff:ff
```

The information is similar to what you see when you enter ip address show, but the information about the address setup is missing. The device attributes are displayed in brackets right after the device name.

The following is a list of some possible attributes and their meanings:

Table 6-2 *Device Attributes*

Attribute	Description
UP	The device is turned on. It is ready to transmit packets to and receive packets from the network.
LOOPBACK	The device is a loopback device.
BROADCAST	The device can send packets to all hosts sharing the same network.
POINTOPOINT	The device is connected only to one other device. All packets are sent to and received from the other device.
MULTICAST	The device can send packets to a group of other systems at the same time.
PROMISC	The device listens to all packets on the network, not only to those sent to the device's hardware address. This is usually used for network monitoring.

Device Statistics

You can use the `-s` option with the `ip` command to display additional statistics information about the devices. The command looks like the following:

```
ip -s link show eth0
```

By giving the device name at the end of the command line, the output is limited to one specific device. This can also be used to display the address setup or the device attributes.

The following is an example of the information displayed for the device eth0 (as other options of `ip` such as `address`, the `link` and `show` options can be abbreviated):

```
da2:~ # ip -s li sh dev eth0
2: eth0: <BROADCAST,MULTICAST,UP,LOWER_UP> mtu 1500 qdisc pfifo_fast
state UNKNOWN qlen 1000
    link/ether 00:0c:29:7f:82:69 brd ff:ff:ff:ff:ff:ff
    RX: bytes  packets  errors  dropped overrun mcast
    142999     1398     0       0       0       0
    TX: bytes  packets  errors  dropped carrier collsns
    257183     1077     0       0       0       0
```

Two additional sections with information are displayed for every device. Each of the sections has a headline with a description of the information displayed.

The section starting with **RX** displays information about received packets, and the section starting with **TX** displays information about sent packets.

The sections display the following information:

- **Bytes.** The total number of bytes received or transmitted by the device.
- **Packets.** The total number of packets received or transmitted by the device.

- **Errors.** The total number of receiver or transmitter errors.

- **Dropped.** The total number of packets dropped due to a lack of resources.

- **Overrun.** The total number of receiver overruns resulting in dropped packets. As a rule, if a device is overrun, it means that there are serious problems in the Linux kernel or that your computer is too slow for the device.

- **Mcast.** The total number of received multicast packets. This option is supported by only a few devices.

- **Carrier.** The total number of link media failures due to a lost carrier.

- **Collsns.** The total number of collision events on Ethernet media.

- **Compressed.** The total number of compressed packets.

Change the Current Network Configuration

You can also use the `ip` tool to change the network configuration by performing the following tasks:

- Assign an IP Address to a Device
- Delete the IP Address from a Device
- Change Device Attributes

Assign an IP Address to a Device

To assign an address to a device, use a command similar to the following:

```
da2:~ # ip address add 10.0.0.2/24 brd + dev eth0
```

In this example, the command assigns the IP address 10.0.0.2 to the device eth0. The network mask is 24 bits long, as determined by the /24 after the IP address. The `brd +` option sets the broadcast address automatically as determined by the network mask.

You can enter `ip address show dev eth0` to verify the assigned IP address. The assigned IP address is displayed in the output of the command line. You can assign more than one IP address to a device.

Delete the IP Address from a Device

To delete the IP address from a device, use a command similar to the following:

```
da2:~ # ip address del 10.0.0.2/24 dev eth0
```

In this example, the command deletes the IP address 10.0.0.2 from the device eth0. Use `ip a s eth0` to verify that the address was deleted.

Change Device Attributes

You can also change device attributes with the `ip` tool. The following is the basic command to set device attributes:

```
ip link set device attribute
```

The possible attributes are described in Device Attributes. The most important attributes are up and down. By setting these attributes, you can enable or disable a network device.

To **enable** a network device (such as eth0), enter the following command:

```
da2:~ # ip link set eth0 up
```

To **disable** a network device (such as eth0), enter the following command:

```
da2:~ # ip link set eth0 down
```

Set Up Routing with the ip Tool

You can use the ip tool to configure the routing table of the Linux kernel. The routing table determines the path IP packets use to reach the destination system.

When using the ip command to set up routing, you need to be able to

- View the Routing Table
- Add Routes to the Routing Table
- Delete Routes from the Routing Table
- Save Routing Settings to a Configuration File

NOTE: Routing is a complex topic; this objective covers only the most common routing scenarios.

View the Routing Table

To view the current routing table, enter ip route show. For most systems, the output looks similar to the following:

```
da1:~ # ip route show
172.17.0.0/16 dev eth0  proto kernel  scope link  src 172.17.8.101
169.254.0.0/16 dev eth0  scope link
127.0.0.0/8 dev lo  scope link
default via 172.17.8.1 dev eth0
```

Every line represents an entry in the routing table. Each line in the example is shown and explained below:

- **172.17.0.0/16 dev eth0 proto kernel scope link src 172.17.8.101**

  This line represents the route for the local network. All network packets to a system in the same network are sent directly through the device eth0.

- **169.254.0.0/16 dev eth0 scope link**

This line shows a network route for the 169.254.0.0 network. Hosts can use this network for address auto configuration.

SLES 11 automatically assigns a free IP address from this network when no other device configuration is present. The route to this network is always set, especially when the system itself has no assigned IP address from that network.

- **127.0.0.0/8 dev lo scope link**

  This is the route for the loopback device.

- **default via 172.17.8.1 dev eth0**

  This line is the entry for the default route. All network packets that cannot be sent according to the previous entries of the routing table are sent through the gateway defined in this entry.

Depending on the setup of your machine, the content of the routing table varies. In most cases, you have at least two entries in the routing table:

- One route to the local network to which the system is connected

- One route to the default gateway for all other packets

Add Routes to the Routing Table

The following are the most common tasks you complete when adding a route:

- Set a Route to the Locally Connected Network

- Set a Route to a Different Network

- Set a Default Route

Set a Route to the Locally Connected Network

The following command sets a route to the locally connected network:

```
da2:~ # ip route add 172.17.0.0/16 dev eth0
```

The system in this example is in the 172.17.0.0 network. The network mask is 16 bits long (255.255.0.0). All packets to the local network are sent directly through the device eth0.

Set a Route to a Different Network

The following command sets a route to a different network:

```
da2:~ # ip route add 192.168.1.0/24 via 172.17.8.100
```

All packets for the 192.168.1.0 network are sent through the gateway 172.17.8.100.

Set a Default Route

The following command sets a default route:

```
da2:~ # ip route add default via 172.17.8.1
```

Packets that cannot be sent according to previous entries in the routing table are sent through the gateway with an IP address of 172.17.8.1.

Delete Routes from the Routing Table

To delete an entry from the routing table, use a command similar to the following:

```
da2:~ # ip route delete 192.168.1.0/24 dev eth0
```

This command deletes the route to the 192.168.1.0 network assigned to the device eth0.

Save Routing Settings to a Configuration File

Routing settings made with the ip tool are lost when you reboot your system. Settings have to be written to configuration files to be restored at boot time.

Routes to the directly connected network are automatically set up when a device is started. All other routes are saved in the `/etc/sysconfig/network/routes` configuration file.

The following shows the content of a typical configuration file:

```
192.168.1.0 172.17.8.100 255.255.255.0 eth0
default 172.17.8.1 - -
```

Each line of the configuration file represents an entry in the routing table. Each line is explained below:

- `192.168.1.0 172.17.8.100 255.255.255.0 eth0`

    All packets sent to the 192.168.1.0 network with the network mask 255.255.255.0 are sent to the gateway 172.17.8.100 through the eth0 device.

- `Default 172.17.8.1 - -`

    This entry represents a default route. All packets that are not affected by the previous entries of the routing table are sent to the gateway 172.17.8.1. It is not necessary to fill out the last two columns of the line for a default route.

To apply changes to the routing configuration file, you need to restart the affected network device with the `ifdown` and `ifup` commands.

Save Device Settings to a Configuration File

All device configuration changes you make with `ip` are lost when the system is rebooted. To restore the device configuration automatically when the system is started, the settings need to be saved in configuration files.

The configuration files for network devices are located in the `/etc/sysconfig/network/` directory. If the network devices are set up with YaST, one configuration file is created for every device. For Ethernet devices, the filenames consist of `ifcfg-` and then the name of the device., such as `ifcfg-eth0`.

We recommend that you set up a device with YaST first and make changes in the configuration file. Setting up a device from scratch is a complex task, because the hardware driver would also need to be configured manually.

The content of the configuration files depends on the configuration of the device. To change the configuration file, you need to know how to do the following:

- Configure a Device Statically

- Configure a Device Dynamically with DHCP

- Start and Stop Configured Interfaces

Configure a Device Statically

The content of a configuration file of a statically configured device is similar to the following:

```
BOOTPROTO='static'
STARTMODE='auto'
NAME='nForce2 Ethernet Controller'
ETHTOOL_OPTIONS=''
BROADCAST=''
IPADDR='172.17.8.101/16'
MTU=''
NETWORK=''
REMOTE_IPADDR=''
USERCONTROL='no'
```

The configuration file includes several lines. Each line has an option and a value assigned to that option, as explained below:

- **BOOTPROTO='static'.** Determines the way the device is configured. There are two possible values:

    - **static.** The device is configured with a static IP address.

    - **dhcp.** The device is configured automatically with a DHCP server.

- **STARTMODE='auto'.** Determines how the device is started. This option can use the following values:

    - **auto.** The device is started at boot time or when initialized at runtime.

    - **manual.** The device must be started manually with `ifup`.

    - **ifplugd.** The interface is controlled by ifplugd.

- **ETHTOOL_OPTIONS=''.** The `ethtool` utility is used for querying settings of an Ethernet device and changing them (for instance, setting the speed or half/full duplex mode). The manual page for ethtool lists the available options.

  If you want ethtool to modify any settings, list the options here. If no options are listed, ethtool is not called.

- **BROADCAST=''.** Broadcast address of the network. If empty, the broadcast address is derived from the IP address and the netmask, according to the configuration in `/etc/sysconfig/network/config`.

- **IPADDR='172.17.8.101/16'.** IP address of the device.

- **NETWORK=''.** Address of the network itself.

- **REMOTE_IPADDR=''.** Required only if you are setting up a point-to-point connection.

- **MTU=''.** Specifies a value for the MTU (Maximum Transmission Unit). If you don't specify a value, the default value is used. For an Ethernet device, the default is 1500 bytes.

The `/etc/sysconfig/network/ifcfg.template` file contains a template that you can use as a base for device configuration files. It also has comments explaining the various options.

Configure a Device Dynamically with DHCP

If you want to configure a device by using a DHCP server, you set the `BOOTPROTO` option to `dhcp`.

When the device is configured by DHCP, you don't need to set any options for the network address configuration in the file. If there are any IP address settings, they are set in addition to the settings from the DHCP server.

Start and Stop Configured Interfaces

To apply changes to a configuration file, you need to stop the corresponding interface and start it again. You can do this with the `ifdown` and `ifup` commands.

For example, entering `ifdown eth0` disables the device eth0. `ifup eth0` enables eth0 again. When the device is restarted, the new configuration is read from the configuration file.

NOTE: Configuring the interfaces with IP addresses, routes, etc., with the `ip` tool requires an existing device setup, including a correctly loaded kernel module. This is usually done at boot time by udev. If you want more information on this topic, read `/etc/sysconfig/hardware/README.hwcfg_and_device_initialisation` and the references listed in that file.

Use Additional Tools to Configure Network Settings

In addition to the `ip` command, a Linux system has several other command line tools that can be used to configure the network setup. You need to be able to

- Use the ifconfig Tool to Configure Network Settings

- Use the iwconfig Tool to Configure Wireless Network Settings
- Use the route Tool to Configure the Routing Table

Use the ifconfig Tool to Configure Network Settings

In older Linux versions, the `ifconfig` tool was used instead of the `ip` tool to configure network settings, but has since been replaced in the scripts used to set up the network configuration by the `ip` tool. Because the `ifconfig` command is still available on SLES 11 and other current distributions, the following paragraphs explain its use.

To use the `ifconfig` command you need to be able to

- Use the ifconfig Command to View the Network Configuration
- Use the ifconfig Command to Change the Network Configuration

Use the ifconfig Command to View the Network Configuration

The `ifconfig` command without any options displays the current interface configuration:

```
da1:~ # ifconfig
eth0      Link encap:Ethernet  HWaddr 00:0C:29:7F:82:69
          inet addr:172.17.8.101  Bcast:172.16.255.255
Mask:255.255.0.0
          inet6 addr: fe80::20c:29ff:fe7f:8269/64 Scope:Link
          UP BROADCAST RUNNING MULTICAST  MTU:1500  Metric:1
          RX packets:1142 errors:0 dropped:0 overruns:0 frame:0
          TX packets:665 errors:0 dropped:0 overruns:0 carrier:0
          collisions:0 txqueuelen:1000
          RX bytes:114327 (111.6 Kb)  TX bytes:129265 (126.2 Kb)
          Interrupt:19 Base address:0x2024

lo        Link encap:Local Loopback
          inet addr:127.0.0.1  Mask:255.0.0.0
          inet6 addr: ::1/128 Scope:Host
          UP LOOPBACK RUNNING  MTU:16436  Metric:1
          RX packets:10517 errors:0 dropped:0 overruns:0 frame:0
          TX packets:10517 errors:0 dropped:0 overruns:0 carrier:0
          collisions:0 txqueuelen:0
          RX bytes:5485504 (5.2 Mb)  TX bytes:5485504 (5.2 Mb)
```

To view the configuration of a specific device only, add the device name to the command, such as `ifconfig eth0`. The `ifconfig -a` command shows all interfaces, including those that are down.

Use the ifconfig Command to Change the Network Configuration

The basic syntax of the ifconfig command looks as follows:

```
ifconfig interface address options
```

To configure the IP address of an interface, you would use ifconfig in the following manner:

```
ifconfig eth0 192.168.1.10 broadcast 192.168.1.255
netmask 255.255.255.0
```

If eth0 had already an IP address assigned, it is replaced by the new one. To assign a second IP address to the interface, you have to add a designation to the device as shown in the following example:

```
ifconfig eth0:1 10.0.0.10 broadcast 10.0.255.255 netmask
255.255.0.0
```

You can remove the above IP address again with the following command:

```
ifconfig eth0:1 del 10.0.0.10
```

Use the iwconfig Tool to Configure Wireless Network Settings

The iwconfig command is similar to the ifconfig command, but dedicated to wireless interfaces.

iwconfig without options beyond the interface name displays the current settings, as in the following:

```
da-laptop:~ # iwconfig eth0
eth0      unassociated  ESSID:off/any  Nickname:"ipw2100"
          Mode:Managed  Channel=0  Access Point: Not-Associated
          Bit Rate:0 kb/s   Tx-Power:16 dBm
          Retry short limit:7   RTS thr:off   Fragment thr:off
          Encryption key:off
          Power Management:off
          Link Quality:0  Signal level:0  Noise level:0
          Rx invalid nwid:0  Rx invalid crypt:0  Rx invalid frag:0
          Tx excessive retries:0  Invalid misc:0   Missed beacon:0
```

In the above example there is no access to a wireless network.

With iwconfig you can set parameters specific to wireless devices, including ESSID, mode, encryption key, and transmit power.

Use the route Tool to Configure the Routing Table

The route command is used to display and change the kernel routing table.

Without options it displays the current routing table. Use the -n option to display numerical addresses, as shown in the following:

```
da10:~ # route -n
Kernel IP routing table
Destination   Gateway       Genmask         Flags Metric Ref    Use Iface
172.17.0.0    0.0.0.0       255.255.0.0     U     0      0        0 eth0
192.168.2.0   172.17.8.100  255.255.255.0   UG    0      0        0 eth0
169.254.0.0   0.0.0.0       255.255.0.0     U     0      0        0 eth0
127.0.0.0     0.0.0.0       255.0.0.0       U     0      0        0 lo
0.0.0.0       172.17.8.1    0.0.0.0         UG    0      0        0 eth0
```

The following command will add a route to the 10.0.0.0/16 network via the router with the IP address 172.17.8.254:

```
route add -net 10.0.0.0 netmask 255.255.0.0 gw
172.17.8.254
```

You can delete that route again with the following command:

```
route del -net 10.0.0.0 netmask 255.255.0.0 gw
172.17.8.254
```

The default route is set with the following command:

```
route add default gw 172.17.8.1
```

Configure the Hostname and Name Resolution

The system hostname and your network's name resolver can be set manually. In this objective, you learn how to do the following:

- Set the Host and Domain Name
- Configure Name Resolution

Set the Host and Domain Name

The hostname is configured in the /etc/HOSTNAME file. The content of the file is similar to the following:

```
da1.digitalairlines.com
```

The file contains the fully qualified domain name of the system. In this case, da1.digitalairlines.com.

Configure Name Resolution

Name resolution is needed to translate host and domain names into IP addresses and vice versa. The components involved on a Linux machine are:

- The /etc/hosts File
- The /etc/resolv.conf file
- The /etc/nsswitch.conf File

The /etc/hosts File

The `/etc/hosts` file contains IP addresses and corresponding host names. Usually it only contains the IP addresses and host name of the machine it resides on, but you can add other entries to it as needed. A typical hosts file found on SLES 11 looks similar to the following:

```
#
# hosts          This file describes a number of hostname-to-address
#                mappings for the TCP/IP subsystem.  It is mostly
#                used at boot time, when no name servers are running.
#                On small systems, this file can be used instead of a
#                "named" name server.
# Syntax:
#
# IP-Address  Full-Qualified-Hostname   Short-Hostname
#

127.0.0.1       localhost
127.0.0.2       da1.digitalairlines.com da1

# special IPv6 addresses
::1             localhost ipv6-localhost ipv6-loopback

fe00::0         ipv6-localnet

ff00::0         ipv6-mcastprefix
ff02::1         ipv6-allnodes
ff02::2         ipv6-allrouters
ff02::3         ipv6-allhosts
```

The /etc/resolv.conf file

The `/etc/resolv.conf` file defines the search prefix and the nameservers to use. The content of the file is similar to the following:

```
search digitalairlines.com
nameserver 172.17.8.1
nameserver 172.16.8.1
nameserver 172.15.8.1
```

The file contains two types of entries:

- **search.** The domain name in this option is used to complete incomplete hostnames. For example, if you look up the host name da3, the name is automatically completed to the fully qualified domain name da3.digitalairlines.com.

- **nameserver.** Every entry starting with `nameserver` is followed by an IP address of a name server. You can configure up to three name servers. If the first name server fails, the next one is used.

The /etc/nsswitch.conf File

The `/etc/nsswitch.conf` (name service switch) file defines the sequence in which the various databases are queried. The file looks similar to the following:

```
#
# /etc/nsswitch.conf
#
# An example Name Service Switch config file. This file should be
# sorted with the most-used services at the beginning.
#
# The entry '[NOTFOUND=return]' means that the search for an
# entry should stop if the search in the previous entry turned
# up nothing. Note that if the search failed due to some other reason
# (like no NIS server responding) then the search continues with the
# next entry.
#
# Legal entries are:
#
#       compat                 Use compatibility setup
#       nisplus                Use NIS+ (NIS version 3)
#       nis                    Use NIS (NIS version 2), also called YP
#       dns                    Use DNS (Domain Name Service)
#       files                  Use the local files
#       [NOTFOUND=return]      Stop searching if not found so far
#
# For more information, please read the nsswitch.conf.5 manual page.
#

# passwd: files nis
# shadow: files nis
# group:  files nis

passwd: compat
group:  compat

hosts:          files dns
networks:       files dns
...
```

The hosts: entry is the one relevant for host name resolution. It specifies that to resolve a host name, the /etc/hosts file is consulted first (files), and if there is no applicable entry in the /etc/hosts file, the query is sent to a DNS server (dns).

Exercise 6-2 **Configure the Network Connection Manually**

In this exercise, you learn how to manually configure network settings.

You will find this exercise at the end of the chapter.

(End of Exercise)

Objective 4   Troubleshoot Networking Issues

After the network is configured, you might want to test the network connection by doing the following:

- Test Network Connections with ping

- Trace Network Packets with traceroute

- Test Service Availability with telnet

- View Connection Information with netstat

- Using dig to Test DNS Name Resolution

Test Network Connections with ping

The `ping` command lets you check network connections between two hosts in a simple way. If the ping command works, then both the physical and logical connections are correctly set up between the two hosts.

The ping command sends special network packets to the target system and waits for a reply. In the simplest scenario, you use ping with an IP address:

```
ping 10.0.0.10
```

You can also use the host name of the target system instead of an IP address. The output of ping looks similar to the following:

```
PING 10.0.0.10 (10.0.0.10) 56(84) bytes of data.
64 bytes from 10.0.0.10: icmp_seq=1 ttl=60 time=2.95 ms
64 bytes from 10.0.0.10: icmp_seq=2 ttl=60 time=2.16 ms
64 bytes from 10.0.0.10: icmp_seq=3 ttl=60 time=2.18 ms
64 bytes from 10.0.0.10: icmp_seq=4 ttl=60 time=2.08 ms
```

Each line of the output represents a packet sent by ping. ping keeps sending packets until it is terminated by pressing Ctrl+c.

The output displays the following information:

- Size of an ICMP datagram (64 bytes)

- IP address of the target system (from 10.0.0.10)

- Sequence number of each datagram (seq=1)

- TTL (TTL, time to live) of the datagram (ttl=60)

- Amount of time that passes between the transmission of a packet and the time a corresponding answer is received (time=2.95 ms). This time is also called the *Round Trip Time*.

If you get an answer from the target system, you can be sure that the basic network device setup and routing to the target host works.

The following table provides some options for ping you can use for advanced troubleshooting:

Table 6-3   *ping Options*

Option	Description
-c *count*	Specifies the number of packets to be sent. After this number has been reached, ping is terminated.
-I *interface*	Specifies the network interface to be used on a computer with several network interfaces.
-i *seconds*	Specifies the number of seconds to wait between individual packet shipments. The default setting is 1 second.
-f	(Flood ping) Packets are sent one after another at the same rate as the respective replies arrive. Only root can use this option. For normal users, the minimum time is 200 milliseconds.
-l *preload*	(Lowercase L) sends packets without waiting for a reply.
-n	The numerical output of the IP address. Address resolutions to hostnames are not carried out.
-t *ttl*	Sets the Time To Live for packets to be sent.
-w *maxwait*	Specifies a timeout in seconds, before ping exits, regardless of how many packets have been sent or received.
-b	Sends packets to the broadcast address of the network.

Trace Network Packets with *traceroute*

The `traceroute` diagnostic tool is primarily used to check the routing between different networks. To achieve this task, traceroute sends packets with an increasing TTL value to the destination host, whereby three packets of each value are sent.

Traceroute also uses UDP packets, which are called *datagrams*.

First, three datagrams with a TTL=1 are sent to the host, then three packets with a TTL=2, and so on. Every time a datagram passes through a router, its TTL is reduced by one.

When the TTL reaches zero (0), the datagram is discarded and a message is sent to the sender. Because the TTL is increased by one every three packets, traceroute can collect information about every router on the way to the destination host.

You normally include a hostname with the traceroute command, as in the following:

```
traceroute slc.digitalairlines.com
```

It is also possible to use an IP address instead of the hostname. The output of traceroute looks similar to the following:

```
da1:~ # traceroute slc.digitalairlines.com
traceroute to slc.digitalairlines.com (192.168.2.1), 30 hops max, 40
byte packets
1 da1.digitalairlines.com (17.17.8.101) 0 ms 0 ms 0 ms
2 muc.digitalairlines.com (192.168.1.254) 14 ms 18 ms 14 ms
3 slc.digitalairlines.com (192.168.2.1) 19 ms * 26 ms
```

The first line of the output displays general information about the traceroute call. Each of the lines that follow represent a router on the way to the destination host. Each router is displayed with the hostname and IP address.

Traceroute also displays information about the round trip times of the three datagrams returned by each router. An asterisk(*) indicates that no response was received from the router. The last line of the output represents the destination host itself.

NOTE: in addition to `traceroute`, you can also use the `tracepath` command. The functionality of the two tools is very similar.

Test Service Availability with telnet

As its name implies, the use of the `telnet` command is to establish a Telnet connection to another host. Once logged in on the remote host, you can work on the remote host as if you were working at a console at the remote location. The main disadvantage of Telnet in comparison to SSH (secure shell) is that the connection is not encrypted.

In addition to its primary purpose, the telnet command can be used to test the availability of TCP-based services by adding the port you want to connect to. If you are able to connect to a remote service, such as a Web server, you know that the network setup and routing are correct.

When you connect to a service using the `telnet` command, you can usually view the banner information the server sends, as shown in the following example:

```
da1:~ # telnet localhost 22
Trying 127.0.0.1...
Connected to localhost.
Escape character is '^]'.
SSH-2.0-OpenSSH_5.1
^[^]
telnet> quit
Connection closed.
da1:~ #
```

The SSH server sends the `SSH-2.0-OpenSSH_5.1` string. Because you cannot create an actual SSH session manually, your only choice is to press ^] to return to the telnet prompt and to enter quit to end the session.

If you are able to "speak" the protocol of the service you are contacting, such as HTTP, SMTP, or POP3, you can get some more information, as shown in the following example using HTTP:

```
da1:~ # telnet localhost 80
Trying 127.0.0.1...
Connected to localhost.
Escape character is '^]'.
GET /index.html HTTP/1.1
host: localhost

HTTP/1.1 200 OK
Date: Thu, 06 Aug 2009 11:23:18 GMT
Server: Apache/2.2.10 (Linux/SUSE)
Last-Modified: Sat, 20 Nov 2004 20:16:24 GMT
ETag: "5b9f-2c-3e9564c23b600"
Accept-Ranges: bytes
Content-Length: 44
Content-Type: text/html

<html><body><h1>It works!</h1></body></html>Connection closed by
foreign host.
```

After entering the HTTP commands `GET / HTTP/1.1` and `host: localhost` followed by an empty line, the Web server sends back the requested HTML document. After a few moments the Web server closes the connection.

View Connection Information with netstat

You can use the `netstat` command at the shell prompt to find out which network ports are open on your system. You can also view a list of connections that have been established through these ports. The following options can be used to customize the output of netstat:

Table 6-4   *netstat Options*

Option	Description
-p	Show processes (When run by a normal user, only that user's processes are shown. `netstat` run as root shows all processes.)
-a	Show listening and non-listening sockets (all)
-t	Show TCP information
-u	Show UDP information
-n	Do not resolve hostnames
-e	Display additional information (extend)
-r	Display routing information

The output of the command varies, depending on the options used. Using the `-patune` options, netstat shows the following information:

```
da10:~ # netstat -patune
Active Internet connections (servers and established)
Proto Recv-Q Send-Q Local Addr Foreign Addr    State   User   Inode
PID/Program name
tcp        0      0 0.0.0.0:111   0.0.0.0:*     LISTEN 0      7552
3260/rpcbind
tcp        0      0 127.0.0.1:80 127.0.0.1:38243 SYN_RECV 0 0
-
tcp        0      0 0.0.0.0:22    0.0.0.0:*     LISTEN 0      9733
4007/sshd
tcp        0      0 127.0.0.1:631 0.0.0.0:*     LISTEN 0      8811
3674/cupsd
tcp        0      0 127.0.0.1:25  0.0.0.0:*     LISTEN 0      9224
3941/master
tcp        0      0 127.0.0.1:6010 0.0.0.0:*    LISTEN 0      14199
4492/1
tcp        0      0 127.0.0.1:6011 0.0.0.0:*    LISTEN 0      25868
14862/2
tcp        0      0 127.0.0.1:38243 127.0.0.1:80 ESTABLISHED 0 25928
14896/telnet
...
```

Using dig to Test DNS Name Resolution

Performing DNS lookups is a routine task for network administrators. The Domain Information Groper (`dig`) performs a DNS lookup and finds detailed information about the queried nameservers.

You can specify that `dig` use a certain domain nameserver just use the nameservers that are listed in the `resolv.conf` file.

Shown below is the `dig` output when querying novell.com.

```
da1:~ # dig novell.com

; <<>> DiG 9.5.0-P2 <<>> novell.com
;; global options:  printcmd
;; Got answer:
;; ->>HEADER<<- opcode: QUERY, status: NOERROR, id: 52196
;; flags: qr rd ra; QUERY: 1, ANSWER: 1, AUTHORITY: 0, ADDITIONAL: 0

;; QUESTION SECTION:
;novell.com.        IN   A

;; ANSWER SECTION:
novell.com.    43157   IN   A   130.57.5.70

;; Query time: 43 msec
;; SERVER: 192.168.1.1#53(192.168.1.1)
;; WHEN: Thu Aug 12 12:04:00 2010
;; MSG SIZE  rcvd: 44
```

Following is the `dig` output when no nameserver or domain is specified:

```
da1:~ # dig

; <<>> DiG 9.5.0-P2 <<>>
;; global options:  printcmd
;; Got answer:
;; ->>HEADER<<- opcode: QUERY, status: NOERROR, id: 22039
;; flags: qr rd ra; QUERY: 1, ANSWER: 13, AUTHORITY: 0, ADDITIONAL: 0

;; QUESTION SECTION:
;.            IN   NS

;; ANSWER SECTION:
.         36633   IN   NS   j.root-servers.net.
.         36633   IN   NS   m.root-servers.net.
.         36633   IN   NS   c.root-servers.net.
.         36633   IN   NS   i.root-servers.net.
.         36633   IN   NS   k.root-servers.net.
.         36633   IN   NS   h.root-servers.net.
.         36633   IN   NS   b.root-servers.net.
.         36633   IN   NS   g.root-servers.net.
.         36633   IN   NS   l.root-servers.net.
.         36633   IN   NS   a.root-servers.net.
.         36633   IN   NS   f.root-servers.net.
.         36633   IN   NS   e.root-servers.net.
.         36633   IN   NS   d.root-servers.net.

;; Query time: 48 msec
;; SERVER: 192.168.1.1#53(192.168.1.1)
;; WHEN: Thu Aug 12 12:05:05 2010
;; MSG SIZE  rcvd: 228
```

Performing a DNS lookup with `dig` will extract for you as little or as much information as you want.

You can use the following options with `dig` (use `dig -h` to display all options available).

```
da1:~ # dig -h
Usage:  dig [@global-server] [domain] [q-type] [q-class] {q-opt}
            {global-d-opt} host [@local-server] {local-d-opt}
            [ host [@local-server] {local-d-opt} [...]]
Where:  domain    is in the Domain Name System
...
```

`dig` can be used in a batch mode operation, reading from a file you create. `dig` can issue multiple lookups to gather information from sites queried. Below are sample results for several different types of queries.

The following is a query for IPv4 address information. This is the default, it is therefore not necessary to specify the A record as query type.

```
da1:~ # dig www.novell.com

; <<>> DiG 9.5.0-P2 <<>> www.novell.com
;; global options:  printcmd
;; Got answer:
;; ->>HEADER<<- opcode: QUERY, status: NOERROR, id: 24712
;; flags: qr rd ra; QUERY: 1, ANSWER: 1, AUTHORITY: 13, ADDITIONAL: 0

;; QUESTION SECTION:
;www.novell.com.                          IN       A

;; ANSWER SECTION:
www.novell.com.          13595   IN       A        130.57.5.25

;; AUTHORITY SECTION:
.                        143082  IN       NS       l.root-servers.net.
...

;; Query time: 2 msec
;; SERVER: 192.168.1.1#53(192.168.1.1)
;; WHEN: Thu Dec  9 18:14:53 2010
;; MSG SIZE  rcvd: 259
```

The following is a query for ptr record information.

```
da1:~ # dig 25.5.57.130.in-addr.arpa ptr

; <<>> DiG 9.5.0-P2 <<>> 25.5.57.130.in-addr.arpa ptr
;; global options:  printcmd
;; Got answer:
;; ->>HEADER<<- opcode: QUERY, status: NOERROR, id: 411
;; flags: qr rd ra; QUERY: 1, ANSWER: 1, AUTHORITY: 12, ADDITIONAL: 0

;; QUESTION SECTION:
;25.5.57.130.in-addr.arpa.        IN       PTR

;; ANSWER SECTION:
25.5.57.130.in-addr.arpa. 41763 IN       PTR      www.novell.com.

;; AUTHORITY SECTION:
arpa.                     46754  IN       NS       h.root-servers.net.
...
```

If the nameserver is listening on some port other than 53, you can add the -p **portnumber** option.

The following is a query for IPv6 information.

```
da1:~ # dig www.ipv6.org AAAA

; <<>> DiG 9.5.0-P2 <<>> www.ipv6.org AAAA
;; global options:  printcmd
;; Got answer:
;; ->>HEADER<<- opcode: QUERY, status: NOERROR, id: 49148
;; flags: qr rd ra; QUERY: 1, ANSWER: 2, AUTHORITY: 10, ADDITIONAL: 0

;; QUESTION SECTION:
;www.ipv6.org.                    IN       AAAA

;; ANSWER SECTION:
www.ipv6.org.          3285    IN       CNAME    shake.stacken.kth.se.
shake.stacken.kth.se.  3286    IN       AAAA
2001:6b0:1:ea:202:a5ff:fecd:13a6

;; AUTHORITY SECTION:
se.                    155925  IN       NS       c.ns.se.
...
```

This is a query for IPv6 reverse lookup information:

```
da1:~ # dig
6.a.3.1.d.c.e.f.f.f.5.a.2.0.2.0.a.e.0.0.1.0.0.0.0.b.6.0.1.0.0.2.ip6.
arpa ptr

; <<>> DiG 9.7.1-P2 <<>>
6.a.3.1.d.c.e.f.f.f.5.a.2.0.2.0.a.e.0.0.1.0.0.0.0.b.6.0.1.0.0.2.ip6.
arpa ptr
;; global options: +cmd
;; Got answer:
;; ->>HEADER<<- opcode: QUERY, status: NOERROR, id: 54568
;; flags: qr rd ra; QUERY: 1, ANSWER: 1, AUTHORITY: 6, ADDITIONAL: 0

;; QUESTION SECTION:
;6.a.3.1.d.c.e.f.f.f.5.a.2.0.2.0.a.e.0.0.1.0.0.0.0.b.6.0.1.0.0.2.ip6.
arpa. IN PTR

;; ANSWER SECTION:
6.a.3.1.d.c.e.f.f.f.5.a.2.0.2.0.a.e.0.0.1.0.0.0.0.b.6.0.1.0.0.2.ip6.
arpa. 3571 IN PTR igloo.stacken.kth.se.

;; AUTHORITY SECTION:
ip6.arpa.                  43777   IN       NS       b.ip6-servers.arpa.
...
```

The following is a query for cname information.

```
da1:~ # dig www.ipv6.org cname

; <<>> DiG 9.5.0-P2 <<>> www.ipv6.org cname
;; global options:  printcmd
;; Got answer:
;; ->>HEADER<<- opcode: QUERY, status: NOERROR, id: 30934
;; flags: qr rd ra; QUERY: 1, ANSWER: 1, AUTHORITY: 6, ADDITIONAL: 0

;; QUESTION SECTION:
;www.ipv6.org.                   IN      CNAME

;; ANSWER SECTION:
www.ipv6.org.           3600    IN      CNAME   shake.stacken.kth.se.

;; AUTHORITY SECTION:
org.                    41176   IN      NS      d0.org.afilias-nst.org.
...

;; Query time: 1813 msec
;; SERVER: 192.168.1.1#53(192.168.1.1)
;; WHEN: Thu Dec  9 18:21:53 2010
;; MSG SIZE  rcvd: 202
```

The following is a query for mx record information.

```
da1:~ # dig novell.com mx

; <<>> DiG 9.5.0-P2 <<>> novell.com mx
;; global options:  printcmd
;; Got answer:
;; ->>HEADER<<- opcode: QUERY, status: NOERROR, id: 62281
;; flags: qr rd ra; QUERY: 1, ANSWER: 3, AUTHORITY: 13, ADDITIONAL: 0

;; QUESTION SECTION:
;novell.com.                     IN      MX

;; ANSWER SECTION:
novell.com.       86400   IN      MX      2 prv-mx.provo.novell.com.
novell.com.       86400   IN      MX      2 prv1-mx.provo.novell.com.
novell.com.       86400   IN      MX      2 prv2-mx.provo.novell.com.

;; AUTHORITY SECTION:
.                 142882  IN      NS      m.root-servers.net.
...
```

The following is a query for soa information.

```
da1:~ # dig novell.com soa

; <<>> DiG 9.5.0-P2 <<>> novell.com soa
;; global options:  printcmd
;; Got answer:
;; ->>HEADER<<- opcode: QUERY, status: NOERROR, id: 33960
;; flags: qr rd ra; QUERY: 1, ANSWER: 1, AUTHORITY: 13, ADDITIONAL: 0

;; QUESTION SECTION:
;novell.com.                    IN      SOA

;; ANSWER SECTION:
novell.com.            20891   IN      SOA     ns.novell.com.
bwayne.novell.com. 2010120202 7200 900 604800 21600

;; AUTHORITY SECTION:
.                      142510  IN      NS      f.root-servers.net.
...
```

As you can see, a `dig` query can produce a large amount of information. Depending on your requirements, dig can be a very useful utility when troubleshooting networking configuration issues.

Objective 5   Configure DHCP

The Dynamic Host Configuration Protocol (DHCP) is used to provide hosts with IP addresses and other information on the network, such as DNS servers to be used, routings, and domain names.

The following is introduced:

- DHCP Server
- DHCP Client

DHCP Server

To configure a Linux machine as a DHCP server, the dhcp-server packages must be installed.

When the DHCP server (dhcpd) starts, it reads the configuration parameters from the `/etc/sysconfig/dhcpd` and `/etc/dhcpd.conf` files.

Before you start the DHCP server, you need to set the `DHCPD_INTERFACE` variable in the `/etc/sysconfig/dhcpd` file, such as `DHCPD_INTERFACE="eth0"`. The other variables can usually remain unchanged.

The `/etc/dhcpd.conf` file contains the information the DHCP server needs to configure the clients.

Global definitions are made at the top of the configuration file. The parameters defined here apply to all subsequent sections unless they are explicitly overwritten in the respective sections. The entries in the configuration file belong to two categories:

- **Parameter statements.** They describe how to do something (for example, define how long an IP address is leased to a client), whether to do something (for example, whether IP addresses should be assigned to unknown clients), or which parameters should be provided to clients (for example, the IP address of the default gateway).

- **Declarations.** They describe the topology of the network (for example, they can describe the clients or provide the address ranges from which to serve clients).

Each statement has to be terminated by a semicolon (";").

In case of an error in the configuration file, dhcpd will not start but will print out an error message. This message can be used to locate the error in the configuration syntax.

A simple `/etc/dhcpd.conf` file could look like the following:

```
# /etc/dhcpd.conf

ddns-update-style none;
default-lease-time 14400;
max-lease-time 172800;

option domain-name "digitalairlines.com";
```

```
option domain-name-servers 172.17.8.1;
option routers 172.17.8.1;
subnet 172.16.0.0 netmask 255.255.0.0 {
    range 172.16.9.100 172.16.9.120;
}
```

The entries above have the following significance:

- **ddns-update-style.** The DHCP server can be configured to update the information in the DNS server when the server issues an IP address to a client. Setting this to none disables this feature.

- **default-lease-time.** The DHCP server issues IP addresses to the clients with a certain lifetime in seconds (14400 seconds equals 4 hours).

  Toward the end of this lifetime, the clients connect to the server again to renew the current IP address or to get a new one.

- **max-lease-time.** The DHCP client can request a lifetime when it requests an IP address. The value of max-lease-time (in seconds) defines the maximum the server grants, even if the client requests a longer lifetime for the IP address.

- **option domain-name.** The domain name of the clients served by this DHCP server.

- **option domain-name-servers.** The IP address of the DNS server the client should use for name resolution

- **option routers.** The default gateway for the clients within the network

- **subnet.** This describes the network topology. The range specifies which IP addresses will be assigned to the clients. You can specify options specific for this subnet that would override options set above this subnet declaration.

The DHCP server can also be configured with YaST by selecting **Network Services > DHCP Server** in the *YaST Control Center*. When this YaST module is started for the first time, a configuration wizard is started, enabling a simple, basic configuration in four steps.

Information, such as which IP address was assigned to which MAC address and when it expires, is kept in the /var/lib/dhcp/db/dhcpd.leases file.

NOTE: For more information on how to configure dhcpd, see the manual page
man dhcpd, man dhcpd.conf and man dhcp-options.

The DHCP Server is started with the rcdhcpd start command. If there are errors in your configuration, the DHCP server won't start, and an error message will give you some hint where to look for the error in the /etc/dhcpd.conf file. Correct the error and start the server again. To stop the DHCP server, use the rcdhcpd stop command.

To make sure the server starts when the system boots, use the chkconfig dhcpd on command.

DHCP Client

To run a Linux host as a DHCP client, a corresponding daemon must be installed on the machine. The DHCP client daemon (dhcpcd) is included in the standard installation. An alternative included on the SLES 11 installation media is the dhcpclient from ISC (Internet System Consortium), the corporation that also publishes the BIND DNS server and ISC DHCP server.

To configure the DHCP client, the host must be instructed to obtain its IP address from a DHCP server. This is done with YaST (***Network Devices > Network Card***). When the network interface is configured to use DHCP to get the IP address, the scripts that set up the network interface start dhcpcd.

Information on the lease is kept in `/var/lib/dhcpcd/`. The file `dhcpcd-eth`*x*`.info` contains the information in human readable format. To look at it, use the `cat /var/lib/dhcpcd/dhcpcd-eth`*x*`.info` command.

Objective 6   Understand the iptables Command

The Linux kernel allows filtering of IP packets according to various rules. Packets can be accepted, dropped, or otherwise handled depending on various criteria. This makes it possible to include Linux computers as components of firewalls.

The iptables command can be used to configure IPv4 packet filtering and Network Address Translation (NAT). To work with iptables, you need to

- Understand Packet Filters

- Understand iptables Basics

- Get Familiar with Basic iptables Syntax

Rules set with the iptables command are lost when the machine is rebooted. They are therefore usually written to scripts that are integrated into the runlevel configuration (see init Scripts and Runlevel Directories). Writing such scripts is beyond the scope of this course.

NOTE: The `ip6tables` command is used to configure rules for IPv6 packets.

Understand Packet Filters

Packet filters are rule sets that allow or forbid IP packets based on criteria such as IP addresses, port numbers, and protocols. There are two types of packet filters:

- Static Packet Filters

- Dynamic (Stateful) Packet Filters

Static Packet Filters

A static packet filter does not use any information from previous packets or any application data within the packet to decide what to do with a packet. As far as the filter is concerned, every packet is completely independent of any other packet.

Let's have a look at an FTP connection to illustrate this. When transferring files using FTP, there are always two connections:

- The control connection from the client to port 21 on the server.

- The connection from port 20 on the server to a high port on the client (active FTP) or from a high port on the client to a high port on the server (passive FTP).

The information on the ports is exchanged within the control connection. If you want to allow FTP transfers through your packet filter, you need to allow

- A connection originating from a high port of the client to port 21 of the server

- A connection originating from port 20 of the server to any port above 1024 on the client (for active FTP)

    or

- A connection originating from any port above 1024 on the client to any port above 1024 on the server (for passive FTP)

However, the filter rules do not care whether or not the connection from port 20 of the server is a legitimate FTP data transfer in answer to a request on port 21. Therefore, with these rules anyone can open connections to the high ports of clients, as long as they originate at port 20. This leaves the high ports of the clients unprotected if you want to allow active FTP.

With passive FTP, the problem is the same on the server side. To allow passive FTP, a packet filter that should protect the server has to allow all connections from the high ports of clients to the high ports on the server.

When filtering TCP connections, static packet filters allow some control on the direction of the connection. You can allow packets with only the syn-flag in one direction (from the inside) while rejecting them when they come from the outside. (The first packet of the TCP handshake has only the syn-flag set.)

The packets following the first one in either direction have to be allowed as well for a successful connection.

Rejecting packets with only the syn flag set from the outside prevents the TCP handshake and thus the TCP connection.

This is not possible with UDP, because there is no handshake and no flags are set. This makes it virtually impossible to effectively filter UDP connections with static packet filters, short of blocking them completely.

Dynamic (Stateful) Packet Filters

A stateful packet filter uses information about previous packets and, to some extent, application data within the packets to decide what should happen with a packet.

Let's have a look again at an FTP connection to illustrate this.

In the beginning, only a connection from the client to port 21 of the server is allowed by a filter rule. Everything else—an answer from the server to the client as well as any connections from port 20 of the server to the client—is forbidden.

The first packet from the client to the server changes the filter rules to allow packets in answer to this first packet and any subsequent packets. To be allowed, they must correspond exactly to the first packet.

After the three-way handshake, the port to be used for the data transfer is transmitted within the control connection. The stateful packet engine reads this information from the data section within the packets of the control connection and configures the filter to allow exactly that data connection. But unlike static packet filtering, this rule is not port 20 of any server to any high port of the client, but only port 20 of this particular server to exactly port x on the client.

After a specific time without traffic elapses, the additional rules allowing these connections are removed from the filter. Only initial connections from the client to port 21 remain allowed.

The advantage of this is that, in general, no connections from port 20 of servers to the high ports of clients are allowed. This blocks any traffic originating from port 20 without a corresponding previous connection to port 21 on the same server. The same holds true for passive FTP. Only the single data connection corresponding to the control connection is allowed for a certain amount of time.

This mechanism can also be used to control UDP traffic. Rules can be set that allow packets from the outside only after a packet from the inside starts the connection. Therefore, stateful packet filtering allows you to control UDP connections much better than static filtering does.

Understand iptables Basics

`iptables` is the program used to control the packet filtering capabilities of the netfilter framework in the Linux kernel.

You use the iptables program to set or delete the packet filter rules. Because of the many ways packets can be handled, the syntax of iptables is rather complex.

To understand iptables, you need to understand:

- Chains
- Policies
- Basic Syntax

Chains

Rules are organized in a chain. Within a chain, the rules are checked one after the other until a rule matches. If no rule matches, a default action is taken. This default action is referred to as the policy of the chain.

There are several chains. The main built-in chains are

- INPUT
- OUTPUT
- FORWARD

The following figure and explanation are from packet-filtering-HOWTO-6.html (http://www.netfilter.org/documentation/HOWTO/packet-filtering-HOWTO-6.html):

Figure 6-9   *iptables Chains*

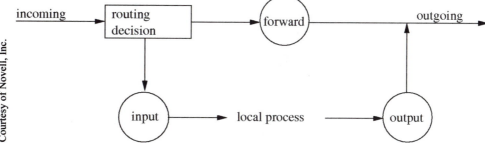

Courtesy of Novell, Inc.

The following describes the process:

1. When a packet comes in (for example, through the Ethernet card), the kernel first looks at the destination of the packet: This is called routing.

2. If the packet is destined for this computer, the packet passes downwards in the diagram to the INPUT chain.

   If it passes this, any processes waiting for that packet will receive it.

3. Otherwise, if the kernel does not have forwarding enabled or if it doesn't know how to forward the packet, the packet is dropped.

   If forwarding is enabled and the packet is destined for another network interface (if you have another one), then the packet goes rightwards on the diagram to the FORWARD chain.

   If it is ACCEPTed, it will be sent out.

4. Finally, a program running on the computer can send network packets.

   These packets pass through the OUTPUT chain immediately: If it says ACCEPT, then the packet continues out to whatever interface it is destined for.

Policies

The policy decides what happens to a packet that did not match a rule in the chain. The policy could either be to accept the packet or to drop it.

Two approaches are possible:

- Everything is forbidden, except if explicitly allowed.
- Everything is allowed, except if explicitly forbidden.

From a security viewpoint, only the first approach is valid.

To set the policy, use the -P option:

```
iptables -P FORWARD DROP
```

Basic Syntax

iptables is called with various options to specify a rule. If a rule matches, the target of the rule is executed, usually accepting, rejecting, or dropping the packet.

After a match, the subsequent rules are usually not checked. Therefore, the sequence of the rules in the chain is of critical importance.

iptables options let you

- Add and delete rules.

  The following commands are possible:

  - -A. Add a rule to the end of the chain.
  - -D. Delete a rule.

- □   **-R.** Replace a rule.

- □   **-I.** Insert a rule.

  For instance, to insert a rule at position 3 of the chain, enter

  ```
  iptables -I INPUT 3 ...
  ```

- ■   Manipulate whole chains.

  The following commands are possible:

  - □   **-F.** Delete (flush) all rules from a chain.

  - □   **-Z.** Zero the byte counter of a chain.

  - □   **-L.** List the rules of a chain (add -v for more information).

  - □   **-N.** Create a user-defined (new) chain.

  - □   **-E.** Rename a user-defined chain.

  - □   **-X.** Delete an empty user-defined chain.

- ■   Define matching rules.

  Matches can be based, for instance, on interfaces, ports, or IP addresses.

  Not every possible option has to be specified. If an option (the destination port, for example) is not specified, it is not taken into consideration.

  - □   Specify the interface: `-i` for input, `-o` for output: `-i eth0`

    `-o` cannot be used in the INPUT chain; `-i` is not possible in the OUTPUT chain.

  - □   Specify the protocol: `-p TCP`, `-p UDP`

    The protocol can be specified with its abbreviation or the number of the protocol from `/etc/protocols`. Both lower and upper case are acceptable.

  - □   Specify source and/or destination IP: `-s 1.2.3.4`, `-d 192.168.0.0/24`

  - □   Specify source and/or destination port: `--sport 1024:65535`, `--dport 80`

    You can specify a single port or port ranges (***start:end***). The port you put in the rules depends on the service you want to access. `/etc/services` lists the ports and the service that can usually be found on that port.

    While UDP and TCP usually have the same service on the same port, this is not necessarily so. See Ports and Port Numbers for frequently used ports and the services associated with them.

  Additional matches can be used with the option `-m`.

- ■   Set the target.

  The target specifies what happens to a packet that matches a rule.

After a match, subsequent rules (with the exception of LOG) are not checked. The target is given after the option -j (jump). Possible targets are

- **ACCEPT.** Depending on the chain, the packet is forwarded, delivered to a local process, or sent out via a network interface.

- **REJECT.** The packet is discarded and, depending on the type of packet, a message (default: ICMP port unreachable) is sent to the source of the packet.

- **DROP.** The packet is silently discarded.

- **LOG.** Unlike with other rules, the packet continues down the chain after it matches a logging rule. Therefore, if you want to log packets that are rejected or dropped, put a logging rule right before the rule dropping the packet.

  Logging packets, especially rejected ones, is useful. When writing your rules, a log can be used to debug your script, and when your rules are in force, a log can give you an idea of what packets hit your packet filter.

  Packets are usually logged in /var/log/firewall. But you can configure syslog to log them into a file of their own.

- **A user-defined chain.** User-defined chains are not covered in this course.

The following are some examples of iptables rules:

- To block all incoming packets on eth1 with a source IP of 10.*x.x.x*, enter

  ```
  iptables -A INPUT -i eth1 -s 10.0.0.0/8 -j DROP
  ```

  The rule is added at the end of the chain (-A).

- To reject all incoming TCP packets on eth1 with a source IP of 10.*x.x.x*, enter

  ```
  iptables -A INPUT -i eth1 -p tcp -s 10.0.0.0/255.0.0.0
  -j REJECT
  ```

  The default for REJECT is to send an ICMP Port Unreachable message, if applicable. (For example, no ICMP messages are sent in response to certain ICMP messages.)

- To specify the ICMP message (or a TCP reset) to be sent, enter

  ```
  -j REJECT --reject-with type
  ```

  Replace *type* with the ICMP message you want sent (icmp-proto-unreachable, icmp-host-unreachable, or tcp-reset, for example).

- To accept all incoming ICMP packets on eth1, enter

  ```
  iptables -A INPUT -i eth1 -p icmp -j ACCEPT
  ```

NOTE: You should not indiscriminately block all ICMP packets on your firewall. If you consider blocking them at all, you should only block certain types of packets; otherwise, network performance could suffer.

Candidates for blocking are timestamp request and reply, information request and reply, address mask request and reply, and redirect.

In any event, you should allow fragmentation-needed messages. Put a rate limit on the others, if you want, or just accept them. You can get a list of types by using iptables -p ICMP --help.

- To accept all outgoing TCP packets to port 80, enter

  ```
  iptables -A OUTPUT -p tcp --dport 80 -j ACCEPT
  ```

  Usually a second rule is needed to take care of the packets received in answer.

- To accept all incoming TCP packets from port 80 (not only the syn-bit set, ! is used to negate an option), enter

  ```
  iptables -A INPUT -p tcp ! --syn --sport 80 -j ACCEPT
  ```

- To log a packet, use the LOG target. To make the log entries more informative, a string that appears in the log file should be entered in the rule:

  ```
  iptables -A INPUT -p tcp --syn --dport 25 -j LOG --log-prefix "SMTP traffic: "
  ```

  This produces the following entry in /var/log/firewall when a new connection is made to port 25:

  ```
  Apr 14 12:01:02 dal kernel: SMTP traffic: IN=eth0 OUT=
  MAC=00:11:11:c2:35:f4:00:11:25:82:d7:f9:08:00 SRC=192.168.1.4
  DST=10.0.0.10 LEN=60 TOS=0x10 PREC=0x00 TTL=64 ID=8108 DF PROTO=TCP
  SPT=1984 DPT=25 WINDOW=5840 RES=0x00 SYN URGP=0
  ```

Exercise 6-3   ***Get Familiar with Basic iptables Syntax***

The purpose of this exercise is to familiarize you with the iptables syntax and to show the effect of some iptables rules.

You will find this exercise at the end of the chapter.

(End of Exercise)

Summary

Objective	Summary
Understand TCP/IP and Linux Network Terms	The protocol used to connect computers within the Internet is TCP/IP.
	Each computer has a unique 32-bit IP address. TCP and UDP use port numbers to be able to address specific applications.
	ARP is used to associate IP addresses with MAC addresses.
	ICMP is used to transmit error and other messages relating to the transmission of IP packets.
	The following terms are used for the Linux network configuration: ■ Device ■ Interface ■ Link ■ Address ■ Broadcast ■ Route
Manage the Network Configuration Information from YaST	The YaST module for configuring the network card and the network connection can be found at ***Network Devices > Network Settings***.
	The following details are then needed to integrate the network device into an existing network: ■ Method of network setup ■ Static IP address ■ Network mask ■ Hostname ■ Name server ■ Routing (gateway)
	After you save the configuration with YaST, the Ethernet card should be available in the computer. You can verify this with the `ip address show` command.

Objective	Summary
Manage the Network Configuration with Command Line Tools	You can perform the following tasks with the ip tool: ■ Display the IP address setup: `ip address show` ■ Display device attributes: `ip link show` ■ Display device statistics: `ip -s link show` ■ Assign an IP address: `ip address add` *IP_address/netmask* `brd + dev` *device_name* ■ Delete an IP address: `ip address del` *IP_address* `dev` *device_name* ■ View the routing table: `ip route show` ■ Add routes to the routing table: `ip route add` *network*/*netmask* `dev` *device_name* ■ Delete routes from the routing table: `ip route del` *network*/*netmask* `dev` *device_name* The configuration files for network devices are located in `/etc/sysconfig/network/`. Configured devices can be enabled with `ifup` *device_name* and disabled with `ifdown` *device_name*. The configuration for the routing table is located in the `/etc/sysconfig/network/routes` file. The hostname is configured in the `/etc/HOSTNAME` file. Name resolution is configured in the `/etc/resolv.conf` file. One line specifies the search domain; the others list up to three available name servers.
Troubleshoot Networking Issues	Frequently used command line tools available to test the network connection are ■ **ping.** You can test whether another host in the network is reachable. ■ **traceroute.** You can test the routing in the network. ■ **telnet.** The telnet command can be used for Telnet connections; it can also be used to check the availability of TCP-based services. ■ **netstat.** The netstat command is used to list available services bound to sockets and the state of IP connections.

Objective	Summary
Configure DHCP	The dhcpd configuration is contained in the `/etc/sysconfig/dhcpd` and `/etc/dhcpd.conf` files.
	The `/etc/sysconfig/dhcpd` file contains an entry for the network interface on which the DHCP server listens.
	The `/etc/dhcpd.conf` file contains a number of entries that describe the network topology, influence the behavior of the server, or contain information transmitted to the clients.
	The entries in the `/etc/dhcpd.conf` file belong to two categories:
	■ Parameter statements
	■ Declarations
	The records of the IP addresses already given are written to the `/var/lib/dhcp/db/dhcpd.leases` file.
	The configuration file for each network interface is located in the `/etc/sysconfig/network/` directory. This file contains the values with which a network card should be activated.
	To configure a Linux host as a DHCP client, software packages, like the dhcpcd must be installed on the machine (included in the standard installation).
	Options for the DHCP client are stored in the `/etc/sysconfig/network/dhcp` file.
Understand the iptables Command	Packet filters control the IP traffic mainly based on information found in TCP/IP headers.
	`iptables` is the program used to control the filtering capabilities of the Linux kernel.
	Rules can be defined based on IP address, protocol, port, and interface. Rules can discard packets entirely, accept them, or reject them with an error code.

Key Terms

/etc/dhcpd.conf – The file that lists the IP configuration information that the DHCP daemon provides to network computers.

/etc/HOSTNAME – A file that contains the name of the host.

/etc/hosts – A local file that contains host names and their respective IP addresses.

/etc/nsswitch.conf – A file that lists the order that programs will use when attempting to connect to databases and files.

/etc/resolv.conf – A file that lists up to three DNS servers and which may be contacted to resolve a remote host name to an IP address.

/etc/sysconfig/dhcpd – The main configuration file for the DHCP daemon.

/etc/sysconfig/network – The directory that contains most network configuration information.

/etc/sysconfig/network/ifcfg-template – A template file that may be used to create the TCP/IP configuration for a network interface.

/etc/sysconfig/network/routes – A file that stores static routes for use on the system.

Address Resolution Protocol (ARP) – A part of the TCP/IP protocol suite that resolves IP addresses to physical hardware addresses.

arp command – Used to view and clear the ARP cache on a computer.

chain – A component of IP tables that identifies the direction of traffic that packet filters can match.

datagram – A unit of information sent on a UDP/IP network.

default gateway – The router that connects a network to other networks. Packets whose destination networks are not included in the routing table are sent to the default gateway.

default route – See default gateway.

DHCP client – A computer that obtains IP configuration from a DHCP server on the network.

DHCP server – A computer that provides IP configuration to other computers on the network.

dig command – Used to test DNS name resolution.

DNS server – A server that contains records for hosts on a network. It may be queried to resolve a host name to an IP address.

domain – A portion of DNS.

Domain Name System (DNS) – The naming system used on the Internet. Each host is identified by a host name and domain name.

Dynamic Host Configuration Protocol (DHCP) – A protocol that is used to assign TCP/IP configuration information to a host on the network.

dynamic packet filter – A packet filter that uses information from other packets to determine whether a packet should be allowed or denied.

Ethernet – The standard method used to access network media today. Most network adapters on networks use Ethernet.

firewall – A software feature that allows a host to drop IP packets that meet a certain criteria set by packet filters.

hardware address – See Media Access Control (MAC) address.

host – A computer or device that can communicate on a network.

ifconfig command – Used to view, configure, and manage IP addresses on a network interface.

ifdown command – Used to deactivate a network interface.

ifup command – Used to activate a network interface.

Internet Control Message Protocol (ICMP) – A part of the TCP/IP protocol suite that is used to relay information about network communications.

Internet Protocol (IP) – A part of the TCP/IP protocol suite used to send packets of data on a TCP/IP or UDP/IP network.

Internet Protocol (IP) address – A unique address used to identify a computer on a TCP/IP network.

ip command – Used to view, configure, and manage network interfaces and the routing table.

IP tables – The software components on a Linux system that provide firewall capabilities.

ip6tables command – Used to configure IPv6 packet filters on a Linux system.

iptables command – Used to configure IPv4 packet filters on a Linux system.

IPv4 – The current version of the TCP/IP protocol suite.

IPv6 – A new version of the TCP/IP protocol suite that contains a larger address space and improvements to routing and security.

iwconfig command – Used to view, configure, and manage IP addresses on a wireless network interface.

Local Area Network (LAN) – A series of computers that are connected to each other in close proximity (e.g., within the same building).

loopback – An IP address that refers to the local host.

Media Access Control (MAC) address – A hardware address that is assigned to network interfaces and used to uniquely identify it to other network interfaces on the same LAN.

name server – See DNS server.

netmask (network mask) – See subnet mask.

netstat command – Displays the routing table as well as network and network interface statistics for the local computer.

network service – A user or daemon process that provides functionality for other computers on the network.

node – See host.

packet – A unit of information sent on a TCP/IP network.

packet filter – Sets of rules that are used to determine whether an IP packet should be allowed or denied by a computer.

ping command – Used to test network connectivity using ICMP.

policy – A component of IP tables that identifies the action that is taken on a packet that matches a packet filter.

port – A number that uniquely identifies a network service running on a computer.

protocol – The format used by packets of information as they are sent across a network. They can be routable or nonroutable as well as connection-oriented or connectionless.

route command – Used to view and modify the routing table.

router – A device that is used to relay packets from one network to another.

routing – The process of sending IP packets from one IP network to another.

routing table – A table that is stored on each host and which contains a list of local and remote networks and routers.

socket – An established network connection between two hosts. TCP uses STREAM sockets, whereas UDP uses DGRAM sockets.

stateful packet filter – See dynamic packet filter.

static packet filter – A packet filter that does not use information from other packets to determine whether a packet should be allowed or denied.

subnet mask – A number used to determine which portions of an IP address represent the network and host.

telnet command – Used to obtain a shell on a remote UNIX or Linux system without encryption. It can also be used to interact with network services on remote hosts.

traceroute command – Used to identify the route an IP packet takes to a remote host.

transmission media – The media used to connect computers together on a LAN.

Transport Control Protocol (TCP) – A part of the TCP/IP protocol suite that provides reliable connection-oriented communication between hosts on a network.

Transport Control Protocol/Internet Protocol (TCP/IP) – A suite of protocols that are used to communicate with other computers on a network.

User Datagram Protocol (UDP) – A part of the TCP/IP protocol suite that provides fast but unreliable (connectionless) communication between hosts on a network.

Wide Area Network (WAN) – A series of computers that are connected to each other across large distances (e.g., the Internet).

Chapter Exercises

Exercise 6-1   ***Manage the Network Configuration Information from YaST***

Up to now, your system got all network configuration information via DHCP. In this exercise, you change all the important information into static values.

Use the `ip` command to find out which ip address you are currently using on eth0. Also note your current host name. Then change the network configuration to static IP addresses, using the values you found.

This exercise is performed on the da-host server.

Detailed Steps to Complete the Exercise

Do the following:

1. Open a terminal window.

2. Enter `ip address show`, `ip route show`, and `cat /etc/resolv.conf` to list the following information for your SLES 11 server (record it here for future reference):

   - IP address:

   - Hostname:

   - Default gateway:

   - Name server:

3. Close the terminal window.

4. From the main menu, select ***System > Yast***.

5. Enter the root password novell, then select ***Continue*** or press Enter.

6. Start the network card module by selecting ***Network Devices > Network Settings***.

7. In the Global Options tab, make sure that ***Traditional Method with ifup*** is selected.

8. (Conditional) If you need to change the settings to ***Traditional Method with ifup***, select ***OK***.

   You are returned to *Yast* and must return to ***Network Settings***.

9. In the Overview tab, make sure your network card is selected, then select ***Edit***.

10. Make sure that the ***Address*** tab is activated.

11. Switch the setup by selecting ***Statically assigned IP address***.

12. In the IP Address field, enter the *IP address* from Step 2.

13. In the Subnet mask field, enter **255.255.255.0**.

14. In the Hostname field, enter da-host.

15. Select ***Next***.

    You are returned to the ***Network Settings*** window.

16. In the *Hostname/DNS* tab, verify the hostname is **da-host**.

17. In the Domain Name field, enter **digitalairlines.com**.

18. In the Name Server 1 field, enter the *IP address* of your DNS server.

19. If there are values in the other *Name Server* text fields, remove them.

20. In the Domain Search field, enter **digitalairlines.com**.

21. If there are values in the other *Domain Search* text fields, remove them.

22. Select *OK*.

23. Select *Routing*.

24. In the Default Gateway field, enter the *IP address* of your Internet gateway.

25. Select *OK*.

26. Close the YaST Control Center.

27. To test your network connection, start the web browser Firefox and try to connect to www.novell.com (http://www.novell.com).

(End of Exercise)

Exercise 6-2   Configure the Network Connection Manually

The purpose of this exercise is to familiarize you with manually configuring network settings. You use the `ip` command to find out the current settings for IP address, routes, and mac address; you use the `ip` command to add a second IP address to eth0 manually; and you add the new address to the configuration file.

This exercise is done on the da1 virtual machine.

Detailed Steps to Complete the Exercise

Do the following:

1. If necessary, power on your da1 virtual server and log in as geeko with a password of **novell**.

2. Open a terminal window and `su` – to root using a password of **novell**.

3. Enter `ip address show eth0`.

4. Under eth0, find the line starting with `inet` and record the IP address with the subnet mask displayed in that line:

   - IP address:

   - Subnet mask:

5. Enter

   `ip route show`

   Notice that a default gateway has not been assigned.

6. Enter

   `ip link show eth0`

7. Find the line starting with `link/ether` and record the MAC address of the network card:

   - MAC address:

8. Enter the following command at the shell prompt:

   `ip address add 172.17.8.201/16 brd + dev eth0`

9. View the new configuration by entering the following command:

   `ip address show eth0`

   You should see two IP addresses.

10. In the terminal window, enter

    `cd /etc/sysconfig/network`

11. Open the `ifcfg-eth0` file in a text editor by entering `vi ifcfg-eth0` at the shell prompt.

12. Add the following lines to the file:

    `IPADDR_2='172.17.8.201/16'`

13. Save the file and close the editor.

14. Reboot your da1 virtual machine by entering `init 6` at the shell prompt.

   Wait while the system reboots.

15. After rebooting, log in as geeko with a password of **novell**.

16. Open a terminal window.

17. Change to root using the `su -` command and a password of **novell**.

18. Verify that the network configuration loaded correctly by entering the following commands:

   `ip address show eth0`

   You should see two IP addresses.

(End of Exercise)

Exercise 6-3   ***Set iptables Rules on the Command Line***

The purpose of this exercise is to show you how iptables is used and the effect the commands have.

Create rules to block incoming and outgoing ICMP messages. View the rules, test them using ping, and then delete them.

Create a rule that prevents others from connecting to your ssh server; use one with the target DROP, test it, and then delete it; create a new rule with the target REJECT, test again, note any difference, and then delete it.

You will set the rules on the da1 virtual machine and test them from your da-host server.

Detailed Steps to Complete the Exercise

Do the following:

1. On da-1, open a terminal window and `su` – to root with a password of novell.

2. Determine if any rules have been set already by entering

   ```
   iptables -v -L -n
   ```

3. If there are any rules in the INPUT, OUTPUT, or FORWARD chain, delete them by entering

   ```
   iptables -F
   ```

4. From da-host, `ping` your da1 virtual machine.

5. Set a rule blocking all ICMP packets to your computer coming from other computers by entering

   ```
   iptables -A INPUT -i eth0 -p icmp -j DROP
   ```

   (This is only an example. Blocking all ICMP messages is generally not advisable.)

6. View the current ruleset by entering

   ```
   iptables -v -L -n
   ```

7. From da-host, `ping` your da1 virtual machine. You should not see any responses.

8. Delete the rule you set in Step 5 by entering

   ```
   iptables -D INPUT -i eth0 -p icmp -j DROP
   ```

9. Set a rule blocking all ICMP packets from your computer to other computers by entering

   ```
   iptables -A OUTPUT -o eth0 -p icmp -j DROP
   ```

10. From da-host, send an echo request to your da1 virtual machine.

    From da1, `ping` da-host (171.17.8.1). (You will notice a slightly different output of the `ping` command compared to Step 7 above.)

11. Delete the rule you set in Step 9 by entering

    ```
    iptables -D OUTPUT -o eth0 -p icmp -j DROP
    ```

12. Set a rule blocking all ICMP packets in the FORWARD chain by entering

    ```
    iptables -A FORWARD -p icmp -j DROP
    ```

    As there is only one NIC in your virtual machine, you cannot test this rule.

    However, you can test if this rule affects traffic to and from da1 (which it shouldn't) by pinging da1 from da-host and da-host from da1.

13. Flush your ruleset by entering

    ```
    iptables -F
    ```

14. Find out what happens when you use ssh from da-host to da1 by entering

    ```
    ssh geeko@172.17.1.101
    ```

    When asked if you are sure you want to continue connecting, enter yes. Then enter the password novell. After you have successfully logged in, log out again by pressing Ctrl+D.

15. Create an iptables rule that drops incoming TCP packets addressed to port 22 (SSH) by entering

    ```
    iptables -A INPUT -i eth0 -p tcp --dport 22 -j DROP
    ```

16. Try again to log in to da1 using ssh and notice how the results differ from the results in Step 14.

17. Change the rule from Step 15 to use REJECT as its target instead of DROP.

    You can either delete the rule and create a new one, or replace the rule by entering

    ```
    iptables -R INPUT 1 -i eth0 -p tcp --dport 22 -j REJECT
    ```

18. View the current ruleset by entering

    ```
    iptables -v -L -n
    ```

19. Try again to ssh to da1 from da-host and find out if there is any difference to before. If yes, why is that?

20. Change the rule from Step 17 to REJECT with a TCP reset, instead of the ICMP message port unreachable, by entering (on one line)

    ```
    iptables -R INPUT 1 -i eth0 -p tcp --dport 22 -j REJECT
    --reject-with tcp-reset
    ```

21. View the current ruleset by entering

    ```
    iptables -v -L -n
    ```

22. Again connect to da1 from da-host using ssh and find out if you get different results.

23. Flush your ruleset by entering

    ```
    iptables -F
    ```

(End of Exercise)

Review Questions

1. What must each computer have in order to participate on a TCP/IP network as well as contact hosts on remote networks by name? (Choose all that apply.)
   a) IP address
   b) netmask
   c) DNS server
   d) default gateway

2. What IPv4 address is reserved for loopback?

3. What name is used to identify the first wired Ethernet network interface in Linux?

4. What file stores the list of DNS servers that your computer can contact to resolve hostnames into IP addresses?
   a) /etc/resolv.conf
   b) /etc/sysconfig/network/scripts
   c) /etc/dns.sysconfig
   d) /etc/sysconfig/network/ifcfg-dns

5. At what TCP/IP layer does the IP protocol exist?
   a) The network access layer
   b) The Internet layer
   c) The transport layer
   d) The application layer

6. What **ifconfig** command can you use to configure the IP address 192.168.1.1 and default subnet mask on your first wired Ethernet network interface?

7. Which of the following commands may be used to view IP configuration? (Choose all that apply.)
   a) ifshow eth0
   b) ip address show
   c) ifconfig -a
   d) ifstat eth0

8. What file contains the information used to configure your second wired Ethernet network interface at boot time?

9. What line would you configure in the file described in Question 10 to obtain an IP configuration from a DHCP server?

10. You need to find the port number that is used by a particular network service. What file can you look in?
    a) /etc/host.conf
    b) /etc/sysconfig/network/services
    c) /etc/services
    d) /etc/nsswitch.conf

11. Which two commands could you type at a command prompt to add a route to the 188.16.0.0 network via the router 192.168.1.254?
    a) ip route add 188.16.0.0/16 via 192.168.1.254
    b) route add 188.16.0.0 via 192.168.1.254
    c) ip route add gw 192.168.1.254 via 188.16.0.0/16
    d) route add —net 188.16.0.0 netmask 255.255.0.0 gw 192.168.1.254

12. What file could you use to configure the static route configured in Question 13 for use with all network interfaces on your system?

13. What command could you use to send five ICMP requests to the host 192.168.1.254?

14. What command could you use to test DNS name resolution for the www.yahoo.com host name?

15. What option to the netstat command could you use to display the routing table?

16. Which of the following commands can be used to test network connectivity issues? (Choose all that apply.)
    a) netstat
    b) ping
    c) traceroute
    d) telnet

17. Which of the following files contains the IP subnet information and options that have been issued to DHCP clients?
    a) /etc/dhcpd.conf
    b) /etc/sysconfig/dhcpd
    c) /var/lib/dhcp/db/dhcpd.leases
    d) /etc/dhcp.conf

18. Which chain can contain rules that pertain to traffic that is destined for the local computer?
    a) LOCAL
    b) INPUT
    c) OUTPUT
    d) FORWARD

19. What command can you use to prevent your Linux router from forwarding any traffic?

20. Which target in an iptables command will drop a packet and send a message to the original host?
    a) DROP
    b) LOG
    c) MESSAGE
    d) REJECT

Discovery Exercises

Practicing Network Interface Commands

Log in to tty1 as the **root** user and perform the following actions in order. For each action, write the command(s) that you used. When finished, log out of tty1.

1. Configure your first Ethernet adapter such that your IP address is 10.10.10.x (where x is a unique student number assigned by your instructor).

2. View your IP configuration.

3. Deactivate and reactivate your first Ethernet adapter.

4. View your IP configuration. What file does this configuration come from?

Configuring IP Aliases

A single network interface can be configured to use multiple IP addresses. Log in to tty1 as the **root** user and perform the following actions in order. Where applicable, write down the command(s) that you used for each action. When finished, log out of tty1.

1. Run the command **ifconfig eth0:1 10.10.10.x** (where x is a unique student number assigned by your instructor). This will configure an IP alias for your first Ethernet adapter such that your first virtual IP address is 10.10.10.x.

2. View your IP configuration.

3. Use the **ping** command to verify both IP addresses bound to eth0.

4. Deactivate and reactivate your first Ethernet adapter.

Routing Commands

Log in to tty1 as the **root** user and perform the following actions in order. For each action, write the command(s) that you used. When finished, log out of tty1.

1. View the routing table and write down the IP address of your default gateway.

2. Create a route to the 42.0.0.0 network via your default gateway using the **route** command.

3. Create a route to the 43.0.0.0 network via your default gateway using the **ip** command.

4. Explain why you haven't created incorrect routes in 2. and 3.

5. View the routing table to verify your routes.

6. Remove all routes from your system.

SECTION 7   Configure Applications and Services

This section covers various services that are frequently offered by Linux servers and are part of the objectives of the LPIC Level One exam.

Objectives

1. Configure the Samba Server
2. Configure the Apache Web Server
3. Enable an FTP Server
4. Configure Electronic Mail
5. Configure a CUPS Server
6. Configure a DNS Server with BIND
7. Configure the NTPD
8. Enable xinetd
9. Configure the Proxy Server Squid

Objective 1   Configure the Samba Server

Using Samba, a Linux system can be configured as a file and print server for Linux, Mac OSX, and Windows workstations. Essentially, Samba allows your Linux system to emulate a Windows server. Users can access shared directories and printers on the Linux server just as they would on a Windows server. You can configure Samba as a domain controller. You can even join an Active Directory domain.

The key to making all of this work is the fact that Samba uses the Server Message Block (SMB) protocol. To fully implement Samba, you need to have a solid understanding of SMB. In this objective, you learn the following:

- Understand the Server Message Block Protocol
- Configure a Simple File Server with Samba
- Configure Local Samba Authentication
- Use Samba's Client Tools
- Configure and Access a Samba Server

Understand the Server Message Block Protocol

The Server Message Block (SMB) protocol is used to allow access to files and printers. To help you understand the SMB protocol, the following topics are covered:

- SMB Overview
- NetBIOS Overview
- How SMB Communications Work
- How Samba Works

SMB Overview

The earliest version of the SMB protocol was developed by IBM in the 1980s. The protocol was later integrated natively into the Windows desktop and server operating systems. SMB has also been integrated into Linux/UNIX as well. Using the Samba package, a Linux server can also support native Windows clients.

The SMB protocol implements **sharing**. Shared resources, such as directories and printers, are referenced using the Universal Naming Convention (UNC). UNC uses the following syntax to identify a share:

```
\\server_name\share_name
```

For example, if you had a SLES 11 server named DA1 with Samba configured, you could create a directory named /home/shared as a place for network users to store their files. Using Samba, you could share this directory with the share name shared. To reference the share, you would use a UNC of \\DA1\shared.

You can also use a URL to reference an SMB share, as shown below:

```
smb://server_name/share_name
```

SMB operates at the Application and Presentation layers of the OSI model. The role of SMB is to provide clients with access to the file system and printers on a server. SMB uses the internal security of the server file system to determine what the client can and cannot do.

NetBIOS Overview

Because it's an upper-layer protocol, SMB can't operate alone. It must be implemented in conjunction with a middle-layer protocol. The most common implementation is to use SMB in conjunction with Network Basic Input/Output System (NetBIOS) protocol on top of IP.

NetBIOS was originally developed in the mid-1980s and is used as the basic networking protocol for the Windows operating system. NetBIOS operates at the Session layer of the OSI model. As such, it has no routing capabilities. To make NetBIOS routable, you have to use it in conjunction with a Network-layer protocol, such as IPX or IP.

This relationship is shown in the figure below:

Figure 7-1   *The Relationship Between SMB, NetBIOS, TCP, and IP*

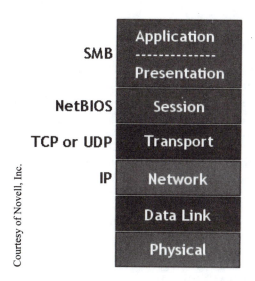

As you know, IP uses a numerical IP address to uniquely identify each network host. NetBIOS, on the other hand, uses a 16-byte, 15-character alphanumeric name to uniquely identify network hosts.

The very last byte of a NetBIOS name (called the *NetBIOS Suffix*) is not used for the name value. Instead, it is used to identify the type of host. A workstation will have a value of 00 (hex). A server will have a hex value of 20. A Primary Domain Controller (PDC) or a Backup Domain Controller (BDC) will have a hex value of 1C.

Any given system can have both a NetBIOS name and a hostname. These two names are completely separate. Because NetBIOS works on top of IP, you need to be able to resolve NetBIOS names into IP addresses, just as you need to resolve hostnames and DNS names into IP addresses.

In NetBIOS, name resolution is done using a Windows Internet Naming Service (WINS) server. A WINS server works much like a DNS server. When a NetBIOS computer is booted on the network, it does the following:

- If a WINS server is detected on the network, the NetBIOS computer registers itself with the server on startup.

  If its NetBIOS name is not already in use, the WINS server puts the system's name and IP address in its database. All other NetBIOS hosts can send queries to the WINS server to resolve the NetBIOS name into an IP address.

- If a WINS server is not detected, the NetBIOS computer will simply broadcast its NetBIOS name on the network when it boots.

  If another system is already using that NetBIOS name, an error will be generated indicating that a name conflict exists.

  Hosts still need to be able to resolve NetBIOS names into IP addresses. To do this without a WINS server, a NetBIOS host that needs to contact another host sends out a broadcast. The host with the requested NetBIOS name responds back with its IP address.

How SMB Communications Work

When you attempt to open an SMB connection, the NetBIOS protocol is used to establish a connection at the Session layer between the sending and receiving systems. Once a NetBIOS session has been established, clients and servers communicate with each other at the upper layers of the OSI model with the SMB protocol, using Server Message Blocks (SMBs).

SMBs contain commands that establish communications and manipulate shared directories, files, and printers. SMBs work on a command/response model.

Consider the following SMB session: A user on a workstation needs to create a file on a server, add content to the file, and save it. The SMB commands and responses required to do this include the following:

1. The client sends an SMBNegProt command to the server. This tells the server which dialect of SMB it's using.

NOTE: There are many different SMB protocol versions and dialects.

---

2. The server sends an SMBNegProt response back to the client, agreeing on the dialect to be used.

3. The client sends an SMBSessetup command to the server. This SMB contains the username and password of the user.

4. If the username and password are valid, the server responds with an SMBSessetup response reporting that the user is authenticated.

5. The client sends an SMBtcon command. This tells the server which share it wants to use.

6. The server responds with an SMBtcon response, telling the client that it has been granted permission to use the share.

7. The client sends an SMBmknew command. This SMB tells the server to create a new file.

8. The server sends an SMBmknew response after the file has been created.

9. The client sends an SMBopen command that tells the server to open the file that was just created.

10. The client sends an SMBread command. The server responds with the requested file.

    At this point, the user can work on the open file from the client workstation.

11. When the editing is complete, the file is saved and closed. The client sends an SMBwriteclose command.

12. The server system writes the file to disk and closes it.

In addition to the SMBs discussed in the example above, many other commands can be used when working with shared resources on the server, including the following:

- **SMBcopy.** Copies files

- **SMBmove.** Moves files

- **SMBsplopen.** Opens a print spool for printing

How Samba Works

The Samba service on a SLES 11 system allows Samba clients to connect to shared directories and printers on your server. You can use Samba for the following purposes:

- Provide file and print services for Samba clients (such as Windows, OSX, and Linux workstations).

- Act as a domain controller for Windows clients.

- Integrate into an existing Windows domain for authentication purposes.

The server side of Samba consists of two daemons:

- **nmbd.** Handles all NetBIOS-related tasks. It can also provide a WINS server.

- **smbd.** Provides file and print services for clients in the network.

In addition, to integrate the Samba server into a Windows environment, Samba also provides the following services and utilities:

- **winbind.** Integrates a Linux system into a Windows authentication system, such as Active Directory. Essentially, it allows Windows domain users to function as local Linux users.

- **nmblookup.** Used for NetBIOS name resolution and testing.

- **smbclient.** Provides access to SMB file and print services.

Configure a Simple File Server with Samba

SLES 11 includes Samba version 3.2.7. You can find more information about the Novell/SUSE Samba packages at en.opensuse.org/Samba (http://en.opensuse.org/Samba).

To set up a simple file server with Samba, you need to be familiar with the following tasks:

- Installing Samba on the Server

- Use the Samba Configuration File

Installing Samba on the Server

To configure a file server, the following Samba packages need to be installed:

- **samba.** Main Samba package. It contains the Samba server software.

- **samba-client.** Contains the Samba client tools.

- **samba-doc (optional).** Provides additional documentation about Samba.

NOTE: The samba and samba-client packages are installed by default during the installation of SLES 11.

You can verify that the packages are installed with the `rpm -q samba` and `rpm -q samba-client` commands. If they are installed, rpm displays the installed version; if they are not, an error message informs you that the package is not installed.

You can start the Samba daemons with the following commands in a terminal window as root:

```
rcnmb start
rcsmb start
```

To start the Samba services automatically when the system is booting, enter the following commands in a terminal window as root:

```
insserv nmb
insserv smb
```


Use the Samba Configuration File

The Samba service is configured in the `/etc/samba/smb.conf` file. The options in this file are grouped into several sections. Each section starts with a keyword in square brackets.

In this part of the course, you learn how to set up a simple file server with Samba. You need to be able to

- Configure General Server Options

- Share Users' Home Directories

- Configure Shares

- Share Printers

- Test the Samba Configuration

Configure General Server Options

The first task you need to be familiar with is configuring general server options in the smb.conf file. The general server configuration section starts with the keyword [global]. The following is an example of a basic global section:

```
[global]
    workgroup = DigitalAirlines
    netbios name = DA1
    security = user
    server string = DA1 File Server
```

The entries of the global section in this example are described below:

- **workgroup = DigitalAirlines.** Defines the name of the workgroup or domain the Samba server will participate in.

- **netbios name = DA1.** Used to manually set the NetBIOS name of the Samba server. If you don't include this parameter, the NetBIOS name will default to the server's hostname.

- **security = user.** Determines how a client has to authenticate itself when accessing a share. This option can have the following values:

    - **share.** (Deprecated) Authentication is handled on a per-share basis. Each share in the system is assigned its own password. Client systems can access the share by simply providing the share's password. Usernames are not checked.

    - **user.** Authentication is handled on a per-user basis. An SMB client must first authenticate with a valid username and password to the Samba server before it is allowed to access shared resources on the server. This is the default value if the security option isn't explicitly included in smb.conf.

    - **server.** Specifies that the client must provide a username and password when it connects to the server. Samba contacts another SMB server in the network to validate the password. This is usually used in a workgroup configuration.

   ❑ **domain.** All authentication processes are handled by a remote primary domain controller or a backup domain controller. This value is usually used in a domain configuration.

   ❑ **ads.** Specifies that Samba act as domain member of an ADS realm to validate the username and password.

  ■ **server string.** Provides a description of the Samba server that will be displayed in My Network Places for Windows clients. This text string can contain any value you want. If you don't include this parameter, smbd will default to a description of Samba *samba_version_number*.

In addition to the above, you can also include the following global server options, if required for your particular implementation:

  ■ **encrypt passwords.** Configures smbd to use encrypted passwords. This should be enabled (which also is the default) because every version of Windows since Windows 98 requires encrypted passwords.

  ■ **passdb backend.** Identifies where Samba user accounts are stored.

  ■ **wins server.** Specifies the IP address of your network's WINS server.

  ■ **wins support.** If your network doesn't already have a WINS server on your network, set this parameter to yes. This will enable WINS by running the nmbd daemon on your server.

  ■ **username map.** Specifies a file that is used to map SMB client usernames to local server usernames. By default, this is /etc/samba/smbusers.

NOTE: There are many other parameters that you can optionally include in the [global] section of the smb.conf file. See the smb.conf man page to learn more.

Share Users' Home Directories

Next, you need to know how to share users' home directories. By default, the smb.conf file is pre-configured to share user home directories in the [homes] section. An example is shown below:

```
[homes]
    comment = Home Directories
    valid users = %S, %D%w%S
    browseable = No
    read only = No
    inherit acls = Yes
```

This section of the smb.conf file automatically shares the home directories of the users on your server. A user can access his or her share using the following UNC:

```
\\server_name\username
```

For example, if your Linux username were rt and you accessed your Samba server from a Windows workstation, you would see a share named rt, as shown below:

Figure 7-2 *Viewing Shared Home Directories*

Courtesy of Novell, Inc.

Configure Shares

In addition to sharing home directories, you can also share other directories in the server's file system. You do this by adding a share definition to the `smb.conf` file for each directory on your file server that will be shared. The following example defines a simple share:

```
[data]
    comment = Data
    path = /srv/samba/data
    read only = Yes
    guest ok = Yes
```

The entries in this example are described below:

- **[data].** Defines the identifier for the share. The share in this example can be accessed with the following UNC:

  `\\da1\data`

- **comment = Data.** Defines a comment that displays additional information about the share. The comment is displayed when you browse the network with Windows Explorer.

- **path = /srv/samba/data.** Sets the path in the local file system that the share points to. Verify that the local user accounts who need access to the files in this share have been granted the appropriate file system rights.

- **read only = Yes.** Specifies that the client accessing the share is not allowed to modify, delete, or create any files. This is the default value used if this parameter is not included in the share definition.

- **guest ok = Yes.** Specifies that a password is **not** required to access the share.

Depending upon your needs, you could also include the following:

- **browseable.** Specifies whether or not the share can be browsed in My Network Places on Windows systems. If you don't include this parameter, a default value of yes is assumed.

- **writeable.** If set to yes, users may create or edit files in the shared directory, as long as the file system permissions assigned to the directory allow it.

- **public.** If set to yes, users can connect to the shared directory without a password using the nobody system user account. This option is used only with share-level security. The default value for this option is no.

- **valid users.** Restricts access to the share to a specified list of users. Separate usernames with a comma (,).

NOTE: There are many other parameters that you can optionally include when defining a share in the smb.conf file. See the smb.conf man page to learn more.

Share Printers

You can also use Samba to share the printers configured on your SLES 11 server. This is a significant benefit for users who use Windows workstations. By default, the Windows operating system isn't compatible with network CUPS printers.

Using Samba, however, Windows users can send print jobs to your SLES 11 server and have them print on your CUPS printers. Samba accepts print jobs from SMB clients and spools them to a local spool directory. When the entire print job has been received, Samba runs a local print command and passes the spooled file to it. The local printing system then processes the print job and sends it to the printer.

By default, the smb.conf file is pre-configured to share all configured printers in the [printers] section. If this section exists within the smb.conf files, users can connect to any printer in the Samba host's printcap file. On startup, Samba creates a printer share for every printer defined in the printcap file. The [printers] section contains settings that are applied by default to all Samba printers on the server.

A sample [printers] section is shown below:

```
[printers]
    comment = All Printers
    path = /var/tmp
    printable = Yes
    create mask = 0600
    browseable = No
```

The options in this file are explained below:

- **comment = All Printers.** Causes the specified comment to be shown next to the share in Network Neighborhood (or with the `net view` command).

- **path = /var/tmp.** Defines the directory that will be used to spool print jobs.

- **printable = Yes.** When set to `Yes`, this option allows client systems to create spool files for printing in the directory defined above. This value must exist within [printers]; otherwise, the Samba daemon won't start.

- **create mask.** Sets the necessary POSIX permissions to the directory.

- **browseable = No.** Makes the [printer] share itself invisible in the list of available shares in Network Neighborhood. Individual shared printers, however, are still visible. This option should always be set to `No` if `printable = yes`.

In addition to the above options, you can also use the following options, as appropriate:

- **guest ok = Yes.** Allows anonymous guest printing to the printer. No password is required. The guest account maps to the nobody user account and print jobs are sent as this user. Otherwise, the user must first authenticate to the Samba service to send a print job.

- **public = Yes.** Performs the same function as `guest ok = Yes`.

- **read only = Yes.** Allows users to spool print jobs to the defined directory but prevents normal write operations in this directory.

- **writable = No.** Performs the same function as `read only = Yes`.

In addition to the [printers] section, you can also add several printing-related options to the [global] section of the `smb.conf` file. These include the following:

- **load printers.** If you include this parameter in your `smb.conf` file, all printers defined in the `/etc/printcap` file will automatically be shared. If you use this parameter, you do not need to define separate shares for your printers. Each automatically created printer share will use the configuration options found in the `[printers]` section of the `smb.conf` file.

- **printing.** Defines the type of printing system that will be shared by Samba. The possible values are `CUPS`, `LPRNG`, `PLP`, `SYSV`, `AIX`, `HPUX`, `QNX`, `SOFTQ`, and `BSD`. Usually you will use `CUPS` for this parameter.

- **show add printer wizard.** If set to `Yes`, this option causes the ***Add Printer*** icon to appear in the Printers folder of the Samba server's share in Network Neighborhood. The Add Printer Wizard lets you upload a printer driver to the `[print$]` share and associate it with a printer.

- **max print jobs.** Sets the maximum number of print jobs that can be active on the Samba server at any one time.

- **printcap name.** Tells Samba where to look for a list of available printer names. By default, this is `cups`.

- **printer admin.** Specifies a user or group (identified with @) that are allowed to add drivers and set printer properties. The root user is always a printer admin.

NOTE: You can configure Samba to support the uploading and downloading of printer drivers. This is done with the `[print$]` share in the `smb.conf` file. See the printing section in the `/usr/share/doc/packages/samba/Samba3-HOWTO.pdf` file.

Test the Samba Configuration

After you have configured your `smb.conf` file, you need to restart the Samba server daemons for the changes to take effect. However, before doing so, you should use the `testparm` command at the shell prompt to test the syntax of your Samba configuration file. When you do, you should see output similar to the following:

```
da1:~ # testparm
Load smb config files from /etc/samba/smb.conf
Processing section "[homes]"
Processing section "[profiles]"
Processing section "[users]"
Processing section "[groups]"
Processing section "[printers]"
Processing section "[print$]"
Processing section "[data]"
Loaded services file OK.
Server role: ROLE_STANDALONE
Press enter to see a dump of your service definitions
```

In this example, no errors were found. If there were any errors in the file, the command would display the errors grouped by configuration sections.

An interesting option for `testparm` is `--section-name` **section_name**, which tests only the specified section. This can be very useful when you have a very long `smb.conf`.

Configure Local Samba Authentication

Samba can authenticate users in various ways: it can use a local Samba user data base, an LDAP directory, a domain controller, or an Active Directory database.

In this manual, only the local user database is covered. You need to

- Understand the /etc/samba/smb.conf File
- Configure Samba to Require User Authentication

Understand the /etc/samba/smb.conf File

It's important to recognize that Samba maintains its own database of user accounts that are used to authenticate to the service. The user accounts in your `/etc/passwd` file are not directly used by Samba. However, they can be mapped over to your Samba database of user accounts.

By default, the `/etc/samba/smbpasswd` file is used by Samba to store user accounts, but it does not have any users defined. To populate the smbpasswd file with user accounts, you use the smbpasswd utility at the shell prompt. To do this, complete the following:

1. Open a terminal session and switch to root using the su – command.

NOTE: If you run smbpasswd as any user other than root, it can be used to manage the smbpasswd account only for the current user.

---

2. At the shell prompt, enter smbpasswd -a *username*.

3. When prompted, enter a password for the Samba user account.

   While not required, many administrators prefer to use the same password for both the Samba user account and the Linux user account.

Once done, the user account is added to the /etc/samba/smbpasswd file, as shown below:

```
# This file is the authentication source for Samba if 'passdb backend'
# is set to 'smbpasswd' and 'encrypt passwords' is 'Yes' in the
# [global] section of /etc/samba/smb.conf
#
# See section 'passdb backend' and 'encrypt passwords' in the manual
# page of smb.conf for more information.
geeko:1000:XXXXXXXXXXXXXXXXXXXXXXXXXXXXXXXXX:55DB0294BC42D6E1B81AE2B5C
7F2943F:[U           ]:LCT-49D5D363:
```

To remove a user from the file, you use the smbpasswd -x *username* command at the shell prompt.

To disable a user, you use the smbpasswd -d *username* command at the shell prompt.

To reactivate a disabled account, you use the smbpasswd -e *username* command.

To change a user's Samba password, you use smbpasswd *username* at the shell prompt.

The /etc/samba/smbusers file is used by Samba to map usernames from client systems to user accounts on the local server. The following syntax is used:

```
unix_name = smb_name
```

This file is not included in the default configuration.

Configure Samba to Require User Authentication

In the [data] share definition presented in the previous objective, guest access to the share was allowed, as shown below:

```
[data]
     comment = Data
     path = /srv/samba/data
     read only = Yes
     guest ok = Yes
```

In most situations, you will want to reconfigure this share with a higher level of security. The first task is to ensure the security option in the [global] section in the smb.conf file is set to **security = user**, as shown below:

```
[global]
     workgroup = DigitalAirlines
     netbios name = DA1
     security = user
     server string = DA1 File Server
```

This forces users to authenticate when a client attempts to connect to the Samba server. However, once they do, your users have access to every share defined in the `smb.conf` file. Usually, this is not acceptable.

More than likely, you will want to restrict access to a given share to a specific set of users. You can use the valid users option within the share definition to specify which Samba users are allowed access to the share.

In the following, the guest ok option has been replaced with the `valid users` option to restrict `[data]` share access to only the tux user:

```
[data]
     comment = Data
     path = /srv/samba/data
     read only = no
     valid users = tux
```

You can specify one or more users with this option. Multiple usernames must be separated by commas.

Changing the `read only` option to a value of `No` makes the share writable. The option `writeable = yes` has the same effect.

IMPORTANT: The underlying UNIX permissions have to also allow write access; if they do not, a user cannot write files via Samba.

You can also use groups with the valid users option. Group names must begin with @, for example @accounting. Remember that all group members must be Samba-enabled with the `smbpasswd` command.

The following example configures the `[data]` share so that it is readable and writable by all members of the accounting group:

```
[data]
     comment = Accounting Data
     path = /srv/samba/data
     read only = no
     valid users = @accounting
     force user = tux
     force group = accounting
```

In this example, several options have been modified or added:

- **valid users = @accounting.** Allows all users who are in the accounting group to access the share.

- **force user = tux.** Forces Samba to perform all file operations in the share as the tux user, which can be very useful. For example, using this option allows you to set your POSIX permissions in the file system for the tux user and have those permissions automatically applied to every other user who is allowed to access the share.

- **force group = accounting.** Forces the Samba server to perform all file operations using the accounting group.

Use Samba's Client Tools

Although Samba is commonly used to provide Windows workstations with access to Linux servers, Linux workstations can also access Samba shares. Samba provides a variety of tools that you can use to access shares from a Linux system. These tools can be used to access a Samba server or a native Windows server.

In this objective, you learn how to use these tools. The following tasks are addressed:

- Use nmblookup
- Use smbclient
- Mount Samba Shares in the Linux File System

Use nmblookup

With the nmblookup tool, you can resolve NetBIOS names into IP addresses. In the following example, the IP address for the Samba server with the NetBIOS name da1 is looked up:

```
geeko@da-host:~> nmblookup da1
querying da1 on 172.17.8.255
172.17.8.101 da1<00>
```

In the first line of the output, nmblookup states that it is querying the server name with a broadcast to 172.17.8.255. In the second line of the output, it displays the result of the query. In this case, the system with a NetBIOS name of DA1 has an IP address of 172.17.8.101.

NOTE: If the system you are querying is not in the same subnet, the name cannot be resolved with a broadcast query. Instead, nmblookup must use a WINS server to resolve the name. For more information, see the man page for nmblookup.

Use smbclient

With the smbclient tool, you can access shares on a Samba server. It's also a very useful tool for testing your Samba server configuration.

You can perform several tasks with smbclient:

- Browse Shares Provided by a Samba Server
- Access Files Provided by a Samba Server
- Send Print Jobs to Samba Printers

Browse Shares Provided by a Samba Server

The smbclient utility can be used to display a list of shares offered by a Samba server. To do this, enter the following command at the shell prompt:

```
smbclient -L //server_name
```

When smbclient asks for your password, press Enter to proceed. The output of smbclient will appear similar to the following:

```
geeko@da-host:~> smbclient -L //da1
Enter geeko's password:
Domain=[DIGITALAIRLINES] OS=[Unix] Server=[Samba 3.2.7-1.3-2042-SUSE-
CODE11]

        Sharename       Type       Comment
        ---------       ----       -------
        profiles        Disk       Network Profiles Service
        users           Disk       All users
        groups          Disk       All groups
        print$          Disk       Printer Drivers
        data            Disk       Data
        IPC$            IPC        IPC Service (DA1 File Server)
Domain=[DIGITALAIRLINES] OS=[Unix] Server=[Samba 3.2.7-1.3-2042-SUSE-
CODE11]

        Server                     Comment
        ---------                  -------

        DA1                        DA1 File Server

        Workgroup                  Master
        ---------                  -------

        DIGITALAIRLINES
```

The `smbclient` utility first displays all available shares on the Samba server. The IPC$ share provides information about the other shares available on the SMB server. The lower part of the smbclient output provides workgroup information.

The `smbclient` command can be very valuable for testing purposes. After you have set up a share, you can use `smbclient` to test the availability of the share.

Some shares are not browseable without authentication. In this case, you can pass a username to smbclient, as in the following example:

```
smbclient -L //server_name -U username
```

With these options, `smbclient` connects to the server with the specified username and prompts for the corresponding password.

Access Files Provided by a Samba Server

You can also use `smbclient` to access a share on a server. To do this, you need to supply the share name along with the server name (without the `-L` option).

In the following example, `smbclient` connects to the share data on the Samba server named da1:

```
smbclient //da1/data
```

A username can also be supplied with the `-U` option. After `smbclient` has connected to a share, it displays the following prompt:

```
smb: \>
```

At this point, `smbclient` can be used like a command line FTP client. Some more commonly used commands include the following:

- **ls:** Displays the contents of the current directory.
- **cd:** Changes to a directory.
- **get:** Copies a file from the share to the current working directory.
- **put:** Copies a file to the share. The share must be writable to use this command.

Send Print Jobs to Samba Printers

You can also use `smbclient` to send print jobs to shared Samba printers. Use the following syntax:

```
smbclient //server_name/shared_printer_name -c "print file_to_print"
```

The `-c` option performs the given command automatically after the connection to the server has been established. You can also enter the print command on the smb:\ command line after you have connected to the server.

Mount Samba Shares in the Linux File System

In addition to accessing shared files with smbclient, you can also mount a remote Samba share into the local file system, much like an NFS export. This is done using the mount command:

```
mount -t cifs //server_name/share_name  /mount_point
```

For example:

```
mount -t cifs //da1/data /mnt/samba
```

In this example, the data share on the da1 Samba server is mounted into the /mnt/samba directory. The -t cifs option specifies that the resource to be mounted is an SMB share.

If the share requires authentication, you can also supply a username, as in the following:

```
mount -t cifs -o username=geeko //da1/data /mnt/samba
```

You will be prompted for the password.

It is also possible to provide the password in the command, as in the following:

```
mount -t cifs -o username=geeko,password=novell //da1/data /mnt/samba
```

However, the password will be visible in the password history. If you use the /etc/fstab file to mount the file system, every user on the system could view the password. The solution is to provide the password in the /etc/samba/smbfstab file that is only readable for the system administrator. The equivalent to the above command line would look similar to the following:

```
# /etc/samba/smbfstab
# This file allows you to mount SMB/ CIFS shares during system boot
# while hiding passwords to other people than root. Use /etc/fstab for
# public available services. You have to specify at least a service
# name and a mount point. Current default vfstype is smbfs.
#
# Possible vfstypes are smbfs and cifs.
#
# The options are explained in the manual page of smbmount and
# mount.cifs.
#
# service      moint-point  vfstype options

//da1/data    /mnt/samba    cifs     username=geeko,password=novell
```

Exercise 7-1   *Configure and Access a Samba Server*

In this exercise, you learn how to configure a basic samba share. You then access the share with `smbclient` and you mount a Samba share in the file system of a Linux workstation.

You will find this exercise at the end of the chapter.

(End of Exercise)

Objective 2   Configure the Apache Web Server

In this objective, you learn how to set up a basic Apache Web Server on SLES 11. To set up Apache, you need to be familiar with the following:

- Set Up a Basic Web Server with Apache
- Configure Virtual Hosts
- Limit Access to the Web Server
- Troubleshoot a Web Server Installation
- Create Dynamic Content
- Configure a Virtual Host

Set Up a Basic Web Server with Apache

To set up a basic Web server with Apache, you need to

- Understand How a Web Server Works
- Install Apache Web Server
- Use the Apache Configuration Files
- The Default Apache Configuration

Understand How a Web Server Works

There are a variety of Web server packages that you can use on Linux but, by far, the most popular is the Apache Web Server. Most of the Web servers you access on the Internet are actually running some version of Apache.

Web servers provide much of the functionality we associate with the Internet today. A Web server's job is to send Web pages, graphics, and other files to clients requesting them.

A Web server can transfer just about any type of file between the server and the client. However, the most common type of file used with a Web server are Hyper-Text Markup Language (HTML) documents. An HTML document is a text file written using HTML markup coding that tells the Web browser how the information should be formatted and displayed.

When a user's Web browser receives an HTML file from the Web server, it interprets the marked-up text from the file and displays it on the screen. The information in the file is reformatted and displayed according to the markup information it contains.

The files that comprise a Web site are saved in a separate directory in the file system of the system running the Web server daemon. This directory is called the **document root** or **root directory**. On SLES 11, the Apache Web server's document root is the `/srv/www/htdocs` directory (you can configure a different directory as document root for Apache).

Communications between the Web browser and the Web server are accomplished using the IP protocol in conjunction with the Hyper Text Transfer Protocol (HTTP). HTTP is a request/response protocol used by the Web browser to get information from the Web server.

The browser initiates the request by establishing a TCP/IP communication session between the client system and the Web server, which runs on TCP port 80 by default. The Web server then listens for the browser to tell it what information it wants. The browser does this by sending a request message to the Web server, which responds with the requested files.

The request message consists of the following:

- **Request method.** Specifies the resource being requested from the server. The HTTP protocol defines several request methods, including the following:

  - **GET.** Requests the specified resource.

  - **POST.** Submits data to the Web server to be processed.

  - **PUT.** Uploads a resource to the Web server.

  - **DELETE.** Deletes a specified resource from the Web server, if permitted.

  - **OPTIONS.** Requests the HTTP methods the Web server supports.

- **HTTP headers.** Define the characteristics of the requested data, such as acceptable content types, character sets, encodings, languages, etc.

- **Message body.** This is optional.

When using a Web browser, you use a Uniform Resource Locator (URL) to access the Web server. The URL is used by your browser to specify the exact information you need from the Web server as well as how it is to be retrieved. The syntax for a URL is shown below:

```
protocol://domain_name_or_IP:port/directory/filename
```

The protocol portion of the URL specifies the protocol the browser will use to retrieve information. When accessing a Web server, you use either the HTTP or HTTPS protocol.

The HTTP protocol transfers information from the Web server using unencrypted communications. This level of security may be acceptable for many Web pages, but the transfer of sensitive information requires transmissions to be encrypted.

For sensitive information, such as credit card numbers or personal information, you should use the HTTPS protocol. HTTPS uses standard HTTP, but it also uses the Secure Socket Layer (SSL) protocol to encrypt the data before sending it. Only the sender and receiver have keys that can decrypt the information.

After specifying the protocol in the URL, you next specify the domain name or IP address of the Web server you want to access. After the address, you can optionally specify the TCP port where the Web server is running. For example:

```
http://www.digitalairlines.com:81
```

This tells the browser to access port 81 on www.digitalairlines.com. Web browsers default to port 80 if you don't specify a port number in the URL. Therefore, a port number is required only if the service you are accessing is running on a port other than 80 (HTTP) or 443 (HTTPS).

You can also specify the filename that you want to retrieve from the Web server by appending it to the end of the URL. For example:

```
http://www.digitalairlines.com/index.html
```

This parameter is optional. Web servers are usually configured such that, if no filename is specified in the URL, it sends a file named `index.html` by default. If you want to request a specific file, however, you need to include it in the URL.

In addition to delivering data to the Web browser, a Web server can perform tasks such as limiting access to specific Web pages, logging access to a file, and encrypting the connection between a server and browser.

Install Apache Web Server

To install Apache on your SLES 11 system, you need to install the following packages:

- **apache2.** Basic Web server software.

- **apache2-prefork.** Additional Apache package that influences the multiprocessing behavior of the Web server.

- **apache2-example-pages (optional).** Sample HTML pages.

- **apache2-doc (optional).** Apache Web server documentation.

The easiest way to do this is to run YaST, access the Software Management module, and install the *Web and LAMP Server* pattern. This is shown in the figure below:

Figure 7-3   *Installing Apache Web Server in YaST*

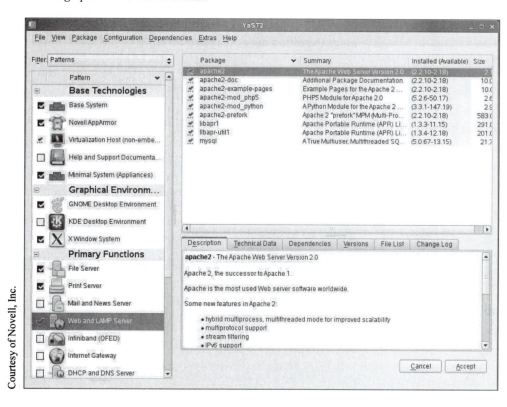

Courtesy of Novell, Inc.

When you install the Web and LAMP Server pattern, YaST automatically resolves dependencies for you and may prompt you to install one or more additional packages. If this is the case, be sure to install the additional packages by selecting *Continue*.

After installing the required software, you need to start the Apache Server service on your SLES 11 system. You do this by opening a terminal window, switching to root, and then entering the following command at the shell prompt:

```
rcapache2 start
```

or

```
/etc/init.d/apache2 start
```

You can verify that Apache is running by entering one of the following at the shell prompt:

```
rcapache2 status
```

or

```
/etc/init.d/apache2 status
```

If you need to stop Apache, you can enter one of the following to stop the Web server:

```
rcapache2 stop
```

or

```
/etc/init.d/apache2 stop
```

If you want the Web server to start automatically every time the server is booted, enter the following at the shell prompt:

```
insserv apache2
```

This command causes Apache to be automatically started at runlevels 3 and 5.

To test the Web server after installation, open a Web browser on your SLES 11 server desktop and enter the following URL:

```
http://localhost
```

If Apache was installed correctly and the apache2-example-pages package is installed, the browser should display the following page:

Figure 7-4   *Testing the Web Server*

If your SLES 11 system is connected to the network, you can access the Web server remotely from other hosts by opening a browser and then accessing the following URL:

```
http://IP_address or DNS_name
```

By default, Apaches stores the documents it serves in the document root `/srv/www/htdocs`.

You can replace the files from the apache2-example-pages package in the document root directory with your own Web server content. Simply create your own content and copy it to `/srv/www/htdocs`.

However, be aware that the Apache daemon must have at least read access to your Web server content files. Apache runs as the wwwrun user on SLES 11. Therefore, you need to make sure that wwwrun has read access to the files in the document root directory, using the `chmod` command as needed.

When creating your Web server content, you can create subdirectories within the document root. If you do, you can access those subdirectories by adding the name of the subdirectory to your URLs:

http://*server_address*/*subdirectory*/

If a filename is not included in the URL, Apache looks for a file with the name index.html in the specified directory.

NOTE: You can change the name of the default file in the Apache configuration files.

Use the Apache Configuration Files

The Apache Web server is configured using a variety of configuration files located in /etc/apache2/. To configure the Apache Web server, you need to be familiar with the following:

- Location of the Apache Configuration Files
- Basic Rules for Apache Configuration Files

Location of the Apache Configuration Files

The configuration of the Apache Web Server is spread among several configuration files located in the /etc/apache2/ directory. These files are shown below:

Figure 7-5   *Apache Web Server Configuration Files*

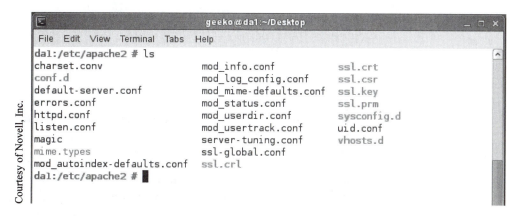

The following are some of the more important Apache configuration files:

- **httpd.conf:** The main Apache configuration file.

- **default-server.conf:** Contains the basic Web server configuration. However, options set in this file can be overwritten by options in other configuration files.

- **vhost.d/:** Directory that contains configuration files for virtual hosts. You will learn more about virtual hosts later in this section.

- **uid.conf.** Sets the user and group ID used by Apache. By default, Apache uses the wwwrun user and the www group.

- **listen.conf.** Specifies the IP addresses and ports the Apache daemon is listening on. By default, Apache listens on all interfaces on port 80.

- **server-tuning.conf.** Used to fine tune the performance of the Apache daemon. The default values in this file are usually appropriate for most installations. However, if your Web server must handle a large number of simultaneous requests, you can adjust the values in this file to increase performance.

- **error.conf.** Configures the behavior of Apache when a request cannot be handled correctly.

- **ssl-global.conf.** Configures the encryption of connections with SSL.

- **/etc/sysconfig/apache2.** This file contains variables that are used to create apache2 configuration files in `/etc/apache2/sysconfig.d/`.

Basic Rules for Apache Configuration Files

The options contained within the Apache configuration files are called **directives**. Directives are case insensitive, which means that "include" is interpreted the same as "Include," but arguments to directives such as paths and filenames, are often case sensitive.

Directives can be grouped so that they apply only to a specific Web server directory instead of the entire server. For example, in the following the directives are applied only to the `/srv/www/htdocs` directory:

```
<Directory "/srv/www/htdocs">
    Options None
    AllowOverride None
    Order allow,deny
    Allow from all
</Directory>
```

Notice in this example that the directives are nested within the `<Directory "/srv/www/htdocs">` and `</Directory>` tags, which limits their application to only the `/srv/www/htdocs` directory.

You can use the # character to indicate comments in the configuration file. All lines starting with a # are ignored by the Apache daemon.

Whenever you modify an Apache configuration file, you need to reload the Web server to have the change applied. This is done by entering the following command at the shell prompt (as root):

```
rcapache2 reload
```

This command forces the Apache daemon to reload its configuration files without stopping and restarting. Some changes, such as changing the port the server listens on, will require you to stop and restart the Apache daemon. This is done by entering the following command at the shell prompt (as root):

```
rcapache2 restart
```

After making changes to the Apache configuration files, you can verify that your modifications use the correct syntax by entering the following command at the shell prompt (as root):

```
apache2ctl configtest
```

If the syntax is correct, the command displays a "Syntax OK" message.

On other distributions, such as Debian, the `apache2ctl` command (`apachectl start`, `apachectl stop`, `apachectl graceful` [a special way or restarting the server], `apachectl restart`) can also be used to control Apache2. Its use is very similar to the `rcapache2` command on SLES11. While the apache2ctl command exists on SLES11 as well, using `rcapache2` or the `/etc/init.d/apache2` init script is the recommended way to control the Apache Web server on SLES 11.

The Default Apache Configuration

The default Apache Web server configuration is defined in the `/etc/apache2/default-server.conf` file. A sample default-server.conf file is shown below:

```
DocumentRoot "/srv/www/htdocs"
<Directory "/srv/www/htdocs">
    Options None
    AllowOverride None
    Order allow,deny
    Allow from all
</Directory>
Alias /icons/ "/usr/share/apache2/icons/"
<Directory "/usr/share/apache2/icons">
    Options Indexes MultiViews
    AllowOverride None
    Order allow,deny
    Allow from all
</Directory>
ScriptAlias /cgi-bin/ "/srv/www/cgi-bin/"
<Directory "/srv/www/cgi-bin">
    AllowOverride None
    Options +ExecCGI -Includes
    Order allow,deny
    Allow from all
</Directory>
<IfModule mod_userdir.c>
    UserDir public_html
    Include /etc/apache2/mod_userdir.conf
    #AliasMatch ^/users/([a-zA-Z0-9-_.]*)/?(.*) /home/$1/public_html/
$2
</IfModule>
Include /etc/apache2/conf.d/*.conf
Include /etc/apache2/conf.d/apache2-manual?conf
```

The following table provides an overview of some of the more important directives used in the default-server.conf file:

Table 7-1   *default-server.conf Directives*

Directive	Description
DocumentRoot	Specifies the document root directory used by the Web server.
<Directory "***dir_name***"> </Directory>	All directives listed within this block apply only to the specified directory.
Options	With this directive additional options can be applied to logical blocks like directories.
AllowOverride	Determines whether directives are allowed to be overwritten by a configuration option found in a .htaccess file in a directory.
Alias "*fakename*" "*realname*"	Allows you to create an alias to a directory.
ScriptAlias	Allows you to create an alias to a directory containing scripts for dynamic content generation.
I<IfModule ***module_name***> </IfModule>	The directives within this block only apply if the module module_name is loaded. The modules apache loads are specified in the `APACHE_MODULES` variable in `/etc/sysconfig/apache2`.

In most cases, the default settings in this file are suitable for most installations and don't need to be modified. The `default-server.conf` file that is installed by default contains comments that explain the respective entries.

NOTE: An overview of all Apache directives can be found at http://httpd.apache.org/docs/2.2/mod/directives.html (http://httpd.apache.org/docs/2.2/mod/directives.html).

Configure Virtual Hosts

Now that you understand how to configure the default Apache Web server, you are ready to create virtual hosts. To use the virtual host feature of Apache, you need to do the following:

- Understand Virtual Hosts
- Configure a Virtual Host

Understand Virtual Hosts

In its default configuration, the Apache Web server can be reached from a browser using the following URLs:

- `http://localhost` (from the computer where the Web server is running)
- `http://web_server_IP_address`
- `http://web_server_hostname`

For all of these URLs, Apache serves the files located in the document root directory.

This configuration works well for a basic Web server. However, Apache can also be configured to host multiple virtual Web servers on the same physical server system. These virtual Web servers are called virtual hosts.

This allows you to host Web servers for multiple domains on the same system. For example, suppose your organization has its own domain: www.digitalairlines.com.

In addition, your organization wants to allow local subsidiaries to present themselves with their own domain:

- www.ditigalairlines-slc.com
- www.digitalairlines-la.com

Using just the basic Apache configuration, you would have to set up three separate servers to host the three domains. Fortunately, using virtual domains, you can set up a virtual host for each domain on the same server. Each domain is accessed using its domain name on port 80.

To access a virtual host, a separate DNS entry is needed for every virtual host on the Apache Web server. The following outlines the steps of sending a request to the virtual host www.ditigalairlines-slc.com:

1. The Web browser requests the IP address of the host www.ditigalairlines-slc.com from a DNS server.

2. The browser uses the IP address to request a file from the Apache Web server listening on the IP address of www.ditigalairlines-slc.com.

3. In the HTTP request, the browser includes the host name of the server it wants to reach.

4. Apache uses the host name contained in the request from the browser to determine the corresponding virtual host and delivers the requested data from that host.

Configure a Virtual Host

To create a virtual host, you need to create a configuration file in the `/etc/apache2/vhosts.d/` directory. The name of the configuration file has to end with `.conf`.

You can use the `vhost.template` file in the `/etc/apache2/vhosts.d/` directory as a template for your virtual host configuration file. You need to edit the following directives in the template:

Table 7-2   *Virtual Host Directives*

Directive	Description
ServerAdmin	Type the e-mail address of the virtual host system administrator here.
ServerName	Type the host name of the virtual host as it is configured in the DNS record.

Directive	Description
DocumentRoot	Set the document root directory of the virtual host. The directory and the files in the directory must be readable by the wwwrun user.
ErrorLog	Type a filename for the error log.
CustomLog	Type a filename for the log file.
ScriptAlias	Set the ScriptAlias to a directory of your choice. The directory must not be under the DocumentRoot of the virtual host. If you don't need scripts for dynamic content creation, delete this directive.
<Directory "script_dir">	If you've set a ScriptAlias, you have to specify the directory which contains the script files. If you are not using a ScriptAlias, you can delete this directive.
<Directory "document_root">	You need to modify the path name of this directive to your document root path.

After customizing the virtual host file, you need to reload the Apache daemon. You also need to make sure the DNS record for the domain has been updated so that the virtual host domain name resolves correctly.

In addition to the above, you need to activate name-based virtual hosting in /etc/apache2/listen.conf. Remove the comment sign in front of one the lines starting with NameVirtualHost, as shown in the following:

```
...
# Use name-based virtual hosting
#
# - on a specified address / port:
#
#NameVirtualHost 12.34.56.78:80
#
# - name-based virtual hosting:
#
#NameVirtualHost *:80
#
# - on all addresses and ports. This is your best bet when you are on
#   dynamically assigned IP addresses:
#
NameVirtualHost *
```

Limit Access to the Web Server

By default, Apache allows Web server data access to all network hosts that can reach the server. This configuration is appropriate for public Web servers. However, there may be times when you need to restrict access to the content on the Web server to specific users or hosts. This can be done in two ways:

- Limit Access by Network Address
- Require User Authentication

Limit Access by Network Address

If you need to limit access to Web server content to specific network hosts, you can add directives to your configuration file that limit access based on a host's IP address or domain name. You can use the following directives to limit access to the Web server based on host address:

Table 7-3   *Apache Configuration File Directives for Restricting Access Based on IP Address*

Directive	Description
allow	IP addresses or networks listed after this directive are allowed to access the Web server.
deny	IP addresses or networks listed after this directive are not allowed to access the Web server.
order	This directive sets the order in which the allow and deny directives are evaluated.

These directives must be added within a `<Directory>` block. This causes Apache to restrict access to all data in that directory as well as its subdirectories based on the parameters you supply.

For example, suppose you wanted to restrict access to the data in the `/srv/www/htdocs` directory on the Web server to hosts on the `10.0.0.0/24` network only. You could add the following directive:

```
<Directory "/srv/www/htdocs">
    Order deny,allow
    Deny from all
    Allow from 10.0.0.0/24
</Directory>
```

The lines in the directive above do the following:

- **<Directory "/srv/www/htdocs">.** Starts the directory block. The directives within the block apply only to the `/srv/www/htdocs` directory on the Web server.

- **Order deny,allow.** Determines the order in which the allow and deny directives are evaluated. You have the following options:

  - **Deny,Allow.** Deny directives are evaluated before the allow directives. Access is allowed by default. Any client which does not match a deny directive or does match an allow directive is allowed access to the server.

  - **Allow,Deny.** Allow directives are evaluated before the deny directives. Access is denied by default. Any client which does not match an allow directive or does match a deny directive is denied access to the server.

- **Deny from all.** Deny directive is evaluated first and, in this case, access is denied for all clients.

  You can use the following options with the deny and allow directives:

  - **all.** Applies to all hosts.

  ❏ **A (partial) domain-name.** Applies to hosts whose names match the given expression (such as novell.com). Only complete domain components are matched. For example, specifying novell.com would match www.novell.com but *not* foonovell.com.

  ❏ **A full IP address.** Applies to a specific IP address (such as 10.0.0.23).

  ❏ **A partial IP address.** Applies to IP addresses starting with the specified IP address fragment (such as 10.0.0).

  ❏ **A network/netmask pair.** Applies to IP addresses matching to the given network/netmask pair (such as 10.0.0.0/255.255.255.0).

  ❏ **A network/CIDR specification.** Applies to IP addresses matching to the given CIDR expression (such as 10.0.0.0/24).

- **Allow from 10.0.0.0/24.** This allow directive is evaluated after the deny directive. In this case, hosts in the network 10.0.0.0/24 are allowed access.

- **</Directory>.** Ends the directory block.

Require User Authentication

By limiting access to certain network addresses, you control the hosts that can access the Web server. However, you have no control over who is using the host.

To rectify this, Apache also allows you to restrict access based on username. This is called basic authentication. Basic authentication requires users to log in before they can access the data on the Web server.

Before you can configure Apache to use basic authentication, you first have to create user accounts for the Web server daemon. This is done using the `htpasswd2` command line utility. The following command creates a password file for Apache to use named `/etc/apache2/htpasswd` and adds a new user account named tux.

```
htpasswd2 -c /etc/apache2/htpasswd tux
```

When you add a user to the htpasswd file for the first time, you have to call `htpasswd2` with the `-c` option to initially create the file. You can use a different location for the password file, but you have to make sure that it's readable by the wwwrun user. It also must not reside within the document root of the Web server.

The `htpasswd2` utility prompts you for a password for the user as you create the user account.

If you want to add more users, use the following command:

```
htpasswd2 /etc/apache2/htpasswd username
```

To delete a user from the password file, use the following command:

```
htpasswd2 -D /etc/apache2/htpasswd username
```

After you have created your htpasswd file and added your user accounts, you next need to configure Apache to prompt for a password when accessing restricted data.

To do this, you need to add the following lines to the <Directory> block for the directory that you want to restrict:

```
AuthType Basic
AuthName "Restricted Files"
AuthUserFile /etc/apache2/htpasswd
Require user tux
```

The directives above do the following:

- **AuthType Basic.** Sets the authentication method (to `Basic` authentication, in this case).

- **AuthName "Restricted Files".** Sets the name of the authorization realm for the directory. This realm is sent to the client so that the user knows which username and password to use. If the realm name contains spaces, it must be enclosed in quotation marks, as shown in the example above. It must also be accompanied by the `AuthType`, `Require`, and `AuthUserFile` directives.

- **AuthUserFile /etc/apache2/htpasswd.** Specifies the password file used for the restricted directory.

- **Require user tux.** Lists the users from the password file who are allowed to access the directory. You can add more than one user by separating the usernames with spaces, or you can use the following directive:

  ```
  Require valid-user
  ```

  This defines that *any* valid username in the password file is granted access (if he enters the correct password).

Putting the authentication directives in the configuration file as above is the preferred approach. However, there is an alternative way to configure authentication by writing the authentication configuration into an `.htaccess` file in the directory where you want to control access.

You would choose this approach if you want to give those who are allowed to maintain the content of the Web space the permission to administer access to it, without allowing them to change the Apache configuration directly. A disadvantage of this approach is that every time a file is read in the document directory, the `.htaccess` file in this and every directory above it has to be read as well, which can impact performance.

To allow the use of `.htaccess` files for user authentication, the following directive has to be included in a Directory block:

```
AllowOverride AuthConfig
```

This allows you to specify the access permissions in an `.htaccess` file in the respective directory or one of its subdirectories. This file would contain similar lines to the ones shown above:

```
AuthType Basic
AuthName "Restricted Files"
AuthUserFile /etc/apache2/htpasswd
Require valid-user
```

The use of .htaccess files is not limited to authentication; other aspects of the Apache configuration can be configured as well. Search for the AllowOverride directive in the Apache documentation for more information.

NOTE: The password is transferred cleartext over the network. For critical applications, you should configure SSL encryption. This is discussed in the next objective.

Troubleshoot a Web Server Installation

The obvious way to test a Web server installation is to start a Web browser such as Firefox and enter the Web server's URL. If you see the expected Web page, you can assume that the basic functionality of the Web server is intact.

Sometimes you need tools that allow you to test the response of a Web server from the command line, and you need to be able to locate errors in the configuration of the Web server when the response is not as intended. To troubleshoot the Web server installation, you need to be able to

- Test Web Server Access with Telnet
- Fetch Web Pages from the Command Line
- View Apache Log Files

Test Web Server Access with Telnet

You can use a Telnet client to find out if a Web server is up and running. A Telnet client is generally available on Linux and Windows systems; however, you have to know how to "speak" HTTP.

The following shows how to connect to a Web server with a Telnet client:

```
geeko@da-host:~> telnet www.google.com 80
Trying 209.85.129.104...
Connected to www.google.com.
Escape character is '^]'.
GET / HTTP/1.1
host: www.google.com

HTTP/1.1 302 Found
Location: http://www.google.de/
Cache-Control: private
Content-Type: text/html; charset=UTF-8
Set-Cookie:
PREF=ID=0aba7796adab4d95:TM=1245665890:LM=1245665890:S=XyiVMTWoZuhk4
XUH; expires=Wed, 22-Jun-2011 10:18:10 GMT; path=/;
domain=.google.com
Date: Mon, 22 Jun 2009 10:18:10 GMT
Server: gws
Content-Length: 218

<HTML><HEAD><meta http-equiv="content-type" content="text/
html;charset=utf-8">
<TITLE>302 Moved</TITLE></HEAD><BODY>
<H1>302 Moved</H1>
The document has moved
<A HREF="http://www.google.de/">here</A>.
</BODY></HTML>
Connection closed by foreign host.
geeko@da-host:~>
```

The explanation of the above is as follows:

- **telnet www.google.com 80.** By default, the Telnet client connects to port 23 of the given host. To access a different port, add that port after the host name.

  The next lines inform you that the telnet client connected to www.google.com (IP address 209.85.129.104) and that you can return to a telnet prompt by pressing Ctrl+]. At the prompt enter **quit** to return to the shell prompt.

- **GET / HTTP/1.1.** You specify the HTTP command (GET), the resource you want to access (/ in this case; if you want to access a specific file, enter the path and file name), and the HTTP protocol version.

- **host: www.google.com.** This HTTP header line tells the Web server which host you want to access. This is necessary if different virtual hosts are hosted at the same IP address. You can enter further HTTP header lines, or press Enter twice to receive the response of the Web server.

- **HTTP/1.1 302 Found.** This and the following lines are HTTP headers sent by the Web server and, separated by an empty line, the content of the Web page.

- **Connection closed by foreign host.** The Web server closed the connection.

Fetch Web Pages from the Command Line

While Telnet offers a quick way to test if a Web server is up and accessible, it is not the ideal command line tool to fetch Web or FTP pages. If you want to fetch one or several Web pages, you can use one of the following tools:

- **wget.** The `wget` command can be used to fetch single Web pages or entire Web sites by automatically following the links contained in Web pages. It can also get files from FTP servers. The basic syntax is

  `wget <options> protocol://www.example.com/path/file`

  Useful options include `-r` (follow links) and `-l <number>` to define the maximum number of levels to follow, to avoid getting too much data. See the wget manual page for all available options.

  The `/etc/wgetrc` and the `~/.wgetrc` files allow you to specify options in a configuration file.

- **curl.** `curl` is a tool to transfer data from or to a server, using one of the supported protocols (HTTP, HTTPS, FTP, FTPS, SCP, SFTP, TFTP, DICT, TELNET, LDAP or FILE). The command is designed to work without user interaction.

  Unlike wget, curl can also be used to upload files to FTP servers.

- **w3m.** `w3m` is a text-based Web browser.

View Apache Log Files

The location of the Apache log files is defined in the Apache configuration. On SLES 11, the default log files are

- **/var/log/apache2/access_log.** For each page served to clients, an entry is written to the log file. The entry includes IP address of the client, time and date of the request, the HTTP method used, and the file requested.

- **/var/log/apache2/error_log.** This file contains any error messages, such as a file request for a file that doesn't exist, invalid URIs, or errors during server startup.

Should the Apache server not behave as expected, a review of the log files often helps to locate the source of the error.

Create Dynamic Content

While in the beginning of the World Wide Web most HTML pages were static, more and more content is now created dynamically. Many Web sites, such as search engines, create HTML pages on the fly in response to user input. Others, such as Web mail sites or portal pages, allow individual users to customize what they see after they log in.

A multitude of technologies exists to create dynamic content. In this course, we touch three aspects of dynamic content creation that are listed in the LPIC Level One objectives (SQL) or were listed in CompTIA's Linux+ objectives (PHP and CGI) before they endorsed LPIC Level One:

- MySQL
- PHP
- Common Gateway Interface

MySQL

MySQL is a relational database management system (RDBMS) that is frequently used in the background of Web applications. In fact, its use is so frequent that an acronym exists for setups that include Linux, Apache, MySQL, and PHP (or Perl): LAMP.

MySQL is a Client/Server system, meaning that there is a server running the database that is accessed by any number of clients to query or change data within the database. As the name MySQL implies, it supports the Structured Query Language (SQL), a standardized language to query and change data in a database system.

A relational database system consists of tables that contain data and relations between the data. You could, for instance, have a database with a table of addresses, a table of products, and a table of orders, pointing to the addresses and products in the first two tables.

There are entire books about MySQL server on the market. This objective only covers the setup of the MySQL server software. You need to understand

- The MySQL Server (mysqld)
- The mysql Client Program
- Managing SQL Data

The MySQL Server (mysqld)

The MySQL server (mysqld) is contained in the **mysql** package. When you install that package with YaST, the **mysql-client** package is automatically installed as well. You can also choose the Web server and LAMP pattern which includes MySQL.

The global configuration for the MySQL daemon `mysqld`, as well as the administration tools, is contained in the `/etc/my.cnf` file. Individual settings for the administration tools can be written to `~/.my.cnf`.

When you start the server for the first time, the following message is displayed:

```
da1:~ # rcmysql start
Creating MySQL privilege database...
Installing MySQL system tables...
OK
Filling help tables...
OK
PLEASE REMEMBER TO SET A PASSWORD FOR THE MySQL root USER !
To do so, start the server, then issue the following commands:
/usr/bin/mysqladmin -u root password 'new-password'
/usr/bin/mysqladmin -u root -h da1.digitalairlines.com password 'new-
password'

Alternatively you can run:
/usr/bin/mysql_secure_installation

which will also give you the option of removing the test
databases and anonymous user created by default.  This is
strongly recommended for production servers.

See the manual for more instructions.

...
```

We recommended that you set a root password. If you omit to set a password with the `mysqladmin` commands shown above, your data on the server are unprotected and any user could log in as root and change or delete them.

You start the server with the `/etc/init.d/mysql start` command. The server is stopped using the `/etc/init.d/mysql stop` command. On SLES 11, `/usr/sbin/rcmysql` is a link that points to `/etc/init.d/mysql` and can be used as well.

The mysql Client Program

The `mysql` client program allows you to administer the database. You can administer access permissions as well as create, view, change, and delete databases, tables, and entries in the tables.

Using the `mysql` program, you can test if your MySQL server is active and responds as expected, as shown in the following:

```
da1:~ # mysql -p
Enter password:
Welcome to the MySQL monitor.  Commands end with ; or \g.
Your MySQL connection id is 5
Server version: 5.0.67 SUSE MySQL RPM

Type 'help;' or '\h' for help. Type '\c' to clear the buffer.
```

```
mysql> SHOW DATABASES;
+--------------------+
| Database           |
+--------------------+
| information_schema |
| mysql              |
| test               |
+--------------------+
3 rows in set (0.00 sec)mysql> USE mysql;
Database changed
mysql> SHOW TABLES;
+--------------------------+
| Tables_in_mysql          |
+--------------------------+
| columns_priv             |
| db                       |
| func                     |
| help_category            |
| help_keyword             |
| help_relation            |
| help_topic               |
| host                     |
| proc                     |
| procs_priv               |
| tables_priv              |
| time_zone                |
| time_zone_leap_second    |
| time_zone_name           |
| time_zone_transition     |
| time_zone_transition_type|
| user                     |
+--------------------------+
17 rows in set (0.00 sec)

mysql> SELECT * FROM user;
+-----------+------+----------
...
```

At the mysql prompt, you can enter SQL commands to create and query databases, tables, or entries within tables. The connection uses port 3306.

If you only want to test if the MySQL server is up, you can also use the `telnet` command to connect to port 3306, as shown in the following:

```
da1:~ # telnet localhost 3306
Trying ::1...
telnet: connect to address ::1: Connection refused
Trying 127.0.0.1...
Connected to localhost.
Escape character is '^]'.
4
5.0.67(N1J^{qF,J~\2$\&DbDltConnection closed by foreign host.
da1:~ #
```

5.0.67 is the version of the MySQL server.

Database users usually do not use the `mysql` command itself. Users access database applications, such as Web applications, that use SQL in the background.

NOTE: If you want to learn more about MySQL, http://dev.mysql.com/ (http://dev.mysql.com/) is a good starting point.

Managing SQL Data

SQL or Structured Query Language is a computer database language used for the management of relational database management systems (RDBMS). It is used for data storage, data query, data updates, data retrieval, and data manipulation, as well as for schema creation, schema modification, and access control of data.

Working with an SQL database has become necessary in many of today's Linux systems. Administrators must understand how to manipulate, query, or use other basic SQL commands. This section will discuss the basic SQL commands and the manipulation of data.

Basic SQL database commands allow the administrator flexibility in updating and performing the general tasks associated with the organization's database. The following commands are some of the most common ones that you will use when interacting with nearly every SQL DBMS.

If a company, for example, Novell Inc., used a table called BrainShare2010 to assign people a date and location to be at during BrainShare 2010, with columns that included Firstname, Lastname, Email, Phone, Assignment, Date, and Time, it might look similar to this:

First Name	Last Name	Email	Phone	Assignment	Date	Time a.m./p.m.
David	Manager	DManager@Novell.com	801-111-1111	DevTable	3/22-25	8-5
Adam	Teamlead	ATeamlead@Novell.com	801-111-2222	DevTable	3/22-25	8-5
Shirley	Certdata	SCertdata@Novell.com	801-111-3333	CertTable	3/22-25	9-6

Using the following command syntax to add entries to this table.

INSERT	Create new row(s) in a table with new data. Use either syntax:
Syntax:	INSERT INTO "table_name" VALUES ('value1', 'value2', 'value3', '…')
Syntax:	INSERT INTO "table_name" (column1, column2, column3, …)
	VALUES ('value1', 'value2','value3', '…')
	NOTE: number of columns and values must match to prevent error.

Usage: INSERT INTO BrainShare2010 (Firstname, Lastname, Email, Phone, Assignment, Date, Time)

Values ('Randy', 'Testdev', 'RTestdev@Novell.com', '801-111-4444',

'TestTable','3/22-24','9am-6pm')

Results:

First Name	Last Name	Email	Phone	Assignment	Date	Time
David	Manager	DManager@ Novell.com	801-111-1111	DevTable	3/22-25	8am-5pm
Adam	Teamlead	ATeamlead@ Novell.com	801-111-2222	DevTable	3/22-25	8am-5pm
Shirley	Certdata	SCertdata@ Novell.com	801-111-3333	CertTable	3/22-25	9am-6pm
Randy	Testdev	RTestdev@ Novell.com	801-111-4444	TestTable	3/22-24	9am-6pm

UPDATE   Change data in existing database. Use WHERE to specify row(s).

Syntax: UPDATE "table_name"

SET Column1 = value1, Column2 = value2, Column3 = value3

WHERE column = value

Usage: UPDATE BrainShare2010

SET Date = '3/22-25'

WHERE Lastname = "Testdev" AND Firstname = 'Randy'

Results: Date entry for Randy Testdev is changed from 3/22-24 to 3/22-25. No other change is made to data. Not specifying WHERE will change all date entries.

SELECT   Select some or all data from an SQL database table.

Syntax: SELECT Column1, Column2, Column3, …

FROM table_name

Usage: SELECT Firstname, Lastname, Phone

FROM BrainShare2010

Results   All Firstname, Lastname, and Phone entries for all employees will be selected

DELETE   Remove data from an SQL database table. Use with WHERE.

Syntax:	DELETE FROM table_name
	WHERE Column = Value
Usage:	DELETE FROM BrainShare2010
	WHERE Phone = 801-111-1111
Results:	Data entries specified with WHERE are deleted. If WHERE is not used, ALL entries from all rows and columns in the table are removed.

WHERE	Select data based on column name specified, as with SELECT above. An example is selecting all users (4) with a Lastname of Ecord, using a table called ClientList, as in the following:
Usage:	SELECT Lastname
	FROM ClientList
	WHERE Lastname = 'Ecord'
Results:	All four users with Lastname of Ecord are selected from the table ClientList.

An SQL database can be queried using statements, functions, and keywords. Using these, you can group information from tables, sort the data from tables, and even join information from two tables.

When the Novell employees work their assigned hours during BrainShare 2010 and the actual hours worked are entered into a database, the sum total of the hours worked by all can be extracted from the database entries, as well as the total worked by each individual employee.

Using the SQL GROUP BY statement along with functions such as SUM will provide a way to group the resulting dataset by database table column's. For example, suppose that Dave Manager created along with the BrainShare2010 table, another table called BrainShareHours that tracked and calculated the actual hours worked by employees at the event.

Using the example database table below, we can use SUM to extract the total number of hours worked and then use GROUP BY get each employee's total hours spent working.

Table 7-4   *Hours Worked*

Employee	Date	Hours	Assignment
Dave Manager	3/22/09	8	Developer's Table
Shirley Certdata	3/22/09	8	Certification Table
Randy Testdev	3/22/09	8	Test Development
Dave Manager	3/23/09	9	Developer's Table
Adam Teamlead	3/23/09	9	Developer's Table
Shirley Certdata	3/23/09	8	Certification Table

Employee	Date	Hours	Assignment
Adam Teamlead	3/24/09	8	Developer's Table
Randy Testdev	3/24/09	8	Test Development
Dave Manager	3/24/09	9	Developer's Table
Randy Testdev	3/25/09	10	Test Development
Shirley Certdata	3/25/09	8	Certification Table
Dave Manager	3/25/09	10	Developer's Table

SUM total of all hours worked by employees during BrainShare

Syntax:	SELECT SUM (Column) FROM table_name
Usage:	SELECT SUM (Hours) FROM BrainShareHours

SUM total of all hours worked by employees individually at BrainShare

Syntax:	SELECT Column, SUM (Column) FROM table_name GROUP BY Column
Usage:	SELECT Employee, SUM (Hours) FROM BrainShareHours GROUP BY Employee
Results:	By the use of the statement GROUP BY, the number of hours worked by each employee can be gathered by extracting all hours worked for each individual employee.

ORDER BY	This will sort the SQL data results by the use of its columns. Looking at our first table, BrainShare2010, Dave Manager has now decided to SELECT all employees working at BrainShare 2010 and sort them by Lastname. Notice use of the wildcard *.
Syntax:	SELECT * FROM table_name ORDER BY Column
Usage:	SELECT * FROM BrainShare2010 ORDER BY Lastname

First Name	Last Name	Email	Phone	Assignment	Date	Time
Shirley	Certdata	SCertdata@Novell.com	801-111-3333	CertTable	3/22-25	9am-6pm
David	Manager	DManager@Novell.com	801-111-1111	DevTable	3/22-25	8am-5pm

First Name	Last Name	Email	Phone	Assignment	Date	Time
Adam	Teamlead	ATeamlead@ Novell.com	801-111-2222	DevTable	3/22-25	8am-5pm
Randy	Testdev	RTestdve@ Novell.com	801-111-4444	TestTable	3/22-24	9am-6pm

To reverse the order displayed, you must use the SQL Keyword DESC for descending order. Add DESC after the ORDER BY clause, such as in the following:

Syntax:	SELECT * FROM table_name ORDER BY Column DESC
Usage	SELECT * FROM BrainShare2010 ORDER BY Lastname DESC

First Name	Last Name	Email	Phone	Assignment	Date	Time
Randy	Testdev	RTestdve@ Novell.com	801-111-4444	TestTable	3/22-24	9am-6pm
Adam	Teamlead	ATeamlead@ Novell.com	801-111-2222	DevTable	3/22-25	8am-5pm
David	Manager	DManager@ Novell.com	801-111-1111	DevTable	3/22-25	8am-5pm
Shirley	Certdata	SCertdata@ Novell.com	801-111-3333	CertTable	3/22-25	9am-6pm

If nothing is specified as to how to order a data set, a data set is alphabetically ordered by default (default assumes ASC, not DESC).

To sort by more than one column, you must specify the columns in the ORDER BY listing, such as in ORDER BY Lastname, Phone.

JOIN	Use this whenever extracting data results from two or more tables, where a relationship exists between the specified columns in the tables.
	Consider the following two tables, BrainShare2010 (modified) and the BrainShareTravel table which Dave set up to record employee travel expenses for the event.
	Adding the common column fields of EID (EmployeeID) to both tables, Dave can now extract the information he requires from them.

Column headings were adjusted due to width requirements for this document; however, we will use the Firstname, Lastname columns in our SQL command.

BrainShare 2010

EID	First Name	Last Name	Email	Phone	Assnmnt.	Date	Time
7000	David	Manager	DManager@ Novell.com	801-111-1111	DevTable	3/22-25	8am-5pm
7001	Adam	Teamlead	ATeamlead@ Novell.com	801-111-2222	DevTable	3/22-25	8am-5pm
7002	Shirley	Certdata	SCertdata@ Novell.com	801-111-3333	CertTable	3/23-24	9am-6pm
7003	Randy	Testdev	RTestdve@ Novell.com	801-111-4444	TestTable	3/22-24	9am-6pm
7004	James	Instruct	JInstruct@ Novell.com	801-111-5555	CNITable	3/21-25	8am-7pm

BrainShare Travel

EID	Employee Name	Dates	Travel Mileage
7000	David Manager	3/22-25	420
7001	Adam Teamland	3/22-25	410
7002	Shirley Certdata	3/23-25	317
7003	Randy Testdev	3/22-24	309
7004	James Instruct	3/21-25	

As shown, both tables have the common column field called EID. We will use that field to extract the information from both tables by matching each of their EID columns.

We will extract the Firstname, Lastname, and the Travel Mileage each employee has accumulated during their travel to and from the BrainShare 2010 Conference held in Salt Lake City, Utah.

Syntax:
```
SELECT 1st_table_name.Column, 1st_table_name.Column,
SUM(2nd_table_name.Column,) AS new_name
FROM 1st_table_name JOIN 2nd_table_name
ON 1st_table_name.Column, = 2nd_table_name.Column
GROUP BY 1st_table_name.Column, 1st_table_name.Column
```

Syntax
```
SELECT BrainShare2010.Firstname, BrainShare2010.Lastname,
SUM(BrainShareTravel.TravelMileage) AS MilesPerEmployee
FROM BrainShare2010 JOIN BrainShareTravel
ON BrainShare2010.EID = BrainShareTravel.EID
GROUP BY BrainShare2010.Firstname, BrainShare2010.Lastname
```

Firstname	Lastname	MilesPerEmployee
David	Manager	420
Adam	Teamlead	410
Shirley	Certdata	317
Randy	Testdev	309

Two types of SQL JOIN can be used, INNER JOIN and OUTER JOIN. Without either keyword (INNER or OUTER) being used, the default used is INNER JOIN which would be JOIN.

If a match exists between columns in both tables, INNER JOIN will select the data from all rows matching. If an employee did not record any mileage as shown above with the employee James Instruct, this employee will not be listed in the resulting SQL query table.

Using OUTER JOIN, you can extract and list all employees whether or not they have entered mileage. Depending on which table you want to select rows from, you can use the sub-types LEFT JOIN or RIGHT JOIN (OUTER does not need to be used with either of these in most databases).

If selecting all the rows from the first table listed after the FROM clause, whether there are matches or not, you would use LEFT JOIN. If selecting all rows, even those that have no matches, from the second table after the FROM clause, you would use RIGHT JOIN.

The syntax after the FROM clause to select all rows from the BrainShare2010 table would be

FROM BrainShare2010 LEFT JOIN BrainShareTravel

Any Employee not having entries matching the BrainShareTravel TravelMileage column would have an entry of NULL in place of an empty cell.

Firstname	Lastname	MilesPerEmployee
David	Manager	420
Adam	Teamlead	410
Shirley	Certdata	317
Randy	Testdev	309
James	Instruct	NULL

PHP

PHP is a very popular scripting language for Web applications. In this objective, you learn how to install PHP on SLES 11. The following topics are addressed:

- Understand How PHP Works

- Install PHP

- Test the PHP Installation

Understand How PHP Works

PHP is a scripting language used in conjunction with the Apache Web server. it accepts PHP code as its input and uses it to output HTML documents. Because of the way it operates, PHP is considered a server-side scripting language, meaning the processing of the script is done by the server running the Web server, not the client Web browser.

To install a PHP Web application, the script files need to be copied into the document root of the Web server. PHP files usually have an extension of `.php`.

A PHP application can be started by accessing the PHP file with a URL such as `http://www.mydomain.com/application.php`. The Web server then opens the PHP file. However, instead of sending it directly to the browser, it is passed through the PHP interpreter first.

The PHP interpreter runs the PHP script in the file and passes the dynamically generated HTML output through the Web server to the browser. The end user never sees the PHP application code.

The PHP interpreter is implemented as an Apache extension module. You could also run PHP applications directly using the Common Gateway interface, but this is not covered in this course.

The following is an overview of the PHP architecture:

Figure 7-6   *PHP Framework*

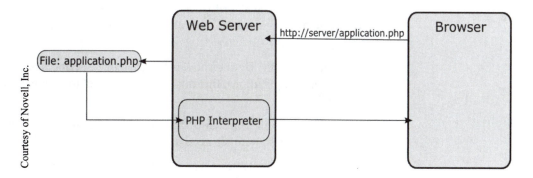

Install PHP

On SLES 11, the PHP components are split into several software packages. You need at least the following packages for a basic PHP Web application server:

- **php5**: Core PHP interpreter and libraries.

- **apache2_mod_php5**: PHP module for Apache.

If you search for **php** in YaST's Software Management module, you'll notice that there are many more PHP packages available, as shown below:

Figure 7-7   *PHP Packages*

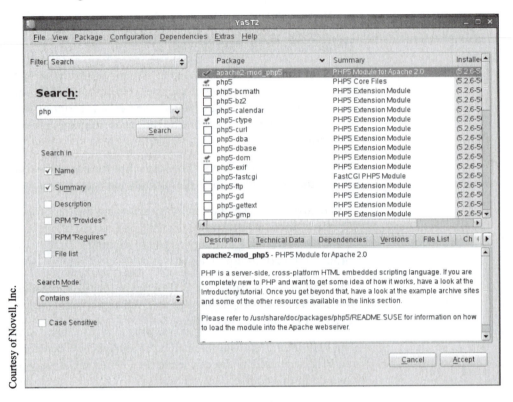

Courtesy of Novell, Inc.

These modules extend the functionality of PHP. Which packages you need depends on the requirements of the PHP application you would like to run.

The PHP interpreter has several configuration options that can be adjusted in the `/etc/php5/apache2/php.ini` file. However, the default configuration should be used in most situations. The following are a few of the options available in this file:

- **memory_limit.** Defines how much memory a script is allowed to use. For complex applications, this might need to be set to a higher value. The default is 8 MB.

- **max_execution_time.** Sets the maximum execution time, in seconds. Complex applications sometimes need a longer execution time. The default is 30 seconds.

- **display_errors.** Determines whether errors or warning messages are displayed in the HTML output. For production systems, this option should be set to `Off`, while on a development system it is useful to set it to `On`. The default is `Off`.

- **register_globals = Off.** Whether or not to register the GET, POST, and certain other variables as global variables. You should do your best to write your scripts so that they do not require `register_globals` to be on. Using form variables as globals can easily lead to possible security problems, if the code is not very well thought of.

After installing PHP packages, you have to restart Apache with the `rcapache2 restart` command.

Test the PHP Installation

A PHP installation can be easily tested by creating a file somewhere in the document root of the Web server with the following content:

```
<?PHP
phpinfo();
?>
```

This content is a simple PHP application. Calling the `phpinfo()` function outputs a Web page with information on the PHP installation. When you request this file in a Web browser, a page similar to the following is displayed:

Figure 7-8   *Testing the PHP Server*

PHP Version 5.2.6	

System	Linux da10 2.6.27.19-5-pae #1 SMP 2009-02-28 04:40:21 +0100 i686
Build Date	Feb 25 2009 17:38:24
Configure Command	'./configure' '--prefix=/usr' '--datadir=/usr/share/php5' '--mandir=/usr/share/man' '--bindir=/usr/bin' '--with-libdir=lib' '--includedir=/usr/include' '--sysconfdir=/etc/php5/apache2' '--with-config-file-path=/etc/php5/apache2' '--with-config-file-scan-dir=/etc/php5/conf.d' '--enable-libxml' '--enable-session' '--with-mm' '--with-pcre-regex=/usr' '--enable-xml' '--enable-simplexml' '--enable-spl' '--enable-filter' '--disable-debug' '--enable-inline-optimization' '--disable-rpath' '--disable-static' '--enable-shared' '--program-suffix=5' '--with-pic' '--with-gnu-ld' '--with-system-tzdata=/usr/share/zoneinfo' '--with-apxs2=/usr/sbin/apxs2' '--disable-all' '--disable-cli'
Server API	Apache 2.0 Handler
Virtual Directory Support	disabled
Configuration File (php.ini) Path	/etc/php5/apache2
Loaded Configuration File	/etc/php5/apache2/php.ini
Scan this dir for additional .ini files	/etc/php5/conf.d
additional .ini files parsed	/etc/php5/conf.d/ctype.ini, /etc/php5/conf.d/dom.ini, /etc/php5/conf.d/hash.ini, /etc/php5/conf.d/iconv.ini, /etc/php5/conf.d/json.ini, /etc/php5/conf.d/tokenizer.ini, /etc/php5/conf.d/xmlreader.ini, /etc/php5/conf.d/xmlwriter.ini
PHP API	20041225
PHP Extension	20060613
Zend Extension	220060519

Courtesy of Novell, Inc.

NOTE: If you want to learn more about PHP, visit the PHP home page at www.php.net (http://www.php.net/).

Common Gateway Interface

PHP is by far not the only way to generate dynamic content. Using the Common Gateway Interface (CGI), external content-generating programs can interact with

Apache. The PERL script language is frequently used for CGI programs, but CGI programs are not limited to a certain programming language.

There are two steps to take to allow the execution of CGI programs:

1. Define a ScriptAlias.

    A ScriptAlias directive looks like this:

    ```
    ScriptAlias /cgi-bin/ /srv/www/cgi-bin/
    ```

    This example is taken from the `default-server.conf` configuration file. It means that everything within the local directory `/srv/www/cgi-bin/` will be considered a CGI program, and it can be accessed from the `/cgi-bin/` directory on the Web server, such as `http://www.digitalairlines.com/cgi-bin/my-cgi.pl`.

    NOTE: You can also allow the execution of CGI scripts in certain directories, as shown in the following configuration example:

    ```
    <Directory /srv/www/htdocs/somedir>
        Options +ExecCGI
        AddHandler cgi-script .cgi .pl
    </Directory>
    ```

    This would allow the execution of scripts with a `.cgi` or `.pl` extension in the `somedir` directory.

    ---

2. Write a CGI program.

    Writing a CGI program differs mainly in two things from any other programming:

    - The output of your program has to be preceded by a MIME-type header, followed by an empty line separating the HTTP header from the actual content.

    - The output of your program has to be HTML or some other format a browser can display.

    A very simple program could look like this:

    ```
    #!/usr/bin/perl
    print "Content-type: text/html\n\n";
    print "Hello, World.";
    ```

    After saving this script to `/srv/www/cgi-bin/myfirstcgi.pl` and making it executable with the `chmod 755 /srv/www/cgi-bin/myfirstcgi.pl` command, you can execute it from a browser using the URL `http://localhost/myfirstcgi.pl`.

    Another way to deliver dynamic content is the use of a web application server such as Apache Tomcat. Apache Tomcat is an implementation of the Java Servlet and JavaServer Pages technologies to execute Java code on Web servers. (While both the Apache Web server and Apache Tomcat contain "Apache" in their name, they are independent of each other and shouldn't be confused.)

Exercise 7-2   *Configure a Virtual Host*

In this exercise, you configure a virtual host for accounting.digitalairlines.com and the hr.digitalairlines.com Web sites on your da-host server.

You will find this exercise at the end of the chapter.

(End of Exercise)

Objective 3   Enable an FTP Server

To enable an FTP server on SLES 11, you need to understand the following:

- The Role of an FTP Server
- How FTP Works
- Advantages of PureFTPd Server
- Install of PureFTPd
- Configure of PureFTPd
- Access an FTP Server
- Manage of PureFTPd Logs
- Configure Anonymous PureFTPd Access

The Role of an FTP Server

As the name indicates, the File Transfer Protocol (FTP) enables the transfer of files from one computer to another. Today, FTP is used mainly for file transfer on the Internet, while internal networks usually rely on NFS or SMB for file transfers.

The following basic features are supported by FTP and available to the user:

- Sending, receiving, deleting, and renaming files
- Creating, deleting, and changing directories
- Transferring data in binary or ASCII mode

An FTP server allows access after authentication against a password database. As a rule, these are the /etc/passwd and /etc/shadow files. Depending on the FTP server software used, other authentication systems, such as NIS or LDAP, are possible.

The PureFTPd FTP server also supports authentication against its own password database, which is independent from the /etc/passwd and /etc/shadow files.

In addition, guest access can be set up as anonymous FTP (aFTP). Generally, users logging in to aFTP use **anonymous** or **ftp** as their username and use their e-mail address as the password.

The address is normally not checked for correctness, although some servers check the syntax and require an entry in the format **user@hostname.domain**. An anonymous user is normally given access to a restricted directory tree (a chroot environment).

How FTP Works

The FTP protocol uses the TCP transport protocol. FTP uses two TCP connections between the client and the server, one for commands and the other for data.

The first of these connections sends FTP commands from the client to the server. To begin an FTP session, the client addresses the FTP command channel on port 21 of the server. The client then sends its commands to the FTP server.

For the actual file transfer, or in response to certain commands like `ls`, FTP uses the second TCP connection, which is created only when data is ready for transfer.

There are two different types of data transfer:

- **Active data transfer.** The FTP client offers the FTP server an unprivileged TCP port for the data channel connection. The server then initializes the data channel from its port 20 to the port offered by the client.

Figure 7-9   *Active FTP*

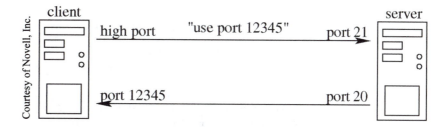

- **Passive data transfer.** The FTP client informs the FTP server that it wants to use a passive data transfer using the PASV command.

  The FTP server then offers the FTP client an unprivileged TCP port for a data channel connection and the client initializes the data channel to the port offered by the server.

Figure 7-10   *Passive FTP*

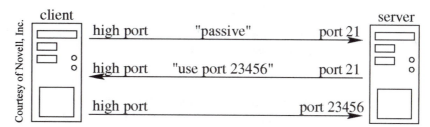

Passive FTP transfer avoids the need of having to allow incoming connections on the client. This makes it easier for firewall administrators on the client side to establish a secure configuration.

Advantages of PureFTPd Server

SLES 11 includes two FTP servers, the Very Secure FTP daemon vsftpd and the PureFTPd FTP server. Several other FTP servers are available for Linux, such as the standard FTP server, in.ftpd, the FTP server from Washington University, wu.ftpd, and proftpd, but these are not included with SLES 11.

PureFTPd has several features that make it stand out from other FTP servers:

- Consistent use of chroot environments
- Uncomplicated configuration of virtual FTP servers

- Virtual users independent of the system users listed in the `/etc/passwd` file
- Configuration via command line parameters or with a configuration file

Install of PureFTPd

You can install the PureFTPd server with the YaST Software Management module by selecting the pure-ftpd package.

After installation, you configure the FTP server manually by editing the `/etc/pure-ftpd/pure-ftpd.conf` configuration file.

You can run PureFTPd server using one of the following methods:

- **From the command line.** Enter `pure-ftpd` *options* (such as `pure-ftpd -B -e`). If you start pure-ftpd this way, no configuration file is used.

NOTE: For details on the possible pure-ftpd options, enter `pure-ftpd --help` or read pure-ftpd's manual page using the command `man pure-ftpd`.

- **From a start script.** Enter `/etc/init.d/pure-ftpd start` (or `rcpure-ftpd start`). To stop the PureFTPd service, enter `rcpure-ftpd stop`.

  The `/etc/pure-ftpd/pure-ftpd.conf` configuration file is parsed by the Perl script `/usr/sbin/pure-config-args` to translate the parameters in the configuration file to command line options.

  These options are then passed to the `/usr/sbin/pure-ftpd` daemon.

  If you want pure-ftpd to be initialized upon startup, you need to set symbolic links by entering the following:

  `insserv /etc/init.d/pure-ftpd`

- **From xinetd.** If you want to start PureFTPd via xinetd, you need to edit the `/etc/xinetd.d/pure-ftpd` file and add the required options, as in the following example:

```
# default: off
# description: The ftpd server serves FTP connections. It uses
# normal, unencrypted usernames and passwords for authentication.
# This ftpd is the pure-ftpd.
#    ** NOTE ** when using pure-ftpd from xinetd the arguments to
#    control it's behaviour should be added here in this file in
#    the "server_args" line since the configuration file
#    /etc/pure-ftpd.conf is only for standalone pure-ftpd.
#    The command "/usr/sbin/pure-config-args /etc/pure-ftpd.conf"
#    will print the arguments needed for behaviour like standalone
#    pure-ftpd.

service ftp
{
    socket_type = stream
    server = /usr/sbin/pure-ftpd
    server_args = -A -i
```

```
                    protocol = tcp
                    user = root
                    wait = no
                    disable = yes
          }
```

Because the `pure-ftpd.conf` configuration file is not parsed or evaluated when PureFTPd is started via xinetd, all the required options must be given in the `/etc/xinetd.d/pure-ftpd` file as server arguments in the `server_args` line.

Configure of PureFTPd

To perform basic configuration tasks for the PureFTPd server, you need to know how to do the following:

- Configure Anonymous FTP
- Configure FTP for Authorized Users

Configure Anonymous FTP

To configure anonymous FTP for PureFTPd, you need to have an FTP user and home directory (such as `/srv/ftp/`) in the `/etc/passwd` file (exists by default in SLES 11).

Unlike other FTP servers, however, you do not need to create any subdirectories (such as bin) in the home directory.

The following is an example of a simple `pure-ftpd.conf` file:

```
# Cage in every user in his home directory
ChrootEveryone            yes

# Don't allow authenticated users - have a public anonymous FTP only.
AnonymousOnly             yes

# Disallow anonymous users to upload new files (no = upload is allowed)
AnonymousCantUpload       yes

# Fork in background
Daemonize                 yes
```

With this configuration file, it is possible to log in only as an anonymous user, regardless of what username is given. It is not possible to change to a directory above `/srv/ftp/`, and no files can be uploaded to the server—only downloads are possible. The server detaches from the terminal it is started in (`Daemonize yes`).

The equivalent command on the command line would be `pure-ftpd -A -e -i -B`

If you want anonymous users to be able to upload files to the server, the configuration file would look like the following:

```
# Cage in every user in his home directory
ChrootEveryone            yes

# Don't allow authenticated users - have a public anonymous FTP only.
AnonymousOnly             yes

# Allow anonymous users to upload new files
AnonymousCantUpload       no

# Disallow downloading of files owned by "ftp", ie.
# files that were uploaded but not validated by a local admin.
AntiWarez                 yes

# Never overwrite files. When a file whose name already exists is
# uploaded, it gets automatically renamed to file.1, file.2, file.3,
...
AutoRename                yes
```

You have to allow write access to the `/srv/ftp/` directory using the `chown ftp /srv/ftp` command, and you have to make sure the permissions are set properly using the `chmod 755 /srv/ftp` command.

The `AntiWarez` option is recommended because the server could otherwise be misused to handle undesirable (or even illegal) data.

Files uploaded to the server belong to the user ftp, but files of the user ftp cannot be downloaded from the server because of this option. The administrator must change the owner of the file (to root, for instance) using the `chown` command before this is possible.

The last line ensures that a file that might already exist is not overwritten. Instead, a new file is created with a number at the end (such as `file.1`).

The equivalent command on the command line would be `pure-ftpd -A -e -s -r`.

Configure FTP for Authorized Users

Configuring an FTP server for authorized users is important for those who are hosting Web sites. Individual customers maintain their own pages in directories which they alone have access to.

The following is an example configuration in which no anonymous FTP access is allowed and where all users are limited to their home directory:

```
# Cage in every user in his home directory
ChrootEveryone            yes

# Disallow anonymous connections. Only allow authenticated users.
NoAnonymous               yes
```

The equivalent command on the command line would be `pure-ftpd -A -E`.

To run the server in the background, add the `-B` option on the command line or `Daemonize yes` to the configuration file.

If you want to modify the above configuration so that certain users are not confined in a chroot environment (for example, members of a group ftpadmin with the GID 500), you could enter the following:

```
# Cage in every user in his home directory
ChrootEveryone          no

# If the previous option is set to "no", members of the following group
# won't be caged. Others will be. If you don't want chroot()ing anyone,
# just comment out ChrootEveryone and TrustedGID.
TrustedGID              500

# Disallow anonymous connections. Only allow authenticated users.
NoAnonymous             yes
```

The equivalent command on the command line would be `pure-ftpd -a 500 -E`.

To run the server in the background, add the **-B** option on the command line or `Daemonize yes` to the configuration file.

IMPORTANT: Users listed in the `/etc/ftpusers` file, such as root and other system accounts, cannot log in to the FTP server.

Access an FTP Server

Any current browser can be used to access an FTP server to download files. However, not every browser is capable of uploading files. Dedicated graphical FTP clients exist, but often a command line client is good enough.

Once you have logged in to an FTP server with your user name (or the username anonymous) and your password (or your e-mail address as your password), you can use the following commands, using a command line client:

Table 7-5 *Frequently Used FTP Commands*

Command	Purpose
ls	List directory content.
cd	Change directory on the FTP server.
lcd	Change your local working directory.
pwd	Print working directory.
ascii	Switch to ascii mode, use for text files only. This mode takes care of the differences between carriage return/line feed conventions on different operating systems.
binary	Switch to binary mode, use for all non-text files. Transferring binary files in ascii mode can lead to corrupted files.

Command	Purpose
put *file*	Upload a file from your local directory to the FTP server.
get *file*	Download a file from the FTP server to your local file system.
bye	End the FTP session.
help	Lists the available commands.
help *command*	Shows a brief explanation of *command*.

The following shows a typical FTP session:

```
geeko@da1:~> ftp da-host
Trying 172.17.8.1...
Connected to da-host.digitalairlines.com.
220-Welcome to Pure-FTPd.
220-You are user number 1 of 10 allowed.
220-IPv6 connections are also welcome on this server.
220 You will be disconnected after 15 minutes of inactivity.
Name (da-host:root): geeko
331 User geeko OK. Password required
Password:
230-User geeko has group access to:  users     video     dialout
230 OK. Current restricted directory is /
Remote system type is UNIX.
Using binary mode to transfer files.
ftp> ls
229 Extended Passive mode OK (|||30093|)
150 Accepted data connection
drwxr-xr-x   27 geeko     users          4096 Jun 24 15:41 .
drwxr-xr-x   27 geeko     users          4096 Jun 24 15:41 ..
...
drwxr-xr-x    7 geeko     users          4096 Apr  6 13:23 Exercises
ftp> cd Exercises/Section_03
250 OK. Current directory is /Exercises/Section_03
ftp> get newuser.ldif
local: newuser.ldif remote: newuser.ldif
229 Extended Passive mode OK (|||30076|)
150 Accepted data connection
100%
|**********************************************************************
***************************|    218        1.28 MB/s     00:00 ETA
226-File successfully transferred
226 0.000 seconds (measured here), 1.40 Mbytes per second
218 bytes received in 00:00 (389.90 KB/s)
ftp> bye
221-Goodbye. You uploaded 0 and downloaded 1 kbytes.
221 Logout.
geeko@da1:~>
```

Manage of PureFTPd Logs

PureFTPd sends its messages to the syslog daemon, so these messages appear in the usual log files.

It is also possible for PureFTPd to write its own log files in various formats. The option for this is `-O format:logfile`, where `format` can be `clf` (Common Log Format, a format similar to that used by the Apache Web server), `stats` (special output format, designed for log file analysis software), or `w3c` (special output format parsed by most commercial log analyzers).

Suitable entries already exist in the `/etc/pure-ftpd/pure-ftpd.conf` configuration file. You need to remove the comment symbol (#) to activate the entry.

The following is an example entry:

```
AltLog              clf:/var/log/pureftpd.log
```

Exercise 7-3   Configure Anonymous PureFTPd Access

In this exercise, you configure anonymous FTP access with the permission to upload files.

You will find this exercise at the end of the chapter.

(End of Exercise)

Objective 4   Configure Electronic Mail

Electronic Mail is one of the most important Internet services today for businesses and it is certainly one of the more complex systems to configure.

As if this complexity weren't enough, if you misconfigure your e-mail server, you might inadvertently create a so-called open relay, a mail server that delivers mail from anyone to anyone. This might lead to your mail server being black listed, making it virtually impossible for you to send e-mails—which has an immediate negative impact on your company and might be difficult to correct quickly.

In this objective, the following topics are described:

- Understand E-Mail Protocols and Programs
- Postfix
- Sendmail
- qmail and Exim
- The mail Command
- Using ~/.forward Files
- Send Mail and Configure Postfix

Understand E-Mail Protocols and Programs

E-mail is an abbreviation of Electronic Mail and denotes the Internet message format (defined in RFC 822) and how e-mail messages are sent.

To understand e-mail, you need to understand:

- The Simple Mail Transfer Protocol
- The Three Mail Agents

The Simple Mail Transfer Protocol

Sending e-mail is governed by the Simple Mail Transfer Protocol (SMTP). SMTP is defined in RFC 821. Since its creation in 1982, it has undergone numerous extensions, such as the MIME format (RFC 2045) and SMTP Service Extensions (RFC 1869). SMTP has the following characteristics:

- There is a direct TCP connection between the sending and the receiving server.
- The task of SMTP is only the transmission of e-mails between mail servers.
- The SMTP sender (client) and the SMTP recipient (server) communicate through readable plain text commands. The sender transmits various commands to the recipient and controls the course of the communication as a whole.

    The recipient acknowledges the messages and gives the status of command processing with a corresponding reply code.

    Every message is confirmed. The sender starts transmitting the next command only when it has received a confirmation for the previous command.

The commands are

- **HELO.** Used by the SMTP sender to open a connection to an SMTP recipient and followed by the full host name.

- **MAIL FROM:.** Initializes transmission of an e-mail message.

  In the simplest case, the MAIL command takes the sender's e-mail address (reverse-path) as an argument.

- **RCPT TO:.** Sets the recipient's address (forward-path) for an item of mail.

  If the mail should be sent to several recipients at the same time, this command is repeated for each recipient.

- **DATA.** Tells the SMTP mailer that anything that follows is the content of the mail.

  The end of the mail content is indicated by line feed and a single dot on a separate line.

- **VRFY.** Verifies a user ID.

  This causes the SMTP recipient to check the validity of the address given as an argument.

- **EXPN.** (Expand.) Instructs the SMTP recipient to treat the argument as a mailing list.

- **RSET.** Resets all the information previously stored about the SMTP recipient.

- **HELP.** Takes as its argument any other SMTP command.

  A page of tips about how to use the corresponding instruction will be displayed.

- **NOOP.** Causes the SMTP recipient to answer with an **OK (no operation)**.

- **QUIT.** Ends the connection between the SMTP sender and recipient.

NOTE: Commands can be written in lowercase or uppercase—SMTP commands are not case sensitive. Not all mail servers implement all commands.

- Messages can be forwarded, for example, if an address has changed.

The text below shows a typical example of an SMTP session, using some of the commands listed above, and a Telnet client to connect to port 25 (the standard mail server port):

```
geeko@da10:~ > telnet da2.digitalairlines.com 25
Trying 10.0.0.2...
Connected to da2.digitalairlines.com.
Escape character is '^]'.
220 da2.digitalairlines.com ESMTP Postfix
HELO da10.digitalairlines.com
250 digitalairlines.com
MAIL FROM:<tux@da10.digitalairlines.com>
250 OK
RCPT TO:<information@digitalairlines.com>: Recipient
address rejected: User unknown in local recipient table
RCPT TO:<info@digitalairlines.com>
250 OK
DATA
354
Start mail input; end with <CR><LF>.<CR><LF>
Hello,
from today, I will no longer be sending e-mails with KMail,
but only with the program Telnet.
Tux
.
250 OK: queued as AD86A16199
QUIT
221 Bye
Connection closed by foreign host.
geeko@da1:~ >
```

The Three Mail Agents

Programs that process Internet e-mail messages are called agents.

There are three types of agents that interact in a specific sequence:

- Mail Transfer Agents
- Mail Delivery Agent
- Mail User Agent
- The Mail Cycle

Mail Transfer Agents

E-mails are passed by the e-mail software to a Mail Transfer Agent (MTA). The MTA sends them to a recipient MTA, which determines if the destination address exists locally. If it does, the recipient MTA passes the mail to a Mail Delivery Agent (MDA). If the address does not exist locally, the recipient MTA either sends the message back to the sending MTA, or it sends the message to another MTA, which passes it to yet another MTA or an MDA.

Well-known MTAs are

- Postfix (the default mail server in SLES 11)
- Sendmail

- Exim
- Qmail

Mail Delivery Agent

The MTA specifies for which local user the message is intended and passes it to a Mail Delivery Agent (MDA), which stores it in the proper location.

A well-known MDA is the Procmail program.

Mail User Agent

The Mail User Agent (MUA) is the program the e-mail user uses to read and write e-mails. It displays messages stored by the MDA and passes new messages to an MTA.

The MUA can access stored messages in three different ways:

- By mail access protocols (such as IMAP or POP3)
- Remotely by file access protocols
- Through access to local files

In the early days of e-mail, the coding of messages was limited to 7-bit ASCII and therefore offered only rudimentary options for the message layout.

Since then, e-mail has expanded to include special characters, such as accents or German umlauts, HTML text, and file attachments with arbitrary content.

You can exchange all types of files using e-mail. The MIME format (Multipurpose Internet Mail Extensions), defined in RFC 1341, regulates the correct exchange of arbitrary file types.

E-mail clients also know how to display certain MIME formats. For example, an HTML text sent by e-mail can be passed to a browser for display, or a PNG graphics file can be displayed in a graphics display program.

The Mail Cycle

The following figure shows the mail cycle and how the different types of mail agents interact:

Figure 7-11   *The Mail Cycle*

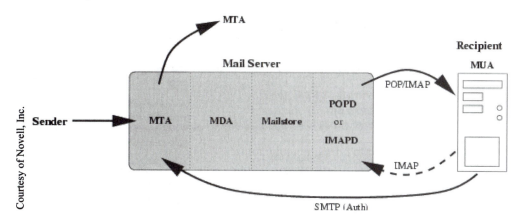

When an MTA receives an e-mail, it checks first if the recipient of the e-mail is an existing user on the local machine. If the e-mail is not for a local user, the MTA sends it to another MTA (either a so-called relay host or to the mail server responsible for the destination domain).

If the e-mail is for a local user, the MTA hands it over to the MDA which stores the mail in the mailbox of the respective user. From there, the e-mail can be retrieved using the POP3 or the IMAP protocol.

If POP3 is used, the e-mail is transferred to the client computer. Depending on the settings on the client computer, it can be kept or it can be deleted on the server.

If IMAP is used, all e-mails are kept on the server and the MUA only checks e-mails on this server. The e-mails stay on the server and are only transferred to the client computer for reading.

When sending e-mail, the MTA can be configured to ask the MUA for authentication of the user. This can be used to prohibit sending spam e-mails via this MTA.

Each recipient MTA leaves a "received" entry in the header of the message sent, with the latest entry at the top. These entries allow you, to some extent, to trace back where a message came from (the actual hostnames and IP addresses in the following example have been changed to fictive addresses):

```
Return-Path: <bo-bubtgerbwt0m3zaxb1mtd9z7mh3pzh@mx.example.com>
Received: from murder ([unix socket])
    by mailx (Cyrus v2.3.11) with LMTPA;
    Fri, 26 Jun 2009 11:25:43 +0200
X-Sieve: CMU Sieve 2.3
Received: from mailx.digitalairlines.com (localhost [IPv6:::1])
  by mailx.digitalairlines.com (Postfix) with ESMTP id 85D00928F4
  for <geeko@localhost>; Fri, 26 Jun 2009 11:25:43 +0200 (CEST)
Received: from fwmx.someisp.com [192.168.134.25]
  by mailx.digitalairlines.com with POP3 (fetchmail-6.3.9-rc2)
  for <geeko@localhost> (single-drop); Fri, 26 Jun 2009 11:25:43 +0200
(CEST)
Received: from mail.subd.someisp.com (mail.subd.someisp.com
[172.18.27.50])
    by mhead702 with LMTP;
```

```
          Fri, 26 Jun 2009 11:21:11 +0200
X-Sieve: CMU Sieve 2.3
Received: from examplehost.provider.com ([172.17.228.76]) by
mail.subd.someisp.com
   with esmtp id 1MK7cK-0wDPxQ0; Fri, 26 Jun 2009 11:21:08 +0200
Received: from examplehost.provider.com (localhost [127.0.0.1])
   by examplehost.provider.com (Postfix) with ESMTP id 5E98E47E70
   for <geeko@digitalairlines.com>; Fri, 26 Jun 2009 11:21:06 +0200
(CEST)
X-Greylist: delayed 971 seconds by postgrey-1.27 at examplehost; Fri,
26 Jun 2009 11:21:05 CEST
Received: from mta.news.example.net (mta.news.example.net
[10.11.12.13])
   by examplehost.provider.com (Postfix) with SMTP id 1AE6A47E1D
   for <geeko@digitalairlines.com>; Fri, 26 Jun 2009 11:21:04 +0200
(CEST)
...
```

Postfix

The standard mail server in SLES 11 is Postfix. Postfix was written as an alternative to the widely known MTA Sendmail.

The author of Postfix, Wietse Venema, had various objectives in the development of Postfix, the most important being that Postfix should be fast, easy to administer, and secure, and should behave as far as possible in a manner compatible with Sendmail.

The result is a modular mail server software that comes with human-readable, well commented configuration files that make the mail server configuration relatively easy. To understand Postfix and to be able to perform basic mail server administration tasks, you need to be familiar with the following:

- Components of the Postfix Program Package

- The Postfix Master Daemon

- The Main Configuration

- Lookup Tables

- Postfix Tools

Components of the Postfix Program Package

During the Postfix installation, files are saved to various locations on a SLES 11 system. These locations can be grouped according to the following criteria:

- **/etc/aliases**. This is the only Postfix configuration file in /etc/. It has the same format as the aliases file for the MTA Sendmail and contains local address aliases.

- **/etc/postfix/**. All configuration files (except /etc/aliases) defining Postfix mail processing are in this directory.

Normally, the Postfix administrator is the only one who can make changes to these files.

- **/usr/lib/postfix/.** This directory contains all the programs needed directly by Postfix. To be more precise, these are the Postfix binaries.

  These programs are not accessed directly by the system administrator.

- **/usr/sbin/.** This directory contains the administration programs for maintaining and manually controlling Postfix.

  An administrator uses these programs during maintenance work.

- **/usr/bin/.** This directory contains symbolic links with the names `mailq` and `newaliases`.

  Both links point to the `/usr/sbin/sendmail` program that provides a Sendmail-compatible administration interface for Postfix.

- **/var/spool/postfix/.** This directory contains the queue directories for Postfix and the `etc/` and `lib/` directories for Postfix processes that run in a chroot environment.

  If the variables `POSTFIX_CHROOT` and `POSTFIX_UPDATE_CHROOT_JAIL` in `/etc/sysconfig/postfix` are set to `yes`, these two directories are set up by the following command:

  ```
  SuSEconfig --module postfix
  ```

- **/usr/share/man/man[1|5|8]/.** These directories contain the manual pages for the Postfix binaries, the configuration files, and the administration programs.

- **/usr/share/doc/packages/postfix-doc/.** After the installation of the postfix-doc package, this contains documentation for Postfix.

  The `html/` subdirectory contains a detailed description about Postfix and a very useful FAQ in HTML format.

The Postfix Master Daemon

The Postfix master daemon `/usr/lib/postfix/master` is started directly by Postfix when the system is booted and is terminated only when the system goes down or if Postfix is stopped.

The Postfix master daemon is normally configured once only as the e-mail system is set up and is usually never changed.

The master daemon monitors the entire mail system:

- It controls and monitors individual Postfix processes.

- It adheres to configured resource limits, which were defined in the `master.cf` file.

- It restarts killed Postfix processes.

The Postfix master daemon is configured in the `/etc/postfix/master.cf` file. Each line in the file contains an entry for one Postfix process. The behavior of each process is defined by the configuration in the respective line.

The Main Configuration

All other configuration definitions (apart from the configuration of processing rules in lookup tables) are set in the `/etc/postfix/main.cf` file.

On SLES 11, the most common parameters of this file can be modified using variables in the `/etc/sysconfig/mail` and `/etc/sysconfig/postfix` files.

Postfix is one of the last services where `SuSEconfig` generates the actual configuration file from files located in `/etc/sysconfig/`.

The `/etc/sysconfig/mail` file is used for general configurations that are not specific to Postfix and are also used for Sendmail.

For the MTA to operate correctly, you need to set the following values in the `/etc/sysconfig/mail` file:

1. The domain name of outgoing mails needs to be entered in the `FROM_HEADER` variable. If this variable is not set, the host name (FQDN) will be used.

2. The variable `SMTPD_LISTEN_REMOTE` needs to be set to `yes` for Postfix to listen on port 25 for incoming mail.

   Otherwise, only e-mail from the local host will be accepted, as postfix will bind to the loopback interface only.

By means of the `/sbin/SuSEconfig` script, both settings and the entries in the `/etc/sysconfig/postfix` file are translated into suitable parameters in the `/etc/postfix/main.cf` file.

If you do not want `SuSEconfig` to generate this configuration file, set the variable `MAIL_CREATE_CONFIG` in the `/etc/sysconfig/mail` file to `no`.

The entries in the `/etc/postfix/main.cf` configuration file consist of key-value pairs, such as the following:

```
...
# Specify an explicit list of network/netmask patterns, where the
# mask specifies the number of bits in the network part of a host
# address.
#
# You can also specify the absolute pathname of a pattern file instead
# of listing the patterns here. Specify type:table for table-based
lookups
# (the value on the table right-hand side is not used).
#
mynetworks = 172.17.8.0/24, 127.0.0.0/8
#mynetworks = $config_directory/mynetworks
#mynetworks = hash:/etc/postfix/network_table
...
```

WARNING: If the same value appears twice in the file, which can be the case when using SuSEconfig to administer Postfix, a later entry overwrites an earlier one.

Lookup Tables

Lookup tables contain rules for processing e-mails within the overall Postfix system. These tables are activated by variables in the file `/etc/postfix/main.cf`. The tables are defined as `/etc/postfix/`*`lookup-table`*.

After a lookup table has been defined, it needs to be converted to the required format (usually in the form of a hash table) using the `postmap` command. This is done by entering `postmap hash:/etc/postfix/`*`lookup-table`*.

The structure of lookup tables is subject to the following general rules:

- Blank lines or lines that begin with a # are not interpreted as command lines.

- Lines that begin with a space are regarded as a continuation of the previous line.

The following example shows a `sender_canonical` lookup-table:

```
# The sender_canonical_maps parameter specifies optional address
# mapping lookup tables for envelope and header SENDER addresses.
#
# For example, you want to rewrite the SENDER address user@ugly.domain
# to user@pretty.domain, while still being able to send mail to the
# RECIPIENT address user@ugly.domain.
# See man 5 canonical,  /etc/postfix/canonical or
# /etc/postfix/sample-canonical.cf for more details

geeko@digiair-internal.com geeko@digitalairlines.com
tux@digiair-internal.com   tux@digitalairlines.com
```

Depending on the lookup table, it is also possible to use regular expressions or to use IP addresses instead of domain names.

NOTE: A manual page exists for every lookup table: `man 5` *`lookup-table`*.

Postfix uses the following lookup tables:

- **access lookup table.** You can use the `/etc/postfix/access` lookup table to reject or allow e-mail from defined senders. The smtpd daemon evaluates this table when e-mail arrives.

- **canonical lookup table.** You can use the `/etc/postfix/canonical` lookup table to rewrite sender and recipient addresses of incoming and outgoing e-mails. Both the header and the envelope are rewritten. The cleanup daemon reads this table when an e-mail arrives.

- **recipient_canonical lookup table.** You can use the `/etc/postfix/recipient_canonical` lookup table to convert recipient addresses of incoming and outgoing e-mails. The cleanup daemon evaluates this table when an e-mail arrives before the generic lookup table `/etc/postfix/canonical` is evaluated.

- **sender_canonical lookup table.** You can use the `/etc/postfix/sender_canonical` lookup table to rewrite sender addresses of incoming and outgoing e-mails (for outgoing e-mail: *login@host.internal*.com to *firstname.surname@mycompany*.com, for instance). The cleanup daemon reads this table when an e-mail arrives before the generic lookup table `/etc/postfix/canonical` is read.

- **relocated lookup table.** You can use the `/etc/postfix/relocated` lookup table to return the corresponding bounce e-mail to the sender, with a note of the new address of the desired addressee, if that addressee no longer exist on this system.

- **transport lookup table.** You can use the `/etc/postfix/transport` lookup table to define e-mail routing for special e-mail address ranges.

- **virtual lookup table.** You can use the `/etc/postfix/virtual` lookup table to set up e-mail for a number of domains with separate user names.

- **aliases lookup table.** The `/etc/aliases` lookup table is used to define aliases. You cannot redirect e-mails to mailboxes on other hosts or domains.

Postfix Tools

Apart from the previously mentioned tools, Postfix also has a whole range of other useful administration tools that can make life considerably easier for a postmaster.

This section briefly introduces the administration tools for Postfix:

- **newaliases.** Converts the `/etc/aliases` ASCII file to the hash table `/etc/aliases.db`.

- **mailq.** Lists all e-mails in the mail queues that have not yet been sent.

- **postalias.** Converts the `/etc/aliases` ASCII file to the hash table `/etc/aliases.db`. Same as `newaliases`.

- **postcat.** Displays the contents of a file from the queue directories in a readable form.

- **postconf.** Without any parameters, this tool displays the values of all variables defined in the `/etc/postfix/main.cf` file, as well as the default values used for all variables that are not defined in the configuration file.

  To modify variables directly, enter `postconf -e key=value`. These changes are automatically integrated in the `main.cf` file.

- **postdrop.** This is run automatically by the `sendmail` command, if `sendmail` cannot write any files to the maildrop directory because of missing world-writeable permissions. It saves the forwarded e-mail as sgid maildrop.

- **postfix.** Enables configuration errors to be found (`postfix check`), forces e-mail from the deferred queue to be delivered immediately (`postfix flush`), or rereads the Postfix configuration files (`postfix reload`).

- **postmap**. Generates the hash tables for the lookup tables in the `/etc/postfix/` directory.

- **postsuper**. Checks the file structure in the queue directories and removes unneeded files and directories (`postsuper -s`) or deletes files and directories that have been left after a system crash and are useless (`postsuper -p`).

   Individual e-mail messages can be removed from the mail queues with `postsuper -d ID`.

   In general, `postsuper` removes all files that are not normal files or directories (such as symbolic links).

NOTE: For more information on these tools, see the manual page
`man 1 `***`postfix_tool`***.

Sendmail

Probably the best known MTA is Eric Allman's Sendmail.

Sendmail has the reputation of being one of the most complex, if not *the* most complex, programs to administer.

To understand Sendmail, you need to know the following:

- Installation and Start
- Further Useful Programs for Sendmail
- Configuration Files for Sendmail

Installation and Start

Before installing sendmail, stop postfix with the `rcpostfix stop` command and uninstall postfix.

In SLES 11, Sendmail is installed using YaST. To do this, select the **sendmail** package and confirm that the installation should proceed. To start Sendmail automatically the next time the system is booted, enter

`insserv /etc/init.d/sendmail`

In addition, the FQDN should be entered in the `/etc/sysconfig/mail` file in the line FROM_HEADER.

To start Sendmail manually in SLES 11, enter

`rcsendmail start`

To stop the Sendmail server, enter

`rcsendmail stop`

As with Postfix, all activities of Sendmail are logged in the `/var/log/mail` file.

Further Useful Programs for Sendmail

The following are useful programs for Sendmail:

- **mailq**. Reports the contents of the e-mails waiting in the mail queue to be delivered.

- **newaliases**. Produces a hash table for the `/etc/aliases` file.

- **mailstats**. Produces statistics on e-mails received and delivered.

- **makemap**. Produces hash tables important for Sendmail, such as the one for the access table.

Configuration Files for Sendmail

Sendmail's configuration is distributed across several files. Sendmail's main configuration file is `/etc/sendmail.cf`. This file configures almost every aspect of Sendmail's behavior.

There are a few other configuration files that, unlike `/etc/sendmail.cf`, are relatively easy to understand and configure, such as the files found in the `/etc/mail/` directory since Sendmail version 8.9. In practice, these files almost always meet all the configuration needs and enable a simple but adequate configuration of Sendmail.

These files, such as `/etc/mail/genericstable`, are readable with a text editor, but they need to be converted to a hash table so Sendmail can also understand them. The hash tables are located in the same directory as the configuration files and have the same names, but with the ending `.db`. The procedure for converting a single configuration file to a hash table is always described at the end of the section describing the respective file.

In SLES 11, all of these configuration files can also be converted to the corresponding hash table by entering

```
SusSEconfig --module sendmail
```

or

```
/sbin/conf.d/SuSEconfig.sendmail
```

The following sections cover the Sendmail configuration files:

- The /etc/sysconfig/mail Configuration File
- The /etc/sysconfig/sendmail Configuration File
- The /etc/sendmail.cf Configuration File
- The /etc/mail/access Configuration File
- The /etc/mail/genericstable Configuration File
- The /etc/mail/virtusertable Configuration File

- The /etc/mail/mailertable Configuration File
- The /etc/aliases Configuration File

The /etc/sysconfig/mail Configuration File

The `/etc/sysconfig/mail` file contains entries that are relevant to both Sendmail and Postfix. You have to specify two settings for the MTA to function correctly:

- Enter the FQDN in the variable `FROM_HEADER`.

- Set the variable `SMTPD_LISTEN_REMOTE` to `Yes`. Otherwise, only e-mails from the local host will be accepted.

The `/etc/sysconfig/mail` file is SUSE-specific and does not necessarily exist on other distributions.

The /etc/sysconfig/sendmail Configuration File

The `/etc/sysconfig/sendmail` file in SLES 11 offers additional parameters specific to Sendmail. Each parameter is described with a comment. After changing parameters, you must run `SuSEconfig` to translate the entries in `/etc/sysconfig/sendmail` to entries in the appropriate configuration files used by sendmail.

The `/etc/sysconfig/sendmail` file is SUSE-specific and does not necessarily exist on other distributions.

The /etc/sendmail.cf Configuration File

The `/etc/sendmail.cf` file comprises macro definitions and rule set definitions, arranged into classes.

For example, the local host name is defined by the **Cw** macro in the **C** class. Therefore, **Cwlocalhost da10.digitalairlines.com** defines Sendmail's host name.

Rule sets provide the means to modify e-mails in Sendmail while they are being processed before delivery (such as changes to the header or checking for spam addresses).

The following is an example for defining rule sets:

```
# check sender address: user@address, user@, address
R<$+> $+ < @ $* > $: @<$1> <$2 < @ $3 >> $| <F:$2@$3> <U:$2@> <H:$3>
R<$+> $+ $: @<$1> <$2> $| <U:$2@>
R@ <$+> <$*> $| <$+> $: <@> <$1> <$2> $| $>SearchList <+From> $| <$3>
R<@> <$+> <$*> $| <$*> $: <$3> <$1> <$2>  reverse result
```

This rule set defines how incomplete addresses in the mail header should be processed.

As a general rule, you do not edit the `/etc/sendmail.cf` file directly.

On a SLES 11 system, you either use YaST to configure sendmail, or you edit `/etc/sysconfig/mail` and `/etc/sysconfig/sendmail` and run the SuSEconfig script.

On other systems, you edit a `sendmail.mc` file, a file consisting of M4 macros that are converted to the actual `sendmail.cf` file by the `m4` command.

The /etc/mail/access Configuration File

The `/etc/mail/access` file defines the hosts, networks, and domains whose mails are relayed via this server. Each line of the file contains a rule for the forwarding of e-mails.

The first column contains an e-mail address, a domain name, or a network address. The second column is separated from the first by a tab and contains a keyword or an SMTP reply code that defines the action for this line.

If an SMTP reply code is used, an extra optional message text can be given that will be sent to the e-mail sender when this rule is activated.

The e-mail address, domain name, or network address, in conjunction with one of the following keywords or an SMTP code, defines the action for all e-mails that match the entry in the first column:

- **OK**. Mails are accepted, even if a reject rule exists.
- **REJECT**. Mails are rejected. The sender receives an error message.
- **RELAY**. Mails are forwarded if no other reject rules exist.
- **DISCARD**. Mails are discarded. The sender is not informed.
- **ERROR:"Reply-Code text-message"**. The defined text is sent back to the sender of an e-mail if a specific reply code occurs.

The `/etc/mail/access` configuration file needs to be converted to a hash table, which can then be evaluated by the mail server.

To convert the file to the hash table, enter (as the user root)

```
makemap hash -f /etc/mail/access.db < /etc/mail/access
```

The /etc/mail/genericstable Configuration File

`/etc/mail/genericstable` modifies the sender address for outgoing e-mail. This is most commonly needed at a mail gateway between a local network and the Internet, where the local e-mail addresses are not the same as the official Internet e-mail addresses.

Each line of the file contains a rule for an e-mail address. The value in the first column defines the original sender address and the value in the second column is the address that is supposed to appear on outgoing mail. The two columns are separated by tabs.

After changing the `/etc/mail/genericstable` file, enter the following (on one line) to create the required hash table:

```
makemap hash -f /etc/mail/genericstable.db < /etc/mail/
genericstable
```

The /etc/mail/virtusertable Configuration File

`/etc/mail/virtusertable` allows the recipient address to be changed for incoming mails. Each line of this file contains a conversion rule for an e-mail recipient address.

The first column contains a complete e-mail address (user@domain) or just the recipient domain. The second column contains the value that should replace the corresponding recipient address.

`/etc/mail/virtusertable` enables Sendmail to host the same e-mail addresses for different domains in that it readdresses e-mails to different local or remote e-mail addresses.

After changing `/etc/mail/virtusertable`, enter the following (on one line) to create the required hash table:

```
makemap hash -f /etc/mail/virtusertable.db < /etc/mail/
virtuserstable
```

The /etc/mail/mailertable Configuration File

`/etc/mail/mailertable` defines the routing for outgoing e-mail messages. Each line contains the definition of a route for an address range.

The first column contains a target host or a target domain. All e-mails that fall within this range are sent via the route defined in the second column. The routing can be defined as UUCP, SMTP, or local delivery. The columns are separated by tabs.

After changing `/etc/mail/mailertable`, enter the following (on one line) to create the required hash table:

```
makemap hash -f /etc/mail/mailertable.db < /etc/mail/
mailertable
```

The /etc/aliases Configuration File

The `/etc/aliases` file (the alias database) allows the definition of e-mail aliases. It is a plain-text file with one e-mail alias per line. This e-mail alias can be totally fictitious, but must point to an existing e-mail address or at least to another already known e-mail alias.

The file has two columns:

- The first column contains the new e-mail alias, followed by a colon (such as maillist:).

- The second column is separated from the first by one or more tabs and contains a list, separated by commas, of real e-mail recipient addresses on which the new alias is based.

You can edit `/etc/aliases` in a text editor. To translate it into the required hash table, run the `newaliases` command as the user root.

qmail and Exim

In addition to postfix and sendmail, you also need to be familiar with the qmail and Exim MTAs, as discussed in the following:

- qmail
- Exim

qmail

qmail is frequently used as a replacement for sendmail. Some consider it a more secure mail server than sendmail. qmail was released to the public domain in 2007, but due to an unusual license agreement, it is considered non-free depending on which guideline is used.

qmail uses a modular architecture comprised of mutually untrusting components. For an example, the SMTP queue manager uses credentials that are different from the SMTP listener component.

Many administrators consider qmail to be easier to use than other Linux e-mail servers. For example, it has the ability to employ user-controlled wildcards. When addressing mail to "user-wildcard" for a qmail server, the message will be delivered to separate mailboxes. Using this with mailing lists and spam management allows users to publish multiple e-mail addresses.

Two protocols introduced by qmail are Quick Mail Queuing Protocol (QMQP) and the Quick Mail Transport Protocol (QMTP). QMQP allows the sharing of e-mail queues among different e-mail hosts. QMTP is a transmission protocol whose performance is better than SMTP, using fewer transmissions in comparison.

qmail uses the maildir format which allows it to deliver mail to Mbox mailboxes. Maildir takes an individual e-mail message and splits it into separate files. By doing this, maildir avoids problems with concurrency and locking. qmail can also be used safely with NFS.

Exim

Another MTA is Exim. Exim is an SMTP mail server similar in function to sendmail, but with a very different configuration and setup.

Exim does not include features such as address books, iMAP4, POP3, shared calendars, and group scheduling that are found in other mail systems. To deploy groupware features with Exim, additional software must be installed. If advanced features found in other systems such as GroupWise or Lotus Notes are needed, then Exim would most likely not be the best choice for an MTA.

Exim does, however, include many advanced configuration features which have made it attractive to large Linux installations, such as ISPs. For example, it is capable of processing millions of messages per day.

It also has the ability to store lists of domains, hosts, and users in text files, databases, and even LDAP directories. Exim's current version is 4.71 and is available from numerous websites.

Exim includes documentation which contains instructions for installing, configuring, and using Exim. You should also take note of the Exim filter specification documents that are available. The default path for the Exim installation is `/usr/sbin/sendmail` or `/usr/lib/sendmail`, depending upon your distribution.

Exim messages have a message-id assigned using a syntax of *xxxxxx-xxxxxx-xx*. The message-id is made up of alpha-numeric characters that may be upper- or lower-cased. Most commands used to manage message logging or the message queue use the message-id. For every message in the spool directory, there are three files.

The `/var/spool/exim/msglog` directory contains message logging information. Each message has a corresponding file that is named with the same as the message-id. The `/var/spool/exim/input` directory contains files that are also named using the message-id and an additional suffix which designate them as either envelope headers (-H) or message data (-D).

The mail Command

Some programs send status mail messages or notes to the user root. Depending on how your server is configured, you might not have a graphical mail client installed on the server to read them. In this case it is helpful to understand how to use the mail command to read e-mails.

If you log in at a virtual terminal, you get a notification if there are mail messages for you, as shown in the following:

```
da1 login: root
Password:
You have new mail in /var/mail/root.
Last login: Mon Jun 29 07:58:21 2009 from da-host.digitalairlines.com
da1:~ #
```

To read these messages, you can use the `mail` command, as shown in the following:

```
da1:~ # mail
Heirloom mailx version 12.2 01/07/07.  Type ? for help.
"/var/mail/root": 2 messages 2 new
>N  1 geeko@da-host.digi  Mon Jun 29 08:03   20/858     Testmail
 N  2 geeko@da-host.digi  Mon Jun 29 08:08   20/858     Testmail
?
```

The prompt for mail is a "?". At the prompt, use the following commands:

Table 7-6   *Mail Commands*

Command	Purpose
t *message_list*	Type (display) messages.
n	Display the next message.
e *message_list*	Edit messages.
f *message_list*	Give headlines of messages.
d *message_list*	Delete messages.
u *message_list*	Undelete messages.
R *message_list*	Reply to message senders.
r *message_list*	Reply to message senders and all recipients.
m *user_list*	Send mail to specific users.
q	Quit and save read, but undeleted, messages in mbox.
x	Quit and do not remove system mailbox.

A message_list consists of integers, ranges of integers, or user names separated by spaces. If omitted, mail uses the last message typed. A user_list consists of user names or aliases separated by spaces. Aliases are defined in .mailrc in your home directory.

You can also use the mail program on the command line to send e-mail. The simplest form of using mail is

mail ***mail_address***

Instead of ***mail_address*** you can enter a username of someone on your local machine. (For sending messages to users other than the local users, you need to configure a mail server on your local host.)

mail first asks you for the subject of the mail. After this, you can enter the body of your message. To finish the text, enter a single full stop in the last line, as shown in the following:

```
geeko@da1:~ > mail root
Subject: A simple Mail
This is just a test mail.
The body of the text ends with an single full stop.
.
```

mail confirms the end of the text body with EOT (end of text) and sends the mail immediately.

The following are the most important options when invoking mail:

Table 7-7   *Mail Options*

Option	Description
-a *file*	Attach the given *file* to the message.
-b *list*	Send blind carbon copies to *list*. *list* should be a comma-separated list of names.
-c *list*	Send carbon copies to *list* of users.
-q *file*	Start the message with the contents of the specified *file*. Can be given in send mode only.
-s *subject*	Specify *subject* on command line (only the first argument after the −s flag is used as a subject; be careful to quote subjects containing spaces).
-R *address*	Specify reply-to *address* on command line. Only the first argument after the −R flag is used as the address.
-f	Read e-mails that are stored in the ~/mbox file. With −f, mail opens this file to read these old e-mail messages.

Using ~/.forward Files

Users often need to forward their messages to another account, their own or another user's. To do this, you can use a .forward file. This file allows users to forward their mail without assistance from the help desk or e-mail administrator. Most Linux MTAs look for a .forward file in the home directory of the forwarding user.

The .forward file contains the address where mail messages should be forwarded to. To do this, create the file .forward and enter the *username* or *e-mail address* using the following syntax:

username	If user is a local user
emailuser@domain.tld	If it is going to an Internet address

For example, if the user geeko needs to forward his mail to a local user named tux, he could configure forwarding by doing the following in his home directory:

To create the file, type	vi .forward
To forward email to tux, type	tux
To save and exit vi, type	:wq
To verify file creation, type	ls -a .forward
To view the file text, type	cat .forward

To forward e-mail to the Internet address geeko@digitalairlines.com, the geeko user could do the following in his home directory:

To create the file, type	vi .forward
To forward email to geeko type	geeko@digitalairlines.com

To save and exit vi, type	:wq
To verify file creation, type	ls -a .forward
To view the file text, type	cat .forward

If you need to forward mail messages to both an internal username and an Internet address, use the syntax of: *user, emailuser*@*domain*.com.

When the file contents are read, the system treats the entry as an alias for that user's e-mail. This causes all e-mail to be forwarded to the alias e-mail address, it will not be delivered to the user's normal mailbox.

Exercise 7-4   Send Mail and Configure Postfix

In this exercise, you use the mail command to send and read mail and you make some basic changes to the Postfix configuration.

You will find this exercise at the end of the chapter.

(End of Exercise)

Objective 5 Configure a CUPS Server

SLES 11 uses CUPS (Common UNIX Printing System) to provide print services. CUPS is based on the Internet Printing Protocol (IPP). This protocol is supported by most printer manufacturers and operating systems. IPP is a standardized printer protocol that enables authentication and access control.

This objective covers the configuration of locally connected and remote printers using the CUPS Web interface, and the management of print queues using CUPS command line tools. It also includes a look at the CUPS configuration and log files.

- The CUPS Web Interface

- Manage Print Jobs and Queues

- Understand How CUPS Works

- Manage a CUPS Server

The CUPS Web Interface

You can access the Web interface of the CUPS server by using the Local URL **http://***IP_Address***:631**.

The main menu is shown in the following figure:

Figure 7-12   *CUPS Web Interface: Welcome*

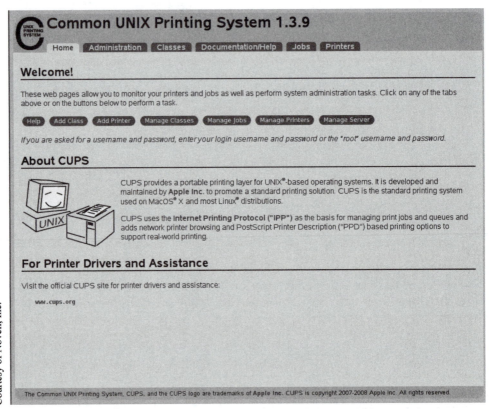

Courtesy of Novell, Inc.

The top navigation bar is available on all pages.

To manage printers and jobs or to modify the current settings, you have to authenticate. Depending on what you want to do, you have to authenticate as the owner of the job you want to modify, or as administrator of the CUPS server (by default, this is the root user).

The navigation bar at the top includes the following tabs:

- Administration
- Classes
- Documentation/Help
- Jobs
- Printers

Administration

In the Administration module (**http://localhost:631/admin**), you can perform all administration tasks:

Figure 7-13   *CUPS Web Interface: Administration*

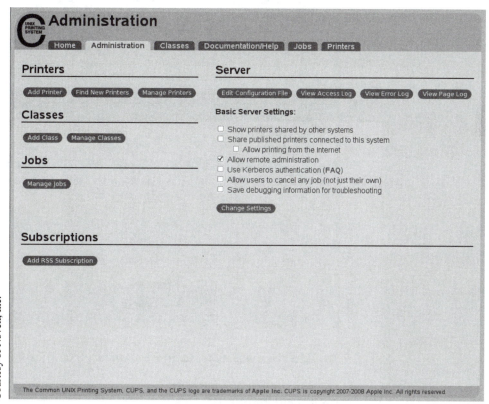

- **Printers:** Here you can add and find new printers. The ***Manage Printers*** button opens the same page as the ***Printers*** tab at the top of the page.

- **Classes:** Here you can add a printer class. The *Manage Classes* button opens the same page as the *Classes* tab at the top of the page.

- **Jobs:** The *Manage Jobs* button opens the same page as the *Jobs* tab at the top of the page.

- **Server:** The *Basic Server Settings* section allows you to make specific changes by selecting or deselecting the respective configuration options.

  The *Edit Configuration File* button opens a dialog that allows you to edit the /etc/cups/cupsd.conf file directly.

  The buttons referring to different logs open the respective logs in a browser window.

Classes

In the Classes module (**http://localhost:631/classes**), you can manage existing printer classes.

Figure 7-14   *CUPS Web Interface: Classes*

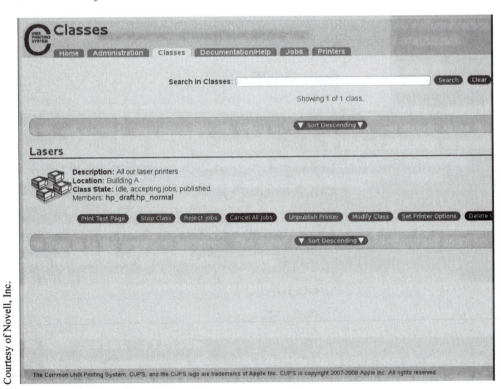

Courtesy of Novell, Inc.

To add a class, select the *Administration* tab, then click the *Add Class* button.

Documentation/Help

The Web interface allows you to quickly access documentation and help for different aspects of CUPS, as shown in the following:

Figure 7-15   *CUPS Web Interface: Help*

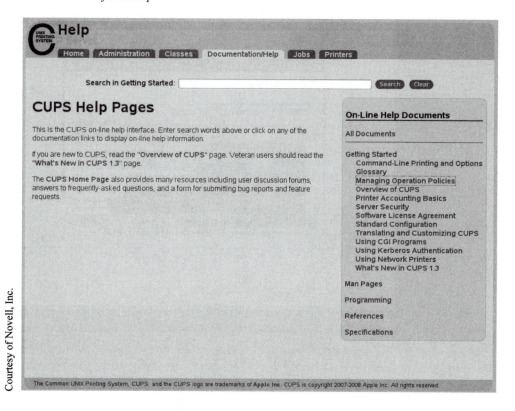

Jobs

In the Jobs module (**http://localhost:631/jobs**), you can switch between the view of the completed jobs or the view of the active jobs.

Figure 7-16   *CUPS Web Interface: Jobs*

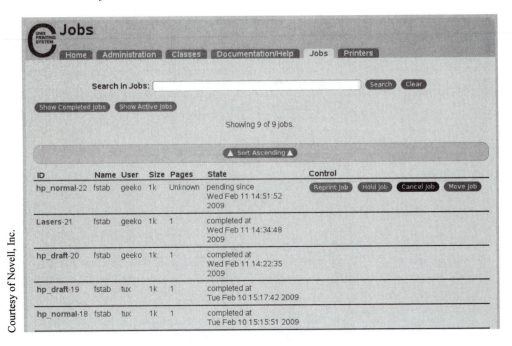

To switch between the two views, select **Show Completed Jobs** or **Show Active Jobs**. Select **All Jobs** to view active and complete jobs.

If any jobs are in the queue, you can also

- Hold the job.

- Cancel the job.

The management dialog is the same as the dialog you get when you select **Manage Jobs** in the Administration interface.

Printers

In the **Printers** module (http://localhost:631/printers), you can do the following:

- Print a test page.

- Stop/start the printer.

- Reject/accept print jobs.

- Modify the printer configuration.

- Set printer options (paper size, resolution, and banner).

- Delete the printer configuration.

- Set a printer as default printer.

- Set users that are allowed to print.

The dialog is shown in the following:

Figure 7-17   *CUPS Web Interface: Printers*

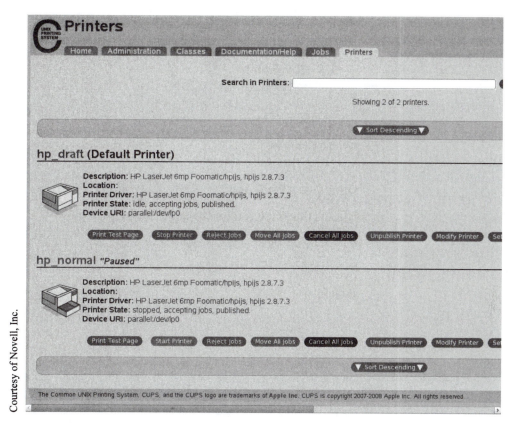

Selecting a printer entry shows information on the print jobs for that printer.

The configuration dialog is the same as the dialog you get when you select *Manage Printers* in the Administration module.

Manage Print Jobs and Queues

CUPS comes with several command line tools to start, stop, and modify print queues. The command line tools for the CUPS printing system and their man pages are included in the cups-client package.

The manual pages are also accessible using the CUPS Web interface. To access this interface from SLES 11, open a browser and point to the local http page at **http://localhost:631/help/**.

The CUPS tools allow you to use commands according to two different styles or conventions:

- Berkeley (these commands are identical to those used with the LPRng printing system)

- System V

Compared with Berkeley style, System V provides a somewhat more extensive range of features for printer administration.

To manage printer queues, you need to know how to do the following:

- Generate a Print Job
- Display Information on Print Jobs
- Cancel Print Jobs
- Manage Queues
- Configure Queues
- Start and Stop CUPS

Generate a Print Job

Use the following commands to generate a print job:

- Berkeley: `lpr -P queue file`
- System V: `lp -d queue file`

Example:

```
lpr -P color chart.ps
```

or:

```
lp -d color chart.ps
```

With these commands, the `chart.ps` file is submitted to the color queue.

If no queue is specified, the job is printed to the default queue.

The `-o` parameter needs to be used whenever any additional print options are specified:

```
lpr -P lp -o duplex=none order.ps
```

or:

```
lp -d lp -o duplex=none order.ps
```

This submits the `order.ps` file to the lp queue and also disables duplex printing for the corresponding device (`duplex=none`). To view possible options, enter `lpoptions -l -d queue` (see Configure Queues).

You have to give the command in a slightly different form to print through a remote queue:

- Berkeley: `lpr -P queue -H server file`
- System V: `lp -d queue -h server file`

Example:

```
lpr -P lp -H da10.digitalairlines.com /etc/motd
```

or

```
lp -d lp -h da10.digitalairlines.com /etc/motd
```

This submits the `/etc/motd` file to the lp queue located on the da10.digitalairlines.com print server.

NOTE: For more information on these command line tools, enter `man lpr` and `man lp`.

Display Information on Print Jobs

Use the following commands to display print job information:

- Berkeley: `lpq -P` *queue*
- System V: `lpstat -o` *queue* `-p` *printer*

To display active print jobs of the default queue, use the `lpq` command, as shown in the following:

```
geeko@da10:~ # lpq
draft is ready and printing
Rank    Owner    Job     File(s)    Total Size
active   root     14       fstab      1024 bytes
```

To list the same information in a slightly different format, use `lpq -l`.

To display the print jobs of another queue, enter the `-P` *queue*, as shown in the following:

```
geeko@da10:~ # lpq -P printer
printer is ready
no entries
```

To display the active print jobs of all available queues, enter `lpq -a`, as shown in the following:

```
geeko@da10:~ # lpq -a
no entries
```

To actualize the output in a fixed interval, enter

`lpq -P` *queue* `+seconds`

The following shows the output of `lpstat -o` *queue* `-p` *queue*. The `lpstat -a` command shows information on the accepting state:

```
da10:~ # lpstat -o draft -p draft
draft-6      root      1024    Wed Feb  4 16:06:53 2009
printer draft now printing draft-0.   enabled since Wed Feb  4
16:06:53 2009
Connected to host, sending print job...
geeko@da10:~ # lpstat -a
draft accepting requests since Tue Feb  3 14:11:08 2009
ps accepting requests since Wed Feb  4 16:19:43 2009
```

NOTE: For more information on these commands, enter `man lpq` and `man lpstat`.

Cancel Print Jobs

Use the following commands to cancel a print job:

- Berkeley: `lprm -P` *queue jobnumber*
- System V: `cancel [-h server] queue-jobnumber`

NOTE: For more information on these commands, enter `man lprm` and `man cancel`.

Manage Queues

In addition to controlling single jobs in a queue, you can also control the queue itself:

- Disable printing on a queue while jobs can still be sent to it by entering `cupsdisable` *destination*.

  Queues that are disabled still accept jobs for printing but won't actually print any files until they are enabled again.

  Disabling a print queue is useful if a printer malfunctions and you need time to fix the problem.

- Start printing again on a queue that is disabled by entering `cupsenable` *destination*.

  If there are any queued print jobs, they are printed after the printer is enabled.

- Stop accepting print jobs on a queue by entering `/usr/sbin/reject` *destination*.

  With the `/usr/sbin/reject` command, the printer finishes the print jobs in the queue but rejects any new print jobs.

  This command is useful for times when you need to perform maintenance on a printer and the printer will not be available for a significant period of time.

NOTE: `lpstat -a` shows information on the accepting state of the queues.

- Accept print jobs again on a queue that rejected them by entering `/usr/sbin/accept` *destination*.

  By using this command, you can reset the print queue to begin accepting new print jobs. If the queue is also disabled, actual printing starts only after enabling the queue again.

NOTE: The commands `cupsdisable`, `cupsenable`, and `reject` are all links pointing to `/usr/sbin/enable`.

Configure Queues

Printer-specific options that affect the physical aspects of the output are stored in the PPD (PostScript Printer Description) file for each queue in the `/etc/cups/ppd/` directory.

PPD is the computer language that describes the properties (such as resolution) and options (such as duplex unit) of PostScript printers. These descriptions are necessary to use the various printer options in CUPS.

During the installation of SLES 11, a lot of PPD files are pre-installed. In this way, even printers that do not have built-in PostScript support can be used.

If a PostScript printer is configured, the best approach is to get a suitable PPD file and store it in the `/usr/share/cups/model/` directory. You can then select the PPD file during the installation. If the model does not show up, select ***Add Driver*** in the ***Add New Printer Configuration*** dialog (Figure 2-8) and follow the simple steps to add the PPD file to the database.

Users can see the current settings of a local queue by entering

`lpoptions -p` *queue* `-l`

NOTE: The sequence of options is important. If you specify `-l` first, the settings of the default queue are listed, no matter what you specify after `-p`.

The output of this command has the following structure:

`option/string: value value value ...`

The following is an example:

```
da10:~ # lpoptions -l
HalftoningAlgorithm/Halftoning Algorithm: Accurate *Standard WTS
REt/REt Setting: Dark Light *Medium Off
TonerDensity/Toner Density: 1 2 *3 4 5
Duplex/Double-Sided Printing: *DuplexNoTumble DuplexTumble None
Manualfeed/Manual Feed of Paper: Off On
InputSlot/Media Source: *Default Tray1 Tray2 Tray3 Tray4 Envelope
Manual Auto
Copies/Number of Copies: *1 2 3 4 5 6 7 8 9 10 11 12 13 14 15 16 ...
PageSize/Page Size: *A4 Letter 11x17 A3 A5 B5 Env10 EnvC5 EnvDL
EnvISOB5 EnvMonarch Executive Legal
PageRegion/PageRegion: A4 Letter 11x17 A3 A5 B5 Env10 EnvC5 EnvDL
EnvISOB5 EnvMonarch Executive Legal
Resolution/Resolution: 75x75dpi *150x150dpi 300x300dpi 600x600dpi
Economode/Toner Saving: *Off On
LowToner/Behaviour when Toner Low: *Continue Stop
```

The * symbol in front of a value indicates the currently active setting. The significance of some of these options is as follows:

- **REt/REt Setting**: (Resolution Enhancement) Includes three modes to improve the quality of dark, light, and medium print jobs.

  Generally, the difference in print quality is small.

- **TonerDensity/Toner Density:** Specifies the quantity of toner (1=little, 5=much).

- **Duplex/Double-Sided Printing:** Disables or enables double-sided printing, assuming that your printer supports duplex printing.

- **InputSlot/Media Source:** If your printer has different paper trays, lets you select the tray for your print job.

- **Copies/Number of Copies:** Specifies the number of copies printed.

- **PageSize/Page Size:** Specifies the physical size of the paper in the selected paper tray.

- **PageRegion/PageRegion:** Normally equals the page size. This option is read by the PostScript interpreter.

- **Resolution/Resolution:** Specifies the resolution used for the print queue.

- **Economode/Toner Saving:** Used to enable economode to save toner, but the quality of prints degrades.

- **LowToner/Behaviour when Toner Low:** Specifies whether the printer continues or stops printing when the toner gets low.

To change any of the options for a local queue, enter a command with the following syntax:

```
lpoptions -p queue -o option=value
```

The following command changes the page size of the lp queue to Letter:

```
lpoptions -p lp -o PageSize=Letter
```

However, the range of users affected by the new settings varies, depending on which user has actually changed the settings:

- If a normal user (such as geeko) enters a command as above, the changes apply only to that user and are stored in the `~/.cups/lpoptions` file (in the user's home directory).

- If root enters the command, changes apply to all users on the corresponding host.

  They are then used as default and stored in the `/etc/cups/lpoptions` file.

  The PPD file of the queue, however, is not modified by this.

There is a way for root to change the defaults in the PPD file of any local queue. Such changes would apply network-wide to all users submitting print jobs to the corresponding queue.

To achieve this, enter (as root)

```
lpadmin -p queue -o option=value
```

For example, to set the default page size for the lp queue, enter

```
lpadmin -p lp -o PageSize=Letter
```

CUPS provides collections of printers called printer classes. Jobs sent to a class are forwarded to the first available printer in the class. You can also use the `lpadmin` command to

- Define classes of printers or queues.

- Edit such classes (by adding a queue to a class or deleting a queue from a class).

- Delete classes.

For example, to add a queue to a class, enter

```
lpadmin -p queue -c class
```

If the class does not exist yet, it will be automatically created.

To remove a queue from a class, enter

```
lpadmin -p queue -r class
```

If the class will be empty (with no other queues left in it) as a result of such a command, it will be deleted automatically.

To see which queues belong to which class on a given host, look at the `/etc/cups/classes.conf` file.

NOTE: For more information on all the available options of `lpadmin`, enter `man lpadmin`.

You can also get information on the commands covered above in a browser by opening **http://localhost:631/help/** in a browser (notice it's a location found locally on your SLES 11 machine) and then selecting Man Pages.

Start and Stop CUPS

As the root user, you can start or stop cupsd manually with the following commands:

- `/etc/init.d/cups start` *or* `rccups start`

- `/etc/init.d/cups stop` *or* `rccups stop`

If you make changes manually to the `/etc/cups/cupsd.conf` file, you need to restart the daemon by entering `/etc/init.d/cups restart` or `rccups restart`.

Understand How CUPS Works

To understand how CUPS works, you need to understand the following:

- Steps of the Printing Process

- Print Queues

- Log Files

- Configuration File

Steps of the Printing Process

The printing process involves the following steps:

1. A print job is submitted by a user or program.

2. The file destined for the printer is stored in a print queue, which creates two files per print job in the `/var/spool/cups/` directory.

   One of the files contains the actual data to print. The other one contains information about the print job; for example, it might contain the identity of the user who created the print job and the printer to use.

3. The cupsd printer daemon acts as the print spooler. It is responsible for watching all print queues and for starting the filters required to convert data into the printer-specific format.

4. The conversion of print data is done in the following way:

   a. The data type is determined using the entries in `/etc/cups/mime.types`.

   b. Subsequently, data is converted into PostScript using the program specified in `/etc/cups/mime.convs`.

   c. After that, the `pstops` program (`/usr/lib/cups/filter/pstops`) is used to determine the number of pages, which is written to `/var/log/cups/page_log`.

   d. CUPS uses other filtering capabilities of `pstops` as needed, depending on the options set for the print job.

   For instance, the `psselect` option of `pstops` makes it possible to limit the printout to a certain selection of pages, while the `ps-n-up` option of `pstops` allows several pages to be printed on one sheet.

e. If the selected printer is not a PostScript printer, cupsd will start the appropriate filter to convert data into the printer-specific format.

One of these filter programs is `/usr/lib/cups/filter/cupsomatic` which, in turn, relies on ghostscript for conversion.

Filters are responsible for processing all printer-specific options, including resolution, paper size, and others.

f. For the actual transfer of the data stream to the printer device, CUPS uses another type of filter, or back end, depending on how the printer is connected to the host.

These back ends are found in the `/usr/lib/cups/backend/` directory:

```
da10:~ # ls /usr/lib/cups/backend/
canon   hpfax   lpd         serial   socket
epson   http    parallel    smb      usb
hp      ipp     scsi        snmp
```

5. Once the print job has been transferred to the printer, the print spooler deletes the job from the queue and starts processing the next job. When the job is deleted, the print data file in `/var/spool/cups/` is removed.

The file that has information about the print job is not deleted. The filename for the first print job is labeled c00001. The number in each of the following print jobs is increased by one.

The following is a schematic representation of the filtering process:

Figure 7-18   *CUPS Filtering Process*

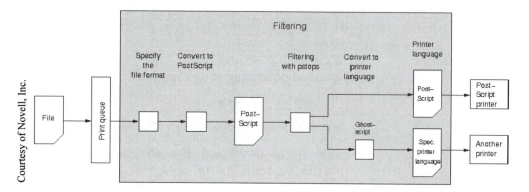

Print Queues

With CUPS, printer devices are addressed using print queues. Rather than being sent directly to the printer, print jobs are sent to a print queue associated with the device. On a print server, each print queue is registered with its name in the `/etc/cups/printers.conf` file.

Among other things, this file defines which queues the printer is addressed through, how it is connected, and which interface it is connected to.

Several print queues can be defined for one printer, as in the following example:

```
# Printer configuration file for CUPS v1.3.9
# Written by cupsd on 2009-02-05 14:06
<DefaultPrinter hp_draft>
Info HP LaserJet 6mp Foomatic/hpijs, hpijs 2.8.7.3
DeviceURI parallel:/dev/lp0
State Idle
StateTime 1233839191
Accepting Yes
Shared Yes
JobSheets none none
QuotaPeriod 0
PageLimit 0
KLimit 0
OpPolicy default
ErrorPolicy stop-printer
</Printer>
<Printer hp_normal>
Info HP LaserJet 6mp Foomatic/hpijs, hpijs 2.8.7.3
DeviceURI parallel:/dev/lp0
State Idle
StateTime 1233839040
Accepting Yes
Shared Yes
JobSheets none none
QuotaPeriod 0
PageLimit 0
KLimit 0
OpPolicy default
ErrorPolicy stop-printer
</Printer>
...
```

For instance, in the case of color printers, it can be useful to have two queues, one for black-and-white printing of text documents and one for color printing.

The following explains some entries in /etc/cups/printers.conf:

- **<DefaultPrinter queuename>**. The entry for the default printer.

- **<Printer hp_draft>** and **<DefaultPrinter hp_normal>**. The queues as defined for the "HP LaserJet 6mp" printer.

- **State Idle.** Currently, this print queue does not have any print jobs.

- **Accepting Yes.** The queue is accepting print jobs.

- **JobSheets none none.** Starting and ending banner will not be printed.

Each existing queue has its own configuration file, which is stored on the print server in the /etc/cups/ppd/ directory.

These files contain settings to configure the paper size, the resolution, and other settings.

By contrast, on the client side the names of queues are registered in the /etc/printcap file:

```
da10:~ # cat /etc/printcap
# This file was automatically generated by cupsd(8) from
# the /etc/cups/printers.conf file.  All changes to this
# file will be lost.
hp_normal|HP LaserJet 6mp Foomatic/hpijs, hpijs
2.8.7.3:rm=da10.digitalairlines.com:rp=hp_normal:
hp_draft|HP LaserJet 6mp Foomatic/hpijs, hpijs
2.8.7.3:rm=da10.digitalairlines.com:rp=hp_draft:
```

This file is generated and updated automatically by cupsd and is relevant for a number of applications (such as OpenOffice.org) that use the entries in it to list the available printers in their printer selection dialogs.

NOTE: You should not change the /etc/printcap file manually.

Log Files

The log files of CUPS are stored in the /var/log/cups/ directory.

CUPS writes three different log files. You should be familiar with the following files and know how to change the log level for troubleshooting:

- The access_log File
- The error_log File
- The page_log File
- Set the Log Level to Record Errors

The access_log File

The access_log file lists each HTTP resource that is accessed by a Web browser or CUPS/IPP client.

Lines in the log file look like the following:

```
localhost - - [05/Feb/2009:14:18:22 +0100] "POST / HTTP/1.1" 200 416
CUPS-Get-Printers successful-ok
localhost - - [05/Feb/2009:14:18:22 +0100] "POST / HTTP/1.1" 200 416
CUPS-Get-Classes successful-ok
localhost - - [05/Feb/2009:14:18:22 +0100] "POST / HTTP/1.1" 200 75
CUPS-Get-Default successful-ok
localhost - - [05/Feb/2009:14:18:22 +0100] "POST /printers/hp_normal
HTTP/1.1" 200 982 Print-Job successful-ok
```

The entries in the lines (from left to right) are explained below:

- The **host** field contains the name of the host (in the example: localhost).
- The **group** field always contains "-" in CUPS.

- The **user** field contains the authenticated username of the requesting user.

  If a username and password are not supplied for the request, this field contains – (as in the example).

- The **date-time** field shows the date and time of the request in local time (in this example: [05/Feb/2009:14:18:22 +0100]).

  The format is [*DD/MON/YYYY:HH:MM:SS +ZZZZ*], where *ZZZZ* is the time zone offset in hours and minutes from coordinated universal time (UTC).

- The **method** field is the HTTP method used (such as GET, PUT, and POST).

- The **resource** field is the filename of the requested resource. Possible resources are

  - /

  - /admin/

  - /printers/

  - /jobs/

- The **version** field is the HTTP version used by the client.

  For CUPS clients, this is always HTTP/1.1.

- The **status** field contains the HTTP result status of the request.

  Usually it is 200, but other HTTP status codes are possible. For example, 401 indicates unauthorized access.

- The **bytes** field contains the number of bytes in the request.

  For POST requests, the bytes field contains the number of bytes that were received from the client.

The error_log File

The `error_log` file lists messages (such as errors and warnings) from the scheduler:

```
I [05/Feb/2009:14:18:22 +0100] [Job 14] Adding start banner page
"none".
I [05/Feb/2009:14:18:22 +0100] [Job 14] Adding end banner page
"none".
I [05/Feb/2009:14:18:22 +0100] [Job 14] File of type text/plain
queued by "root".
I [05/Feb/2009:14:18:22 +0100] [Job 14] Queued on "hp_normal" by
"root".
I [05/Feb/2009:14:18:22 +0100] [Job 14] Started filter /usr/lib/cups/
filter/texttops (PID 28773)
I [05/Feb/2009:14:18:22 +0100] [Job 14] Started filter /usr/lib/cups/
filter/pstops (PID 28774)
I [05/Feb/2009:14:18:22 +0100] [Job 14] Started filter /usr/lib/cups/
filter/foomatic-rip-hplip (PID 28775)
I [05/Feb/2009:14:18:22 +0100] [Job 14] Started backend /usr/lib/
cups/backend/parallel (PID 28776)
I [05/Feb/2009:14:18:24 +0100] [Job 14] Completed successfully.
```

The entries in the lines (from left to right) are explained below:

- The **level** field contains the type of message:
    - **E.** An error occurred.
    - **W.** The server was unable to perform an action.
    - **I.** Informational message.
    - **D.** Debugging message.

- The **date-time** field contains the date and time of the entry (for example, when a page started printing).

    The format of this field is identical to the date-time field in the `access_log` file.

- The **message** field contains a free-form text message.

The page_log File

The `page_log` file lists each page that is sent to a printer.

```
hp_normal root 14 [05/Feb/2009:14:18:23 +0100] 1 1 - localhost
```

The entries in the lines (from left to right) are explained below:

- The **printer** field contains the name of the printer that printed the page (in this example: hp_normal).

    If you send a job to a printer class, this field contains the name of the printer that was assigned the job.

- The **user** field contains the name of the user that submitted this file for printing.

- The **job-id** field contains the job number of the page being printed (in this example: 14).

- The **date-time** field contains the date and time the page started printing.

    The format of this field is identical to the date-time field in the `access_log` file.

- The **page-number** field contains the number of pages (in this example: 1).

- The **num-pages** field contains the number of copies (in this example: 1).

    For printers that cannot produce copies on their own, the num-pages field will always be 1.

- The **job-billing** field contains a copy of the job-billing attribute provided with the IPP create-job or print-job requests or if none was provided, it will contain –.

- The **hostname** field contains the name of the host that originated the print job (in this example: localhost).

Set the Log Level to Record Errors

Messages from cupsd are written to the `/var/log/cups/error_log` file. With the default log level info, only requests and status changes are logged to the file.

If you want errors recorded, you need to change the LogLevel option in the cupsd `/etc/cups/cupsd.conf` configuration file:

```
# Log general information in error_log - change "info" to "debug" for
# troubleshooting...
LogLevel info
```

For debugging and troubleshooting, set the log level to `debug` or `debug2`. After changing the configuration, restart CUPS by entering `rccups restart`.

Configuration File

The CUPS configuration file is `/etc/cups/cupsd.conf`. It has a format similar to that of the Apache web server configuration file.

Various options are used to configure the server itself, as well as to configure filtering, networking, browsing, and access.

Exercise 7-5   Manage a CUPS Server

In this exercise, you add a printer via the Web frontend of CUPS (even though no printer is physically available at your workstation) and use command line tools to print and to manage queues.

You will find this exercise at the end of the chapter.

(End of Exercise)

Objective 6   Configure a DNS Server with BIND

The Domain Name System (DNS) is one of the most important network services. Without DNS, it would be difficult, if not impossible, to work with networked computers.

To configure a DNS server (also called a **name server**) using BIND (Berkeley Internet Name Domain), the most popular DNS software, you need to do the following:

- Understand the Domain Name System
- Install and Configure the BIND Server Software
- Configure a Caching-Only DNS Server
- Configure a Master Server
- Configure DNS Clients
- Use the rndc Command
- Query DNS Servers with Command Line Tools
- Find More Information on DNS
- Configure a DNS Server

Understand the Domain Name System

To understand the basics of name resolution with DNS, you need to know the following:

- How Name Resolution Worked in the Early Days of the Internet
- The Internet Domain Concept
- How Name Servers Work
- Query DNS

How Name Resolution Worked in the Early Days of the Internet

Computers communicate with each other by using IP addresses, but for humans it is more simple to address a computer by using its name. This requires some kind of conversion that provides computers with IP addresses when a user enters a computer name.

In the early days of the Internet, when there were relatively few computers connected to each other, a file was maintained at the Network Information Center (NIC) of the Stanford Research Institute (SRI) in California that provided exactly this conversion.

Whenever system administrators added a new computer to the Internet or changed the name of an already connected computer, these changes were sent by e-mail to the SRI-NIC where they were written to a file called `hosts.txt`.

Every system administrator worldwide had to copy this file by FTP and distribute it to all computers for which he was responsible.

This procedure had several weak points:

- **Load.** Requests to the SRI-NIC created considerable network traffic. Additionally, the computer on which the file was located soon became completely overloaded.

- **Name collisions.** Each computer name could be assigned only once worldwide. Although the NIC was able to assign unique IP addresses, it had no influence over the choice of names.

- **Consistency.** It was very difficult to guarantee the consistency of a file which was distributed worldwide. When a version of the `hosts.txt` file reached a computer, it could already be out of date.

- **Scalability.** As the number of computers grew, maintenance work became much greater.

In 1984, Paul Mockapetris created a powerful solution: the Domain Name System (or DNS). DNS is a distributed database system that allows local administration of areas and guarantees unique computer names worldwide. Its hierarchical structure is very similar to the tree structure of the Linux file system.

The Internet Domain Concept

DNS consists of several domains that can be divided into subdomains. The top level of this structure is the root domain. It is represented simply by a dot ("."). There are several computers worldwide that act as root name servers. The first layer below the root domain is built by the top-level domains (TLDs).

In the early days of DNS there were seven TLDs:

- **.com** for commercial institutions (such as novell.com and suse.com)

- **.edu** for educational institutions and research institutes (such as harvard.edu and stsci.edu)

- **.gov** for institutions of the U.S. government (such as nasa.gov and whitehouse.gov)

- **.int** for international institutions (such as un.int and ecb.int)

- **.mil** for military institutions (such as army.mil and navy.mil)

- **.net** for institutions that provide and manage network infrastructure (such as internic.net and att.net)

- **.org** for noncommercial institutions (such as eso.org and eff.org)

.arpa was used as a TLD, while the ARPAnet transferred from host files to DNS. The Advanced Research Projects Agency Network (ARPAnet) developed by ARPA of the U.S. Department of Defense was the world's first operational packet switching network, and the progenitor of the global Internet. All computers from the ARPAnet were later put into the other TLDs. The arpa TLD still has a special meaning which will be explained later in this section.

These TLDs are also known as generic TLDs. Other TLDs for individual countries, such as .de for Germany, .uk for the United Kingdom, and .ch for Switzerland, were also defined.

Recently, TLDs such as .info or .biz have been added. Each of these TLDs is administered by its own institution (the Network Information Center or NIC).

Part of the Internet namespace is shown in the following:

Figure 7-19   *The DNS*

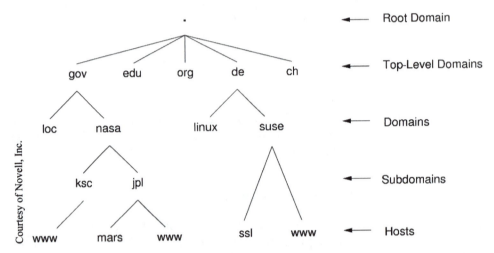

The complete computer name or fully qualified domain name (FQDN) is made up from the host name of the computer, the domain name and possibly subdomains, and the name of the TLD.

Examples of FQDNs are

- www.suse.de

- mars.jpl.nasa.gov

- mail.novell.com

To be precise, all these names end with a dot (such as www.suse.de.), indicating the root domain. But as a rule, the dot normally is not used.

How Name Servers Work

Domains are administered locally instead of using a global authority. Each domain has its own administration point (in practice, many domains are administered from one location).

For each domain there is one DNS server (or name server) defined as being "in charge" of its domain. This server is known as the master server, and it is the authority for this domain (providing authoritative answers).

This authoritative information is important, because DNS servers also temporarily store information on other domains in a cache and can pass this information on, with the note that it is a non-authoritative answer.

There are other DNS servers called slave servers for the domain that distribute the load and serve as backups. Slave servers keep a copy of the information on the master server and update this information at regular intervals. This update is called zone transfer.

The following describe the DNS server types available:

Table 7-8   *Types of DNS Servers*

Server Type	Description
Master server	Has the main responsibility for a domain. Gets its data from local files (or a directory service).
Slave server	Gets its data from the master server using zone transfer.
Caching-only server	Queries data from other DNS servers and stores the information in the cache until its expiration date. All replies are non-authoritative.
Forwarding server	All queries the server cannot answer authoritatively are forwarded to other DNS servers.

Query DNS

Various programs are involved in processing a request to the DNS database. The first is the *resolver*. This is a set of library routines used by various programs.

The resolver makes a request to a DNS server, interprets the answer (real information or error message), and sends back this information to the program that called it up.

If the DNS server receives a request from a resolver, one of two things happens:

- If the DNS server is the authority for the requested domain, the DNS server provides the required information to the resolver (the authoritative answer).

- If the DNS server is not the authority for the required domain, the DNS server queries the responsible authority for the request domain and gives the result to the resolver.

The data is stored in the cache of the DNS server. If there is another request for this data later, the DNS server can provide it immediately (a non-authoritative answer). All data has a timestamp and time-to-live (TTL) information. When the TTL expires, the information is deleted from the cache.

Assume that your DNS server wants to find the IP address of the computer www.suse.de. To do this, the DNS server first makes a request to one of the DNS servers of the root domain. Each DNS server knows the servers of the root domain, such as a.root-servers.net. The root server's answer contains the address of a name server for the .de TLD, such as a.nic.de.

Our DNS server then asks a.nic.de for the authority of the domain suse.de and receives as an answer the computer ns.suse.de (one of the DNS servers responsible for suse.de).

In a third step, this DNS server is queried and returns the IP address of the SUSE web server. This answer is returned by our DNS server to the requesting resolver.

This procedure is illustrated in the following figure:

Figure 7-20   *DNS Query Procedure*

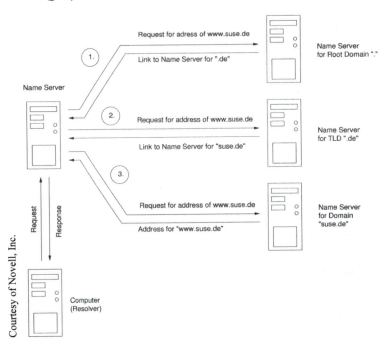

The DNS servers for the root domain play a very important role in name resolution. To alleviate the server load due to queries, every DNS server stores the information received from other names servers in its cache. When queries are made, this information is sent without querying the root DNS server anew. However, root DNS servers are very busy despite this caching mechanism. Several thousand queries per second is nothing unusual.

Install and Configure the BIND Server Software

To run a DNS server, you need to install the following packages:

- **bind.** The BIND server software (version 9 in SLES 11)

- **bind-chrootenv.** Chroot environment for BIND server.

- **bind-utils.** Utilities to query and test BIND (included in standard installation).

After installation, BIND can be used without changes to the configuration as a caching-only DNS server (see Configure a Caching-Only DNS Server for details). You can start the server using the following command:

```
rcnamed start
```

To stop a running server, use the following command:

```
rcnamed stop
```

To have the DNS server start automatically at boot time, use the following command:

```
insserv named
```

This creates the necessary links in the runlevel directories.

By default, the name server runs in a chroot environment (NAMED_RUN_CHROOTED="yes" in /etc/sysconfig/named).

The /etc/named.conf configuration file and the /etc/rndc.key file plus any files listed in the NAMED_CONF_INCLUDE_FILES variable in the /etc/sysconfig/named file are copied to the respective subdirectories in /var/lib/named/. For example, the BIND /etc/named.conf configuration file is copied to /var/lib/named/etc/named.conf.

To disable the chroot environment, set the NAMED_RUN_CHROOTED variable in /etc/sysconfig/named to no.

NOTE: For security reasons, chroot should always be used.

Configure a Caching-Only DNS Server

A caching-only DNS server does not manage its own databases but merely accepts queries and forwards them to other DNS servers. The supplied replies are saved in the cache.

The DNS server configuration is defined in the /etc/named.conf file. You can use the example file that is installed with the DNS package as a configuration file for a caching-only server.

The following example shows the beginning of a simple configuration:

```
# /etc/named.conf
#
# This is a sample configuration file for the name server BIND 9.
# It works as a caching only name server without modification.
#
# A sample configuration for setting up your own domain can be found in
# /usr/share/doc/packages/bind/sample-config.
#
# A description of all available options can be found in
# /usr/share/doc/packages/bind/misc/options.

options {
```

```
                    # The directory statement defines the name server's
                    # working directory
                    directory "/var/lib/named";
};
...
```

Lines beginning with a hash sign ("#") are comments and will be ignored.

The global options are defined in the options block at the beginning of the file. The directory option specifies the directory where the database files (or zone files) are located. Normally, this is /var/lib/named/. With this option, you specify filenames for the database files with a relative path (no absolute path required).

The global options are followed by the definition of the database files for the domains managed by the DNS server. Several entries are needed for basic DNS server functions such as those provided by a caching-only server.

Three entries are needed for every DNS server:

- The entry for the root DNS servers (not needed for BIND 9 because it has the list of root DNS servers compiled into the software).

- The forward resolution for localhost.

- The reverse resolution for the network 127.0.0.0 (localhost).

The following are examples of these entries:

```
# The following zone definitions don't need any modification.
# The first one is the definition of the root name servers.
# The second one defines localhost while the third defines
# the reverse lookup for localhost.

zone "." in {
        type hint;
        file "root.hint";
};

zone "localhost" in {
        type master;
        file "localhost.zone";
};

zone "0.0.127.in-addr.arpa" in {
        type master;
        file "127.0.0.zone";
};
```

IMPORTANT: If you omit any needed semicolons within the configuration file, BIND won't start.

The zone entry for the root DNS servers contains a reference to a file containing the addresses of the root DNS servers. This file (root.hint) and those for the resolution of localhost (localhost.zone and 127.0.0.zone) are part of the bind package.

The structure of these files is explained later.

These entries are used to forward queries to the DNS server directly to the root DNS servers. However, this resolution method can be very slow and puts an unnecessary burden on the root name servers.

This problem can be solved by specifying a name server with a lot of information in its cache (such as the name server of your internet service provider) as forwarder. In most cases, queries will be answered much faster this way.

You can define such DNS servers in the options block in the /etc/named.conf file, as in the following:

```
options
{
    directory "/var/lib/named";
    forwarders {
        10.0.0.254;
    };
};
```

You can enter up to three DNS server addresses. Queries that cannot be resolved by the local DNS server itself are forwarded to one of the specified DNS servers.

If these DNS servers cannot be reached, the queries are sent directly to the root DNS servers.

Configure a Master Server

The following are the tasks you need to complete to configure a master DNS server for your domain:

- Adapt the Main Server Configuration File

- Create the Zone Files

- Create Additional Resource Records

- Understand Slave Servers

Adapt the Main Server Configuration File

You can use the configuration of the caching-only DNS server as basis to configure a DNS server that contains its own information files. The caching-only configuration already contains the global entries for the directory and the forwarders entries (which can be omitted) in the options block. The file also contains the mandatory entries for the root servers and the resolution of localhost.

The global options are followed by definitions for the database files (or zone files) for the domains this DNS server serves. At least two files are necessary for each domain:

- A file for forward resolution (allocating an IP address to a computer name)

- A file for reverse resolution (allocating a computer name to an IP address)

If several subnets belong to a domain, then one file for each of these networks must be created for reverse resolution.

Each definition begins with the instruction **zone** (this is why the database files are also known as zone files), followed by the name of this zone.

For forward resolution, this is always the domain name. For reverse resolution, the network prefix of the IP address must be given in reverse order (172.17.8.0 becomes 8.17.172.) to which the suffix in-addr.arpa is added (8.17.172.in-addr.arpa).

The zone name is always followed by an "in" for Internet. (DNS servers can administer information on different name spaces, not only that of the Internet. Other name spaces are, however, practically never used.

The text in curly brackets defines the type of DNS server (e.g., master) for this zone and the name of the zone file.

The entries for a domain digitalairlines.com and a network 172.17.8.0/24 look like the following:

```
#
# forward resolution for the domain digitalairlines.com
#
zone "digitalairlines.com" in {
    type master;
    file "master/digitalairlines.com.zone";
};
#
# reverse resolution for the network 172.17.8.0
#
zone "8.17.172.in-addr.arpa" in {
    type master;
    file "master/172.17.8.zone";
};
```

Create the Zone Files

The two files for the domain localhost and the file for the root DNS servers are always included in the installation. You do not need to change these files; however, you must create the files required for the actual domain.

The `/var/lib/named/master/` directory is used for the database files of a master server.

You need to know the following to manually create the zone files:

- The Zone File Structure
- The /var/lib/named/master/digitalairlines.com.zone File
- The /var/lib/named/master/172.17.8.zone File
- The /var/lib/named/localhost.zone File
- The /var/lib/named/127.0.0.zone File

The Zone File Structure

Each of the database files consists of a series of entries, or resource records. The syntax of these records is always as follows:

reference [TTL] class type value

The following describes each part of a record:

- **reference.** The reference to which the record refers. This can be a domain (or subdomain) or a standalone computer (name or IP address).

- **TTL.** The Time-To-Live value for the record. If this is not present, a default TTL value is used. This determines how long other name servers store this information in their cache.

- **class.** The class of the record. For TCP/IP networks, this is always IN (internet).

- **type.** The type of the record. The most important types are listed in the table below:

- **value.** The value of the record. The value depends on the type of record, as listed below.

Table 7-9 *DNS Record Types*

Record Type	Meaning	Value
SOA	Start of Authority (term for the authority)	Parameter for the domain
NS	DNS server	Name of one of the DNS servers for this domain
MX	Mail exchanger	Name and priority of a mail server for this domain
A	Address	IP address of a computer
AAAA	IPv6 Address	IPv6 address of a computer
PTR	Pointer	Name of a computer
CNAME	Canonical name	Alias name for a computer
TXT	Text	Additional information

NOTE: Individual entries must always start in the first column with the reference. If an entry does not start in the first column, the reference is taken from the previous entry.

The /var/lib/named/master/digitalairlines.com.zone File

Unlike earlier versions of BIND, BIND 9 requires you to specify at the top of the file a default TTL for all information. This value is used whenever the TTL has not been explicitly given for an entry.

You define the TTL with the following instruction:

```
;
; definition of a standard time to live, here: two days
;
$TTL 172800
```

IMPORTANT: In this file, the semicolon is used as a comment sign.

In this example, the TTL is given in seconds. It can be given in other units as well, such as 2D for two days. Other units are M (minutes), H (hours), and W (weeks).

This is followed by the definition of the SOA (Source of Authority) entry that specifies which DNS server has the authority for this domain:

```
;
; SOA Entry
;
digitalairlines.com. IN SOA da1.digitalairlines.com.
hostmaster.digitalairlines.com. (
    2009092601; serial number
    1D          ; refresh (one day)
    2H          ; retry (two hours)
    1W          ; expiry time (one week)
    3H          ; "negative" validity (three hours)
)
```

The domain to which this entry refers (digitalairlines.com in the example) is listed first. The domain name must end with a dot. If a name does not have a trailing dot, the name of the domain is added (which would lead to an error).

The name of the DNS server is listed after the SOA entry (in this example, da1.digitalairlines.com with a dot at the end). Alternatively, you could write da1 (without a dot at the end), and the domain name digitalairlines.com would be added after the name.

Next comes the e-mail address of the person who is responsible for the administration of the DNS server. The "@" usually used in e-mail addresses must be replaced by a dot (so the e-mail address in this example is hostmaster.digitalairlines.com). This is necessary because @ has a special meaning as an abbreviation. You should use a generic e-mail address here (e.g., hostmaster.digitalairlines.com) instead of an individual e-mail address.

The next entry is a serial number. Any number can be used, but normally the date and a version number are used. After any change to the data in this file, the serial number has to be increased.

Slave servers use this number to determine whether or not they need to copy this zone file. If the serial number on the master server is greater than that on the slave server, the file is copied.

The serial number is followed by time information (the first three entries listed here are only important for slave servers):

- The first entry causes a slave server to query a master server after this amount of time, to see if there is a new version of the files (in the example, this is 1D or one day).

- If the slave server cannot reach the master server, the next time entry specifies at what intervals new attempts should be made (in the example, this is 2H or two hours).

- If the master server is not reached for a longer period of time, the third time entry specifies when the slave server should discard its information on this zone (in the example, this is 1W or a week).

  The basic idea here is that it is better not to pass on any information than to pass on outdated information.

- The fourth entry defines how long negative responses from the DNS server are valid. Each requesting server stores responses in its cache, even if a computer name could not be resolved (in the example, this is 3H or 3 hours).

These time definitions are followed by the name or IP address of the computer that is responsible for this domain as the DNS server. In all cases, the master server must be entered here. If slave servers are used, they should also be entered, as in the following:

```
;
; entry for the name server
;
digitalairlines.com.     IN NS    da1.digitalairlines.com.
                         IN NS    da2.digitalairlines.com.
```

The name of the domain can be omitted at this point. Then the name from the previous entry (the SOA entry) is taken.

The remainder of this file lists the IP addresses that are allocated to computer names. This is done with A (address) entries, as in the following:

```
;
; Allocation of IP addresses to host names
;
da1             IN A     172.17.8.101
da-host         IN A     172.17.8.1
...
```

The /var/lib/named/master/172.17.8.zone File

The file for reverse resolution contains similar entries as the file for forward resolution. At the beginning of the file, there is the definition of a default TTL and an SOA entry.

In the SOA and NS entries, the IP address of the network is written in reverse order:

```
; Database file for the domain digitalairlines.com:
; reverse resolution for the network 172.17.8.0
;
; Definition of a default TTL, here: two days
;
$TTL 172800
;
; SOA entry
;
8.17.172.in-addr.arpa. IN SOA da1.digitalairlines.com.
hostmaster.digitalairlines.com. (
     2009092601; serial number
     1D          ; refresh (one day)
     2H          ; retry (two hours)
     1W          ; expiry time (one week)
     3H          ; "negative" validity(three hours)
                          )
; Entry for the name server
;
                IN NS    da1.digitalairlines.com.
                IN NS    da2.digitalairlines.com.
```

The remainder of this file lists the host names that are allocated to IP addresses, this time with the PTR (Pointer) entry, as in the following:

```
;
; Allocation of host names to IP addresses
;
1               IN PTR  da-host.digitalairlines.com.
101             IN PTR  da1.digitalairlines.com.
...
```

The following two files must exist for the local computer. These are part of the bind package and should not be modified.

The /var/lib/named/localhost.zone File

The following is an example of the /var/lib/named/master/localhost.zone file:

```
$TTL 1W
@               IN SOA  @    root (
                             42              ; serial (d. adams)
                             2D              ; refresh
                             4H              ; retry
                             6W              ; expiry
                             1W )            ; minimum

                IN NS        @
                IN A         127.0.0.1
```

In this example, the "@" character is used as an abbreviation (this is the reason why it must be replaced by a dot in the e-mail address in the database files).

Using "@" instead of the domain name causes the file /etc/named.conf to be read to see which domain this file is responsible for.

In this case, it is localhost, which is also used for the name of the DNS server (this is why "@" appears several times in the file).

The /var/lib/named/127.0.0.zone File

In this file, the abbreviation "@" is also used. But here, the computer name must be given explicitly with localhost (remember the dot at the end):

```
$TTL 1W
@               IN SOA          localhost.      root.localhost. (
                                42              ; serial (d. adams)
                                2D              ; refresh
                                4H              ; retry
                                6W              ; expiry
                                1W )            ; minimum

                IN NS           localhost.
1               IN PTR          localhost.
```

Create Additional Resource Records

Apart from the resource records already discussed (SOA, NS, A, PTR), there are MX and CNAME resource records, which are used to do the following:

- Define Mail Servers for the Domain
- Assign Aliases for Computers

Define Mail Servers for the Domain

To be able to use e-mail addresses in the form geeko@digitalairlines.com, the e-mail server responsible for the domain must be defined. This is done with an MX (Mail Exchange) entry in the database file for forward resolution, after the DNS server entry:

```
digitalairlines.com.    IN MX   0 mail
                        IN MX   10 da1
                        IN MX   10 da5
```

If an e-mail is now sent to the address geeko@digitalairlines.com, the computer sending the mail asks the DNS server which computer is the mail server and is sent the list of the MX entries in return.

Several mail servers can be listed. On the basis of their priorities, it is then decided to which computer the e-mail is sent. The priority of mail servers is defined by the number next to MX; the lower this number, the higher the priority.

In this example, the computer mail.digitalairlines.com has the highest priority (therefore, it is the primary mail server). da1.digitalairlines.com and da5.digitalairlines.com both have the same priority.

If the mail server with the highest priority cannot be reached, the mail server with the second-highest priority is used. If several mail servers have the same priority, then one of them is chosen at random. An address entry must be made for each mail server.

Assign Aliases for Computers

If you want a computer to be reached by more than one name (such as addressing a computer as da30.digitalairlines.com and www.digitalairlines.com), then corresponding aliases must be given.

These are the CNAME (canonical name) entries in the database file for forward resolution:

```
da30          IN A     10.0.0.30
www           IN CNAME da30
```

NOTE: The names of the mail servers for the domain (MX entry) cannot be alias names, since some mail servers cannot handle this correctly.

Understand Slave Servers

To guarantee reliable operation, at least one more DNS server besides the master server is required. It receives the zone information from the DNS master server and can take over part of the load from the master. But it is especially important in case the DNS master server is not available. The configuration of a slave server is not covered in this course.

Configure DNS Clients

To instruct a computer to use a certain DNS server, the information on this server has to be written to the /etc/resolv.conf file. This can be done using YaST (during installation or at any time later) or by editing this file with any text editor.

The /etc/resolv.conf file looks similar to the following:

```
search digitalairlines.com
nameserver 172.17.8.1
```

Normally, this file has the following two types of entries:

- **search.** A list of domains (or subdomains) is provided after this keyword. Several domain names are entered on one line. This allows only the host name to be used to resolve to the correct IP address. The host name is expanded by the domain names specified here until a matching IP address is found.

  For example, if you provide digitalairlines.com and atl.digitalairlines.com as domain names after the **search** entry, when looking up a host named "server" this name is expanded to server.digitalairlines.com and server.atl.digitalairlines.com. The first matching IP address is returned. If both of these host names exist, you have to specify the FQDN to resolve both IP addresses.

- **nameserver.** The keyword **nameserver** specifies the IP address of a DNS server to use. You can have up to three entries, but each of them must only contain one server address. If several entries of this type exist, the second DNS server is queried when the first does not answer, and the third one is queried if both previous servers do not respond.

Another important file for the clients is /etc/nsswitch.conf. It applies to all programs that use the resolver functions of the current GNU C Library (glibc6). (The predecessor of this file is /etc/host.conf, which applies to older versions of the GNU C Library.) This file configures the name service switch, which is responsible for resolving host names, network names, users, and groups.

The relevant part for resolving host names looks like the following:

```
#/etc/nsswitch.conf
...
hosts:          files dns
networks:       files dns
...
```

Both entries shown here define that the first attempt to resolve a host name is done using the /etc/hosts file. If this fails, a DNS server is queried to resolve the name. The same applies to the resolution of network names, using /etc/networks first.

Use the rndc Command

rndc is a utility that allows you to control the name server over a TCP connection. Its commands require a key for authentication. On SLES 11 this key is generated when the bind package is installed and it is written to the /etc/rndc.key file. The content of the file looks similar to the following:

```
key "rndc-key" {
        algorithm hmac-md5;
      secret "pjBZbfuWI70VERC8j5isq1Zlpo+r4y70Skm4HYjjmLixgp+nkpte3j
Vn0+1MzJZrlosBobQuYNdqx34b7jHhsQ==";
};
```

The rndc command is called within the /etc/init.d/named script to generate the status report when the script is called with the status parameter, or to stop the server when it is called with the stop parameter.

You can use the rndc stats command to write the named statistics to a file, by default to /var/lib/named/var/log/named.stats. The rndc reload command causes named to reread its configuration and zone files. To view the possible control commands that can be used with rndc, enter rndc without any parameters.

By default, rndc can only be used on the machine where named is running. If you want to control named from remote, edit the /etc/named.d/rndc-access.conf file according to the comments given in that file and add the rndc-access.conf file name to the NAMED_CONF_INCLUDE_FILES variable in the /etc/sysconfig/named file. After a restart of named you can control named remotely, for instance to get it to reload its configuration. The content of the rndc.key file needs to be available on the remote computer—use the -k key-file -s server options when using rndc remotely.

Query DNS Servers with Command Line Tools

Several command line tools are available to query a DNS server. These include the following:

- The host Command
- The dig Command
- The nslookup Command
- The hostname command

The host Command

The most important command to query a DNS server is the host command. The general syntax is host *computer nameserver*. The following example shows how it is used:

```
da10:~ # host da-host
da-host.digitalairlines.com has address 172.17.8.1
da10:~ # host 172.17.8.101
101.8.17.172.in-addr.arpa domain name pointer
da1.digitalairlines.com.
...
```

If a name server address is not provided, host contacts the servers listed in /etc/resolv.conf. If you want to use another DNS server, you have to provide its IP address with the command.

By default, host returns the IP address or the host name, depending on which information is given. If you want to query domain information, you need to use the -t option with the type of information required, as in the following:

```
da10:~ # host -t ns novell.com
novell.com name server ns.wal.novell.com.
novell.com name server ns2.novell.com.
novell.com name server ns.novell.com.
da10:~ # host -t mx novell.com
novell.com mail is handled by 2 prv2-mx.provo.novell.com.
novell.com mail is handled by 2 prv-mx.provo.novell.com.
novell.com mail is handled by 2 prv1-mx.provo.novell.com.
da10:~ # host -t soa novell.com
novell.com has SOA record ns.novell.com. bwayne.novell.com.
2009070101 7200 900 604800 21600
```

In this example, the host names of the DNS servers, the mail servers, and the SOA entry for the domain novell.com are requested.

The dig Command

A more verbose command is `dig`, which is normally used to troubleshoot DNS problems. The general syntax is

```
dig  @nameserver  computer  type  query_options
```

The options are listed in the following table:

Table 7-10   *dig Options*

Option	Description
nameserver	The IP address or name of the DNS server that should be queried. If not specified, dig checks all DNS servers listed in `/etc/resolv.conf`.
computer	The resource record to look up (such as a host name, an IP address, or a domain name).
type	The type of resource record to be returned, such as A (IP address), NS (DNS server), MX (mail exchanger), -x (pointer), or ANY (all information).
query_options	Defines how the query is done and the results are displayed. Each query option starts with a +.

The most important difference between `host` and `dig` is that dig does not use the domain list from `/etc/resolv.conf` by default to expand the host name. This means that the FQDN or IP address of the host must be specified. If the domain list should be used, use `+search`.

The following example demonstrates the use of `dig`:

```
da10:~ # dig ripe.net ns

; <<>> DiG 9.5.0-P2 <<>> ripe.net ns
;; global options:  printcmd
;; Got answer:
;; ->>HEADER<<- opcode: QUERY, status: NOERROR, id: 22348
;; flags: qr rd ra; QUERY: 1, ANSWER: 4, AUTHORITY: 0, ADDITIONAL: 7

;; QUESTION SECTION:
;ripe.net.                        IN      NS

;; ANSWER SECTION:
ripe.net.               166934   IN      NS      ns-pri.ripe.net.
ripe.net.               166934   IN      NS      ns3.nic.fr.
ripe.net.               166934   IN      NS      sunic.sunet.se.
ripe.net.               166934   IN      NS      sns-pb.isc.org.

;; ADDITIONAL SECTION:
ns3.nic.fr.             167273   IN      A       192.134.0.49
ns3.nic.fr.             139762   IN      AAAA    2001:660:3006:1::1:1
sunic.sunet.se.         84724    IN      A       192.36.125.2
sunic.sunet.se.         85720    IN      AAAA    2001:6b0:7::2
ns-pri.ripe.net.        172336   IN      A       193.0.0.195
sns-pb.isc.org.         171392   IN      A       192.5.4.1
sns-pb.isc.org.         171570   IN      AAAA    2001:500:2e::1

;; Query time: 73 msec
;; SERVER: 172.17.8.1#53(172.17.8.1)
;; WHEN: Fri Jul  3 08:30:23 2009
;; MSG SIZE  rcvd: 291
```

The **QUESTION SECTION** shows what was queried and the **ANSWER SECTION** shows the response: a list of DNS servers of the domain ripe.net.

The IP addresses of certain DNS servers are listed under **ADDITIONAL SECTION**. The address in the last line is an IPv6 address (**2001:500:2e::1**).

Data about the query, such as the duration of the query (**Query time**), the server that answered the query (**SERVER**), and the date of the query (**WHEN**) are listed at the end of the output.

Using dig to Test DNS Name Resolution lists some more examples of the use of the `dig` command.

The nslookup Command

The `nslookup` (name service lookup) command is older than the dig and host commands. It might be removed from future releases of the BIND utilities. But it can still be used in current releases to query the DNS database for the IP address or name of a server on the network.

The basic syntax for the `nslookup` command is

```
nslookup server_name/IP_address nameserver
```

For example, entering `nslookup da1.digitalairlines.com` would return information showing the IP address of the server answering the query and the name and address of the server being looked up, as shown in the following:

```
da10:~ # nslookup da-host.digitalairlines.com
Server:         172.17.8.101
Address:        172.17.8.101#53
Name:   da-host.digitalairlines.com
Address: 172.17.8.1
```

The hostname command

The `hostname` command does not query the DNS server; however, it can be used to display the hostname of the machine, the domain it belongs to (-d option), and its Fully Qualified Domain Name (FQDN) (-f option).

Find More Information on DNS

If there are syntax errors in one of the configuration or zone files, BIND writes verbose messages to the `/var/log/messages` file. These messages also contain information on the filename and the line in which the error occurs.

If there is an error, the processing of the file is interrupted at this point (that is, errors later in the file are not detected now).

NOTE: For more information on BIND and DNS, see the BIND home page at http://www.isc.org/sw/bind/ (http://www.isc.org/sw/bind/).

Exercise 7-6   Configure a DNS Server

In this exercise, you learn how to configure a DNS server.

You will find this exercise at the end of the chapter.

(End of Exercise)

Objective 7   Configure the NTPD

Many network services, like directory services, as well as forensic investigations that need to correlate log entries on different machines, rely on uniform time settings across all computers within the network.

To implement uniform time settings on all computers in a network, all computers must be able to access at least one time server so clocks will synchronize.

There are two ways of synchronizing the time on a SLES 11: `netdate` and NTP (Network Time Protocol). To configure and synchronize the time, you need to understand the following:

- Time Overview

- Synchronize Time with hwclock or netdate

- The Network Time Protocol (NTP)

- Synchronize Time with NTP

- Configure ntpd

Time Overview

To configure and synchronize time on a SLES 11, you need to understand the following fundamental concepts:

- Hardware Clock and System Clock

- GMT (UTC) and Local Time

- Time Configuration Files

Hardware Clock and System Clock

There are two main clocks in a Linux system:

- **Hardware clock.** Clock that runs independently of any control program running in the CPU. It even runs when you turn off the server.

  This clock is part of the ISA (Industry Standard Architecture) standard and is commonly called the hardware clock. It is also called the time clock, the RTC (Real Time Clock), the BIOS clock, or the CMOS (Complementary Metal-oxide Semiconductor) clock.

  The term *hardware clock* is used on Linux systems to indicate the time set by the hwclock utility.

- **System time.** Time kept by a clock inside the Linux kernel. It is driven by a timer interrupt (another ISA standard).

  System time is meaningful while Linux is running on the server. System time is the number of seconds since 00:00:00 January 1, 1970 UTC (or the number of seconds since 1969).

On a Linux server, it is the system time that is important. The hardware clock's basic purpose is to keep time when Linux is not running. The system time is synchronized to the hardware clock when Linux boots. After that, Linux uses only the system time.

Once the system time is set on the Linux server, it is important that you do not use commands such as `date` or `netdate` to adjust the system time without considering the impact on applications and network connections.

For a Linux server connected to the Internet (or equipped with a precision oscillator or radio clock), the best way to regulate the system clock is with `ntpd`.

For a standalone or intermittently connected machine, you can use `adjtimex` instead to at least correct systematic drift (man adjtimex lists the options).

You can set the hardware clock (with a command such as `hwclock`) while the system is running. The next time you start Linux, it will synchronize with the adjusted time from the hardware clock.

The Linux kernel also maintains a concept of a local time zone for the system. Some programs and parts of the Linux kernel (such as file systems) use the kernel time zone value. An example is the vfat file system. If the kernel timezone value is wrong, the vfat file system reports and sets the wrong time stamps on files.

However, programs that care about the time zone (perhaps because they want to display a local time for you) almost always use a more traditional method of determining the time zone such as using the `/etc/localtime` file and the files in the `/usr/share/zoneinfo/` directory.

GMT (UTC) and Local Time

On startup, Linux reads the time from the computer's local hardware (CMOS) clock and takes control of the time. The hardware clock can be set using one of the following:

- **UTC (Universal Time Coordinated).** This time is also referred to as GMT (Greenwich Mean Time). For this setting, the variable HWCLOCK in the `/etc/sysconfig/clock` file has the value `-u`.

- **Local time.** If the hardware clock is set to the local time, the variable HWCLOCK in the `/etc/sysconfig/clock` file has the value `--localtime`.

Choosing GMT as the hardware time makes it easier to coordinate a large number of computers in different places (especially if the computers are located in different time zones).

Time Configuration Files

The current time (system time) is calculated with the help of the variable TIMEZONE in the `/etc/sysconfig/clock` file, which also handles the required changes between daylight saving time and standard time.

The following is an example of the settings in `/etc/sysconfig/clock`:

```
HWCLOCK="--localtime"
SYSTOHC="yes"
TIMEZONE="Europe/Berlin"
DEFAULT_TIMEZONE="US/Eastern"
```

By means of the variable TIMEZONE, the time configured on the local host (= system time) is set in the /etc/localtime file, a copy of the respective timezone file from /usr/share/zoneinfo/. The /usr/share/zoneinfo/ directory is a database of all time zones. SYSTOHC="yes" makes sure the current system time is written to the hardware clock when the system shuts down.

NOTE: In SLES 9, there used to be a symbolic link (/usr/lib/zoneinfo/localtime) pointing to /etc/localtime. This link does not exist anymore in SLES 10 and SLES 11, even though it might still be mentioned in /etc/sysconfig/clock.

Synchronize Time with hwclock or netdate

To synchronize time between network servers with hwclock or netdate, you need to know how to

- Use hwclock
- Use netdate

Use hwclock

hwclock is a tool used to access the hardware clock. You can display the current time, set the hardware clock to a specified time, set the hardware clock to the system time, and set the system time from the hardware clock.

You can also run hwclock periodically to insert or remove time from the hardware clock to compensate for systematic drift (where the clock consistently gains or loses time at a certain rate if left to run).

hwclock uses several methods to get and set hardware clock values. The normal way is to initialize an I/O process to the device special file /dev/rtc (RTC: Real Time Clock), which is maintained by the rtc device driver.

However, this method is not always available. The rtc driver is a relatively recent addition to Linux and is not available on older systems.

On older systems, the method of accessing the hardware clock depends on the system hardware.

NOTE: For additional details on how the system accesses the hardware clock and other hwclock options, enter man hwclock in a terminal window.

Some of the more commonly used options with hwclock include the following:

Table 7-11   *Options of the hwclock Command*

Option	Description
-a or --adjust	Adds or subtracts time from the hardware clock to account for system drift (enter `man hwclock` for details).
-r or --show	Displays the current time of the hardware clock. The time is always shown in local time, even if you keep your hardware clock set to UTC time.
-s or --hctosys	Sets the system time to the current hardware clock time. It also sets the kernel's timezone value to the local time zone as indicated by the TZ variable.
--set --date=newdate	Sets the hardware clock to the date given by the `--date` option. For example: `hwclock --set --date="9/22/09 16:45:05"`
-v or --version	Displays the version of hwclock.
-w or --systohc	Sets the hardware clock to the current system time.

You can also view the hardware clock time by entering `cat /proc/driver/ rtc`.

Use netdate

To set up the system time once only, you can use the `netdate` command as follows:

`netdate` ***timeserver1 timeserver2*** `. . .`

where ***timeserver*** represents a time server on the network or the Internet that offers the time service on UDP port 37.

After querying the time servers, the netdate client compares the server times with its own time.

Time differences are then sorted into groups to determine which is the largest group of servers with an identical time (within certain limits). The first computer in the group is then used to update the time on the local server.

To synchronize the time to a specific external time source, you enter `netdate` ***time_source***, as in the following:

`netdate ptbtime1.ptb.de`

In this case, the client queries the time server at the Physikalisch-Technische Bundesanstalt (PTB) in Braunschweig, Germany.

You then need to set the hardware clock to the system clock time by entering `hwclock --systohc` or `hwclock -w`.

NOTE: A simple way to implement time synchronization with `netdate` and `hwclock` is to use a script that is run regularly by cron.

The Network Time Protocol (NTP)

The disadvantage of using netdate is that it causes jumps of the system time into the past or the future compared to the current system time. NTP provides a means to avoid such jumps by slightly speeding or slowing system time, thus (within limits) keeping the time continuum of the system time while adjusting it.

As the networking environment continues to expand to include mixed operating system environments, time synchronization is becoming more dependent on NTP.

To configure NTP on SLES 11, you need to understand the following:

- The Network Time Protocol
- Stratum
- NTP Daemon (ntpd)
- NTP Terms
- How the NTP Daemon Works

NOTE: For more information on NTP, visit www.ntp.org (http://www.ntp.org).

The Network Time Protocol

NTP is an industry standard protocol that uses UDP on port 123 to communicate between time servers and time clients.

An NTP server uses the NTP protocol to provide time information to other servers or to workstations on the network.

An NTP client is a computer that understands the Network Time Protocol and gets time information from an NTP server. A time client can also, in turn, act as a time server for other servers and client workstations on the network.

Any computers on your network with Internet access can get time from NTP servers on the Internet. NTP synchronizes clocks to the UTC standard, the international time standard.

NTP not only corrects the time, but it also keeps track of consistent time variations and automatically adjusts for system time drift on the client. This reduces the network traffic and it keeps the client clocks more stable, even when the network is down.

Stratum

NTP introduces the concept of a stratum. Stratum x is used as a designation of the location of the servers in the NTP tree hierarchy.

Stratum 1 is the first (highest) level in the hierarchy. It denotes servers that adjust their time by means of some external reference time source (such as GPS [Global Positioning System], an atomic clock, or radio).

Servers that synchronize their time to stratum 1 servers are denoted as stratum 2, and those that use stratum 2 servers to synchronize their time are denoted as stratum 3, and so on until you reach a stratum level of 16 (the maximum allowed).

Differences between stratum 2 and stratum 1 servers are normally very small and, for the majority of users, unnoticeable.

The following figure depicts the stratum hierarchy.

Figure 7-21   *Stratum Hierarchy*

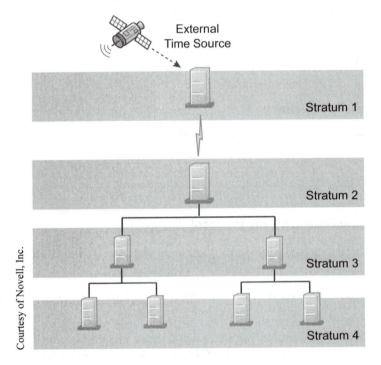

Generally only one server in a network communicates with an external time provider. This reduces network traffic across geographical locations and minimizes traffic across routers and WANs.

NTP Daemon (ntpd)

The NTP distribution in the **ntp** package includes ntpd, the NTP daemon. This daemon is used by both the time server and the time client to give and to obtain time, respectively.

The ntpd process is designed to adjust time continuously, making the time adjustments very small.

ntpd can also limit the drift of the system clock based on historical data, even when an external time server is unavailable.

The ntpd process requires little resource overhead. This allows NTP to be easily deployed on servers hosting other services, even if the servers are heavily loaded.

ntpd uses the following approaches to avoid sudden time changes:

- Regularly corrects the local computer clock on the basis of collected correction data.

- Continuously corrects the local time with the help of time servers in the network.

- Enables the management of local reference clocks, such as radio-controlled clocks.

NTP Terms

To configure and adjust NTP, you need to understand the following terms:

- **Drift.** During operation, ntpd measures and corrects incidental clock frequency errors and writes the current value to a file under `/var/lib/ntp/drift/`.

  If you start and stop ntpd, the daemon initializes the frequency from this file. This helps prevent a potentially long interval to relearn the frequency error.

- **Jitter.** This is the estimated time error of the peer clock (the delta between the client and server since the last poll).

How the NTP Daemon Works

After the NTP Daemon is started, it automatically synchronizes the system time with a time server on an ongoing basis. The correction takes place in small increments by expanding or compressing the system time (not abruptly, as when `netdate` and `hwclock` are used).

Transactions between the client and the server occur about once per minute, increasing the interval between transactions gradually to once per 17 minutes under normal conditions. Poorly synchronized clients will tend to poll more often than well synchronized clients.

The client uses the information it gets from the server or servers to calibrate its clock. This consists of the client determining how far its clock is off and adjusting its time to match that of the server.

To allow clocks to quickly achieve high accuracy yet avoid overshooting the time with large time adjustments, NTP uses a system where large adjustments occur quickly and small adjustments occur over time.

For small time differences (less than 128 milliseconds), NTP uses a gradual adjustment. This is called *slewing*. For larger time differences, the adjustment is immediate. This is called *stepping*.

If the difference between system time and the reference server at the start of the NTP daemon is larger than about 17 minutes, the NTP daemon is aborted. You can change this behavior by starting ntpd with the option `-g` (the default on SLES 11). This option makes sure the system time is adjusted in one jump after the start of the daemon.

If the inaccuracy of a clock becomes too significant (off by more than about 17 minutes) while NTP is running, NTP aborts the NTP daemon, with the assumption that something has gone wrong with either the client or the server. (This behavior is independent of the option -g used to start the NTP daemon.)

Because NTP averages the results of several time exchanges to reduce the effects of variable latency, it might take several minutes for NTP to even reach consensus on what the average latency is.

It often takes several adjustments (and several minutes) for NTP to reach synchronization. In the long run, NTP tries to decrease the amount of polling it does by making the clock on each system become more accurate.

Because of the algorithm that the NTP daemon uses, it is best to synchronize with multiple servers to help protect the client from an incorrect or downed server. In many environments, it is unlikely that an NTP server failure will be noticed quickly.

Synchronize Time with NTP

To synchronize network time with NTP, you need to know how to do the following:

- Configure the NTP Server
- Start and Stop the NTP Server
- Monitor the NTP Server

Configure the NTP Server

As soon as you start ntpd on a host, it serves as an NTP server and can be queried via NTP. You configure the NTP server either by using the YaST NTP Configuration module, or by editing the NTP configuration files /etc/ntp.conf and /etc/sysconfig/ntp and starting the NTP server from the command line.

You need to know how to

- Configure the NTP Server Using YaST
- Configure the NTP Server Using the Command Line

Configure the NTP Server Using YaST

YaST provides an NTP Configuration module to configure the NTP daemon on SLES 11. The server can, as client, synchronize with an existing NTP server and act, in turn, as an NTP server to other clients.

To configure the NTP with YaST, start YaST and select *Network Services > NTP Configuration*. From a terminal you can start the module directly as root by entering yast2 ntp-client.

The *Advanced NTP Configuration* dialog appears.

Figure 7-22   *Advanced NTP Configuration, General Settings*

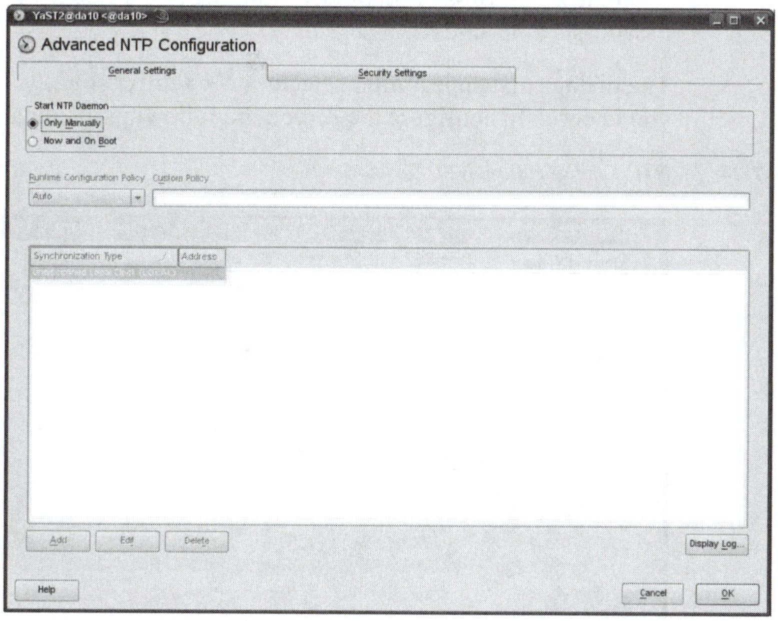

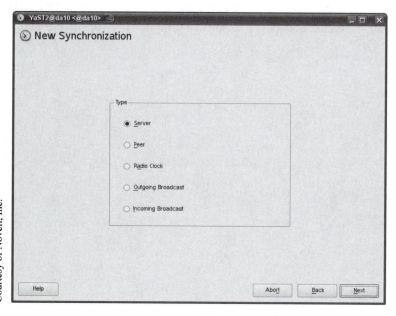

Courtesy of Novell, Inc.

On the *General Settings* tab, you configure the NTP daemon to start each time you boot your system by selecting *Now and On Boot*.

Once you select Now and On Boot, you can click the *Add* button. The *New Synchronization* dialog appears:

Figure 7-23   *NTP Configuration, New Synchronization*

Courtesy of Novell, Inc.

Here you specify whether you want to synchronize to a time Server, a Peer (a specialized relationship to another machine that can act as server or as client; see

/usr/share/doc/packages/ntp-doc/confopt.html), a Radio Clock, or an Incoming Broadcast. Select Outgoing Broadcast if you want your server to send broadcasts to its clients.

The dialogs that appear after selecting **Next** differ slightly, depending on the option you choose. To configure the server, the following dialog appears:

Figure 7-24   *NTP Configuration, NTP Server Settings*

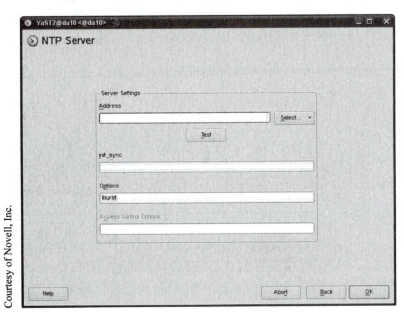

Courtesy of Novell, Inc.

You can enter the Fully Qualified Domain Name or the IP address manually, or select **Select ... > Public NTP Server** and choose from a list of public NTP servers. The dialog allows you to select a time server close to your geographical location:

Figure 7-25   *NTP Configuration, Select Public NTP Server*

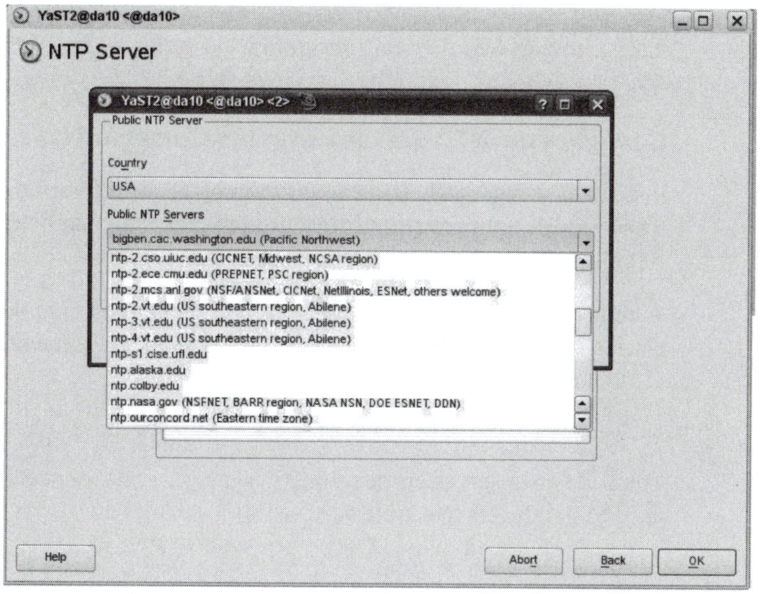

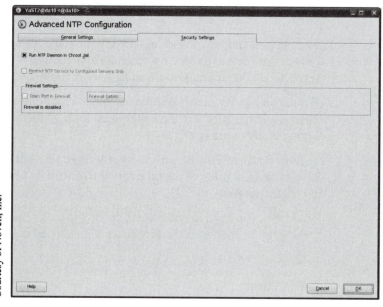

Courtesy of Novell, Inc.

The information in parenthesis tells you which clients the NTP server serves according to its policy. You should choose a server that is near you and allows you to use it.

Select your time server and click **OK**. The server will appear in the *General Settings* overview.

The *Security Settings* tab offers additional configuration options:

Figure 7-26   *Advanced NTP Configuration, Security Settings*

Courtesy of Novell, Inc.

You can choose to run ntpd in a change root environment and open the NTP port in the firewall if the firewall is active.

After clicking **OK**, the configuration is written to `/etc/ntp.conf` and `/etc/sysconfig/ntp`, and the service is started.

Configure the NTP Server Using the Command Line

Instead of using YaST, you can edit the NTP configuration files directly. The `/etc/ntp.conf` configuration file is used by the NTP daemon; variables defined in the `/etc/sysconfig/ntp` file are used by the `/etc/init.d/ntp` start script.

When editing the `/etc/ntp.conf` file, you need to make sure that the following entries exist for the local clock, which is used if the time server is not available:

```
server 127.127.1.0              # local clock (LCL)
fudge  127.127.1.0 stratum 10   # LCL is unsynchronized
```

The following server entries in `/etc/ntp.conf` concern the time servers that are used to get the current time:

```
## Outside source of synchronized time
server timeserver1.example.com
server timeserver1.digitalairlines.com
```

There are two possible methods of synchronization between the time server and the client:

- **Polling.** With polling, the client asks the server for the current time.

  Polling starts at one-minute intervals. If the time interval is determined to be trustworthy, the interval is reset to once every 1024 seconds.

  You can set the minimum and maximum limits of the polling in `/etc/ntp.conf`, as in the following:

  ```
  server timeserver1.example.com minpoll 4 maxpoll 12
  ```

  The minpoll and maxpoll values are interpreted as powers of 2 (in seconds). The default settings are 6 (26 = 64 seconds) and 10 (210 = 1024 seconds), respectively. Values between 4 and 17 are permitted.

- **Broadcasting.** By means of broadcasting, the server sends the current time to all clients, and the clients receive the signal through the `broadcastclient` option in their ntpd.conf.

  In large networks, traffic caused by polling can be significant. In this case, you might want to configure the time server to distribute time information by sending broadcast packets.

  To do this, you need to enter the following in `/etc/ntp.conf` on the server (where the IP address is the broadcast address used in the network):

  ```
  broadcast 172.17.255.255
  ```

  On the client:

```
disable auth
broadcastclient
```

For reasons of security, broadcast-based synchronization should be used together with an authentication key so that the client accepts information only from trustworthy time servers. See the documentation in `authopt.html` and `miscopt.html` in the `/usr/share/doc/packages/ntp-doc/` directory (package ntp-doc).

You also need to include the name for the drift file and log file in `/etc/ntp.conf`, as in the following:

```
driftfile /var/lib/ntp/drift/ntp.drift
logfile /var/log/ntp
```

The drift file contains information that describes how the hardware clock drifts. When the daemon ntpd is started for the first time, this file does not exist. It takes about 15 minutes for the daemon to gather enough information to create the file.

The `/etc/sysconfig/ntp` file contains variables that are used to configure the way the daemon is started, as shown in the following:

```
## Path:          Network/NTP
## Description:    Network Time Protocol (NTP) server settings
## Type:          string
## Default:       "-g -u ntp:ntp"
#
# Additional arguments when starting ntpd. The most
# important ones would be
# -u user[:group]   to make ntpd run as a user (group) other than root.
#
NTPD_OPTIONS="-g -u ntp:ntp"

## Type:          yesno
## Default:       yes
## ServiceRestart: ntp
#
# Shall the time server ntpd run in the chroot jail /var/lib/ntp?
#
# Each time you start ntpd with the init script, /etc/ntp.conf will be
# copied to /var/lib/ntp/etc/.
#
# The pid file will be in /var/lib/ntp/var/run/ntpd.pid.
#
NTPD_RUN_CHROOTED="yes"
```

If you want, for instance, to limit NTP communication to a certain interface, you change the NTPD_OPTIONS variable:

```
NTPD_OPTIONS="-g -u ntp:ntp -I eth0"
```

Start and Stop the NTP Server

You can start the NTP daemon by entering `rcntp start` (or `/etc/init.d/ntp start`). You can check the status of ntpd by entering `rcntp status`. To stop the NTP Daemon, use `rcntp stop`.

In SLES 10 and earlier, the start script called the `ntpdate` program to initially set the system time before starting ntpd. In SLES 11, this is no longer the case, because the NTP daemon is now able to deal with time differences greater than 1000 seconds, provided it is started with the `-g` option. The use of `ntpdate` is deprecated in the current version of NTP.

If the time difference between the NTP server and its time source is greater than 1000 seconds, the time is adjusted with one jump, as shown in the following excerpt from the `/var/log/ntp` log file (note the change of the system time in the last line):

```
da10:~ # tail -f /var/log/ntp
...
22 Jan 16:44:12 ntpd[11507]: synchronized to LOCAL(0), stratum 10
22 Jan 16:44:12 ntpd[11507]: kernel time sync status change 0001
22 Jan 16:45:16 ntpd[11507]: synchronized to 192.168.1.15, stratum 3
23 Jan 14:54:11 ntpd[11507]: time reset +78898.715082 s
```

NOTE: If you want to set the time of a SLES 11 machine once with no NTP daemon running, use the `sntp` program as replacement for ntpdate. Enter `man sntp` in a terminal window to learn about its syntax.

To start NTP automatically when the system is booted, you need to create the symbolic links in the respective runlevel directories by entering `insserv ntp`.

If any changes are made to the `ntp.conf` file, you need to restart ntpd using the command `rcntp restart`.

After the `/etc/ntp.conf` file has been read by ntpd, the client sends a request to the server (its time provider), and the server sends back a time-stamped response, along with information such as its accuracy and stratum. Other computers can now, in turn, use it as their time server.

NOTE: For time requests of other kinds (such as time servers for netdate) to be processed, the services must be made available by means of inetd or xinetd. For this reason, the prepared entries for daytime and time must be enabled for UDP and TCP in the configuration file of inetd or xinetd.

Monitor the NTP Server

Different tools allow you to get information on the status of the NTP server. You need to know how to

- Trace the Time Source with ntptrace

- Query the NTP Daemon Status

Trace the Time Source with ntptrace

The NTP distribution includes the `ntptrace` program. `ntptrace` is an informational tool that traces the source of time that a time consumer is receiving. It can be a useful debugging tool.

The following is an example of ntptrace output:

```
da10:~ # ntptrace
localhost: stratum 3, offset 0.000723, synch distance 1.18225
tick.east.ca: stratum 2, offset 1.601143, synch distance 0.06713
tock.usask.ca: stratum 1, offset 1.712003, synch distance 0.00723,
refid 'TRUE'
```

The `ntptrace` output lists the client name, its stratum, its time offset from the local host, the synchronization distance, and the ID of the reference clock attached to a server, if one exists.

The synchronization distance is a measure of clock accuracy, assuming that it has a correct time source.

Query the NTP Daemon Status

To verify that the time server is working properly, you can enter `ntpq -p`. The command queries the status of the ntpd daemon and returns information similar to the following:

```
da10:~ # ntpq -p
   remote        refid     st t when poll reach   delay   offset  jitter
==============================================================================
 LOCAL(0)      LOCAL(0)  10 l   15   64    1   0.000   0.000   0.008
*ptb1.ptb.de   .PTB.      1 u   14   64    1  27.165   2.348   0.001
 ntp2.ptb.de   .PTB.      1 u   13   64    1  26.159   0.726   0.001
```

Displayed information includes the following:

- **remote.** Hostname or IP address of the time server.

- **refid.** Type of reference source (0.0.0.0 = unknown).

- **st.** Stratum value for the server.

- **when.** Number of seconds since the last poll.

- **poll.** Number of seconds between two polls.

- **reach.** Indicates if the time server was reached in the last poll attempt. Reach begins with the value 0 when you start ntpd.

  For every successful attempt, a 1 is added to the binary register on the right. The maximum value of 377 means that the server was reachable in the last eight requests.

- **delay.** Time between the ntpd request and the arrival of the answer (in milliseconds).

- **offset.** Difference between the reference time and the system time (in milliseconds).

- **jitter.** Size of the discrepancies between individual time comparisons (in milliseconds).

An asterisk (*) in front of a server name means that this server is the current reference server with which system time is compared. If this server cannot be reached, then the server that is marked with a plus sign (+) is used.

Exercise 7-7   Configure ntpd

In this exercise, you configure your server to get time information from another server.

You will find this exercise at the end of the chapter.

(End of Exercise)

Objective 8   Enable xinetd

Services can run either standalone, meaning they listen on a port themselves, or via "super-server" xinetd (or inetd on some older Linux distributions). In this case, the xinetd acts as a mediator of connection requests for a series of services.

It accepts the connection requests, starts the required service, and passes the request to the newly started server process. After the connection between the client and the server is terminated, the server process is removed from memory.

Starting services through inetd or xinetd has both advantages and disadvantages. The most significant advantage is saving resources (especially memory), since a server process is started only when it is needed. A disadvantage, however, is that a delay occurs while the required service is loaded, started, and connected.

As a rule, you want to use inetd or xinetd only for services that are occasionally (not permanently) needed on the server. Some of the services run traditionally by inetd or xinetd include Telnet and FTP.

SLES 11 uses xinetd as "super-server." Because inetd is listed in the LPIC Level One objectives, it is described as well, despite the fact that it is not available on the SLES 11 DVD.

In this objective, you learn how to enable the Extended Internet Daemon (xinetd) and the Internet Daemon (inetd) by reviewing the following:

- Configure xinetd with YaST
- Manage xinetd Manually
- Configure inetd
- Configure xinetd

Configure xinetd with YaST

To configure the services mediated by xinetd, you can use the YaST Network Services (xinetd) module. Start the **YaST Control Center** and then select **Network Services > Network Services (xinetd)**. Or open a terminal window, su – to root, and then enter yast2 inetd.

NOTE: The YaST module to configure xinetd is called inetd because in the past, the default super daemon on SUSE Linux was inetd, not xinetd.

Enable the xinetd super daemon by selecting **Enable**. This activates the *Currently Available Services* list. You can add, edit, or delete services in the list:

Figure 7-27   *Network Service Configuration (xinetd)*

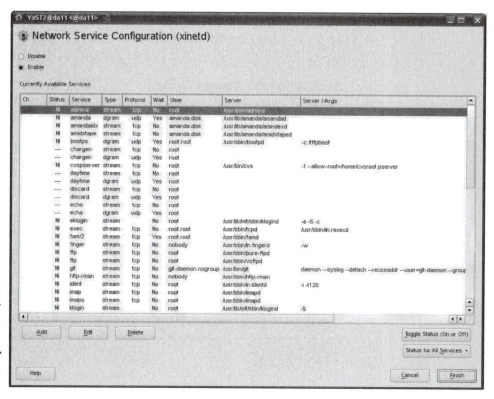

Courtesy of Novell, Inc.

NOTE: To manage the services available through xinetd (except for enabling services such as Telnet or FTP) requires a skill set beyond the objectives of this course. This is especially true of configuring services with *Edit*.

Notice that some services are off (---), while others are not installed (NI).

To configure a service, select the service and then select *Toggle Status (On or Off)*.

If a service is not installed, it will be installed. The word "On" appears in the Status column. An "X" appears in the Changed (Ch) column to indicate that the service has been edited and will be changed in the system configuration.

You can change the status of all installed services to On or Off by selecting *Status for All Services > Activate All Services* or *Status for All Services > Deactivate All Services*.

When you finish configuring the services, save the configuration setting and start the xinetd daemon by selecting *Finish*.

Manage xinetd Manually

To manage xinetd manually, you need to know how to do the following:

- Start, Stop, and Restart xinetd
- Configure xinetd

- Configure Access Control
- Configure Log Files
- Configuring TCP Wrappers

Start, Stop, and Restart xinetd

The default installation of SLES 11 includes the xinetd package. To have the daemon automatically activated at boot, enter `insserv xinetd`.

xinetd is controlled by the `/etc/init.d/xinetd` script. `/usr/sbin/rcxinetd` is a link to this script. You can start and stop the daemon by entering `rcxinetd start` or `rcxinetd stop`. You can find out whether or not the daemon is activated by entering `rcxinetd status`.

Additionally, xinetd can be influenced by signals sent with kill or killall. The following table lists some of the signals that can be used with xinetd:

Table 7-12   *Signals Used with xinetd*

Signal	Number	Description
SIGHUP	1	xinetd re-reads the configuration file and stops listening on ports of services that are no longer available and/or binds to ports now available according to the new configuration.
SIGQUIT	3	Causes xinetd termination.
SIGUSR1	10	Causes an internal state dump (the default dump file is `/var/run/xinetd.dump`).
SIGTERM	15	Terminates all running servers before terminating xinetd.
SIGIO	29	Causes an internal consistency check to verify that the data structures used by the program have not been corrupted.

Configure xinetd

The configuration of xinetd is distributed across several files. `/etc/xinetd.conf` lists general options, while files in `/etc/xinetd.d/` contain the configuration of specific services provided via xinetd. These files are included into the xinetd configuration by an include statement at the end of `/etc/xinetd.conf`.

To configure xinetd, you need to understand the following:

- The File /etc/xinetd.conf
- The Directory /etc/xinetd.d/

- Internal Services

- chkconfig

The File /etc/xinetd.conf

In SLES 11, the `/etc/xinetd.conf` file contains only general options, no service configurations. The following is the syntax of `/etc/xinetd.conf` for the default configuration parameters of xinetd:

```
defaults
    {
            key operator parameter parameter. . .
    }
```

Operators include =, −=, and +=. Most attributes (keys) support only the operator =, but you can include additional values to some attributes by entering += or remove them by entering −=.

The defaults entry in the configuration file is optional and allows you to set defaults such as the following:

```
defaults
{
        log_type         = FILE /var/log/xinetd.log
        log_on_success   = HOST EXIT DURATION
        log_on_failure   = HOST ATTEMPT
#        only_from        = localhost
        instances        = 30
        cps              = 50 10
}
includedir /etc/xinetd.d
```

The configurations for `log_type` and instances will be overwritten if something else has been defined in the individual service entries. For all other attributes, the default configurations are combined with the values set in the services.

The `log_type` statement can define whether (as in the example) the output is written directly to a log file (`/var/log/xinetd.log`) or forwarded to the daemon syslog (such as `log_type = SYSLOG daemon`).

The `log_on_success` and `log_on_failure` keys configure what should be recorded in the log file, depending on whether the connection to a network service succeeds or fails.

The `instances` key can be used to limit the maximum possible number of daemons for each service, which protects the machine from either intentional or accidental overload due to too many simultaneous connections (Denial of Service attempts).

`cps` stands for connections per second. The first value (50) is the maximum number of connections per second that can be handled. The second value (10) is the wait period before accepting new connections after the maximum has been exceeded (helpful in mitigating Denial of Service attacks).

The directive `includedir /etc/xinetd.d` prompts xinetd to search all files in the directory `/etc/xinetd.d/` for the configuration of services.

The Directory /etc/xinetd.d/

The `/etc/xinetd.d/` directory has a separate configuration file for every service. The main advantage of splitting the configuration in several files is improved transparency.

The syntax for configuring network services in these files is similar to the one used for the options in `/etc/xinetd.conf` above:

```
service service_name
     {
            key operator parameter parameter. . .
            key operator parameter parameter. . .
     }
```

The following is an example of the configuration of the finger service:

```
# default: off
# description: The finger server answers finger requests.
# Finger is a protocol that allows remote users to see
# information such as login name and login time for
# currently logged in users.
service finger
{
        socket_type      = stream
        protocol         = tcp
        wait             = no
        user             = nobody
        server           = /usr/sbin/in.fingerd
        server_args      = -w
        disable          = yes
}
```

The significance of the keywords in the example is as follows:

Table 7-13   *xinetd Configuration Parameters*

Keyword	Description
disable	Disables the service if set to `yes`.
protocol	Specifies the protocol (usually tcp or udp) used by the corresponding network service. The protocol must be listed in the `/etc/protocols` file.
server	Specifies the absolute path name of the daemon to start.
server_args	Specifies which parameters to pass to the daemon when it starts.
socket_type	Specifies the type of socket (stream, dgram, raw, or seqpacket).
user	Indicates which user ID the daemon will start under. The user name must be listed in the `/etc/passwd` file.

Keyword	Description
wait	Specifies whether xinetd must wait for the daemon to release the port before it can process further connection requests for the same port (Yes: single-threaded) or not (No: multithreaded).

NOTE: For a description of all possible parameters, in a terminal window enter `man xinetd.conf`.

Internal Services

Certain services (such as echo, time, daytime, chargen, and discard) are provided by xinetd itself without calling another program. These are called internal services and are labeled in the configuration as follows:

```
type = INTERNAL
```

Without this line, xinetd assumes that external services are involved. With services such as echo, which are both TCP- and UDP-based services, you not only specify the respective `socket_type`, but you also need to identify the service in the ID field in such a way that it is properly distinguished from other services.

The following two examples show this for echo.

Echo over TCP:

```
# /etc/xinet.d/echo
# default: off
# description: An echo server. This is the tcp version.

service echo
{
        type            = INTERNAL
        id              = echo-stream
        socket_type     = stream
        protocol        = tcp
        user            = root
        wait            = no
        disable         = yes
        FLAGS           = IPv6 IPv4
}
```

Echo over UDP:

```
# /etc/xinet.d/echo-udp
# default: off
# description: An echo server. This is the udp version.

service echo
{
        type            = INTERNAL UNLISTED
        id              = echo-dgram
        socket_type     = dgram
        protocol        = udp
        user            = root
```

```
wait            = yes
disable         = yes
port            = 7
FLAGS           = IPv6 IPv4
}
```

chkconfig

The `chkconfig program` can be used to list services covered by xinetd:

```
da10:~ # chkconfig -l
...
xinetd based services:
        chargen:        off
        chargen-udp:    off
        daytime:        on
        daytime-udp:    on
        echo:           off
...
```

It can also be used to turn services on and off:

```
da10:~ # chkconfig daytime
daytime  xinetd
da10:~ # chkconfig daytime off
da10:~ #
da10:~ # chkconfig daytime
daytime  off
```

Configure Access Control

The xinetd daemon recognizes four parameters used to control access:

- **only_from.** Lets you define which hosts can use which service. You can specify IP addresses (such as 192.168.1.1, 192.168.1.0, or 192.168.), network addresses (IP address with network mask), network names, or hostnames. For IPv6 addresses, you have to specify the complete address or a network address with netmask.

  You can define this parameter in the defaults or service section.

- **no_access.** Lets you define which hosts are excluded from access. The specification follows the same rules as outlined in `only_from`.

  You can define this parameter in the defaults or service section.

- **access_time.** Lets you define when the service is available (in 24-hour format).

  You can define this parameter in the defaults or service section.

- **disabled.** Lets you completely shut off a server. This also applies to logging access attempts.

  The following is an example for the attribute disabled:

```
disabled = finger
```

With this setting, the service finger is switched off completely. If a computer tries to access the service, the attempt is not even logged.

This `disabled` parameter can be used only in the defaults section. (Within a service section, the corresponding parameter to use is `disable`. Note the missing **d** at the end!)

The following is an example for the Telnet service:

```
# default: off
# description: Telnet is the old login server which is
#  INSECURE and should therefore not be used. Use secure
#  shell (openssh). If you need telnetd not to
#  "keep-alives" e.g. if it runs over an ISDN uplink,
#  add "-n". See 'man telnetd' for more details.

service telnet
{
        socket_type     = stream
        protocol        = tcp
        wait            = no
        user            = root
        server          = /usr/sbin/in.telnetd
        server_args     = -n
        only_from       = 192.168.0.3   192.168.0.7
        only_from       += 192.168.0.10 192.168.0.12
        only_from       += 192.168.1.0/24
        no_access       = 192.168.1.10
        flags           = IDONLY
        access_times    = 07:00-21:00
#        disable = yes
}
```

These settings result in the following:

- Access is permitted for machines with the following IP addresses:

  192.168.0.3
  192.168.0.7
  192.168.0.10
  192.168.0.12
  192.168.1.0-255

- Access is denied to the host with the IP address 192.168.1.10.

- The service is available from 7:00 a.m. to 9:00 p.m.

If you place high demands on access monitoring, you can tighten the security level even more by using the INTERCEPT and IDONLY parameters in the flags entry.

If the USERID parameter was set in the log_on_access and log_on_failure entries, IDONLY then makes sure that a connection to the network service is permitted only when the user identification service (such as identd) of the host requesting the network service issues the user ID.

If the INTERCEPT parameter has been entered as well, xinetd also attempts to make sure that an authorized host is on the other end of already existing connections—that the connection has not been intercepted.

However, connection monitoring does not function with multithreaded or internal xinetd services. In addition, it puts a heavy burden on the network connection and the performance of the network service.

Configure Log Files

Almost every intruder has to make several attempts and needs some time before achieving success. To protect your server, you not only need hacker-resistant software, but you also need log files that the system administrator can use to detect unauthorized login attempts.

Because of this, it does not make sense to only deter unauthorized access attempts. To maintain optimal system security, you also need to record failed and unauthorized connection attempts.

To shut off a service but still retain its logging functions, configure only_from without using any additional parameters (such as the following):

```
only_from     =
```

Logging through xinetd is controlled by the log_type statement along with the log_on_success and log_on_failure attributes.

These let you record from which host and for how long an access attempt was made, and which user was using the service (if the remote host supports this feature).

In addition, you can also log the circumstances of how and why the network service was used. However, even the best log does not mean much if you do not check it on a regular basis for failed connection attempts.

Configuring TCP Wrappers

If you enable a particular service using its configuration file in the /etc/ xinetd.d/ directory, any host can connect to it using the xinetd daemon.

However, you will probably want to control access to these network services, perhaps limiting access to specific hosts while denying access to everyone else. In this situation, you need to configure these services to use *TCP Wrappers*. TCP Wrappers are used by xinetd to start and run the network services using a set of configuration files that you can use to specify who can and can't access the service.

First you must enable TCP Wrappers in each service's configuration file in /etc/ xinetd.d. Do the following:

1. Verify that the **tcpd** package has been installed.

2. Open the appropriate configuration file for the service in a text editor.

3. Comment out the existing server = line in the file.

4. Add following line:

```
server          = /usr/sbin/tcpd
```

This will cause the tcpd daemon to be started instead of the service daemon itself when the service is requested.

5. Add the following line:

```
server_args        =/path/daemon
```

This tells the tcpd daemon to run the specified daemon. For example:

```
server             = /usr/sbin/tcpd
server_args        =/usr/sbin/in.telnetd
```

In this example, the /etc/xinetd.d/telnet file has been modified to run the Telnet daemon within a TCP wrapper.

6. Save the file and restart the xinetd daemon.

Once done, you need to configure the appropriate access controls. The tcpd daemon uses the /etc/hosts.allow and /etc/hosts.deny files to specify the hosts that can access the services it controls. As their file names imply, any host listed in /etc/hosts.allow is allowed access while hosts in /etc/hosts.deny are not. The syntax for both files is the same. First specify the service and then the corresponding hosts, as shown below:

service: hostnames

Be aware that hosts.deny is processed first, followed by hosts.allow. Any configuration in hosts.allow takes precedence over any conflicting directive in hosts.deny. Accordingly, the best practice for controlling access is to first explicitly deny access to the service for all hosts in /etc/hosts.deny. For example, to deny access for all hosts to the Telnet service, you would enter the following:

```
in.telnetd: ALL
```

Then edit the /etc/hosts.allow file and add entries to provide access to specific hosts. For example, in the example below, access has been granted to the Telnet service to hosts with the IP addresses of 172.17.8.10 and 172.17.8.102:

```
in.telnetd: 172.17.8.10, 172.17.8.102
```

If an unauthorized host tries to connect, the request fails.

Configure inetd

The configuration of inetd is carried out by default via the /etc/inetd.conf file. This file contains the instructions for the services which are started by inetd if a connection request is made.

Each line of this configuration file describes a service to be maintained and is put together as follows:

service_name socket_type protocol flags user server_path arguments

The entries have the following significance:

- **service_name.** A valid symbolic service name, corresponding to an entry from the file /etc/services or, for RPC-based services, to an entry from the file /etc/rpc.

  By default, inetd binds to all sockets. If you want inetd to bind to a specific IP address only, add it to the service name separated by a colon, such as 192.168.1.1:ftp

- **socket_type.** Describes the type of network socket, usually stream or dgram. Further possible entries are raw, rdm, or seqpacket.

- **protocol.** A valid symbolic entry of the protocol used in the file /etc/protocols (usually tcp or udp). For RPC services, rpc/tcp or rpc/udp is entered here.

- **flags.** Valid entries are wait and nowait. For TCP-based services, the value nowait is always used. UDP-based services can be configured here with the value wait, if they are capable of processing all incoming datagrams via one socket (single-threaded server). One option is to give a number (nowait.number), which defines the maximum number of connection requests that can be processed in one minute. The default for this value is 40.

- **user.** This entry should contain the user name with whose permission the service is run. It is also possible to specify a group here (user.group).

- **server_path.** This entry specifies the complete path name and file name of the program inetd starts when a connection request is made. For a number of internal services of inetd (echo, discard, chargen, daytime, and time), the value internal must be entered.

- **arguments.** The entry arguments contains all arguments (including the name of the server: argv[0]), which are passed to the server when it starts.

As an example, here is an extract from an /etc/inetd.conf file, containing typical entries:

```
#...

# These are standard services.
#
# ftp stream tcp nowait root /usr/sbin/tcpd in.ftpd
ftp stream tcp nowait root /usr/sbin/tcpd vsftpd

#...

# swat is the Samba Web Administration Tool
# swat stream tcp nowait.400 root /usr/sbin/swat swat

#...
```

NOTE: /usr/sbin/tcpd is the TCP wrapper program that can be configured with the /etc/hosts.allow and /etc/hosts.deny files to restrict access to a service.

Exercise 7-8   Configure xinetd

In this exercise, you configure xinetd to provide the Telnet and Finger services.

You will find this exercise at the end of the chapter.

(End of Exercise)

Objective 9   Configure the Proxy Server Squid

Squid is the most widely used proxy server for the HTTP protocol. Squid is open source software developed by the Squid project (www.squid-cache.org (http://www.squid-cache.org/)).

HTTP is one of the most frequently used Internet transfer protocols. The major field of application is the transfer of web pages and their related data (HTML, images, and other files such as multimedia files).

When a web page is transferred, the client needs to make a request for each component of the page. A component could be an HTML file, a graphic file, and maybe a Flash or JavaScript file.

When clients are configured to use a proxy server, they send their requests to the proxy server instead of the actual target web server. The proxy makes a request to the actual server on behalf of the client and forwards the data to the client. In most cases, the proxy saves the requested data and uses this data when another client has the same request. This is called caching.

Not all content that is transferred over HTTP is suitable for caching. Pages that are generated by a script or that are personalized for the user viewing the page are usually not cached. Therefore, a web server response usually contains the header fields Pragma and Cache-Control, which determine if a page can be cached. HTTP requests from clients can contain header fields that tell a proxy to not deliver data from its cache but to fetch the data from the target web server.

With its clients, Squid speaks only HTTP. However, it is possible to encapsulate other protocols such as FTP or GOPHER into HTTP requests. Squid can handle these requests and connect to the target servers in their native protocol. Because of this feature, Squid is sometimes also called an FTP proxy. This is incorrect, because all FTP requests need to be encapsulated into HTTP by the browser.

As a caching proxy server, Squid is used as a gateway to connect an internal network to the Internet. On one side Squid works as a firewall, separating the internal and the external network. On the other side, Squid caches the transferred data and reduces the load on the Internet connection.

An intercepting (or transparent) proxy server is very similar to a standard (caching) proxy server. Squid separates the involved networks and stores content in its cache. But unlike a standard proxy, no specific client (web browser) configuration is required to use the proxy. Intercepting proxying does not work for HTTPS connections.

Install Squid on SLES 11

Squid is shipped as an RPM package with SLES 11. To install it, you need to select the squid package in the YaST Software Manager. You can also install the squidGuard package, which contains additional content and access control filters for Squid.

After you have installed and configured Squid, you can start it by entering

```
rcsquid start
```

To start Squid automatically at boot time, you can add it to the init process by entering

```
insserv squid
```

Understand the Squid Configuration File

The configuration file for Squid (`/etc/squid/squid.conf`) is fully documented with extensive comments; the comments are placed directly in the file.

Only a few entries in this file need to be adjusted to configure basic proxy server functionality; most parameters can be left with the default values. The default values will also be used if no other value is given or if the entry is prefaced with a comment sign.

Control Access to Squid

In the simplest possible setup, anyone who can reach the network interface where the proxy is listening can use the Squid proxy to access web sites. However, Squid can also be used to control access to web sites.

The default configuration contains some reasonable default settings that can be used as a base for your own setup. Like options in the config file, the `acl` setup is well commented.

Squid offers very powerful access management, which lets you allow or deny access to the proxy as well as control which sites are visited when and by whom, based on parameters such as

- IP/Network addresses of clients or Web servers

- Week day and time of the day

- Content type

- Transfer protocol

The access management of Squid is based on two different tag types in the squid.conf file:

- **acl (Access Control List).** Defines a condition that is matched against the incoming HTTP requests.

- **http_access.** Determines whether access is allowed or denied when a given `acl` condition matches.

Access control management in Squid is based on two tasks: Defining `acl` tags and defining `http_access` tags for these acls.

Let's assume you have the following lines in your squid.conf file:

```
acl all src 0.0.0.0/0.0.0.0
acl allowed_clients src 172.17.0.0/16

http_access allow allowed_clients
http_access deny all
```

Two ACLs are defined. Each `acl` line consists of the following components:

acl ***acl_name acl_type acl_string*** [***acl_string*** ...]

- **acl_name.** Works as an identifier when the condition is later used in an http_access statement. You can choose any name, but it cannot use spaces or special characters.

- **acl_type.** One of the ACL types that Squid supports. The type `src` in the example refers to the IP or network address of the client that makes a request to Squid. The available acl types, such as `src`, `dst`, `srcdomain`, or `dstdomain`, are listed in the configuration file.

- **acl_string.** Defines the condition that is matched against the requests. If more than one string is given, the ACL matches when one of the strings matches (OR). (Note: Some ACL types have only one string.)

  Instead of one or several strings, a filename could be given. Instead of listing the strings in one line in `/etc/squid/squid.conf`, the file would list the strings line by line:

  `acl offlimits dstdomain "/etc/squid/forbidden-sites.list"`

In the example, the two acl lines have the following meaning:

`acl all src 0.0.0.0/0.0.0.0`

This acl, named `all`, matches the IP address of the requesting client (`src`). The acl string 0.0.0.0/0.0.0.0 matches any IP address.

`acl allowed_clients src 172.17.0.0/16`

This acl line, with the name `allowed_clients`, matches all requests coming from the network with the network address 172.17.0.0/16.

The last two lines of our example are http_access tags. They have the following basic structure:

http_access ***allow/deny acl_name***

Following the http_access tag, you have either an allow or a deny statement, depending what you want to do with the line. The ***acl_name*** used to allow or deny access to the proxy is listed after the allow/deny statement. If two acl names are given, the line matches when both acl_name entries match (AND).

In the example, this means the following:

Two acl lines are defined, one that only matches requests from the 172.17.0.0/16 network and one that matches every request.

`http_access allow allowed_clients`

The first http_access line allows access to the proxy for every request that matches the `allowed_clients` acl. Thus, it allows every request from the 172.17.0.0/16 network.

```
http_access deny all
```

The second http_access line denies access to every request that matches the `all` acl. Thus, access is denied to every request.

The `http_access` lines are processed from top to bottom. Once a line and its ACL matches, the given access rule (`allow` or `deny`) is applied and any subsequent `http_access` tags are not taken into consideration.

Assume that a client from the 172.17.0/16 network tries to access the proxy server in the example. The first `http_access` line matches and access is allowed; the second `http_access` line is not processed at all.

When someone outside the 172.17.0.0/16 network tries to access the proxy, the first `http_access` line does not match and the second line is processed. This line denies access to every request with the result that this request is not allowed.

When no `http_access` line matches a request, the default access rule is the opposite of the last found `http_access` line. An allow turns into a deny and a deny turns into an allow.

To avoid confusion, you should always have an `http_access` line at the end of your configuration that matches every request, such as `http_access deny all` as above. This line sets the default (allow/deny) when no other acl matches.

Summary

Objective	Summary
Configure the Samba Server	Using Samba, a Linux system can be configured as a file and print server for Linux, Mac OSX, and Windows workstations.
	Essentially, Samba allows your Linux system to emulate a Windows server. Users can access shared directories and printers on the Linux server just as they would on a Windows server.
	The Samba service is configured in the `/etc/samba/smb.conf` file.
	The options for storing your Samba users include `/etc/samba/smbpasswd` and LDAP.
	Linux workstations can access Samba shares. Samba client tools include `nmblookup`, `smbclient`, and the `mount` command.
Configure the Apache Web Server	The Apache Web server is configured by several files in the `/etc/apache2/` directory. In the default configuration, the document root directory is `/srv/www/htdocs`, and the `/var/log/apache2/` directory contains the Apache log files.
	Virtual hosts allow Apache to serve several domains from the same IP address.
	Access to the Web server can be limited based on various criteria, including client IP address and user name.
	PHP is often used to create dynamic content. The Common Gateway Interface (CGI) allows the use of other programming languages as well.
Enable an FTP Server	FTP is a widely used file transfer protocol. It uses two TCP connections, one for control commands and one for the data transfer.
	Various FTP servers are available. PureFTPd has the advantage of a flexible configuration and the reputation of being secure.
	It can be configured via a configuration file or command line options.

Objective	Summary
Configure Electronic Mail	E-mails are passed by the user's e-mail software to the MTA. The MTA sends them to a recipient MTA.
	The MTA specifies which local user the received message is intended for and passes this to an MDA, which stores it in the right location.
	The MUA reads saved messages and passes new messages to the MTA. The MUA is the interface between the MDA and the user.
	E-mails are passed by the user's e-mail software to the MTA.
	You can use the `mail` command to read the messages. You can also use the mail program as a mail client on the command line.
	Postfix is the default mail server software installed on SLES 11.
	The Postfix master daemon is configured via the `/etc/postfix/master.cf` file. Each line in the file contains an entry for one Postfix process.
	All further configuration definitions (apart from the configuration of processing rules in lookup tables) are set in the `/etc/postfix/main.cf` file.
	Lookup tables contain rules for processing e-mail within the overall Postfix system.
	Various utilities are provided with Postfix, such as `mailq` to view the mail queue, `postsuper` to administer mail queues, and `postconf` to change the Postfix configuration.

Objective	Summary
Configure a CUPS Server	The Common UNIX Printing System (CUPS) is the default printing system used in SLES 11.
	CUPS can be used to print on local or remote printers. The protocol used is IPP, but other protocols are also supported.
	You can enter the CUPS Web front end at http://localhost:631/ or http://IP_Address:631.
	The Web interface allows the administration of all aspects of CUPS, including managing printers, viewing log files, or editing the /etc/cups/cupsd.conf file.
	Printers are addressed using print queues.
	CUPS tools allow you to use commands according to
	■ Berkeley (LPRng) style, such as lpr, lpq, and lprm.
	■ System V style, such as lp, lpstat, and cancel.
	To list the current settings of a local queue, enter lpoptions -p queue -l
Configure a DNS Server with BIND	DNS is a distributed database used to translate host names into IP addresses.
	On SLES 11, you can use the BIND software to set up your own DNS server.
	A caching-only DNS server is not responsible for a domain; it just forwards requests to other name servers and caches the result for later requests.
	A master server is responsible for a domain. It provides authoritative information about this domain.
	The BIND configuration is stored in the /etc/named.conf file
	DNS server information is stored in zone files that usually reside in the /var/lib/named/master directory.
Configure the NTPD	To implement a uniform time on all computers in a network, all computers must have access to at least one time server.
	The ntp package contains the ntpd time server to get the time from another time server as well as provide time to other machines on the network via NTP.

Objective	Summary
Enable xinetd	The Extended Internet Daemon (xinetd) is used to start various network services like FTP or POP3 when a connection is made to the respective port.
	The xinetd configuration is contained in the `/etc/xinetd.conf` file and in individual files for the various services in the `/etc/xinetd.d/` directory.
	Configuration can be done with the YaST Network Services Module, an editor and, to a certain extent, the `chkconfig` command.
Configure the Proxy Server Squid	Squid is the most commonly used application-level gateway for the HTTP protocol. It can perform tasks like caching, logging, and filtering.
	Browsers need to be configured to use Squid.
	Squid's configuration is contained in the `/etc/squid/squid.conf` file. The configuration file contains variables, which are also called *tags*. The `acl` and `http_access` tags are used for access control management.

Key Terms

. (root domain) — The root domain of DNS.

.htaccess — A file that contains directory-specific restrictions for the Apache Web server.

/etc/aliases — Contains mail aliases for user accounts.

/etc/apache2/default-server.conf — The file that contains the default Apache configuration if the same parameters are not overridden in other Apache configuration files.

/etc/apache2/httpd.conf — The main Apache configuration file.

/etc/cups/cupsd.conf — The main CUPS configuration file.

/etc/cups/lpoptions — The file that stores system-wide print options set by the root user.

/etc/cups/ppd — The directory that stores the active PPD files used for a particular printer.

/etc/cups/printers.conf — Contains CUPS printer definitions.

/etc/hosts.allow — A text file used by tcpd listing hosts that are allowed to connect to network daemons.

/etc/hosts.deny — A text file used by tcpd listing hosts that are not allowed to connect to network daemons.

/etc/inetd.conf — The main configuration file for inetd.

/etc/localtime — A file that stores time and time zone information.

/etc/mail/genericstable — A Sendmail configuration file that modifies the sender address for outgoing e-mail.

/etc/mail/mailertable — A Sendmail configuration file that defines the routing for outgoing e-mail.

/etc/named.conf — A file that lists the type of zones hosted on the DNS server and the location of the zone files.

/etc/ntp.conf — The main NTP server and client configuration file.

/etc/postfix/main.cf — The main configuration file for the Postfix MTA.

/etc/postfix/master.cf — The configuration file for the Postfix master daemon.

/etc/printcap — Stores a list of print queues on a print client.

/etc/pure-ftpd/pure-ftpd.conf — The main configuration file for PureFTPd.

/etc/samba/smb.conf — The main Samba configuration file.

/etc/sendmail.cf — The main Sendmail configuration file.

/etc/squid/squid.conf — The main configuration file for Squid.

/etc/sysconfig/clock — A file that is used to configure how the Linux kernel obtains its time information.

/etc/sysconfig/ntp — A file that stores variables used when starting and stopping the NTP daemon.

/etc/xinetd.conf — The main configuration file for xinetd. It loads configuration files from the /etc/xinetd.d directory.

/etc/xinetd.d — The directory that stores most xinetd configurations.

/srv/ftp – The default anonymous FTP home directory used by PureFTPd.

/srv/www/htdocs — The default document root directory in Apache on an SLES system.

/usr/lib/postfix/master — The Postfix master daemon.

/usr/share/cups/model — The directory that stores sample PPD files used for a particular printer.

/usr/share/zoneinfo – A directory that stores time zone information.

/var/lib/named — The directory that stores zone files in SLES.

/var/log/apache2/access_log — An Apache log file that stores information about network access requests.

/var/log/apache2/error_log — An Apache log file that stores Apache daemon errors and invalid access.

/var/log/cups/access_log — A CUPS log file that stores information about network print requests.

/var/log/cups/error_log — A CUPS log file that stores information about the CUPS daemon.

/var/log/cups/page_log — A CUPS log file that stores information about each page sent to a CUPS printer.

/var/spool/cups — The default print queue directory in SLES.

~/.forward — An MTA file used to configure e-mail handling options.

~/.lpoptions — The file that stores user-defined print options.

accept command — Allows print jobs to enter the print queue.

Address record (A or AAAA) — A DNS record that identifies hosts within a domain. A is used for IPv4 and AAAA is used for IPv6.

adjtimex command – Used to adjust time drift on network computers.

Apache — The default Web server software in SLES.

apachectl command — Used to start, stop, and restart Apache as well as check its configuration files for errors.

ARPANET — The network that led to the development of the Internet. It stands for Advanced Research Projects Agency Network.

authoritative answer — A name resolution response from a DNS server where the DNS server contained the appropriate record in its zone database.

Berkeley Internet Name Domain (BIND) — The reference implementation for DNS.

broadcasting — A process whereby an NTP server sends time information to an NTP client periodically.

cache — An area of memory that stores information obtained from resolving DNS names. Entries are kept in the cache for the time period specified by the TTL.

caching-only server — A DNS server that is not authoritative for any zones. It only answers DNS queries where the answers come from other DNS servers.

cancel command — Used to remove a print job from the print queue.

Canonical NAME (CNAME) — An alias for another record in DNS.

Common Gateway Interface (CGI) – A standard interface that is used by scripting and programming languages when interacting with a Web server.

Common Internet File System (CIFS) — The most recent version of the SMB protocol.

Common Unix Printing System (CUPS) — The default printing system in SLES.

cupsdisable command — Prevents print jobs in the print queue from being sent to the printer.

cupsenable command — Allows print jobs in the print queue to be sent to the printer.

CUPS Web Interface — A series of CUPS administration utilities that may be accessed using a web browser on port 631.

curl command — Used to interact with different Internet services such as Web and FTP services.

directive — A configuration parameter within an Apache configuration file.

DNS server — A server that responds to DNS lookup requests.

document root — The directory that stores Web content on a Web server.

domain — The name in DNS that identifies a division of an organization.

Domain Name System (DNS) – A standard structure and set of services on the Internet that are used to provide name resolution for Internet hosts.

drift – The difference in time between two time servers.

Exim — A common MTA on Linux systems.

File Transfer Protocol (FTP) – The most common protocol used to transfer files on the Internet.

forward resolution — A name resolution request that desires the IP address for a particular FQDN.

forwarding server — A DNS server that forwards any DNS queries it cannot resolve to another DNS server on the network.

ftp command — Used to connect to a remote FTP server and transfer files.

fully qualified domain name (FQDN) — A complete name that identifies a host computer in DNS. It consists of a host name (or computer name) followed by subdomain/domain names and a TLD (e.g., www.west.afr ica.com).

hardware clock — The clock that runs on a computer's motherboard.

host command — Used to resolve DNS names.

hostname command — Used to display the local host name.

htpasswd command — Used to create and modify entries in an Apache password file.

hwclock command — Used to view and set the hardware clock from within Linux.

Hyper-Text Markup Language (HTML) — The format used by Web pages.

inetd — The Internet Super Daemon used to start other network daemons on Linux systems.

Internet Message Access Protocol (IMAP) — A protocol used to obtain e-mails from an e-mail server.

Internet Printing Protocol (IPP) — A printing protocol that allows print jobs to be sent across the Internet using HTTP.

jitter — The estimated time error for another time server.

lookup table — A file that contains rules for processing e-mails for the Postfix MTA.

lp command — Used to create a print job.

lpadmin command — Used to create and manage CUPS printers.

lpoptions command — Used to create or change printing options, such as resolution.

lpq command — Used to view print jobs in the print queue.

lpr command — Used to create a print job.

lprm command — Used to remove a print job from the print queue.

lpstat command — Used to view print jobs in the print queue.

mail command — An MUA available on most Linux systems.

Mail Delivery Agent (MDA) — A server program that stored e-mail in a mailbox for access by MUAs.

Mail eXchanger (MX) — A DNS record that identifies the e-mail servers for a domain.

mailq command — Lists mail in the Postfix/Sendmail mail queue.

mailstats command — Displays Sendmail e-mail statistics.

Mail Transfer Agent (MTA) — A server program that relays e-mail on the Internet.

Mail User Agent (MUA) — An e-mail reader program.

makemap command — Generates lookup tables for Sendmail information.

master server — A DNS server that contains a read-write copy of the zone database.

Multipurpose Internet Mail Extensions (MIME) — A standard used for attaching files to e-mails.

MySQL — A RDBMS commonly used on Linux systems.

mysqladmin command — Used to configure and manage the MySQL RDBMS.

mysql command — Used to configure and manage MySQL databases.

mysqld — The MySQL daemon.

named — The DNS/BIND daemon in Linux.

name resolution — The process where an FQDN is associated with its IP address.

name server — See DNS server.

Name Server (NS) — A DNS record that identifies a DNS server that is authoritative for the zone.

NetBIOS — A Windows protocol that uses unique, 15-character computer names to identify network hosts.

netdate command — Used to view and set the system date and time from another computer on the network.

Network Time Protocol (NTP) — A protocol used on the Internet to synchronize time and date information.

newaliases command — It converts the plain text /etc/aliases file into the /etc/aliases.db database file for use by the system.

nmbd — The NetBIOS name daemon on a Linux system.

nmblookup command — Displays NetBIOS computer names for hosts.

non-authoritative answer — A name resolution response from a DNS server where the DNS server had to query other DNS servers in order to find the appropriate record.

nslookup command — Used to resolve DNS names.

ntpd — The NTP daemon.

ntpdate command — Used to view, synchronize, and set time information using NTP.

ntpq command — Used to query the NTP daemon and return status information.

ntptrace command — Lists the source(s) of NTP information on an NTP client.

PHP — A popular scripting language for Web applications. It stands for Personal Home Page.

PoinTeR (PTR) — A DNS record that identifies the FQDN associated with an IP address for reverse resolution.

polling – A process whereby an NTP client asks an NTP server for the current time.

postalias command — A postfix program that performs the same function as the newaliases command.

postcat command — Displays contents of files in the Postfix mail queue.

postconf command — Displays and sets Postfix variables.

postdrop command — Creates files in the postdrop directory.

Postfix — The default MTA on SLES Linux systems.

postfix command — Checks for Postfix configuration problems.

postmap command — Generates lookup tables for Postfix information.

Post Office Protocol (POP) — A protocol used to obtain e-mails from an e-mail server. POP3 is the latest version of POP.

PostScript Printer Description (PPD) — A printing for mat that is widely used by many printers and printing systems.

postsuper command — Cleans up unused files in the Postfix queue directories.

Procmail — A common MDA on Linux systems.

PureFTPd — The FTP service used by SLES.

Qmail — A common MTA on Linux systems.

queue — A directory used to store print jobs before they are sent to the physical printer.

Quick Mail Queuing Protocol (QMQP) — A qmail protocol that allows the sharing of e-mail queues among different email hosts.

Quick Mail Transport Protocol (QMTP) — A qmail protocol that provides e-mail transport between computers.

reject command — Prevents print jobs from entering the print queue.

relational database management system (RDBMS) — a set of software that is designed to store information in related tables.

resolver — A host that requests name resolution using DNS.

reverse resolution — A name resolution request that desires the FQDN for a particular IP address.

rndc command – Used to view and control a DNS name server over a TCP connection.

Samba — A set of services in Linux that provides the SMB and CIFS protocols for file and printer sharing with Windows computers.

Secure Socket Layer (SSL) – A common encryption technology used by Internet protocols.

Sendmail — A common MTA on Linux systems.

Server Message Block (SMB) — A file- and printer-sharing protocol used by Windows systems.

Simple Mail Transfer Protocol (SMTP) — The protocol used to send e-mails to MTAs on the Internet.

slave server — A DNS server that contains a read-only copy of the zone database obtained from a master server via a zone transfer.

smbclient command — Used to view and access Windows file and printer shares.

SMBcopy command — Used to copy files across the network using the SMB protocol.

smbd — The Samba file and printer sharing daemon on a Linux system.

SMBmove command — Used to move files across the network using the SMB protocol.

smbpasswd command — Sets a Windows-formatted password for Linux user accounts.

SMBsplopen command — Used to open a print connection across the network using the SMB protocol.

Squid — A proxy server that is commonly used on Linux systems.

Start Of Authority (SOA) — A DNS record that identifies zone-specific information and zone transfer settings.

stratum — A label that identifies how far a time server is from a real-time time source (e.g., atomic clock).

Structured Query Language (SQL) — A protocol and format used to access, modify, and store information in RDBMSs.

subdomain — The name in DNS that identifies a division of an organization and which exists under the domain and TLD.

SuSEconfig — A script that generates configuration files from source files located in the /etc/ sysconfig directory.

system time — The time that is used by the Linux kernel.

TCP wrapper (tcpd) — A small program that is used to start network daemons via inetd or xinetd. It provides additional secur ity by using the /etc/hosts.allow and /etc/hosts.deny files to control access.

testparm command — Checks the syntax of /etc/samba/smb.conf.

Time To Live (TTL) — The amount of time a name resolution result is cached on the computer. The default TTL is set in the SOA in the zone file on the DNS server.

top-level domain (TLD) — The first level of names underneath the root domain in DNS.

TXT (Text) — A DNS record that contains additional information.

Uniform Resource Locator (URL) — A naming convention and format used to access Internet resources.

Universal Naming Convention (UNC) — A naming convention and format used to access SMB shared resources.

virtual host — An additional Web site that is hosted by an Apache Web server.

w3m command — A text-based Web browser.

wget command — Used to retrieve Web pages from Web and FTP servers.

winbind — A service that integrates Samba with Active Directory services.

Windows Internet Naming Service (WINS) — A network service that resolves NetBIOS names to IP addresses.

workgroup — A name that identifies a group of computers in a Windows network that are not part of a domain.

xinetd — The Extended Internet Super Daemon used to start other network daemons on Linux systems. It is the default Internet Super Daemon used in SLES.

zone — A specific domain in DNS that is represented by file on a DNS server that contains the records used for name resolution.

zone transfer — The process whereby a master DNS server sends zone information to a slave DNS server.

Chapter Exercises

Exercise 7-1   *Create a Basic Samba Share*

In this exercise, you learn how to configure a basic samba share. You then access the share with smbclient and you mount a Samba share in the file system of a Linux workstation. This exercise has four parts.

In the first part of the exercise, you configure the Samba server on da-host as a member of the digitalairlines workgroup and to use user-level security.

In the second part of the exercise, you create the /srv/samba/geeko-data directory and create a share named geeko-data.

In the third part of the exercise, you access the geeko-data share on da-host using the smbclient utility on da1.

In the fourth part of the exercise, you mount the geeko-data share on da-host to the file system of your da1server.

Detailed Steps to Complete the Exercise

- Part I: Configure the Samba Server

- Part II: Create the [geeko-data] Share

- Part III: Access a Share with smbclient

- Part IV: Mount a Share in the File System

Part I: Configure the Samba Server

In this part of the exercise, you configure global settings for the Samba service on da-host.

Complete the following:

1. In YaST on da-host, select *Network Services > Samba Server*.

2. In the *Workgroup or Domain Name* field, type digitalairlines, then select *Next*.

3. Under *Samba Server Type*, select *Not a Domain Controller*, then select *Next*.

4. On the *Start-Up* tab, select the following options:

    - *During Boot*

    - *Open Port in Firewall* (if necessary)

5. Select the *Identity* tab.

6. In the *NetBIOS Hostname* field, type da-host.

7. Select *WINS Server Support*.

8. Deselect *Retrieve WINS Server via DHCP*, then select *Use WINS for Hostname Resolution*.

9. Select *Advanced Settings > Expert Global Settings*.

    Confirm the warnings by clicking *OK*.

10. Verify that security is set to *user* and that printing is set to *cups*.

11. Select *OK*.

12. Select *OK* to close the *Samba Configuration* module.

Part II: Create the [geeko-data] Share

In this part of the exercise, you create a share named `geeko-data` that points to the `/srv/samba/geeko-data` directory.

Complete the following:

1. Create the `/srv/samba/geeko-data` directory on da-host:

   a. At the shell prompt, (as root) enter `mkdir -p /srv/samba/geeko-data`.

   b. Create a test file in the directory by entering `touch /srv/samba/geeko-data/my_file` at the shell prompt.

   c. To adjust the permissions assigned to the directory and file to allow access by the geeko user, at the shell prompt enter

   `chown -R geeko: /srv/samba/geeko-data/`

2. Create the `[geeko-data]` share by doing the following:

   a. In YaST, select *Network Services > Samba Server*.

   b. On the *Shares* tab, select *Add*.

   c. On the *New Share* screen, enter the following information:

      - Share Name: **geeko-data**
      - Share Description: **Geeko's Data Directory**
      - Share Path: **/srv/samba/geeko-data**

   d. Select *OK*.

   e. With the geeko-data share selected, select *Edit*.

   f. On the *Share geeko-data* screen, select *Add*.

   g. In the *Selected Option* drop-down list, select *valid users*, then select *OK*.

   h. In the *valid users* field, enter **geeko**, then select *OK*.

   i. Select *OK* to close the *Share geeko-data* dialog.

   j. Select *OK* to close the *Samba Configuration*.

3. Close YaST.

4. Open a terminal window, enter `su -` (password **novell**), and view the samba configuration by entering

   `less /etc/samba/smb.conf`

5. Test the configuration of the Samba server and the `[geeko-data]` share by entering `testparm` at the shell prompt.

You should see no error messages.

6. Press Enter to see a dump of your share defintions.

7. To add geeko to the smbpasswd database, enter

   ```
   smbpasswd -a geeko
   ```

   When prompted for the password, enter **novell** (twice).

Part III: Access a Share with smbclient

To access a share with smbclient, complete the following:

1. Switch to your da1server.

2. If necessary, log in as your **geeko** user with a password of **novell**.

3. Open a terminal session.

4. Verify that the Samba server is responding to SMB requests by entering `smbclient -L //da-host` at the shell prompt.

5. When prompted for a password, press Enter.

   You should see a list of shares on da-host, including the geeko-data share.

6. Access the data share by entering `smbclient -U geeko //da-host/geeko-data` at the shell prompt.

7. When prompted for a password, enter **novell**.

   You should see the **smb:** prompt displayed.

8. List the content of the share by entering `ls` at the smb:\ prompt.

   You should see the `my_file` file that you created earlier.

9. Copy the `my_file` file to the current directory by entering `get my_file` at the **smb:** prompt.

10. Exit smbclient by entering `exit`.

11. Enter `ls`.

    You should see the `my_file` file in the `ls` output.

Part IV: Mount a Share in the File System

To mount a share in the file system, complete the following:

1. In a terminal window on your da1 server, switch to root using the `su -` command and a password of **novell**.

2. Mount the data share in the `/mnt` directory by entering the following command at the shell prompt:

   ```
   mount -t cifs -o username=geeko //172.17.8.1/geeko-
   data /mnt
   ```

When prompted for a password, enter **novell**.

3. At the shell prompt, enter `mount`.

   You should see that `//172.17.8.1/geeko-data` is mounted on `/mnt`.

4. Display the content of the mounted share by entering `ls /mnt/` at the shell prompt.

   You should see the `my_file` file.

5. Unmount the share by entering `umount /mnt` at the shell prompt.

6. Close your terminal window.

(End of Exercise)

Exercise 7-2   Configure a Virtual Host

In this exercise, you configure virtual hosts for the accounting.digitalairlines.com and hr.digitalairlines.com Web sites on your da-host server.

Create their document roots in `/srv/www/accounting` and `/srv/www/hr` directories, and create their `accounting.conf` and `hr.conf` configuration files in the `/etc/apache2/vhosts.d/` directory. Change `/etc/apache2/listen.conf` to support name-based virtual hosting and include the two domains in `/etc/hosts`, pointing to 172.17.8.1.

Detailed Steps to Complete the Exercise

Complete the following on da-host:

1. In the YaST Control Center, select *Software > Software Management*.

2. From the *Filter* drop-down list, select *Patterns*.

3. Mark the *Web and LAMP Server* pattern and click *Accept*.

4. In the *Automatic Changes* screen, select *Continue*.

   Wait while the packages are installed.

5. When installation is complete, close YaST.

6. Open a terminal window and switch to root using the `su -` command and a password of **novell**.

7. Open the `/etc/apache2/listen.conf` file in an editor and remove the comment sign in front of the following line:

   ```
   NameVirtualHost *:80
   ```

   Save the file and close the editor.

8. Create directories for the virtual hosts by entering the following (as root) at the shell prompt:

   ```
   mkdir /srv/www/accounting
   mkdir /srv/www/hr
   ```

9. As root, using an editor of your choice, create the `/srv/www/accounting/index.html` file with the following content:

   ```
   <html>
       <head>
           <title>Accounting Intranet Server</title>
       </head>
       <body>
           <h1>Accounting Intranet</h1>
           Under construction.
       </body>
   </html>
   ```

   Save the file and close the editor.

Create a /srv/www/hr/index.html file with similar content for the hr web site.

NOTE: You can use the accounting-index.html and hr-index.html files from the Exercises/Section_07 directory on the *Novell's Guide to the LPIC-1 Certification Using SUSE Linux Enterprise Server 11* Course CD.

---

10. As root in the terminal window, change to the /etc/apache2/vhosts.d/ directory and copy the virtual host template file by entering

```
cp vhost.template accounting.conf
```

11. Edit the accounting.conf file so it looks like the following:

```
<VirtualHost _default_:80>
      ServerAdmin webmaster@digitalairlines.com
      ServerName accounting.digitalairlines.com
      DocumentRoot /srv/www/accounting
      ErrorLog /var/log/apache2/accounting.digitalairlines.com-
error_log
      CustomLog /var/log/apache2/accounting.digitalairlines.com-
access_log combined
      UseCanonicalName On
      ScriptAlias /cgi-bin/ "/srv/www/cgi-bin"
      <Directory "/srv/www/cgi-bin">
            AllowOverride None
            Options +ExecCGI -Includes
            Order allow,deny
            Allow from all
      </Directory>
      <Directory "/srv/www/accounting/">
            Options Indexes FollowSymLinks
            AllowOverride None
            Order allow,deny
            Allow from all
      </Directory>
</VirtualHost>
```

12. Copy the accounting.conf file to hr.conf and edit it so it fits the requirements of the hr.digitalairlines.com domain.

NOTE: You can find the accounting.conf and hr.conf configuration files in the Exercises/Section_07 directory on the *Novell's Guide to the LPIC-1 Certification Using SUSE Linux Enterprise Server 11* Course CD.

---

13. For testing purposes, add accounting.digitalairlines.com and hr.digitalairlines.com to the /etc/hosts file.

As root, open the /etc/hosts file in an editor of your choice, and add the following lines at the bottom of the file:

```
172.17.8.1 accounting.digitalairlines.com accounting
172.17.8.1 hr.digitalairlines.com hr
```

14. Test the syntax of your configuration file by entering `apache2ctl configtest` at the shell prompt.

The command should return a `Syntax OK` message. If not, inspect your configuration to identify and fix any errors. (If you see a "Could not open configuration file /etc/apache2/sysconfig.d/include.conf" message, you can ignore it; this file will be created automatically when Apache is started in the next step.)

15. Start the Apache daemon by entering `rcapache2 start` at the shell prompt.

16. To make sure Apache starts automatically, use the command `insserv apache2`.

17. Test your virtual host.

   a. Start Firefox on da-host by selecting ***Computer > Firefox***.

   b. Access the Accounting virtual host by entering **http:// accounting.digitalairlines.com/** in the URL field of the Firefox browser.

   You should see the *Accounting Intranet* page that you created earlier.

   c. Access the HR virtual host by entering **http://hr.digitalairlines.com/** in the URL field of the Firefox browser.

   You should see the *HR Intranet* page that you created earlier.

   d. Close Firefox and any open terminal windows.

(End of Exercise)

Exercise 7-3   Configure Anonymous PureFTPd Access

In this exercise, you configure anonymous FTP access with the permission to upload files.

Make sure that the files cannot be downloaded again without permission from the system administrator. Test your setup by uploading a file and trying to download it again. As a system administrator, allow users to download the file; then try again to do so.

Detailed Steps to Complete the Exercise

Do the following on da1:

1. Open a terminal window, then su – to root (password: **novell**).

2. Install the pure-ftpd package if it is not yet installed:

    rpm -q pure-ftpd || yast -i pure-ftpd

3. Open the /etc/pure-ftpd/pure-ftpd.conf file in an editor.

    Allow anonymous users to upload files to the FTP server by changing the AnonymousCantUpload parameter to no.

4. To make sure that files which are owned by the user ftp cannot be downloaded, verify that AntiWarez is set to yes.

5. When you finish, save the file and close the editor.

6. Start the PureFTPd server by entering rcpure-ftpd start.

7. Change the ownership of the /srv/ftp directory to the user ftp by entering

    chown ftp /srv/ftp

8. Log in by entering ftp localhost; log in using the name **ftp**.

9. Verify that you can upload files as the anonymous ftp user.

    a. Change to binary transfer mode by entering bin.

    b. Upload the /usr/lib/rpm/gnupg/suse-build-key file by entering the following:

        lcd /usr/lib/rpm/gnupg
        put suse-build-key.gpg

    c. Try to download the file by entering the following:

        get suse-build-key.gpg

        You should see a message that the file has not yet been approved for download.

    d. Exit the FTP session by entering bye.

10. Verify that the file was uploaded by entering

    cd /srv/ftp

    ls -l.

The file is listed.

11. Change ownership of the file and make sure that the FTP server can access the file:

    `chown geeko /srv/ftp/suse-build-key.gpg`

    `chmod 444 /srv/ftp/suse-build-key.gpg`

12. Change to your home directory by entering `cd`.

13. Enter `ftp localhost`, log in with the username **ftp**, and again try to download the `suse-build-key.gpg` file.

    This should succeed now.

14. Close the ftp client by entering `bye`.

15. Close the terminal window.

(End of Exercise)

Exercise 7-4   *Send Mail and Configure Postfix*

In this exercise, you use the `mail` command to send and read mail, and you make some basic changes to the Postfix configuration. This exercise has two parts.

In the first part, use the `mail` command to send an e-mail message to root and to read e-mail.

In the second part, you send mail in the local network. First, you edit the Postfix `/etc/postfix/main.cf` configuration file on da-host to accept mail from the 172.17.0.0/16 network and to masquerade the domain name of the sender for normal users. Then you edit the `/etc/postfix/main.cf` configuration file on da1 to forward mail addressed to external recipients to da-host. Test your configuration by sending an e-mail message from da1 to joe@example.com, using the `mail` command.

Detailed Steps to Complete the Exercise

- Part I: Use the mail Command
- Part II: Configure Postfix to Send Mail in the Local Network

Part I: Use the mail Command

Do the following on da-host:

1. Open a terminal window and enter `mail root`.

2. Enter the subject:

   `My first e-mail with mail.`

3. Enter the following two lines of text (press Enter after each line):

   ```
   I have just installed SUSE Linux Enterprise Server 11
   on my computer and am ready for administration training.
   ```

   When you finish, press Ctrl+d.

4. Change to the root account by entering `su  -` (password **novell**).

5. Enter `mail`.

   In the last line of the list you should find the mail message you just sent to root.

6. To read the message, enter the number in the second column of the table.

7. Delete the message by entering `d` and the number of the message (such as `d  4`).

8. Quit mail by entering `q`.

9. Verify that the message was deleted by entering `mail`, then exit `mail` by entering `q`.

Part II: Configure Postfix to Send Mail in the Local Network

Do the following:

1. On da-host, open a terminal window and enter `su` – to get root permissions. When prompted, enter the root password **novell**.

2. Stop the postfix daemon by entering

   `rcpostfix stop`

3. Open the `/etc/postfix/main.cf` file in a text editor.

   Scroll to the settings at the end of the file.

4. To accept mail only from the local network, modify the following options as shown below:

   `inet_interfaces = 172.17.8.1, localhost`

   `mynetworks_style = subnet` (should already be set)

   `smtpd_recipient_restrictions = permit_mynetworks, reject_unauth_destination` (on one line)

5. To rewrite the sender addresses and remove the host name, modify the following options as shown below:

   `masquerade_exceptions = root` (should already be set)

   `masquerade_domains = digitalairlines.com`

6. Save the file and close the editor.

7. Start Postfix by entering

   `rcpostfix start`

8. Start your da1 virtual server if it is not already running.

9. On da1, stop the postfix daemon by entering

   `rcpostfix stop`

10. Open the `/etc/postfix/main.cf` file in a text editor.

    Scroll to the settings at the end of the file.

11. To deliver external mail to the relay host da-host, edit the following option:

    `relayhost = 172.17.8.1`

12. To rewrite the sender addresses and remove the host name, modify the following options as shown below:

    `masquerade_exceptions = root` (should already be set)

    `masquerade_domains = digitalairlines.com`

    Save the file and close the editor.

13. Start Postfix by entering

    rcpostfix start

14. To generate a test e-mail message, enter

    `mail joe@example.com.`

    Enter the subject and some text and finish the e-mail message by doing the following:

    Press Enter.

    Type . (dot).

    Press Enter.

15. As root in a terminal window on da-host, enter `mailq`.

    As your classroom network is most likely not set up to deliver mail to the outside and there is no MX record for the example.com domain, you should see an entry for the e-mail message you just created. If not, have a look at the `/var/log/mail` file on da1 and da-host to find out what happened to the e-mail message.

16. Using the Queue ID displayed in the output of the `mailq` command, delete the e-mail message from the queue by entering

    `postsuper -d queue_ID`

17. Enter `mailq` to verify the mail has been deleted from the queue.

(End of Exercise)

Exercise 7-5   *Manage a CUPS Server*

In this exercise, add a printer via the Web frontend of CUPS (even though no printer is physically available at your workstation) and use command line tools to print and to manage queues.

In the first part of the exercise, using the web interface, add a network printer, the model being HP LaserJet 4050, and its name "Fictive."

In the second part of the exercise, use the `lpr` and `lp` commands to print the `/etc/hosts` file to the queue hplj4. View the jobs using `lpq` and `lpstat`. Delete the first job using `lprm`.

Detailed Steps to Complete the Exercise

- Part I: Add a Printer Using the Web Interface
- Part II: Manage Printers from the Command Line

Part I: Add a Printer Using the Web Interface

Do the following on da-host:

1. Start a Web browser on your workstation.

2. Enter **http://localhost:631/** as the URL in your browser window.

3. Select the *Administration* tab.

4. To add the (nonexistent) printer, select *Add Printer*.

5. Under *Name*, type **Fictive**.

6. Under *Location*, type **Nowhere**.

7. Under *Description*, type **This printer does not exist.**

8. Select *Continue*.

   If there is a warning message from the browser about sending information over an unencrypted connection, select *Continue*.

   After some time (usually short, but it can also take several minutes), a *Device for Fictive* dialog appears.

9. From the Device pull-down menu, select *AppSocket/HP JetDirect*, then select *Continue*.

   The *Device URI for Fictive* dialog appears.

10. As Device URI, enter

    socket://172.17.8.250:9100

    Select *Continue*.

    The *Make/Manufacturer for Fictive* dialog appears.

11. From the *Make/Manufacturer for Fictive* pull-down menu, select *HP*, then select *Continue*.

The *Model/Driver for Fictive* dialog appears.

12. From the *Model/Driver* list, select one of the *HP LaserJet 4050 Series Postscript (recommended) (en)* drivers, then select *Add Printer*.

13. In the *Authentication* dialog, type root as the username and novell as the password.

14. Select *OK*.

15. You should get the following message:

   Printer Fictive has been added successfully.

   After a few moments, the *Fictive: Options installed* page appears. Review the available options.

16. Select the *Printers* tab to see the new printer in the list.

Part II: Manage Printers from the Command Line

Do the following on da-host:

1. Open a terminal window.

2. Send a print job to the Fictive printer using the Berkeley printer commands.

   a. Send the /etc/hosts file to be printed by entering

   ```
   lpr  -P  Fictive  /etc/hosts
   ```

   b. View the print queue for hplj4 by entering the following Berkeley command:

   ```
   lpq  -P  Fictive
   ```

3. Send a print job to the Fictive printer using the System V printer commands.

   a. Send the /etc/hosts file to the printer by entering

   ```
   lp  -d  Fictive  /etc/hosts
   ```

   b. View the print queue for hplj4 by entering the following Berkeley command:

   ```
   lpstat  Fictive
   ```

4. At the terminal window, cancel the first print job by entering the following Berkeley command (use the jobnumber displayed in Step 2b above):

   ```
   lprm  -P  Fictive  jobnumber
   ```

5. Enter lpstat Fictive.

   The first print job has been deleted.

6. Check the status of the printer by entering

   ```
   lpc  status
   ```

(End of Exercise)

Exercise 7-6   *Configure a DNS Server*

In this exercise, you learn how to configure a DNS server.

Install the BIND software on da-host and configure two zones, one for digitalairlines.com, and one for the reverse lookup for the 172.17.0.0/16 network.

Detailed Steps to Complete the Exercise

Do the following on da-host:

1. From the YaST Control Center, select *Software > Software Management*.

2. From the *Filter* drop-down menu, select *Search*.

3. In the *Search* field, enter bind, then select *Search*.

4. On the right, select the *bind* and the *bind-chrootenv* package.

5. Select *Accept*; insert the *SUSE Linux Enterprise Server 11* installation DVD as needed.

    When installation is complete close the YaST Control Center.

6. Open a terminal window and su - to root (password **novell**).

7. Rename the /etc/named.conf file to /etc/named.conf.orig, by entering

    ```
    mv /etc/named.conf /etc/named.conf.orig
    ```

8. Create a new configuration file named /etc/named.conf with the following content:

    ```
    # /etc/named.conf: Configuration of the master name server

    options {

    # Where are the files located?
        directory "/var/lib/named";

    # Forwarding requests to the classroom server if there is one
    #     forwarders { 192.168.2.1; };

    };

    # Definition of root zone
    zone "." in {
        type hint;
        file "root.hint";
    };

    # Definition of the zone localhost
    zone "localhost" in {
        type master;
        file "localhost.zone";
    ```

```
};
zone "0.0.127.in-addr.arpa" in {
    type master;
    file "127.0.0.zone";
};
```

NOTE: You can find the above `named.conf` file in the `Exercises/Section_07/` directory on the *Novell's Guide to the LPIC-1 Certification Using SUSE Linux Enterprise Server 11* Course CD.

---

9. Conditional: If there is a name server for the classroom, ask the instructor for its IP address and configure the forwarders line to match the following:

   ```
   forwarders {x.x.x.x;};
   ```

   Make sure that you delete the comment character from the beginning of the forwarders line.

10. Add the following two zone statements after the existing zone statements:

    ```
    zone "digitalairlines.com" in {
        type master;
        file "master/digitalairlines.com.zone";
    };

    zone "0.0.10.in-addr.arpa" in {
        type master;
        file "master/10.0.0.zone";
    };
    ```

    Save and close the file.

11. Create a new `/var/lib/named/master/digitalairlines.com.zone` file with the following content:

    ```
    $TTL 172800

    digitalairlines.com. IN SOA da-host.digitalairlines.com.
    hostmaster.digitalairlines.com. (
                2009081201 ; serial, todays date + todays serial
                1D         ; refresh
                2H         ; retry
                1W         ; expire
                3H         ; minimum
                )
            IN NS da-host.digitalairlines.com.
    da-host    IN A 172.17.8.1
    da1        IN A 172.17.8.101
    da2        IN A 172.17.8.102
    ```

    The SOA record (including hostmaster.digitalairlines.com) must be on a single line.

    Use the current date and "01" as the serial number (such as 2009121401).

NOTE: You can use the `digitalairlines.com.zone` file from the `Exercises/Section_07/` directory on the *Novell's Guide to the LPIC-1 Certification Using SUSE Linux Enterprise Server 11* Course CD as a template.

Save and close the file.

12. Create a new `/var/lib/named/master/172.17.zone` file with the following content:

```
$TTL 172800
17.172.in-addr.arpa. IN SOA da-host.digitalairlines.com.
hostmaster.digitalairlines.com. (
            2009081201 ; serial, todays date + todays serial
            1D         ; refresh
            2H         ; retry
            1W         ; expire
            3H         ; minimum
            )

            IN NS da-host.digitalairlines.com.

8.1         IN PTR da-host.digitalairlines.com.
8.101       IN PTR da1.digitalairlines.com.
8.102       IN PTR da2.digitalairlines.com.
```

The SOA record (including hostmaster.digitalairlines.com) must be on a single line.

Use the current date and "01" as the serial number (such as 2009121401).

NOTE: You can use the `172.17.zone` file from the `Exercises/Section_07/` directory on the *Novell's Guide to the LPIC-1 Certification Using SUSE Linux Enterprise Server 11* Course CD as a template.

Save and close the file.

13. Open a second terminal window and `su -` to root (password **novell**).

14. To view the end of the `/var/log/messages` file and any new entries added to it, enter

```
tail -f /var/log/messages
```

15. Switch to the first terminal window and start bind by entering

```
rcnamed start
```

If there are errors in the `/etc/named.conf` file, they are displayed in the output (with specific references and line numbers). The named daemon will not start until these errors are fixed.

16. From the second terminal window, watch the log output of bind for any messages such as Unknown RR Type or File Not Found.

If any errors occur, fix them and restart bind.

17. From the first terminal window, start bind automatically when the system is booted by entering

```
insserv named
```

18. Open the `/etc/resolv.conf` file in a text editor.

19. Delete all existing `nameserver` entries and add the following entry:

```
nameserver 172.17.8.1
```

Save and close the file.

20. Repeat Step 18 and Step 19 on da1.

21. Verify that your DNS server works by entering

```
host da2.digitalairlines.com
```

This should display the IP address of 172.17.8.102.

(End of Exercise)

Exercise 7-7   Configure ntpd

In this exercise, you configure your server to get time information from another server.

Set up an NTP server on your machine that gets its time from a server on the Internet. (If you do not have Internet access, you can still do the exercise, but your time won't be synchronized with an external server.)

Detailed Steps to Complete the Exercise

Do the following on da-host:

1. At a terminal window, `su -` to root (password: **novell**).

2. View the system date and time by entering `date`.

   Record the time:

3. View the hardware clock time by entering `hwclock`.

4. Configure the NTP server with YaST.

   a. Start the YaST Control Center and select *Network Services > NTP Configuration*.

      The *Advanced NTP Configuration* dialog appears.

   b. Under **Start NTP daemon**, on the **General Settings** tab, select **Now and On Boot**.

   c. Make sure the **Runtime Configuration Policy** is set to **Auto**, then click **Add**.

      The *New Synchronization* dialog appears.

   d. Select **Server** as the type, then click **Next**.

      The *NTP Server* dialog appears.

   e. In the **Server Settings** pane, select **Public NTP Server** from the drop-down menu.

      The *Public NTP Server* dialog appears.

   f. From the **Country** drop-down menu, select your country or a country geographically near your country.

   g. From the **Public NTP Servers** drop-down menu, select a public NTP server that, according to its policy, allows you to use it as time source.

      Click **Test** to test its availability. The result depends on the Internet connectivity of your course environment. Confirm the test result by clicking **OK**.

   h. Click **OK > OK**.

      You are returned to the *Advanced NTP Configuration* dialog.

   i. Save the NTP configuration by clicking **OK**.

5. At the terminal window, view the status of the NTP time synchronization by entering `rcntp status`.

The output will vary, depending on the time passed since ntpd was started and whether or not the NTP server you configured can actually be reached from your computer.

6. View the log of the NTP server by entering

   ```
   tail -f /var/log/ntp
   ```

   Stop tail by pressing Ctrl+c.

7. View the changes made to the `/etc/ntp.conf` file by entering
   ```
   less /etc/ntp.conf
   ```

   Notice that the NTP server is the server you selected earlier.

8. Check the hardware clock time by entering `hwclock`.

9. Set the hardware clock from the system time by entering the following:

   ```
   hwclock --systohc
   ```

10. Check the new hardware clock time by entering `hwclock`.

11. Close all open windows.

(End of Exercise)

Exercise 7-8   Configure xinetd

In this exercise, you configure xinetd to provide the Telnet and Finger services. This exercise has two parts.

In the first part of this exercise, use the YaST Network Services (xinetd) module to set up a Telnet server on your computer.

In the second part, install the Finger service, and edit its configuration in `/etc/xinetd.d/` to activate the service.

Detailed Steps to Complete the Exercise

- Part I: Enable xinetd Services with YaST
- Part II: Enable an xinetd Services Manually

Part I: Enable xinetd Services with YaST

Do the following on da-host:

1. Start the YaST Control Center and select **Network Services > Network Services (xinetd)**.

   The *Network Services Configuration (xinetd)* dialog appears.

2. Select **Enable**.

   A list of currently available services becomes active.

3. Scroll down and select the service **telnet (*Server: /usr/sbin/in.telnetd*)**, then set the service to **On** by selecting **Toggle Status (On or Off)**.

   If the telnet-server package is not yet installed, it will be installed now. Insert the *SUSE Linux Enterprise Server 11* installation DVD as needed and select **Install**.

4. Save the configuration to the system by selecting **Finish**.

5. Test the configuration.

   a. Open a terminal window and telnet to localhost by entering `telnet localhost`.

   b. Log in as geeko (password: **novell**).

   c. Log out by entering `exit`.

   d. On da1, open a terminal window and telnet to da-host.digitalairlines.com by entering

      `telnet 172.17.8.1`

   e. Log in as geeko (password: **novell**).

   f. Log out by entering `exit`.

Part II: Enable an xinetd Services Manually

Enable the finger server on da-host by doing the following:

1. At a terminal window, `su -` to root (password: **novell**).

2. Install the finger-server package if it is not yet installed:

   `rpm -q finger-server || yast -i finger-server`

3. At the terminal window, edit the `/etc/xinetd.d/finger` file by entering

   `vi /etc/xinetd.d/finger`

4. At the bottom of the file, change the `disable = yes` setting to the following:

   `disable = no`

5. Save the changes and close vi.

6. Restart the service xinetd by entering `rcxinetd restart`.

7. Test the Finger service by doing the following:

   a. On da1, open a terminal window.

   b. Get the finger information available at da-host by entering

      `finger @172.17.8.1`

   c. Get the finger information available for a specific user by entering

      `finger geeko@172.17.8.1`

8. Optional: Change the Finger configuration to allow access only at certain times during the day. Test your configuration.

9. Stop the service xinetd by entering `rcxinetd stop`.

(End of Exercise)

Review Questions

1. What two commands can you run to activate changes made to the /etc/samba/smb.conf file?
    a) smbclient --restart
    b) rcsmb restart
    c) nmbclient --restart
    d) rcnmb restart

2. What command can you use to check the /etc/samba/smb.conf file for errors?

3. What command may be used to mount the acctg shared directory on the server arfa to the local /mnt director y using SMB?

4. What is the default document root directory on an SLES system for the Apache Web server?

5. What Apache directive is used to set the IP address and port for an Apache virtual host?
    a) Listen
    b) NameVirtualHost
    c) VirtualHostIP
    d) VirtualHost

6. What file can contain directory-specific access restrictions for Apache?
    a) htpasswd
    b) AllowOverride
    c) .htaccess
    d) ht.conf

7. What hosts are allowed to connect to the following directory?
    ```
    <Directory /var/www/website>
    Order allow,deny
    Deny from all
    </Directory>
    ```
    a) All hosts
    b) No hosts
    c) Only hosts that can perform reverse DNS lookups
    d) Only hosts that are listed in the <Allowedhosts> section

8. What Apache file is used to log web server hits?
    a) custom_log
    b) access_log
    c) server_log
    d) error_log

9. Which command can you use to insert new entries into MySQL database tables?
    a) mysql
    b) mysqladmin
    c) dbadmin
    d) dbsql

10. Which of the following are technologies that can be used to generate dynamic content with the Apache Web server? (Choose all that apply.)
    a) CGI programs
    b) PERL
    c) PHP
    d) NTP

11. What is the main configuration file for the PureFTPd FTP server?

12. What is the default anonymous home directory for the FTP server on SLES?

13. What FTP command can be used to change the current working directory on the FTP client?

14. Which of the following are common MTAs in Linux? (Choose all that apply.)
    a) Postfix
    b) Procmail
    c) mail
    d) Sendmail

15. What two protocols do MUAs typically use to retrieve e-mails from across the network?

16. What protocol does an MUA typically use to send e-mails to an MTA?

17. You have recently modified the /etc/aliases file. What command can you run to update your MTA with the changes?
    a) newaliases
    b) alias
    c) postsuper
    d) mailq

18. What file can you place in your home directory to create a forwarder entry for your e-mail?

19. Which command may be used to create printer classes?
    a) cupsadmin
    b) lpadmin
    c) lpstat
    d) cupsd

20. When you try to send a print job to the printer p1, you receive an error message stating that the print queue is unavailable. What command can you use to allow print jobs to enter the print queue for p1?

21. What address would you use in your web browser to administer your local CUPS server?

22. What CUPS log stores remote printing requests?

23. What is the TLD for www.sample.domain.com?

24. What determines the default length of time that a name resolution result is cached on your computer?
    a) The resolver settings in IP properties
    b) The search line in /etc/resolv.conf
    c) The TTL in the SOA record on the DNS server
    d) The NS record on the DNS server in the TLD

25. Which packages must you have installed for your computer to function as a DNS server? (Choose all that apply.)
    a) bind
    b) bind-chrootenv
    c) bind-utils
    d) bind-named

26. What record in a DNS zone file is used to map names to IP addresses for hosts on the network?
    a) SOA
    b) NS
    c) MX
    d) A

27. How does a slave DNS server know that changes have been made on the master DNS server?
    a) By broadcasting to the master DNS server
    b) By querying the serial number in the SOA on the master DNS server
    c) By receiving a zone notification from the master DNS server
    d) By obtaining an NS record from the master DNS server

28. What of the following are valid commands for testing DNS name resolution? (Choose all that apply.)
    a) nslookup
    b) dig
    c) testparm
    d) host

29. What command can you run to manually synchronize your time with the NTP time sources listed in /etc/ntp.conf?
    a) netdate
    b) ntpd
    c) ntpq
    d) ntpdate

30. What term refers to the hop distance that a time server is from a real-time time source such as an atomic clock?

31. What xinetd file could you edit to configure the telnet daemon?
    a) /etc/telnet.d
    b) /etc/inetd
    c) /etc/xinetd.d/telnet
    d) /etc/xinetd

32. Provided that your xinetd daemon is configured to use TCP wrappers for telnet connections, what lines could you add to the /etc/hosts.allow and /etc/hosts.deny files to allow only the host arfa the ability to use the telnet utility when connecting to your server? (Choose two answers.)
    a) /etc/hosts.allow: in.telnetd: arfa
    b) /etc/hosts.allow: in.telnetd: ALL
    c) /etc/hosts.deny: in.telnetd: arfa
    d) /etc/hosts.deny: in.telnetd: ALL

33. What two tags are used in the /etc/squid/squid.conf file to control access to Web content? (Choose two answers.)
    a) access_list
    b) acl
    c) http_access
    d) allow_list

Discovery Exercises

Testing Apache File System Restrictions

Ensure that the Apache Web server is installed on your system and started. Log into the GNOME desktop as **geeko** and enter the URL of **http://127.0.0.1** in your Web browser to view the default Web page.

Next, log into tty1 as the **root** user and view the contents of the **/etc/apache2/uid.conf** file (this is referenced by the /etc/apache2/httpd.conf file). Next, view the ownership and permissions on the /srv/www/htdocs/index.html file. Can the Apache daemon read its contents?

Next, change the permissions on the **/srv/www/htdocs/index.html** file to **600** (rw-------), switch back to tty7 and refresh your Web page (http://127.0.0.1). What error do you receive and why?

When finished, switch back to tty1, change the permissions on the **/srv/www/htdocs/index.html** file to **644** and log out of the terminal. Switch back to tty7, refresh your Web page to ensure that it can be read by the Apache daemon, and log out of the GNOME desktop.

Hosting Personal Web Pages using Apache

Ensure that the Apache Web server is installed on your system and started. Next, log into tty1 as the **root** user and view the contents of the **/etc/apache2/mod_user.conf** file (this is referenced by the /etc/apache2/httpd.conf file). Take specific note of the comments that indicate the default configuration that allows for personal Web pages. What directory is used by default within each user's home directory for personal Web pages?

Log into the GNOME desktop as **geeko** and open a GNOME terminal. Create a **public_html** directory under geeko's home directory. Inside this directory, create an **index.html** file that contains the following lines using thevieditor, and save your changes when finished:

```
<html><body>
<h1> My sample Web page! </h1>
</body></html>
```

Next, open your Web browser and navigate to the URLhttp://127.0.0.1/~geekoto test your personal Web page.

Testing Postfix using Telnet

SMTP is a command-based protocol used to relay e-mail across the Internet. As a result, it is easy to test its functionality using telnet.

Log into tty1 as the **root** user and type **telnet localhost 25** to interact with the network service listening on TCP port 25. Can you tell that you are interacting with Postfix? Next, perform the following actions:

- Type **EHLO** to verify ESMTP support
- Type **HELO** to verify SMTP support
- Type **mail from: billy.gates@microsoft.com** to create a new e-mail from Bill Gates
- Type **rcpt to: geeko** to specify that the geeko user on your local system is the recipient
- Type **data**
- Type **Hello World**
- Type **.** to finish the e-mail
- Type **quit** to end the telnet session.

When finished, switch to the **geeko** user and check geeko's mail using the **mail** command. Is your message there? Delete the message and quit the mail utility when finished.

Configuring a Basic Samba Domain Controller

Use the Internet to research the steps required to use your Samba server as a Windows NTdomain controller. Next, log in to tty1 as the root user and configure your Samba service as a domain controller by editing your /etc/samba/smb.conf file. The minimum lines required in this file are:

```
[global]
        domain logons = yes
        security = user
        encrypt passwords = yes
        wins support = yes
        netbios name = (your NetBIOS name)
        workgroup =(put your domain name here)
[netlogon]
        path=/netlogon (create this directory with permissions 777)
        public = no
        writable = no
        locking = no
```

Next, create a new user on the system (**useradd −m testuser**) and give the user an encrypted password in the samba database (**smbpasswd testuser**). Then, add computer accounts for each Windows computer that will be joining the domain on your Linux computer by adding a line to /etc/passwd and /etc/shadow that lists the computer name followed by a $ character, as shown below:

```
/etc/passwd sample line:
        clientcomputer name$:x:5000:5000::/dev/null:/bin/false
/etc/shadow sample line:
        clientcomputer name$:*:6445::::::
```

When finished, test your configuration by joining a Windows client to the domain and testing domain logon. Log out of tty1 on your Samba server when finished.

SECTION 8   Understand Security-Related Tools

In this section, you learn how to perform security-related administrative tasks using various tools and you learn how to configure remote access solutions for SLES 11.

Objectives

1. Manage and Secure the Linux User Environment

2. Provide Secure Remote Access with OpenSSH

3. Configure User Authentication with PAM

4. Ensure File Integrity

5. Use Security-Related Utilities

6. Understand SELinux

Objective 1   Manage and Secure the Linux User Environment

As a system administrator of SLES 11, you need to know how to manage and secure the user environment on Linux. In this objective, the following topics are addressed:

- Manage Use of root
- Delegate Administrative Tasks with sudo
- Set Defaults for New User Accounts
- Configure Security Settings
- Limiting Resources with ulimit
- Configure sudo
- Configure the Password Security Settings

Manage Use of root

You should carefully manage how you use the root user account on your system. Remember that root has full access to the entire system. When doing day-to-day work, you should log in as a normal user and switch to root **only** to perform tasks that require root permissions. When done, you should switch back to your normal user account.

To switch between a normal user and root while performing administrative tasks, you can do the following:

- Switch to Another User with su
- Switch to Another Group with newgrp
- Start Programs as Another User from GNOME

Switch to Another User with su

You can use the su (switch user) command to assume the UID of root or of other users on the Linux system. The following is the syntax for using su:

```
su options [-] user argument
```

For example, to change to the user geeko, you enter su geeko; to change to the user root, you enter su root or su (without a username). If you want to start a login shell with root's environment variables applied, you can enter su -.

NOTE: Root can change to any user ID without knowing the password of the user.

To return to your previous user ID, enter exit.

To change to the user root and execute a single command, use the -c option:

```
geeko@da1:~> su - -c "grep geeko /etc/shadow"
```

NOTE: For additional information on the su command, enter `su --help` at the shell prompt.

Switch to Another Group with newgrp

A user can be a member of many different groups but can have only one **effective** (current) group at any one time. Normally this is the **primary group**, which is specified in the `/etc/passwd` file. If a user creates directories or files, then they belong to the user and to the user's effective group.

You can change the effective group GID with the `newgrp` or `sg` command (such as `sg video`). Only group members can perform this group change unless a group password is defined. In this case, any user that knows the group password can make the change, too. You can undo the change (return to the original effective GID) by entering `exit` or by pressing Ctrl+d.

Start Programs as Another User from GNOME

In GNOME you can start any program with a different UID (as long as you know the password), using the `gnomesu` program.

On the GNOME desktop, open a command line dialog by pressing Alt+F2, then enter `gnomesu`. You are prompted for the root password. After entering it, a terminal window appears. The path is still that of the user logged in to GNOME; if you need the standard environment for root, enter `su -` in the terminal window.

You can specify a different user than root and also start a program directly with the following syntax: `gnomesu -u user command`. If the command is not in the path of the user logged in to GNOME, you have to enter the full path, like `gnomesu /sbin/yast2`, which starts YaST after the root password is entered.

NOTE: For some programs, you do not need to use `gnomesu` after pressing Alt+F2; for instance, when you enter `yast2`, you are automatically prompted for the root password.

Delegate Administrative Tasks with sudo

Sometimes it is necessary to allow a normal user access to a command which can be run only by root. For example, you might want a co-worker to take over tasks such as shutting down the computer and creating users while you are on vacation. To do this, you could just give them your root user's password. However, this represents a significant security risk.

It would be better to provide root-level access to only the commands you want them to be able to run **without** giving them the root password. This can be done using `sudo`.

The default configuration of sudo in SLES 11 requires the knowledge of the root password. If you know the root password, you do not need to use sudo for administrative tasks. Its use, nevertheless, has the advantage that the executed commands are logged to `/var/log/messages` and that you do not need to retype the password for each command (as with the `su -c` command), because it is cached for several minutes by sudo.

```
geeko@da1:~ > sudo /sbin/shutdown -h now

We trust you have received the usual lecture from the local System
Administrator. It usually boils down to these three things:

    #1) Respect the privacy of others.
    #2) Think before you type.
    #3) With great power comes great responsibility.

root's password:
```

You can change the configuration of sudo so that it asks for the user password instead of the root password. To do this, put a comment sign (#) in front of the following two lines in /etc/sudoers using the visudo command:.

```
# In the default (unconfigured) configuration, sudo asks for the root
# password. This allows use of an ordinary user account for
# administration of a freshly installed system. When configuring
# sudo, delete the two following lines:
Defaults targetpw # ask for the password of the target user i.e. root
ALL ALL=(ALL) ALL # WARNING! Only use this together with 'Defaults
                  # targetpw'!
```

Using visudo, you can specify which commands a user can or cannot enter by configuring the /etc/sudoers file. The following is the general syntax of an entry in the configuration file:

user/**group host** = **command1, command2** ...

For example

```
geeko ALL = /sbin/shutdown
```

In this example, the user geeko is able to carry out the /sbin/shutdown command with the permissions of root on all computers (ALL). Being able to specify the computer in /etc/sudoers allows you to copy the same file to different computers without having to grant the same permissions on all computers involved.

The /etc/sudoers file can also be configured with aliases to define who can do what as root. The following aliases are used:

- **User_Alias.** Users who are allowed to run commands.

- **Cmnd_Alias.** Commands that users are allowed to run.

- **Host_Alias.** Hosts that users are allowed to run the commands on.

- **Runas_Alias.** User names that commands may be run as.

You need to use User_Alias to define an alias containing the user accounts (separated by commas) you want to allow to run commands:

```
User_Alias alias = users
```

For example, to create an alias named POWERUSERS that contains the tux and geeko user accounts, you would enter the following in the /etc/sudoers file:

```
User_Alias POWERUSERS = tux, geeko
```

All alias names must start with a capital letter.

You next need to use Cmnd_Alias to define an alias that contains the commands (using the full path) that you want the users defined in User_Alias to be able to run. You can separate multiple commands with commas.

For example, if your users are developers that need to be able to kill hung processes from time to time, you could define an alias named KPROCS that contains the kill and killall command, as shown below:

```
Cmnd_Alias KPROCS = /bin/kill, /usr/bin/killall
```

Next, you need to use Host_Alias to specify which systems the users can run the commands on. For example, to let them run the commands on a system named da1, you would use the following:

```
Host_Alias HOSTS = da1
```

Finally, you need to assemble these aliases together to define exactly what will happen. The syntax is

User_Alias Host_Alias = (user) Cmnd_Alias

Using the aliases defined above, you could allow the specified users to run the specified commands on the specified hosts as root by entering the following:

```
POWERUSERS HOSTS = (root) KPROCS
```

This sample configuration is shown below:.

```
User_Alias      POWERUSERS = tux, geeko
Cmnd_Alias      KPROCS = /bin/kill, /usr/bin/killall
Host_Alias      HOSTS = da1
POWERUSERS      HOSTS = (root) KPROCS
```

To exit the visudo editor, press Esc and then enter :exit. The visudo utility checks your syntax and informs you if you have made any errors. At this point, the users you defined can now execute the commands you specified as root by entering sudo *command* at the shell prompt.

For example, the geeko user could kill a process named top owned by root by entering sudo killall top at the shell prompt, as shown below:

```
geeko@da1:~> sudo killall top
geeko's password:
geeko@da1:~>
```

After supplying the geeko user's password, the process is killed. If you run the sudo command again from within the same terminal session, you won't be prompted for the user's password again for some time (5 minutes unless changed in the /etc/sudoers file).

YaST includes the Sudo module, which you can also use to configure the `sudoers` file. Start YaST, then select **Security and Users > Sudo**. By default, a list of your sudo rules is displayed, as shown below:

Figure 8-1   *YaST Sudo Module*

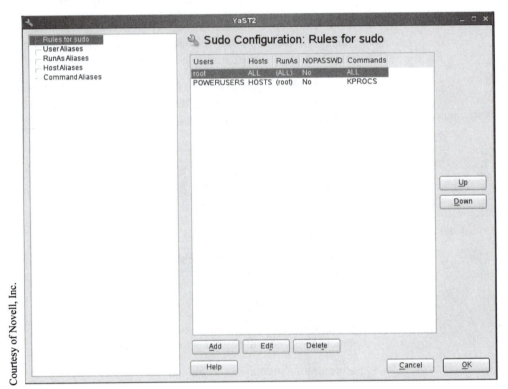

Courtesy of Novell, Inc.

Using the Sudo module in YaST, you configure your User_Aliases using the **User Alias** link, your Host_Aliases using the **Host Alias** link, and your Cmnd_Aliases using the **Command Alias** link. Then you use the **Rules for sudo** link to construct your sudo rules.

Set Defaults for New User Accounts

Another aspect of user security that you should consider is specifying default settings for new users when they are created. You can use YaST to select default settings to be applied to new user accounts.

In YaST, select **Security and Users > User Management**. You can also start the User Management module directly from a terminal window by entering `yast2 users`. Select the **Defaults for New Users** tab. The following is displayed:

Figure 8-2   *User and Group Administration in YaST*

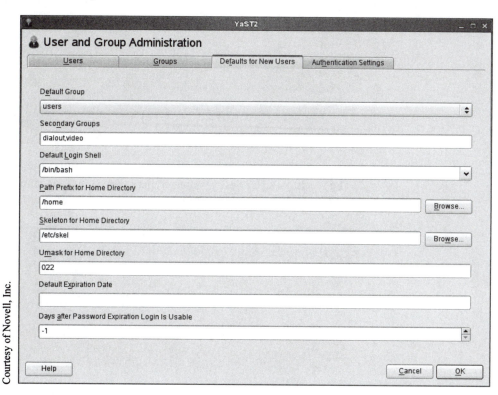

Courtesy of Novell, Inc.

To define the default settings that will be applied to new users when they are created, edit the information in the following fields:

- **Default Group.** Select the primary (default) group.

- **Secondary Groups.** Specify a list of secondary groups (separated by commas) to assign to the user.

- **Default Login Shell.** From the drop-down list, select the default login shell (command interpreter) from the shells installed on your system.

- **Path Prefix for Home Directory.** Specify the initial path prefix for a new user's home directory. The user's name will be appended to the end of this value to create the default name of the user's home directory. This is /home by default.

- **Skeleton Directory.** Specify the skeleton directory. The contents of this directory will be copied to the user's home directory when you add a new user.

- **Default Expiration Date.** Specify the date when the user account is disabled. The date must be in the format *YYYY-MM-DD*. Leave the field empty if this account never expires.

- **Days after Password Expiration Login Is Usable:** Enables users to log in after passwords expire. Set how many days login is still allowed after a password expires. Enter -1 for unlimited access.

Save the configuration settings by selecting *OK*. The values are written to the /etc/default/useradd file:

```
da1:~ # cat /etc/default/useradd
GROUP=100
HOME=/home
INACTIVE=-1
EXPIRE=
SHELL=/bin/bash
SKEL=/etc/skel
GROUPS=video,dialout
CREATE_MAIL_SPOOL=no
```

You can also use the `useradd` command line utility to view or change the defaults. The `--show-defaults` option displays the options shown above. The `--save-defaults` option, followed by an option with a value, changes them:

```
da1:~ # useradd --save-defaults -d /export/home
da1:~ # useradd --show-defaults
GROUP=100
HOME=/export/home
INACTIVE=-1
EXPIRE=SHELL=/bin/bash
SKEL=/etc/skel
GROUPS=video,dialout
CREATE_MAIL_SPOOL=no
```

The manual page for `useradd` lists the possible options.

Configure Security Settings

Next, you need to consider your system's security settings. YaST provides the *Local Security* module, which lets you configure the following local security settings for your SLES 11 system:

- Password settings
- Boot configuration
- Login settings
- User creation settings
- File permissions

To meet the requirements of your organization's security policies and procedures, you can select from (or modify) three preset levels of security. You can also create your own customized security settings.

You can access the Security Settings module from the YaST Control Center by selecting *Security and Users > Local Security*, or by entering `yast2 security` in a terminal window. When you do, the *Security Overview* window is displayed:

Figure 8-3   *YaST Security Overview*

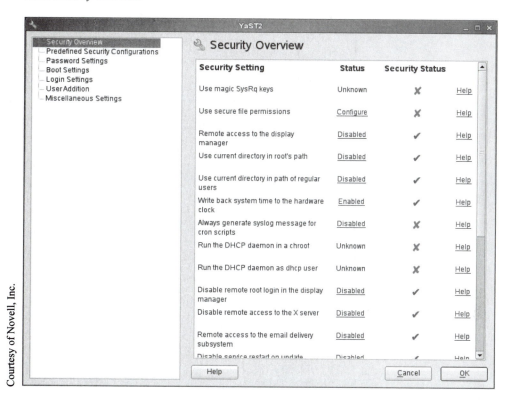

Courtesy of Novell, Inc.

This screen provides you with an overview of your system's security settings. If desired, you can select a specific setting in the *Security Overview* and modify it.

You can also use this module to select one of several preset security configurations. To do this, select **Predefined Security Configuration**. The following is displayed:

Figure 8-4   *YaST Local Security Configuration*

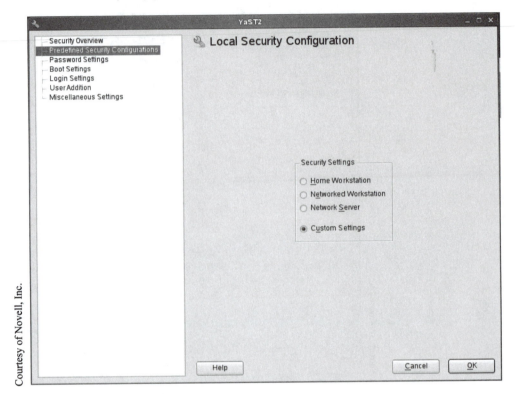

Courtesy of Novell, Inc.

You can select from the following preset security configurations in this screen:

- **Home Workstation.** For a home computer that is not connected to any type of a network. This option represents the lowest level of local security.

- **Networked Workstation.** For a computer connected to any type of a network or the Internet. This option provides an intermediate level of local security.

- **Network Server.** For a computer that provides any type of service (network or otherwise). This option enables a high level of local security.

You can also select *Custom Settings* to create your own configuration.

By selecting one of the three predefined security levels and then clicking *OK*, you apply the chosen security level. If you want to customize your configuration, select *Custom Settings*. Then, on the left, select the parameter you want to modify.

For example, to modify your password security settings, select *Password Settings*. The following is displayed:

Figure 8-5   *YaST: Password Settings*

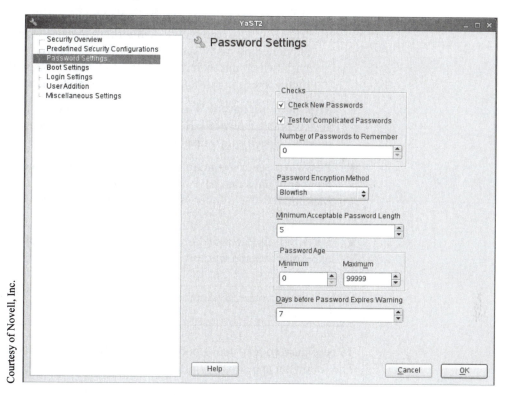

Courtesy of Novell, Inc.

In this dialog, you can edit the default system password requirements. You can modify the following settings (they are mainly stored in `/etc/login.defs`, but some values are also stored in `/etc/default/passwd` and `/etc/security/pam_pwcheck.conf`):

- **Check New Passwords.** Enforces password checking. It verifies that passwords cannot be found in a dictionary and are not a name or any other simple, common word.

- **Test for Complicated Passwords.** Enables additional password checks. Passwords should be constructed using a mixture of uppercase and lower case characters as well as numbers. Special characters, such as ;, (, or =, may be used, too, but could be hard to enter on a different keyboard layout. This makes it very difficult to guess the password.

- **Number of Passwords to Remember.** Number of user passwords to store. Users are prevented from reusing a stored password. Specify 0 if passwords should not be stored.

- **Password Encryption Method.** Select one of the following encryption methods:

    - **DES.** Lowest common denominator. It works in all network environments, but it restricts you to passwords no longer than eight characters. If you need compatibility with other systems, select this method.

❏ **MD5.** Allows longer passwords and is supported by all current Linux distributions, but not necessarily by other systems or older software.

❏ **Blowfish.** Uses the blowfish algorithm to encrypt passwords. It is not yet supported by many systems. A lot of CPU power is needed to calculate the hash, which makes it difficult to crack passwords with the help of a dictionary. It is the default encryption method used on SLES 11.

- **Minimum Acceptable Password Length.** Minimum number of characters for an acceptable password. If a user enters fewer characters, the password is rejected. Specifying 0 disables this check.

- **Password Age.** Minimum and maximum password ages. Minimum refers to the number of days that have to elapse before a password can be changed again. Maximum is the number of days after which a password expires and must be changed.

- **Days Before Password Expires Warning.** Number of days before password expiration when a warning is issued to the user.

NOTE: Although root receives a warning when setting a bad password, root can still set it despite the above settings.

To configure your system's boot security settings, select **Boot Settings** on the left. The following appears:

Figure 8-6   *YaST Boot Settings*

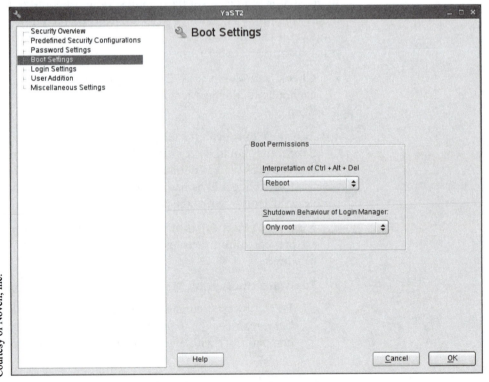

In this dialog, you can select the following boot settings (which update the `/etc/inittab` file):

- **Interpretation of Ctrl + Alt + Del.** When someone at the console presses the Ctrl+Alt+Del keystroke combination, the system usually reboots. You can change this behavior using the following options:

  □ **Ignore.** Sometimes you want to have the system ignore this keystroke combination, especially when the system serves as both workstation and server. Nothing happens when the Ctrl+Alt+Del keystroke combination is pressed.

  □ **Reboot.** System reboots when the Ctrl+Alt+Del keystroke combination is pressed.

  □ **Halt.** System is shut down when the Ctrl+Alt+Del keystroke combination is pressed.

- **Shutdown Behavior of Login Manager.** Use this option to determine who is allowed to shut down the computer from GNOME or KDE.

  □ **Only Root.** To halt the system, the root password has to be entered.

  □ **All Users.** Everyone, even remotely connected users, can halt the system.

  □ **Nobody.** Nobody can halt the system.

  □ **Automatic.** If the `PERMISSION_SECURITY` variable in `/etc/sysconfig/security` is set to `"easy local"`, it is the same as **All Users**, for all other settings it is **Only Root**.

For a server system you should use **Only Root** or **Nobody** to prevent normal users from halting the system accidentally or deliberately.

If you want to customize your login security settings, select *Login Settings* on the left. The following dialog appears:

Figure 8-7 *YaST Login Settings*

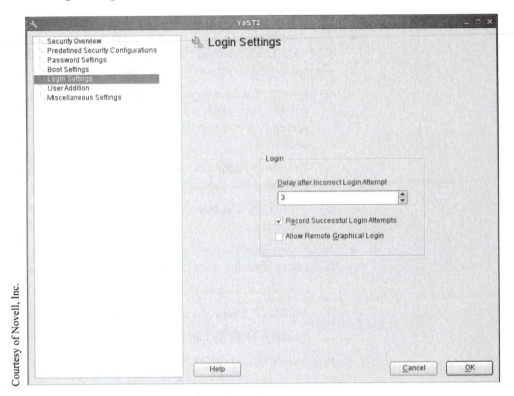

Courtesy of Novell, Inc.

In this dialog, you can specify the following login settings, which are stored in /
etc/login.defs:

- **Delay After Incorrect Login Attempt.** Following a failed login attempt, there is typically a waiting period of a few seconds before another login is possible. This makes it more difficult for password crackers to log in.

  This option lets you adjust the time delay before another login attempt. The default is 3 seconds, which is a reasonable value.

- **Record Successful Login Attempts.** Recording successful login attempts can be useful, especially in warning you of unauthorized access to the system (such as a user logging in from an unusual location).

  Select this option to record successful login attempts in the /var/log/wtmp file. You can use the last command to view who logged in at what time.

- **Allow Remote Graphical Login.** Allows other users access to your graphical login screen via the network. Because this type of access represents a potential security risk, it is disabled by default.

If you want to customize user addition settings, select ***User Addition*** on the left. The following dialog appears:

Figure 8-8   *YaST Security Settings: User Addition*

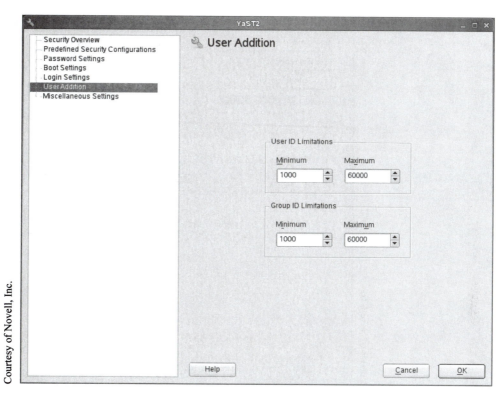

Courtesy of Novell, Inc.

In this dialog, you can configure the following ID settings, which are also stored in `/etc/login.defs`:

- **User ID Limitations.** Specify a minimum and maximum value to configure a range of possible user ID numbers. New users will receive a UID from within this range.

- **Group ID Limitations.** Specify a minimum and maximum value to configure a range of possible group ID numbers.

You can also configure miscellaneous security settings by selecting ***Miscellaneous Settings*** on the left. The following appears:

Figure 8-9   *YaST Security Settings: Miscellaneous Settings*

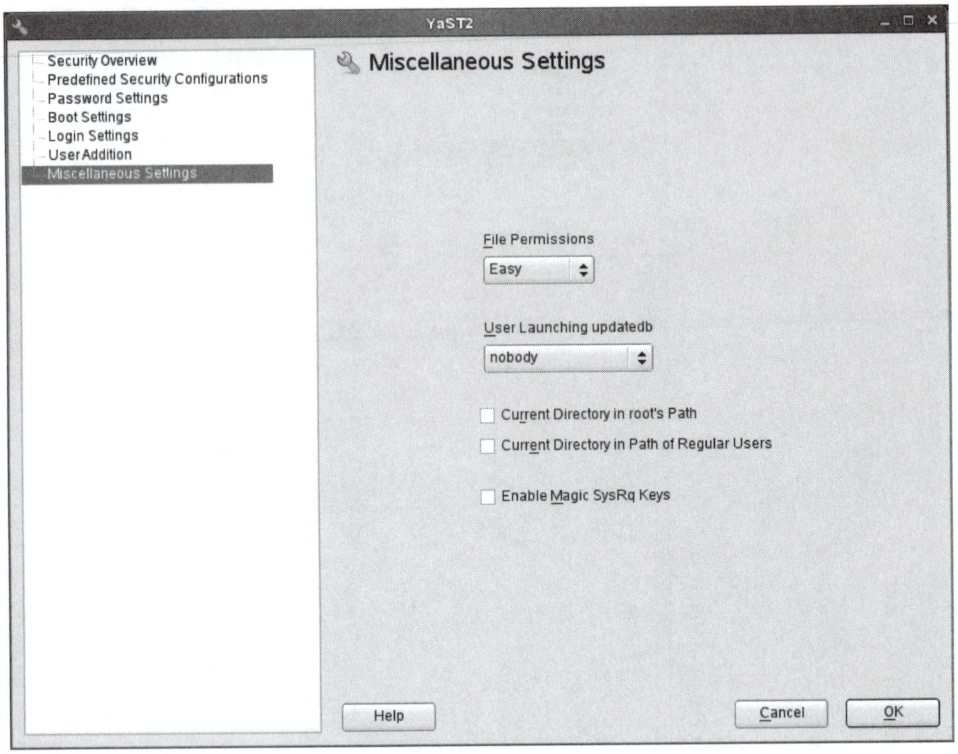

Courtesy of Novell, Inc.

In this dialog, you can select the following global security settings:

- **File Permissions.** Settings for the permissions of certain system files are configured in `/etc/permissions.easy`, `/etc/permissions.secure`, or `/etc/permissions.paranoid`. You can also add your own rules to the `/etc/permissions.local` file. Each file contains a description of the file syntax and purpose of the preset.

  Settings in files in the `/etc/permissions.d/` directory are included as well. This directory is used by packages that bring their own permissions files.

  From the drop-down list, select one of the following:

  - **Easy.** Allows read access to most of the system files by users other than root.

  - **Secure.** Ensures certain configuration files (such as `/etc/ssh/sshd_config`) can be viewed only by the user root. Some programs can only be launched by root or by daemons, not by an ordinary user.

  - **Paranoid.** Creates an extremely secure system. All SUID/SGID-Bits on programs are cleared. If you use this option, be aware that some programs might not work correctly because users no longer have the correct permissions to access certain files.

  This sets these permissions according to the settings in the respective `/etc/permissions*` files. This fixes files with incorrect permissions, whether they were set accidentally or changed by intruders.

- **User Launching updatedb.** If the `updatedb` program is installed, it automatically runs on a daily basis or after booting. It generates a database (locatedb) where the location of each file on your computer is stored.

  You can search this database from the command line using the `locate` utility, which is an alternative to the find command.

  From the drop-down list, select one of the following:

  - **nobody.** Any user can find only the paths in the database that can be seen by any other (unprivileged) user.

  - **root.** All files in the system are added into the database.

- **Current Directory in root's Path** and **Current Directory in the Path of Regular Users.** If you deselect these options (the default), users must always launch programs in the current directory by adding ". /" (such as `. /configure`).

  If you select these options, the dot (".") is appended to the end of the search path for root and users, allowing them to enter a command in the current directory without appending ". /".

  Selecting these options can be very dangerous because users can accidentally launch unknown programs in the current directory instead of the usual system-wide files.

  This configuration is written to `/etc/sysconfig/suseconfig`.

- **Enable MagicSysRq Keys.** Gives you some control over the system even if it crashes (such as during kernel debugging). For details, see `/usr/src/linux/Documentation/sysrq.txt`.

  This configuration is written to `/etc/sysconfig/sysctl`.

When you finish configuring security settings, save the settings by clicking **OK**.

Limiting Resources with ulimit

You can use the `ulimit` command to configure limits on system resources. It can be used to view or set the shell's resource usage limits.

NOTE: The limits set with `ulimit` only affect programs launched from the shell prompt.

The syntax for using ulimit is as follows:

```
ulimit options limit
```

You can use the following options with ulimit:

- File size limits:

  - `-c`: Sets the maximum size of core files. By setting this limit to 0, core dumps are disabled.

  - `-f`: Sets the maximum size of files created by the shell.

  - `-n`: Sets the maximum number of open file descriptors.

- Process time and number limits:
  - -t: Sets the maximum amount of cpu time (in seconds).
  - -u: Sets the maximum number of processes available to a single user.
- Memory size limits:
  - -d: Sets the maximum size of a process's data segment.
  - -l: Sets the maximum size that may be locked into memory.
  - -m: Sets the maximum resident set size.
  - -s: Sets the maximum stack size.
- Hard and soft limits:
  - -H: Sets a hard resource limit.
  - -S: Sets a soft resource limit.

You can also use the -a option to simply view current limits. For example, the limits associated with the geeko user are shown below:

```
geeko@da1:~> ulimit -a
core file size          (blocks, -c) 0
data seg size           (kbytes, -d) unlimited
scheduling priority             (-e) 0
file size               (blocks, -f) unlimited
pending signals                 (-i) 8192
max locked memory       (kbytes, -l) 64
max memory size         (kbytes, -m) 812600
open files                      (-n) 1024
pipe size            (512 bytes, -p) 8
POSIX message queues     (bytes, -q) 819200
real-time priority              (-r) 0
stack size              (kbytes, -s) 8192
cpu time               (seconds, -t) unlimited
max user processes              (-u) 8192
virtual memory          (kbytes, -v) 2005040
file locks                      (-x) unlimited
```

In the example below, core dumps are disabled by setting the maximum size of core dump files to 0:

```
geeko@da1:~> ulimit -c 0
```

Exercise 8-1   Configure sudo

In this exercise, you practice configuring `sudo`.

You will find this exercise at the end of the chapter.

(End of Exercise)

Exercise 8-2   Configure the Password Security Settings

In this exercise, you practice changing security settings.

You will find this exercise at the end of the chapter.

(End of Exercise)

Objective 2   Provide Secure Remote Access with OpenSSH

In the past, remote connections between Linux systems were established using the Telnet protocol. This allowed remote users to log in to a Linux system and run commands from the shell prompt as if they were sitting at the system's console.

However, Telnet had a serious shortcoming. It offered no safeguards in the form of encryption or other security mechanisms against eavesdropping. When you logged in to the remote system using a Telnet client, your username and password (as well as any data written to the terminal) could be easily sniffed and captured.

Because of this, Telnet is no longer widely used to provide remote access. It is replaced by OpenSSH. OpenSSH works in much the same manner as Telnet, providing remote access to the Linux shell prompt. However, OpenSSH encrypts the data as it is transferred between systems.

The Secure SHell (SSH) suite was developed to provide secure communications between systems by encrypting authentication information (your username and a password) as well as all the data exchanged between the hosts.

With SSH, the data flow can still be captured by a third party, but the contents are encrypted and cannot be decoded into plain text unless the encryption key is known.

The OpenSSH package is installed on SLES 11 by default. The OpenSSH package includes programs such as `ssh`, `scp`, and `sftp`. You can use these commands as alternatives to the traditional Telnet, rlogin, rsh, rcp, and ftp programs.

To provide secure remote access on a network with the OpenSSH version of SSH, you need to understand the following:

- Cryptography Basics
- SSH Features and Architecture
- Configure the SSH Server
- Configure the SSH Client
- SSH-Related Commands
- Public Key Authentication Management
- Practice Using OpenSSH

Cryptography Basics

Cryptography involves the procedures and techniques used to encrypt data and prove the authenticity of data. An encryption algorithm is used to convert clear text into cipher text using a key. The key is the information required to encrypt and decrypt data.

Two types of encryption procedures are used:

- Symmetric Encryption
- Asymmetric Encryption

Symmetric Encryption

With symmetric encryption, the same key is used for encryption and decryption. If this secret key is known, then all data encrypted with that key can be decrypted.

An important feature of an encryption procedure is the length of the key. A symmetric key with a length of 40 bits (1,099,511,627,776 possibilities) can be broken with brute force methods in a short amount of time. Currently, 128-bit (or longer) symmetric keys are considered secure.

Basically, the longer the length of the encryption key, the more secure the data transmission, provided there is no cryptographic flaw in the encryption algorithm.

The following are some of the more important symmetric encryption technologies that you need to be familiar with:

- **DES (Data Encryption Standard).** Standardized in 1977, DES is the foundation of many encryption procedures (such as UNIX/Linux passwords). The key length is 56 bits.

  However, in January 1999, the EFF (Electronic Frontier Foundation) decrypted a text encrypted with DES in 22 hours using brute force (trying one possible key after the other). Therefore, a key with a length of 56 bits is no longer secure—messages protected with such a key can be decrypted in a short time.

- **Triple-DES.** Extension of DES, using DES three times. Depending on the variant used, the effective key length offered is 112 or 168 bits.

- **IDEA.** Algorithm with a key length of 128 bits. This algorithm has been patented in the USA and Europe (its noncommercial use is free).

- **Blowfish.** Algorithm with a variable key length of up to 448 bits. It was developed by Bruce Schneier. It is unpatented and license-free and it can be freely used by anyone.

- **AES (Advanced Encryption Standard).** Successor to DES.

  In 1993, the National Institute of Standards and Technology (NIST) decided that DES no longer met today's security requirements, and it organized a competition for a new standard encryption algorithm. The winner of this competition was announced on October 2, 2000, and is the Rijndael algorithm, which supports key lengths of 128, 192, or 256 bits.

The main advantage associated with symmetric encryption is that it can efficiently encrypt and decrypt data. Its main disadvantage is that key distribution and management can be difficult.

Asymmetric Encryption

In an asymmetric encryption there are two keys—a private key and a public key. Data that has been encrypted with the private key can be decrypted only with the public key. Data encrypted with the public key can be decrypted only with the private key.

The main advantage of asymmetric encryption is the fact that key management is relatively easy. The public key can be distributed freely. However, asymmetric procedures tend to be much slower than symmetric procedures.

As a result, symmetric and asymmetric procedures are often combined. In fact, SSH uses a combination of both procedures. For example, a key for symmetric encryption can be transmitted through a channel encrypted asymmetrically.

Some important asymmetric cryptographic procedures include the following:

- **RSA.** The name is derived from the surnames of its developers: Rivest, Shamir, and Adleman. Its security is mainly based on the fact that it is easy to multiply two large prime numbers, but it is difficult to regain the factors from this product.

- **DSA.** (Digital Signature Algorithm) A US Federal Government standard for digital signatures.

- **Diffie-Hellman.** This key exchange describes a method to establish cryptographic keys securely without having to send the keys across insecure channels. Such a key can then be used as a secret key in symmetric encryption.

Keys for asymmetric encryption need to be much longer than those used for symmetric procedures. For example, the minimum key length currently considered secure with RSA is 1024 bits.

SSH Features and Architecture

SSH is a secure, remote transmission protocol. To effectively use SSH, you need to understand the following:

- SSH Features
- SSH Protocol Versions
- SSH Authentication Mechanism Configuration

SSH Features

The secure shell not only provides all the functionality of Telnet, rlogin, rsh and rcp, but it also includes some features of FTP. SSH supports the protection of X11 and any TCP connections by routing them through a cryptographically secure channel.

The following lists the basic functionality provided by SSH:

- Login from a remote host
- Interactive or non-interactive command execution on remote hosts
- File copy between different network hosts and optional support for compressing data
- Cryptographically secured authentication and communication across insecure networks
- Automatic and transparent encryption of all communication
- Complete substitution of the "r" utilities: rlogin, rsh, and rcp

- Port forwarding

- Tunneling

SSH not only encrypts the traffic and authenticates the client, it also authenticates the involved servers. Various procedures are available for server authentication.

In SLES 11, the Open Source implementation of SSH (OpenSSH) is used. OpenSSH is available as open source because it does not use any patented algorithms.

By default, the OpenSSH server is not activated when you install SLES 11, but it can be easily activated during or after installation.

NOTE: For more details on OpenSSH functionality, see www.openssh.org/ (http://www.openssh.org/).

SSH Protocol Versions

The following versions are currently available for the SSH protocol:

- Protocol Version 1 (SSH1)

- Protocol Version 2 (SSH2)

NOTE: SSH1 and SSH2 are used for convenience in referencing the protocol versions in this section. They are not official designations of the protocol versions.

Protocol Version 1 (SSH1)

The following illustrates the process SSH1 uses to transmit data over a secure connection:

Figure 8-10   *SSH Protocol Version 1*

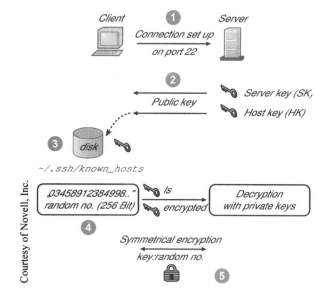

Courtesy of Novell, Inc.

The following describes the steps in this process:

1. The client establishes a connection to the server (port 22).

    In this phase, the SSH client and the server agree on the protocol version and other communication parameters.

2. The SSH server works with the following RSA key pairs and transmits the public keys to the client:

    *   **Long-life host key pair (HK).** Consists of a public host key (`/etc/ssh/ssh_host_key.pub`) and a private host key (`/etc/ssh/ssh_host_key`) that identify the computer.

        This long-life key pair is identical for all SSH processes running on the host.

    *   **Server process key pair (SK).** This key pair is created at the start of each server process. It consists of a public server key and a private server key that are changed at specific intervals (normally once an hour).

        This pair is never stored in a file. These dynamic keys help prevent an attacker from being able to decrypt recorded sessions, even if the attacker can break into the server and steal the long-life key pair.

3. The client checks to see if the public host key is correct.

    To do this, it compares the host key with keys in the `/etc/ssh/ssh_known_hosts` or `~/.ssh/known_hosts` files. If these files do not contain the key, depending on the configuration, the connection is terminated or the user is asked how to proceed.

4. The client generates a 256-bit random number, encrypts this using the public keys of the SSH server, and sends it to the server.

5. The server is now in a position to decrypt the random number because it possesses the secret key.

6. This random number is the key for the symmetric encryption that now follows.

NOTE: The random number is also referred to as the session key.

Now, when the user types his or her password, it is protected by the encrypted connection.

Protocol Version 2 (SSH2)

SSH protocol version 1 does not have a mechanism to ensure the integrity of a connection. This allows attackers to insert data packets into an existing connection (an insertion attack).

SSH2 provides features to avoid such attacks. These are referred to as HMAC (Keyed-Hash Message Authentication Code) and are described in detail in RFC 2104.

NOTE: You should use SSH1 only if SSH2 is not available.

The following illustrates the process SSH2 uses to transmit data over a secure connection:

Figure 8-11   *SSH Protocol Version 2*

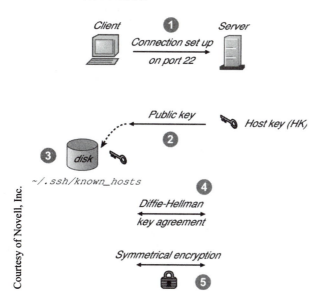

The following describes the steps in this process:

1. A connection is established between the server and client as described for SSH1.

2. The server now contains a key pair (DSA or RSA), the public and private host key.

    The private key files are /etc/ssh/ssh_host_rsa_key (RSA) and /etc/ssh/ssh_host_dsa_key (DSA), respectively.

3. As with SSH1, the host key is compared with the keys in the /etc/ssh/ssh_known_hosts and ~/.ssh/known_hosts files.

4. A Diffie-Hellman key agreement then follows, through which client and server agree on a secret session key without having to send the key across the wire.

5. As with SSH1, communication is ultimately encrypted symmetrically.

The main difference between SSH1 and SSH2 is the mechanisms within the protocol that guarantee the integrity of the connection. A keyed-hash message authentication code (HMAC) is used for this purpose. The mechanism for the session key agreement (Diffie-Hellman) is different as well.

To see which SSH version an SSH server supports, you can log in to port 22 using a Telnet client. The following shows the potential responses from the server:

Table 8-1   *SSH Banners and SSH Protocols*

Protocol	Server Response
SSH1 only	SSH-1.5-OpenSSH...

Protocol	Server Response
SSH1 and SSH2	SSH 1.99-OpenSSH...
SSH2 only	SSH-2.0-OpenSSH...

The following is an example of a Telnet connection on port 22:

```
da10:~ # telnet da20 22
Trying 172.17.8.120...
Connected to da20.
Escape character is '^]'.
SSH-1.99-OpenSSH_4.2
```

In the OpenSSH server configuration file (`/etc/ssh/sshd_config`), the Protocol parameter defines which protocol versions are supported.

For example, Protocol 2,1 in the configuration file would indicate SSH2 and SSH1 are both supported, but preference is given to SSH2. If SSH2 is not available, then SSH1 is used. You can also specify the version to use when starting the clients (such as `ssh -1` for SSH1).

SSH Authentication Mechanism Configuration

The SSH server can decrypt the session key generated and encrypted by the client only if it also has the private key. If the server does not have this key, communications end at this point.

To ensure security, the client needs to be able to verify that the public host key of the server really belongs to the server.

SSH currently does not support directory services (such as LDAP) or certificates (such as with SSL) for public key management. This means that anyone, even a potential attacker, can easily create a random key pair and include it in the authentication dialog.

When you first contact an unknown server, it is possible to learn its host key. When you do, the SSH client writes this key to the local key database. The following is an example of an initial SSH connection to a computer whose host key is unknown:

```
geeko@da50:~ > ssh geeko@da10
The authenticity of host 'da10 (172.17.8.110)' can't be established.
RSA key fingerprint is
ea:79:90:9a:d4:bf:b6:a2:40:ee:72:56:f8:d9:e5:76.
Are you sure you want to continue connecting (yes/no)? yes
Warning: Permanently added 'da10,172.17.8.110' (RSA) to the list of
known hosts.
```

If you answer the question with **yes**, the host key is saved in the `~/.ssh/known_hosts` file.

Several mechanisms are available on the server side to authenticate clients. The mechanisms allowed by the server are specified in its `/etc/ssh/sshd_config` configuration file.

The following describes the two most important mechanisms, with the appropriate configuration parameters for `/etc/ssh/sshd_config` in parentheses:

- **Public Key (RSA/DSA) Authentication**

  (sshd_config: RSAAuthentication for SSH1)
  (sshd_config: PubkeyAuthentication for SSH2)

  Authentication through a public key procedure is the most secure method. In this case, the user proves knowledge of his or her private key (and, thus, his or her identity) through a challenge-response procedure, which can be run automatically using the SSH agent.

- **Password Authentication**

  (sshd_config: PasswordAuthentication)

  This authentication procedure takes place through a POSIX user password. The transfer of the password is encrypted.

After successful authentication, a work environment is created on the server. For this purpose, environment variables are set (`TERM` and `DISPLAY`), and X11 connections and any possible TCP connections are redirected.

NOTE: The redirection of the X11 connections works only if the `DISPLAY` variable set by SSH is not subsequently changed by the user. The SSH daemon must appear to the X11 applications as a local X11 server, which requires a corresponding setting of `DISPLAY`.

In addition, the program `xauth` (used to edit and display the authorization information used in connecting to the X server) must exist. This program is in the xf86 package.

The `X11Forwarding` parameter in the SSH server configuration file (`/etc/ssh/sshd_config`) determines whether or not the graphical output is forwarded when the client requests it. If you want to use X forwarding, you must set the parameter to `Yes` and you must start the SSH client with the `-X` option.

Configure the SSH Server

The `/etc/ssh/sshd_config` file is the SSH server (sshd) configuration file. Some of the more commonly used options in this file include the following:

Table 8-2   */etc/ssh/sshd_config Options*

Option	Description
AllowUsers	Allows SSH login only for users listed. It is followed by a space-separated list of users.
DenyUsers	Denies SSH login to users listed. It is followed by a space-separated list of users.

Option	Description
Protocol	Specifies the protocol versions supported. (Default: 2)
ListenAddress	Specifies the local addresses that sshd should listen on. The syntax is *IP_address:port*
Port	Specifies the port number that sshd listens on. The default is 22. Multiple options of this type are permitted.
PasswordAuthentication	Specifies whether password authentication is allowed. If you want to disable it, set this to `no` and also set UsePAM to `no`.
UsePAM	Enables the Pluggable Authentication Module interface.

NOTE: For additional information on SSH server configuration options, enter `man sshd` and `man sshd_config` at the shell prompt.

Configure the SSH Client

In addition to configuring the SSH server, you also need to configure the SSH client on the client system. You do this by editing the `/etc/ssh/ssh_config` file. Each user can edit his or her individual settings in the `~/.ssh/config` file.

If you want to constrain client connections to only SSH servers whose keys have already been added to the `~/.ssh/known_hosts` or `/etc/ssh/ssh_known_hosts` files, you can set the StrictHostKeyChecking option in the client configuration file (`~/.ssh/config`) to `yes`.

This prevents the SSH client from simply adding new keys from unknown servers to `~/.ssh/known_hosts` when connecting to unknown servers. Any new keys have to be added manually using an editor. In this configuration, connections to a server whose key has changed are refused.

Starting with SSH version 1.2.20, three values are allowed for StrictHostKeyChecking:

- yes
- no
- ask

The default setting is `ask`, which means that the user is asked for permission before a new key is entered.

The precedence of SSH client configuration options is as follows:

1. Command line options
2. `~/.ssh/config`
3. `/etc/ssh/ssh_config`

NOTE: For additional information on SSH client configuration options, enter `man ssh_config` at the shell prompt.

SSH-Related Commands

The following are commonly used SSH-related client commands:

Table 8-3   *SSH-Related Commands*

Command	Description
ssh	SSH client command line utility. SSH can be used as a replacement for rlogin, rsh, and Telnet. slogin is a symbolic link to ssh.
	Every user should use ssh instead of Telnet.
scp	Copies files securely between two computers using ssh. It replaces the rcp utility.
sftp	Offers an interface similar to the ftp command line utility. You can view files on the remote machine with the `ls` command and transfer files using the `put` and `get` commands.
ssh-keyscan	Gathers the public ssh host keys from several SSH servers. The gathered keys are displayed on the standard output.
	This output can then be compared with the key in `/etc/ssh/ssh_known_hosts` and be included in the file.
ssh-keygen	Generates public/private key pairs. Use the `-t` option to specify the type (`rsa1`, `rsa`, or `dsa`)
ssh-agent	Handles private keys. It is used to respond to challenges (challenge response) from the server, which simplifies authentication.
ssh-add	Registers new keys with the ssh-agent.

The basic syntax for ssh is `ssh options host command`. The basic syntax for scp is `scp options source_file destination_file`.

The following are examples of using `ssh` and `scp`:

- Example 1:

```
geeko@da10:~> ssh da20.digitalairlines.com
```

In this example, you connect to the da20.digitalairlines.com system via the SSH client and are automatically logged in as the user geeko.

- Example 2:

```
geeko@da10:~> ssh tux@da20.digitalairlines.com
```

or

```
geeko@da10:~> ssh -l tux da20.digitalairlines.com
```

In this example, you connect to the da20.digitalairlines.com system via the SSH client and log in as the user tux.

- Example 3:

```
geeko@da10:~> ssh root@da20.digitalairlines.com shutdown -h now
```

In this example, you use the SSH client to remotely shut down da20.digitalairlines.com.

- Example 4:

```
geeko@da10:~> scp da20.digitalairlines.com:/etc/HOSTNAME ~
```

In this example, you copy the /etc/HOSTNAME file from da20.digitalairlines.com to your home directory on the local system.

- Example 5:

```
geeko@da10:~> scp /etc/motd da20.digitalairlines.com:
```

In this example, you copy the local /etc/motd file to your home directory on da20.digitalairlines.com.

- Example 6:

```
geeko@da10:~> ssh -X da20.digitalairlines.com
```

In this example, you connect to da20.digitalairlines.com from da10 via SSH. The connection is established with a graphical X11 tunnel, which allows X11 applications started on the da20.digitalairlines.com system to be displayed on da10.

- Example 7:

```
geeko@da10:~> ssh-keyscan da50
```

In this example, the host key is read from the da50 system. The results are shown in the following:

```
geeko@da10:~> ssh-keyscan da50
# da50 SSH-1.99-OpenSSH_4.2da50 1024 35
14763075313887762890721211435182838711560983853623973900394164593
32178917967536904026039322601801087591319766718758610486673209117
06379693377112828949660003683832...
geeko@da10:~> ssh-keyscan -t rsa da50
# da50 SSH-1.99-OpenSSH_4.2
da50 ssh-rsa
AAAAB3NzaC1yc2EAAAABIwAAAIEA3Nj0qGKjyGCBBhn487sMtAzyRFq9QPK9ZcPiI
LSNPugTGbG9Y7+ta68JLAS+Bxp4yZGNhtw5tdnM3sRYWCj6KbjtzjdibuVUGv9xdd
rq8tUHl8x3y2SY48JA9Yozl057QIT3VPp/
cv5YFYPAlPttNQf0DIbpLkNlNuXTrhbfIsE=
```

SSH can also be used to protect unencrypted traffic, such as POP3 communications, by tunnelling it through an SSH connection. The following examples illustrate this:

- Example 1:

```
geeko@da10:~> ssh -L 4242:da20.digitalairlines.com:110
geeko@da20.digitalairlines.com
```

In this example, you forward the connection coming in on port 4242 of your local host da10 to port 110 (POP3) of the remote host da20 via an SSH tunnel. This is called port forwarding.

By using port forwarding through an SSH tunnel, you can set up an additional secure channel for connections between the local host and a remote host.

NOTE: Privileged ports (0–1024) can be forwarded only by root.

- Example 2:

```
geeko@da10:~> ssh -R 4242:da10.example.com:110
geeko@da20.digitalairlines.com
```

In this example, you forward port queries addressed to a port of a remote host to the port of the local host. This is called reverse port forwarding.

In the above example, queries coming in on port 4242 of the remote host da20.digitalairlines.com are reverse-tunneled via SSH to port 110 of the local host da10.

If the host you want to forward to cannot be reached directly through SSH (for example, because it is located behind a firewall), you can establish a tunnel to another host running SSH. This is shown in the following example.

- Example 3:

```
geeko@da10:~> ssh -L 4242:da20.digitalairlines.com:110
geeko@da30.digitalairlines.com
```

In this example, you forward incoming connections on port 4242 of your local host da10 to the remote host da30.digitalairlines.com by way of an SSH tunnel. This host then forwards the packets to port 110 (POP3) of the host da20.digitalairlines.com by using an unencrypted connection.

Public Key Authentication Management

Besides password authentication, you can also authenticate using a public key procedure. Protocol version 1 supports only RSA keys. Protocol version 2 provides authentication through both RSA and DSA keys.

To manage public key authentication, you need to be familiar with the following concepts and procedures:

- Public Key Authentication Process
- Create a Key Pair
- Configure and Use Public Key Authentication

Public Key Authentication Process

To use public key authentication, the public key of the user has to be stored in the home directory of the user account being accessed on the server. These public keys are stored on the server in the ~/.ssh/authorized_keys file. The corresponding private key must be stored on the client computer.

With the keys stored in the appropriate places, the following occurs in the public key authentication process:

1. The client informs the server which public key is being used for authentication.

2. The server checks to see if the public key is known.

3. The server encrypts a random number using the public key and transfers this to the client.

4. Only the client is able to decrypt the random number with its private key.

5. The client sends the server an MD5 checksum that it has calculated from the number.

6. The server also calculates a checksum and, if they are identical, the user has authenticated successfully.

7. If public key authentication fails and password authentication is allowed, the user is asked for the login password.

The secret key should be protected by a passphrase. Without passphrase protection, simply owning the file containing the private key is sufficient for a successful authentication. However, if the key is additionally protected with a passphrase, the file is useless if you do not know the passphrase.

Create a Key Pair

You create a key pair with the ssh-keygen command. A different key is used for SSH1 and for SSH2. For this reason, you need to create a separate key pair for each version.

You use the -t *keytype* option to specify the type of key:

- ssh-keygen -t rsa1 generates a key pair for SSH1

- ssh-keygen -t rsa and ssh-keygen -t dsa are used to create key pairs for ssh2.

The keys are stored in the `~/.ssh` directory. For SSH1, the default for these files is `~/.ssh/identity` (private key) and `~/.ssh/identity.pub` (public key). For SSH2, the default files are `~/.ssh/id_rsa` and `~/.ssh/id_dsa`, respectively, plus the corresponding public key files with the `.pub` extension.

The following example shows how a key pair for the protocol version 2 is generated using the `-t` option (required) to generate a DSA key pair:

```
geeko@da10:~> ssh-keygen -t dsa
Generating public/private dsa key pair.
Enter file in which to save the key (/home/geeko/.ssh/id_dsa):
Enter passphrase (empty for no passphrase):
Enter same passphrase again:
Your identification has been saved in /home/geeko/.ssh/id_dsa.
Your public key has been saved in /home/geeko/.ssh/id_dsa.pub.
The key fingerprint
is:ef:73:c6:f6:8a:ff:9d:d1:50:01:cf:07:65:c5:54:8b
geeko@da10:~>
```

Configure and Use Public Key Authentication

For authentication using RSA or DSA keys, you need to copy the public key to the server and then append the public key to the `~/.ssh/authorized_keys` file.

For example, you can copy the key to the server with the `scp` command, as in the following:

```
geeko@da10:~> scp .ssh/id_dsa.pub da50:geeko-pubkey
```

The key should then be added to the `~/.ssh/authorized_keys` file in such a way that the existing keys are not overwritten, as in the following:

```
geeko@da10:~> ssh da50
Password:
Last login: Tue May 30 12:03:29 2006 from da10.digitalairlines.com
geeko@da50:~> cat geeko-pubkey >> ~/.ssh/authorized_keys
geeko@da50:~> exit
geeko@da10:~>
```

NOTE: The `ssh-copy-id` utility can be used to simplify the above steps of copying the key to the other computer and appending it to `~/.ssh/authorized_keys`. For more information, enter `man ssh-copy-id` at the shell prompt.

You can now launch the client to see if authentication with the DSA key works properly, as shown in the following:

```
geeko@da10:~> ssh da50
Enter passphrase for key '/home/geeko/.ssh/id_dsa':
Last login: Tue May 30 12:03:40 2006 from da10.digitalairlines.com
geeko@da50:~>
```

You can use the `-i` option to enter the filename for a private key with a different name or location.

When authentication is done with keys, the passphrase is required when logging in to the server or when copying with scp. If you mistype your passphrase three times, you are asked for your usual login password. (The sshd configuration allows you to change this behavior; see Table 8-2.)

The `ssh-agent` can be used to avoid having to type this passphrase upon each connection. When you first start the ssh-agent, you need to enter the passphrase using the `ssh-add` command. After that, the ssh-agent monitors all SSH requests and provides the required private key as necessary.

The ssh-agent serves as a wrapper for any other process (such as for a shell or the X server). The following example shows the start of a Bash through the ssh-agent:

```
geeko@da10:~> ssh-agent bash
geeko@da10:~> ssh-add .ssh/id_dsa
Enter passphrase for .ssh/id_dsa:
Identity added: .ssh/id_dsa (.ssh/id_dsa)
```

For all `ssh` or `scp` commands entered from this shell (for which a key authentication is configured), the agent will automatically provide the private key.

You can also use the ssh-agent with a graphical login. When you log in to the graphical interface, an X server is started. If you log in by using a display manager, the X server loads the `/etc/X11/xdm/sys.xsession` file.

For the ssh-agent to start automatically when an X server starts, you simply enter the following parameter in the sys.xsession file:

`usessh="yes"`

This entry is already set by default in SLES 11.

After entering the `yes` parameter, the ssh-agent starts automatically the next time the user logs in to the graphical interface. The agent running in the background must be given the passphrase once, as in the following:

```
geeko@da10:~> ssh-add .ssh/id_dsa
Enter passphrase for .ssh/id_dsa:
Identity added: .ssh/id_dsa (.ssh/id_dsa)
```

For subsequent connections in which authentication takes place with the public key procedure, a passphrase now no longer has to be given. This ssh-agent takes care of the private keys.

When the X server is terminated, the ssh-agent is also closed. The passphrase is never stored in a file; the private keys are stored in memory by the ssh-agent only until the user has logged out again.

Exercise 8-3   *Practice Using OpenSSH*

In this exercise, you learn how to establish SSH connections between computers and how to use SSH with public key authentication.

You will find this exercise at the end of the chapter.

(End of Exercise)

Objective 3   Configure User Authentication with PAM

A key aspect of administering user access and security is configuring user authentication with PAM. In this objective, you learn how to do this. The following topics are addressed:

- How PAM Works
- PAM Configuration Files
- PAM Configuration File Syntax
- PAM Configuration File Examples
- Secure Password Guidelines
- PAM Documentation Resources
- RADIUS
- Two-Factor Authentication
- Configure PAM Authentication

How PAM Works

Linux uses Pluggable Authentication Modules (PAM) in the authentication process as a layer between users and applications. A Linux system administrator can use these modules to configure the way programs should authenticate users.

PAM provides system-wide access to applications through authentication modules. Individual applications do not need to include their own authentication routines. PAM takes care of that task for them.

For example, when a user logs in to a Linux system from a virtual terminal, the user runs a process called `login`. The login process requests the user's login name and password. The password is encrypted and then compared with the encrypted password stored in an authentication database via PAM. If the encrypted passwords are identical, login grants the user access to the system by starting the user's login shell.

If other authentication procedures, such as smart cards, are used, all programs that perform user authentication must be able to work with these smart cards. Before PAM was introduced, each individual application, such as login, FTP, or SSH, would have to be extended to support the smart card reader.

Fortunately, PAM makes things easier. PAM creates a software bridge with clearly defined interfaces between applications (such as `login`) and the current authentication mechanism. If you install a smart card reader, you can install a new PAM module to enable authentication using this new device. After adjusting the PAM configuration for your applications, they can make use of this new authentication method.

The following figure illustrates the role of PAM:

Figure 8-12   *PAM*

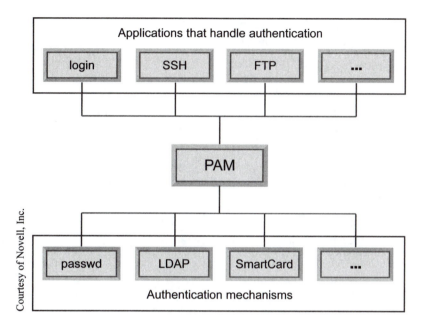

Third-party vendors can also supply additional PAM modules to enable specific authentication features for their products, such as the PAM modules that enable Novell's Linux User Management (LUM) authentication with eDirectory.

PAM Configuration Files

PAM provides a variety of modules—each one with a different purpose. For example, one module checks the password, another verifies the location the system is accessed from, and another reads user-specific settings.

Every program that uses PAM authentication has its own configuration file in the /etc/pam.d directory. Each file is named after the service is represents. For example, the configuration file for the passwd program is called /etc/pam.d/passwd.

There is one special configuration file in this directory named other. This file contains default configuration parameters that are used if no application-specific file is found.

In addition, there are global configuration files for most PAM modules in /etc/security/. These files define the exact behavior of the PAM modules. Examples include pam_env.conf, pam_pwcheck.conf, pam_unix2.conf, and time.conf.

Every application that uses a PAM module actually calls a set of PAM functions. These functions are implemented in modules which perform the authentication process according to the information in the various configuration files and then return the result to the calling application.

PAM Configuration File Syntax

Each line in a PAM configuration file contains three columns plus optional arguments, as shown below:

Figure 8-13   *PAM Modules*

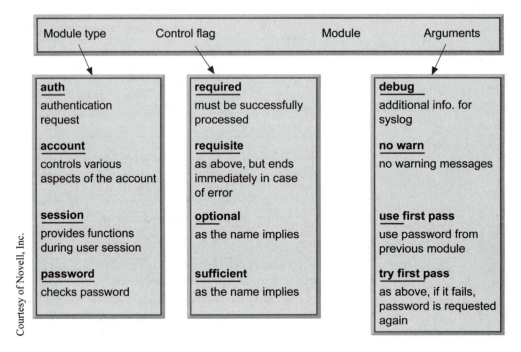

The following describes the purpose of each column:

- **Module Type.** There are four types of PAM modules:
    - **auth.** Provides two means for authenticating the user:
        - Establish that the user is who he claims to be by instructing the application to prompt the user for a password or other means of identification.
        - Grant group membership or other privileges through credential-granting properties.
    - **account.** Performs non-authentication account management tasks.

      They are typically used to restrict or permit access to a service based on the time of day, currently available system resources (such as the maximum number of users), or even the location of the user (such as limiting root login to the console).
    - **session.** Performs tasks that need to be done before users can be given access to a service or after a service is provided.

      This could include logging user information or mounting directories.
    - **password.** Update the authentication token associated with the user. Typically, there is one module for each challenge/response-based authentication (auth) module type.

- **Control Flag.** Indicates how PAM will react to the success or failure of the module it is associated with.

  Since modules of the same type can be executed in a series (called stacking), the control flags determine the relative priority of each module.

  The Linux PAM library uses the following control flags in the following ways:

  - **required.** A module with this flag must be successfully processed before the authentication can proceed.

    After the failure of a module with the required flag, all other modules with the same flag are processed before the user receives a message about the failure of the authentication attempt. This prevents users from knowing at what stage their authentication failed.

  - **requisite.** A module with this flag must also be processed successfully. If successful, other modules are subsequently processed, just like modules with the required flag.

    However, if it fails, the module gives immediate feedback to the user and no further modules are processed.

    You can use the requisite flag as a basic filter, checking for the existence of certain conditions that are essential for a correct authentication.

  - **optional.** The failure or success of a module with this flag does not have any direct consequences.

    You can use this flag for modules that are intended only to display a message (such as telling a user that mail has arrived) without taking any further action.

  - **sufficient.** After a module with this flag has been successfully processed, the application receives an immediate message about the success and no further modules are processed (provided there was no preceding failure of a *required* module).

    The failure of a module with the sufficient flag has no direct consequences. All subsequent modules are processed in their respective order.

  - **include.** This is not really a control flag but indicates that the keyword in the next column is to be interpreted as a filename relative to `/etc/pam.d/` that should be included at this point.

    The purpose of include files is to simplify changes concerning several applications. The file included has to have the same structure as any other PAM configuration file.

- **Module.** The PAM modules are located in the `/lib/security/` directory. Every filename of a module starts with the prefix `pam_`. You do not need to include the path as long as the module is located in the default directory (`/lib/security/`).

NOTE: For all 64-bit platforms supported by SLES 11, the default directory is `/lib64/security/`.

Some PAM modules can be used for multiple module types. For example, `pam_unix2.so` can be used for both auth and password.

- **Arguments (options).** You can include options in this column for the module, such as **debug** (enables debugging) or **nullok** (allows the use of empty passwords).

PAM Configuration File Examples

The default configuration file for the login program on SLES 11 is `/etc/pam.d/login`. An example is shown below:

```
da1:~ # cat /etc/pam.d/login
#%PAM-1.0
auth       requisite     pam_nologin.so
auth       required      pam_securetty.so
auth       include       common-auth
account    include       common-account
password   include       common-password
session    required      pam_loginuid.so
session    include       common-session
session    required      pam_lastlog.so   nowtmp
session    optional      pam_mail.so standard
session    optional      pam_ck_connector.so
```

As an example of the files included in the above configuration, the `/etc/pam.d/common-auth` file looks like this:

```
da1:~ # cat /etc/pam.d/common-auth
#%PAM-1.0
#
# This file is autogenerated by pam-config. All changes
# will be overwritten.
#
# Authentication-related modules common to all services
#
# This file is included from other service-specific PAM config files,
# and should contain a list of the authentication modules that define
# the central authentication scheme for use on the system
# (e.g., /etc/shadow, LDAP, Kerberos, etc.). The default is to use
# the traditional Unix authentication mechanisms.
#
auth       required      pam_env.so
auth       required      pam_unix2.so
```

The modules perform the following tasks (not all are included in the above configuration):

- **auth required pam_securetty.so**

  Checks the `/etc/securetty` file for a list of valid login terminals. If a terminal is not listed in that file, the login is denied from that terminal. This concerns only the root user.

- **auth required pam_env.so**

  Used to set additional environment variables. The variables can be configured in the `/etc/security/pam_env.conf` file.

- **auth required pam_unix2.so**

  Used during the authentication process to validate the login and password provided by the user.

- **auth required pam_nologin.so**

  If the `/etc/nologin` file exists, its content is displayed when a user tries to log in and login is denied for all but the root user.

- **account required pam_unix2.so**

  In this entry, the `pam_unix2.so` module is used again but, in this case, it checks whether the password of the user is still valid or if the user needs to create a new one.

- **password required pam_pwcheck.so**

  Entry for a module of the type password. It is used when a user attempts to change the password. In this case, the module `pam_pwcheck.so` is used to check if a new password is secure enough.

  You can use the `nullok` argument to allow users to change an empty password; otherwise, empty passwords are treated as locked accounts.

- **password required pam_unix2.so nullok use_first_pass use_authtok**

  Also necessary when changing a password. It encrypts (or hashes, to be more exact) the new password and writes it to the authentication database.

  `nullok` has the same significance as described above for `pam_pwcheck.so`. With the `use_first_pass` argument, pam_unix2 uses the password from a previous module, for instance `pam_pwcheck.so`, and aborts with an error if no authentication token from a previous module is available. The `use_authtok` argument is used to force this module to set the new password to the one provided by the previously stacked password module.

- **session required pam_unix2.so**

  Uses the session component of the **pam_unix2.so** module. Without arguments, this module has no effect; with the `trace` argument, it uses the syslog daemon to log the user's login.

- **session required pam_limits.so**

  Sets resource limits for the users that can be configured in the `/etc/security/limits.conf` file.

- **session required pam_mail.so**

  Displays a message if any new mail is in the user's mail box. It also sets an environment variable pointing to the user's mail directory.

Secure Password Guidelines

Even the best security setup for a system can be defeated if users choose passwords that can be easily guessed.

A common attack frequently used against Linux systems is called a dictionary attack. This type of attack uses a password-cracking program that identifies passwords by simply trying one word after another from a dictionary file, including some common variations of these words. With today's computing power, a simple password can be cracked within minutes.

Therefore, a password should never be a word which could be found in a dictionary. A good, secure password should always be at least eight characters long and contain numbers along with uppercase characters.

To determine if users' passwords fulfill this requirement, you can enable a special PAM module to test a password first before a user can set it. This module is called `pam_pwcheck.so` and uses the cracklib library to test the security of passwords. By default, this PAM module is enabled on SLES 11.

If a user enters a password that is not secure enough, the following message is displayed:

```
Bad password: too simple
```

and the user is prompted to enter a different one.

You can also use dedicated password check programs, such as John the Ripper (www.openwall.com/john/ (http://www.openwall.com/john/)).

PAM Documentation Resources

The following PAM documentation is available in the `/usr/share/doc/packages/pam/` directory:

- **READMEs:** In the top level of this directory are some general README files. The `modules/` subdirectory holds `README` files for the available PAM modules.

- **Linux-PAM System Administrators' Guide:** Includes everything that a system administrator should know about PAM.

  The document discusses a range of topics, from the syntax of configuration files to the security aspects of PAM. The document is available in PDF, HTML, or plain text format.

- **Linux-PAM Module Writers' Manual:** Summarizes the topic from the developer's point of view, with information about how to write standard-compliant PAM modules. It is available in PDF, HTML, or plain text format.

- **Linux-PAM Application Developers' Guide:** Includes everything needed by an application developer who wants to use the PAM libraries. It is available in PDF, HTML, or plain text format.

There are also manual pages for some PAM modules, such as `pam_unix2`.

RADIUS

RADIUS (Remote Authentication Dial-In User Service) is a networking protocol that provides centralized authentication, authorization, and accounting (AAA):

■ Authentication: Users or devices have to authenticate before they are granted access to a network.

■ Authorization: After successful authentication, users or devices are authorized to access certain services in the network.

■ Accounting: The usage of these services by users or devices is accounted.

The RADIUS protocol can authenticate users on systems such as 802.1x (WiFi), dialup, PPPoE, VPNs, VoIP, and many others. Supported back-end databases are, among others, MySQL, PostgreSQL, Oracle, Novell eDirectory, OpenLDAP, Microsoft Active Directory.

On SLES 11, RADIUS can be configured using the server and client from the FreeRADIUS project. Using the corresponding module for PAM, users can authenticate against this server.

Two-Factor Authentication

Normally, authenticating a user is done via verifying one piece of information (e.g., a password). This piece of information is called an authentication factor.

Two-factor authentication requires two pieces of information to verify a user. In addition to something the user knows (e.g., a password or other secret information), the user is requested to prove his or her identity by something the user has or is.

Pieces of information the user has can be something like a smart card or a USB stick containing certain information. Pieces of information the user is can be verified by using something like a fingerprint, a voice print, or an iris scan.

Two-factor authentication always requires information you know and information you have or are. Using a smart card and a fingerprint is not considered two-factor authentication because the mechanism to prove you know something would be missing.

Exercise 8-4   *Configure PAM Authentication*

In this exercise, you practice configuring PAM authentication.

You will find this exercise at the end of the chapter.

(End of Exercise)

Objective 4   Ensure File Integrity

It is important to ensure and verify file integrity, especially when you download software packages. Only unmodified packages, which contain the original signature or checksum from the package creator, should be considered secure.

There are several commands available which can be used to check the integrity of a file. The provider of the file runs one or more of these and provides you with the correct value. After downloading the files, you run the corresponding commands and verify the signature or checksum.

In this objective, you will learn the following:

- Compute a Checksum Using the MD5 Algorithm
- Computing a Checksum Using the SHA1 Algorithm
- Check the Signature of a File Using gpg

Compute a Checksum Using the MD5 Algorithm

To compute a checksum of a file using the MD5 algorithm, use the md5sum command:

```
da1:~ # md5sum /etc/passwd
8e550f426c54c53b10418f384955d0da   /etc/passwd
```

This checksum has to be compared character by character with the checksum provided. In case you want to provide files for others to verify, you need to publish this checksum together with the filename.

If you have multiple files to verify, you can write the filenames together with the checksums in a file and use this file to verify the integrity:

```
da1:~ # md5sum /etc/passwd /etc/shadow /etc/group > /tmp/md5
da1:~ # cat /tmp/md5
8e550f426c54c53b10418f384955d0da   /etc/passwd
ff2a25e0e610b96ef33206bf75d941fd   /etc/shadow
bf9124d27633dc4a7095fbc86485ccc7   /etc/group
da1:~ # md5sum -c /tmp/md5
/etc/passwd: OK
/etc/shadow: OK
/etc/group: OK
```

If the file has been modified, you will see messages similar to the following example:

```
da1:~ # md5sum -c /tmp/test
/etc/motd: FAILED
md5sum: WARNING: 1 of 1 computed checksum did NOT match
```

NOTE: The correct MD5 checksum only proves that the file has not been altered (e.g., damaged during download).

Computing a Checksum Using the SHA1 Algorithm

To compute a checksum using the SHA1 algorithm, use the `sha1sum` command. The usage is very similar to the `md5sum` command:

```
da1:~ # sha1sum /etc/passwd /etc/shadow /etc/group > /tmp/sha1
da1:~ # sha1sum -c /tmp/sha1
/etc/passwd: OK
/etc/shadow: OK
/etc/group: OK
da1:~ # sha1sum /etc/passwd
56beaffdcf57153b389652cc96307e5e6e4398ff  /etc/passwd
```

NOTE: The correct SHA1 checksum only proves that the file has not been altered (e.g., damaged during download).

Check the Signature of a File Using gpg

`gpg` is the OpenPGP part of the GNU Privacy Guard (GnuPG). It is a tool providing digital encryption and signing services using the OpenPGP standard. On SLES 11, `gpg2` is used instead of `gpg`. It can be called by the `gpg` command (which is a symbolic link to `gpg2`) as well.

To be able to verify digitally signed files, `gpg2` needs to know about the public keys which have been used to sign the files. With SLES 11, several public keys are copied to the home directory of the root user during installation. These keys can be listed:

```
da1:~ # gpg --list-keys
/root/.gnupg/pubring.gpg
------------------------
pub   1024R/307E3D54 2006-03-21 [expires: 2010-05-05]
uid                  SuSE Package Signing Key <build@suse.de>

pub   1024D/9C800ACA 2000-10-19 [expires: 2010-05-05]
uid                  SuSE Package Signing Key <build@suse.de>
sub   2048g/8495160C 2000-10-19 [expires: 2010-05-05]
```

If you want to verify a file which has been signed with an unknown key, the result will be something like this:

```
da1:~ # gpg --verify Apache/httpd-2.2.13.tar.gz.asc
gpg: Signature made Thu Aug  6 06:31:54 2009 CEST using RSA key ID
B55D9977
gpg: Can't check signature: No public key
```

You first have to include the key to your key ring (`/root/.gnupg/pubring.gpg`). The ID of the public key is shown in the output (B55D9977 in the example). You can get this key from a so-called keyserver, e.g., pgpkeys.mit.edu (http://pgpkeys.mit.edu):

```
da1:~ # gpg --keyserver pgpkeys.mit.edu --recv-key B55D9977
gpg: requesting key B55D9977 from hkp server pgpkeys.mit.edu
gpg: key B55D9977: public key "William A. Rowe, Jr. <wrowe@rowe-
clan.net>" imported
gpg: no ultimately trusted keys found
gpg: Total number processed: 1
gpg:               imported: 1  (RSA: 1)
```

The key is now known and can be used for the verification:

```
da1:~ # gpg --verify Apache/httpd-2.2.13.tar.gz.asc
gpg: Signature made Thu Aug  6 06:31:54 2009 CEST using RSA key ID
B55D9977
gpg: Good signature from "William A. Rowe, Jr. <wrowe@rowe-clan.net>"
gpg:                 aka "William A. Rowe, Jr. <wrowe@apache.org>"
gpg:                 aka "William A. Rowe, Jr.
<william.rowe@springsource.com>"
gpg: WARNING: This key is not certified with a trusted signature!
gpg:          There is no indication that the signature belongs to the
owner.
Primary key fingerprint: B1B9 6F45 DFBD CCF9 7401  9235 193F 180A
B55D 9977
```

In this case the line containing "Good signature" shows that the integrity of the file could be proven. However, it cannot be proven that the key used for the verification really belongs to the person who is named here (in this case, William A. Rowe).

NOTE: You have to make sure that any keys you import to your key ring really belong to the person they claim they belong to. For more information about how to trust public keys, visit www.gnupg.org (http://www.gnupg.org) or www.dewinter.com/gnupg_howto/english/ GPGMiniHowto.html (http://www.dewinter.com/gnupg_howto/english/GPGMiniHowto.html).

If you are using RPM packages for installing software, these can be verified using the rpm command:

```
da1:~ # rpm -v --checksig Snort/snort-2.8.4.1-1.1.i586.rpm
Snort/snort-2.8.4.1-1.1.i586.rpm:
    Header V3 DSA signature: OK, key ID ee454f98
    Header SHA1 digest: OK (e78e76a3d97433bb0bff297349f4bf5f9483cb60)
    MD5 digest: OK (79269c79bddc5da4400f1cee9c2359ce)
    V3 DSA signature: OK, key ID ee454f98
```

If a package is provided from SUSE/Novell, the public keys are already included in the RPM database:

```
da1:~ # rpm -qa gpg-pub*
gpg-pubkey-a1912208-446a0899
gpg-pubkey-ee454f98-47965b54
gpg-pubkey-0dfb3188-41ed929b
gpg-pubkey-9c800aca-481f343a
gpg-pubkey-307e3d54-481f30aa
gpg-pubkey-3d25d3d9-36e12d04
gpg-pubkey-7e2e3b05-4816488f
gpg-pubkey-307e3d54-481f30aa
gpg-pubkey-b37b98a9-486b702f
```

More information about the key is available using the `rpm -qi` command:

```
da1:~ # rpm -qi gpg-pubkey-307e3d54-481f30aa
Name          : gpg-pubkey            Relocations: (not
relocatable)
Version       : 307e3d54                  Vendor: (none)
Release       : 481f30aa              Build Date: Wed Aug 12
08:56:16 2009
Install Date: Wed Aug 12 08:56:16 2009   Build Host: localhost
Group         : Public Keys           Source RPM: (none)
Size          : 0                        License: pubkey
Signature     : (none)
Summary       : gpg(SuSE Package Signing Key <build@suse.de>)
Description :
-----BEGIN PGP PUBLIC KEY BLOCK-----
Version: rpm-4.4.2.3 (beecrypt-4.1.2)

mIsERCAdXQEEAL7MrBTz+3SBWpCm2ae2yaDqV3ezQcs2JlvqidJVhsZqQe9/jkxiKTE
XF/+BlQSiebunRI7oo3+9U8GyRCgs1sf+yRQWMLzZqRaarzRhw9w+IhledtqYl6/U2J
dp6d7RzlRliJdJ/VtsfXj2ef7Dwu7elOVSsmaBdtAAYptChTdVNFIFBhY2thZ2UgU2l
ZyBLZXkgPGJ1aWxkQHN1c2UuZGU+iLgEEwECACICGwMECwcDAgMVAgMDFgIBAh4BAhe
HzCqBQkHwXpNAAoJEOOlw2Awfj1UvWgEAIRoxE8S6jQB7S43SVcX06FHJeUJ/m+1ErI
TYrR/8qsDjTgrttgb+nBHkIjNhCCLAuR8sWj3CxsUMH2fayryNnwZEWGqnzo7Jtt4Rl
pHYonFjfoJyFUZjJ7Mhw7/TuOWx20FrzqBi8tbHx8pd7Fa5lCUgopVtMh6GR
-----END PGP PUBLIC KEY BLOCK-----
```

If you want to add more keys, you can do so with the following command:

rpm --import *keyfile*

where ***keyfile*** is the file containing the public key.

NOTE: Before adding public keys you need to verify that they belong to the user or organization they claim to belong to.

Objective 5   Use Security-Related Utilities

This objective describes the functionality of several security-related utilities. The following topics are discussed:

- Scan Open Ports with nmap

- Use Wireshark to Analyze Network Traffic

- Detect Vulnerabilities Using OpenVAS

- Use Snort for Intrusion Detection

- Check File System Integrity with Tripwire

For the LPIC Level One exam, you only need to have a basic knowledge of these utilities and what they are used for.

Scan Open Ports with nmap

nmap is a tool used to scan open ports on a system. You can use nmap to scan remote hosts as well as your local host. The simplest way is to call nmap without any options:

```
da1:~ # nmap da2

Starting Nmap 4.75 ( http://nmap.org ) at 2009-08-18 17:01 CEST
Interesting ports on da2.digitalairlines.com (10.0.0.2):
Not shown: 996 closed ports
PORT     STATE SERVICE
22/tcp   open  ssh
25/tcp   open  smtp
80/tcp   open  http
111/tcp  open  rpcbind
MAC Address: 00:19:D1:B5:A2:B4 (Intel)

Nmap done: 1 IP address (1 host up) scanned in 0.21 seconds
```

The man page for nmap provides a lot of information about different scanning options. The next example calls nmap with the option -A to enable OS and version detection, script scanning, and traceroute. The -T4 option provides faster execution.

```
da1:~ # nmap -A -T4 da5

Starting Nmap 4.75 ( http://nmap.org ) at 2009-08-18 17:05 CEST
Interesting ports on da5.digitalairlines.com (10.0.0.5):
Not shown: 991 closed ports
PORT       STATE       SERVICE     VERSION
22/tcp     open        ssh         OpenSSH 4.2 (protocol 2.0)
53/tcp     open        domain      ISC BIND 9.3.4
80/tcp     open        http        Apache httpd 2.2.3 ((Linux/SUSE))
|   robots.txt: has 1 disallowed entry
|_  /
|_  HTML title: Site doesn't have a title.
111/tcp    open        rpcbind
|   rpcinfo:
|   100000  2              111/udp  rpcbind
|   100005  1,2,3         657/udp  mountd
|   100003  2,3,4        2049/udp  nfs
|   100024  1           32770/udp  status
|   100021  1,3,4       32770/udp  nlockmgr
|   100000  2              111/tcp  rpcbind
|   100005  1,2,3         658/tcp  mountd
|   100003  2,3,4        2049/tcp  nfs
|   100024  1           57494/tcp  status
|_  100021  1,3,4       57494/tcp  nlockmgr
427/tcp    open        svrloc?
631/tcp    open        ipp         CUPS 1.1
2049/tcp   open        rpcbind
3000/tcp   filtered    ppp
3128/tcp   open        http-proxy Squid webproxy 2.5.STABLE12
MAC Address: 00:15:17:72:12:8A (Intel Corporate)
Device type: general purpose
Running: Linux 2.6.X
OS details: Linux 2.6.13 - 2.6.20
Network Distance: 1 hop

OS and Service detection performed. Please report any incorrect
results at http://nmap.org/submit/ .
Nmap done: 1 IP address (1 host up) scanned in 21.90 seconds
```

You can use the scanlog daemon to detect if somebody is doing a port scan on your systems. Simply install the package and run the service. If `scanlogd` detects a (possible) port scan, corresponding warning messages are written to the `/var/log/messages` file.

NOTE: Scanning ports on remote systems can be considered preparation for an attack. Please keep this in mind before scanning systems on the Internet.

NOTE: For more information on nmap, visit www.nmap.org (http://www.nmap.org/).

Use Wireshark to Analyze Network Traffic

Wireshark (formerly called Ethereal) is a tool used to analyze the traffic in a network.

Another network analyzer is `tcpdump`, but Wireshark provides a graphical user interface that can be used to define filters to analyze and investigate the packets collected.

Wireshark sets the defined network interface to the so-called promiscuous mode, meaning that the interface collects every packet, whether it is destined for this interface or for another interface in the network.

NOTE: To set the network interface to the promiscuous mode, Wireshark needs to be started as the root user.

To capture all network traffic, simply select the interface to be used from the *Capture* menu. Wireshark displays all traffic immediately when it is detected:

Figure 8-14   *Wireshark*

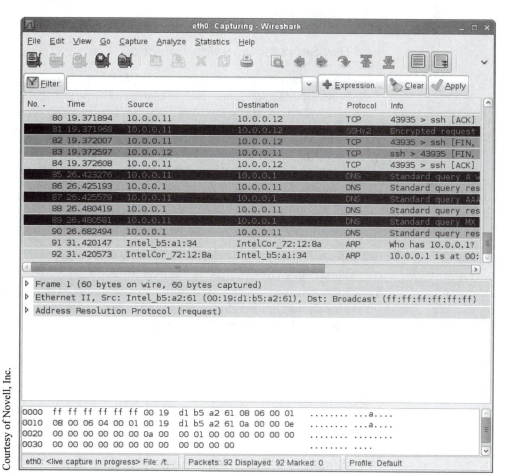

Courtesy of Novell, Inc.

NOTE: For more information on WireShark, visit www.wireshark.org (http://www.wireshark.org/).

Detect Vulnerabilities Using OpenVAS

The Open Vulnerability Assessment System (OpenVAS) is a fork of the well-known vulnerability scanner Nessus. In 2005, the Nessus license changed from open source to proprietary. OpenVAS was forked from the last open source version of Nessus.

Neither OpenVAS nor Nessus are included in SLES 11. If you want to have a deeper look at OpenVAS, you can download RPM packages from the openSUSE Build Service at software.opensuse.org/search (http://software.opensuse.org/search).

OpenVAS consists of two components:

- OpenVAS server: This is the scanner that runs vulnerability scans against target hosts and delivers the results. Scans are defined using plug-ins which are updated to contain recently discovered security holes.

- OpenVAS client: This is a terminal and GUI application used to control the OpenVAS server, perform vulnerability scans, and manage the result of the scans.

NOTE: For more information, visit the OpenVAS Web site at www.openvas.org (http://www.openvas.org).

Use Snort for Intrusion Detection

Snort is an intrusion detection system (IDS) based on attack signatures. It is the most sophisticated open source IDS available. It scans the network traffic for any pattern of a known attack via the network.

SLES 11 does not contain Snort. If you want to have a look at Snort, you can download the RPM packages from the openSUSE Build Service at software.opensuse.org/search (http://software.opensuse.org/search).

You need to connect the computer running Snort to the network in a way that it can monitor all network traffic, e.g., to the monitor port of a switch. An advantage of Snort is that you can monitor an entire network with one host.

Known attacks can be detected, but the ability to detect unknown attacks is limited. Similar to a virus scanner, Snort requires to use up-to-date signatures. The Web site www.snort.org (http://www.snort.org) offers a paid subscription to obtain rules as soon as they are developed. Registered users can obtain these rules five days later for free. Provided you have the necessary know-how, you can also create your own rules.

The basic configuration is done in `/etc/sysconfig/snort` and `/etc/snort/snort.conf`. The rules are also kept in the `/etc/snort/` directory. Snort is started via the script `/etc/init.d/snort`.

NOTE: For more information, visit the Snort web site at www.snort.org (http://www.snort.org).

Check File System Integrity with Tripwire

Tripwire (officially called **Open Source Tripwire** because commercial versions are available as well) is a tool used to check modifications on file systems. It can be configured to send an alert when any properties of certain files have been modified. These properties can be permissions, ownership, size, time stamps, and others.

When Open Source Tripwire is initialized, it scans the configured file systems and stores the information found for each file in a database. This first collection of information is then used to compare the properties of files at a later time. If there are any changes, the user is informed. Open Source Tripwire does not store whole files in the database but only hashes.

Tripwire is not included in SLES 11. If you want to have a deeper look at this utility, you can download the RPM packages from the openSUSE Build Service at software.opensuse.org/search (http://software.opensuse.org/search).

NOTE: For more information on Tripwire, visit www.tripwire.com (http://www.tripwire.com). Open Source Tripwire is available at sourceforge.net/projects/tripwire/ (http://sourceforge.net/projects/tripwire/).

Objective 6   Understand SELinux

NOTE: This section is included because the CompTIA Linux+ objectives listed it before CompTIA endorsed LPIC Level One, but SELinux is not part of the LPIC Level One objectives. However, the information was not removed with the revision of the course following the endorsement of LPIC Level One by CompTIA for Linux+, because some students might still find the information useful.

Security Enhanced Linux (SELinux) is an extension of the Linux kernel used to provide a variety of security policies. It is based on mandatory access control (MAC). MAC means that every time a process tries to access a resource, additional rules (policies) are evaluated to decide if access is granted or denied.

Originally developed by the National Security Agency (NSA), SELinux is part of many current Linux distributions. In SLES 11, it is provided as a so called Technology Preview. That means that the technology is provided, but it is currently not supported. Novell also does not provide any examples or any rules to be used with SELinux.

The configuration of SELinux is quite complex, making it easy to misconfigure the system.

If you want to have a look at SELinux, you first need to switch off AppArmor by using `insserv -r boot.apparmor`.

SELinux has three modes it can be in:

- **Enforcing.** SELinux policy is enforced. SELinux denies access based on SELinux policy rules.

- **Permissive.** SELinux policy is not enforced. SELinux does not deny access, but denials are logged for actions that would have been denied if running in enforcing mode.

- **Disabled.** SELinux is disabled.

To set up policy rules, two packages have to be installed: **policycoreutils** and **checkpolicy**. Additional packages (libraries) will be installed automatically when you install these packages using YaST. Additionally, you may want to install the **selinux-doc** package, which contains documentation (to be found in the `/usr/share/doc/selinux-doc/` directory).

To enable SELinux on the system, you have to provide the following kernel parameter at the boot prompt (or, after thorough testing, add this to the GRUB configuration file): `selinux=1`.

For the reasons mentioned above, we do not cover the configuration of SELinux in this course.

Summary

Objective	Summary
Manage and Secure the Linux User Environment	You should use the root account only when absolutely necessary. You can grant other users limited root-level access using tools like `sudo`, `su`, or `gnomesu`.
	Defaults for user accounts and other security-relevant settings can be configured using the YaST Local Security module.
	The configuration settings are written to various files, the most pertinent being files in `/etc/default/` and the `/etc/login.defs` file.
Provide Secure Remote Access with OpenSSH	The SSH suite was developed to provide secure transmission by encrypting the authentication strings (usually a login name and a password) and all other data exchanged between the hosts.
	SLES 11 installs the OpenSSH package by default. The package includes programs such as `ssh`, `scp`, and `sftp` as alternatives to Telnet, rlogin, rsh, rcp, and FTP.
Configure User Authentication with PAM	Linux uses Pluggable Authentication Modules (PAM) in the authentication process as a layer that communicates between applications and the authentication system.
	Within the PAM framework, there are four different module types:
	■ Auth
	■ Account
	■ Session
	■ Password
	Control flags govern what happens on success or failure of a module:
	■ Required
	■ Requisite
	■ Sufficient
	■ Optional
	Files in `/etc/pam.d/` are used to configure PAM, with additional configuration options in files in `/etc/security/` for certain modules.

Objective	Summary
Ensure File Integrity	Files can have the same size and the same name, but still be different, if only in a few bits. The following tools allow you to establish if a file has been altered compared to a reference file: ■ `md5sum` ■ `sha1sum` ■ `gpg`
Use Security-Related Utilities	The following tools can help you to find out what services are listening on which ports, if vulnerabilities exist on a server, if there is unwanted network traffic, or if files have been altered compared to a previous point in time: ■ `nmap` ■ `wireshark` ■ `OpenVAS` ■ `snort` ■ `tripwire`
Understand SELinux	Security Enhanced Linux (SELinux) is an extension of the Linux kernel used to provide a variety of security policies. It is based on mandatory access control (MAC). Originally developed by the National Security Agency (NSA), SELinux is part of many current Linux distributions. In SLES 11, it is provided as a so-called Technology Preview. That means that the technology is provided, but it is currently not supported.

Key Terms

/etc/default/passwd — A file that contains system password requirements.

/etc/pam.d — The directory that stores application-specific PAM configuration and restriction information.

/etc/permissions.easy — A file that lists the least secure file permission restrictions for system files.

/etc/permissions.local — A file that lists user-defined file permission restrictions for system files.

/etc/permissions.paranoid — A file that lists the most secure file permission restrictions for system files.

/etc/permissions.secure — A file that lists secure file permission restrictions for system files.

/etc/security – The directory that stores PAM global configuration files.

/etc/ssh/ssh_config — The system-wide ssh client program configuration file.

/etc/ssh/sshd_config — The Secure Shell daemon configuration file.

/etc/sudoers — A file that lists the users who are allowed to run certain commands as other users.

/lib/security – The directory that stores PAM modules.

/var/log/wtmp — A data file that lists successful login attempts.

~/.ssh/config – A file that stores user-specific options for use with the ssh client program.

Advanced Encryption Standard (AES) — One of the most common symmetric encryption algorithms used today.

asymmetric encryption — An encryption method that uses an encryption key to encrypt data and a different encryption key to decrypt the same data.

Blowfish — A common symmetric encryption algorithm. It is often used to encrypt Linux passwords.

Data Encryption Standard (DES) — A common symmetric encryption algorithm. It is often used to encrypt Linux passwords.

Diffie-Hellman (DH) — A common asymmetric encryption algorithm used today.

Digital Signature Algorithm (DSA) — A common asymmetric encryption algorithm used today. Its primary use is to generate digital signatures.

effective group — See **primary group.**

gnomesu command — Used to run programs as another user. It is part of the GNOME desktop environment.

GNU Privacy Guard (GnuPG) — A technology that provides asymmetric cryptography for a variety of network technologies.

gpg command — A symbolic link to the **gpg2 command.**

gpg2 command — Used to generate and validate GnuPG keys and data.

IDEA — A common symmetric encryption algorithm.

Intrusion Detection System (IDS) — A software system designed to check for evidence of security threats and breaches.

Keyed-Hash Message Authentication Code (HMAC) — An authentication technology used to validate the sender and receiver of data transmission in version 2 of Secure Shell.

last command — Displays the most recent users who have logged in to the system from entries in /var/log/wtmp.

mandatory access control (MAC) — A system that allows access to resources based on a set of security policies.

md5sum command — Used to calculate an MD5 hash from a file.

Message Digest 5 (MD5) — An hash algorithm used to encrypt Linux passwords.

nmap command — Used to scan open ports on a local or remote system.

Open Source Tripwire — See **Tripwire.**

OpenSSH — An implementation of Secure Shell on Linux systems.

Open Vulnerability Assessment System (OpenVAS) — A program that may be used to monitor security settings on network computers for vulnerabilities.

Pluggable Authentication Modules (PAM) — A software subsystem on Linux systems that manages the access to system data by user applications.

primary group — The group specified for a user in the /etc/passwd file that becomes the group owner on newly created files and directories.

private key — An asymmetric encryption key that is commonly used to decrypt data and generate digital signatures.

public key — An asymmetric encryption key that is commonly used to encrypt data and validate digital signatures.

Remote Authentication Dial-In User Service (RADIUS) — A network service that provides centralized authentication and tracking.

Rivest, Shamir, Adleman (RSA) — A common asymmetric encryption algorithm used today.

r utilities — A term that refers to the legacy rlogin, rsh, and rcp network utilities that have been replaced by Secure Shell.

scanlogd — A daemon that is used to detect and log remote port scanning attempts.

scp command — Used to transfer files across the network using Secure Shell.

Secure Hash Algorithm 1 (SHA1) — A common hash algorithm used by various network and software technologies.

Security Enhanced Linux (SELinux) — A set of software components and kernel extensions that provide security-related policy control on a Linux system.

sftp command — A Secure Shell replacement for the traditional FTP client program.

sg command — Used to change the primary group used by a Linux user within the current shell session. It is functionally equivalent to the newgrp command.

sha1sum command — Used to calculate an SHA1 hash from a file.

Snort — A common network based IDS used to identify network traffic attacks.

ssh-add command — Used to register new Secure Shell keys with ssh-agent.

ssh-agent — A software component used to respond to requests that require use of the local Secure Shell private key.

ssh-keygen command — Used to generate Secure Shell public/private key pairs.

ssh-keyscan command — Used to gather Secure Shell public keys from other servers.

sudo command — Used to run commands as another user via entries in /etc/sudoers.

symmetric encryption — An encryption method that uses the same encryption key to encrypt and decrypt data.

tcpdump command — Used to analyze the network traffic on a local network interface.

Triple-DES — An extension of DES that uses the DES algorithm three times.

Tripwire — A common host based IDS used to identify changes to key system files.

two-factor authentication — An login method that requires users use two different forms of identification.

ulimit command — Used to configure limits on system resources.

updatedb command — Updates the file and directory database used by the locate and slocate commands.

visudo command — Used to edit the entries in the /etc/sudoers file.

Wireshark — A common graphical network traffic analyzer for Linux systems.

Chapter Exercises

Exercise 8-1   *Configure sudo*

In this exercise, you practice configuring `sudo`.

Configure `sudo` to allow the geeko user to kill processes on da-host as root.

Detailed Steps to Complete the Exercise

Complete the following on da-host:

1. Open a terminal window and switch to root using the `su` – command and password **novell**.

2. At the shell prompt, enter `visudo`.

3. Scroll down to the "Defaults targetpw..." line.

4. Comment out the following lines by placing a # at the beginning of the following lines:

   ```
   Defaults targetpw    # ask for the password of the target user i.e.
   root

   ALL     ALL=(ALL) ALL    # WARNING! Only use this together with
   'Defaults targetpw'!
   ```

5. Define a User_Alias named POWERUSERS that contains the geeko user account by adding the following line to the end of the file:

   ```
   User_Alias        POWERUSRES = geeko
   ```

6. Define a Cmnd_Alias named KPROCS that contains the kill and killall commands by adding the following line to the end of the file:

   ```
   Cmnd_Alias        KPROCS = /bin/kill, /usr/bin/killall
   ```

7. Define a Host_Alias named HOSTS that contains the da1 host by adding the following line to the end of the file:

   ```
   Host_Alias        HOSTS = da-host
   ```

8. Using the aliases defined above, allow the geeko user to run the specified commands on da1 as root by adding the following line to the end of the file:

   ```
   POWERUSERS HOSTS = (root) KPROCS
   ```

9. Press Esc, then save your changes and exit the editor by entering `:exit`.

10. Test your configuration by doing the following:

    a. At the shell prompt (as root), enter `top` to start the top process running.

    b. Open a new terminal window.

    c. At the shell prompt in the new terminal window (as geeko), enter `sudo killall top`.

    d. When prompted, enter geeko's password of **novell**.

    You should see that top is unloaded in the first terminal window.

(End of Exercise)

Exercise 8-2   ***Configure the Password Security Settings***

In this exercise, you practice changing security settings.

Change the password hash algorithm from blowfish to MD5 and change the default behavior when Ctrl+Alt+Del is pressed to halting the machine.

Detailed Steps to Complete the Exercise

Complete the following on da-host:

1. In a terminal window, check the setting for the Ctrl+Alt+Del keystroke in the /etc/inittab file by entering

   `grep ctrlaltdel /etc/inittab`

   Note the current setting:

   _____

2. Start YaST by selecting ***Computer > YaST*** and entering a password of novell.

3. Select ***Security and Users > Local Security***.

   The Security Overview dialog appears.

4. On the left, select ***Predefined Security Configurations***.

5. Make sure ***Custom Settings*** is selected.

6. On the left, select ***Password Settings***.

7. From the ***Password Encryption Method*** drop-down list, select ***MD5***.

8. On the left, select ***Boot Settings***.

9. From the ***Interpretation of Ctrl + Alt + Del*** drop-down list, select ***Halt***.

10. Apply the new security settings by clicking ***OK***, then close YaST.

11. To test the change, you must first activate the new configuration.

    This can be done either by rebooting the system or by entering (as root) `init q`, which reloads the /etc/inittab file. You will do the latter:

    a. In the terminal window, `su -` to root using a password of novell.

    b. Reload the /etc/inittab file by entering `init q`.

12. Verify that the Ctrl+Alt+Del setting has changed by entering

    `grep ctrlaltdel /etc/inittab`

    Notice that the setting is now `shutdown -h` instead of what you noted in Step 1.

13. If your da1 virtual server is running, shut it down.

14. Test this setting by changing to a virtual terminal (Ctrl+Alt+F1) and pressing Ctrl+Alt+Del.

    The system shuts down instead of restarting.

15. Power the da-host machine back on and log in as geeko.

(End of Exercise)

Exercise 8-3   *Practice Using OpenSSH*

In this exercise, you learn how to establish SSH connections between computers and how to use SSH with public key authentication. This exercise has two parts.

In the first part, do the following:

- Log in remotely to your da1 server as root.

- Remotely execute the `ps aux` command on DA1 without logging in to the server.

- Copy the `/etc/hosts` file from DA1 to your `/tmp` directory.

- Copy the `/etc/hosts` file from your workstation to the home directory of geeko on DA1.

- Using sftp, copy the `/bin/date` file from DA1 to `/home/geeko` on your workstation.

In the second part of the exercise, do the following:

- Create an ssh-key pair and add the public key to the `~geeko/.ssh/authorized_keys` file on your da1 server and note the difference between logging in with and without a public key.

- Use ssh-agent to cache the private key and log in again to your da1 server as geeko.

- Change the server configuration to allow only public key authentication.

Detailed Steps to Complete the Exercise:

- Part I: Log In to a Remote Computer
- Part II: Perform Public Key Authentication

Part I: Log In to a Remote Computer

Do the following:

1. If necessary, start your da1 virtual machine.

2. Log in to da1 from da-host by doing the following:

   a. On da-host, open a terminal window and enter

      `ssh -l geeko da1.digitalairlines.com`

   b. When prompted to continue, enter **yes**.

   c. When prompted, enter a password of **novell**.

      You are now logged in to the da1 server as geeko.

   d. Log out by entering `exit`.

3. Check the processes running on the da1 server by entering the following at the shell prompt of your workstation:

   `ssh -l geeko da1.digitalairlines.com ps aux`

4. When prompted, enter a password of **novell**.

   A list of all processes currently running on da1 is displayed.

5. Copy the `/etc/hosts` file on your da1 server to the `/tmp` directory on your workstation by entering the following at the workstation shell prompt:

   `scp geeko@da1.digitalairlines.com:/etc/hosts /tmp/`

6. When prompted, enter a password of **novell**.

7. At the shell prompt, enter `ls /tmp`.

   You should see the hosts file from the da1 server in your `/tmp` directory.

8. Copy the `/etc/hosts` file on your workstation to geeko's home directory on your da1 server by entering the following:

   `scp /etc/hosts geeko@da1.digitalairlines.com:`

9. When prompted, enter a password of **novell**.

10. Verify that the file was copied by doing the following:

    a. Switch to your da1 server.

    b. If necessary, log in as geeko with a password of **novell**.

    c. Double-click the **geeko's Home** icon on the desktop.

       You should see the hosts file from the workstation in the geeko user's home directory.

    d. Switch back to your workstation.

11. Use sftp to connect to your da1 server as geeko by entering:

    `sftp geeko@da1.digitalairlines.com`

12. When prompted, enter a password of **novell**.

13. Copy the `/bin/date` program from the da1 server to geeko's home directory on your workstation by entering:

    `get /bin/date /home/geeko/`

14. Quit `sftp` by entering `exit`.

15. At the shell prompt, enter `ls /home/geeko`.

    Verify that the date program has been copied to the geeko user's home directory.

Part II: Perform Public Key Authentication

Complete the following:

1. In a terminal window on da-host, generate an RSA key pair by doing the following:

   a. At the terminal window, enter `ssh-keygen -t rsa`.

   b. Accept the default location for the key (`/home/geeko/.ssh/id_rsa`) by pressing Enter.

    c. When prompted, enter a passphrase of **novell**.

      Information about your key pair, such as the location of your identification and the public key, is displayed.

2. Add the RSA public key to the geeko user's `~/.ssh/authorized_keys` file on da1 by doing the following:

    a. Copy the file to the home directory of geeko on the da1 server by entering the following (in one line) in the terminal window on da-host:

```
scp ~/.ssh/id_rsa.pub
geeko@da1.digitalairlines.com:
```

    b. When prompted, enter a password of **novell**.

    c. Using ssh, log in as geeko to your da1 server by entering

```
ssh -l geeko da1.digitalairlines.com
```

    d. When prompted, enter a password of **novell**.

    e. Enter `ls -al`.

    f. If an .ssh directory does not exist, then create it by entering

```
mkdir .ssh
```

    g. Copy the public key to the `~/.ssh/authorized_keys` file by entering

```
cat id_rsa.pub >> .ssh/authorized_keys
```

3. Log out from the da1 server by entering `exit`.

4. Using ssh, log in to your da1 server as geeko by entering

```
ssh -l geeko da1.digitalairlines.com
```

You are prompted for a passphrase to unlock the private key.

5. Log in by entering **novell**, then log out by entering `exit`.

6. To avoid having to enter the passphrase on every use of `ssh`, start the ssh-agent by entering `ssh-agent bash`.

7. Add your private key to the agent for authentication by entering

```
ssh-add ~/.ssh/id_rsa
```

8. When prompted, enter a passphrase of **novell**.

9. Using `ssh`, log in as geeko to your da1 server by entering

```
ssh -l geeko da1.digitalairlines.com
```

This time you are not prompted for a password or passphrase.

10. Switch to user root by entering `su -` followed by a password of **novell**.

11. At the shell prompt, enter `vi /etc/ssh/sshd_config`.

12. Do the following:

    a. Enter **/PasswordAuthentication** to locate the PasswordAuthentication line.

    b. Make sure it is set to **no**.

    c. Enter **/UsePAM** to locate the UsePAM line.

    d. Change the value of UsePam from yes to **no**.

    e. Save the file and close the editor.

13. Restart sshd by entering `rcsshd restart`.

14. Enter `ssh geeko@localhost`.

15. When prompted to continue connecting, enter **yes**.

You should see an error message and no prompt for a password.

16. Using the `vi` editor, undo the changes made in Step 12, then restart sshd.

17. Log out as root by entering `exit`.

18. Log out from da1 by entering `exit`.

(End of Exercise)

Exercise 8-4   ***Configure PAM Authentication***

In this exercise, you practice configuring PAM authentication.

You will create a file that prevents all normal users (such as geeko) from logging in and you will test the system.

Detailed Steps to Complete the Exercise

Complete the following on da-host:

1. From the graphical desktop, switch to virtual console 3 by pressing Ctrl+Alt+F3.

2. Log in as root with a password of **novell**.

3. Create a `/etc/nologin` file by entering the following command at the shell prompt:

   `echo No login possible > /etc/nologin`

4. Switch to virtual console 4 by pressing Alt+F4.

5. Attempt to log in as geeko.

   A "No login possible" and a "Login incorrect" message are displayed, indicating that you cannot log in to the system.

6. Switch back to virtual console 3 by pressing Alt+F3.

7. View the last lines of the file `/var/log/messages` by entering the following at the shell prompt:

   `tail /var/log/messages`

   Look for the "FAILED LOGIN" message for geeko that indicates the failed login attempt.

8. Edit the `/etc/pam.d/login` configuration file by doing the following:

   a. At the shell prompt, enter `vi /etc/pam.d/login`.

   b. Add a # sign to the beginning of the following line:

      `auth      requisite      pam_nologin.so`

      This PAM module checks to see if the `/etc/nologin` file exists. If it does, it does not allow regular users to log in by returning a failed status.

      Now that this line is commented out, PAM will not check for the file. This means that all users can log in, even if the file exists.

   c. Save the file by entering `:w`.

9. Test the modified PAM configuration file:

   a. Switch to virtual console 4 by pressing Alt+F4.

   b. Attempt to log in as geeko with a password of **novell**.

      You are able to log in because PAM no longer checks for the `/etc/nologin` file.

   c. Log out as geeko by entering `exit`.

10. Edit the file `/etc/pam.d/login` to uncomment the pam_nologin.so line:

   a. Switch to virtual console 3 by pressing Alt+F3.

   b. In the vi editor, press Ins.

   c. Uncomment the pam_nologin.so line (by removing the # sign you entered before) so it looks like the following:

   ```
   auth      requisite      pam_nologin.so
   ```

   d. Press Esc, then save the file and exit vi by entering `:wq`.

11. On virtual console 4, try logging in again as geeko.

   Again, you receive a "Login incorrect" message.

12. Press Alt+F3.

13. Delete the `/etc/nologin` file by entering `rm /etc/nologin` at the shell prompt.

14. Press Alt+F4.

15. Try again to log in as geeko with a password of **novell**.

   Because the `/etc/nologin` file no longer exists, user login is enabled again.

16. Log out as geeko by entering `exit`.

17. Press Alt+F3.

18. Log out as root by entering `exit`.

19. Return to the server desktop by pressing Alt+F7.

(End of Exercise)

Review Questions

1. Which command(s) may be used to change to the root user and start a new shell? (Choose all that apply.)
   a) su - root
   b) su root
   c) su -
   d) su

2. What line in /etc/sudoers could you use to allow the user dgrant to execute the /sbin/useradd program as the root user on the computer ARFA?

3. Why is it best to use the **visudo** command to edit the /etc/sudoers file rather than the **vi** editor?
   a) It checks for syntax errors
   b) It checks your permissions to create entries in the file first
   c) It allows you to save changes to the file
   d) It allows any user to edit the file

4. What option to the **useradd** command can be used to display the current system defaults for user creation?

5. Which of the following can be configured using the Local Security module of YaST? (Choose all that apply.)
   a) Login settings
   b) Boot configuration
   c) Password settings
   d) File permissions

6. What algorithm is used by default in SLES to encrypt passwords stored on the system?
   a) MD5
   b) DES
   c) 3DES
   d) Blowfish

7. What file should you modify to restrict files in the /home directory from running with the SUID bit?
   a) /etc/permissions.easy
   b) /etc/permissions.secure
   c) /etc/permissions.paranoid
   d) /etc/permissions.local

8. What option to the **ulimit** command can be used to limit the number of processes that a user can run in their environment concurrently?

9. Which of the following are good security practices? (Choose all that apply.)
   a) Assigning only necessary file system permissions
   b) Using passwords that are three characters long or longer
   c) Disabling unused network services
   d) Updating network software

10. Which of the following algorithms are asymmetric? (Choose all that apply.)
    a) RSA
    b) DES
    c) AES
    d) DH

11. What file in stores cached Secure Shell encryption keys from other systems that your user account has contacted in the past?

12. You would like to configure the settings used by your Secure Shell daemon on your computer. What file must you edit?

13. Which of the following commands may be gather public host keys from other computers on the network running the Secure Shell daemon?
    a) ssh-keygen
    b) ssh-keyscan
    c) ssh-agent
    d) ssh-get

14. You need to modify the restrictions that are enforced by PAM on your Linux system. Which directory holds the file or files that you need to modify?
    a) /etc/security
    b) /etc/pam
    c) /etc/pam.d
    d) /etc/security.d

15. You have downloaded a file from the Internet. The Web site that you downloaded the file from lists the SHA1 hash for the file. What command can you run on the downloaded file to determine the SHA1 hash to ensure that the file was downloaded successfully?

16. Which of the following may be used to check your system for weak passwords?
    a) nmap
    b) Wireshark
    c) OpenVAS
    d) Tripwire

17. Which of the following Linux Intrusion Detection Systems scans your system to detect changes to system files?
    a) Tripwire
    b) Snort
    c) nmap
    d) OpenVAS

18. What SELinux mode only logs information about access requests that match restrictions in a policy rather than enforce the restrictions?

Discovery Exercises

Configuring a File Based Intrusion Detection System

Log in to the GNOME desktop as the **geeko** user and download the latest version of Open Source Tripwire and related documentation for the SLES 11 platform from http://sourceforge.net.

In a terminal run as the **root** user, extract the Tripwire file and follow the instructions in the documentation file to install and configure Tripwire on your system. When finished, perform a system scan using Tripwire to create a file checksum database. Next, modify the **/etc/login.defs** file. Use Tripwire again to check your system against this database to see if any files have changed (you should notice /etc/login.defs at minimum). Log out of your system when finished.

Using sudo to Grant Process Permissions

Log in to tty1 as the **root** user and edit the **/etc/sudoers** file (using **visudo**) and add the following line to the bottom of the file:
geeko ALL = (root) /usr/bin/killall

When finished, save your changes and quit the vi editor. What does this line do?

Use the **su** command to switch the **geeko** user and run the **sudo killall -9 bash** command. Type geeko's password for confirmation. Why were you successful?

Configuring Local Security

Log in to the GNOME desktop as the geeko user and run the YaST program as the root user. Next, use the Local Security module to set custom security settings for your computer to perform the following actions. Log out of your system when finished.

1. Require that passwords be a minimum of eight characters long, be checked against dictionary words, and be difficult to guess.

2. Store passwords using the Blowfish encryption algorithm again (you changed this to MD5 in a previous exercise).

3. Expire passwords every 42 days. Users should be warned five days before expiry.

4. Restrict the ability to shut down the system from the GDM to the root user.

5. Record failed login attempts, and set a delay after two invalid login attempts.

6. Set secure file permissions.

7. Allow the current directory in the path statement for all users.

When finished, compile a list of files that were modified on the system to achieve these settings.

Symbols